Comparative Analysis of Hindu, Buddhist and Jain Philosophies

Comparative Analysis of Hindu, Buddhist and Jain Philosophies

Hinduism Buddhism Jainism

Prof. (Dr) Jai Pai Paul Dudeja

KALPAZ

ISBN: 978-93-5324-940-3 (HB)

First Published, 2022

Published by

Kalpaz Publications
C-30, Satyawati Nagar,
Delhi – 110052
Ph.: 011-47034999, 9811692060
www.kalpazpublications.com
E-mail: kalpaz@hotmail.com

Printed at: Gyan Press, Delhi.

Contents

SECTION - 5: COMPARISON BETWEEN HINDU, BUDDHIST AND JAIN PHILOSOPHIES

Preface

Dear Readers,

I am extremely happy to see this book titled, **"Comparative Analysis of Hindu, Buddhist and Jain Philosophies"** in your hands. It is my firm belief that you have chosen to read this book with a specific aim in mind, and I assure you that you will not be disappointed.

One can divide this voluminous book consisting of 37 chapters, into **five broad sections**. The **first section** (chapter 1) consists of 'Introduction'. The **second section** consisting of 18 chapters (chapters 2-19), deals with **Hindu Philosophy.** The **third section,** consisting of 8 chapters (chapters 20-27) describes the **Buddhist Philosophy**. The **fourth section,** consisting of 8 chapters (chapters 28-35) deals with **Jain Philosophy**. The **fifth section,** consisting of 2 chapters (chapters 36-37) compares the philosophical aspects (similarities and differences) between these religions.

Chapter 1, titled "Introduction and Overview" gives an overview of the entire book. Readers are advised to go through this chapter in order to get a flavour of the rest of the book.

As discussed earlier, Section-2 is on "**Hindu Philosophy**" and is discussed in chapters 2-19.

Chapter 2, titled "Introduction to Hindu Philosophy" classifies six schools of Indian philosophy: Sāmkhya, Yoga, Vaisheshika, Nyāya, Mīmāṃsā, and Vedānta Philosophy. Each of these six philosophies are discussed in the subsequent chapters.

Chapter 3, titled "Samkhya Philosophy" describes this philosophy in detail.

Chapter 4, titled "Yoga Philosophy" is a detailed coverage of this topic. Subsequent four chapters describe each of the four systems of Yoga. **Chapter 5,** titled "Karma Yoga Philosophy" describes this philosophy in detail. **Chapter 6,** titled " Bhakti Yoga Philosophy" is a detailed coverage of this topic. **Chapter 7,** titled "Raja Yoga Philosophy" describes this philosophy in detail; and finally **Chapter 8,** titled "Jnana Yoga Philosophy" is a detailed coverage of the fourth system of Yoga.

Resuming with the six schools of Hindu philosophy, **Chapter 9,** titled "Nyaya Philosophy" is a detailed coverage of this topic. **Chapter 10,** titled "Vaisheshika Philosophy" describes this philosophy in detail. **Chapter 11,** titled "Purva Mimansa Philosophy" is a detailed coverage of this topic.

Vedanta Philosophy is discussed in **Chapter 12.** Main Schools of Vedanta: Bhedabheda Vedanta, Advaita Vedanta, Vishishtadvaita Vedanta, Dvaita Vedanta, and Suddhadvaita Vedanta, are discussed in **Chapters 13-17,** respectively.

Chapter 18, titled "Neo-Vedanta" discusses a practical and modern version of Vedanta, which appeals to modern generations including the westerners. Swami Vivekananda was the main proponent of this philosophy.

Chapter 19, titled "Kashmir Shaivism Philosophy", though not directly a part of six schools of Hindu philosophy, has nevertheless left a deep impact on the psyche of a large number of seekers. It, therefore, finds a separate mention in this chapter.

Section-3 is on "**Buddhist Philosophy**" and is discussed in chapters 20-27.

Chapter 20, titled "Introduction to Buddhist Philosophy" is an overview of Buddhist Philosophy. This is followed by specific chapters on Buddhism. **Chapter 21,** titled "The Four Noble Truths and Eightfold Path" discusses the basic tenets of Buddhism, and is described in the beginning. **Chapter 22,** titled "Theravada Philosophy" is one of the main schools of philosophy; the other one being, "Mahayana Philosophy", which is discussed in detail in **Chapter 23. Chapter 24,** titled "Vajrayana Philosophy", which mainly deals with "Tantric Buddhism", and is very popular in Tibet, is discussed here. **Chapter 25,** is titled the "Concept of Karma and Rebirth in Buddhism". **Chapter 26,** titled "Pure Land Buddhism" is a tradition of Buddhist teachings that are focused on the Buddha Amitābha. The final chapter in Buddhism (**Chapter 27**), that is titled "Taking Refuge in the Three Jewels in Buddhism" describes the importance of three jewels in Buddhism: (i) The Buddha, (ii) The Dharma, and (iii) The Sangha.

Section-4 is on "**Jain Philosophy**" and is discussed in chapters 28-35.

Chapter 28, titled "Introduction to Jain Philosophy" is an overview of Jain Philosophy. **Chapter 29,** titled "Svetambara and Digambara Sects in Jainism" describes the two classifications of Jains: Svetambaras (white-robed) and Digambara (naked). **Chapter 30,** titled "Anekantavada Philosophy in Jainism". This is the core philosophy of Jainism that distinguishes it from Hinduism and Buddhism. **Chapter 31,** is titled "Agamas and Purvas in Jainism". **Chapter 32,** is titled

"Ratnatraya (Three Jewels) in Jainism". These three jewels are different from those in Buddhism and are: ((i) Samyak darśana (Right View), (ii) Samyak jnana (Right Knowledge), and (iii) Samyak charitra (Right Conduct). **Chapter 33,** titled "Mahavratas and Vratas in Jainism". There are five maha vratas (great vows) for monks and nuns, and twelve vows prescribed for lay people in Jainism. **Chapter 34** is titled "Mula Sutras in Jainism". There are four mula (fundamental) sutras in Jainism, viz, Daśavaikālika-sūtra, Uttarādhyayana-sūtra, Āvaśyaka-sūtra, and Piṇḍa-niryukti and Ogha-niryukti. The final chapter in Jain Philosophy, that is, **Chapter 35,** is titled "Moksha (Liberation) in Jainism". It discusses the path to Liberation and Nirvana in Jainism.

Section-5 (chapters 36-37) is on "**Comparative Analysis between Hindu, Buddhist and Jain Philosophies**". **Chapter 36** is titled "Similarities between Hindu, Buddhist and Jain Philosophies" and **Chapter 37** is titled "Differences between Hindu, Buddhist and Jain Philosophies".

The author sincerely believes that a book of this nature comparing the similarities and differences between the three major Asian religions (that is, Hinduism, Buddhism and Jainism) will add to the value and knowledge of the eager readers. It will be useful as a text book for the students, a reference source for the research scholars studying comparative philosophies of religions, and finally to a large section of general readers across the globe.

I would gratefully and open heartedly love to receive any encouraging/ critical comments as well as feedback from my dear readers at my Email ID: drjpdudeja@gmail.com

Sincerely

2022 **Prof. (Dr.) Jai Pai Paul Dudeja**

Acknowledgements

The seeds of my interest in 'ancient culture' were sown more than sixty years ago by my revered parents, **Late (Dr) Shanti Sawrup Dudeja and Late (Mrs.) Jai Devi Dudeja**. I, therefore, bow to them, wherever they are in the other world. Besides this, I have had the good fortune of learning at the feet of great saints, monks and nuns in Hinduism, Buddhism and Jainism. Any words of gratitude for them will not do justice for the tremendous knowledge and experiences shown by these enlightened souls.

I have greatly benefitted in going through the books and articles referred in the 'Bibliography' of this Book. I gratefully acknowledge these authors for enhancing my understanding on the subject matter of this book.

Last but not the least, my greatest admiration is reserved for **Mrs. Rita Dudeja**, **my wife**, my best friend and my constant source of inspiration, for all my ventures and endeavours like this and many others.

2022 **Prof. (Dr) Jai Pai Paul Dudeja**

SECTION - 1: INTRODUCTION

Chapter - 1

Introduction and Overview

1.1 What is Religion?

The word Religion comes from the Latin word 'religio', which consists of two words, viz., 're' (meaning: back) and 'ligare' (meaning: to bring or bind): that which binds the soul back to God is religion. Religion shows the way for the attainment of God-realisation.

Religion satisfies the deep inward craving in man who is not always content with leading merely an animal existence and wants spiritual consolation, solace, peace and salvation. Man cannot live by bread alone. A time comes in the life of many of us when mere worldly prosperity does not satisfy us and we hanker after something more. And that something more is to follow the path of religion.

Religion is the human beings' relation to that which they regard as holy, sacred, absolute, spiritual, divine, or worthy of especial reverence. It is also commonly regarded as consisting of the way people deal with ultimate concerns about their lives and their fate after death. In many traditions, this relation and these concerns are expressed in terms of one's relationship with or attitude toward gods or spirits; in more humanistic or naturalistic forms of religion, they are expressed in terms of one's relationship with or attitudes toward the broader human community or the natural world. In many religions, texts are deemed to have scriptural status, and people are esteemed to be invested with spiritual or moral authority. Believers and worshippers of religion participate in and are often enjoined to perform devotional or contemplative practices such as prayer, meditation, or particular rituals. Worship, moral conduct, right belief, and participation in religious institutions are among the constituent elements of the religious life.

1.2 What is the Purpose of Religion?

The purpose of the practice of a religion is to pursue the goals of salvation for oneself and others, and (if there is a God) to render due worship and obedience to God. Different religions have different understandings of salvation and God. It is rational for someone to pursue these goals by following religious practices or rituals, in so far as they judge that it would be greatly worthwhile to achieve those goals and in so far as they judge that it is to some degree possible that they will attain them by following the way of that religion.

1.3 What is Theology?

Theology deals with thinking about religious beliefs in a rational manner but it presumes faith. Theology examines the human experience of faith, and how different people and cultures express it. Theologians examine the many different religions of the world and their impact on society. Today we are more aware than ever of the profound influence religion has on us, even if we do not follow it ourselves. Understanding this can help us understand the laws, wars, traditions and morals of our own society and that of others. Theologians employ reason to make their beliefs appear more clearly and to wherever possible have beliefs satisfy the dictates of reason. Theologians begin with a set of beliefs as foundational or fundamental and in some sense not subject to possible disbelief or to truly critical analysis. Philosophers examine and look for all assumptions and suppositions of any system of thought or belief. For philosophers there are no ideas to be accepted on faith.

The study of theology is part philosophy, part history, part anthropology, and also something entirely its own. Theologians have the complex job of thinking about and debating the nature of God. Studying theology means taking on challenging questions about the meaning of religion. It also requires being able to compare different religions in a knowledgeable, analytical and balanced way.

1.4 Philosophy of Religion

Philosophy of religion deals with questions that involve religion and religious ideas from a philosophically neutral perspective (as opposed to theology which begins from religious convictions). Traditionally, religious questions were not seen as a separate field from philosophy proper, the idea of a separate field only arose in the 19th century. Issues in the philosophy of religion include the existence of God, the relationship between reason and faith, questions of religious epistemology, the relationship between religion and science, how to interpret religious experiences, questions about the possibility of an afterlife, the problem of religious language and the existence of souls and responses to religious pluralism and diversity.

1.5 What is the difference between Philosophy and Religion?

Philosophy (from Greek: philosophia, 'love of wisdom') is the study of general and fundamental questions, such as those about existence, reason, knowledge, values, religion, mind, and language. Philosophy is the most critical and comprehensive thought process developed by human beings. It is quite different from religion in that where Philosophy is both critical and comprehensive, religion is comprehensive but not necessarily critical. Religion attempts to offer a view of all of life and the universe and to offer answers to most, if not all, of the most basic and important questions which occur to humans all over the planet. The answers offered by religion are not often subject to the careful scrutiny of reason and logic. Indeed many religious beliefs defy logic and seem to be unreasonable. Religion has its basis in belief. Philosophy, on the other hand, is a critic of belief and belief systems. Philosophy subjects what some would be satisfied in believing to severe examination. Philosophy looks for rational explications and justifications for beliefs. Philosophy has its basis in reason.

Philosophy of Religion is a rational thought about religious issues and concerns without a presumption of the existence of a deity or reliance on acts of faith.

Philosophers examine the nature of religion and religious beliefs. Philosophers have focused on ideas related to the existence and nature of the deity because that idea is central to some religions. Philosophy of Religion centres on arguments or proofs for the existence of god and explications of apparent inconsistencies in the description of the nature of god.

In the last century philosophers around the world have refocused their examinations onto the nature of religious beliefs, religious language and the religious mindset. Indeed, some philosophers have entered into critical reflection and dialogue on the nature or essence of religion itself. Philosophy examines the issues related to the existence and nature of the deity and considers the nature of religious belief.

Philosophy is one of life's noblest pursuits; although its wisdom is the reward of few, it ought to be the aspiration of all. If a philosophy is going to satisfy the intellectual life of the modern world, its conclusions must be able to withstand the acid test of analysis in the dry light of reason. Nothing can be taken for granted; the necessity of every assumption must be established. It must be capable of explaining all things from the Great Absolute to a blade of grass; it must not contradict the facts of experience, conceptual or perceptual. Its hypothesis must satisfy all the demands of our nature; it must account for all types of experience: waking, dreaming, sleeping, and those moments which are claimed by the religious ascetic during his deep contemplation. It must be realistic as well as idealistic; it must not be a brutal materialism, worshipping facts and figures and ignoring values, idealising science and denying spirituality. Nor must it be predominantly a philosophy of values which evades and ignores all connection with facts. It must be comprehensive enough to account for every new discovery of science; it must embrace all the concepts of religion and other philosophical systems. All ideas must receive recognition and find their proper place within the border of its synthesis; every fact of the universe, every aspect of life, every content of experience must immediately fall within the scope of its mold. The March of Science must justify it at every step.

Philosophy and religion are related. By general understanding, religion is composed of a set of morals, rules, principles, and ethics that serve to guide one's way of living. Philosophy, on the other hand, is a bigger domain of discipline that tackles many concepts like: metaphysics, the search for the ultimate truth, knowledge, and life itself.

Although the two are the same in having to deal with man's life, they are still very different in various aspects like the presence of observed rituals across all world religions and the absence of such in philosophy, because the latter only deals more with how people should think. So, an individual cannot be entirely religious withut performing certain rituals stipulated by his or her religion while this same person can still be philosophical even without engaging in some religious rituals.

Another distinction between the two is the strength of belief. Religion puts an emphasis on one's belief as the core of his religiosity. This connects to the concept of faith – the strong belief in something even if there's no empirical evidence of such a thing or phenomenon existing. Philosophy, by contrast, will only believe if a certain subject under argument is proven to be true by using tested means of reasoning. If there's no clearly identifiable and explainable reason for such, then it is not immediately accepted as the truth.

Religion, although considered as a subset of philosophy, involves many supernatural beliefs and superstitions, some of which are already too hard to believe that philosophers constantly argue against. Nevertheless, some philosophers (especially those from the East) happen to be strong believers in faith as well. Thus, they believe in the meanings hidden in religion and its practices that help man understand himself and the truth of life much better than someone who has no religion or who has no belief in such.

1.6 What is the difference between Theology and Philosophy?

Philosophy is about the person and what one thinks in one's own mind. Existence, knowledge, value, reason, mind, language, much of these ideas are in the perspective of what humans view in life are in the domain of philosophy. There can be differences in philosophies as there are a variety of worldviews. There can be a debate with differing views and we come to reconcile those differences, acknowledging that everyone has their own perspective of what they think, and some can change what they think and others may not change their thinking as they believe to be firm in their position. Everyone is a philosopher when they have their own philosophy.

Theology is about God and how a person understands or believes in God. Theology centralises on God - what God thinks, what the will of God is, and the system of belief in God. Theologies are many a time grounded on holy texts, not individual views. Theologians interpret holy texts to understand what God speaks to people and establish the relationship between the believer and the deity. The nature of God and the religious belief is what a person investigates to find truth in the core of their beliefs. The debate with theology is not too much about which religion is right but which interpretation within the religion is right and true. Theologians learn the reasons why their religion is right and true through the branch of apologetics, defending the faith from its objections. Of the different religions, we come to a discussion of understanding the different theologies to discover the truth. Theology does not ask whether God is real or not but assumes God exists and understand who God is. As a believer, you are a theologian, and believers ought to have the right theology.

Philosophy and theology clash with each other in some ways. Theology may influence one's philosophy, but the truth of theology is independent of any person's philosophy. Meaning, theology is a type of philosophy but philosophy is not theology. Going back to the definition, philosophy is about a person and theology is about God and what both think in perspective. One's theology can change one's philosophy, but one's philosophy cannot change the truth of their theology and belief. Mixing one's philosophy and theology together becomes a philosophy. In other words, a person's individual view cannot compromise with their religion as a believer. Theology is a systematic belief regardless of a person's views because theology seeks objective answers whereas philosophy can often seek subjective answers if not guided by correct and logical thinking. For philosophy, you can think whatever you want. For theology, you have a way of thinking.

The similarities between philosophy and theology are that both hold beliefs and worldviews. But ultimately, both use knowledge, reason, and the mind to discover the truth.

1.7 Which are the Major Indian Religions?

Religions originating in the Indian subcontinent include Hinduism, Buddhism, Jainism, and Sikhism, out of which the first three religions will be discussed in this book. The theologies and philosophies of these religions have several concepts in common, such as dharma, karma, maya and samsara.

1.7.1 Hinduism

Hinduism originated on the Indian subcontinent and was related to many other religious traditions outside the subcontinent, in places like ancient Central Asia and ancient Iran. It is considered by some to be the world's oldest extant major religion. Some consider Hinduism to originate from the Indus Valley Civilisation along with animism of the pre-Harappan migrants as well as the Indo-Aryan migrants. Hinduism contains a vast body of scripture, divided as revealed (*shruti*) and remembered (*smriti*), expounding on dharma, or religious living. Hindus consider the Vedas and the Upanishads as being among the foremost in authority, importance and antiquity. The Bhagavad Gītā, a treatise excerpted from the Mahabharata, is sometimes called a summary of the spiritual teachings of the Vedas. It is difficult to identify any universal belief or practice in Hinduism, although prominent themes include: Dharma, Saṃsara, Karma, and Moksha. Hinduism is sometimes called a polytheistic religion, but this is an oversimplification. Hinduism includes a diverse collection of schools whose beliefs span monotheism, polytheism, pantheism, monism and even atheism. For instance, the Advaita Vedanta school holds that there is only one causal entity (Brahman), which manifests itself into all the various living and non-living forms that we observe, whereas traditions such as Vaishnavism and Shaivism worship Vishnu and Shiva in a relatively more monotheistic sense (caused by a differentiation between the para-brahman and atman). A number of scholars even consider the Samkhya school of thought to have atheistic leanings.

Hinduism is the religion of the Hindus, a name given to the Universal Religion which hailed supreme in India. It is the oldest of all living religions. This is not founded by any prophet. Buddhism, Christianity and Islam owe their origin to the prophets. Their dates are fixed. But no such date can be fixed for Hinduism. Hinduism is not born out of the teachings of particular prophets. It is not based on a set of dogmas preached by a particular set of teachers. It is free from religious fanaticism. Hinduism is also known by the names Sanatana-Dharma and Vedic-Dharma. Sanatana-Dharma means eternal religion. Hinduism is as old as the world itself. Hinduism is the mother of all religions. Hindu scriptures are the oldest in the world.

Vedic-Dharma means the religion of the Vedas (Rig Veda, Sama Veda, Yajur Veda, and Atharva Veda). The Vedas are the foundational scriptures of Hinduism. The ancient Rishis and sages of India have expressed their intuitive spiritual experiences (*Aparoksha-Anubhuti*) in the Upanishads. These experiences are direct and infallible. Hinduism regards the spiritual experiences of the Rishis of yore as its authority. The priceless truths that have been discovered by the Hindu Rishis and sages through millennia and constitute the glory of Hinduism.

1.7.1.1 Orthodox (Āstika) Schools or Systems of Hindu Philosophy

Orthodox (astika) schools, originally called Sanatana Dharma, are collectively referred to as Hinduism in modern times. The ancient Vedas are their source and scriptural authority. Hinduism consists of the following six systems of philosophy and theology:

(i) Samkhya, (ii) Yoga, (iii) Nyaya, (iv) Vaishesika, (v) Purva Mimansa, and (vi) Vedanta or Uttara Mimansa. These systems are said to have been founded by sages Kapila, Patanjali, Gautama Muni, Konada, Jaimini and Vyasa, respectively.

- **(i) Samkhya (Kapila):** Samkhya is the oldest of the orthodox philosophical systems, and it postulates that everything in reality stems from purusha (self, soul or mind) and prakriti (matter, creative agency, energy). Purusha cannot be modified or changed while prakriti brings change in all objects.
- **(ii) Yoga (Patanjali):** Yoga literally means the union of two principal entities. Yogic techniques control body, mind and sense organs, thus considered as a means of achieving freedom or mukti. This freedom could be attained by eight stages (*ashta yoga*) practising (i) self-control (yama), (ii) observation of rules (niyama), (iii) physical postures (asana), (iv) breath control (pranayama), (v) choosing an object (pratyahara), (vi) fixing the mind (dharna), (vii) concentrating on the chosen object (dhyana), and (viii) complete dissolution of self, merging the mind and the object (Samadhi). Yoga admits the existence of God as a teacher and guide.
- **(iii) Nyaya (Gautama Muni):** Nyaya Philosophy states that nothing is acceptable unless it is in accordance with reason and experience

(scientific approach). Nyaya is considered as a technique of logical thinking. Nyaya Sutras say that there are four means of attaining valid knowledge: perception, inference, comparison, and verbal testimony.

(iv) Vaisheshika (Kanada): The basis of this school's philosophy is that all objects in the physical universe are reducible to a finite number of atoms and Brahman is regarded as the fundamental force that causes consciousness in these atoms. Vaisheshika system is considered as the realistic and objective philosophy of universe. The reality, according to this philosophy, has many bases or categories which are substance, attribute, action, genus, distinct quality and inherence. Vaisheshika thinkers believe that all objects of the universe are composed of five elements–earth, water, air, fire and ether (akasha).

They believe that God is the guiding principle. The living beings were rewarded or punished according to the law of karma, based on actions of merit and demerit.

The Vaisheshika and Nyaya schools eventually merged because of their closely related metaphysical theories (Vaisheshika only accepted perception and inference as sources of valid knowledge).

(v) Purva Mimamsa (Jaimini): This philosophy encompasses the Nyaya-vaisheshika systems and emphasises the concept of valid knowledge. According to Purva Mimamsa philosophy, Vedas are eternal and possess all knowledge, and religion means the fulfilment of duties prescribed by the Vedas. It says that the essence of the Vedas is Dharma. By the execution of Dharma, one earns merit which leads one to heaven after death.

(vi) Vedanta: The Vedanta, or **Uttara Mimamsa**, school concentrates on the philosophical teachings of the **Upanishads** (mystic or spiritual contemplations within the Vedas), rather than the Brahmanas (instructions for ritual and sacrifice). The school separated into **six sub-schools**, each interpreting the texts in its own way and producing its own series of sub-commentaries:

1. **Advaita (Adi Shankara):** It states that both the individual self (Atman) and Brahman are the same, and knowing this difference causes liberation.
2. **Visishtadvaita (Ramanuja):** It believes that all diversity is subsumed to a unified whole.
3. **Dvaita (Madhvacharya):** It considers Brahman and Atman as two different entities, and Bhakti as the route to eternal salvation.

4. **Dvaitadvaita (Nimbarka):** It states that the Brahman is the highest reality, the controller of all.
5. **Shuddhadvaita (Vallabhacharya):** It states that both God and the individual self are the same, and not different.
6. **Achintya Bheda Abheda (Chaitanya Mahaprabhu)**: It emphasises that the individual self (Jīvatman) is both different and not different from Brahman.

1.7.1.2 Unorthodox (Nāstika) Schools or Systems of Hindu Philosophy

Schools that do not accept the authority of Vedas are by definition unorthodox (Nāstika) systems. The following schools belong to heterodox schools of Indian Philosophy.

1. **Cārvāka**, a materialism school that accepted the existence of free will. According to Brihaspati, Charvaka is a materialistic, sceptical and atheistic school of thought. According to Charvaka, there is no other world. Hence, death is the end of humans and pleasure is the ultimate object in life. It is also known as the Lokayata Philosophy- the philosophy of masses.
2. **Ājīvika,** a materialism school that denied the existence of free will.
3. **Buddhism,** a philosophy that denies existence of ātman (soul, self) and is based on the teachings and enlightenment of Gautama the Buddha.
4. **Jainism,** a philosophy that accepts the existence of the ātman (soul, self), and is based on the teachings and enlightenment of twenty-four teachers known as tirthankaras, with Rishabha as the first and Mahavira as the twenty-fourth tirthankara.

1.7.2 Buddhism

Buddhism is a non-theistic religion (no belief in a creator god), also considered a philosophy and a moral discipline, originating in India in the 6th and 5th centuries BCE. It was founded by the sage Siddhartha Gautama (the Buddha l. c. 563 - c. 483 BCE) who, according to legend, had been a Hindu prince. It is based on the Four Noble Truths and the Eightfold Path as its central principles. According to the scriptures, the Four Noble Truths were revealed by the Buddha in his first sermon after attaining enlightenment. The schools of Buddhism are typically divided into Theravada and Mahayana. In academic circles, Mahayana is further divided into East Asian and Tibetan Buddhism. Buddhism teaches that someone who becomes enlightened without instruction is a Buddha. The primary goal of Buddhism is the liberation of the practitioner from samsara. Buddhists hold this to be the solution to the problem of suffering.

Some key Buddhism beliefs include:

- Followers of Buddhism don't acknowledge a supreme god or deity. They instead focus on achieving enlightenment—a state of inner peace and wisdom. When followers reach this spiritual echelon, they're said to have experienced nirvana.
- The religion's founder, Buddha, is considered an extraordinary man, but not a god. The word Buddha means "enlightened."
- The path to enlightenment is attained by utilising morality, meditation and wisdom. Buddhists often meditate because they believe that it helps awaken the truth.
- There are many philosophies and interpretations within Buddhism, making it a tolerant and evolving religion.
- Some scholars don't recognise Buddhism as an organised religion, but rather, a "way of life" or a "spiritual tradition."
- Buddhism encourages its people to avoid self-indulgence but also self-denial. It follows a middle path.
- Buddha's most important teachings, known as The Four Noble Truths, are essential to understanding the religion.
- Buddhists embrace the concepts of karma (the law of cause and effect) and reincarnation (the continuous cycle of rebirth).
- Followers of Buddhism can worship in temples or in their own homes.
- Buddhist monks, or bhikkhus, follow a strict code of conduct, which includes celibacy.
- There is no single Buddhist symbol, but a number of images have evolved that represent Buddhist beliefs, including the lotus flower, the eight-spoked dharma wheel, the Bodhi tree and the *swastika* (an ancient symbol whose name means "well-being" or "good fortune" in Sanskrit).

1.7.3. Jainism

Jainism is the religion of the followers of the Jinas or Tirthankaras (torch bearers and spiritual teachers of dharma). Parsvanatha and Mahavira, the 23rd and 24th Tirthankaras respectively, revived the Jain religion and re-organised the shraman sangha. Jains highlight the practice of austerity. Jain philosophy states that the jiva, or soul, can escape the cycle of rebirth and death by freeing itself from karmic bondages. When nothing remains but the purity of the jiva, that person is called a jina, or winner, which is the origin of the term Jain. Karma is viewed as an accumulation that burdens the soul, causing attachment and suffering. Ahimsa, or non-violence, is central to Jain faith, philosophy and practice. It is interpreted very strictly as prohibiting all forms of harm to other living beings. Due to this, Jainism requires a strict vegetarian lifestyle. Ahimsa also applies to speaking, as one's words can cause harm and suffering.

Jainism is an ancient religion from India that teaches that the way to liberation and bliss is to live lives of harmlessness and renunciation.

The essence of Jainism is the concern for welfare of every being in the universe and for the health of the universe itself. Some of the features of Jainism are given here-as-under:

- Jains believe that animals and plants, as well as human beings, contain living souls. Each of these souls is considered of equal value and should be treated with respect and compassion.
- Jains are strict vegetarians and live in a way that minimises their use of the world's resources.
- Jains believe in reincarnation and seek to attain ultimate liberation - which means escaping the continuous cycle of birth, death and rebirth so that the immortal soul lives for ever in a state of bliss.
- Liberation is achieved by eliminating all karma from the soul.
- Jainism is a religion of self-help.
- There are no gods or spiritual beings that will help human beings.
- The three guiding principles of Jainism, the 'three jewels', are right belief, right knowledge and right conduct.
- The supreme principle of Jain living is non-violence (ahimsa).
- This is one of the 5 mahavratas (the 5 great vows). The other mahavratas are non-attachment to possessions, not lying, not stealing, and sexual restraint (with celibacy as the ideal).
- **Lord Mahavira**, the 24th Tirthankara, is regarded as the man who gave Jainism its present-day form.
- The texts containing the teachings of Mahavira are called the Agamas.
- Jains are divided into two major sects; the Digambara (meaning "sky clad") sect and the Shvetambara (meaning "white clad") sect.
- Jainism has no priests. Its professional religious people are monks and nuns, who lead strict and ascetic lives.

1.8 Comparison between Hindu, Buddhist and Jain Philosophies

1.8.1 Comparison between Hindu and Buddhist Philosophies

1.8.1.1 Differences between Hindu and Buddhist Philosophies

(i) Places of Worship:

Hindus: The places of worship of Hindus are known as Temples.

Buddhists: The places of worship of Buddhists are known as Buddhist monasteries, shrines, temples.

(ii) Founder:

Buddhists: Buddha is the founder of Buddhism. Buddhists consider Buddha as the all-transcending sage and highest teacher.

Hindus: Among some sections of Hindus, they consider Buddha as the 9th avatar of Vishnu.

(iii) Spiritual Leader:

Buddhists: Tibetan Buddhism has a foremost Spiritual Leader. The title given to the foremost spiritual leader is ***the Dalai Lama***. Dalai Lama is the title given by Tibetan people to the supreme spiritual leader of Yellow Hat or Gelug school of Tibetan Buddhism.

Hindus: Hinduism does not have a concept of having the foremost Spiritual Leader.

(iv) Male and Female Monks:

Buddhism: In Buddhism Male Monks are known as Bhikkhus and Female Monks are known as Bhikkhunis. The Monastic Communities in Buddhism are known as Sangha.

Hindus: In Hinduism male monks are known as Yogis, Sages, Rishis, Gurus, Priests, Swamis, and female monks are known as Sanyasini, Sadhvi, Svāmini.

(v) Branches and Denominations:

Buddhists: The two major branches of Buddhism are Hinayana (Theravada) and Mahayana.

Hindus: The four largest denominations of Hinduism are Shaktism, Shaivism, Vaishnavism and Smartism.

(vi) Primary Languages:

Buddhism: The primary language used by Theravada tradition was the Pali language. The primary language used by Mahayana and Vajrayana traditions is Sanskrit.

Hinduism: Sanskrit is the primary sacred language of Hinduism. Most of the works of Hindu Philosophy were written in Sanskrit language.

(vii) Festivals and Holy Days:

Buddhism: Some of the most important festivals of Buddhists are Vesak (Buddha's birthday), Parinirvana Day (also known as Nirvana day), Buddha Purnima, Ullambana, Uposatha, Losar (celebrated by Tibetan Buddhists), etc.

Hinduism: Holy Days in Hinduism are plenty. There are many important days for worshipping different Gods, some of the most important holy days are Ganesh Chaturthi, Mahashivaratri, Ram Navami, Krishna Janmashtami, Navaratri, Durga Puja, etc.

(viii) Scriptures:

Buddhism: Some of the most important scriptures are Tripitaka and Gandhara Texts. Tripitaka are composed of three sections: Commentaries, Discipline and Discourses.

Hinduism: Some of the most important scriptures of Hinduism are Vedas, Bhagavad Gita, Ramayana, Upanishads, Puranas.

(ix) Symbols:

Buddhism: Some of the most important symbols in Buddhism are Conch, Dharmachakra – it is a wheel of dharma, fish, lotus, vase, victory banner, parasol etc.

Hinduism: Some of the most important symbols of Hinduism are Om, Swastika etc.

(x) Married Life:

Buddhism: Buddhism does impart advice on how to maintain a cordial and happy married life. However, Buddhism does not treat marriage as a religious duty. Buddhists monks and nuns follow celibacy all their lives.

Hinduism: As per Hinduism, man can marry once. However, in ancient India and in Mythologies there are cases of a man having multiple wives.

(xi) Origin:

Buddhism: Buddhism originates from Buddha. Buddha achieved enlightenment at Bodh Gaya, at Gaya district located in Bihar, India. The first teachings of Buddha were delivered at a Deer Park in Sarnath. Origins can be traced to 563 B.C.E.

Hinduism: Hinduism began in Indian subcontinent, even before 3000 B.C.E.

(xii) Vedas:

Buddhism: Vedas were rejected by Buddha as per the dialogues given in Nikayas.

Hinduism: In Hinduism, Vedas are considered as the most important scriptures.

(xiii) Goal:

Buddhism: The goal of Buddhism is to bring lasting, unconditional happiness.

Hinduism: The goal of Hinduism is freedom from the cycle of birth and rebirth; and ultimately attain moksha or liberation from birth and rebirth.

1.8.1.2 Similarities between Hindu and Buddhist Philosophies

1. There is idol worship in both Buddhism (Mahayana) and Hinduism.
2. Both Buddhism and Hinduism give equal rights to men and women. There is no discrimination against women in either religion.
3. Atheists can take part in religious activities, there will be no restrictions.
4. Both the religions originated from Indian Subcontinent.

1.8.2 Comparison between Hindu and Jain Philosophies

1.8.2.1 Differences between Hindu and Jain Philosophies

(i) Creation:

Hinduism: Hinduism believes the Universe was created by Brahma, the creator.

Jainism: Jainism does not believe that the universe was created by one God Brahma, rather Jainism believes the Universe itself is eternal and powerful. Jainism believes it was never created as it is eternal.

(ii) Soul vs Supreme Soul:

Hinduism: As per Hinduism, Soul was separated from Supreme Soul (Paramatma) and the main purpose of life is to attain moksha, that is, merger of Soul back into supreme soul.

Jainism: As per Jainism, every soul itself is supreme Soul, hence the objective of life is to separate soul from bad karma (sinful actions) and attain moksha.

(iii) Non-violence vs Violence:

Hinduism: Hinduism also believes in non-violence, however if violence is absolutely necessary to achieve victory over evil, then it is permitted. Mahabharata and Ramayana are good examples.

Jainism: Jainism does not believe in violence; it strongly believes only in non-violence.

(iv) Sects and Denominations:

Hinduism: The 4 largest denominations of Hinduism are: Shaktism, Shaivism, Vaishnavism and Smartism.

Jainism: The 2 important sects of Jainism are Shvetambara and Digambara.

(v) Holy Days and Festivals:

Hinduism: Holy Days in Hinduism are plenty. There are many important days for worshipping different Gods, some of the most important holy days are Ganesh Chaturthi, Mahashivaratri, Ram Navami, Krishna Janmashtami, Navaratri, Durga Puja etc.

Jainism: Some of the most important Jain festivals are Paryushana, Mahavira Janma Kalayanak, Ashtanhika Parv, Nandishwar Ashtanika, Maun agiyaras, Mahamastabhisheka etc.

(vi) Worship:

Hinduism: In Hinduism many Gods are worshipped, most prominent are Ganapathi, Shiva, Vishnu, Lakshmi, Saraswati, Parvati, Hanuman, Kartikeya etc.

Jainism: In Jainism, 24 Tirthankars, besides some celestial beings are worshipped as Demi Gods. Mahavira was the 24th Thirthankara of Jainism.

(vii) Casteism:

Hinduism: Hinduism has different castes and classes.

Jainism: In Jainism there is no division of followers on the basis of castes and class.

(viii) Vegetarian vs Non-Vegetarian Diet:

Hinduism: In Hinduism one can find people strictly following vegetarian diets as well as people who consume non-vegetarian diets.

Jainism: In Jainism it is strictly forbidden from having non-vegetarian diets including eggs.

(ix) Sacred Scriptures:

Hinduism: In Hinduism Vedas, Upanishads, Smritis etc are considered sacred.

Jainism: In Jainism, Vedas and other religious books of Hinduism are not accepted. Jainism has their own sacred scriptures like Agamas and Sutras.

(x) Animal Sacrifice:

Hinduism: In Hinduism, animal sacrifices were mostly associated with Shaktism; animal sacrifices were done in ancient times. However, Puranas and Gita forbid animal sacrifice.

Jainism: Animal sacrifices are strictly prohibited in Jainism.

(xi) Stages of Human Life:

Hinduism: Hinduism has 4 stages of life: Brahmacharya (student life), Grihastha Ashram (householders life), Vanaprastha Ashram (searching for truth), and the final stage Sanyasa Ashram. As per Hinduism, spirituality must be pursued in the last 2 stages of Human life. One has to follow Dharma at all stages, but focus on salvation is at the last 2 stages.

Jainism: Jainism does not have different stages of human life; the main focus of entire life is to attain liberation and must be strictly spiritual.

1.8.2.2 Similarities between Hindu and Jain Philosophies

1. Both Hinduism and Jainism believe in reincarnation, i.e., cycle of birth and death.
2. Both Hinduism and Jainism believe in non-violence,
3. Both Hinduism and Jainism emphasise on consuming vegetarian diet.
4. Both religions give importance to meditation.
5. Followers of both the religions celebrate festivals like Diwali.
6. Both religions have the same concepts like Moksha, Samsara, Karma; although the precise meaning may be different.

1.8.3 Comparison between Jain and Buddhist Philosophies

1.8.3.1 Differences between Jain and Buddhist Philosophies

Jainism has developed and refined the non-violence (Ahimsa) doctrine to an extraordinary degree where it is an integral part of the Jain culture. Jain vegetarianism, for example, is driven by the principle of not harming any animals and both lay and mendicants are predominantly vegetarian. In Buddhism, Mahayana monks in China, Japan, Korea and Vietnam are vegetarian; however, vegetarianism is not required for lay Buddhists. In Theravada monastic tradition, a monk should eat whatever is placed in his bowl when receiving food.

Although both Buddhists and Jain had orders of nuns, Buddhist Pali texts record the Buddha saying that a woman has the ability to obtain nirvana in the dharma and Vinaya. According to Digambara Jains, women are capable of spiritual progress but must be reborn as a man in order to attain final spiritual liberation. The religious texts of the Śvētāmbara mention that liberation is attainable by both men and women.

Jains believe in the existence of an eternal Jiva (soul), whereas Buddhism denies the concept of self (jiva) or soul (atman), proposing the concept of no-self (anatta) instead.

The Anekantavada doctrine is another key difference between Jainism and Buddhism. The Buddha taught the Middle Way, rejecting extremes of the answer "it is" or "it is not" to metaphysical questions. The Mahavira, in contrast, accepted both "it is" and "it is not", with "perhaps" qualification and with reconciliation.

Jainism discourages monks and nuns from staying in a single place for a long time, with the exception of 4 months in the rainy season (chaturmas). Thus, most of the time the Jain monks and nuns keep wandering, staying in a place for just a few days. Some Theravada Buddhist monks also observe vassa rules, but often they stay in one monastery.

1.8.3.2 Similarities between Jain and Buddhist Philosophies

In Jainism, the way of liberation is the ford (tirtha), and Tirthankaras "those making the ford" (from samsara to moksha) are supreme teachers. Same concept is found in Buddhism which says that through enlightenment (bodhi) an individual crosses the river of samsara and attain liberation. Both religions deny the existence of a creator god. Buddhism and Jainism evince a shared belief in the existence of geographical regions beyond the parameters of Bharatavarsha (ancient India), access to which could not be gained by ordinary human beings.

Karakandu, a Pratyekabuddha in both Jainism and Buddhism, is a rare personality that is shared between Jainism and Buddhism. The Jain text Isibhasiyam mentions, Vajjiyaputra Mahakashyap and Sariputra among the rishis.

The Jain community (or Jain sangha) consists of monastics, munis (male ascetics) and aryikas (female ascetics) and householders, śhrāvaks (laymen) and śrāvakīs (laywomen). Buddhism has a similar organisation: the community consists of renunciate bhikkhus and bhikkhunis and male and female laypersons, or śrāvakas and śrāvikas, who take limited vows.

Jain and Buddhist iconography can be similar. In north India, the sitting Jain and Buddhist images are in padmasana, whereas in South India both Jain and Buddhist images are in ardha-padmasana (also termed virasana in Sri Lanka). However, the Jina images are always samadhi mudra, whereas the Buddha images can also be in bhumi-sparsha, dharam-chakra-pravartana and other mudras. The standing Jain images are always in khadgasana or kayotsarga asana.

The topics introduced in this chapter will be discussed in detail in the rest of the book.

SECTION - 2: HINDU PHILOSOPHY

Chapter - 2

Introduction to Hindu Philosophy

In the ancient times, it had been accepted that man can know metaphysical truths by direct experience. He need not depend upon speculation, inference, or faith. The literature is replete with the writings of such great men who have been said to know the whole truth of Nature and human existence, and the teachings of these men have been set forth in the philosophical systems of ancient India.

All systems of Hindu Philosophy are in complete agreement that the purpose of philosophy is the extinction of sorrow and suffering and that the method is by the acquisition of knowledge of the true nature of things which aims to free man from the bondage of ignorance, which is the cause of human suffering. In this light, Hindu philosophy is seen as an art of life and not a theory about the universe, for it is the means of attaining the highest aspirations of man. It is not for the discovery, but for the understanding of Truth.

Hindu philosophy encompasses the philosophies, world views and teachings of Hinduism that emerged in Ancient India. These include six schools or systems (shad-darshana) – (i) Samkhya, (ii) Yoga, (iii) Nyaya, (iv) Vaisheshika, (v) Mimamsa and (vi) Vedanta (or Uttara Mimansa).

In Indian tradition, the word used for philosophy is Darshana. This word comes from the Sanskrit root *drish* (to see, or to experience).

These systems have many characteristics in common. They all grew out of the Upanishads, the philosophical portion of the Vedas, which is accepted as the supreme authority; they are delivered in the Sutra style, that is as aphorisms; as such, they are extremely concise, avoiding all unnecessary repetition and employing a rigid economy of words, making it difficult to understand them correctly in their original form without the use of commentaries, for they use many of the same terms, but each system gives its own meaning to the use of the term. They rest their conclusions on several common concepts: all accept the eternal cycle of Nature which is without beginning and end, and which consists of vast periods of creation, maintenance, and dissolution; all accept the principle of regeneration of the soul that maintains that life and death are but two phases of a single cycle to which the soul is bound and to which it clings because of ignorance of the true nature of things; all accept Dharma as the moral law of the universe that accounts for these eternal cycles of Nature, as well as the destiny of the human soul; all agree that knowledge is the path to freedom and that Yoga is the method to attain final liberation.

These six systems are also called the Astika (theistic) philosophical traditions and are those that accept the Vedas as an authoritative, important source of knowledge. Ancient and medieval India was also the source of philosophies that share philosophical concepts but rejected the Vedas, and these have been called nāstika (heterodox or non-orthodox) Indian philosophies. Nāstika Indian philosophies include Buddhism, Jainism, Cārvāka, Ājīvika, and others.

Hindu philosophy also includes several sub-schools of theistic philosophies that integrate ideas from two or more of the six orthodox philosophies, such as the realism of the Nyāya, the naturalism of the Vaiśeṣika, the dualism of the Sāṅkhya, the non-dualism and knowledge of Self as essential to liberation of Advaita, the self-discipline of Yoga and the asceticism and elements of theistic ideas. Examples of such schools include Pāśupata Śaiva, Śaiva siddhānta, Pratyabhijña, Raseśvara and Vaiṣṇava. Some sub-schools share Tantric ideas with those found in some Buddhist traditions. The ideas of these sub-schools are found in the Puranas and Āgamas.

Each school of Hindu philosophy has extensive epistemological literature called pramāṇaśāstras, as well as theories on metaphysics, axiology, and other topics.

2.1 Classifications in Hindu Philosophy

2.1.1 Āstika and nāstika

In the history of India, the six orthodox schools had emerged before the start of the Common Era, and some schools emerged possibly even before the Buddha. Some scholars have questioned whether the orthodox and heterodox schools classification is sufficient or accurate, given the diversity and evolution of views within each major school of Indian philosophy, with some sub-schools combining heterodox and orthodox views.

Since ancient times, Indian philosophy has been categorised into āstika and nāstika schools of thought. The orthodox schools of Indian philosophy have been called ṣaḍ-darshana ("six systems"). This schema was created between the 12th and 16th centuries by Vedantins.

2.1.1.1 Āstika

There are six āstika (orthodox) schools of thought. Each is called a darśana, and each darśana accepts the Vedas as authority. Each astika darsana also accepts the premise that Atman (soul, eternal self) exists. The āstika schools of philosophy are:

(i) **Samkhya** – A strongly dualist theoretical exposition of consciousness and matter. Agnostic with respect to God or the gods.

(ii) **Yoga** – A monotheistic school which emerged from Samkhya and emphasises practical use of Samkhya theory: meditation, contemplation and liberation.

(iii) **Nyāya or logic** – The school of epistemology which explores sources of knowledge.

(iv) **Vaiśeṣika** – An empiricist school of atomism.

(v) **Mīmāṃsā** – An anti-ascetic and anti-mysticist school of orthopraxy. This school deals with the correct interpretation of the verses in Vedas.

(vi) **Vedānta** – The last segment of knowledge in the Vedas, or jñānakhāṇḍa (section of knowledge). Vedanta is also referred as Uttara-Mimamsa. Vedānta came to be the dominant current of Hinduism in the post-medieval period.

The **Samkhya of Kapila** enumerates in a still more elaborate manner into the nature of the phenomenal world as an evolution from the "interplay" of Purusha and Prakriti, the twin primordial principles, the cosmic subject or observer (Iswara) and the cosmic object or energy (Avyakta) and lists a total of 25 basic entities. It further establishes that there are three primary all-pervading fields called gunas (Sattva, Rajas and Tamas) that by their mutual interactions make up the entire phenomenal universe of things and beings inhabiting space-time.

The Yoga system of Patanjali sheds light on how the individual can go beyond the clutches of the nature made up of the three gunas and can attain a blissful state of perfect knowledge and power (Jnana and Siddhi) called Samadhi by the practice of protracted meditation. The relationship of the Individual with God is now left to be rationally established.

The Nyaya system of sage Gautama gives us the research methodology, so to say, basing on which we can gain right knowledge (Pramana) about everything: by empirical observations (Pratyaksha), by doing rational analysis (Anumana), by building analogous theoretical models (Upamana) and by taking recourse to the knowledge documented (Shabda) by previous authentic investigators (i.e., "statements of seers" in vedic era and "papers by peers" in scientific era) regarding the phenomena concerned. This is precisely the scientific method that is universally followed today.

The Vaisheshika of Kanada classifies the basic categories and the fundamental substances (Padarthas) and enumerates their various attributes, interactions and functions, which is akin to the roles that Physics and Chemistry play in modern day sciences.

The Purva (prior) Mimansa of Jaimini (disciple of Vyasa) treats of the methods of sacrificial works or Karma for the attainment of any desired end and holds Karma as the sole determinant of the destiny of the individual.

The Vedanta system or Uttara (later) Mimansa of Vyasa (also known as Vadarayana) codified in the Vedanta sutras or Brahma Sutras points out the methods of liberation (Moksha) of the individual by attainment of Jnana or knowledge of the Highest Self (Brahman), which is defined as Sat-Chit-Ananda, existence-consciousness-Bliss, Absolute and irrefutably establishes the identity of the individual with the supreme Absolute at the most fundamental level.

2.1.1.2 Nāstika

Schools that do not accept the authority of the Vedas are nāstika philosophies, of which four nāstika (heterodox) schools are prominent:

(i) **Cārvāka,** a materialism school that accepted the existence of free will.

(ii) **Ājīvika,** a materialism school that denied the existence of free will.

(iii) **Buddhism,** a philosophy that denies existence of ātman (soul, self) and is based on the teachings and enlightenment of Gautama Buddha.

(iv) **Jainism,** a philosophy that accepts the existence of the ātman (soul, self), and is based on the teachings and enlightenment of twenty-four teachers known as tirthankaras, with Rishabha as the first and Mahavira as the twenty-fourth.

2.1.1.3 Other schools

Besides the major orthodox and non-orthodox schools, there have existed syncretic sub-schools that have combined ideas and introduced new ones of their own. The medieval scholar Vidyaranya (1238–1317 CE), in his book 'Sarva-Darshana-Samgraha', includes the following, along with Buddhism and Jainism, as sub-schools of Hindu philosophy:

- **Pashupata Shaivism**, developed by Nakulisa;
- **Shaiva Siddhanta**, the theistic Samkhya school;
- **Pratyabhijña**, the recognitive school of Kashmir Shaivism, Trika;
- **Raseśvara**, a Shaiva school that advocated the use of mercury to reach immortality;
- The **Ramanuja** school;
- The **Pūrṇaprājña** (Madhvācārya) school;
- The **Pāṇinīya**.

The above sub-schools introduced their own ideas while adopting concepts from orthodox schools of Hindu philosophy such as realism of the Nyāya, naturalism of Vaiśeṣika, monism and knowledge of Self (Atman) as essential to liberation of Advaita, self-discipline of Yoga, asceticism and elements of theistic ideas. Some sub-schools share Tantric ideas with those found in some Buddhist traditions.

2.2 Epistemology or Pramana

Epistemology is called pramāṇa. It has been a key, much debated field of study in Hinduism since ancient times. Pramāṇa is a Hindu theory of knowledge and discusses the valid means by which human beings can gain accurate knowledge. The focus of pramāṇa is how correct knowledge can be acquired, how one knows, how one doesn't, and to what extent knowledge pertinent about someone or something can be acquired.

2.2.1 Six Pramāṇas

Ancient and medieval Hindu texts identify six pramāṇas as correct means of accurate knowledge and truths:

(i) Pratyakṣa – Direct perception;

(ii) Anumāṇa – Inference or indirect perception;

(iii) Upamāṇa – Comparison and analogy;

(iv) Arthāpatti – Postulation, derivation from circumstances;

(v) Anupalabdi – Non-perception, absence of proof; and

(vi) Shabda – Word, testimony of past or present reliable experts.

Each of these are further categorised in terms of conditionality, completeness, confidence and possibility of error, by the different schools. The schools vary on how many of these six are valid paths of knowledge. For example, the Cārvāka nāstika philosophy holds that only one (perception) is an epistemically reliable means of knowledge, the Samkhya school holds that three are (perception, inference and testimony), while the Mīmāṇsā and Advaita schools hold that all six are epistemically useful and reliable means to knowledge.

2.3 Sāmkhya Philosophy

Samkhya is the oldest of the orthodox philosophical systems in Hinduism, with origins in the 1st millennium BCE. It is a rationalist school of Indian philosophy, and had a strong influence on other schools of Indian philosophies. Sāmkhya is an enumerationist philosophy whose epistemology accepted three of six pramāṇas as the only reliable means of gaining knowledge. These were pratyakṇa (perception), anumāṇa (inference) and shabda (Āptavacana, word/testimony of reliable sources).

Samkhya was founded by Kapila who is considered the Father of Hindu Philosophy. This system comprehends the universe as a sum total of twenty-five categories. In no way does it discard the basic realities of the previous system. It only shows that they are not final, in the same way that the breaking down of the atom to electrons and protons did not discard the existence of the atom, but only showed that it was not the last possible reduction of matter. It shows that all derived things in this world are not produced from the nine realities, but from two realities, Spirit and Matter, which are considered as the Ultimate Realities. It discards the creation of the Vaiseshika system and shows that all things are evolved out of pre-existing material which is the static background of the universe and which simply unfolds itself as a rose unfolds from its seed.

Samkhya school espouses dualism between consciousness and matter. It regards the universe as consisting of two realities: Purusha (consciousness) and prakriti (matter). Jiva (a living being) is that state in which purusha is bonded to prakriti in some form. This fusion, state the Samkhya scholars, led to the emergence of buddhi (awareness, intellect) and ahankara (individualised ego consciousness, "I-maker"). The universe is described by this school as one created by Purusha-Prakriti entities infused with various permutations and combinations of variously enumerated elements, senses, feelings, activity and mind.

Samkhya philosophy includes a theory of gunas (qualities, innate tendencies, psyche). Guna, it states, are of three types: Sattva being good, compassionate, illuminating, positive, and constructive; Rajas Guna is one of activity, chaotic, passion, impulsive, potentially good or bad; and Tamas being the quality of darkness, ignorance, destructive, lethargic, negative. Everything, all life forms and human beings, state Samkhya scholars, have these three gunas, but in different proportions. The interplay of these gunas defines the character of someone or something, of nature and determines the progress of life. Samkhya theorises a pluralism of souls (Jeevatmas) who possess consciousness. Samkhya has historically been theistic or non-theistic, and there has been debate about its specific view on God.

The Samkhya karika, one of the key texts of this school of Hindu philosophy, opens by stating its goal to be "three kinds of human suffering" and means to prevent them. The text then presents a distillation of its theories on epistemology, metaphysics, axiology and soteriology. For example, Samkhya karika states that:

From the triad of suffering, arises this inquiry into the means of preventing it.

That is useless – if you say so, I say: No, because suffering is not absolute and final. – Verse 1

The Guṇas (qualities) respectively consist in pleasure, pain and dullness, are adapted to manifestation, activity and restraint; mutually domineer, rest on each other, produce each other, consort together, and are reciprocally present. – Verse 12

Goodness is considered to be alleviating and enlightening; foulness, urgent and persisting; darkness, heavy and enveloping. Like a lamp, they cooperate for a purpose by union of contraries. – Verse 13

There is a general cause, which is diffuse. It operates by means of the three qualities, by mixture, by modification; for different objects are diversified by influence of the several qualities respectively. – Verse 16

Since the assemblage of perceivable objects is for use (by man); Since the converse of that which has the three qualities with other properties must exist (in man); Since there must be superintendence (within man); Since there must be some entity that enjoys (within man); Since there is a tendency to abstraction (in man), therefore soul is. – Verse 17

The soteriology in Samkhya aims at the realisation of Purusha as distinct from Prakriti; this knowledge of the Self is held to end transmigration and lead to absolute freedom (kaivalya).

2.4 Yoga Philosophy

In Indian philosophy, Yoga is, among other things, the name of one of the six āstika philosophical schools. The Yoga philosophical system aligns closely with the dualist premises of the Samkhya school. The Yoga school accepts Samkhya psychology and metaphysics, but is considered theistic because it accepts the concept of personal god (Ishvara), unlike Samkhya. The epistemology of the Yoga school, like the Sāmkhya school, relies on three of six prāmaṇas as the means of gaining reliable knowledge: pratyakṇa (perception), anumāṇa (inference) and shabda (āptavacana, word/testimony of reliable sources).

The universe is conceptualised as a duality in Yoga school: purusha (consciousness) and prakriti (matter); however, the Yoga school discusses this concept more generically as "seer, experiencer" and "seen, experienced" than the Samkhya school.

A key text of the Yoga school is the Yoga Sutras of Patanjali. Patanjali may have been, as Max Müller explains, "the author or representative of the Yoga-philosophy without being necessarily the author of the Sutras." Hindu philosophy recognises many types of Yoga, such as rāja yoga, jñāna yoga, karma yoga, bhakti yoga, tantra yoga, mantra yoga, laya yoga, and hatha yoga.

The Yoga school builds on the Samkhya school theory that jñāna (knowledge) is a sufficient means to moksha. It suggests that systematic techniques/practice (personal experimentation) combined with Samkhya's approach to knowledge is the path to moksha. Yoga shares several central ideas with Advaita Vedanta, with the difference that Yoga is a form of experimental mysticism while Advaita Vedanta is a form of monistic personalism. Like Advaita Vedanta, the Yoga school of Hindu philosophy holds that liberation/freedom in this life is achievable, and that this occurs when an individual fully understands and realises the equivalence of Atman (soul, self) and Brahman.

2.5 Vaisheshika

The Vaisheshika philosophy is a naturalist school. It is a form of atomism in natural philosophy. It postulates that all objects in the physical universe are reducible to paramāṇu (atoms), and that one's experiences are derived from the interplay of substance (a function of atoms, their number and their spatial arrangements), quality, activity, commonness, particularity and inherence. Knowledge and liberation are achievable by complete understanding of the world of experience, according to Vaisheshika school. The Vaisheshika darśana is credited to Kaṇāda Kaśyapa from the second half of the first millennium BCE. The foundational text, the Vaisheshika Sūtras 1.1.1–1.1.4, say as follows:

Dharma is that from which results the accomplishment of Exaltation and of the Supreme Good. The authoritativeness of the Veda arises from its being an exposition of dharma. The Supreme Good results from knowledge, produced from a particular dharma, of the essence of the Predictable,

Substance, Attribute, Action, Genus, Species and Combination, by means of their resemblances and differences.

The Vaisheshika school is related to the Nyāya school but features differences in its epistemology, metaphysics and ontology. The epistemology of the Vaisheshika school, like Buddhism, accepted only two means to knowledge as reliable – perception and inference. The Vaisheshika school and Buddhism both consider their respective scriptures as indisputable and valid means to knowledge, the difference being that the scriptures held to be a valid and reliable source by Vaisheshika were the Vedas.

Vaisheshika metaphysical premises are founded on a form of atomism, that reality is composed of four substances (earth, water, air, and fire). Each of these four are of two types: atomic (paramāṇu) and composite. An atom is, according to Vaisheshika scholars, that which is indestructible (anitya), indivisible, and has a special kind of dimension, called "small" (aṇu). A composite, in this philosophy, is defined to be anything which is divisible into atoms. Whatever human beings perceive is composite, while atoms are invisible. The Vaisheshika stated that size, form, truths and everything that human beings experience as a whole is a function of atoms, their number and their spatial arrangements, their guṇa (quality), karma (activity), sāmānya (commonness), vishesha (particularity) and amavāya (inherence, inseparable connectedness of everything).

2.6 Nyāya Philosophy

The Nyāya school is a realist āstika philosophy. The school's most significant contributions to Indian philosophy were its systematic development of the theory of logic, methodology, and its treatises on epistemology. The foundational text of the Nyāya school is the Nyāya Sūtras of the first millennium BCE. The text is credited to Aksapada Gautama and its composition is variously dated between the sixth and second centuries BCE.

Nyāya epistemology accepts four out of six prāmaṇas as reliable means of gaining knowledge: pratyakṇa (perception), anumāṇa (inference), Upamāṣa (comparison and analogy) and shabda (word, testimony of past or present reliable experts).

In its metaphysics, the Nyāya school is closer to the Vaisheshika school than the others. It holds that human suffering results from mistakes/defects produced by activity under wrong knowledge (notions and ignorance). Moksha (liberation), it states, is gained through right knowledge. This premise led Nyāya to concern itself with epistemology, that is, the reliable means to gain correct knowledge and to remove wrong notions. False knowledge is not merely ignorance to Naiyayikas; it includes delusion. Correct knowledge is discovering and overcoming one's delusions, and understanding the true nature of the soul, self and reality. The Nyāya Sūtras 1.1.3–1.1.9 say:

Perception, Inference, Comparison and Word – these are the means of right knowledge.

Perception is that knowledge which arises from the contact of a sense with its object and which is determinate, unnameable and non-erratic.

Inference is that knowledge which is preceded by perception, and is of three kinds: a priori, a posteriori, and commonly seen.

Comparison is the knowledge of a thing through its similarity to another thing previously well known.

Word is the instructive assertion of a reliable person.

It [knowledge] is of two kinds: that which is seen, and that which is not seen.

Soul, body, senses, objects of senses, intellect, mind, activity, fault, transmigration, fruit, suffering and release – are the objects of right knowledge.

2.7 Mīmāṃsā Philosophy

The Mīmāṃsā school is a form of philosophical realism. Key texts of the Mīmāṃsā school are the Purva Mimamsa Sutras of Jaimini. The classical Mīmāṃsā school is sometimes referred to as Pūrva Mīmāṃsā or Karmamīmāṃsā in reference to the first part of the Vedas.

The Mīmāṃsā school has several sub-schools defined by epistemology. The Prābhākara sub-school of Mīmāṃsā accepted five means to gaining knowledge as epistimetically reliable: pratyakṣa (perception), anumāṇa (inference), upamāṇa (comparison and analogy), arthāpatti (postulation, derivation from circumstances), and shabda (word, testimony of past or present reliable experts). The Kumārila Bhaṭṭa sub-school of Mīmāṃsā added a sixth way of knowing to its canon of reliable epistemology: anupalabdi (non-perception, negative/cognitive proof).

The metaphysics of the Mīmāṃsā school consists of both atheistic and theistic doctrines, and the school showed little interest in systematic examination of the existence of God. Rather, it held that the soul is an eternal, omnipresent, inherently active spiritual essence, then focussed on the epistemology and metaphysics of dharma. To them, dharma meant rituals and duties, not devas (gods), because devas existed only in name.

The Mīmāṃsākas held that the Vedas are "eternal authorless infallible", that Vedic vidhi (injunctions) and mantras in rituals are prescriptive karya (actions), and that the rituals are of primary importance and merit. They considered the Upanishads and other texts related to self-knowledge and spirituality to be of secondary importance, a philosophical view that the Vedanta school disagreed with.

Mīmāṃsā gave rise to the study of philology and the philosophy of language. While their deep analysis of language and linguistics influenced other schools, their views were not shared by others. Mīmāṃsākas considered the purpose and power of language was to clearly prescribe the proper, correct and right. In contrast, Vedantins extended the scope and value of language as a tool to also describe, develop and derive. Mīmāṃsākas considered orderly, law-driven, procedural life as the central purpose and noblest necessity of dharma and society, and divine (theistic) sustenance means to that end. The Mimamsa school was influential and foundational to the Vedanta school, with the difference that Mīmāṃsā developed and emphasized karmakāṇḍa (the portion of the shruti which relates to ceremonial acts and sacrificial rites, the early parts of the Vedas), while the Vedanta school developed and emphasised jñānakāṇḍa (the portion of the Vedas which relates to knowledge of monism, the latter parts of the Vedas).

2.8 Vedānta Philosophy

Vedanta was founded by Badariiyana. It is an inquiry into the nature of the Ultimate Principle (Brahman). The Vedānta school built upon the teachings of the Upanishads and Brahma Sutras from the first millennium BCE and is the most developed and best-known of the Hindu schools. The epistemology of the Vedantins included, depending on the sub-school, five or six methods as proper and reliable means of gaining any form of knowledge: pratyakṣa (perception), anumāṇa (inference), upamāṇa (comparison and analogy), arthāpatti (postulation, derivation from circumstances), anupalabdi (non-perception, negative/cognitive proof) and shabda (word, testimony of past or present reliable experts). All of these have been further categorised by each sub-school of Vedanta in terms of conditionality, completeness, confidence and possibility of error.

The emergence of the Vedanta school represented a period in which a more knowledge-centred understanding began to emerge, focusing on jnana (knowledge) driven aspects of the Vedic religion and the Upanishads. These included metaphysical concepts such as ātman and Brahman, and an emphasis on meditation, self-discipline, self-knowledge and abstract spirituality, rather than ritualism. The Upanishads were variously interpreted by ancient- and medieval-era Vedanta scholars. Consequently, the Vedanta separated into many sub-schools, ranging from theistic dualism to non-theistic monism, each interpreting the texts in its own way and producing its own series of sub-commentaries.

2.8.1 Advaita Vedanta Philosophy

Advaita literally means "not two, sole, unity". It is a sub-school of Vedanta, and asserts spiritual and universal non-dualism. Its metaphysics is a form of absolute monism, that is all ultimate reality is interconnected oneness. This is the oldest and most widely acknowledged Vedantic school. The foundational texts of this school are the Brahma Sutras and the early Upanishads from the 1st millennium BCE. Its first great consolidator was the 8th century scholar Adi Shankara, who continued the line of thought of the Upanishadic teachers, and that of his teacher's teacher Gaudapada. He wrote extensive commentaries on the major Vedantic scriptures and is celebrated as one of the major Hindu philosophers from whose doctrines the main currents of modern Indian thought are derived.

According to this school of Vedanta, all reality is Brahman, and there exists nothing whatsoever which is not Brahman. Its metaphysics includes the concept of māyā and ātman. Māyā connotes "that which exists, but is constantly changing and thus is spiritually unreal". The empirical reality is considered as always changing and therefore "transitory, incomplete, misleading and not what it appears to be". The concept of ātman is of soul within each person, each living being. Advaita Vedantins assert that ātman is same as Brahman, and this Brahman is within each human being and all life, all living beings are spiritually interconnected, and there is oneness in all of existence. They hold that dualities and misunderstanding of māyā as the spiritual reality that matters is caused by ignorance, and are the cause of sorrow, suffering. Jīvanmukti (liberation during life) can be achieved through Self-knowledge, the understanding that ātman within is same as ātman in another person and all of Brahman – the eternal, unchanging, entirety of cosmic principles and true reality.

2.8.2 Vishishtadvaita Philosophy

Ramanuja (c. 1037–1137) was the foremost proponent of the philosophy of Vishishtadvaita or qualified non-dualism. Vishishtadvaita advocated the concept of a Supreme Being with essential qualities or attributes. Vishishtadvaitins argued against the Advaitin conception of Brahman as an impersonal empty oneness. They saw Brahman as an eternal oneness, but also as the source of all creation, which was omnipresent and actively involved in existence. To them the sense of subject-object perception was illusory and a sign of ignorance. However, the individual's sense of self was not a complete illusion since it was derived from the universal beingness that is Brahman. Ramanuja saw Vishnu as a personification of Brahman.

2.8.3 Dvaita Philosophy

Dvaita refers to a theistic sub-school in Vedanta tradition of Hindu philosophy. Also called as Tattvavāda and Bimbapratibimbavāda, the Dvaita sub-school was founded by the 13th-century scholar Madhvacharya. The Dvaita Vedanta school believes that God (Vishnu, supreme soul) and the individual souls (jīvātman) exist as independent realities, and these are distinct.

Dvaita Vedanta is a dualistic interpretation of the Vedas, espouses dualism by theorising the existence of two separate realities. The first and the only independent reality, states the Dvaita school, is that of Vishnu or Brahman. Vishnu is the supreme Self, in a manner similar to monotheistic God in other major religions. The distinguishing factor of Dvaita philosophy, as opposed to monistic Advaita Vedanta, is that God takes on a personal role and is seen as a real eternal entity that governs and controls the universe. Like Vishishtadvaita Vedanta sub-school, Dvaita philosophy also embraced Vaishnavism, with the metaphysical concept of Brahman in the Vedas identified with Vishnu and the one and only Supreme Being. However, unlike Vishishtadvaita which envisions ultimate qualified nondualism, the dualism of Dvaita was permanent. Salvation, in Dvaita, is achievable only through the grace of God Vishnu.

2.8.4 Dvaitādvaita (Bhedabheda) Philosophy

Dvaitādvaita was proposed by Nimbarka, a 13th-century Vaishnava Philosopher from the Andhra region. According to this philosophy there are three categories of existence: Brahman, soul, and matter. Soul and matter are different from Brahman in that they have attributes and capacities different from Brahman. Brahman exists independently, while soul and matter are dependent. Thus, soul and matter have an existence that is separate yet dependent. Further, Brahman is a controller, the soul is the enjoyer, and matter the thing enjoyed. Also, the highest object of worship is Krishna and his consort Radha, attended by thousands of gopis; of the Vrindavan; and devotion consists in self-surrender.

2.8.5 Shuddhādvaita

Shuddhādvaita is the "purely non-dual" philosophy propounded by Vallabha Acharya (1479–1531). The founding philosopher was also the guru of the Vallabha sampradaya ("tradition of Vallabha") or Puṣṭimarga, a Vaishnava tradition focused on the worship of Krishna. Vallabhacharya enunciates that Brahman has created the world without connection with any external agency such as Māyā (which itself is His power) and manifests Himself through the world. That is why Shuddhadvaita is known as 'Unmodified transformation' or 'Avikṛta Pariṇāmavāda'. Brahman or Ishvara desired to become many, and he became the multitude of individual souls and the world. The Jagat or Maya is not false or illusionary, the physical material world is. Vallabha recognises Brahman as the whole and the individual as a 'part' (but devoid of bliss) like sparks and fire.

2.8.6 Achintya Bheda Abheda

Chaitanya Mahaprabhu (1486–1534), stated that the soul or energy of God is both distinct and non-distinct from God, whom he identified as Krishna, Govinda, and that this, although unthinkable, may be experienced through a process of loving devotion (bhakti). He followed the Dvaita concept of Madhvacharya. This philosophy of "inconceivable oneness and difference".

2.9. Nāstika Classification of Schools

2.9.1 Charvaka Philosophy

The Charvaka school is one of the nāstika or "heterodox" philosophies. It rejects supernaturalism, emphasises materialism and philosophical scepticism, holding empiricism, perception and conditional inference as the proper source of knowledge. Charvaka is an atheistic school of thought. It holds that there is neither afterlife nor rebirth, all existence is mere combination of atoms and substances, feelings and mind are an epiphenomenon, and free will exists.

Brihaspati is sometimes referred to as the founder of Charvaka (also called Lokayata) philosophy. Much of the primary literature of Charvaka, the Barhaspatya sutras (ca. 600 BCE), however, are missing or lost. Its theories and development has been compiled from historic secondary literature such as those found in the shastras, sutras and the Indian epic poetry as well as from the texts of Buddhism and from Jain literature. The Tattvôpaplava-siṁha by the sceptic philosopher Jayarāśi Bhaṭṭa has been considered by many scholars to be an unorthodox Charvaka text.

One of the widely studied principles of Charvaka philosophy was its rejection of inference as a means to establish valid, universal knowledge, and metaphysical truths. In other words, the Charvaka epistemology states that whenever one infers a truth from a set of observations or truths, one must acknowledge doubt; inferred knowledge is conditional.

2.9.2 Shaivism Philosophy

Early history of Shaivism is difficult to determine. However, the Śvetāśvatara Upanishad (400 – 200 BCE) is considered to be the earliest textual exposition of a systematic philosophy of Shaivism. Shaivism is represented by various philosophical schools, including non-dualist (abheda), dualist (bheda), and non-dualist-with-dualist (bhedābheda) perspectives. Vidyaranya in his works mentions three major schools of Shaiva thought—Pashupata Shaivism, Shaiva Siddhanta and Pratyabhijña (Kashmir Shaivism).

2.9.2.1 Pāshupata Shaivism

Pāshupata Shaivism (Pāśupata, "of Paśupati") is the oldest of the major Shaiva schools. The philosophy of Pashupata sect was systematised by Lakulish in the 2nd century CE. Paśu in Paśupati refers to the effect (or created world), the word designates that which is dependent on something ulterior. Whereas, Pati means the cause (or principium), the word designates the Lord, who is the cause of the universe, the pati, or the ruler. Pashupatas disapproved of Vaishnava theology, known for its doctrine servitude of souls to the Supreme Being, on the grounds that dependence upon anything could not be the means of cessation of pain and other desired ends. They recognised that those depending upon another and longing for independence will not be emancipated because they still depend upon something other than themselves. According to Pāshupatas, soul possesses the attributes of the Supreme Deity when it becomes liberated from the 'germ of every pain'.

Pāshupatas divided the created world into the insentient and the sentient. The insentient was the unconscious and thus dependent on the sentient or conscious. The insentient was further divided into effects and causes. The effects were of ten kinds: the earth, four elements and their qualities, colour etc. The causes were of thirteen kinds, the five organs of cognition, the five organs of action, the three internal organs, intellect, the ego principle and the cognising principle. These insentient causes were held responsible for the illusive identification of Self with non-Self. Salvation in Pāshupata involved the union of the soul with God through the intellect.

2.9.2.2 Shaiva Siddhanta

Considered normative Tantric Shaivism, Shaiva Siddhanta provides the normative rites, cosmology and theological categories of Tantric Shaivism. Being a dualistic philosophy, the goal of Shaiva Siddhanta is to become an ontologically distinct Shiva (through Shiva's grace). This tradition later merged with the Tamil Shaiva movement and expression of concepts of Shaiva Siddhanta can be seen in the bhakti poetry of the Nayanars.

2.9.2.3 Kashmir Shaivism

Kashmir Shaivism arose during the eighth or ninth century CE in Kashmir and made significant strides, both philosophical and theological, until the end of the twelfth century CE. It is categorised by various scholars as monistic idealism (absolute idealism, theistic monism, realistic idealism, transcendental physicalism or concrete monism). It is a school of Shaivism consisting of Trika and its philosophical articulation Pratyabhijña.

Even though, both Kashmir Shaivism and Advaita Vedanta are non-dual philosophies which give primacy to Universal Consciousness (Chit or Brahman), in Kashmir Shaivisim, as opposed to Advaita, all things are a manifestation of this Consciousness. This implies that from the point of view of Kashmir Shaivisim, the phenomenal world (Shakti) is real, and it exists and has its being in Consciousness (Chit). Whereas, Advaita holds that Brahman is the reality (pure consciousness) and it is inactive (nishkriya) and the phenomenal world is an appearance (māyā). The objective of human life, according to Kashmir Shaivism, is to merge in Shiva or Universal Consciousness, or to realise one's already existing identity with Shiva, by means of wisdom, yoga and grace.

In some of the chapters to follow, we shall discuss six āstika (orthodox) schools of Hindu philosophy and also Shaivism.

Chapter - 3

Samkhya Philosophy

3.1 Introduction to Samkhya Philosophy

Sāṃkhya (or sāṅkhya, also transliterated as samkhya and sankhya, respectively, is a Sanskrit word that, depending on the context, means 'to reckon, count, enumerate, calculate, deliberate, reason, reasoning by numeric enumeration, relating to number, rational'. In the context of ancient Indian philosophies, Samkhya refers to the philosophical school in Hinduism based on systematic enumeration and rational examination.

The Samkhya is the oldest school of Hindu Philosophy, for it is the first attempt to harmonise the philosophy of the Vedas through reason. The unique position of the Samkhya in the history of thought is the fact that it expounds by careful reflection the first systematic account of the process of cosmic evolution which attempts to comprehend the universe as a sum total of twenty-five categories. This exposition is no mere metaphysical speculation, but is a purely logical account based on the scientific principles of conservation, transformation and dissipation of energy.

The Samkhya is held to be the most notable attempt in the realm of pure philosophy. The term Samkhya is derived from the word Samkhya, "number." This name is used because the Samkhya enumerates the principles of cosmic evolution by rational analysis; and in the philosophical sense, the term is used because this system teaches discriminative knowledge which enables us to distinguish between Spirit and Matter.

The founder of the Samkhya was Kapila. Very little is known of this renowned sage and there is much controversy as to his actual date; however, the weight of authority places him in the sixth century BC. According to history, his father's name was Kardama, and his mother's name was Devahuti. His father was a Rishi (inspired sage), but Kapila was believed to have learned the rudiments of philosophy and the nature of the soul from his mother. A likeness of Kapila is carved in the cave temple of Anuradhapura in Ceylon. The latter part of his life was passed on an island called Sagara, situated in the mouth of the Ganges River ninety miles from

Calcutta (Kolkata). Each year on the last day- of the Hindu month Magha (January-February), thousands of devotees visit the place where Kapila meditated and gave the fruits of his meditations to his disciples. In this manner the tradition of his life is still kept. Throughout India the memory of Kapila is worshipped as a Great Sage and Philosopher.

As an astika school, though Samkhya believes in the authority of the Vedas yet the popular Samkhya is very much silent about the existence of God. It is rather known as a dualistic system in Indian philosophical tradition, which accepts two ultimate principles, i.e. prakriti and purusha. The Samkhya system is called Nir-Isvara (Godless) Samkhya. It is atheistical. The Samkhyas do not believe in Isvara. They do not accept Isvara (God). The creation produced by Prakriti has an existence of its own, independent of all connection with the particular Purusha to which it is united. So the Samkhyas say that there is no need for an intelligent Creator of the world, or even of any superintending power.

This is a mistake; according to the Vedanta, Prakriti is always under the control of the Lord. It cannot do anything by itself. The Lord gazes at Prakriti. Then alone it is put in motion, and it begins to create. Prakriti is non-intelligent. An intelligent Creator alone can have a thought-out plan for the universe. Prakriti is only a helper (Sahakari). This is the theory of Vedanta.

The Samkhya adopts the theory of evolution and involution. The cause and effect are the undeveloped and developed states of one and the same substance. There is no such thing as total destruction. In destruction, the effect is involved into its cause. That is all.

3.2 Purpose of Samkhya Philosophy

The purpose of the Samkhya is to provide that knowledge which will forever remove the cause of misery and thereby release the soul from its bondage. According to this system misery is threefold: (i) adhyatmika, i.e., proceeding from intrinsic causes, such as disorders of the body and mind; (ii) adhibhautika, i.e., proceeding from extrinsic causes, such as other men, beasts, birds, or inanimate objects; and (iii) adhidaivika, i.e., proceeding from supernatural causes, such as the influence of the atmosphere or planets. It is undisputed that misery constitutes the real torment of the soul. The problem arises, how to terminate misery? If known means were sufficient, there would be no need to seek further, but all known means fail to be absolute. Medicine cannot cure forever, no more than a banquet can banish hunger for all time; therefore, it is necessary to search for that knowledge which will forever terminate misery. The Samkhya argues that if misery is an attribute of the soul, there is no need to seek further, but it is universally agreed that the soul is free and devoid of all suffering; therefore, misery must belong to the body. The misery of the soul is said to be caused by its intimate association with the body. When the true nature of the soul is understood, bondage will no longer exist, and the soul will be forever free from all suffering. Bondage is claimed to be purely an illusion caused by incorrect knowledge of the true nature of things. The release and bondage of the soul depend solely upon knowledge and ignorance; therefore, it is believed that discriminative knowledge will forever release the soul from all misery.

3.3 Philosophy of Samkhya

For the purpose of study, the Samkhya postulates two ultimate realities, (i) Spirit (Purusha) and (ii) Matter (Prakrti), to account for all experience. They exist as logical principles and serve as the source out of which all things evolve. The Samkhya views the evolution of matter from its cosmic cause as a process of unfolding, a projection of potentialities into realities according to fixed laws that can be understood and controlled by man. This chain of causation is based on the fundamental tenet of the Samkhya that creation is impassible, for something cannot come out of nothing; change implies something to change; whatever is, always is, and whatever is not, never is.

For the sake of analysis, the Samkhya divides the process of cosmic evolution into twenty-five categories which are classified under four headings:

1. That which is neither produced nor produces.
2. That which is not produced but produces.
3. Those which are produced and do produce.
4. Those which are produced and do not produce.

- The first is called Purusha (Cosmic Spirit). It is the unevolved which does not evolve, the uncaused which is not the cause of any new mode of being.
- The second is called Prakriti (Cosmic Substance). It is the unevolved which does evolve, the uncaused cause of phenomenal existence.
- The third group consists of seven categories called evolvents, which are caused and serve as causes for new modes of being. They are Mahat (Cosmic Intelligence), Ahamkara (Individuating Principle) and five Tanmatras (Subtle Elements).

- The fourth group consists of sixteen categories called evolutes which are caused, but do not serve as causes for new modes of being. They are Manas (Cosmic Mind), five Jiianendriyas (Abstract Knowing-Senses), five Karmendriyas (Abstract Working-Senses), and five Mahabhutas (Sense Particulars).

Samkhya philosophy occupies a key position in the Indian philosophical heritage. The beginnings of the Samkhya system of thought may be discovered in some of the early Upanishads. It has tried to link up the various strands of thought that can be found in the Mahabharata, the Gita, the Puranas and the Caraka-Samhita and also in other relevant Buddhist and Pancaratra texts, which may lead to the conclusion that the Samkhya system of thought must have passed through various stages of development, which shaped and reshaped it at various times both theistically and atheistically.

3.4 25 Tattvas (elements) in Samkhya Philosophy

Samkhya (sometimes Sankhya, often translated as "enumeration" or "perfect declaration") is one of the schools of classical Indian Philosophy – and possibly, one of the earliest. It is thought to have developed from dualist teachings in the Upanishads. It has been a strong influence in the development of Yoga and it is possible that it was studied by the Buddha. Patanjali's Yoga Sutras also shows traces of Samkhya influences. The most well-known Samkhya text is the Samkhya-karika of Isvarakrisna.

Samkhya is characterised by a reliance on traditional doctrine and a form of rational enquiry into the nature of reality and human existence. Samkhya is often presented as nontheistic, as opposed to Yoga, which is theistic.

3.4.1 Purusha and Prakriti

The Samkhya doctrine is basically dualist, regarding the universe as consisting of two eternal and distinct realities – Purusha (Consciousness) and Prakriti (material existence). Purusha is sometimes referred to as the "Transcendental Self" or Eternal Witness. It is absolute, independent, and – above all experience – unknowable. Prakriti – "The Seen" – is matter – unconscious and transient; composed of the three gunas – that which multiplies.

Everything in the world – all physical events, all experiences – comes from Prakriti. This includes self-consciousness, intellectual activity and emotions. Everything in the universe (with the exception of Purusha) is composed of varying degrees of the three "primary strands" – the Gunas: sattva, rajas and tamas. Sattva is illuminating, Rajas is activating, and Tamas imposes limitations and restrictions. These three qualities are continually transforming, and are inseparable from each other.

Purusha (as "Pure Consciousness") cannot create anything of its own accord. It is only when Purusha 'witnesses' Prakriti that the world comes into being and things are presented to consciousness. The union (samyoga) of these two principles is mutually beneficial: Purusha is given something to "see" and Prakriti gains the illumination of consciousness.

Purusha is the witness-consciousness. It is absolute, independent, free, imperceptible, unknowable through other agencies, above any experience by mind or senses and beyond any words or explanations. It remains pure, "nonattributive consciousness". No appellations can qualify purusha, nor can it substantialised or objectified. Unmanifest prakriti is infinite, inactive, and unconscious, and consists of an equilibrium of the three guṇas ('qualities, innate tendencies'), namely sattva, rajas, and tamas. When prakriti comes into contact with Purusha this equilibrium is disturbed, and Prakriti becomes manifest, evolving twenty-three tattvas, namely intellect (buddhi, mahat), ego (ahamkara) mind (manas); the five sensory capacities; the five action capacities; and the five "subtle elements": "modes of sensory content" (tanmatras), from which the five "gross elements": "forms of perceptual objects" emerge, giving rise to the manifestation of sensory experience and cognition.

The Samkhyas constantly hammer on the theme that no pain, no suffering, no bondage ever belongs to Purusha. Purusha is eternally free, never bound, never released. And because they thoroughly reveal the nature of Purusha, their word, Samkhya doctrine is described as the Samkhya, thorough revealer. Purusha is considered as the conscious principle, a passive enjoyer (bhokta) and the prakriti is the enjoyed (bhogya). Samkhya believes that the purusha cannot be regarded as the source of inanimate world, because an intelligent principle cannot transform itself into the unconscious world. It is a pluralistic spiritualism, atheistic realism and uncompromising dualism.

Jiva ('a living being') is that state in which purusha is bonded to prakriti. Human experience is an interplay of purusha-prakriti, purusha being conscious of the various combinations of cognitive activities. The end of the bondage of Purusha to prakriti is called liberation or kaivalya by the Samkhya school.

3.4.2 The Tattvas

In the Samkhya doctrine there are 25 Tattvas:

1. Purusha (Transcendental Self)

2. The uncreated (unmanifest) Prakriti (primordial nature)
3. Mahat/Buddhi (intellect)
4. Ahamkara (ego, consciousness of self)
5. Manas (mind)

6-10. The five sense-organs

11-15. The five motor-organs

16-20. The five subtle elements

21-25. The five gross elements

Tattvas 3-25 evolve from primordial nature. All of the Tattvas account for the totality of the universe as a whole, and of each individual human being.

3.4.3 The Antahkarana and the Powers

3.4.3.1 Buddhi

Buddhi is the principle of reflective discrimination. It is through the activity of Buddhi that all things are known, classified or understood. One might say that it is Buddhi's "task" to distinguish between Purusha and Prakriti.

3.4.3.2 The Bhavas

In Samkhya, the Buddhi is divided into bhavas – states of being, which are illustrative of particular modes of action. The bhavas are sattvic or tamasic: thus Virtue (dharma), Knowledge (jnana), Nonattachment (viraga) and Power (aishvarya) are sattvic bhavas, and Non-virtue (adharma), Ignorance (Ajnana), Attachment (raga) and Weakness (anaishvarya) are tamasic bhavas. These states pervade one's sense of selfhood, and shape the individual's perception of the world, and the kinds of actions that one pursues as a result. For example, a predominance of the raga bhava would result in the constant pursuit of personal desires, whilst a predominance of viraga bhava would result in non-attachment and contentment. Of the Sattvic bhavas, it is Discriminative Knowledge (jnana) which is considered to be that which leads to liberation. Whilst notions of bondage and liberation are concepts of the intellect, the jnana of nonattachment to the body, the sense-experiences, or the mind, the individual becomes gradually aware of the knowledge of the True Self (i.e. the Purusha) and is freed from confusion and false identifications.

3.4.3.3 Ahamkara

Ahamkara ("I"-maker) is the sense of subjective selfhood – that which interprets the activities of the three gunas in a way that understands the "I" as the agent or origin of an experience, i.e. "this is my experience." From the Ahamkara springs the desire to experience the five sense-objects. From the establishment of Ahamkara, its further evolution takes two forms – the production of Manas and the Tanmatras. Out of Manas is formed the five Buddhindriyas; the sense-powers of hearing, touching, seeing, tasting, smelling, and the five Karmendriyas; the action-powers of speaking, grasping, walking, excreting and generating. It is with these ten powers that Manas is able to gratify the desires which arise out of the Ahamkara. Also from the Ahamkara arise the five Tanmatras or qualities of subtle matter: sound, touch, form, taste and smell, which are in turn, the essences of the five Bhutas (gross) or visible elements: Space, Air, Fire, Water, Earth.

Buddhi, Ahamkara and Manas are collectively referred to as the "inner organ" – the Antahkarana. Predominately Sattvic, they determine how the world will be seen.

3.4.4 Liberation

Suffering (caused by ignorance – the ground state of the human condition) is associated with a failure to discriminate between Purusha and Prakriti. The bound self identifies itself with the body and its constituents, such as Manas and Ahamkara. Liberation occurs when one realises that one is distinct from, and not restricted to physical matter. It is the curiosity of the Purusha for experience that leads to the identification with the limitations of Prakriti and thus causes bondage. The Purusha is sometimes likened to an observer who, enchanted by a beautiful dancer, cannot take his eyes off the performer. The Samkhya-approach to Liberation involves examining how perception operates, in order to reverse the world-generating process and allow Pure Consciousness to be released from its bonds.

3.5 Theory of Causation in Samkhya

The Sāṁkhya theory of causation is known as satkāryavāda. It explains the effect exists in its material cause prior to its production. For example, curd was existing in the milk before it comes into existence. Hence, the effect is not a real beginning or a new creation. It is also named as 'parināmavāda'. By refuting this view Nyāyikas said that effect is a new creation, otherwise why we say this is the effect and that was the cause.

The following arguments uphold by Sāmkhya to support the theory satkāryavāda:

(i) If the effect does not exist in the cause prior to its operation, none can bring into existence out of the cause. For example, blue cannot be turned into yellow even by a thousand artists. The effect is related to its cause. Effect is nothing but the manifestation of the cause, as oil will be produced from oil seeds only. Thus, effect pre-exists in the material cause in a latent or un-manifest condition.

(ii) A particular effect can be produced out of a particular material cause. A mud jar can be produced out of clay only; cloth can be produced out of threads only. Thus, it proves that the effects are existing in the cause in a latent condition.

(iii) If the effect is not related to its cause, then every effect would arise from every cause. But this does not happen. Every effect does not arise from every cause. For example, butter cannot be produced from sands, waters, or oils. It is produced from milk only.

(iv) The effect pre-exists in the cause since it can be produced by a potent cause only. A potent cause has causal energy to produce a particular effect. The causal energy in this case is inferred from the perception of the effect. If the effect is not existent in the cause, then the causal energy can't be related to it. If the causal energy is unrelated to the effect, then any effect will arise from any cause. Hence, the effect must be pre-existent in its potent cause only.

(v) The effect pre-exists in the cause since it is identical in nature with its cause. The effect is not different from the cause. The cause is existent and therefore, the effect cannot be nonexistent. Hence, effect inheres in its cause. This is so because there is no identity between entity and non-entity.

There cannot be any production of something out of nothing. That which is not, cannot be developed into that which is. The production of what does not already exist potentially is impossible like a horn on a man, because there must, of necessity, be a material out of which a product is developed, and because everything cannot occur everywhere at all times, and also because anything possible must be produced from something competent to produce it.

That which does not exist cannot be brought into existence by an agent. It would be useless to grind groundnut, unless the oil existed in it. The same force applied to sand or orange would not express groundnut oil. The manifestation of the oil is a proof that it was contained in the groundnut and consequently, a proof of the existence of the source from which it is derived. The effect truly exists beforehand in its cause. This is one of the central features of the Samkhya system of philosophy. Cause is a substance in which the effect subsists in a latent form. Just as the whole tree exists in a latent or dormant state in the seed, so also the whole world exists in a latent state in Prakriti, the Avyakta (unevolved), or the Avyakrita (undifferentiated). The effect is of the same nature as the cause. The effect or product is not different from the material of which it is composed.

3.6 The Samkhya Karika

Though Isvarakrsna's Sarhkhya Karika is the first available systematic popular text of Samkhya, still Isvarakrsna is not the founder of this system. Tradition accepts Kapila as the founder of this system and his Samkhya-Sutra as the original text. There is a vast chronological gap between Kapila's original Samkhya and Isvarakrsna's Samkhya-Karika. It is generally agreed that Kapila flourished around the 8th century BC and he must have composed Samkhya-Sutra which is unfortunately not available at present. With the Samkhya Karika we emerge from the region of conjecture and doubt, and arrive at the classic statement of the doctrine of the Samkhya philosophy. It is admittedly by far the most brilliant account of the system.

According to the Karika, the end of the Samkhya philosophy is to discover the means of removing the three-fold misery of the world, that is, the sorrows brought on us by ourselves, those brought by others, and those inflicted by fate. The removal of misery cannot be achieved either empirically or by devotion to religious practices. Good fortune on earth is perishable, and moreover it is not positive pleasure but freedom from misery that the wise man seeks. The practice of religion, again, is insufficient; the performance of sacrifice not only involves the slaying of victims which offends against the rule of non-injury, but the rewards of such actions are transitory, and the performer must fall back again, after the enjoyment of the fruit of his deeds in yonder world, into an earthly existence : moreover, the result of such actions leads to prove not to the freedom from pain which is the ideal of the sage. The statement of the object of the system is of importance in that it brings out clearly the fundamental pre-suppositions on which the Samkhya, like the other philosophical systems, rests. It is assumed as self-evident that the world is a condition of misery, that the soul is subject to transmigration, and that there is some degree of truth at least in the Vedic tradition. Whatever the origin of the doctrines in question, the first two assumptions are of universal validity for all schools of Indian thought, with and the Samkhya makes no effort to establish their validity. The third assumption is of much less importance from the philosophical point of view, for unlike the first two it has no real effect on the substance of the Samkhya philosophy.

Following are some of the extracts from Samkhya karika:

Du:kha traya abhighātāj jijñāsā thad abhighātake hetho

Drishti sā apārthā chenna aikāntha atyantha atho abhāvāth (1)

Meaning: Investigating the triad of interactive stresses shows that such interactive modes of stresses exist but it would not have been detectable, had it not been for the existence of the synchronised - perpetual - dynamic - unmanifest state of existence (of the substratum).

Drishtamm anumānam āptavacanam ca sarva pramana siddhatvāt
Trividham pramānamam ishtam Prameya iddhi: pramānād dhi (4)

Meaning: Siddhi or conclusive holistic proof is arrived at by a process of logical and theoretical analysis of information from observations, inferences and axiomatic principles. When such holistic conclusions are further condensed by using the three-fold analytical process with appropriate rationale and theory, it is established as a conclusive axiomatic theorem.

Sāmānya atha asthu drishtād atīndriyānām pratītir
Anumānāt tasmād api ca siddham paroksham apt agamāt siddham (6)

Meaning: And in the case of phenomenon that is imperceptible, mobile, expansive and hence undetectable, inferential method using holistic, deductive, logical, verification technique to mentally experience phenomenon, is known as Siddhi.

Asad karanād upādāna grahanāth sarva sambhava
Abhavat śaktasya śakya aranāt kārana bhava ca satkāryam (9)

Meaning: It is an error of logic to accept that continuous or all possible modes of action (manifestation) are possible without a physical cause; the ability to act in all possible ways must be due to the existence of a cause, therefore it becomes an axiomatic rule.

Explanation: Theoretically it is impossible to accept all modes of manifestation or events are possible without a cause. The most rigorous logic compels the acceptance of fundamental substratum if observable phenomena exist. Since it is an axiomatic fact that phenomena exists it automatically proves that a substratum of space must exist even if it is not detectable. This principle of logical verification by axiomatic concepts does not exist in Physics and hence space as a vacuous void is accepted as a reality. It means there is a hidden cause in every effect.

Mathematical description of internal field force as a spectrum

Sutra 23 of this book states the following:

Adhyavasāyo buddhir dharmo jñānam virāg eaiśvaryam
ātvikam etad rupam hāmasam asmad viparyastam (23)

Meaning: Defined by axiomatic process, any constant and continuing stress as the potential in the simultaneous or static state, undergoes a phase change, acceleration is produced by expansion of the volumetric form. The reverse process when acceleration reduces and undergoes a phase change it attains the compressed state of continuing stress as a potential in the static state. orders.

Explanation: An extraordinary theorem that defines through axiomatic rules that only a constant and continuing state of stress creates the potential state. The change from that state through expansion creates the acceleration of those stresses into an increasing volumetric form. When this expanded volumetric form is compressed by the same stresses acting in the reverse, it compresses and when that is continued and becomes constant it becomes a potential in the simultaneous state of compression. In other words change in the state of stresses creates the potential or accelerative states as a change in the volumetric form as either in compression or in expansion mode.

Sutra 24 of this book states the following:

Abhimāno ahankārah tasmād dvividhah pravartate rāg
Ekādaśakas ca ganas tanmātrah pañcakaścaiva (24)

Meaning: Self-potential, as compressed stresses in the simultaneous state and self-action, as the expansion due to accelerating stresses, form the dual mode of initiating an oscillatory state that creates the spectrum of stresses forming the field force, which accelerate and decelerate as an alternating wave form. Since the stresses are in the simultaneous state, forming the self-potential, only through calculations, by using the axiomatic Dharmic law, the value of the self-potential can be arrived at as eleven orders thus leaving five orders forming each set, from the sixteen orders.

Explanation: This theorem defines the spectrum of stresses radiated in the expanding mode referred to in Sutra 23. This is an axiomatic derivation of the electromagnetic field force in space. The sixteen orders of stress levels released (Sutra 23) in the expanding form must polarise into two sets of 8 orders in each alternating phase of compression and expansion. Since space is volumetric then each volumetric form will take 3 orders of stress levels and therefore in the expanding phase it will add up to 8+3=11 and in the compressive phase reduce to 8-3 = 5. Therefore, the expanding phase will consist of eleven orders of stress levels creating the acceleration and reduce to 5 orders of stress levels in the compressive phase. In Physics, the eleven orders correspond to the electric field force as permittivity and the five orders as the magnetic field force as permeability.

Sarvam pratyapa bhoga yasmāt purushasya sādhayati buddhih
saiva ca viśin ishti punah pradhān purushāntaram sūkshamam (37)

Meaning: A comprehensive and extraordinary use can be made in the following way. The potential of the Purusha can be attained from the minute coherent state hidden inside the Purusha by repeated precisely triggered inputs to initiate the primary interactions.

Explanation: This theorem is an extraordinary derivation that describes the process of extracting energy from space by triggering input of energy to create primary or large-scale interactions that would yield a large amount of energy that could be used. It is a process that is similar to nuclear fission but this is applies to unrestrained space.(The Rigveda's first shloka contains this theorem with 25-digit numerical proof)

Purusha artha hetu kam idam nimitta naim-ittika prasangena
Prakrater vibhut vayogān natavad vyavatithishtathe lingam(42)

Meaning: The synchronised and coherent state of the nuclear core forms the target potential to attract the oscillatory interactions to synchronise and superposition itself circumferentially, simultaneously, similar to the movements in a dance, which increases and strengthens resonant state of the interactions.

Explanation: This theorem defines the process of acquiring a coherent state as being due to the state of nucleus, which creates the potential to draw inward or attract the oscillatory interactive states to adhere to the surface circumferentially in a harmonic and resonant state that exchanges its activity to form and be absorbed by the nucleary passive or static state. The nucleus, though formed by absorbing the interactive states, because it attains a coherent state by absorbing the activities, it creates a low potential or unitary count state towards which the active states get drawn to it and gets absorbed.

Purusha tatra jarā marana kritam prāpnoti cetanam purushah
lingasya vini vritheh tasmād duhkham svabhāven (55)

Meaning: Therefore, the interactive process of decaying and dying interactive stresses creates the dynamic state of the Purusha at the nuclear core through absorption of stresses. The diminishing vorticular interactive activity by the process of super positioning continues until the minimised interactions is absorbed to form the coherent state through the self, similar interactive mode of action.

Explanation: The principle of the formation of the nuclear core is a self-similar process of merging by absorption. As the interactive stresses diminish, decay and die out, the dwindling counts are absorbed at the boundary of the nuclear core to form a coherent state by super-positioning of the decaying quanta through an absorption process following the rules of self-similar merging of stresses. The decreasing interactive stress count increases in turn the inflow or gravitational acceleration towards the "static" core. Hence gravitation is ubiquitous.

Iti esha prakrithi kritho mahad ādi viśeshabhūta paryantah
prati purusha vimokshān arth svārth iva parārth ārambhah (56)

Meaning: The interactive oscillatory activity is initiated and perpetuated from the intense fundamental activity at the source to the final coherent superposed massive state at the isolated the nuclear boundary where the self-potential balances with the reactive potential to initiate the cyclic activity.

Explanation: Referring to sutra 55, the process of how the nuclear region is isolated and yet the interactions continue as an oscillatory interaction. The intense force from the boundary is directed towards the nuclear core and its reaction initiates the cyclic process from the start again. The oscillation starting from the boundary as an intense inward going action towards the nucleus is drawn towards it by its self-potential which isolates it but the rebounding reaction initiates the cycle from the starting point again.

3.7 Samkhya Philosophy in Mahabharata

The Mahabharata appears to have attached the greatest importance to Samkhya system. Critics are of the opinion that the matters, relating to Samkhya, are far more elaborate than those relating to other systems. The epic mentions several Samkhyacharyas, e.g. Jaigisavya, Asita, Devala, Yajnavalkya, Asuri, Panchasikha, Kapila etc. Of them, Yajnavalkya has been accorded the most exalted position and his teaching has been adumbrated in some detail. Panchasikha has been stated to have taken great pains to disseminate the knowledge of Samkhya through a succession of disciples. Samkhya has been proclaimed as the repository of all kinds of salutary knowledge enshrined in the Vedas, Puranas, and Yoga etc.

The elements of Samkhya are scattered in the epic. As regards padarthas of Samkhya, the epic mentions eightfold prakriti and sixteen vikriti. Prakriti comprises avyakta, mahat, ahamkara, Prithvi, vayu, akasa, aap and jyoti. Here the mulaprakrti and its vikritis, mahat etc. are called by the common name prakriti. Vikriti comprises the five sensory organs, five motor organs, five subtle elements as well as the mind. Critic says, the Samkhya order of evolution has been mentioned in the epic. Over and above the aforesaid 24 tattvas, admitted in Samkhya, twenty-fifth one has been added; that is purusha. One vital difference between Samkhya philosophy, specially, Classical Samkhya and the Mahabharata is that while God has no place in the former, the latter has accepted God as the twenty-sixth tattva over and above all others. All this may indicate that it was a period when reflection was very busy on the Samkhya problems.

3.8 Samkhya Philosophy in Bhagavad Gita

Bhagavad-Gita, the most sacred book of Hindu religion contains considerable Samkhya materials. Chapter-II of Bhagavad-Gita is known as Samkhya-Yoga, chapter-XIII is designated as prakriti-purusha-viveka-yoga. In the Gita, the word 'Samkhya' has been used in many contexts, but it can be noticed, nowhere it has been used in the sense of Kapila's Samkhya or any other form of Samkhya. There is a reference of the word 'Samkhya' in the second chapter of the Gita, but here, it cannot be interpreted in any manner except "pursuit of true knowledge". In other words, in this context, the word Samkhya is clearly used in the sense of the path of philosophic wisdom, which leads to the realisation of the essential nature of the soul or atman. Sri Krishna's subsequent instruction of the "pursuit of true knowledge" i.e., Jnana Yoga refers actually to Karma-Yoga or the disinterested performance of duties. Samkhya-Yoga or "the path of knowledge" directly destroys ignorance which is the root cause of human misery and is, therefore, meant for those blessed seekers who are endowed with keen intellectual and volitional power for discrimination and renunciation. So, in Gita, the word 'Samkhya' is definitely used in the sense of 'wisdom', as it has been stated that the Samkhyas (wise men) follow the path of knowledge for attaining liberation from the miseries of the world.

Chapter - 4

Yoga Philosophy

4.1 Introduction to Yoga philosophy

The word Yoga is derived from Sanskrit word 'Yog', which means 'Jod' in Hindi or 'Joining' in English. This is joining of 'Jivatama' (Human soul) with 'Parmatma' (God). Through the practice of Yoga, one can have Self-realisation and achieve God. 'Yog' word became Yoga in English. Yoga philosophy is one of the six major orthodox schools of Hinduism. Ancient, medieval and most modern literature often refers to Yoga-philosophy simply as Yoga and it is only at the end of the first millennium CE that Yoga is mentioned as a separate school of thought in Indian texts, distinct from Samkhya.

The Yoga philosophy speaks about the theory and practice for the realisation of the ultimate truth concerning human being and the world. In Vedanta, yoga is understood as 'union', that is, spiritual union of the individual soul with the supreme soul. This view is not explained clearly. Patanjali, who is the founder of the Yoga System says, yoga is a spiritual effort to attain perfection through the control of sense organs, gross body, subtle mind, intellect and ego. It guides to achieve the highest wisdom through spiritual realisation. The systematic collection of ideas of Yoga-philosophy is found in the Yoga Sutras of Patanjali, which has influenced all other schools of Indian philosophy. The Yoga Sutras of Patanjali is a key text of Yoga-philosophy. The metaphysics of Yoga is built on the same dualist foundation as the Samkhya school. The universe is conceptualised as composed of two realities in the Samhkya-Yoga schools: (i) Purusha (witness-consciousness), and (ii) prakriti (mind, cognition, and matter). Jiva (a living being) is considered as a state in which purusha is bonded to prakriti in some form, in various permutations and combinations of various elements, senses, feelings, activity and mind. During the state of imbalance or ignorance, one or more constituents overwhelm the others, creating a form of bondage. The end of this bondage is called liberation, or moksha, by both the Yoga and Samkhya schools of Hinduism, and can be attained by insight and self-restraint. The ethical theory of Yoga-philosophy is based on Yamas and Niyamas, as well as elements of the Guna theory of Samkhya.

The epistemology of Yoga-philosophy, like the Sāmkhya school, relies on three of six Pramanas as the means of gaining reliable knowledge. These include Pratyakṣa (perception), (ii) Anumāṇa (inference) and Shabda (Āptavacana, word/testimony of reliable sources).

Yoga-philosophy differs from the closely related non-theistic/atheistic Samkhya school by incorporating the concept of a "personal, yet essentially inactive, deity" or "personal god" (Ishvara).

Yoga shares several central ideas with the Advaita Vedanta school of Hinduism, with the difference that Yoga philosophy is a form of experimental mysticism, while Advaita Vedanta is a form of monistic personalism. Advaita Vedanta, and other schools of Hinduism, accept, adopt and build upon many of the teachings and techniques of Yoga.

4.1.1 Yoga Practice

The origins of yoga-practice are unclear, but seems to have been developed in the first millennium BCE. Some of its earliest discussions and of proto-Samkhya ideas are found in1st millennium BCE Indian texts such as the Katha Upanishad, the Shvetashvatara Upanishad and the Maitri Upanishad.

The root of the word "Yoga" is found in hymn 5.81.1 of the Rig Veda, a dedication to rising Sun-god in the morning (Savitri), interpreted as "yoke" or "yogically controlled". Seers of the vast illumined seer yogically control their minds and their intelligence.- Rigveda 5.81.1

The Rig Veda, however, does not describe Yoga philosophy with the same meaning or context as in medieval or modern times. Early references to practices that later became part of Yoga-philosophy, are made in Brihadaranyaka Upanishad, the oldest Upanishad, where its translated as, "...having become calm and concentrated, one perceives the self (atman), within oneself. "The practice of pranayama (consciously regulating breath) is mentioned in hymn 1.5.23 of Brihadaranyaka Upanishad (c. ~ 900 BCE), and the practice of pratyahara (withdrawal of the senses) is mentioned in hymn 8.15 of Chandogya Upanishad (c. ~ 800-700 BCE). The Katha Upanishad, dated to be from about the middle of the 1st millennium BCE, in verses 2.6.6 through 2.6.13 recommends a path to Self-knowledge akin to Samkhya, and calls this path Yoga.

Only when Manas (mind) with thoughts and the five senses stand still, and when Buddhi (intellect, power to reason) does not waver, that they call the highest path. That is what one calls Yoga, the stillness of the senses, concentration of the mind. It is not thoughtless heedless sluggishness; Yoga is creation and dissolution. -Katha Upanishad, 2.6.10-1. Yoga-practice is also mentioned in foundational texts of other orthodox schools such as the Vaisheshika Sutras, Nyaya Sutras and Brahma Sutras.

4.2 Separate Darshana

Yoga as a separate school of thought is mentioned in Indian texts from the end of the 1st millennium CE. The systematic collection of ideas of the Yoga school of Hinduism is found in the Yoga Sutras of Patanjali. After its circulation in the first half of the 1st millennium CE, many Indian scholars reviewed it, then published their Bhāṣya (notes and commentary) on it, which together form a canon of texts called the Pātañjalayogaśāstra ("The Treatise on Yoga of Patañjali").

The Yoga Philosophy is closely associated with Samkhya philosophy. The Yoga presents a practical path for the realisation of the self, whereas the Samkhya emphasises the attainment of knowledge of self by means of concentration and meditation. Thus, it won't be incorrect to state that yoga is the practice and Samkhya is its theory. Srimad Bhagavad Gita says that Yoga and Samkhya are the practical and theoretical sides of the same system, respectively. Yoga-philosophy is closely related to the Samkhya school. In both, the foundational concepts include two realities: Purusha and Prakriti. The Purusha is defined as that reality which is pure consciousness and is devoid of thoughts or qualities. The Prakriti is the empirical, phenomenal reality which includes matter and also mind, sensory organs and the sense of identity (self, soul). A living being is held in both schools to be the union of matter and mind. The Yoga school differs from the Samkhya school in its views on the ontology of Purusha, on axiology and on soteriology.

4.2.1 Metaphysics of Yoga-Philosophy

The metaphysics of Yoga-philosophy, again like Samkhya school, is a form of dualism. It considers consciousness and matter, self/soul and body as two different realities. The Samkhya-Yoga system espouses dualism between consciousness and matter by postulating two "irreducible, innate and independent realities: Purusha and Prakriti". While the Prakriti is a single entity, the Samkhya-Yoga schools admit a plurality of the Purusha in this world. Unintelligent, unmanifest, uncaused, ever-active, imperceptible and eternal Prakriti is alone the final source of the world of objects. The Purusha is considered as the conscious principle, a passive enjoyer (bhokta) and the Prakriti is the enjoyed (bhogya). Samkhya-Yoga believes that the Purusha cannot be regarded as the source of inanimate world, because an intelligent principle cannot transform itself into the unconscious world. This metaphysics is a pluralistic spiritualism, a form of realism built on the foundation of dualism.

Yoga-philosophy adopts the theory of Guṇa from Samkhya. Guṇas theory states that three gunas (innate tendency, attributes) are present in different proportions in all beings, and these three are sattva guna (goodness, constructive, harmonious), rajas guna (passion, active, confused), and tamas guna (darkness, destructive, chaotic). These three are present in every being but in different proportions, and the fundamental nature and psychological dispositions of beings is a consequence of the relative proportion of these three gunas. When sattva guna Philosophy predominates an individual, the qualities of lucidity, wisdom, constructiveness, harmonious, and peacefulness manifest themselves; when rajas is predominant, attachment, craving, passion-driven activity and restlessness manifest; and when tamas predominates in an individual, ignorance, delusion, destructive behaviour, lethargy, and suffering manifests. The guṇas theory underpins the philosophy of mind in Yoga school of Hinduism.

The early scholars of Yoga philosophy, posit that the Purusha (consciousness) by its nature is sattva (constructive), while Prakriti (matter) by its nature is tamas (chaotic). They further posit that individuals at birth have Buddhi (intelligence, sattvic). As life progresses and churns this buddhi, it creates asmita or ahamkara (ego, rajasic). When ego in turn is churned by life, manas (temper, mood, tamasic) is produced. Together, buddhi, ahamkara and manas interact and constitute citta (mind) in Yoga school of Hinduism. Unrestrained modification of citta causes suffering. A way of life that empowers one to become ever more aware of one's consciousness and spirituality innate in buddhi, is the path to one's highest potential and a more serene, content, liberated life. Patanjali's Yoga sutra begins, in verse 2 of Book 1, by defining Yoga as "restraining the Citta from Vrittis."

Liberation, like many other schools, is removal of ignorance, which is achieved through discriminative discernment, knowledge and self-awareness. The Yoga Sūtras is Yoga school's treatise on how to accomplish this.

Book 3 of Patanjali's Yogasutra is dedicated to soteriological aspects of yoga philosophy. Patanjali begins by stating that all limbs of yoga are necessary foundation to reaching the state of self-awareness, freedom and liberation. He refers to the three last limbs of yoga as sanyama, in verses III.4 to III.5, and calls it the technology for "discerning principle" and mastery of citta and self-knowledge. In verse III.12, the Yogasutras state that this discerning principle then empowers one to perfect shanti (tranquility) and udita (reason) in one's mind and spirit, through intentness. This leads to one's ability to discern the difference between shabda (word), artha (meaning) and pratyaya (understanding), and this ability empowers one to compassionately comprehend the cry/speech of all living beings. Once a yogi reaches this state of sanyama, it leads to unusual powers, intuition, self-knowledge, freedoms and kaivalya, the soteriological goal of the yogi.

The benefits of Yoga philosophy of Hinduism is then summarised in verses III.46 to III.55 of Yogasutras, stating that the first 5 limbs leads to bodily perfections such as beauty, loveliness, strength and toughness; while the last 3 limbs through sanyama leads to mind and psychological perfections of perceptiveness, one's nature, mastery over egoism, discriminative knowledge of purity, self and soul. This knowledge once reached is irreversible, states Yogasutra's Book 4.

4.3 The Eight-Fold Yoga (Ashtanga Yoga) Path of Patanjali

To get rid of bondage and worldly sufferings and to remove the ignorance that is found within us, we have to conquer our sense organs, mind and even our bodily act. To do so the citta needs to be controlled. In this respect, yoga philosophy prescribes eight-fold path, given by Maharishi Patanjali, which helps to control our passions and craving for worldly pleasures.

This eight-fold path is given as follows:

(i) Yama
(ii) Niyama
(iii) Asana
(iv) Pranayama
(v) Pratyahara
(vi) Dharana
(vii) Dhyana
(viii) Samadhi

Let us discuss these points one after the other in a sequential manner.

4.3.1 Yama

It is the control of mind, body, and speech.

The five yamas are:

(a) Ahimsa: it means to accept the principle of non-violence. It upholds that not to kill or do any injuries to any living beings.

(b) **Satya:** Satya or truth says that to speak the truth and adhere to the truth even in your thinking.

(c) **Asteya:** It upholds the principle of non-stealing. This includes both not desiring on others' wealth and not stealing any goods from others.

(d) **Brahmacharya:** It is known as celibacy. Here one needs to control his/her senses towards the attachment of heavenly pleasures. It restrains somebody for not having sexual life.

(e) **Aparigraha:** It says not to accept and aspire for any sorts of unnecessary lavish things for life enjoyment like gold, diamond, etc.

All these yamas are badly required for the concentration of citta.

4.3.2 Niyama

It speaks about the rules for possessing good conduct. There are five niyamas as follows:

(a) **Sauch:** It says about cleanliness which includes both external cleaning (e.g. bath, pure diet, hair cutting and cleaning, nail cutting etc.) and internal cleaning (e.g. friendliness, empathy, happiness, smile, etc.

(b) **Santosh:** It is understood as contentment. It means to be satisfied with yourself whatever you attain or have. In other words, "what you are, you must be happy with that".

(c) **Tapa**: Tapa or penance includes the power of tolerance. To tolerate extreme and maximum cold and heat, one needs to do the hard practices. And, this is possible through tapa.

(d) **Svadhyaya:** It says one needs to study religious scriptures to develop his/her spiritual knowledge. It is considered as one of the good principles to possess good conduct.

(e) **Iswara Pranidhan:** It says always to remember God as It is the supreme authority and Almighty. One should completely surrender himself/herself to Him. This is a practice which helps for the development of good conduct upholds the yoga philosophy.

4.3.3 Asana

It is an advanced stage of yoga. It speaks about how to do various bodily postures which help to retain concentration of citta and even helps to control the body as well as mind. There are various types of asanas. Among them, a few includes, padmasana, shirsana, chakrasana, garudasana, maurasana, etc.

It is advisable to do regular practice of asanas. The reason is, it not only controls the body as such, it also keeps the body flexible, increases the immunity, and keeps the body free from diseases and make it strong and healthy. By doing regular asanas one can control the different external and internal organs of the body.

4.3.4 Pranayama

This is the fourth stage in the practice of yoga. Pranayama is understood as control of breath. It suggests that practicing pranayama helps the person to control his/her inhaling and exhaling of breath. This helps the citta to remain concentrated and focused. Through pranayama one can control one's body by doing some postures. This makes the practitioner remain healthy and good.

Pranayama has three steps. These are:

(a) Puraka

(b) Kumbhaka

(c) Recaka

The first step puraka includes to take as much air as possible. It is known as inhaling. The second step Kumbhaka means to hold the breath after inhaling as much air as possible and it tries to retain it for half of the time taken in inhaling. The third step 'recaka' states that gradually exhale the air by taking the same time that you had consumed while taking inhalation.

These three steps will gradually accelerate, so that in due course of time the practitioner may control his/her breath which helps the citta to remain concentrated and not disturbed.

4.3.5 Pratyahara

In this stage, the person should control his/her sense organs for not being attracted by the worldly objects. He/she will try to restrain the sense organs for not clinging desperately for the objects of the world. Hence, craving for an object would be ceased. By practicing this yoga, the person can keep his/her mind undisturbed from worldly objects even while living in this planet. To do this practice, it requires strong determination and repression of the senses.

4.3.6 Dharana

Our mind constantly shifts from one object to another. To keep our mind focused in one particular point the person tries to check for its frequency of shifting one object to another is called as dharana. In this stage, the person keeps his/her mind continuously engaged in one object and try to bring back the mind to that particular object if it is shifted to another object as quickly as possible. For example, a person tries to concentrate to the top of the flame of a candle, concentrating on the cap of a water bottle.

4.3.7 Dhyana

It is one step ahead to dharana. In this stage, the aspirant becomes successful to remain concentrated on an object in a longer time. Here, the aspirant realises the whole object by concentrating its one part. This step is known as meditation. It helps to realise the true nature of the citta.

4.3.8 Samadhi

The eighth and the last step of yoga is known as samadhi. This is the apex stage of yoga. In this stage, the aspirant negates the differences between subject and object, realises the true nature of the citta that how it attains the form of the object. Here, the process of concentration and the object becomes one and identical. This stage is known as cessation of modification of the citta.

Samadhi is of two kinds: Samprajnata or sabeeja (attributed samadhi) and asamprajnata or nirbija (attributeless samadhi).

4.3.8.1 Samprajnata (Conscious Samadhi)

In this form of samadhi, the aspirant becomes aware of his/her concentration. When the citta is concentrated on one object, the similar kind of object of modifications occurs in the citta. This is known as conscious samadhi or samprajnata. Concentrating on one object leads to controlling the distracted mind which often attaches to different objects of the world. Thus, it is said that focusing on one object implies dissociating from other objects. Since attachment for worldly pleasures causes suffering, the attention towards a particular object removes worldly sufferings (klesas) and passion for worldly pleasures. This helps to receive the real knowledge of an object and becomes free from law of karma or karmic influx. This (conscious samadhi) is further divided in four types. These are:

(a) Savitarka samadhi (b) Savicara samadhi

(c) Sananda samadhi (d) Sasmita samadhi

(a) Savitarka Samadhi: In this stage, the citta is concentrated on a gross object and clearly identifies it through meditation. For example, meditating to see the top of a nose.

(b) Savicara Samadhi: In this stage, the citta is concentrated on subtle object and assumes its form. For example, concentrating on tanmantras (rupa, rasa, gandha, sabda, sparsha).

(c) **Sananda Samadhi:** In this stage, the citta is concentrated on a sattvika subtler object and produces happiness and joy. It even helps in attaining bliss.

(d) **Sasmita Samadhi:** In this stage, the citta is concentrated on the ego-substance which is identified with the self. Hence, individuality becomes an existent.

4.3.8.2 Asamprajnata (Supra-conscious)

This is the highest form of samadhi. In this stage, there will be no distinction found between subject and object. The worldly attachment and sufferings disappear. Thus, it is known as attribute-less samadhi or nirbija.

Out of these eight stages of yoga, the first five are to be practiced by external means and the remaining three stages are to be practiced by internal means. This is so because the first five stages are merely preparatory to the latter three stages. The last three stages of yoga are directly connected with yoga.

4.4 Yoga Sutras of Patanjali

The eternal concepts of the Yoga Darshana have been codified in a nutshell through his Yoga Sutras. These Sutras must have been composed and then transmitted by the oral tradition since at least 1000 – 1500 BC but came into the written form much later in around 500 BC – 300 AD that is the commonly quoted date for them.

The Patanjali Yoga Sutra consists of short succinct Sutras that run together as if they were making up a garland of pearls on a string. This unique method common to the oral tradition of Yoga helps us grasp the intricacies of Yoga, this greatest science of inner experience. The Sutras were always kept short as they were intended to be learnt, memorised and chanted with reverence and understanding in order to facilitate the development of a deep sense of quiet, inner contemplation. The Yoga Sutras are an efficient tool to help the sincere Sadhaka remember and understand the subtleties of the great art and science of Yoga and were NEVER meant to be a mere instruction manual.

The Sutras are arranged in a logical form and placed into four Padas. The Padas may be said to be the main chapter-wise division of the Yoga Sutras, but we must also consider that the term Pada refers to feet and this may indicate the step-by-step approach advocated by Maharishi Patanjali.

The four Padas are:

(i) **Samadhi Pada:** This chapter is an exploration of the different aspects of Samadhi and gives us a clue about the process of introspective contemplation.

(ii) **Sadhana Pada:** This chapter lays out the path of Yoga Sadhana in the form of a Bahiranga Sadhana though the first five limbs of Ashtanga Yoga.

(iii) **Vibhuti Pada:** This chapter deals with the Antaranga Yoga and details the Siddhis or psychic accomplishments that may be attained through the practice of Samyama on various aspects of the Universe.

(iv) **Kaivalya Pada:** This chapter deals with the attainment of the highest state of Kaivalya (liberation) that ensues when we finally go beyond the Kleshas (afflictions) and Karmas (action-reaction entwinement) to ultimately become 'ONE WITH THE DIVINE'.

4.5 Four Systems of Yoga

Our own life experience reveals that people's natures are varied, according to their archetypes, differing thoughts, feelings and goals. Corresponding to this variety in human nature, there are four Yoga paths that take into account people's inclinations.

Our Self (our Atma) arises from the Supreme Self (Paramatma). The nature of the Supreme Self is bliss (Ananda), and because our inner Self is part of the Supreme, each human being is striving for this in order to be happy. Everybody, whether they believe in God or not, whether they are conscious of it or not, are ultimately striving for happiness, bliss and moksha.

We cannot find true and lasting bliss (Ananda) in the outside world. It lies within our innerself. Real and lasting bliss may only be gained through wisdom, meditation and Divine grace, and will only be achieved by one who searches and strives with a sincere heart. God's grace is everywhere and is available with all of us at all the times, just as the sun always shines even though the sky may be covered by clouds. To realise God and to be conscious of His grace, we must drive away the clouds of ignorance from our consciousness.

The four paths of Yoga lead us to this goal:

(i) **Karma Yoga:** It is the path of action. It deals with the law of cause and effect. Each action has a corresponding reaction, on one's body, mind and consciousness. The outcome of an action is dependent upon its ethical value and the intention with which it was carried out.

Karma means "action," and Karma Yoga is performing action without attachment to the outcome. It is the path of selfless service (Seva). You cease to identify with the ego and all action is seen as an offering to the Divine.

The heart is purified so, egoism, hatred, jealousy, selfishness, and similar negative qualities vanish, creating space for humility, pure love, sympathy, tolerance, and compassion.

Karma Yoga is "doing the right thing,": the process of achieving perfection in action. It means following one's dharma (true purpose) and accepting whatever comes, without expectation of payment, thanks, or recognition.

The Karma Yogi:

- Lives life with passion but remains dispassionate about the outcome.
- Is effortless and graceful in all things.
- Has a loving, friendly nature.
- Is sympathetic, compassionate, and tolerant.
- Rejoices in the success and happiness of others.
- Feels neither above nor beneath anyone.
- Speaks and acts truthfully.

Vedanta also says that Karma Yoga is the Warriors Path and the Yogi should:

- Maintain a strong healthy body.
- Bear insults and compliments, comfort and pain, equally.
- Have faith in him/herself, knowing that the Divine will always love him/her.
- Be adaptable to any situation and able to mix with everyone.
- Have a calm mind.
- Be fearless.

With Karma Yoga, all desires eventually merge into one, which is to ultimately serve the Divine.

(ii) Bhakti Yoga: It is the path of devotion and love for God and for the whole of creation - animals, as well as humans, and all of nature.

Bhakti is the yoga of devotion, ultimately to the Divine, but it can initially be a guru, your family, a friend, or anything that creates strong emotional ties.

In today's world with so much chaos and confusion, it is said that Bhakti is the easiest of the paths. It can be practiced by anyone—regardless of mental or physical abilities—and doesn't involve extensive yogic practices.

Bhakti is the path of love which removes jealousy, hatred, lust, anger, egoism, pride, and arrogance. It replaces those feelings with feelings of joy, divine ecstasy, bliss, peace, and wisdom. "Drowning in a sea of love, where everyone would love to drown." This is Bhakti—drowning in love.

Vedanta says there is a fine thread made of Pure Love (Prem), which connects your heart with the Divine. This thread is the essence of Bhakti. It has been lying dormant in your heart since the beginning of creation, hidden by layers of ignorance and suffering. However, no matter what you do or where you go, this thread, our Divine connection, can never be broken. This is what creates the deep yearning of your Soul for joy and bliss.

Bhakti is to be loved—to be intoxicated with Divine Love. It is the Unity of being in love with Love Itself. Vedanta says, put the emphasis where it belongs—on the Divine Self within each person we come across.

The Bhakti Yogi:

- Asks what is it that I long for at the deepest level of my Being?
- Is pure in thoughts, words, and actions.
- Looks for the Divinity in the ordinary.
- Honours and respects all human being, animals, plants etc.
- Purifies the heart through devotion.
- Sings, dances, chants, and listens to Divine verses.
- Surrenders by being open to everything.
- Acts as a servant, friend, or mother to the Divine in everyone.

(iii) Raja Yoga: It is also known as the "Royal Path of Yoga" or the "Eight Step Path". It is the path of self-discipline and contains, amongst other things, those Yoga techniques that are familiar to us such as Asanas, Pranayama, Meditation and Kriyas.

Raja Yoga means the "Royal Path." Just as a king maintains control over his kingdom, you must maintain control over your own "kingdom"—the vast territory of your mind.

It's the path of meditation, mantras, and techniques. The basic theme of Raja Yoga is that your perception of the Divine Self is obscured by the disturbances of the mind. If the body and mind can be made still and pure; the Self, will instantaneously shine forth.

Raja Yoga is the path most favoured by many because it can be practiced by almost everyone requiring no belief or particular faith. Raja Yoga says to believe only what you find out for yourself through direct experience.

The Raja Yogi:

- Maintains balance in sleep, diet, lifestyle, and work.
- Is in harmony with nature's rhythms.
- Is pure and nonjudgmental.
- Takes responsibility for his/her life.
- Has control over his/her emotions and remains free from worries.
- Avoids distractions.
- Trains the mind through techniques of meditation.

(iv) Jnana Yoga: It is the philosophical path. The focus of this path is to gain the ability to distinguish between reality and unreality. To attain Self-Knowledge through study, practice and experience.

Jnana Yoga is the path of knowledge or, more correctly, wisdom. It is the means to Enlightenment through the process of reason—particularly the process of discrimination between what is real and what is not real, what is true and untrue—through study and self-inquiry.

It is said to be the most difficult path because it uses the mind and intellect to go beyond themselves to finally realise you are One with the Divine. The Upanishads call it the "razor's edge," where the ego is always trying to knock us off. It requires great strength of character, will power, and intellect.

When asked a question, Ramana Maharshi, a great Indian Saint and Jnana Yogi, would often reply, "First ask yourself who is asking the question." Jnana Yoga is the study of the ancient texts and teachings of the Great Masters but, more importantly, it is the study of your own self.

The Jnana Yogi:

- Studies the spiritual texts of his/her traditions.
- Reads the words of the Great Masters.
- Asks the heart the following questions and listens to the answers without judgement or evaluation:

  Who am I?

  What do I want?

  What is my purpose?

  What am I grateful for?

  Is mindful of the surrounding world?

Listens, reflects, contemplates.

Practices discernment and detachment.

Meditates and takes time each day to be silent.

The Jnana Yogi stops worrying about what is being seen but asks, "Why am I seeing it?" Life begins to be seen as a dream.

These four Yoga paths do not represent separate paths. Each path is closely related to the other. When we think of God and are full of love for our fellow-humans and for nature, we are Bhakti Yogis. When we stand by others and help, we are Karma Yogis. When we meditate and perform yoga practices, we are Raja Yogis; and when we reflect upon the meaning of life and are explorers seeking truth and reality, we are Jnana Yogis.

The following four chapters will discuss in detail each of these paths of Yoga.

Chapter - 5

Karma Yoga Philosophy

5.1 Introduction to Karma Yoga

The Bhagavad Gita is the cream of the Vedas. It is the essence of the soul-elevating Upanishads. It is a universal scripture applicable to people of all temperaments and for all times. It is a wonderful book with sublime thoughts and practical instructions on Yoga, devotion, Vedanta and action. It is a marvellous book, profound in thought and sublime in heights of vision. It brings peace and solace to souls that are afflicted by the three fires of mortal existence, namely, afflictions caused by one's own body, those caused by beings around one, and those caused by the fate.

The Gita is divided into three sections, illustrative of the three terms of the Mahavakya of the Sama Veda—"Tat Twam Asi—That Thou Art". In accordance with this view, the first six chapters deal with the path of action or Karma Yoga, that is, the nature of "Thou". It is called the Twam-pada. The next six chapters explain the path of devotion (Bhakti Yoga), the nature of "That". This is called the Tat-pada. The concluding six chapters treat of the path of knowledge (Jnana Yoga), the nature of the middle term "Art". Hence, it is called the Asi-pada, which establishes the identity of the individual soul with the Supreme Soul.

The Gita again and again emphasises that one should cultivate an attitude of non-attachment or detachment. It urges repeatedly that an individual should live in the world like water on a lotus leaf. "He who does actions, offering them to Brahman (God) and abandoning attachment, is not tainted by sin as a lotus leaf by water". To a karma yogi, right action is a form of prayer.

According to Bhagavad Gita, Chapter 2, Verse: 47

Karmanye vadhikaraste Ma Phaleshu Kadachana,
Ma Karmaphalaheturbhurma Te Sangostvakarmani (BG, 2.47)

Meaning: You have a right to perform your prescribed duty, but you are not entitled to the fruits of action. Never consider yourself to be the cause of the results of your activities, and never be attached to not doing your duty.

Explanation: Actions done with expectation of its rewards bring bondage. If you do not crave for them, you get purification of heart and ultimately knowledge of the Self. The word Karma is derived from the Sanskrit Kri, to do; all action is Karma. Technically, this word also means the effects of actions. In connection with metaphysics, it sometimes means the effects, of which our past actions were the causes. But in Karma-Yoga we have simply to do with the word Karma as meaning work. The goal of mankind is knowledge.

This is one of the most significant and popular verses of the Bhagavad Gita that offers deep insight into the spirit of the work and is invariably quoted in discussions of karma yoga. Regarding the science of work, the verse give four instructions: (1) You perform the work without expecting any results; (2) The fruits of your actions are not for pleasure; (3) Pride of doership should be given up while working; (4) Do not be attached to inaction.

Yogasthah kuru karmaani sangam tyaktwaa dhananjaya;
Siddhyasiddhyoh samo bhootwaa samatwam yoga uchyate. (BG, 2.48)

Meaning: Be steadfast in yoga, O Arjuna. Perform your duty and abandon all attachment to success or failure. Such evenness of mind is called yoga.

Explanation: Lord Krishna tells Arjuna that he should act in yoga. And what is that yoga? Yoga means to concentrate the mind upon the Supreme by controlling the ever-disturbing senses. And who is the Supreme? The Supreme is the Lord. And because He Himself is telling Arjuna to fight, Arjuna has nothing to do with the results of the fight. Gain or victory are Krishna's concern; Arjuna is simply advised to act according to the dictation of Krsna. The following of Krishna's dictation is real yoga, and this is practiced in the process called Krishna consciousness. By Krishna consciousness only can one give up the sense of proprietorship. One has to become the servant of Krishna, or the servant of the servant of Krishna. That is the right way to discharge duty in Krishna consciousness, which alone can help one to act in yoga. Arjuna is a kshatriya, and as such he is participating in the varnasrama-dharma institution. It is said in the Visnu Purana that in the varnasrama-dharma, the whole aim is to satisfy Vishnu. No one should satisfy himself, as is the rule in the material world, but one should satisfy Krishna. So, unless one satisfies Krishna, one cannot correctly observe the principles of varnasrama-dharma. Indirectly, Arjuna was advised to act as Krishna told him.

Doorena hyavaram karma buddhiyogaad dhananjaya;
Buddhau sharanamanwiccha kripanaah phalahetavah. . (BG, 2.49)

Meaning: Far lower than the Yoga of wisdom is action, O Arjuna! Seek thou refuge in wisdom; wretched are they whose motive is the fruit.

Explanation: Actions done with evenness of mind is the Yoga of wisdom. Actions performed by one who expects their fruits are far inferior to the Yoga of wisdom wherein the seeker does not seek the fruits. The former leads to bondage, and is the cause of birth and death.

Buddhiyukto jahaateeha ubhe sukrita dushkrite;
Tasmaad yogaaya yujyaswa yogah karmasu kaushalam. . (BG, 2.50)

Meaning: Endowed with wisdom (evenness of mind), one casts off in this life both good and evil deeds; therefore, devote thyself to Yoga; Yoga is skill in action.

Explanation: Actions which are of a binding nature lose that nature when performed with equanimity of mind.

karma-jam buddhi-yukta hi phalam tyaktva manisinah
janma-bandha-vinirmuktah padam gacchanty anamayam (BG, 2.51)

Meaning: The wise, engaged in devotional service, take refuge in the Lord, and free themselves from the cycle of birth and death by renouncing the fruits of action in the material world. In this way they can attain that state beyond all miseries.

Explanation: The liberated living entities seek that place where there are no material miseries.

The Karma-Yogi is the man who understands that the highest ideal is non-resistance, and who also knows that this non-resistance is the highest manifestation of power in actual possession, and also what is called the resisting of evil is but a step on the way towards the manifestation of this highest power, namely, non-resistance. Before reaching this highest ideal, man's duty is to resist evil; let him work, let him fight, let him strike straight from the shoulder. Then only, when he has gained the power to resist, will non-resistance be a virtue.

Chapter 3 of Bhagavad Gita lays focus on Karma Yoga.

Shloka 1 of Chapter 3 says:

arjuna uvaca jyayasi cet karmanas te mata buddhir janardana
tat kim karmani ghore mam niyojayasi kesava (BG, 3.1)

Meaning: Arjuna said: O Janardana, O Kesava, why do You urge me to engage in this ghastly warfare, if You think that intelligence is better than fruitive work?

vyamisreneva vakyena buddhim mohayasiva me
tad ekam vada niscitya yena sreyo 'ham apnuyam (BG, 3.2)

Meaning: My intelligence is bewildered by Your equivocal instructions. Therefore, please tell me decisively what is most beneficial for me.

sri-bhagavan uvaca
loke 'smin dvi-vidha nistha
pura prokta mayanagha
jnana-yogena sankhyanam
karma-yogena yoginaṁ (BG, 3.3)

Meaning: The Supreme Personality of Godhead said: O sinless Arjuna, I have already explained that there are two classes of men who try to realize the self. Some are inclined to understand Him by empirical, philosophical speculation, and others are inclined to know Him by devotional work.

na karmanam anarambhan naiskarmyam puruso 'snute
na ca sannyasanad eva siddhim samadhigacchati (BG, 3.4)

Meaning: Not by merely abstaining from work can one achieve freedom from reaction, nor by renunciation alone can one attain perfection.

Shloka 5:

na hi kascit ksanam api jatu tisthaty akarma-krt
karyate hy avasah karma sarvah prakrti-jair gunaih

Not indeed anyone, even for a moment ever stays without performing action, indeed all are forced to perform action (even) against will (by) prakriti born (originating) gunas.

Shloka 6:

karmendriyani saṃyamya ya aste manasa smaran
indriyarthan vimudhatma mithyacarah sa ucyate

Restraining organs of action, he who sits, but by mind (mentally) thinking (dwelling on) sense objects, (this) deluded person is called a hypocrite.

Shloka 7:

yas tv indriyani manasa niyamyarabhate 'rjuna
karmendriyaih karma-yogam asaktah sa visisyate

But, who controlling sense organs by mind, O Arjuna, begins (engages) by organs of action in karma-yoga, unattached; he is superior.

Shloka 8:

niyatam kuru karma tvam karma jyayo hy akarmanah
sarira-yatrapi ca te na prasiddhyed akarmanah

You (should) perform enjoined actions, (for) action is better than non-action; even body-maintenance cannot be accomplished without action.

Shloka 9:

yajnarthat karmano 'nyatra loko 'yam karma-bandhanah
tad-artham karma kaunteya mukta-sangah samacara

Action for performing sacrifice aside, this world is bound by action (karma); for that (sacrifice) purpose O Kaunteya, free from attachment perform (action).

(NOTE: All actions are binding, other than the actions undertaken for performing yagna (sacrifice). Hence Lord Krishna urges action for performing yagna. It is in this contexts that Mahabharata is known as a yagna, not war.)

Shloka 10:

saha-yajnah prajah srstva purovaca prajapatih
anena prasavisyadhvam esa vo 'stv ista-kama-dhuk

Along with yagna having created mankind, Prajapati said, "by this (yagna) may you bring forth, may this be your desire-full-filler (cow).

Shloka 11:

devan bhavayatanena te deva bhavayantu vah
parasparam bhavayantah sreyah param avapsyatha

May you increase well-being of Devas by this (yagna), may the Divine beings increase your well-being; mutually increasing well-being, supreme happiness you'll achieve.

Shloka 12:

istan bhogan hi vo deva dasyante yajna-bhavitah
tair dattan apradayaibhyo yo bhunkte stena eva sah

The Devas provide you desired enjoyment, having been brought about by yagna; without offering to them these gifts, he who enjoys these (without offering to Devas), he is a thief.

Shloka 13:

yajna-sistasinah santo mucyante sarva-kilbisaih
bhunjate te tv agham papa ye pacanty atma-karanat

Sacrifice-remainder consumer (are) good people, (and) are released from all evils (sins); they consume their own evil, the wicked who cook (only) for their own sake.

Shloka 14:

annad bhavanti bhutani parjanyad anna-sambhavah
yajnad bhavati parjanyo yajnah karma-samudbhavah

From food come (into existence) beings, from rains food originate, from yagna comes rains (rain clouds), (and) yagna originates in karma.

Shloka 15:

karma brahmodbhavam viddhi brahmaksara-samudbhavam
tasmat sarva-gatam brahma nityam yajne pratisthitam

Know that karma originates in Brahman, Brahman (originates) from the imperishable, therefore all-pervading Brahman is ever established in sacrifice.

Shloka 16:

evam pravartitam cakram nanuvartayatiha yah
aghayur indriyaramo mogham partha sa jivati

Thus, set in motion cycle (wheel), he (who) does not cause (help) to turn, (the) malicious (person sunk in) sense-delight, (in) vain, Partha, he lives.

Shloka 17:

yas tv atma-ratir eva syad atma-trptas ca manavah
atmany eva ca santustas tasya karyam na vidyate

He who is delighted only in Self, and is satisfied only by Self, and is contented only with Self, for him the need to act (duty) is not found (does not exist).

Shloka 18:

naiva tasya krtenartho nakrteneha kascana
na casya sarva-bhutesu kascid artha-vyapasrayah

Not indeed of him (any) action with purpose (goal oriented), not in inaction anything whatever, and not for him any purpose or need with beings whatever.

Shloka 19:

tasmad asaktah satatam karyam karma samacara
asakto hy acaran karma param apnoti purusah

Therefore (being) unattached always, perform actions; indeed, being unattached and performing action man attains supreme.

Shloka 20:

karmanaiva hi saṃsiddhiṃ asthita janakadayah
loka-sangraham evapi sampasyan kartum arhasi

By (performing) action only perfection (was) attained (by) Janaka and others, (therefore for) ensuring world maintenance you should act.

Shloka 21:

yad acarati sresthas tat tad evetaro janah
sa yat pramanam kurute lokas tad anuvartate

Whatever actions great man (does) that (thus) do other men, whatever standard he, sets world that follows.

Shloka 22:

na me parthasti kartavyaṃ trisu lokesu kincana
nanavaptam avaptavyam varta eva ca karmani

Not for me Partha (any) prescribed work in three worlds (anything) whatever, nothing unattained (or) to be attained, nevertheless I engage in action.

Shloka 23:

yadi hy aham na varteyam jatu karmany atandritah
mama vartmanuvartante manusyah partha sarvasah

Indeed, if I not (be) engaged ever in action tirelessly, me indeed (will) follow men Partha, everywhere.

Shloka 24:

utsideyur ime loka na kuryam karma ced aham
sankarasya ca karta syam upahanyam imah prajah

These would perish this world not if I should perform action if I; confusion causer I should be (and because of) destruction of these creatures.

Shloka 25:

saktah karmany avidvamso yatha kurvanti bharata
kuryad vidvams tathasaktas cikirsur loka-sangraham

Attached, the unwise, in which way they act, Bharatha (Arjuna), the wise one he should act similarly unattached, desiring (only) for world maintenance.

Shloka 26:

na buddhi-bhedam janayed ajnanam karma-sanginam
josayet sarva-karmani vidvan yuktah samacaran

No fragmentation of intelligence (confusion of mind), (should be) produced (among) the ignorant (who are) attached to work; he (the wise) should cause (them to) delight in all actions (while himself) being yoked to equanimity in performance.

Shloka 27:

prakrteh kriyamanani gunaih karmani sarvasah
ahankara-vimudhatma kartaham iti manyate

All action in nature (are) always performed by the gunas; the fool, confused by ego, "I am the doer", he believes.

Shloka 28:

tattva-vit tu maha-baho guna-karma-vibhagayoh
guna gunesu vartante iti matva na sajjate

But, (those who) know the truth, O mighty armed one (Arjuna) of the (two) roles of gunas and karma; "Gunas, in the Gunas work/act", thus thinking (knowing) are not attached (to actions).

Shloka 29:

prakrter guna-sammudhah sajjante guna-karmasu
tan akrtsna-vido mandan krtsna-vin na vicalayet

Deluded by gunas of the nature (and) attached to actions of gunas; them, of incomplete knowledge and dullards; those with complete knowledge should not unsettle.

Shloka 30:

mayi sarvani karmani sannyasyadhyatma-cetasa
nirasir nirmamo bhutva yudhyasva vigata-jvarah

On Me, all actions, renouncing, on Supreme Self concentrating; free from desire and feelings of 'mine' becoming; fight, (having) rid of fever.

Shloka 31:

ye me matam idam nityam anutisthanti manavah
sraddhavanto 'nasuyanto mucyante te 'pi karmabhih

(Those) men who always practice this opinion of mine, with faith, not sneering, (they too) are freed (from) action (i.e., its bondage).

Shloka 32:

ye tv etad abhyasuyanto nanutisthanti me matam
sarva-jnana-vimudhams tan viddhi nastan acetasah

But, those who sneer, (and) do not follow my opinion; (they) confusing all knowledge; know (them as) lost and stupid.

Shloka 33:

sadrsam cestate svasyah prakrter jnanavan api
prakrtim yanti bhutani nigrahah kim karisyati

According to their own nature, even wise ones strives; being follow (their own) nature; what will restraints accomplish?

Shloka 34:

Indriyasyendriyasyarthe raga-dvesau vyavasthitau
tayor na vasam agacchet tau hy asya paripanthinau

(Between) the sense and (its corresponding) sense-object, attraction-repulsion (love-hate) reside; (do) not come under (their) power (influence); they are his (man's) two stumbling blocks.

Shloka 35:

sreyan sva-dharmo vigunah para-dharmat svanusthitat
sva-dharme nidhanam sreyah para-dharmo bhayavahah

(It is) better (to perform) one's own dharma (even if) deficient than other's dharma well performed; death (performing) one's own dharma is better; other's dharma brings danger.

Shloka 36:

arjuna uvaca

atha kena prayukto 'yam papam carati purusah
anicchann api varsneya balad iva niyojitah

Arjuna said: then impelled by what this evil act (from) man, even unwillingly Varshney (Krishna), (as if) commanded by force.

Shloka 37:

sri-bhagavan uvaca

kama esa krodha esa rajo-guna-samudbhavah
mahasano maha-papma viddhy enam iha vairinam

Sri Bhagavan said : This is desire, this is anger originating in rajo-guna, all-devouring and cause of great hurt (sin); know this to be the enemy.

Shloka 38:

dhumenavriyate vahnir yathadarso malena ca
yatholbenavrto garbhas tatha tenedam avrtam

By smoke fire is covered, as mirror by dust, as membrane covers the embryo, thus man by this (desire and anger) is covered.

Shloka 39:

avrtam jnanam etena jnanino nitya-vairina
kama-rupena kaunteya duspurenanalena ca

The eternal enemy of the wise, covers the intelligence in form of desire, Kaunteya, like an insatiable fire.

Shloka 40:

indriyani mano buddhir asyadhisthanam ucyate
etair vimohayaty esa jnanam avrtya dehinam

The senses, the mind and the intelligence are said to be its (desire's) abode, with these it confuses the embodied, (and his) knowledge/wisdom is obscured.

Shloka 41:

tasmat tvam indriyany adau niyamya bharatarsabha
papmanam prajahi hy enam jnana-vijnana-nasanam

Therefore, controlling your senses first, Bull of Bharatha (Arjuna), destroy this evil, the knowledge-discrimination destroyer.

Shloka 42:

indriyani parany ahur indriyebhyah param manah
manasas tu para buddhir yo buddheh paratas tu sah

Senses are great, it is said, greater than senses is mind, greater than mind is buddhi, that which is greater than buddhi is he (the indweller).

Shloka 43:

evam buddheh param buddhva samstabhyatmanam atmana
jahi satrum maha-baho kama-rupam durasadam

Thus, having known what is greater than buddhi, establishing oneself in Self, kill the enemy mighty-armed-one (Arjuna), in the form of desire that is (otherwise) unapproachable.

The ultimate objective of humankind according to Vedanta is to attain Moksha or liberation from the cycle of birth and death. Indian philosophy advocates that the paths for liberation must be suited to an individual's situation, temperament and disposition. Karma yoga is one of the paths that provide the route to the ultimate liberation.

5.2 Three Types of Karma

As briefly stated earlier, there are three types of karma in the yoga world. These are:

5.2.1 Sanchitta

These are the accumulated works and actions that you have completed in the past. These cannot be changed but can only wait to come into fruition. This is the vast accumulation of karma that encompasses our countless past lifetimes. This comprises every action that you have ever made in your past and present lives.

5.2.2 Prarabdha

Prarabdha is that portion of the past karma that is responsible for the present. These are the ripe and fructuous actions and reactions. The things that you did in the past make you what you are today. It cannot be avoided or changed, but only exhausted by being experienced.

5.2.3 Agami

Agami Karma is the Karma we are creating for ourselves right here in the current moment. It is the action that we create and the choices we make right now, as we live this present lifetime.

All these three aspects of karma blend into each other. "As you think, so shall you be" – our choices and actions of the present moment will become our karma in the future.

The benefits of understanding Karma are that it discourages one from performing unwholesome actions as it will bring about suffering. Instead, it encourages one to perform goodness and kindness, in order to bring happiness as their fruit.

By taking full responsibility for our thoughts and actions, we create our reality. Everything we think or do right now creates the kind of future that is related to those thoughts and actions.

5.3 More on Karma Yoga

Of the classical paths to spiritual liberation in Hinduism, karma yoga is the path of unselfish action. It teaches that a spiritual seeker should act according to dharma, without being attached to the fruits or personal consequences. Karma Yoga, states the Bhagavad Gita, purifies the mind. It leads one to consider dharma of work, and the work according to one's dharma, doing god's work and in that sense becoming and being "like unto god Krishna" in every moment of one's life. According to Lord Krishna in Bhagavad Gita, Karma yoga is the spiritual practice of "selfless action performed for the benefit of others". Karma yoga is a path to reach moksha (spiritual liberation) through work. It is rightful action without being attached to fruits or being manipulated by what the results might be, a dedication to one's duty, and trying one's best while being neutral to rewards or outcomes such as success or failure.

Karma yoga does not mean forfeiture of emotions or desires, rather it means action driven by "equanimity, balance", with "dispassion, disinterest", avoiding "one sidedness, fear, craving, favouring self or one group or clan, self-pity, self-aggrandizement or any form of extreme reactiveness". A Karma yogi acts and does his or her duty, whether that be as a homemaker, mother, nurse, carpenter or garbage collector, with no thought for one's own fame, privilege or financial reward, but simply as a dedication to the Lord.

Karma yoga applies to "any action in any profession or family activities", where the yogi works selflessly to others' benefit. This is in contrast to other forms of yoga which focus on self-development and self-realisation, typically with isolation and meditative introspection. The disinterested action idea is not unique to Hinduism, and similar disinterested non-craving precepts for monks and nuns are also found in Buddhism and Jainism.

A part of the premise of "disinterested action" is that the more one acts with the hope of getting rewards, the more one is liable to disappointment, frustration or self-destructive behaviour. Further, another part of the premise is that the more one is committed to "disinterested action", the more one considers the dharma (ethical dimension), focuses on other aspects of the action, strives to do one's best, and this leads to liberating self-empowerment.

According to Chapter 5 of the Bhagavad Gita, both sannyasa (renunciation, monastic life) and karma yoga are means to liberation. Between the two, it recommends karma yoga, stating that anyone who is a dedicated karma yogi neither hates nor desires, and therefore such as person is the "eternal renouncer".

5.3.1 Karma Yoga in other Hindu Texts

The earliest texts that are forerunners of the karma yoga ideas in the Bhagavad Gita are the ancient Upanishads, such as the Brihadaranyaka Upanishad. Other Vedic texts as well as post-Vedic literature of the Mimamsa school of Hindu philosophy mention karma marga, but these contextually refer to the path of rituals. The Mimamsa ideas, though orthodox, were the fertile grounds on which the later ideas of Karma yoga developed.

Karma yoga is discussed in many other Hindu texts. For example, the section 11.20 of the Bhagavata Purana states that there are only three means to spiritual liberation: jnana yoga (knowledge), karma yoga (action) and bhakti yoga (devotion). Those who are of philosophical bent, prefer the "knowledge path". Those who are inclined to productive application of arts, skills and knowledge, prefer the "karma path". Those who prefer emotional connection, prefer the "devotional path". These three paths overlap, with different relative emphasis.

Discussions on Karma yoga are also found in Chapter 33 of Narada Purana.

Later, new movements within Hinduism added raja yoga as the fourth spiritual path, but this is not universally accepted as distinct to other three.

5.3.2 Karma yoga versus Kriya yoga

Karma yoga is "yoga of action", while kriya yoga is "yoga of ritual action". Kriya yoga is found in tantric texts, and believed by its practitioners to activate chakras and energy centres in the body. In that sense, kriya yoga is a subset of karma yoga.

Chapter - 6

Bhakti Yoga Philosophy

6.1 Introduction to Bhakti Yoga

Bhakti yoga, also called Bhakti marga (literally the path of Bhakti), is a spiritual path or spiritual practice within Hinduism focused on loving devotion towards any personal deity. It is one of the classical paths in Hinduism which lead to Moksha.

The tradition has ancient roots. Bhakti is mentioned in the Shvetashvatara Upanishad where it simply means participation, devotion and love for any endeavour. Bhakti yoga as one of the spiritual paths for salvation is discussed in depth by the Bhagavad Gita.

The personal god varies with the devotee. It may include a god or goddess such as Ganesha, Krishna, Radha, Rama, Sita, Vishnu, Shiva, Shakti, Lakshmi, Saraswati, Parvati, Durga, and Surya among others.

The Bhakti marga involving these deities grew with the Bhakti Movement, starting about the mid-first millennium CE, from Tamil Nadu in South India. The movement was led by the Saiva Nayanars and the Vaisnava Alvars. Their ideas and practices inspired bhakti poetry and devotion throughout India over the 12th-18th century CE. Bhakti marga is a part of the religious practice in Vaishnavism, Shaivism, and Shaktism.

Devotion may also be impersonal as discussed in the book "Narada's Way of Divine Love" written by Swami Prabhavananda.

The Sanskrit word bhakti is derived from the root *bhaj*, which means "divide, share, partake, participate, to belong to". The word also means "attachment, devotion to, fondness for, homage, faith or love, worship, piety to something as a spiritual, religious principle or means of salvation".

The term yoga literally means "union, yoke", and in this context connotes a path or practice for "salvation, liberation". The yoga referred to here is the "joining together, union" of one's Atman (true self) with the concept of Supreme Bṛahman (true Reality).

Bhakti yoga is an Indian tradition of "divine love mysticism", a spiritual path "synonymous for an intimate understanding of oneness and harmony of the eternal individual with the Divine (the universal Being) and all creatures, a constant delight". Bhakti yoga consists of concentrating one's mind, emotions, and senses on the Divine.

6.1.1 Bhakti Yoga in Bhagavad Gita

Bhakti yoga is one of yogas taught in Bhagavad Gita. Bhakti yoga is a devotee's loving devotion to a personal god as the path for spirituality. The other paths are jnana yoga, the path of wisdom where the individual pursues knowledge and introspective self-understanding as spiritual practice, while karma yoga is path of virtuous action (karma) neither expecting reward nor consequence for doing the right thing, or nishkama karma. Raja yoga is the fourth spiritual path.

6.1.2 Bhagavata Purana

The Bhagavata Purana is a popular and influential text in the Vaishnavism traditions, and it discusses Ishvara pranidhana (devotion to a personal god). The Sanskrit text presents various modes of bhakti specifically to incarnations of Vishnu, particularly in terms of "Narayana, Krishna". The Bhakti yoga taught in this text is inspired by Yoga Sutras of Patanjali and Bhagavad Gita, and they focus on "the ultimate truths of the individual self and its loving relationship with a personal god". The presentation in the Bhagavata Purana is not in abstract terms, but through "charming and delightful tales that capture the heart and mind", the goal of Bhakti yoga, states Bryant.

6.1.3 Panchayatana Puja

Panchayatana puja is a form of bhakti found in the Smarta tradition of Hinduism. It consists of the simultaneous worship of multiple deities: Shiva, Vishnu, Shakti, Surya and an Ishta Devata such as Ganesha or Skanda or any personal god of devotee's preference.

Philosophically, the Smarta tradition emphasises that all images (murti) are icons of saguna Brahman, a means to thinking about the abstract Ultimate Reality called nirguna Brahman. The five or six icons are seen by Smartas as multiple representations of the one Saguna Brahman (i.e., a personal God with form), rather than as distinct beings. The ultimate goal in this practice is to transition past the use of icons, then follow a philosophical and meditative path to understanding the oneness of Atman (soul, self) and Brahman – as "That art Thou".

6.1.4 Saiva Siddhanta

The Śaivasiddhānta tradition favours Bhakti yoga, emphasising loving devotion to Shiva. Its theology presents three universal realities: the pashu (individual soul), the pati (lord, Shiva), and the pasha (soul's bondage) through ignorance, karma and maya. The tradition teaches ethical living, service to the community and through one's work, loving worship, yoga practice and discipline, continuous learning and self-knowledge as means for liberating the individual soul from bondage.

6.1.5 Shakti Bhakti

Meerabai is considered one of the most significant saints in the Vaishnava bhakti tradition. Bhakti of goddess is another significant tradition, one found in Shaktism. The theology of oneness and unity of "the divine Goddess and the devotee", their eternal fearless love for each other is a theme found in Devi Gita, a text embedded inside the Devi-Bhagavata Purana. The specific Bhakti yoga practices amongst Shakta are similar to those in other traditions of Hinduism. The Shakta devotion is common in eastern states of India, particularly West Bengal. The personal god here varies, and includes Durga, Tara Ma (Buddhist influence), Kali and to a lesser extent Saraswati, Lakshmi, Bharat Mata (land goddess).

6.1.6 Vaishnava Bhakti

The Bhakti yoga tradition has been historically most associated with Vaishnavism. The personal god here is Vishnu or one of his avatars. In many regions, the loving devotion is either to Vishnu-Lakshmi (god-goddess) together, or through Lakshmi who is considered the shakti of Vishnu. The specific avatar varies by the devotee and region, but the most common are Krishna and Rama.

6.1.7 Chaitanya Mahaprabhu

In the Krishna-oriented traditions of Vaishnavism, the Chaitanya Charitamrita by Krishnadasa Kaviraja interprets the section 7.5.23-24 of Bhagavata Purana to teach nine types of bhaktis sadhana, as follows:

(1) śravaṇa ("listening" to the scriptural stories of Krishna and his companions), (2) kīrtana ("praising"; usually refers to ecstatic group singing), (3) smaraṇa ("remembering" or fixing the mind on Vishnu), (4) pāda-sevana (rendering service), (5) arcana (worshipping an image), (6) vandana (paying homage), (7) dāsya (servitude), (8) sākhya (friendship), and (9) ātma-nivedana (complete surrender of the self).

These nine principles of devotional service were linked to Chaitanya Mahaprabhu as integral to spiritual practice focused on Krishna.

6.1.8 Meher Baba

A movement led by Meher Baba states that "out of a number of practices which lead to the ultimate goal of humanity – God-Realisation – Bhakti Yoga is one of the most important. Almost the whole of humanity is concerned with Bhakti Yoga, which, in simple words, means the art of worship. But it must be understood in all its true aspects, and not merely in a narrow and shallow sense, in which the term is commonly used and interpreted. The profound worship based on the high ideals of philosophy and spirituality, prompted by divine love, doubtless constitutes true Bhakti Yoga".

6.2 Narada Bhakti Sutras

The Narada Bhakti Sutra is a well-known sutra venerated within the traditions of Hinduism, reportedly spoken by the famous sage, Narada. It is a very popular treatise in India on Bhakti Yoga. This treatise is very lucid and practical in its exposition of the birth, growth, development, unfoldment and expression of Bhakti. This is a very useful book for earnest and sincere aspirants who tread the path of devotion. This book is a great standard work on Bhakti Yoga. It contains laconic aphorisms ascribed to Devarishi Narada.

The Holy Rishi Narada propounds the doctrine of love to God, a path which can easily be followed by the ordinary man. It does not demand either great knowledge of philosophy or total renunciation of the world.

The text details the process of devotion (Bhakti), or Bhakti yoga and is thus of particular importance to many of the Bhakti movements within Hinduism. It has received particular attention among the Vaishnava traditions.

In the translation by Swami Prabhavananda there are eighty-four verses arranged in nine chapters. The text covers the following subjects:

Chapter 1 (verses 1-6) provides a definition of bhakti.

Chapter 2 (verses 7-14) stresses the importance of renunciation and self-surrender.

Chapter 3 (verses 15-24) provides exemplars of divine love.

Chapter 4 (verses 25-33) endorses bhakti as the highest goal of human life.

Chapter 5 (verses 34-42) provides suggestions on how to practice divine love.

Chapter 6 (verses 43-50) explains the importance of seeking holy company.

Chapter 7 (verses 51-57) discusses the difference between preparatory and supreme devotion.

Chapter 8 (verses 58-73) covers the forms of divine love.

Chapter 9 (verses 74-84) recommends the practice of ethical virtues and worship of God.

6.2.1 Key Concepts in Narada Bhakti Sutra

Within the text, Narada explains the perfectional stage of pure devotion; the process to achieve this state; gives quotations from other Vedic personalities on the subject matter; things to avoid when developing bhakti; and finally explains the nature of selfless love and the different forms of attachment to the Supreme person.

6.2.2 Pure Devotion

Firstly, bhakti itself is defined as being "the most elevated, pure love for God", which is eternal by nature and through following which one obtains perfect peace and immortality (release from samsara). The symptoms of such devotion are that one no longer has any selfish desires, nor is affected by the dualities of loss or gain for himself being fully content with (and experiencing ecstasy through) the process of bhakti itself. Narada describes that lust is absent in those who execute bhakti purely because they naturally have no personal desires to fulfill.

The aspirant bhakta is encouraged to renounce "social customs" and "religious rituals" and to focus purely on service to God with exclusive dedication, being indifferent to whatever may stand in the way of such service. Activities of social custom and religious rituals that are favourable to devotional service are still promoted but devotional activities are given as "the only means for reaching the perfection of life."

The text then goes on to quote Vyasa, Garga and Sandilya in terms of their opinions on what is bhakti, giving the opinion that all three are correct but declaring in conclusion that "bhakti consists of offering one's every act to the Supreme Lord and feeling extreme distress in forgetting Him". The Gopis (cowherd women) of Vrindavan are given as an example of devotees who display this form of pure bhakti, but warning is also given about 'false devotion' that imitates this perfectional stage. Narada follows this warning by stating, "Furthermore, the Lord dislikes the proud but is pleased with the humble".

6.2.3 Bhakti begets Bhakti

An important point is made in verse 30 in regard to the relationship between bhakti and knowledge: "But the son of Brahma [Narada] says that bhakti is its own fruit". Bhakti is not dependent on anything else for nourishment" being complete in itself, without dependence on the paths of either knowledge or renunciation.

6.2.4 Obtaining Bhakti

The methods initially described for obtaining bhakti are as follows:

- Giving up worldly pleasures and the close company of others who indulge in such activities.
- Worshipping the Supreme Lord ceaselessly.
- Hearing and speaking about the Lord's special qualities and activities.

However, following these three, the text gives the "grace of great souls" or "a small drop of the Lord's grace" as the most important factors in developing true devotion. Saying that such association is so rare and precious that it can only be obtained through the grace of God Himself, thus the instruction is given in verse 42: "Strive, strive only for the association of pure devotees".

6.2.5 Items to avoid

Alongside the acceptance of positive practices in the cultivation of bhakti, the text also describes items which should be avoided by the aspiring bhakta. Intimate dealings with others who are against the path of bhakti or who indulge in sinful habits is described as potentially dangerous for one attempting to purify their consciousness: "Material association is the cause of lust, anger, confusion, forgetfulness, loss of intelligence, and total calamity". It further explains that only one who abandons such material association, serves the sages and becomes selfless in their dealings, renouncing desires for profit or gain, can cross beyond the ocean of illusion. Even the Vedas are given as an object to renounce for one for wants to obtain pure and uninterrupted love for God. In later chapters however an instruction is also given that respect should be shown for all scriptures which promote bhakti (devotion) and an aspirant bhakta should endeavour to follow the instructions of such texts.

6.2.6 The nature of Pure Love

The text states that the true nature of pure love of God is beyond description, but this does not restrict God from revealing it to those who are qualified. Once this pure love is obtained it says that a person "looks only at the Lord, hears only about Him, speaks only of Him, and thinks only of Him". Secondary forms of this love are given as stepping stones which bring one to the perfectional stage, with each stage nearer to perfection being better than those preceding it. It is also stated that perfection is attained much more easily by bhakti than by any other process. The reason is that "bhakti does not depend on any other authority for its validity, being itself the standard of authority. Furthermore, bhakti is the embodiment of peace and supreme ecstasy."

6.2.7 Ultimate Attachment

In conclusion, the sutra gives an instruction to "patiently endure" until the perfectional stage of bhakti becomes manifest, whilst cultivating qualities such as nonviolence, honesty, cleanliness, compassion and faith. Again it is said that the Lord "reveals Himself to His devotees" and that bhakti is the most precious of all possessions.

Next a list of forms of attachment is given, through which a devotee should attain a loving feeling towards God, including :

- attachment to the Lord's qualities,
- attachment to His beauty,
- attachment to worshipping Him,
- attachment to remembering Him,
- attachment to serving Him,
- attachment to dealing with Him as a friend,
- attachment to surrendering one's self completely to Him,
- attachment to being absorbed in thoughts of Him.

Finally a number of devotional figures from Puranic scriptures are quoted as being in agreement with the truth of the process given, including: the Four Kumaras, Vyasa, Śuka, Sandilya, Garga, Vishnu, Kaundinya, Sesha, Uddhava, Aruni, Bali, Hanuman and Vibhishana.

The last verse of the text gives the message that: "Anyone who trusts these instructions spoken by Narada and is convinced by them will be blessed with devotion and attain the most dear Lord. Yes, he will attain the most dear Lord."

6.3 Bhakti Yoga in Bhagavad Gita (Chapter 12)

Shloka 1:

arjuna uvaca

evam satata-yukta ye bhaktas tvam paryupasate
ye capy aksaram avyaktam tesam ke yoga-vittamah

Arjuna said : Thus, constantly steadfast who devotees you worship, and who imperishable and unmanifest, of them which (who) has better knowledge of yoga?

Arjuna inquires: O Krishna, from your descriptions, I notice that there are two kinds of practitioners of yoga : one who steadfastly worship you and those who devote themselves to the imperishable unmanifest. Who according to you among the two have better knowledge and understanding of yoga?

Shloka 2:

sri-bhagavan uvaca

mayy avesya mano ye mam nitya-yukta upasate
sraddhaya parayopetas te me yuktatama matah

Shri Bhagavan said: On me fixing (their) mind those who ever-steadfast in worship; endowed with faith supreme, they are thought to be most-yoked to me.

Shloka 3:

ye tv aksaram anirdesyam avyaktam paryupasate
sarvatra-gam acintyam ca kuta-stham acalam dhruvam

Who imperishable, undefinable, unmanifest, worship, all pervading, unthinkable also unchanging, un-moving steady;

Shloka 4:

sanniyamyendriya-gramam sarvatra sama-buddhayah
te prapnuvanti mam eva sarva-bhuta-hite ratah

Controlling multitude of senses, everywhere even-minded, they too achieve me, (those) rejoicing in welfare of all-beings

Shloka 5:

kleso 'dhikataras tesam avyaktasakta-cetasam
avyakta hi gatir duhkham dehavadbhir avapyate

Pain (exertion) is greater of them, those attached to the unmanifest, unmanifest goal is indeed difficult for the embodied to attain.

Shloka 6:

ye tu sarvani karmani mayi sannyasya mat-parah
ananyenaiva yogena mam dhyayanta upasate

Who, but, all action in me renounce (hold) me supreme, with undistracted yoga me meditate upon and worship.

Shloka 7:

tesam aham samuddharta mrtyu-samsara-sagarat
bhavami na cirat partha mayy avesita-cetasam

Of them, I am deliverer (from) death-rebirth-ocean, without delay, O Partha; (whose) consciousness in me has entered.

Shloka 8:

mayy eva mana adhatsva mayi buddhim nivesaya
nivasisyasi mayy eva ata urdhvam na samsayah

In me alone fix (your) mind, into me let your intelligence enter, (then) you'll dwell in me only, from now on (henceforth) do no doubt.

Shloka 9:

atha cittam samadhatum na saknosi mayi sthiram
abhyasa-yogena tato mam icchaptum dhananjaya

Or if, (you are) not able to hold in place (your) mind steadily in me, (then) by yoga of practice, there on, seek to attain me, Dhananjaya (Arjuna).

Shloka 10:

abhyase 'py asamartho 'si mat-karma-paramo bhava
mad-artham api karmani kurvan siddhim avapsyasi

(If) you are unable to practice also, (then) let (consider) my work (to) be supreme, performing work for my sake, perfection you'll attain.

Shloka 11:

athaitad apy asakto 'si kartum mad-yogam asritah
sarva-karma-phala-tyagam tatah kuru yatatmavan

Or if, (this) also (you are) unable to do, then depending upon my power, abandoning fruits of all actions, there on do (actions) with self-restraint.

Shloka 12:

sreyo hi jnanam abhyasaj jnanad dhyanam visisyate
dhyanat karma-phala-tyagas tyagac chantir anantaram

Superior, indeed, is knowledge than practice, than knowledge meditation (is) superior, than meditation abandoning fruits of actions, from abandonment (follows) peace immediately.

Shloka 13:

advesta sarva-bhutanam maitrah karuna eva ca
nirmamo nirahankarah sama-duhkha-sukhah ksami

A non-hater of all beings, friendly (and) compassionate, freed from attachment, free from ego, same (indifferent) in pain and pleasure, patient.

Shloka 14:

santustah satatam yogi yatatma drdha-niscayah
mayy arpita-mano-buddhir yo mad-bhaktah sa me priyah

Contented always, yogi, self-restrained and firm in resolve, in me entrusted mind and intelligence, who is devoted to me, he is dear to me.

Shloka 15:

yasman nodvijate loko lokan nodvijate ca yah
harsamarsa-bhayodvegair mukto yah sa ca me priyah

From whom the world (does) not shrink, (and) who from (the) world (does) not-shrink, who is freed (from) pleasure-indignation-fear-distress, he too (is) dear (to) me.

Shloka 16:

anapeksah sucir daksa udasino gata-vyathah
sarvarambha-parityagi yo mad-bhaktah sa me priyah

Who (is) disinterested, pure, capable, indifferent, freed-from-anxiety, abandoning all undertakings, (and is) devoted to me, he is dear to me.

Shloka 17:

yo na hrsyati na dvesti na socati na kanksati
subhasubha-parityagi bhaktiman yah sa me priyah

Who (does) not rejoice, nor hate, neither mourns nor expects, (has) abandoned agreeable-disagreeable, (and) he is full of devotion, he is dear to me.

Shloka 18:

samah satrau ca mitre ca tatha manapamanayoh
sitosna-sukha-duhkhesu samah sanga-vivarjitah

Alike (to) foe and friend, (and) in honour and dishonour, same (steady) in cold-heat-pleasure-pain, freed from attachment.

Shloka 19:

tulya-ninda-stutir mauni santusto yena kenacit
aniketah sthira-matir bhaktiman me priyo narah

Similar in praise-censure, taciturn, contented with anything-whatever, homeless, steady-minded, full of devotion, (that) man is dear to me.

Shloka 20:

ye tu dharmamrtam idam yathoktam paryupasate
sraddadhana mat-parama bhaktas te 'tiva me priyah

Who, indeed, this nectar of dharma, as propounded (a fore) worship/ honour full of faith; consider me as Supreme (and) are devoted, they (are) exceedingly dear to me.

6.4 Origin of Narada Bhakti Sutras

Sri Veda Vyasa was staying in his hermitage of Badarikasrama. One day Narada went to the Ashram in the course of his wanderings. Sri Vyasa welcomed the Rishi with due rites and said, "Man seeks freedom etc. But without devotion it is dry. Devotion does not lead directly to the goal. Knowledge bestows freedom, etc. But without devotion, it is dry. Devotion is the only way for attaining salvation. All the others have importance only in so far as they are auxiliary to it. I humbly ask you to explain to me the virtue of devotion."

Narada said, "Your disciple Jaimini has already discussed the problem of action in the Purva Mimamsa. You have yourself completed the enquiry of the problem of knowledge in the Uttara-Mimamsa. Now you have taken up the problem of devotion. Its full explanation will be given by you in your Srimad Bhagavatam. I shall explain Bhakti in the form of Sutras." So saying, Narada delivered a discourse on devotion in 84 aphorisms.

The Bhakti Sutras of Narada number 84 in all. The first twenty-four of them deal with the nature of Bhakti. The next nine Sutras, i.e., 25 to 33 explain why and how the path of Bhakti is superior to Karma, Jnana and Yoga. Sutras 34 to 50 (seventeen in all) describe the methods by which Bhakti may be practiced and developed. The next sixteen Sutras (51 to 66) give a description of the external marks by which Bhakti can be detected in a true devotee. The last 18 Sutras (67 to 84) glorify the great realised souls who are full of devotion to the Lord.

Sutra 2.

Sa twasmin parama prema rupaa.

That (devotion), verily, is of the nature of supreme Love of God.

Sutra 3.

Amruthaswaroopaa cha.

And it is of the nature of Nectar.

Sutra 4.

Yallabdhwa puman siddho Bhavati Amrito Bhavati, Tripto Bhavati.

On attaining it (this supreme love) man becomes perfect, immortal and (fully) satisfied.

Sutra 25.

Saa tu karmajnanayogebhyopyadhikataara.

It (supreme devotion) is again higher than action knowledge and Yoga.

Sutra 26.

Phalarupatwat.

Because of its being of the nature of the result or fruit of all these.

Sutra 27.

Easwarasyapyabhimaanadweshitwat dainyapriyattwattcha.

(Devotion is higher than the others), because God hates egoism and loves humility.

Sutra 28.

Tasya jnanameva Saadhanamityeke.

In the view of some, knowledge (of the object loved) alone is the means to attain (devotion).

Sutra 29.

Annyonyasrayatwamityanye.

Others are of opinion that there is mutual dependence between knowledge and devotion.

Sutra 30.

Svayam phalaroopateti brahnakumaaraa.

Bhakti is its own fruit-thus opines Brahma Kumara (Narada) the son of Brahma.

Sutra 31.

Rajagrihabhojanaa tathaiva drishtatwaat.

For it is seen to be just so in the case of the king's home and dinner.

Sutra 32.

Na Tena Rajaparitosha kshudhasaantirva.

Not by that (by mere knowledge of things) does the king become king, nor does the hungry man become satisfied.

Sutra 33.

Tasmaatsaiva graahyaa mumukshubhihi.

Therefore, the path of devotion alone should be adopted by those who desire salvation.

Chapter - 7

Raja Yoga Philosophy

7.1 Introduction to Raja Yoga (Kingly Science or Kingly Secret)

Observing that Arjuna was a qualified aspirant and endowed with faith, Krishna declares to him the sovereign knowledge and sovereign secret that is to be known by direct experience. He (Krishna) adds that without faith in this knowledge man fails to reach God and is reborn to suffer. Now the Lord proceeds to describe His nature as the eternal, all-comprehensive Truth. He is everything that is invisible and visible. He pervades everything that exists. He creates everything, sustains everything, and when final dissolution takes place, absorbs everything into Himself. He manifests them again when the next creation begins. All beings who are ignorant of this knowledge are caught helplessly in the cycle of birth and death. In the midst of this creation, preservation and dissolution of the universe, the Lord stands as a silent witness, unaffected and unattached. He is the sole director, sustainer and supervisor of His Cosmic Prakriti.

Ignorant beings are not able to recognise the Lord in one who has realised Him. Although these cruel beings assume a human form, their nature is that of demons. The God-realised Mahatma, on the other hand, is a man of knowledge, and perceives Him indwelling all beings and creatures. He beholds the underlying unity of existence in all names and forms. The Lord's divine protection is assured to all those who take refuge in Him. Whatever path a devotee follows, he ultimately reaches Him. He is the goal of the various methods of spiritual practice. Devotion, Sri Krishna emphasises, is the essence of all spiritual discipline. If this supreme element is present, then the devotee is freed from bondage. The Lord observes the motive and degree of devotion. Even the most sinful and diabolical man, if he takes a radical turn towards the path of righteousness and truth, reaches the Lord. Whatever vocation one follows, one can attain the Lord if one seeks earnestly and with loving devotion. The essential thing is to fix the mind on the Lord and dedicate everything unto Him—one's body, mind, actions, emotion and will.

The science of Raja Yoga proposes to put before humanity a practical and scientifically worked-out method of reaching this truth. This study of Raja Yoga takes a long time and constant practice. A part of this practice is physical, but the main part of it is mental.

As stated earlier in Patanjali's Yoga Sutras, Raja Yoga is divided into eight steps. The first is Yama— non-killing, truthfulness, non-stealing, continence, and non-receiving of any gifts. Next is Niyama — cleanliness, contentment, mortification, study, and self-surrender to God. Then comes Asana, or posture; Pranayama, or controlling the vital forces of the body; Pratyahara, or making the mind introspective; Dharana, or concentration; Dhyana, or meditation; and Samadhi, or super-consciousness.

7.2 Raja Yoga in Bhagavad Gita (Chapter 9)

Sri Bhagavaan Uvaacha:

Idam tu te guhyatamam pravakshyaamyanasooyave;
Jnaanam vijnaanasahitam yajjnaatwaa mokshyase'shubhaat.(BG, 9.1)

The Blessed Lord said:

I shall now declare to thee who does not cavil (make petty or unnecessary objections), the greatest secret, the knowledge combined with experience (Self-realisation). Having known this, thou shalt be free from evil.

Raajavidyaa raajaguhyam pavitramidamuttamam;
Pratyakshaavagamam dharmyam susukham kartumavyayam.(BG, 9.2)

This is the kingly science, the kingly secret, the supreme purifier, realisable by direct intuitional knowledge, according to righteousness, very easy to perform and imperishable.

Ashraddhadhaanaah purushaa dharmasyaasya parantapa;
Apraapya maam nivartante mrityusamsaaravartmani. .(BG, 9.3)

Those who have no faith in this Dharma (knowledge of the Self), O Parantapa (Arjuna), return to the path of this world of death without attaining Me!

Mayaa tatamidam sarvam jagadavyaktamoortinaa;
Matsthaani sarvabhootaani na chaaham teshvavasthitah. .(BG, 9.4)

All this world is pervaded by Me in My unmanifest aspect; all beings exist in Me, but I do not dwell in them.

Na cha matsthaani bhootaani pashya me yogamaishwaram;
Bhootabhrinna cha bhootastho mamaatmaa bhootabhaavanah. .(BG, 9.5)

Nor do beings exist in Me (in reality): behold My divine Yoga, supporting all beings, but not dwelling in them, is My Self, the efficient cause of beings.

Yathaakaashasthito nityam vaayuh sarvatrago mahaan;
Tathaa sarvaani bhootaani matsthaaneetyupadhaaraya. .(BG, 9.6)

As the mighty wind, moving everywhere, rests always in the ether, even so, know thou that all beings rest in Me.

Sarvabhootaani kaunteya prakritim yaanti maamikaam;
Kalpakshaye punastaani kalpaadau visrijaamyaham. .(BG, 9.7)

All beings, O Arjuna, enter into My Nature at the end of a Kalpa; I send them forth again at the beginning of (the next) Kalpa!

Prakritim swaamavashtabhya visrijaami punah;
Bhootagraamamimam kritsnamavasham prakritervashaat. .(BG, 9.8)

Animating My Nature, I again and again send forth all this multitude of beings, helpless by the force of Nature.

Na cha maam taani karmaani nibadhnanti dhananjaya;
Udaaseenavadaaseenam asaktam teshu karmasu.(BG, 9.9)

These actions do not bind Me, O Arjuna, sitting like one indifferent, unattached to those acts!

Mayaa'dhyakshena prakritih sooyate sacharaacharam;
Hetunaa'nena kaunteya jagadwiparivartate. .(BG, 9.10)

Under Me as supervisor, Nature produces the moving and the unmoving; because of this, O Arjuna, the world revolves!

Avajaananti maam moodhaah maanusheem tanumaashritam;
Param bhaavamajaananto mama bhootamaheshwaram. .(BG, 9.11)

Fools disregard Me, clad in human form, not knowing My higher Being as the great Lord of (all) beings.

Moghaashaa moghakarmaano moghajnaanaa vichetasah;
Raakshaseemaasureem chaiva prakritim mohineem shritaah. .(BG, 9.12)

Of vain hopes, of vain actions, of vain knowledge and senseless, they verily are possessed of the deceitful nature of demons and undivine beings.

Mahaatmaanastu maam paartha daiveem prakritimaashritaah;
Bhajantyananyamanaso jnaatwaa bhootaadimavyayam. .(BG, 9.13)

But the great souls, O Arjuna, partaking of My divine nature, worship Me with a single mind (with the mind devoted to nothing else), knowing Me as the imperishable source of beings!

Satatam keertayanto maam yatantashcha dridhavrataah;
Namasyantashcha maam bhaktyaa nityayuktaa upaasate. .(BG, 9.14)

Always glorifying Me, striving, firm in vows, prostrating before Me, they worship Me with devotion, ever steadfast.

Jnaanayajnena chaapyanye yajanto maamupaasate;
Ekatwena prithaktwena bahudhaa vishwatomukham. .(BG, 9.15)

Others also, sacrificing with the wisdom-sacrifice, worship Me, the all-faced, as one, as distinct, and as manifold.

Aham kraturaham yajnah swadhaa'hamahamaushadham;
Mantro'hamahamevaajyam ahamagniraham hutam. .(BG, 9.16)

I am the Kratu; I am the Yajna; I am the offering (food) to the manes; I am the medicinal herb and all the plants; I am the Mantra; I am also the *ghee* or melted butter; I am the fire; I am the oblation (a thing presented or offered to God or a god).

Pitaahamasya jagato maataa dhaataa pitaamahah;
Vedyam pavitramonkaara riksaama yajureva cha. .(BG, 9.17)

I am the father of this world, the mother, the dispenser of the fruits of actions, and the grandfather; the (one) thing to be known, the purifier, the sacred monosyllable (Om), and also the *Rig-*, the *Sama-* and *Yajur Vedas.*

Gatirbhartaa prabhuh saakshee nivaasah sharanam suhrit;
Prabhavah pralayah sthaanam nidhaanam beejamavyayam. .(BG, 9.18)

I am the goal, the support, the Lord, the witness, the abode, the shelter, the friend, the origin, the dissolution, the foundation, the treasure-house and the imperishable seed.

Tapaamyahamaham varsham nigrihnaamyutsrijaami cha;
Amritam chaiva mrityushcha sadasacchaahamarjuna. .(BG, 9.19)

(As the sun) I give heat; I withhold and send forth the rain; I am immortality and also death, existence and non-existence, O Arjuna!

Traividyaa maam somapaah pootapaapaa
Yajnairishtwaa swargatim praarthayante;
Te punyamaasaadya surendraloka-
Mashnanti divyaan divi devabhogaan. .(BG, 9.20)

The knowers of the three *Vedas,* the drinkers of Soma, purified of all sins, worshipping Me by sacrifices, pray for the way to heaven; they reach the holy world of the Lord of the gods and enjoy in heaven the divine pleasures of the gods.

Te tam bhuktwaa swargalokam vishaalam

Ksheene punye martyalokam vishanti;
Evam trayeedharmamanuprapannaa
Gataagatam kaamakaamaa labhante. .(BG, 9.21)

They, having enjoyed the vast heaven, enter the world of mortals when their merits are exhausted; thus abiding by the injunctions of the three *(Vedas)* and desiring (objects of) desires, they attain to the state of going and returning.

Ananyaashchintayanto maam ye janaah paryupaasate;
Teshaam nityaabhiyuktaanaam yogakshemam vahaamyaham. .(BG, 9.22)

To those men who worship Me alone, thinking of no other, of those ever united, I secure what is not already possessed and preserve what they already possess.

Ye'pyanyadevataa bhaktaa yajante shraddhayaa'nvitaah;
Te'pi maameva kaunteya yajantyavidhipoorvakam. .(BG, 9.23)

Even those devotees who, endowed with faith, worship other gods, worship Me only, O Arjuna, but by the wrong method!

Aham hi sarvayajnaanaam bhoktaa cha prabhureva cha;
Na tu maamabhijaananti tattwenaatashchyavanti te. (BG, 9.24)

(For) I alone am the enjoyer and also the Lord of all sacrifices; but they do not know Me in essence (in reality), and hence they fall (return to this mortal world).

Yaanti devavrataa devaan pitreen yaanti pitrivrataah;
Bhutaani yaanti bhutejyaa yaanti madyaajino'pi maam. . (BG, 9.25)

The worshippers of the gods go to them; to the manes go the ancestor-worshippers; to the Deities who preside over the elements go their worshippers; My devotees come to Me.

Patram pushpam phalam toyam yo me bhaktyaa prayacchati;
Tadaham bhaktyupahritamashnaami prayataatmanah. . (BG, 9.26)

Whoever offers Me with devotion and a pure mind (heart), a leaf, a flower, a fruit or a little water—I accept (this offering).

Yatkaroshi yadashnaasi yajjuhoshi dadaasi yat;
Yattapasyasi kaunteya tatkurushva madarpanam. (BG, 9.27)

Whatever thou doest, whatever thou eatest, whatever thou offerest in sacrifice, whatever thou givest, whatever thou practiseth as austerity, O Arjuna, do it as an offering unto Me!

Shubhaashubhaphalairevam mokshyase karmabandhanaih;
Sannyaasayogayuktaatmaa vimukto maamupaishyasi. . (BG, 9.28)

Thus, shalt thou be freed from the bonds of actions yielding good and evil fruits; with the mind steadfast in the Yoga of renunciation, and liberated, thou shalt come unto Me.

Samo'ham sarvabhooteshu na me dweshyo'sti na priyah;
Ye bhajanti tu maam bhaktyaa mayi te teshu chaapyaham. (BG, 9.29)

The same am I to all beings; to Me there is none hateful or dear; but those who worship Me with devotion are in Me and I am also in them.

Api chet suduraachaaro bhajate maamananyabhaak;
Saadhureva sa mantavyah samyagvyavasito hi sah. (BG, 30.)

Even if the most sinful worships Me, with devotion to none else, he too should indeed be regarded as righteous, for he has rightly resolved.

Kshipram bhavati dharmaatmaa shashwacchaantim nigacchati;
Kaunteya pratijaaneehi na me bhaktah pranashyati. . (BG, 31.)

Soon he becomes righteous and attains to eternal peace; O Arjuna, know thou for certain that My devotee is never destroyed!

Maam hi paartha vyapaashritya ye'pi syuh paapayonayah;
Striyo vaishyaastathaa shoodraaste'pi yaanti paraam gatim. (BG, 32.)

For, taking refuge in Me, they also, who, O Arjuna, may be of sinful birth—women, Vaisyas as well as Sudras—attain the Supreme Goal!

Kim punarbraahmanaah punyaa bhaktaa raajarshayastathaa;
Anityamasukham lokam imam praapya bhajaswa maam. (BG, 33.)

How much more easily, then the holy Brahmins and devoted royal saints (attain the goal); having obtained this impermanent and unhappy world, do thou worship Me.

Manmanaa bhava madbhakto madyaajee maam namaskuru;
Maamevaishyasi yuktwaivamaatmaanam matparaayanah. (BG, 34.)

Fix thy mind on Me; be devoted to Me; sacrifice unto Me; bow down to Me; having thus united thy whole self with Me, taking Me as the Supreme Goal, thou shalt verily come unto Me.

Chapter - 8

Jnana Yoga Philosophy

8.1 Introduction to Jnana Yoga

Jnana is knowledge. To know Brahman as one's own Self is Jnana. To say, "I am Brahman, the pure, all-pervading Consciousness, the non-enjoyer, non-doer and silent witness," is Jnana. To behold the one Self everywhere is Jnana.

Ajnana is ignorance. To identify oneself with the illusory vehicles of body, mind, Prana and the senses is Ajnana. To say, "I am the doer, the enjoyer, I am a Brahmin, a Brahmachari, this is mine, he is my son," is Ajnana. Jnana alone can destroy Ajnana, even as light alone can remove darkness.

Brahman, the Supreme Self, is neither the doer of actions nor the enjoyer of the fruits of actions. The creation, preservation and destruction of the world are not due to Him. They are due to the action of Maya, the Lord's energy manifesting itself as the world-process.

Just as space appears to be of three kinds – absolute space, space limited by a jar, and space reflected in the water of a jar, – so also there are three kinds of intelligence. They are absolute intelligence, intelligence reflected in Maya, and intelligence reflected in the Jiva (the individual soul). The notion of the doer is the function of intelligence as reflected in the intellect. This, together with the notion of Jiva, is superimposed by the ignorant on the pure and limitless Brahman, the silent witness.

The illustration of space absolute, space limited by a jar and space reflected in water of a jar, is given to convey the idea that in reality Brahman alone is. Because of Maya, however, It appears as three.

The notion that the reflection of intelligence is real, is erroneous, and is due to ignorance. Brahman is without limitation; limitation is a superimposition on Brahman.

The identity of the Supreme Self and the Jiva or reflected self is established through the statement of the Upanishad 'Tat Tvam Asi' –

'That Thou Art'. When the knowledge of the identity of the two arises, then world problems and ignorance, with all their offshoots, are destroyed and all doubts disappear.

Self-realisation or direct intuitive perception of the Supreme Self is necessary for attaining freedom and perfection. This Jnana Yoga or the path of Wisdom is, however, not meant for the masses whose hearts are not pure enough and whose intellects are not sharp enough to understand and practice this razor-edge path. Hence, Karma Yoga and Upasana (Bhakti) are to be practiced first, which will render the heart pure and make it fit for the reception of Knowledge.

8.2 Jnana Yoga in Bhagavad Gita (Chapter 2)

The second Chapter begins with Sanjaya telling Dhritarashtra about the dialogue between Krishna and Arjuna when the latter continues to remain under the spell of melancholy and dejection. Arjuna, with a false sense of renunciation, argues that he would rather live on alms than slay the noble elders like Bhishma and Drona and that even an undisputed sovereignty over all the worlds would not drive away his grief. Arguing thus, he expressed his unwillingness to fight and became silent completely burnt out.

Sanjaya uvaacha

tam tathaa kripayaavishtam ashrupoornaakulekshanam
visheedantam idam vaakyam uvaacha madhusoodanah // 2.1 //

Sanjaya said:

To him who was thus overwhelmed with pity and sorrow and whose eyes were dimmed with tears, Madhusudana (Krishna) spoke these words.

Sri bhagavaan uvaacha

kutastwaa kashmalam idam vishame samupasthitam
anaaryajushtam aswargyam akeertikaram arjuna // 2.2 //

Sri Bhagavan said:

O Arjuna, at this moment of crisis, wherefrom have you got this weakness, un-Aryan like, disgraceful and which is not conducive to the attainment of heaven?

klaibyam maa sma gamah paartha naitattwayyupapadyate
kshudram hridaya daurbalyam tyaktwottishtha parantapa //2.3//

O Partha (Son of Pritha, Kunti), yield not to unmanliness. It does not befit you. Cast off this petty faint-heartedness and arise, O Paranthapa (scorcherer of foes - Arjuna)

Arjuna uvaacha:

katham bheeshmamaham sankhye dronam cha madhusoodana
ishubhih pratiyotsyaami poojaarhaav arisoodana //2.4 //

Arjuna said:

But O Madhusudana, how can I strike Bhishma and Drona with arrows in this battle, for they are worthy of worship, O Arisudana (Destroyer of enemies - Krishna)?

guroon ahatwaa hi mahaanubhaavaan
shreyo bhoktum bhaikshyam apeeha loke
hatwaarthakaamaamstu guroon ihaiva
bhunjeeya bhogaan rudhirapradigdhaan // 2.5 //

It is better to live in this world by begging than to slay these honoured teachers. By slaying them I would enjoy in this world pleasures which are stained with blood.

na chaitad vidmah kataran no gareeyo
yad waa jayema yadi vaa no jayeyuh
yaan eva hatwaa na jijeevishaamas
te'vasthitaah pramukhe dhaartaraashtraah // 2.6 //

I can hardly tell which will be better - to fight or not to fight, that we should conquer them or they should conquer us. The very sons of Dhritarashtra after slaying whom we do not even wish to live stand facing us.

kaarpanya dosho pahata swabhaavah
pricchaami twaam dharma sammoodha chetaah
yacchreyah syaan nischitam broohi tanme
shishyaste'ham shaadhi maam twaam prapannam // 2.7 //

With my nature stricken with weakness of sentimental pity and my mind bewildered about my duty, I request you to tell me for certain what is good for me. I am your disciple. Please teach me. I am seeking refuge in you.

na hi prapashyaami mamaapanudyaad
yacchokam ucchoshanam indriyaanaam
avaapya bhoomaav asapatnam riddham
raajyam suraanaam api chaadhipatyam // 2.8 //

For, even after obtaining an undisputed sovereignty and an affluent kingdom on this earth and lordship over the Gods, I do not see any means of driving away this grief which is drying up my senses.

sanjaya uvaacha

evam uktwaa hrishikesham gudakeshah parantapah
na yotsya iti govindam uktwaa tooshneem babhoova ha // 2.9 //

Sanjaya said:

Having thus spoken to Hrishikesa (Krishna), Arjuna the destroyer of foes (Parantapa), said to Govinda (Krishna), I will not fight and became silent.

tam uvaacha hrisheekeshah prahasanniva bhaarata
senayor ubhayor madhye visheedantam idam vachah // 2.10 //

O descendent of Bharata (Dhritarashtra), then Krishna, as if smiling, spoke these words to him (Arjuna) thus depressed in the midst of the two armies.

sri bhagavaan uvaacha

ashochyaan anvashochastwam prajnaavaadaamshcha bhaashase
gataasoon agataasoomshcha naanushochanti panditaah // 2.11 //

Sri Bhagavan said:

You grieve for those who are not to be grieved for; and yet you speak words of wisdom! The learned do not grieve for the departed and those who have not departed.

na twevaaham jaatu naasam na twam neme janaadhipaah
na chaiva na bhavishyaamah sarve vayam atah param // 2.12 //

It is not that I did not exist before, nor you nor these kings. Nor is it that we shall cease to exist in future.

dehino'smin yathaa dehe kaumaaram yauvanam jaraa
tathaa dehaantara praaptir dheeras tatra na mhuhyati // 2.13 //

Just as in this body the embodied self passes into childhood, youth and old age, so also does he pass into another body; calm man does not grieve at it.

maatraa sparshaastu kaunteya sheetoshna sukha dukhadaah
agamaapaayinonityaas taamstitikshaswa bhaarata //2.14 //

The contacts of the senses with objects, O son of Kunti, which cause heat and cold, pleasure and pain have a beginning and an end; they are impermanent ; endure them bravely, O descendent of Bharata (Arjuna).

yam hi na vyathayantyete purusham purusharshabha
samaduhkha sukham dheeram so'mritatwaaya kalpate // 2.15 //

That calm man who remains unchanged in pain and pleasure, whom these cannot disturb, alone is able, O greatest amongst men, to attain immortality.

naasato vidyate bhaavo naabhaavo vidyate satah
ubhayorapi drishto'ntastwanayos tattwadarshibhih // 2.16 //

The unreal has no existence. The Real never ceases to be (never ceases to exist). Men possessed of the knowledge of the Truth fully know both these.

avinaashi tu tad viddhi yena sarvam idam tatam
vinaasham avyayasyaasya na kaschit kartum arhati // 2.17 //

Know 'That' to be indestructible, by whom all this is pervaded. None can cause the destruction of That, the Imperishable.

antavanta ime dehaa nityasyoktaah shareerinah
anaashino'prameyasya tasmaad yudhyaswa bhaarata // 2.18 //

Only the bodies, of which this eternal, imperishable, and incomprehensible Self is the indweller, are said to have an end. Therefore, O descendent of Bharata (Arjuna), fight.

ya enam vetti hantaaram yashchainam manyate hatam
ubhau tau na vijaaneeto naayam hanti na hanyate // 2.19 //

He who looks on the Self to be the slayer and he who looks on the Self as the slain - neither of them apprehends correctly. The Self neither slays nor is slain.

na jaayate mriyate vaa kadaachin
naayam bhootwaa bhavitaa vaa na bhooyah
ajo nityah shaashwato'yam puraano
na hanyate hanyamaane shareere // 2.20 //

He is never born nor does He ever die; after having been, He again does not cease to be. Unborn, eternal, changeless and ancient. He is not killed when the body is killed.

vedaavinaashinam nityam ya enam ajam avyayam
katham sa purushah paartha kam ghaatayati hanti kam // 2.21 //

Whosoever knows Him to be indestructible, eternal, unborn and immutable, how can that man slay O Arjuna, or cause another to slay?

vaasaamsi jeernaani yathaa vihaaya
navaani grihnaati naro'paraani
tathaa shareeraani vihaaya jeernaa
nyanyaani samyaati navaani dehee // 2.22 //

Just as a man casts off his worn-out clothes and puts on new ones, so also the embodied Self casts off Its worn out bodies and enters that are new.

nainam chhindanti shastraani nainam dahati paavakah
na chainam kledayantyaapo na shoshayati maarutah // 2.23 //

Weapons cannot cut It, nor can fire burn It; water cannot wet It, nor can wind dry It.

acchedyo'yam adaahyo'yam akledyo'shoshya eva cha
nityah sarvagatah sthaanur achalo'yam sanaatanah // 2.24 //

This Self cannot be cut, burnt, wetted or dried up. It is eternal, all-pervading, stable, ancient and immovable.

avyakto'yam achintyo'yam avikaaryo'yam uchyate
tasmaad evam viditwainam naanushochitum arhasi // 2.25 //

The Self is unmanifest, unthinkable and unchangeable. Therefore, knowing it to be as such, you should not grieve.

atha chainam nityajaatam nityam vaa manyase mritam
tathaapi twam mahaabaaho nainam shochitum arhasi // 2.26 //

But even if you think of it as being perpetually born and perpetually dying, even then, O Mighty Armed (Arjuna), you should not grieve.

jaatasya hi dhruvo mrityur dhruvam janma mritasya cha
tasmaad aparihaarye'rthe natwam shochitum arhasi // 2.27 //

Death is sure to happen to that which is born. Birth is sure to happen to that which dies. Birth and death are certainly unavoidable. Therefore, you should not grieve over an inevitable occurrence.

avyaktaadeeni bhootani vyaktamadhyaani bhaarata
avyakta nidhanaanyeva tatra kaa paridevanaa // 2.28 //

Beings are unmanifest in their beginning, manifest in their middle state and unmanifest again in their end, O Arjuna. What is there to grieve about?

aashcharyavat pashyati kashchid enam
aashcharyavad vadati tathaiva chaanyah
aashcharyavacchainam anyah shrinoti
shrutwaapyenam veda na chaiva kaschit // 2.29 //

Some look on the Self as a wonder; some speak of It as a wonder; some hear of It as a wonder; still others, though hearing, do not understand It at all.

dehee nityam avadhyo'yam dehe sarvasya bhaarata
tasmaat sarvaani bhootani na twam shochitum arhasi // 2.30 //

This Self, the indweller in the body of everyone, is always indestructible. O, Arjuna, therefore you should not grieve for any creature.

swadharmam api chaavekshya na vikampitum arhasi
dharmyaaddhi yuddhaachhreyo'nyat kshatriyasya na vidyate // 2.31 //

Further having regard to your duty (your own Dharma) you should not waver, for there is nothing higher for a Kshatriya than a righteous war.

yadåcchayä copapannaà
svarga-dväram apävåtam
sukhinaù kñatriyäù pärtha
labhante yuddham édåçam // 2.32 //

Happy are the Kshatriyas who are called upon to fight in such a battle that comes of itself unsought as an open door to heaven, O Arjuna.

atha cet tvam imaà dharmyaà
saìgrämaà na kariñyasi
tataù sva-dharmaà kértià ca
hitvä päpam avaapsyasi // 2.33 //

If, however, you do not perform your religious duty of fighting, then you will certainly incur sins for neglecting your duties and thus lose your reputation as a fighter.

akértià cäpi bhütäni
kathayiñyanti te 'vyayäm
sambhävitasya cäkértir
maraëäd atiricyate // 2.34 //

People will always speak of your infamy, and for a respectable person, dishonour is worse than death.

bhayäd raëäd uparataà
maàsyante tväà mahä-rathäù
yeñäà ca tvaà bahu-mato
bhütvä yäsyasi läghavam // 2.35 //

The great generals who have highly esteemed your name and fame will think that you have left the battlefield out of fear only, and thus they will consider you insignificant.

aväcya-vädäàç ca bahün
vadiñyanti tavähitäù
nindantas tava sämarthyaà
tato duùkhataraà nu kim // 2.36 //

Your enemies will describe you in many unkind words and scorn your ability. What could be more painful for you?

hato vä präpsyasi svargaà
jitvä vä bhokñyase mahém
tasmäd uttiñöha kaunteya
yuddhäya kåta-niçcayaù // 2.37 //

O son of Kuntī, either you will be killed on the battlefield and attain the heavenly planets, or you will conquer and enjoy the earthly kingdom. Therefore, get up with determination and fight.

sukha-duùkhe same kåtvä
läbhäläbhau jayäjayau
tato yuddhäya yujyasva
naivaà päpam avaapsyasi // 2.38 //

Do thou fight for the sake of fighting, without considering happiness or distress, loss or gain, victory or defeat — and by so doing you shall never incur sin.

eñä te 'bhihitä säìkhye
buddhir yoge tv imäà çåëu
buddhyä yukto yayä pärtha
karma-bandhaà prahäsyasi // 2.39 //

Thus, far I have described this knowledge to you through analytical study. Now listen as I explain it in terms of working without fruitive results. O son of Parthā, when you act in such knowledge you can free yourself from the bondage of works.

nehäbhikrama-näço 'sti pratyaväyo na vidyate sv-alpam
apy asya dharmasya träyate mahato bhayät // 2.40 //

In this endeavour there is no loss or diminution, and a little advancement on this path can protect one from the most dangerous type of fear.

vyavasäyätmikä buddhir ekeha kuru-nandana bahu-çäkhä
hy anantäç ca buddhayo 'vyavasäyinäm // 2.41 //

Those who are on this path are resolute in purpose, and their aim is one. O beloved child of the Kurus, the intelligence of those who are irresolute is many-branched.

8.3 Seven Stages of Jnana

There are seven stages of Jnana or the seven Jnana Bhumikas. **(i)** First, Jnana should be developed through a deep study of Atma Jnana Sastras and association with the wise and the performance of virtuous actions without any expectation of fruits. This is Subheccha or good desire, which forms the first Bhumika or stage of Jnana. This will irrigate the mind with the waters of discrimination and protect it. There will be non-attraction or indifference to sensual objects in this stage. The first stage is the substratum of the other stages. From it the next two stages, viz., **(ii)** Vicharana and Tanumanasi will be reached. Constant Atma Vichara (Atmic enquiry) forms the second stage. **(iii)** The third stage is Tanumanasi. This is attained through the cultivation of special indifference to objects. The mind becomes thin like a thread. Hence the name Tanumanasi. Tanu means thread – threadlike state of mind. The third stage is also known by the name Asanga Bhavana. In the third stage, the aspirant is free from all attractions. If anyone dies in the third stage, he will remain in heaven for a long time and will reincarnate on earth again as a Jnani. The above three stages can be included under the Jagrat state. **(iv)** The fourth stage is Sattvapatti. This stage will destroy all Vasanas to the root. This can be included under the Svapana state. The world appears like a dream. Those who have reached the fourth stage will look upon all things of the universe with an equal eye. **(v)** The fifth stage is Asamsakti. There is perfect non-attachment to the objects of the world. There is no Upadhi or waking or sleeping in this stage. This is the Jivanmukti stage in which there is the experience of Ananda Svaroopa (the Eternal Bliss of Brahman) replete with spotless Jnana. This will come under Sushupti. **(vi)** The sixth stage is Padartha Bhavana. There is knowledge of Truth. **(vii)** The seventh stage is Turiya, or the state of superconsciousness. This is Moksha. This is also known by the name Turiyatita. There are no Sankalpas. All the Gunas disappear. This is above the reach of mind and speech. Disembodied salvation (Videhamukti) is attained in the seventh stage.

8.4 More on Jnana Yoga

The body is composed of the five elements and is unintelligent. It is made up of skin, flesh, blood and bones. It is produced by time, action and the attributes of Sattva, Rajas and Tamas.

The Atman is neither born, nor does it die, nor does it stop or go anywhere. It is neither male nor female nor neuter. It is all-pervading and everlasting. It is one without a second, unblemished like ether, eternal, pure and perfect Knowledge itself.

Sorrow has the body as its cause. The body has Karma for its cause. Action of Karma proceeds from man having the notion of 'I' in the body. The notion of 'I' which is unintelligent is beginningless, having Avidya for its root cause. Egoism is always associated with the reflection of Chitta like a piece of iron heated in fire. Thus, the body becomes independent with the Ahamkara (ego) and becomes possessed of intelligence.

I am the body; this notion arises by force of the connection between the Self and Ahamkara. Worldly life which is the giver of pleasure and pain has for its root this notion of 'I' in the body. On account of this identification of the Atman, which is without modification, with the Ahamkara, with the notion of I am the body, I am the doer of action, the individual soul always acts and is forcibly bound by the results. Possessed of virtue and vice, he wanders up and down. I have surely done much good work through sacrifices, gifts and the rest, and shall therefore go to heaven and enjoy happiness there; thus he thinks. This is a false notion. He enjoys in heaven the celestial happiness for some time, and falls down as soon as the results of his meritorious deeds are exhausted.

So long as there is connection of the Ahamkara or the principle of egoism and the rest with the body and the sense-organs, there are pleasure and pain and transmigratory existence for the self or the knower. Ahamkara is the notion of 'I' and 'mine' in the gross and subtle bodies. The ignorant are attached to the body. They cannot rise above the sense of 'I' and 'mine' in the gross body. The discriminating few men rise above it through Knowledge.

The Samsara or cause of worldly life exists so long as there is any thought of object of sense. When one awakens from the sleep of ignorance taking the unreal for the real, then it ceases to assert itself. The Samsara which has been erroneously imposed on the Self does not go of itself for one, who like a person in a dream cherishes objects of sense.

Non-existence appears to exist through the force of beginningless Avidya or ignorance. Man is agitated through attachment and aversion. The sense of 'I' is the effect of ignorance.

The mind is verily the world. The mind is bondage. The superimposition or identification of the mind with the Atman is the cause of bondage.

Just as a piece of crystal which is in fact colourless takes the red or other colour from the object with which it is brought into contact, so also is the world-process or Samsara due to the contact of the Self with the intellect or the organs of sense. The mind cannot of itself cognise without a cognising Self behind it. The Self on the other hand, making the objects created by the mind as its own, takes the form of the latter like the piece of crystal when it is brought into contact with coloured objects, and thus becomes bound by the attributes of those objects and wanders about in Samsara as if helpless and powerless.

Having first created the attributes of attachment and aversion to actions of diverse kinds, the mind takes in various forms, such as white, red and black (the good, the active and the passive). In this way, the Jiva or the individual soul wanders through the influence of Karma till the period of universal dissolution. At the time of universal dissolution, the Self survives with Vasanas taking impressions of past Karmas attracted under the influence of beginningless Avidya.

When there is universal dissolution, there is no destruction of the individual soul. He remains in a latent form in the Mula (original) Prakriti or Avyakta, which is the condition of the equilibrium of all the three Gunas. At the time of creation, he is born again together with the Vasanas born of the mind. In this way he is forced to go round and round like the wheel for drawing water.

When, through special merit acquired by good Karmas in the past, he gets the company of pious devotees, his mind becomes directed towards the Lord. Then is produced in him faith, which is so difficult of attainment, in hearing stories relating to the Lord. Then comes to him without any trouble Knowledge of the Self. Then through the grace of the preceptor, as well as Knowledge of the meaning of the great sentences, Tat Tvam Asi Thou Art That, and the like, and his own experience, he forthwith realises the distinction between the body, the organs of sense, egoism and the pure Atman and knows himself to be the intelligent and the blissful Self who is one without a second and becomes thenceforth released.

Know yourself, therefore, to be separate from the three bodies and beyond Prakriti. Relinquish all sense of 'I' in the body and become a Sage of Wisdom. Realise your own Self to be free from the conditions of waking, dream and deep sleep, as Truth, Knowledge and Bliss Absolute.

After having discussed two out of six systems of Hindu Philosophy, viz., Samkhya and Yoga, we shall now resume with the remaining four systems of this philosophy, in the chapters to follow.

Chapter - 9

Nyaya Philosophy

9.1 Introduction to Nyaya Philosophy

The Nyaya is the science of logical proof, and furnishes a correct method of philosophical inquiry into the objects and subjects of human knowledge. It is said to be the means to true knowledge about the soul and the realisation of the destiny of man according to the laws of nature. Vatsyayana, the classic commentator on the Nyaya-Sutra, defines it as a "critical examination of the objects of knowledge by means of the canons of logical proof." The Nyaya is also called Tarka vidyā, "science of reasoning," or Vada vidyā, "science of discussion." The founder of the Nyaya was Gautama (Gotama) who is frequently referred to in the literature as Aksapada, "Eye-footed," and Dirghatapas, "Long-penance." It was customary to call one by a name which gave a descriptive characterisation of the individual. In this instance, Gautama probably received these names from his long penances during his periods of study and from the fact that he was customarily seen with his eyes directed toward his feet when walking, which is a natural way to carry the head when contemplating during the course of a stroll. In fact, it is the way one is trained to walk.

The sage Gotama, who should not confused as Gautama Buddha. He is famous as 'Aksapāda'. Nyāya means correct thinking with proper arguments and valid reasoning. Thus, Nyāya philosophy is known as tarkashāstra (the science of reasoning); pramānashāstra (the science of logic and epistemology); hetuvidyā (the science of causes); vādavidyā (the science of debate); and anviksiki (the science of critical study). The Nyāya philosophy as a practitioner and believer of realism seeks for acquiring knowledge of reality.

Nyaya is a Sanskrit word which means justice, equality for all being, especially a collection of general or universal rules. In some contexts, it means model, axiom, plan, legal proceeding, judicial sentence, or judgment. Nyaya could also mean, "that which shows the way" tracing its Sanskrit etymology. In philosophical context, Nyaya encompasses propriety, logic and method.

Nyaya is related to several other concepts and words used in Indian philosophies: Hetu-vidya (science of causes), Anviksiki (science of inquiry, systematic philosophy), Pramana-sastra (epistemology, science of correct knowledge), Tattva-sastra (science of categories), Tarka-vidya (science of reasoning, innovation, synthesis), Vadartha (science of discussion) and Phakkika-sastra (science of uncovering sophism, fraud, error, finding fakes). Some of these subsume or deploy the tools of Nyaya.

Nyaya school's epistemology accepts four out of six Pramanas as reliable means of gaining knowledge – Pratyakṇa (perception), Anumāṇa (inference), Upamāṇa (comparison and analogy) and Śabda (word, testimony of past or present reliable experts). In its metaphysics, Nyaya school is closer to the Vaisheshika school of Hinduism than others. It holds that human suffering results from mistakes/defects produced by activity under wrong knowledge (notions and ignorance). Moksha (liberation), it states, is gained through right knowledge. This premise led Nyaya to concern itself with epistemology, that is the reliable means in gaining correct knowledge and to remove wrong notions. False knowledge is not merely ignorance to Naiyyayikas, it includes delusion. Correct knowledge is discovering and overcoming one's delusions, and understanding true nature of soul, self and reality.

Naiyyayika scholars approached philosophy as a form of direct realism, stating that anything that really exists is, in principle, humanly knowable. To them, correct knowledge and understanding is different from simple, reflexive cognition; it requires Anuvyavasaya (cross-examination of cognition, reflective cognition of what one thinks one knows). An influential collection of texts on logic and reason is the Nyāya Sūtras, attributed to **Akshapada Gautama**, variously estimated to have been composed between 6th century BCE and 2nd century CE.

Nyaya school shares some of its methodology and human suffering foundations with Buddhism; however, a key difference between the two is that Buddhism believes that there is neither a soul nor self; Nyaya school like other schools of Hinduism believes that there is a soul and self, with liberation (moksha) as a state of removal of ignorance, wrong knowledge, the gain of correct knowledge and unimpeded continuation of self.

9.2 Purpose of Nyaya Philosophy

The purpose of the Nyaya is said to enable us to attain the highest end of life, salvation, release, freedom as it is variously referred to.

For this purpose it classifies the different ways in which knowledge is acquired. It teaches that the world consists of the uninterrupted flow of misapprehension, faults, activity, birth and pain. By the cessation of the flow of this chain of consequences will we be freed. The way to break this chain is to obtain a fuller understanding of the true nature of things. When this has been accomplished the faults which consist of a delusion causing us to like and dislike a thing will no longer exist. When this disappears, there will no longer be any desire which is the stimulus for all action. It is claimed that this will free us from rebirth, the cause of all sorrow and suffering, and enable us to achieve the supreme end of life.

This exalted goal is said to be attained by thoroughly realising the four subjects established in the Nyayasutra, namely: (1) the thing to be avoided (i.e., pain), (2) its cause (i.e., desire and ignorance), (3) absolute avoidance, (4) the means of such avoidance (i.e., true knowledge) which is to be secured. These four steps are considered the prime pre-requisites for the attainment of life's highest reward.

The teachings of the Nyaya are believed to enable us to discern the true from the false, and at the same time, to be our greatest protection when our knowledge is still in the process of growth and has not yet matured into the ripened fruit of enlightenment. Today in the search for truth, the doctrine of each new teacher raises doubt as to which is the right path. The seeker of truth centuries before the advent of the Christian era was likewise confronted with the same problem of trying to discern the true from the false. For this very purpose, certain teachings of the Nyaya were laid down so that there would be a rational basis for recognising the Truth. The only difference between those of the past and ourselves was that in those days there were a thousand teachers to every one met today.

9.3 Sixteen Categories (padārthas) in Nyaya Philosophy

The Nyaya metaphysics recognises sixteen padarthas or categories and includes all six (or seven) categories of the Vaisheshika in the second one of them, called prameya.

These sixteen categories are:

(i) pramāṇa (valid means of knowledge or knowledge sources),

(ii) prameya (objects of valid knowledge),

(iii) saṁśaya (doubt),

(iv) prayojana (aim),

(v) dṛṣṭānta (example),

(vi) siddhānta (conclusion or accepted position),

(vii) avayava (members of inferential components),
(viii) tarka (hypothetical/suppositional reasoning),
(ix) nirṇaya (settlement or certainty),
(x) vāda (discussion or debate for truth),
(xi) jalpa (wrangling or disputation),
(xii) vitaṇḍā (cavilling or destructive debate),
(xiii) hetvābhāsa (fallacy or pseudo-proovers),
(xiv) chala (quibbling or equivocation),
(xv) jāti (sophisticated refutation or misleading/futile objections), and
(xvi) nigrahasthāna (point of defeat or clinchers).

9.4 More on Nyaya Philosophy

The Nyaya school of Hinduism developed and refined many treatises on philosophy that widely influenced other schools of Hinduism. Nyaya treated it as theory of knowledge, and its scholars developed it as Pramana-sastras. Pramana, a Sanskrit word, literally is "means of knowledge". It encompasses one or more reliable and valid means by which human beings gain accurate, true knowledge. The focus of Pramana is how correct knowledge can be acquired, how one knows, how one doesn't, and to what extent knowledge pertinent about someone or something can be acquired.

The Naiyayikas (the Nyaya scholars) accepted four valid means (pramaṇa) of obtaining valid knowledge (pramana) - perception (pratyakṣa), inference (anumāna), comparison (upamāna) and word/testimony of reliable sources (śabda). The Nyaya scholars, along with those from other schools of Hinduism, also developed a theory of error, to methodically establish means to identify errors and the process by which errors are made in human pursuit of knowledge. These include Saṁśaya (problems, inconsistencies, doubts) and Viparyaya (contrariness, errors) which can be corrected or resolved by a systematic process of Tarka (reasoning, technique).

9.4.1 Pratyaksha (Perception)

Pratyaksha (perception) occupies the foremost position in the Nyaya philosophy. Perception can be of two types, laukika (ordinary) and alaukika (extraordinary). Ordinary perception is defined by Akshapāda Gautama in his Nyaya Sutra (I,i.4) as a 'non-erroneous cognition which is produced by the intercourse of sense-organs with the objects'.

Indian texts identify four requirements for correct perception: (i) Indriyarthasannikarsa (direct experience by one's sensory organ(s) with the object, whatever is being studied), (ii) Avyapadesya (non-verbal;

correct perception is not through hearsay, according to ancient Indian scholars, where one's sensory organ relies on accepting or rejecting someone else's perception), (iii) Avyabhicara (does not wander; correct perception does not change, nor is it the result of deception because one's sensory organ or means of observation is drifting, defective, suspect), and (iv) Vyavasayatmaka (definite; correct perception excludes judgments of doubt, either because of one's failure to observe all the details, or because one is mixing inference with observation and observing what one wants to observe, or not observing what one does not want to observe).

Ordinary perception to Nyaya scholars was based on direct experience of reality by eyes, ears, nose, touch and taste. Extraordinary perception included yogaja or pratibha (intuition), samanyalaksanapratyaksa (a form of induction from perceived specifics to a universal), and jnanalaksanapratyaksa (a form of perception of prior processes and previous states of a 'topic of study' by observing its current state).

9.4.2 Determinate and Indeterminate Perception

The Naiyyayika maintains two modes or stages in perception. The first is called nirvikalpa (indeterminate), when one just perceives an object without being able to know its features, and the second savikalpa (determinate), when one is able to clearly know an object. All laukika and alaukika pratyakshas are savikalpa, but it is necessarily preceded by an earlier stage when it is indeterminate. Vātsāyana says that if an object is perceived with its name we have determinate perception but if it is perceived without a name, we have indeterminate perception. Indeterminate perception apprehends substance, qualities and actions and universals as separate and indistinct something and also it does not have any association with name, while determinate perception apprehends all these together with a name. There is yet another stage called Pratyabhijñā, when one is able to re-recognise something on the basis of memory.

9.4.3 Anumāna (Inference)

Anumāna (inference) is one of the most important contributions of the Nyaya. It can be of two types: inference for oneself (Svarthanumana, where one does not need any formal procedure, and at the most the last three of their 5 steps), and inference for others (Parathanumana, which requires a systematic methodology of 5 steps). Inference can also be classified into 3 types: Purvavat (inferring an unperceived effect from a perceived cause), Sheshavat (inferring an unperceived cause from a perceived effect) and Samanyatodrishta (when inference is not based on causation but on uniformity of co-existence).

9.4.4 Theory of Inference

The methodology of inference involves a combination of induction and deduction by moving from particular to particular via generality. It has **five steps**, as in the example shown:

(i) There is fire on the hill (called Pratijñā, required to be proved);
(ii) Because there is smoke there (called Hetu, reason);
(iii) Wherever there is smoke, there is fire, e.g. in a kitchen (called Udāhārana, example of vyāpti);
(iv) The hill has smoke that is pervaded by fire (called Upanaya, reaffirmation or application);
(v) Therefore, there is fire on the hill (called Nigamana, conclusion).

In Nyāya terminology for this example, the hill would be called as paksha (minor term), the fire is called as sādhya (major term), the smoke is called as hetu, and the relationship between the smoke and the fire is called as vyapti (middle term).

Hetu further has five characteristics: (1) It must be present in the Paksha, (2) It must be present in all positive instances, (3) It must be absent in all negative instances, (4) It must not be incompatible with the minor term or Paksha, and (5) All other contradictions by other means of knowledge should be absent.

The fallacies in Anumana (hetvābhasa) may occur due to the following:

1. ***Asiddha***: It is the unproved hetu that results in this fallacy. [Paksadharmata]
   - *Ashrayasiddha*: If Paksha [minor term] itself is unreal, then there cannot be locus of the hetu. For example, the sky-lotus is fragrant, because it is a lotus like any other lotus.
   - *Svarupasiddha*: Hetu cannot exist in paksa at all. For example, sound is a quality, because it is visible.
   - *Vyapyatvasiddha*: Conditional hetu. 'Wherever there is fire, there is smoke'. The presence of smoke is due to wet fuel.

2. ***Savyabhichara:*** This is the fallacy of irregular hetu.
   - *Sadharana*: The hetu is too wide. It is present in both sapaksa and vipaksa. 'The hill has fire because it is knowable'.
   - *Asadharana*: The hetu is too narrow. It is only present in the Paksha, it is not present in the Sapaksa and in the Vipaksha. 'Sound is eternal because it is audible'.

- *Anupasamhari*: Here the hetu is non-exclusive. The hetu is all-inclusive and leaves nothing by way of sapaksha or vipaksha. e.g. 'All things are non-ternal, because they are knowable'.

3. ***Satpratipaksa***: Here the hetu is contradicted by another hetu. If both have equal force, then nothing follows. 'Sound is eternal, because it is audible', and 'Sound is non-eternal, because it is produced'. Here 'audible' is counterbalanced by 'produced' and both are of equal force.
4. ***Badhita***: When another proof (as by perception) definitely contradicts and disproves the middle term (hetu). 'Fire is cold because it is a substance'.
5. ***Viruddha***: Instead of proving something it is proving the opposite. 'Sound is eternal because it is produced'.

9.4.5 Upamāna (comparison, analogy)

Upamāna means comparison and analogy. Upamana may be explained with the example of a traveller who has never visited lands or islands with endemic population of wildlife. He or she is told, by someone who has been there, that in those lands you see an animal that sort of looks like a cow, grazes like cow but is different from a cow in such and such way. Such use of analogy and comparison is, state the Indian epistemologists, a valid means of conditional knowledge, as it helps the traveller identify the new animal later. The subject of comparison is formally called upameyam, the object of comparison is called upamānam, while the attribute(s) are identified as sāmānya. Thus, if a boy says "his face is like the moon in charmingness", "his face" is upameyam, the moon is upamānam, and charmingness is sāmānya. The 7th century text Bhaṭṭikāvya in verses 10.28 through 10.63 discusses many types of comparisons and analogies, identifying when this epistemic method is more useful and reliable, and when it is not. In various ancient and medieval texts of Hinduism, 32 types of Upamāna and their value in epistemology are debated.

9.4.6 Śabda (word, testimony)

Śabda means relying on word, testimony of past or present reliable experts. Sabda-pramana means testimony of a reliable and trustworthy person (āptavākya). The schools of Hinduism which consider it epistemically valid suggest that a human being needs to know numerous facts, and with the limited time and energy available, he can learn only a fraction of those facts and truths directly. He must rely on others, his parent, family, friends, teachers, ancestors and kindred members of society to rapidly acquire and share knowledge and thereby enrich each other's lives. This means of gaining proper knowledge is either spoken or written, but through Sabda (words). The reliability of the source is important, and legitimate knowledge can only come from the Sabda of reliable sources.

Testimony can be of two types, Vaidika (Vedic), which are the words of the four sacred Vedas, and Laukika, or words and writings of trustworthy human beings. Vaidika testimony is preferred over Laukika testimony. Laukika-sourced knowledge must be questioned and revised as more trustworthy knowledge becomes available.

9.4.7 Theory of Causation

A *cause* is defined as an unconditional and invariable antecedent of an *effect* and an effect as an unconditional and invariable consequent of a cause. The same cause produces the same effect; and the same effect is produced by the same cause. The cause is *not* present in any hidden form whatsoever in its effect.

The following conditions should be met:

1. The cause must be antecedent [Purva vritti]
2. Invariability [Niyatapurva vritti]
3. Unconditionality [Ananyathasiddha]

Nyaya recognises five kinds of accidental antecedents [Anyathasiddha]

1. Mere accidental antecedent. For example, the colour of the potter's cloth.
2. Remote cause is not a cause because it is not unconditional. For example, the father of the potter.
3. The co-effects of a cause are not causally related.
4. Eternal substances, or eternal conditions are not unconditional antecedents, for example, space.
5. Unnecessary things, for example, the donkey of the potter.

Nyaya recognises three kinds of cause:

1. *Samavayi*, material cause, for example, thread of a cloth.
2. *Asamavayi*, colour of the thread which gives the colour of the cloth.
3. *Nimitta*, efficient cause, for example, the weaver of the cloth.

9.4.8 Anyathakhyativada (Theory of Error)

The Nyaya theory of error is similar to that of Kumarila's Viparita-khyati (see Mimamsa). The Naiyyayikas also believe like Kumarila that error is due to a wrong synthesis of the presented and the represented objects. The represented object is confused with the presented one. The word 'anyatha' means 'elsewise' and 'elsewhere' and both these meanings are brought out in error. The presented object is perceived elsewise and the represented object exists elsewhere. They further maintain that knowledge is not intrinsically valid but becomes so on account of extraneous conditions (paratah pramana during both validity and invalidity).

9.5 On God and Salvation

Early Naiyyayikas wrote very little about Ishvara (literally, the Supreme Soul). Evidence available so far suggests that early Nyaya scholars were non-theistic or atheists. Later, and over time, Nyaya scholars tried to apply some of their epistemological insights and methodology to the question: Does God exist? Some offered arguments against and some in favour.

9.5.1 Arguments that God does not exist

Nyāya Sūtra's Book 4, Chapter 1, verses 19–21, postulates God exists, states a consequence, then presents contrary evidence, and from contradiction concludes that the postulate must be invalid.

The Lord is the cause, since we see that human action lacks results. This is not so since, as a matter of fact, no result is accomplished without human action. Since this is efficacious, the reason lacks force.

—Nyaya Sutra, IV.1.19 - IV.1.21

A literal interpretation of the three verses suggests that Nyaya school rejected the need for a God for the efficacy of human activity. Since human action and results do not require assumption or need of the existence of God, sutra IV.1.21 is seen as a criticism of the "existence of God and theism postulate". The context of the above verses includes various efficient causes. Nyāya Sūtra verses IV.1.22 to IV.1.24, for example, examine the hypothesis that "random chance" explains the world, after these Indian scholars had rejected God as the efficient cause.

9.5.2 Arguments that God exists

Scholars gave the following nine arguments to prove the existence of creative God and also tried to refute the existing objections and questions by atheistic systems of charvaka, mimamsa, buddhists, jinas and samkhya:

(i) Kāryāt (lit. "from effect"): The world is an effect, all effects have efficient cause, hence the world must have an efficient cause. That efficient cause is God.

(ii) Āyojanāt (lit., from combination): Atoms are inactive. To form a substance, they must combine. To combine, they must move.

Nothing moves without intelligence and source of motion. Since we perceive substance, some intelligent source must have moved the inactive atoms. That intelligent source is God.

(iii) Dhṛtyādéḥ (lit., from support): Something sustains this world. Something destroys this world. Unintelligent Adrsta (unseen principles of nature) cannot do this. We must infer that something intelligent is behind. That is God.

(iv) Padāt (lit., from word): Each word has meaning and represents an object. This representational power of words has a cause. That cause is God.

(v) Pratyayataḥ (lit, from faith): Vedas are infallible. Human beings are fallible. Infallible Vedas cannot have been authored by fallible human beings. Someone authored the infallible Vedas. That author is God.

(vi) Shrutéḥ (lit., from scriptures): The infallible Vedas testify to the existence of God. Thus, God exists.

(vii) Vākyāt (lit., from precepts): Vedas deal with moral laws, the rights and the wrongs. These are divine. Divine injunctions and prohibitions can only come from a divine creator of laws. That divine creator is God.

(viii) Samkhyāviśeṣāt (lit., from the specialty of numbers): By rules of perception, only number "one" can ever be directly perceived. All other numbers other than one, are inferences and concepts created by consciousness. When man is born, his mind is incapable of inferences and concepts. He develops consciousness as he develops. The consciousness development is self-evident and proven because of man's ability with perfect numerical conception. This ability to conceive numerically perfect concepts must depend on something. That something is divine consciousness. So God must exist.

(ix) Adṛṣṭāt (lit., from the unforeseen): Everybody reaps the fruits of his own actions. Merits and demerits accrue from his own actions. An Unseen Power keeps a balance sheet of the merit and demerit. But since this Unseen Power is Unintelligent, it needs intelligent guidance to work. That intelligent guide is God.

9.6 Self and Liberation

The Nyāyikas expressed that there are infinite number of individual Self, existing in the universe. All those have perceivable qualities like pleasure, pain, etc. They are eternal and all pervading. According to Nyāya, the self can neither be identified with mind (mānas) nor can be identified with pure consciousness, but understood as consciousness belonging to an individual/subject. This is so because mind is atomic and unperceivable and hence devoid from perceivable qualities. On the other hand, consciousness belongs to the individual self but not same as self. Thus, consciousness is not the self but only an attribute of the self. It is an accidental attribute of the self. The self in its original state has no consciousness and hence devoid of cognition and knowledge. But when it comes to contact with sense organs it acquires consciousness.

Self is regarded as 'I' the knower and it is known through internal perception. Since there is self, there is bondage and hence, aspires for liberation or salvation. Liberation is the state refraining from all kinds of sufferings and bondage which arises because of the self's association with body and sense organs. Nyāyikas uphold association and attachment are the sources of pain and suffering. Hence, as long as self is attached with body and sense organs, it goes through the cycles of birth and death. This implies Nyāyikas believe in law of karma.

Liberation, according to Nyāya, can be achieved when there is cessation of karmic chain or karmic influx. It is a state where self is detached from body and sense organs.

9.7 An Established Tenet (Siddhanta)

It is a dogma resting on the authority of a certain school, hypothesis, or implication.

There are four kinds of dogma:

(1) A dogma of all the schools is defined as a tenet which is not opposed by any school and which is claimed by at least one school; for example, all schools accept earth, water, light, air, and ether as the basic five elements, and smell, taste, colour, touch, and sound as the objects of the five senses.

(2) A dogma peculiar to some school is defined as a tenet which is accepted by similar schools, but rejected by opposite schools; for example, the Samkhya doctrine proceeds on the established premise that "a thing cannot come into existence out of nothing."

(3) A hypothetical dogma is defined as a tenet which, if accepted, leads to the acceptance of another tenet; for example, the acceptance of the doctrine that there is a soul apart from the senses, because it can recognise one and the same object by seeing and touch, implies:

(a) that the senses are more than one; (b) that each of the senses has its particular object; (c) that the soul derives its knowledge through the channels of the senses; and (d) that a substance which is distinct from its qualities is the abode of them. Many other implications could be cited.

(4) An implied dogma is defined as a tenet which is not explicitly declared as such, but which follows from the examination of particulars concerning it, for example, the discussion whether sound is eternal or non-eternal implies that sound is a substance.

9.8 Nyaya Sūtras

The Nyāya Sūtras is an ancient Indian Sanskrit text composed by Aksapāda Gautama, and the foundational text of the Nyaya school of Hindu philosophy. The date when the text was composed, and the biography of its author is unknown, but variously estimated between 6th century BCE and 2nd century CE. The text may have been composed by more than one author, over a period of time. The text consists of five books, with two chapters in each book, with a cumulative total of 528 aphoristic sutras, about rules of reason, logic, epistemology and metaphysics.

The Nyāya Sūtras is a Hindu text, notable for focusing on knowledge and logic, and making no mention of Vedic rituals. The first book is structured as a general introduction and table of contents of sixteen categories of knowledge. Book two is about pramana (epistemology), book three is about prameya or the objects of knowledge, and the text discusses the nature of knowledge in remaining books. It set the foundation for Nyaya tradition of the empirical theory of validity and truth, opposing uncritical appeals to intuition or scriptural authority.

The Nyaya sutras cover a wide range of topics, including Tarka-Vidyā, the science of debate or Vāda-Vidyā, the science of discussion. The Nyāya Sutras are related to but extend the Vaiśeṣika epistemological and metaphysical system. Later commentaries expanded, expounded and discussed Nyaya sutras, the earlier surviving commentaries being by Vatsyayana (c.450–500 CE), followed by the Nyāya Varttika of Uddyotakāra (c. 6th–7th centuries), Vācaspati Miśra's Tātparyatīkā (9th century), Udayana's Tātparyapariśuddhi (10th century), and Jayanta's Nyāyamañjarī (10th century).

The text is written in sutra genre. A sutra is a Sanskrit word that means "string, thread", and represents a condensed manual of knowledge of a specific field or school. Each sutra is any short rule, like a theorem distilled into few words or syllables, around which "teachings of ritual, philosophy, grammar or any field of knowledge" can be woven. Sutras were compiled to be remembered, used as reference and to help teach and transmit ideas from one generation to the next.

The first sutra 1.1.1 of the text asserts its scope and the following sixteen categories of knowledge as a means to gain competence in any field of interest:

Perfection is attained by the correct knowledge about true nature of sixteen categories:

> (i) means of right knowledge (pramāṇa); (ii) object of right knowledge (prameya); (iii) doubt (samsaya); (iv) purpose (prayojana); (v) familiar instance (dṛṣṭānta); (vi) established tenet (siddhānta); (vii) members of an inference (avayava); (viii) reasoning (tarka); (ix) ascertainment or results (nirṃaya); (x) discussion (vāda); (xi) sophistic disputations (jalpa); (xii) cavil (vitaṇḍa); (xiii) fallacies (hetvābhāsa); (xiv) quibbles (chala); (xv) futile rejoinders (jāti); and (xvi) methods of losing an argument (nigrahasthāna).
>
> —Nyayasutra, 1.1.1

These sixteen categories cover many sections of the text. The verse 1.1.2 of the Nyāya Sūtra declares the text's goal is to study and describe the attainment of liberation of soul from wrong knowledge, faults and sorrow, through the application of above sixteen categories of perfecting knowledge.

The Nyaya-sutras assert the premise that "all knowledge is not intrinsically valid", that "most knowledge is not valid unless proven" and "truth exists whether we human beings know it or not". However, the text accepts the foundation that "some knowledge is self-evident" and axiomatic in every field of knowledge, which can neither be proven nor needs proof, such as "I am conscious", "I think" and "soul exists". Furthermore, the text presents its thesis that knowledge is not self-revealing, one must make effort to gain knowledge and this is a systematic process that empowers one to learn correct knowledge, and abandon incorrect knowledge.

The Nyāya sutras asserts and then discusses four reliable means of obtaining knowledge (pramāṇa), viz., Perception, Inference, Comparison and Reliable Testimony.

9.9 Commentaries

The earliest surviving complete bhasya (review and commentary) on Nyaya Sutras is by Vatsyayana. This commentary itself inspired many secondary and tertiary bhasya. Vatsyayana's commentary has been variously dated to be from the 5th century CE, or much earlier around 2nd century BCE. Another often studied surviving commentary on the text is credited to Vacaspati Mishra from about 9th century CE.

Liberation is impossible without knowledge of the real nature of the world. To achieve liberation and to know the soul, one must take shelter of yoga practices, because without this knowledge, knowledge of Reality is not obtained.

— Akṣapada Gautama in Nyayasutra

Other historical Indian commentaries and works inspired by Nyayasutras and which have survived into the modern era, include Nyaya-varttika by 6th century Uddyotakara, Nyaya-bhasyatika by 6th century Bhavivikta, another Nyaya-bhasyatika by 7th century Aviddhakarna, Nyaya-bhusana by 9th century Bhasarvajana, Nyaya-manjari by 9th century Kashmir scholar Jayanta Bhatta, Nyaya-prakirnaka by 10th century Karnata scholar Trilocana, and Nyaya-kandali by 10th century Bengal scholar Sridhara.

Numerous other commentaries are referenced in other Indian historical texts, but these manuscripts are either lost or yet to be found. Starting around 11th to 12th century CE, Udayana wrote a primary work, that built upon and expanded the theories on reason found in Nyayasutras. Udayana's work created the foundation for Navya-Nyaya (new Nyaya) school. The Hindu scholar Gangesa of 13th or 14th century, integrated the Gautama's Nyayasutras and Udayana's Navya-Nyaya work, to create the influential Tattvacintāmaṇi text considered a masterpiece by scholars.

9.10 Futility

It consists in offering objections founded on mere similarity or dissimilarity. The reply is said to be futile if it does not take into consideration the universal connection between the middle term and the major term. Mere similarity or dissimilarity is not sufficient. There are twenty-four kinds of futility which aim at showing an equality of the arguments of two sides. They are as follows:

(1) Balancing the homogeneity.

(2) Balancing the heterogeneity.

(3) Balancing the addition.

(4) Balancing the subtraction.

(5) Balancing the questionable.

(6) Balancing the unquestionable.

(7) Balancing the alternative.

(8) Balancing the reciprocity.
(9) Balancing the co-presence.
(10) Balancing the mutual absence.
(11) Balancing the infinite regression.
(12) Balancing the counter-example.
(13) Balancing the non-produced.
(14) Balancing the doubt.
(15) Balancing the controversy.
(16) Balancing the non-reason.
(17) Balancing the presumption.
(18) Balancing the non-difference.
(19) Balancing the non-demonstration.
(20) Balancing the perception.
(21) Balancing the non-perception.
(22) Balancing the non-eternality.
(23) Balancing the eternality.
(24) Balancing the effect.

9.11 Disagreement in Principle (Nigrahasthana)

It arises when one misunderstands, or does not understand at all. There is no purpose in arguing with one who reveals his utter lack of understanding of the subject of investigation; therefore, one is privileged to stop the argument. Twenty-two occasions of disagreement in principle are listed and discussed in this text. They are as follows:

(1) Hurting the proposition.
(2) Shifting the proposition.
(3) Opposing the proposition.
(4) Renouncing the proposition.
(5) Shifting the reason.
(6) Shifting the topic.
(7) The meaningless.
(8) The unintelligible.
(9) The incoherent.
(10) The inopportune.
(11) Saying too little.
(12) Saying too much.

(13) Repetition.
(14) Silence.
(15) Ignorance.
(16) Non-ingenuity.
(17) Evasion.
(18) Admission of an opinion.
(19) Overlooking the censurable.
(20) Censuring the non-censurable.
(21) Deviating from a tenet.
(22) The semblance of a reason.

9.12 Nyaya and Navyanyaya

Nyāya, and its further development in the Navyanyāya (new Nyāya) in time made immense contributions in the new philosophy. Notice here that arises between earlier- and later-day Nyāya stalwarts. Vaiśeṣika began with a fixed number of padārthas (six, later seven), whereas the Navyanyāya (new Nyāya) school (c. 13th cent.) came to advocate a theory of an almost undetermined number of padārthas.

Navya carries the nuance of "new" "neo" or "nouveau" and may also mean "worthy" or "laudable," but it also has inflected in it nyaya in both senses of logic and new, so there is a double entendre implicated. "Navyanyāya" is the name of the subschool of Nyāya that developed after the 10th century, closer to the era from the 14th to the late 17th century, in about three specific areas in northeast India: Kāśi (Varanasi), Navadvip, and Mithila, where philosophers schooled in the classical Nyāya system interacted with intellectuals and philosophers and learned scholars belonging to different schools of thought, notably Buddhists, moving in and out of Lhasa and Nalanda, Vedāntins, and Jainas.

One may also note that while the Navyanyāya philosophising climaxed in its rationally analytical and logical developments, there is indeed no evidence of deep or engaging reflections on the emotions, on feelings other than those marked to separate out cognitions from the range of human experiences (anubhava). The aesthetic and the sublime seem to find no place in their philosophising either, much less under the rubric of the categories. Did karma ever feature as a possible natural kind or moral universal? This is such a pervasive trope in the tradition that one wonders how it can be so overlooked by the Naiyāyikas.

Chapter 10

Vaisheshika Philosophy

10.1 Introduction to Vaisheshika Philosophy

Vaisheshika or Vaiśeṣika is one of the six schools of Indian philosophy (Vedic systems) from ancient India. In its early stages, the Vaiśeṣika was an independent philosophy with its own metaphysics, epistemology, logic, ethics, and soteriology. Over time, the Vaiśeṣika system became similar in its philosophical procedures, ethical conclusions and soteriology to the Nyāya school of Hinduism, but retained its difference in epistemology and metaphysics.

The epistemology of Vaiśeṣika school of Hinduism, like Buddhism, accepted only two reliable means to knowledge: perception and inference. Vaiśeṣika school and Buddhism both consider their respective scriptures as indisputable and valid means to knowledge, the difference being that the scriptures held to be a valid and reliable source by Vaiśeṣikas were the Vedas.

Vaisheshika school is known for its insights in naturalism. It is a form of atomism in natural philosophy. It postulated that all objects in the physical universe are reducible to paramāṇu (atoms), and one's experiences are derived from the interplay of substance (a function of atoms, their number and their spatial arrangements), quality, activity, commonness, particularity and inherence. Everything was composed of atoms, qualities emerged from aggregates of atoms, but the aggregation and nature of these atoms was predetermined by cosmic forces. Ajivika metaphysics included a theory of atoms which was later adapted in Vaiśeṣika school.

According to Vaiśeṣika school, knowledge and liberation were achievable by a complete understanding of the world of experience.

Hinduism identifies six Pramāṇas as epistemically reliable means to accurate knowledge and to truths: Pratyakṣa (perception), Anumāna (inference), Upamāna (comparison and analogy), Arthāpatti (postulation, derivation from circumstances), Anupalabdhi (non-perception, negative/

cognitive proof) and Śabda (word, testimony of past or present reliable experts). Of these Vaiśeṣika epistemology considered only pratyaksha (perception) and anumāna (inference) as reliable means of valid knowledge.

10.1.1 Pratyaksha

It means perception. It is of two types: external and internal. External perception is described as that arising from the interaction of five senses and worldly objects, while internal perception is described by this school as that of inner sense, the mind. The ancient and medieval texts of Hinduism identify four requirements for correct perception: (i) Indriyarthasannikarsa (direct experience by one's sensory organ(s) with the object, whatever is being studied), (ii) Avyapadesya (non-verbal; correct perception is not through hearsay, according to ancient Indian scholars, where one's sensory organ relies on accepting or rejecting someone else's perception), (iii) Avyabhicara (does not wander; correct perception does not change, nor is it the result of deception because one's sensory organ or means of observation is drifting, defective, suspect), and (iv) Vyavasayatmaka (definite; correct perception excludes judgments of doubt, either because of one's failure to observe all the details, or because one is mixing inference with observation and observing what one wants to observe, or not observing what one does not want to observe). Some ancient scholars proposed "unusual perception" as pramāṇa and called it internal perception, a proposal contested by other Indian scholars. The internal perception concepts included pratibha (intuition), samanyalaksanapratyaksa (a form of induction from perceived specifics to a universal), and jnanalaksanapratyaksa (a form of perception of prior processes and previous states of a 'topic of study' by observing its current state). Further, the texts considered and refined rules of accepting uncertain knowledge from Pratyakṣa-pranama, so as to contrast nirnaya (definite judgment, conclusion) from anadhyavasaya (indefinite judgment).

10.1.2 Anumāna

It means inference. It is described as reaching a new conclusion and truth from one or more observations and previous truths by applying reason. Observing smoke and inferring fire is an example of Anumana. In all except one Hindu philosophies, this is a valid and useful means to knowledge. The method of inference is explained by Indian texts as consisting of three parts: pratijna (hypothesis), hetu (a reason), and drshtanta (examples). The hypothesis must further be broken down into two parts: sadhya (that idea which needs to be proven or disproven) and paksha (the object on which the sadhya is predicated). The inference is conditionally true if sapaksha (positive examples as evidence) are present, and if vipaksha (negative examples as counter-evidence) are absent. For rigor, the Indian philosophies also state further epistemic steps. For example, they demand Vyapti - the requirement that the hetu (reason) must necessarily and separately account for the inference in "all" cases, in both sapaksha and vipaksha. A conditionally proven hypothesis is called a Nigamana (conclusion).

10.2 Categories of Padārtha

According to the Vaisheshika school, all things that exist, that can be cognised and named are padārthas (literal meaning: the meaning of a word), the objects of experience. All objects of experience can be classified into six categories, dravya (substance), guṇa (quality), karma (activity), sāmānya (generality), viśeṣa (particularity) and samavāya (inherence). Later Vaiśeṣikas (Śrīdhara and Udayana and Śivāditya) added one more category abhava (non-existence). The first three categories are defined as artha (which can perceived) and they have real objective existence. The last three categories are defined as budhyapekṣam (product of intellectual discrimination) and they are logical categories.

10.2.1 Dravya (substance; the building blocks):

According to the Vaisesika, substance as an entity possesses qualities and action. It is the inherent or material cause of an effect. The genus of substance (dravyatva) inheres in it. It is not mere conglomeration of qualities and actions. It has a real and objective existence. It differs from qualities and actions because it is their substrate. They inhere in it. It is their substratum. Thus, it is said that a substance is the substrate of qualities and actions. Qualities and actions can be separated from substance. The reason is, they exist in a substance.

Kanada in his sutras enumerates real entities irrespective of whether they can be perceived through the sense organs or not. These are conceivable by the mind of the observer who is central to his world. These are the nine dravyas and these alone describe everything existing in the universe. These are the building blocks of Kanada's world described through their gunas/ attributes and karma/motion. Space is one among these nine and Kanada recognises it as an independent positive entity which is neither absence of matter nor an abstract concept. Every dravya has an identifier.

Linga, which helps identify the specific dravya, besides which it has a unique set of guna/attributes associated with it. (V. Sutra, 1-1-5)

Prithvi: earth, Apas: water, Tejas: Fire vayus: Air, Akasam, kalah: Time, Dik: Space, Atma: Manas: mind Iti, only Dravyani, dravyas.

Earth, water, Fire, Air, Akasa, time, Space, atma, mind are the only nine dravyas (1.1.5.)

The Vaisesika system expresses that a substance is devoid of qualities at the first moment of its production. It possesses qualities at the next moment. Substances, for them, are of two sorts; eternal and non-eternal. The non-eternal substances are:

(i) Earth or Prithivi
(ii) Water or Jal
(iii) Fire or Tej
(iv) Air or Vayu.

The eternal substances are:

(i) Time or Kala
(ii) Space or Dik
(iii) Self or Atma
(iv) Mind or Manas.

Commentary: All the nine mentioned dravyas in the sutra although are translated as earth, water, etc., are not to be understood as the planet earth or the drinking water, etc. These nine dravyas have specific gunas/attributes associated to them like the dravya earth has smell associated as the primary guna/attribute to it. An understanding of dravyas can be arrived at by analysing their attributes and their interacting with the rest of the world. It is important to understand the division of the dravyas.

The first four dravyas: earth, water, fire and air are associated with a sense organ each as sense of smell, taste, sight and touch respectively. Although sound is mentioned as the identifier of akasa - the fifth dravya, which is not translated here as ether.

Time, space, atma and mind are the eternal or nitya dravyas and none of them are perceivable by any of the sense organs is a basic definition in Vaisesika. Although, these four eternal entities can only be conceived by the mind, they are really existent dravyas or entities. Time, space and akasa are incapable of motion (by sutra 5.2.21) and it is only the first four dravyas and mind which are capable of motion. The mind is also not visible (because it is by nature an anu like-fundamental particle, which is not visible by sutra 7.1.23). It is only the first four dravyas which compose the matter world. A sort of motion is applicable only to the matter section of dravyas which are the first four among the nine.

A substance is the material because of its effect. This features states that a substance can have existence without qualities and actions. Qualities and actions in this sense are considered as the non-inherent cause of substance. For example, green colour of threads, which is a quality, is the non-inherent cause of a cloth. In the similar way, an action is also a non-inherent cause, for example, holding a pen. The conjunction relation between fingers and a pen can be separated from each other without losing any significance or identification of fingers and the pen. But this is not possible in case of a substance. Thus, a substance is the inherent cause of an effect. For example, a cloth is made by threads. Without threads a cloth can't exist. Hence, threads are the inherent cause of a cloth. They are the material out of which it is produced. Thus, a substance is an inherent cause of an effect, while quality and action are its non-inherent cause.

In addition to all these substances, Vaisesika added one more, i.e. ether or akasa. Therefore, vaisesika recognises nine substances. The four non-eternal substances with ether or akasa are called 'panchabhuta'. In each of these substances there is one such specific quality that may be perceived by one of the external sense organs. For example, earth has the quality of smell, water that of taste, fire of colour, air of touch, and ether that of sound. These qualities are perceived by the nose, tongue, eyes, skin, and ears respectively. These sense organs are also believed to have originated in earth, water, fire, air and ether.

According to the vaisesika, anything which is composite and hence has parts and is divisible can't be eternal. But the simple, individual, and non-composite is eternal. With these parameters this system has distinguished eternal substances from non-eternal substances. This distinction entails that Vaisesika advocates ontological dualism. This is so because it recognises the existence of souls and material substances, which are irreducible to each other.

10.2.2 Guṇa (quality):

According to the Vaisesika philosophy, quality is that category which subsists in substance but in which no other quality or action can be here. Qualities cannot exist without substance. A quality cannot belong to another quality or action, but only to a substance. Qualities are completely passive and don't produce any objects. A quality is devoid of quality. For example, colour is a quality of the substance. It is not a quality of its odors, tastes, and other qualities. Hence, qualities have no qualities. A quality is devoid of action. An action is caused by a substance. But the quality of a substance is incapable of doing actions. For example, a bird is flying. Here, flying as a motion is caused by the bird but not by the colours of its feathers. Hence, the colours are devoid of motion. Therefore, a quality has no motion. But it seems to be in motion because its substrate is in motion. In addition to all these defining features vaisesika expresses that a quality is non-inherent cause of a substance. The reason as a substance can exist without qualities at the first moment of its production. Qualities are added to it later.

Qualities can be either material or mental and are not necessarily eternal. The vaisesika recognises twenty-four qualities. These are: (1) colour, (2) taste, (3) smell, (4) touch, (5) sound, (6) number, (7) magnitude, (8) distinctness, (9) conjunction, (10) disjunction, (11) nearness, (12) remoteness, (13) cognition, (14) pleasure, (15) pain, (16) desire, (17) aversion, (18) effort, (19) heaviness, (20) fluidity, (21) viscidity, (22) tendency, (23) moral merit, and (24) moral demerit. Further, Vaisesika mentions that these 24 qualities are not counted as an exact number of qualities. This is so because the number would be increased if one wishes to count the subdivisions of qualities. For example, blue, red, yellow, etc. can be recognised as colours subsume under the colour category.

10.2.3 Karma (activity):

Action is physical motion. It resides in a substance like quality. It is dynamic and transient, and not like quality which is static and passive. An action cannot possess another action or quality. Substances are conjoined and separated because of action. The existence of action is independent of being known. It is expressed by a word because it is known, and therefore nameable. Its existence is independent of its knowledge and expression. It resides in a substance which is its substrate.

Action is unconditional, non-inherent cause of substance. It is non-eternal. Hence, it resides in a non-eternal substance.

There are five kinds of action recognised by Vaisesika:

(i) Upward motion (Utksepana);

(ii) Downward motion (Avaksepana);

(iii) Contraction (Akuncana);

(iv) Expansion (Prasarana); and

(v) Gamana (Locomotion).

Upward motion, brings a body into contact with a higher region, e.g. throwing a stone upward. Downward motion brings a body into contact with a lower region, e.g. falling a fruit from the branch of a tree. Contraction brings the parts of a body closer to one another, e.g. clinching fingers of a hand. Expansion makes the part of a body farther from one another, e.g. keeping fingers separate one from the other of a hand. All other kinds of motions are comprised in which locomotion. For example, walking, running, swimming, etc. It is important to remember that there are a few actions cannot be perceived. They can only be inferred through our internal perception. For example, the action of mind.

10.2.4 Sāmānya (generality):

According to the Vaisesika, generality is that category by virtue of which different individuals are grouped together and called by a common name indicating a class, e.g. bird, table, fruit, etc.

The members of such groups have some properties in common. They have some general or common qualities which are to be found in the entire class. For example, the term 'bird' is a general name. It does not refer to this or that bird, but bird in general. Thus, objects or individuals possess similarity because they belong to a general class. The Vaisesika emphasises that universal/general subsists in substances, qualities and actions. They are non-spatial and non-temporal. They are similar to the platonic doctrine of the reality of the ideas. Thus, it is impossible for one universal to subsist in another. If it were then one and the same thing would have contrary natures.

Vaisesika divides generality into three kinds:

(i) Para

(ii) Apara

(iii) Parapara

'Para' is the most comprehensive, such as 'animal'. It is the beinghood which has maximal scope. Apara is the beinghood which has minimal scope. It is the name given to the least comprehensive, such as 'men'. 'Parapara' is the generality which is found between para and apara, such as 'beinghood'. Here the general term 'beinghood' is higher than the general term 'men' and lower than the general term 'animal'. This is so because under animality both beinghood and non-beinghood can be constituted, and under beinghood both 'men', 'women' and other category of general term would be constituted. While considering the generality the Indian Philosophers have subscribed to one or the other of the following three views:

(i) Nominalism: This school of thought states that generality is not an essential quality of the similar objects of a particular group but merely a name. Similarity of the beings belonging to a class and distinguishes it from other classes is only by virtue of the name. The general has no individual or separate existence. Buddhist philosophy has suggested this view. The Buddhist nominalism is known as 'apohavada'.

(ii) ***Conceptualism:*** This school suggests that the general quality has no existence apart from the individuals. The general quality does not come from outside and enter into the individual. Hence, the universal and particular are identical. They cannot be separated from each other. It is the essential quality or the internal form of individuals in general which is apprehended by our mind or intellect. This view is expressed by Jainism and Advaitva Vedantins.

(iii) ***Realism:*** This school emphasises that the general/universal is neither a mental thought nor merely a name. But it has its own existence. It is the generality which brings similarity between different individuals of a group. Thus, it is eternal although pervades in each individual or particular object/being. It is because of the general, individuals are called by the same name. This view is subscribed by both Nyaya-Vaisesikas.

10.2.5 Viśeṣa (particularity):

Particularity is referred to 'individuality' and understood as the opposite of generality. It indicates to the unique and specific individuality of eternal substances which have no parts. These substances are space, time, mind, ether, sound and the atoms of these elements. Thus, it is ultimate and eternal. It is because of particularity that individuals are differentiated and distinguished from each other. This also causes the atoms of the same substances considered separately. Hence, each particular is unique in its nature. A particular is partless, and therefore cannot be divided further. Since each particular is unique in its nature and distinguishable from other particulars, there are enumerable particulars found. Thus, the particulars are eternal, part less and enumerable. They are invisible because we cannot have perceptional cognition to them.

10.2.6 Samavāya (inherence):

Inherence is an inseparable and intimate relation between two entities, one of which is incapable of existing separately or independently apart from the other. Inherence relation is eternal. It cannot be separated from its substrate. For example, colour of a flower, motion in water, smell of earth, etc. Inherence should not be understood mistaken as 'conjunction'. In conjunction, the relation between two substances can be separated. It is momentary and non-eternal, while inherence is eternal. Conjunction is the relationship resulted by the connection of at least two substances but inherence is not resulted by the connection of substances. Inherence is inherent in substance. Conjunction is an external relation whereas inherence is an internal relation to the substance. Two substances are joined in conjunction are capable of existing apart. But in case of inherence relation, it is not possible to exist separate from substance. For example, appleness of an apple. Appleness can't exist apart from apple. So appleness and apple are related with inherence relation. This sort of relation is not found in case of 'conjunction'. Here, two substances can exist separate from each other. For example, 'A pen is on the table'. Here the pen is conjoined with table. In this case, the pen can be separated from table and vice versa. Thus, inherence is not conjunction.

Inherence is not perceptible. It is only inferred. This is so because there is no distinct perceptual cognition of it. For example, the relation between a flower and its colour is an inherence relation which is not perceived. What we perceive are that, the colour of the flower and the flower. But we are not able to perceive their inherence relation. Thus, inherence is unperceivable/ imperceptible.

10.2.7 Non-existence (Abhāva)

Non-existence as the seventh category of vaisesika substance is not mentioned by Kanada. It was added later by his commentators. The Vaisesika upholds that non-existence, like existence is perceivable. Non-existence is the absence of an object. For example, no one can deny the absence of the sun on the dark cloud of a rainy day. Hence, it is a necessary category in Vaisesika system. Non-existence is broadly divided in two sorts:

(a) Sansargabhava

(b) Anyonyabhava

(a) Sansargabhava states the absence of one entity in another. This is symbolically expressed as 'X' is not 'Y'. For example, coolness in fire, squareness in circle, etc.

Sansargabhava is of three kinds. These are:

(i) Pragbhava or antecedent non-existence

(ii) Dhvansabhava or subsequent non-existence

(iii) Atyantabhava or absolute non-existence

(i) **Prāgbhāva:** Pragbhava or antecedent non-existence means the absence of the substance prior to its production or creation. For example, the chair does not exist before the carpenter made it, i.e. prior to its making, the non-existence of the chair is in the wood. Similarly, the absence of the pot in the clay before the clay is made into a pot. Thus, antecedent non-existence has no beginning but it has an end.

(ii) **Dhvansābvhāva:** Dhvansabhava or subsequent non-existence means the absence of the substance after its destruction. For example, the absence of the pot in its pieces after the pot is destroyed. When a pot breaks, we can recreate it from its pieces. Hence, subsequent non-existence has a beginning but it has no end.

(iii) **Atyantabhāva:** Atyantabhava or absolute non-existence means the absence of one thing in another at all times, past, present, and future. For example, the absence of heat in the moon. The absolute nonexistence has neither a beginning nor an end. In short, it is eternal. The absence of colour in space will continue for all time. In this way, absolute non-existence is neither burnt nor destroyed.

(b) Anyonyabhāva: Anyonyabhava is also termed as mutual non-existence. Mutual non-existence means the exclusion of one thing by another. It is the absence of something in some other object. It is symbolically expressed as 'X is not Y'. For example, the table is not a horse. The non-existence of a table in a horse and the non-existence of a horse in a table are mutual non-existence. Anyonyabhava is eternal because two things which are different from each other exclude each other at all times and under all circumstances.

10.3 Vaiśeṣika Sūtra

Vaiśeṣika Sūtra, also called Kanada sutra, is an ancient Sanskrit text at the foundation of the Vaisheshika school of Hindu philosophy. The sutra was authored by the Hindu sage Kanada, also known as Kashyapa. According to some scholars, he flourished before the advent of Buddhism because the Vaiśeṣika Sūtra makes no mention of Buddhism or Buddhist doctrines; however, the details of Kanada's life are uncertain, and the Vaiśeṣika Sūtra was likely compiled sometime between 6th and 2nd century BCE, and finalised in the currently existing version before the start of the common era.

A number of scholars have commented on it since the beginning of common era; the earliest commentary known is the Padartha Dharma Sangraha of Prashastapada. Another important secondary work on Vaiśeṣika Sūtra is Maticandra's Dasha padartha sastra which exists both in Sanskrit and its Chinese translation in 648 CE by Yuanzhuang.

The Vaiśeṣika Sūtra is written in aphoristic sutras style, and presents its theories on the creation and existence of the universe using naturalistic atomism, applying logic and realism, and is one of the earliest known systematic realistic ontologies in human history. The text discusses motions of different kind and laws that govern it, the meaning of dharma, a theory of epistemology, the basis of Atman (self, soul), and the nature of yoga and moksha. The explicit mention of motion as the cause of all phenomena in the world and several propositions about it make it one of the earliest texts on physics.

10.4 Atomic Theory in Sutras of Vaishashika Philosophy

On closer scrutiny it turns out that that one of the Vaisheshika Darshana aphoristically developed by Kanada in the treatise Vaisheshika Sutras (VS), the aphorisms on particularities, has much in common with Modern physics and even in some respects goes beyond it conceptually. It would be interesting to find out the areas of agreement and difference between the two in regard to the various concepts such as the fundamental substances, their general nature, particular properties and also their interactions.

There are 10 chapters containing a total of 368 aphorisms in the Vaisheshika Sutras of Kanada. The six Padarthas (categories) enumerated in the first chapter are dravya (substance), guna (attribute), karma (action), samanya (generality), vishesha (particularlity) and samavaya (inherence).

The 9 substances are Prithvi (earth), Apas (water), Tejas (fire or radiation), vayu (air), akasa (ethereal space), kala (time), Dik (directions or dimensions), Atma (self or soul) and manas (mind). Substances are those which have attributes and actions. Some authors and commentators keep akasha as akasha and translate it as ether and translate Dik as space, but this does not seem logical. The directions are clearly mentioned under the heading Dik in the VS and thus they should mean directions or dimensions. This is reasonable since the astronomy of the Vedas gives us clear indication that the directions were different (anisotropic space) in their contents and impact. The constellations, stars and planets are present in different directions and hence different direction needed to be spelt out.

Definition of Dik: That which gives rise to such (cognition and usage) as "This (is remote, etc.) from this," – (the same is) the mark of space (Sutra 2.2.10).

Space is identified through the fact that it can provide the context to describe objects as being separated spatially. Spatial separation can only apply to matter since eternal dravyas which are incapable of motion can neither be separated nor brought together. Although mind can move, it is invisible. Therefore, all that remains in Kanada's classification of dravyas is matter. The separation is an identifier and the identification is with reference to the observing mind. It is also significant that the displacement of matter is observed relative to another piece of matter.

The essence of this sutra may be rephrased as: mind recognises space when matter is displaced relative to another piece of matter.

Further, based on experimental observations e.g. in Michelson-Morley experiment, modern physics does not any more recognise the existence of a material ether. Currently, ether or space is not considered different from free space or vacuum. In Quantum field theories this vacuum becomes a material entity with many particle-antiparticle pairs continuously being created and annihilated in it. It serves as the source for all matter-energy in the universe. Therefore, akasha, which is physical in vaisheshika must mean physical empty space or vacuum of science, as far as special Relativity is concerned, while Dik should be taken to mean the directions in space. It is only in general relativity that space and time cease to be infinite and eternal entities and are determined by the energy density.

Space in Dravya: Dravyatva (being a dravya) and eternality (of Space are) explained by (the explanation of the same in) Air. (Sutra, 2.2.11).

Space is eternal. It is concluded to be a dravya and that encompasses hypothesis like –

Space is an independent entity :

- It is existent;
- It is unique;
- It is a padartha;
- It has guna/attributes associated with it;
- It can give rise to another dravya;
- It is incapable of motion;
- It is homogenous.

There **are 17 attributes** rupa (colour), rasa (taste), gandha (odour), sparsha (touch), samkhya (number), parimana (dimension), prithaktva (distinctness), samyoga (conjunction), vibhaga (disjunction), paratva (priority), aparatva (posteriority), buddhi (intellect), sukha (pleasure), dukha (pain), ichha (desire or attraction), dvesha (aversion or repulsion) and prayatna (volition or will). The 5 types of action are: utkshepana (throwing up), avakshepana (throwing down), akunchana (contraction), prasarana (expansion) and gamana (movement). In this system, time is the primary cause of everything but it exists only in and for the non-eternal substances (VS-2/2/6). For the eternal ones it does not exist.

A substance has attributes and actions and is an inherent cause. The characteristic attribute of earth is odour, of fire is heat and that of water is coldness. Earth has colour, taste, touch and odour; water has colour, taste and touch; fire has colour and touch; while air has touch only. These first four substances are atomic in character and form basic building blocks of the entire visible universe. Sound is a special attribute associated with space. Time, directions and mind and the self are eternal and not perceivable by the senses, but the eternal mind is atomic in character. Plurality of individuals results from difference in circumstances in which these atomic minds are placed. The self must exist as the ultimate perceiver through the mind (chapters-2&3).

In the 4th chapter, it is mentioned that the eternal are those which are not produced from any causes. They are uncaused existences. The principle of causality is mentioned succinctly by Kanada: Everything (an object, an event or a process) has a cause (Karanabhavat karyabhavaah: VS-4/1/3) and the cause precedes the effect.

The 5th chapter deals with the causes of phenomena and states that gravitational force (gurutva) causes the downward movement (gurutvat patanam: VS-5/1/8 and VS-5/1/18). It is important to note that gurutva is mentioned as the cause of free fall of an object, without any connecting link or the involved therein, and not as an attribute (guna) of the moving object. The movement of the needle towards the magnet (magnetic force), circulation of water in plants i.e. Capillary/ electrostatic forces (VS:-5/2/7), flow of air (pressure/mechanical/electric force), assimilation of food in the body (vital/electric forces), movement of atoms (all fundamental physical forces, will force and karmic force depending on which atoms are being considered), and their mutual interactions are all said to be due to an invisible causative force called adrishta or "the unseen" (Agnerurdhvajvalanam vayostiryakpavanamanunam manasaschaadyam karmadrishtakaritam: VS-5/2/13). These are examples of the karmakaranas or the forces in Vaisheshika which bring about the karmas like gamanam etc.

In the 6th chapter, this adrishta is also said to be responsible for the desires arising in the mind and for the accrual of fruits (merits and demerits) of actions performed by individuals and is therefore the cause behind their births and deaths i.e. conjunction or disjunction of the soul with an atomic mind plus a physical body made up of the atomic first four substances (earth, water, fire, air).

Defining the **atom in chapter-7**, Kanada mentions that they are eternal, a dimensionless point particle (kana), and hence have spherical symmetry (Nityam Parimandalam: VS-7/1/20), but are invisible. One can apply this definition to all the four nitya dravyas. These atoms are to be known only from their effects (Tasya karyam lingam: VS- 4/1/2). The atoms of fire, air, water and earth combine via adrishta to form dvanuka (diads), trayanuka (triads), chaturanauka (tetrads) etc. and thus give rise to the four gross substances which are perceived by us. The subtle difference between objectivity and subjectivity of attributes are also discussed in the 7th chapter.

The last three chapters have very little to offer for a comparative analysis of Vaisheshika and modern physics, and therefore, we just state for the sake of completeness their brief contents. In the 8th chapter the nature of perception, whether it is determinate or not, and the right means of establishing a fact are discussed. In the 9th the function of the intellect in drawing an inference is made clear. In the 10th the different possible types of inference are analysed.

We have separated out the electromagnetic part from the general adrishta and written the rest as 'adrishta' which is responsible for the rest of the functions ascribed to adrishta. Therefore,

Fundamental Force = Adrishta (1)

Adrishta ▶ Gravity + Electric force+ Magnetic Force +Adrishta' (2)

Adrishta'▶ Any other Physical forces + Will force + Karmic Force (3)

The "Will force" is responsible for actions by the mind and the "Karmic force" is responsible for the fruits that are to come to the mind as its effects. These two and any other Physical force that is not explicitly mentioned in the VS by Kanada i.e. neither Gravitational nor Electric nor magnetic, make up the 'Adrishta' as can be inferred from the sutras regarding the actions of the atomic substances. (VS-5/2/13).

Secondly, we have put the substances in two distinct levels in order of their subtlety. The first four atomic substances make up all matter; the next five are at a subtler level. Space, time and directions are discussed in Physics, but the last two i.e. mind and soul are yet to convincingly occupy their rightful place in today's mainstream Physics, although there are indications that they cannot be left out in the cold any longer. Space, time, soul and directions in Vaisheshika are non-atomic and infinite, while the mind is stated to be atomic. With this classification scheme in mind, we will now try to see how far the Vaisheshika tallies with the classification scheme of modern physics for fundamental entities (particles) developed in the 20th century. It is quite surprising that in many respects they are in agreement in regard to the basic concepts and entities involved.

The characteristics of all that can be conceptualised and hence named and defined in the world through comparison and contrast, is the science of Vaisheshika. This includes a conceptual representation of space, and the gross visible matter, which is taken to be constructed out of the varying motions of anu, the most fundamental particle of matter.

The nature of both Space and, anu - the most fundamental particle of matter (sutra 7.1.8) in Vaisheshika are said to be explained in the chapter that discusses nitya/eternal.

According to the Vaiśeṣika school, the trasareṇu are the smallest mahat (perceivable) particles and defined as tryaṇukas (triads). These are made of three parts, each of which are defined as dvyaṇuka (dyad). The dvyaṇukas are conceived as made of two parts, each of which are defined as paramāṇu (atom). The paramāṇus (atoms) are indivisible and eternal, they can neither be created nor destroyed. Each paramāṇu (atom) possesses its own distinct viśeṇa (individuality) and have an inhering relation which is responsible for change and motion.

Kanada has stated in a later chapter (sutra 7.1.8) that both anu and mahat are explained through the nitya/eternal, which must be the reason for all scholars to explain this sutra with an extension to mean the fundamental particle – the anu.

The measure of the partless atoms is known as parimaṇḍala parimāṇa. It is eternal and it cannot generate the measure of any other substance. Its measure is its own absolutely.

The early Vaiśeṣika texts presented the following syllogism to prove that all objects i.e. the four bhūtas, pṛthivī (earth), ap (water), Tejas (fire) and vāyu (air) are made of indivisible paramāṇus (atoms): Assume that the matter is not made of indivisible atoms, and that it is continuous. Take a stone. One can divide this up into infinitely many pieces (since matter is continuous). Now, the Himalayan mountain range also has infinitely many pieces, so one may build another Himalayan mountain range with the infinite number of pieces that one has. One begins with a stone and ends up with the Himalayas, which is a paradox - so the original assumption that matter is continuous must be wrong, and so all objects must be made up of a finite number of paramāṇus (atoms).

Chapter - 11

Purva Mimansa Philosophy

11.1 Introduction to Purva Mimansa

Mīmāṃsā is a Sanskrit word that means "reflection" or "critical investigation" and thus refers to a tradition of contemplation which reflected on the meanings of certain Vedic texts. This tradition is also known as Pūrva-Mīmāṃsā because of its focus on the earlier (pūrva) Vedic texts dealing with ritual actions, and similarly as Karma-Mīmāṃsā due to its focus on ritual action (karma). It is one of six Vedic "affirming" (āstika) schools of Hinduism. This particular school is known for its philosophical theories on the nature of dharma, based on hermeneutics of the Vedas, especially the Brāḥmanas and Saṃhitas. The Mīmāṃsā school was foundational and influential for the Vedāntic schools, which were also known as Uttara-Mīmāṃsā for their focus on the "later" (Uttara) portions of the Vedas, the Upanishads. While both "earlier" and "later" Mīmāṃsā investigate the aim of human action, they do so with different attitudes towards the necessity of ritual praxis.

Mimamsa is a philosophical school (advocating realism) in India which developed the ritualistic aspect of the Vedas. It must be noted that the Vedas depict two different aspects – the ritualistic aspect and speculative aspect. Of the 6 orthodox systems of philosophy (astika darshanas), - Nyaya, Vaisesika, Samkhya and Yoga developed their philosophies independently though owing allegiance to the Vedas. But Mimamsa and Vedanta are two schools which developed the two different aspects of the Vedas. While Mimamsa developed from the ritualistic side, Vedanta developed from the speculative side of the Vedas. In fact, it is because of this reason that philosophers are inclined to name them as Purva Mimamsa (early Mimamsa) and Uttara Mimamsa (later Mimamsa). They were also known as karma Mimamsa and jnana Mimamsa respectively.

Mīmāṃsā has several sub-schools, each defined by its epistemology. The Prābhākara sub-school, which takes its name from the seventh-century philosopher Prabhakara, described the five epistemically reliable means to gaining knowledge: pratyaksha or perception; anumāna or inference; upamāṇa, by comparison and analogy; arthāpatti, the use of postulation and derivation from circumstances; and shabda, the word or testimony of past or present reliable experts. The Bhaṭṭa sub-school, from philosopher Kumārila Bhaṭṭa, added a sixth means to its canon; Anupalabdhi meant non-perception, or proof by the absence of cognition (e.g., the lack of gunpowder on a suspect's hand).

The school of Mīmāṃsā consists of both atheistic and theistic doctrines, but the school showed little interest in systematic examination of the existence of Gods. Rather, it held that the soul is an eternal, omnipresent, inherently active spiritual essence, and focused on the epistemology and metaphysics of dharma. For the Mīmāṃsā school, dharma meant rituals and social duties, not devas, or gods, because gods existed only in name. The Mīmāṃsākas also held that Vedas are "eternal, author-less, [and] infallible", that Vedic vidhi, or injunctions and mantras in rituals are prescriptive kārya or actions, and the rituals are of primary importance and merit. They considered the Upanishads and other texts related to self-knowledge and spirituality as subsidiary, a philosophical view that Vedānta disagreed with.

While their deep analysis of language and linguistics influenced other schools of Hinduism, their views were not shared by others. Mīmāṃsākas considered the purpose and power of language was to clearly prescribe the proper, correct and right. In contrast, Vedāntins extended the scope and value of language as a tool to also describe, develop and derive. Mīmāṃsākas considered orderly, law driven, procedural life as central purpose and noblest necessity of dharma and society, and divine (theistic) sustenance means to that end.

The Mīmāṃsā school is a form of philosophical realism. A key text of the Mīmāṃsā school is the Mīmāṃsā Sūtra of ***Jaimini.***

Jaimini (400 BC) was the author of the Mimamsa Sutra, and the founder of the Mimamsa system. Savarasvamin (300 AD) wrote a commentary called, Savara-Bhasya, in which he criticised the views of the different schools of Buddhism. He started his views on the principal philosophical topics, and raised the Purva Mimamsa to the status of an independent system. Kumarila Bhatta (700 AD), the founder of the Bhatta school of Mimamsa, wrote Slokavartika, Tantravartika and Tuptika. Slokavartika has great philosophical importance. Sucarita Misra wrote a commentary entitled Kasika. Parthassrathi Misra (900 AD) wrote a commentary known as Nyayaratnakara on it, Nyayaratnamala, Tantraratna, and Sastradipika. Vacaspati Misra (1000 AD) wrote Nyayakanika, a commentary on

Mandana Misra's (680-750 AD) Vidhiviveka, and Tattvabindu. Prabhakara Misra (700 AD), the founder of the Prabhakara school of Mimamsa, wrote a commentary entitled Brhati on Savara-Bhasya. Salikanatha Misra (800 AD), wrote a commentary known as Rjuvimalapancika on, Brhati and Prakaranapancika. The third school of Mimamsa was founded by Murari Misra whose works are lost. The Mimamsa is called the Purva Mimamsa, while the Vedanta is called the Uttara Mimamsa. The former is earlier than the latter in the sense that it deals with rituals, while the latter is concerned with knowledge. The performance of rituals leads to the knowledge of the reality. So the Purva Mimamsa, called the Mimamsa, is logically prior to the Uttara Mimamsa or the Vedanta, the former being concerned with Dharma, and the latter, with Brahman. The Mimamsa is also called Karma Mimamsa. It mainly deals with the Vedic injunctions about rituals, the rules of interpretation of the texts, which remove the apparent contradictions among them, and harmonise them with one another, and the philosophical justification of the beliefs underlying ritualism. It believes in the reality of the external world, the reality of the individual souls, and the Law of Karma. It believes in transmigration, heaven and hell, and liberation. It believes in many Gods, who are worshipped through rejects the notion of one God, who creates, preserves and dissolves the world.

11.2 Jaimini

Jaimini is most known for his great treatise Purva Mimamsa Sutras, also called Karma-mimamsa ("Study of Ritual Action"), a system that investigates the rituals in the Vedic texts. The text founded the Purva-Mimamsa school of Ancient Indian philosophy, one of the six Darsanas or schools of Ancient Indian philosophy. His school is considered non-theistic, but one that emphasised rituals parts of the Vedas as essential to Dharma. Jaimini is known for his studies of older rituals part of the Vedas.

Jaimini's guru was Badarayana, the latter founded the Vedanta school of Hindu philosophy, emphasising the knowledge parts of the Vedas, and credited with authoring Brahma Sutras. Both Badarayana and Jaimini quoted each other as they analyzed each other's theories, Badarayana emphasising knowledge while Jaimini emphasizes rituals, sometimes agreeing with each other, sometimes disagreeing, often anti-thesis of the other.

Jaimini's contributions to textual analysis and exegesis influenced other schools of Indian philosophies, and the most studied bhasya (reviews and commentaries) on Jaimini's texts were by scholars named Shabara, Kumarila and Prabhakara.

Dated to ca. the 4th century BCE, the text contains about 3,000 sutras and is the foundational text of the Mimamsa school. The text aims at an exegesis of the Vedas with regard to ritual practice (karma) and religious duty (dharma), commenting on the early Upanishads. Jaimini's Mimamsa is a ritualist (karma-kanda) counter-movement to the Self-knowledge (Atman) speculations of the Vedanta philosophy. His Mimamsa Sutra was commented upon by many, of which Śābara was among the earliest.

Jaimini also wrote a version of the Mahabharata narrated to him by his preceptor Vyasa, but today, only the Ashvamedhika Parva of his work is available.

11.3 Mimansa Darshana (Philosophy)

Mīmāṃsā is one of the six classical Hindu darshanas. It is among the earliest schools of Hindu philosophies. It has attracted relatively less scholarly study, although its theories and particularly its questions on exegesis and theology have been highly influential on all classical Indian philosophies. Its analysis of language has been of central importance to the legal literature of India.

Ancient Mimosa's central concern was epistemology (pramana), that is what are the reliable means to knowledge. It debated not only "how does man ever learn or know, whatever he knows", but also whether the nature of all knowledge is inherently circular, whether those such as foundationalists who critique the validity of any "justified beliefs" and knowledge system make flawed presumptions of the very premises they critique, and how to correctly interpret and avoid incorrectly interpreting dharma texts such as the Vedas. It asked questions such as "what is devata (god)?", "are rituals dedicated to devatas efficacious?", "what makes anything efficacious?", and "can it be proved that the Vedas, or any canonical text in any system of thought, fallible or infallible (svatah pramanya, intrinsically valid)?, if so, how?" and others. To Mīmāṃsā scholars, the nature of non-empirical knowledge and human means to it are such that one can never demonstrate certainty, one can only falsify knowledge claims, in some cases. The Mīmāṃsā school is one of the most distinctively Hindu forms of thinking; it is without real parallel elsewhere in the world.

The central text of the Mīmāṃsā school is Jaimini's Mīmāṃsā Sutras, along with the historically influential commentaries on this sutra by Sabara and by Kumarila Bhatta. Together, these texts develop and apply the rules of language analysis (such as the rules of contradiction), asserting that one must not only examine injunctive propositions in any scripture, but also examine the alternate related or reverse propositions for better understanding. They suggested that to reach correct and valid knowledge it is not only sufficient to demand proof of a proposition, it is important to give proof of a proposition's negative as well as declare and prove one's own preferred propositions. Further, they asserted that whenever perception is not the means of direct proof and knowledge, one cannot prove such non-empirical propositions to be "true or not true", rather one can only prove a non-empirical proposition is "false, not false, or uncertain".

Jaimini, in his Mimamsa Sutra, presents material activity and its results as the whole of reality. He and later proponents of Karma-mimamsa philosophy teach that material existence is endless, that there is no liberation. For Mimamsas, the cycle of karma is perpetual, and the best one can aim for is higher birth among the Devas. Therefore, they hold that the whole purpose of the Vedas is to engage human beings in rituals for creating good karma, and consequently the mature soul's prime responsibility is to ascertain the exact meaning of the Vedas' sacrificial injunctions and to execute them.

Codana-laksano 'rtho dharmah: (Mimamsa Sutra 1.1.2)

Duty is that which is indicated by the injunctions of the Vedas.

Mīmāṃsākas welcome not only the demand for proof of an injunctive proposition such as "Agnihotra ritual leads one to heaven", but suggest that one must examine and prove alternate propositions such as "ritual does not lead one to heaven", "something else leads one to heaven", "there is heaven", "there is no heaven" and so on. Mīmāṃsā literature states that if satisfactory, verifiable proof for all of such propositions cannot be found by its proponents and its opponents, then the proposition needs to be accepted as a part of a "belief system". Beliefs, such as those in the scriptures (Vedas), must be accepted to be true unless its opponents can demonstrate the proof of validity of their own texts or teacher(s) these opponents presume to be prima facie justified, and until these opponents can demonstrate that the scriptures they challenge are false. If they do not try to do so, it is hypocrisy; if they try to do so, it can only lead to infinite regress, according to Mīmāṃsākas. Any historic scripture with widespread social acceptance, according to Mīmāṃsākas, is an activity of communication (vyavaharapravrtti) and is accepted as authoritative because it is socially validated practice, unless perceptually verifiable evidence emerges that proves parts or all of it as false or harmful.

Mīmāṃsākas were predominantly concerned with the central motivation of human beings, the highest good, and actions that make this possible. They stated that human beings seek niratisaya priti (unending ecstatic pleasure, joy, happiness) in this life and the next. They argued that this highest good is the result of one's own ethical actions (dharma), that such actions are what the Vedic sentences contain and communicate, and therefore it important to properly interpret and understand Vedic sentences, words and meaning. Mīmāṃsā scholarship was centrally concerned with the philosophy of language, how human beings learn and communicate with each other and across generations with language in order to act in a manner that enables them to achieve that which motivates them. The Mīmāṃsā school focused on dharma, deriving ethics and activity from the karma-kanda (rituals) part of the Vedas, with the argument that ethics for this life and efficacious action for svarga (heaven) cannot be derived from sense-perception, and can only be derived from experience, reflection and understanding of past teachings.

In every human activity, the motivating force to perform an action is his innate longing for priti (pleasure, happiness), whether at the lowest level or the highest level. At the highest level, it is nothing but an unsurpassed state of priti, which is ensured only by performing ethical actions.

– Sabara, 2nd century Mīmāṃsā scholar

The Mīmāṃsākas subjected to a radical critique, more than two thousand years ago, the notions such as "God," the "sacred text," the "author" and the "anthropocentric ordering of reality".

11.4 Epistemology of Mimansa

In the field of epistemology, later Mīmāṃsākas made some notable contributions. Unlike the Nyaya or the Vaisheshika systems, the Prābhākara sub-school of Mīmāṃsā recognises five means of valid knowledge (Skt. pramāṇa). The Bhaṭṭa sub-school of Mīmāṃsā recognises one additional sixth, namely Anupalabdhi, just like Advaita Vedanta school of Hinduism. These six epistemically reliable means of gaining knowledge are:

11.4.1 Perception (Pratyaksha) of Mimansa Philosophy

Kumarila recognises six Pramanas, viz., perception, inference, comparison, testimony, presumption, and non-apprehension. Prabhakara rejects negation as an independent category, and non-apprehension as the means of knowing it.

Jaimini defines perception as the knowledge produced in the self by the right intercourse of the sense-organs with existing objects. It is produced by real objects existing at present and acting upon the sense-organs. When there is a right intercourse of the sense-organs with their objects, valid perception is produced.

Kumarila says, "Right intercourse is the intercourse of the sense-organs untainted by defects with real objects." Illusions are produced by wrong intercourse. The Mimamsa theory of perception is similar to the Nyaya theory. Only the latter regards the auditory organ as ether limited by the ear-hole, while the former regards it as space limited by the ear-hole. Prabhakara defines perception as direct apprehension which relates to an object, the self, and cognition. In every perception of an object, the self, the cognition, and the object are perceived. This is Prabhakara's doctrine of triple perception. In regard to objects, there is the perception of substances, qualities, and universals due to the intercourse of the sense-organs with them. Cognitions are self-manifest. But the self and an object are not self-manifest, but are manifested by a cognition, which is self-aware and which is not manifested by any other cognition.

Kumarila and Prabhakara both recognise two stages of perception, viz., indeterminate perception and determinate perception. Kumarila defines indeterminate perception as simple apprehension of an object, pure and simple, similar to the apprehension of a baby or a dumb person. It apprehends neither the specific characters nor the generic characters, but an individual object only, which is their substrate. It cannot apprehend the generic characters as generic and the specific characters as specific.

Prabhakara defines indeterminate perception as a simple apprehension of the bare nature of an object. It apprehends a substance, a quality, and a genus as bare existences unrelated to each other just after the sense object-intercourse. Its existence is proved by its self-awareness. It apprehends generic characters and specific characters, but it cannot cognise them as generic and specific, since it is devoid of recollection of other similar and dissimilar objects.

Kumarila defines determinate perception as apprehension of the generic characters of an object as generic, and of its specific characters as specific. It contains an element of recollection of similar and dissimilar objects, and apprehends the community of its object with other similar objects and its distinction from other dissimilar objects. It apprehends an object and its generic and specific properties in a subject predicate relation.

Prabhakara also regards determinate perception as the apprehension of the generic characters and the specific characters of an object as generic and specific respectively. It apprehends its object and its properties in a subject-predicate relation. It apprehends its object as a substance endued with particular qualities and belonging to a certain genus. It contains an element of recollection produced by subconscious impressions. It is immediate apprehension produced by the sense-object-intercourse aided by subconscious impressions.

Kumarila recognises the validity of indeterminate and determinate perception both. Indeterminate perception reveals the bare nature of an object. It is direct apprehension or distinct cognition of an object in itself, unrelated to other objects. Its validity consists in its directness and immediacy; it yields new knowledge not acquired already. Though it is devoid of subject-predicate relation, it is valid. Determinate perception also is valid, since it is direct and immediate knowledge of an object and its properties as related to each other, which is produced by the sense-object-intercourse aided by subconscious impressions.

Prabhakara also regards indeterminate perception as valid, since it is sensuous apprehension of an object unrelated to other objects and devoid of recollection, and since its validity is proved by self-awareness. He regards determinate perception also as valid, because it apprehends the subject-predicate relation between its object and its properties, substance, quality and genus, which is not apprehended by indeterminate.

11.4.2 Inference (Anumana) of Mimamsa Philosophy

Savara defines inference as the knowledge of an unperceived object, which is not present to a sense-organ, from the perception of another object, when a uniform relation has been known to subsist between them. Kumarila explains the relation as invariable concomitance of a sign or reason with a predicate, the former being pervaded by the latter, and being the indicator of the latter, which is indicated.

The sign is called vyapya because it is coextensive with, or narrower than, the predicate in time and place. The predicate is called vyapaka because it is coextensive with, or wider than, the sign in time and place. The unperceived predicate is inferred from the sign perceived in the subject on the ground of the uniform relation between them known already in similar instances.

Smoke was perceived to be accompanied by fire in a kitchen and other similar instances at certain times and in certain places. Smoke is subsequently perceived in a hill exactly in the same form. So the existence of a fire in the same form in a hill is inferred from it. The sign or reason proves the existence of the predicate. The predicate alone (e.g., a fire) is not the object of inference because it is already known. The subject (e.g., a hill) as qualified by the predicate (e.g., a fire) is the object of inference. The subject alone unrelated to the predicate cannot be the object of inference. Nor can the subject and the predicate, singly or collectively, be the object of inference, independently of the other. The subject as qualified by the predicate is inferred from the sign perceived in it. The invariable concomitance, according to Kumarila, is known by repeated observation of concomitance of the two general properties of the reason and the predicate, and sometimes of two particular objects denoted by them, strengthened by the non-observation of contrary instances of their non-concomitance. The observation of concomitance of the reason and the predicate in numerous instances and the non-observation of non-concomitance between them are the means of knowing invariable concomitance. Invariable concomitance is known by induction by simple enumeration.

Does inference involve the fallacy of petitio principii? Kumarila regards novelty as an essential characteristic of valid knowledge. It consists in not being apprehended already. It is objected that inference contains the recollection of invariable concomitance, which apprehends what has already been apprehended, and thus invalidates inference. Kumarila argues that though the concomitance of smoke and fire in a kitchen and the like is certainly known in a general way, yet the relation between the present subject (e.g., a hill) and the predicate (e.g., a fire) is not already known. The hill was not already known, far less its fieriness. What is the novel factor, which was not already apprehended, in the inference? The fieriness of smoky objects is already known in a general way. The generic character of fire is already known. The hill is perceived. But the hill as qualified by a fire was not already known by any means of valid knowledge.

Prabhakara slightly amends savara's definition of inference. He defines it as the knowledge of a predicate in a subject from the perception of a sign or reason on the ground of the knowledge of a uniform relation between them, if the knowledge is not contradicted by another knowledge.

The uniform relation may express inherence, co-inherence in the same substance, causality, and the like. The causal relation between smoke and fire is invariable. The relation between smell and earth is invariable. The relation between taste and colour, which inhere in the same substance is invariable. But the relation between colour and taste is not invariable. Whenever there is taste, there is colour, for instance, in water. But wherever there is colour, there is no taste, for instance, in light. An invariable relation is the ground of inference.

Prabhakara also regards induction by simple enumeration as the ground of invariable concomitance. He considers inference to be valid, since the knowledge of the predicate existing in the subject is in the nature of apprehension, though it is produced by the perception of the sign and the recollection of the invariable concomitance. Prabhakara admits inference for oneself and inference for others. Both consist of three members, viz.,

(i) The thesis or proposition,

(ii) The minor premise which states the reason, and

(iii) Universal major premise which states the uniform relation illustrated by an example.

The proposition should be stated first, but the major premise and the minor premise may be stated in any order. Either the reason or the application may be stated. The conclusion follows necessarily from the general principle of relation between the sign and the predicate. A heterogeneous example is needless, since a homogeneous example is enough to illustrate the general principle.

Savara admits two kinds of inference, viz., pratyaksatodrstasambandha and samanyatodrstasambandha. Kumarila calls them drstasvalaksanavi saya and adrstasvalaksanavisaya. Prabhakara calls them drstasvalaksana and adrstasvalaksana. In the former there is the invariable concomitance between objects which are perceptible, as smoke and fire. In the latter there is the invariable concomitance between a perceptible object and an imperceptible object, as motion of the sun is inferred from its change of position in the sky. Prabhakara regards motion as imperceptible.

11.4.3 Comparison (Upamana)

Savara defines comparison as the knowledge of similarity subsisting in an unperceived object (e.g., a cow) on the perception of a similar object (e.g.. a wild cow). Kumarila defines it as the knowledge of similarity subsisting in a remembered object (e.g., a cow) with an object (e.g., a wild cow) perceived. 'The cow which was perceived by me in the past in a town is similar to this wild cow perceived in a forest at present'. This is an example of comparison.

Prabhakara also defines comparison as the knowledge of similarity subsisting in a remembered object, which arises from the perception of similarity. A person, who perceived a cow in a town in the past, perceives a wild cow in a forest, perceives its similarity with the cow, and then knows the similarity of the remembered cow with the perceived wild cow. The knowledge of similarity of the remembered cow with the perceived wild cow is comparison. Prabhakara's view of comparison is identical with that of Kumarila. Both regard similarity as an object of comparison. Both regard similarity of a remembered object with a perceived object as known by comparison.

Comparison is not perception, since its object known to be similar (e.g., a cow) is not in contact with a sense-organ. Nor is comparison inference, since it does not depend upon the knowledge of invariable concomitance between the two objects, which are similar to each other. It may be reduced to an inference in the following manner. 'The cow is similar to the wild cow, because it is the substrate of similarity with another cow, and whatever is the substrate of similarity with another object is found to be similar to it, as one of the twins is similar to the other'.

This is wrong, because the cow and the wild cow, which are similar to each other, were never perceived together in the past. So comparison is not inference. Nor is it testimony, since it does not depend upon verbal authority. So it is an independent means of valid knowledge.

11.4.4 Presumption (Arthāpatti) of Mimamsa Philosophy

Savara defines presumption as the assumption of an unperceived fact without which inconsistency among perceived facts cannot be reconciled. If we know that Devadatta is alive, and perceive that he is absent from his house, we cannot reconcile his being alive with his nonexistence in his house, unless we assume his existence outside his house. The assumption of this unperceived fact which reconciles two apparently inconsistent well-known facts is presumption. It is also called postulation or implication. Kumarila and Prabhakara differ from each other in their views on presumption. Prabhakara maintains, that there is an element of doubt in presumption. While Kumarila denies its existence in it. There is doubt, according to Prabhakara, as to the truth of the two perceived facts which cannot be reconciled with each other. The assumption of another fact removes the doubt, and reconciles the apparently inconsistent facts.

We know that Devadatta is living, and perceive his absence from his house. This perception generates a doubt about our knowledge that he is living. In order to remove this doubt we assume that he must be outside his house. This presumption removes the doubt as to his living, and reconciles the two apparently inconsistent facts of his living and non-existence in his house. The element of doubt, according to Prabhakara, distinguishes presumption from inference. There is no element of doubt in inference. From the undoubted perception of smoke we can infer the existence of fire. The sign is free from doubt. But the perceived absence of Devadatta from his house leads to the presumption of his living outside his house only when it has made the fact of his living doubtful. Thus, there is doubt in presumption, while there is no doubt in inference. Presumption removes doubt, and reconciles two apparently inconsistent facts, and cannot be regarded as inference.

There is no element of doubt, according to Kumarila, in presumption. We perceive the absence of Devadatta from his house. We know for certain that he is alive. In order to reconcile these two well-known and undoubted facts we assume that he has gone out of his house. Without this assumption the apparent inconsistency between his being alive and his absence from his house cannot be reconciled. If the knowledge of his living were doubtful, it could not be the sound basis of presumption. It removes the mutual inconsistency of two well-ascertained facts. The presumption of a third fact reconciles the two well-known facts perceived, which appear to be inconsistent with each other.

11.4.5 Non-Apprehension (Anupalabdhi) of Mimamsa Philosophy

Kumarila regards non-apprehension as the means of knowing the non-existence of an object, which cannot be known by perception, inference, comparison, testimony and presumption. Nonexistence is real and apprehended by non-apprehension. The non-existence of curd in milk is prior non-existence. The non-existence of milk in curd is posterior non-existence. The nonexistence of a horse in a cow is mutual non-existence. The non-existence of horns in a hare is absolute non-existence. If non-apprehension were not recognised as an independent means of knowledge, there would be the existence of curd in milk, of milk in curd, of a jar in a piece of cloth, and of horns in a hare.

Non-apprehension is non-production of perception and the like, but it is a cognition or a modification of the self. It is a means of valid knowledge, since it cognises non-existence which cannot be known by any other means of valid knowledge. How is the non–existence of jar on the ground cognised? First, the ground, which is the locus of the non-existence of a jar, is perceived. Then the jar, the counter-positive entity of the non-existence, is remembered. Then a purely mental cognition of the non-existence of the jar, which is independent of the sense-object-intercourse, produced. A person first perceives the bare ground, then remembers a jar which existed on it. Then he cognises the non-existence of the jar on the ground by means of non-apprehension. Non-apprehension being negative in character, cannot cognise positive existence. Perception, inference, comparison, testimony and presumption being positive in character, cannot cognize non-existence. Non-apprehension is their negation which cognises the non-existence of their objects. Non-existence is cognised by a means of knowledge similar to itself, or negative in character. It is an object of appropriate non-apprehension. But Prabhakara does not recognise non-apprehension as an independent means of valid knowledge. Nor does he recognise the category of non-existence which may be cognised by non-apprehension. He rejects both non-existence as an ontological reality, and non-apprehension as a distinct mode of knowing it. When we perceive the existence of a jar on the ground, we perceive the existence of the ground as related to the existence of the jar. But when the jar is absent, we perceive the bare ground only. The non-existence of the jar is nothing but the existence of the mere locus, the ground. The perception of the mere locus is erroneously called non-apprehension by Kumarila. The so-called non-apprehension of the non-existence of the jar on the ground is nothing but perception of its mere locus, the bare ground. The perception of the bare ground is a positive cognition due to the contact of a sense-organ with the ground. It is not of a negative character and in the nature of non-apprehension. Every kind of valid knowledge is invariably accompanied by an object. There is no distinct object of non-apprehension, and, consequently, no distinct means of knowing it. So non-apprehension is not an independent means of valid knowledge. Non-existence is not cognised by perception, since there is no intercourse of a sense-organ with it. Nor can it be said to be cognised by indeterminate perception at first, and then remembered by determinate perception.

The non-existence of an object can never be cognised by indeterminate perception, since it is non-relational apprehension. So it cannot be remembered by determinate perception. Nor can non-existence be inferred from the knowledge of a sign, because the invariable concomitance between them is not known. Further, no sign pervaded by non-existence is known. Nor is non-existence known by testimony, comparison and presumption, because in the knowledge of non-existence there is neither knowledge of a verbal statement, nor knowledge of similarity, nor knowledge of inconsistency between two perceived facts which may be reconciled by presumption. It is known by appropriate non-apprehension, which is a distinct means of valid knowledge.

11.4.6 Testimony (Sabda) of Mimamsa Philosophy

Kumarila defines testimony as the knowledge of objects, which are supersensible, derived from sentences by comprehending the meanings of the constituent words. Testimony is verbal authority. He divides testimony into human and superhuman. The former is the testimony of trustworthy persons, while the latter is the testimony of the Vedas. The former is valid, if it is uttered by persons of trustworthy character, while the latter is valid in itself. Again, testimony may either give us knowledge of existing objects, as 'a jar exists'; or, it may direct us to perform an action, as 'bring a jar'. The former gives us the knowledge of existential propositions, while the latter gives us the knowledge of injunctive propositions. Vedic testimony gives us the knowledge of duties. Dharma is supersensible, and cannot be perceived through the sense-organs. Inference, comparison, presumption and non-apprehension also cannot yield the knowledge of Dharma, since they presuppose perception. The knowledge that the performer of the Agni stoma sacrifice will go to heaven cannot be given by them. Vedic testimony is the only source of our knowledge of duties relating to supersensible entities. The Vedic texts which enjoin us to perform certain actions which lead to beneficial results are authoritative. Injunctive sentences in the Vedas are authoritative, and prohibitions are injunctions in disguise. The other Vedic texts are authoritative in so far as they help persons perform their duties.

Kumarila maintains that human testimony is valid, if the sentence is uttered by a person of trustworthy character, and that it is invalid, if it is spoken by a person of untrustworthy character. Human testimony has no intrinsic validity. It may be vitiated by carelessness, deliberate desire to cheat, and other defects of the speakers. But Vedic testimony has intrinsic validity, since the Vedas are impersonal and eternal, and not human compositions tainted with the defects of the speakers.

Non-contradiction is a test of truth. A knowledge, which is contradicted by a subsequent valid knowledge, is invalid. But the Vedic injunctions are never contradicted by any subsequent valid knowledge. The objects denoted by them can never be known by perception, inference and other means of valid knowledge. Hence Vedic testimony is valid in itself. A word consists of letters which are eternal. It denotes a class or genus, and not an individual. It denotes an individual indirectly through a class denoted by it. A word has a permanent relation to an object, which is impersonal. It is neither created by God nor by persons. It is only learnt from the speech and actions of the elders acquainted with the meanings of words.

Prabhakara regards testimony as the knowledge of supersensible objects depending on the knowledge of words. There is no other testimony than scriptural testimony. The supersensible object is Apurva, super-sensuous Ought, Categorical Imperative, or Duty. The entire Vedas are the means of knowing Apurva or Duty. Apurva or the moral command is the object of Vedic testimony, which cannot be known by any other means of valid knowledge. The Vedas are not composed by any person, human or divine. The sentences in the Vedas manifest their meanings by their inherent powers. They enlighten us on Apurva, which is incomprehensible by the human reason. Vedic sentences are intrinsically valid, and always yield valid cognitions, since they are impersonal and devoid of human origin. The entire Vedas which prescribe the Moral Law are intrinsically valid. The Moral Law is Ought or Duty, which is realisable by human volition.

Prabhakara includes human testimony in inference. Sentences uttered by persons cannot by themselves guarantee the real existence of objects which they mean. They often contain great falsehood and are not in harmony with real objects. The validity or the invalidity of a sentence spoken by a person is inferred from the trustworthy or untrustworthy character of the person who utters it. The knowledge of the person is the cause, and the sentence uttered by the person is the effect. The effect is inferred from the cause. So, human testimony is included in inference. Words denote their objects by nature. Their denotative power is natural and permanent, and not determined by convention, human or divine. The Nyaya maintains that God fixes the meanings of words by convention. But the Mimansa does not believe in the conventional meanings of words. They have natural and external relations to the objects denoted by them.

Prabhakara regards the meanings of proper names as fixed by convention, but does not consider the meanings of common words to be determined by convention, which are independent of human agency. The Vedas are neither created by God nor composed by seers they are unproduced and eternal. The words in the Vedic texts denote their proper objects by their Very nature. Their denotative power does not depend on any convention determined by God or men. The Vedas are self-sufficient and independent of all personal agency. They mainly enjoin the performance of certain duties, which generates an Apurva, an invisible subtle potency, leading to a desirable result. No person can have any knowledge of duties independently of the Vedas. Hence the denotative powers of the Vedic words are eternal and independent of conventions, human or divine.

Both Prabhakara and Kumarila maintain that a word denotes a class, and indirectly refers to an individual through it. All injunctions would be meaningless, if words did not refer to classes. The word 'cow' denotes the class 'cow'. The generic idea of 'cow' represents the class 'cow'. A word cannot denote a single individual, an aggregate of individuals, or all individuals. If a single individual only were denoted by it, there could be no eternal relation between it and its object, and no action would be possible, since one could not make sure which individual was meant by the word. Nor can it denote an aggregate of individuals, since all the individuals cannot be known, and, consequently, their aggregate cannot be known. Even if it could be known, the meaning of the word would constantly change, since some individuals are born and others perish. Nor can a word denote all individuals, since they can never be known, and, consequently, its meaning can never be fully comprehended. Hence a word denotes a class at first, then an individual through it.

11.5 Jaimini's Mimansa Sutras

The work is divided into twelve adhyayas (chapters), which are further divided into sixty padas (sections).

The text provides rules for the interpretation of the Vedas and also provides philosophical justifications for the observance of Vedic rituals, by offering meaning and significance of Vedic rituals to attain Moksha.

11.5.1 Commentaries

Over the centuries many commentaries were written on this text, most important being the Śābara Bhāṣya written by Śābara, the only extant commentary on all the 12 chapters of the Mimamsa Sutras of Jaimini. The major commentaries written on the text as well as the Śābara Bhāṣya were by Kumarila Bhatta and Prabhakara Mishra.

Jaimini, in his Mimamsa Sutra, presents material activity and its results as the whole of reality. His Duty is that which is indicated by the injunctions of the Vedas.

11.6 Contents of Mimansa Sutras

Mimamsa Sutra consists of **twelve chapters:**

In the **first chapter** import of the collections of words which have various meanings is discussed. Such as, injunction (vidhi), explanatory passage (arthavada), hymn (mantra), tradition (smriti) etc.

In the **second chapter**, discussions relating to the difference of various rites, refutation of erroneously proofs etc. are held.

In the **third chapter**, sruti, sense of the passage (linga), context (vakya), and their respective weight when in apparent opposition to one another, the ceremonies called pratipatti-karmdni, things mentioned incidentally (anarabhyadhita) and the duties of the sacrifices are expounded.

In the **fourth chapter**, the influence on other rites of the principal and subordinate rites, the fruit caused by the juhu and dice-playing, which forms a subordinate part of the rajasuya sacrifice are explained.

Fifth chapter discusses relative order of various passages of sruti, different parts of sacrifice etc.

In the **sixth chapter**, the persons qualified to offer sacrifices, their obligations, the substitutes for materials used in sacrifices, expiatory rites and the different sacrificial fires are made clear.

In the **seventh and eight chapters,** transference of ceremonies and transference by virtue from one sacrifice to another are discussed.

In the **ninth chapter**, adaptation of hymns when quoted in a new context (uha), and melodies (samans) and mantras are discussed.

In the **tenth chapter**, the discussion revolves around the non-performance of the primary rites and dependent rites, offerings to grahas etc.

In the **eleventh chapter**, there is discussion on tantra (combining several acts one), and avapa (performance of an act more than once).

In the **twelfth chapter**, prasanga, tantra and cumulation of concurrent rites (samuchchaya) is explained.

11.7 Relevance of Mimansa to Ayurveda

Ayurveda traditionally looks back to certain of the six systems of Indian philosophy (the Shad darshanas) for its fundamental concepts. Today, Ayurveda curricula normally only include the first three systems, Nyaya, Vaisheshika and Samkhya, since their concepts are recognised as the foundation of Ayurveda's approach to the human organism. In ancient times, educated people were familiar with all six systems, viz. the three named above, together with Yoga, Purva Mimansa and Uttara Mimansa (Vedanta). All six regard the Vedas as supreme authority, i.e. they were orthodox, or "Astika", systems and were considered relevant to the practice of Ayurveda, itself an "orthodox" system. In contrast, the heterodox, or Nastika systems, principally those due to Charvaka, Buddhists, and Jains, do not acknowledge the authority of the Vedas.

This chapter addresses Maharishi Jaimini's Purva Mimansa and shows how its study has been found valuable in Ayurveda postgraduate study today, in particular, because its logic matures student interpretation and understanding of texts. Ayurveda's own methodology for interpretation of texts is given in Tantrayukti, for which a sound knowledge of grammar is a prerequisite. Details differ from text to text, however, and in cases where Tantrayukti fails, Mimansa may be helpful. Also, certain commentaries on Ayurvedic texts use the perspective of Mimansa.

As one of the six Astik darshanas, Mimansa is a well-recognised school of Indian philosophy. Its nature is not philosophical advocacy. Rather, as a logical system of interpretation of Vedas for carrying out the Vedic rituals, it has practical applications. The word Mimansa derives from the root man meaning "to know". The Mimansa system is oriented toward interpreting Vedic texts used in rituals. It does not apply to Aranyaka or Upanishad texts. Its scope is limited to the Mantra and Brahmana aspects of Veda, for which it elaborates ritualistic aspects. Such elaboration may create apparent controversies or ambiguities. One branch of a Brahman text may describe a ritual in a certain way, while another branch may describe it differently. The chronology of rituals may vary in different texts.

Reflection of the Mimansa system in the interpretation of Ayurvedic texts:

Some texts and commentaries on Ayurvedic texts are suggestive of the Mimansa viewpoint.

1. The "Rasavaisesika texts" are composed entirely in the adhikaran form which is typical of the Mimansa system.
2. Hemadri, in his commentary on the Asthanga hridaya (AH), explains not only the text but also its similarity to other respected texts, a method of classical Mimansa.
3. Elsewhere, Hemadri explains certain potentially controversial things, as in AH Ni. 1/2 where he explains that the terms divided into are respectively related to sansarga and sannipata, rather than to kshaya and kopa, as there are types of vridhi sansarga and of kshaya sannipata described in dosabhediya adhyaya.
4. The Sharngadhara Samhita describes a guduchayadi kwath. The commentator himself here points out a controversy, i.e. guduchi is considered kaphapittahara by Sushruta, so how can the kwath be said to be vatahara. He then explains that guduchi leaves are Kaphapittahara while the stem is vatahara. So, the stem is to be used in this particular kwath and not the leaves.

Chapter - 12

Vedanta Philosophy

12.1 Introduction to Vedanta Philosophy

Vedānta (also Uttara Mīmāṃsā) is one of the six (āstika) schools of Hindu philosophy. Literally meaning "end of the Vedas", Vedanta reflects ideas that emerged from, or were aligned with, the speculations and philosophies contained in the Upanishads, specifically, knowledge and liberation.

The word Vedanta is made of two words :

Veda - refers to the four sacred vedic texts.

Anta - this word means "End".

The word Vedanta literally means the end of the Vedas and originally referred to the Upanishads. Vedanta is concerned with the jñānakāṇḍa or knowledge section of the Vedas which is called the Upanishads.

The denotation of Vedanta subsequently widened to include the various philosophical traditions based on to the Prasthanatrayi. Vedanta contains many sub-traditions on the basis of a common textual connection called the Prasthanatrayi: the Upanishads, the Brahma Sutras and the Bhagavad Gita. Some scholars believe Brahma Sutra of Vyasa is an interpolation from Madyamika school of Buddhism.

All Vedanta schools, in their deliberations, concern themselves with, but differ in their views regarding, ontology, soteriology and epistemology. The main **traditions of Vedanta** are:

(i) **Bhedabheda (difference and non-difference)**, as early as the 7th century CE, or even the 4th century CE. Some scholars are inclined to consider it as a "tradition" rather than a school of Vedanta.

(ii) **Dvaitādvaita or Svabhavikabhedabheda (dualistic non-dualism)**, founded by Nimbarka in the 7th century CE.

(iii) **Achintya Bheda Abheda (inconceivable one-ness and difference)**, founded by Chaitanya Mahaprabhu (1486–1534 CE), propagated by Gaudiya Vaishnava.
(iv) **Advaita (monistic),** most prominent Gaudapada (~500 CE) and Adi Shankaracharya (8th century CE).
(v) **Vishishtadvaita (qualified monism),** prominent scholars are Nathamuni, Yāmuna and Ramanuja (1017–1137 CE).
(vi) **Dvaita (dualism),** founded by Madhvacharya (1199–1278 CE).
(vii) **Suddhadvaita (purely non-dual)**, founded by Vallabha (1479–1531 CE).

Modern developments in Vedanta include **Neo-Vedanta**, and the growth of the **Swaminarayan Sampradaya**. All of these schools, except Advaita Vedanta and Neo-Vedanta, are related to Vaishavism and emphasise devotion, regarding Vishnu or Krishna or a related manifestation, to be the highest Reality. While Advaita Vedanta attracted considerable attention in the West due to the influence of Hindu modernists like Swami Vivekananda, most of the other Vedanta traditions are seen as discourses articulating a form of Vaishnav theology.

The Upanishads may be regarded as the end of Vedas in different senses:

- These were the last literary products of the Vedic period.
- These mark the culmination of Vedic thought.
- These were taught and debated last, in the Brahmacharya (student) stage.

12.2 Common Features of Vedanta Philosophy

Despite their differences, all schools of Vedanta share some common features:

- Vedanta is the pursuit of knowledge into the Brahman and the Ātman.
- The Upanishads, the Bhagavad Gita and the Brahma Sutras constitute the basis of Vedanta (together known as Prasthanatrayi), providing reliable sources of knowledge (Sruti Śabda in Pramana).
- Brahman, c.q. Ishvara (God), exists as the unchanging material cause and instrumental cause of the world. The only exception here is that Dvaita Vedanta does not hold Brahman to be the material cause, but only the efficient cause.
- The self (Ātman/Jiva) is the agent of its own acts (karma) and the recipient of the consequences of these actions.

- Belief in rebirth and the desirability of release from the cycle of rebirths, (moksha).
- Rejection of Buddhism and Jainism and conclusions of the other Vedic schools (Nyaya, Vaisheshika, Samkhya, Yoga, and, to some extent, the Purva Mimamsa.)

12.3 Prasthanatrayi (The Three Sources)

The Upanishads, the Bhagavad Gita and the Brahma Sutras constitute the basis of Vedanta. All schools of Vedanta propound their philosophy by interpreting these texts, collectively called the Prasthanatrayi, literally, three sources.

(i) The Upanishads, or Śruti prasthāna; considered the Sruti, the "heard" (and repeated) foundation of Vedanta.
(ii) The Brahma Sutras, or Nyaya prasthana / Yukti prasthana; considered the reason-based foundation of Vedanta.
(iii) The Bhagavad Gita, or Smriti prasthāna; considered the Smriti (remembered tradition) foundation of Vedanta.

The Brahma Sutras attempted to synthesise the teachings of the Upanishads. The diversity in the teaching of the Upanishads necessitated the systematisation of these teachings. This was likely done in many ways in ancient India, but the only surviving version of this synthesis is the Brahma Sutras of Badarayana.

All major Vedantic teachers, including Shankara, Bhaskara, Ramanuja, Nimbarka, Vallabha, and Madhva have composed commentaries not only on the Upanishads and Brahma Sutras, but also on the Bhagavad Gita. The Bhagavad Gita, due to its syncretism of Samkhya, Yoga, and Upanishadic thought, has played a major role in Vedantic thought.

12.4 Metaphysics of Vedanta

Vedanta philosophies discuss **three fundamental metaphysical categories** and the relations between the three.

(i) Brahman or Ishvara: the ultimate reality;
(ii) Ātman or Jivātman: the individual soul, self; and
(iii) Prakriti/Jagat: the empirical world, ever-changing physical universe, body and matter.

12.4.1 Brahman / Ishvara – Conceptions of the Supreme Reality

Shankara, in formulating Advaita, talks of two conceptions of Brahman: The Para Brahman (higher Brahman) as undifferentiated Being, and a lower (Aparā) Brahman endowed with qualities as the creator of the universe.

(i) **Parā or Higher Brahman:** The undifferentiated, absolute, infinite, transcendental, supra-relational Brahman beyond all thought and speech is defined as parā Brahman, nirviśeṣa Brahman or nirguṇa Brahman and is the Absolute of metaphysics.

(ii) **Aparā or Lower Brahman:** The Brahman with qualities defined as aparā Brahman or saguṇa Brahman. The saguṇa Brahman is endowed with attributes and represents the personal God of religion.

Ramanuja, in formulating Vishishtadvaita Vedanta, rejects nirguṇa – that the undifferentiated Absolute is inconceivable – and adopts a theistic interpretation of the Upanishads, accepts Brahman as Ishvara, the personal God who is the seat of all auspicious attributes, as the One reality. The God of Vishishtadvaita is accessible to the devotee, yet remains the Absolute, with differentiated attributes.

Madhva, in expounding Dvaita philosophy, maintains that Vishnu is the supreme God, thus identifying the Brahman, or absolute reality, of the Upanishads with a personal god, as Ramanuja had done before him. Nimbarka, in his Dvaitadvaita philosophy, accepted the Brahman both as nirguṇa and as saguṇa. Vallabha, in his Shuddhadvaita philosophy, not only accepts the triple ontological essence of the Brahman, but also His manifestation as personal God (Ishvara), as matter and as individual souls.

12.4.2 Relation between Brahman and Jiva / Atman

The schools of Vedanta differ in their conception of the relation they see between Ātman / Jivātman and Brahman / Ishvara:

According to Advaita Vedanta, Ātman is identical with Brahman and there is no difference. According to Vishishtadvaita, Jīvātman is different from Ishvara, though eternally connected with Him as His mode. The oneness of the Supreme Reality is understood in the sense of an organic unity (vishistaikya). Brahman / Ishvara alone, as organically related to all Jīvātman and the material universe is the one Ultimate Reality.

According to Dvaita, the Jīvātman is totally and always different from Brahman / Ishvara. According to Shuddhadvaita (pure monism), the Jīvātman and Brahman are identical; both, along with the changing empirically-observed universe being Krishna.

Epistemology in Dvaita and Vishishtadvaita Vedanta. Advaita and some other Vedanta schools recognise six epistemic means:

12.5 Epistemology

12.5.1 Pramana

Pramāṇa literally means "proof", "that which is the means of valid knowledge". It refers to epistemology in Indian philosophies, and encompasses the study of reliable and valid means by which human beings gain accurate, true knowledge. The focus of Pramana is the manner in which correct knowledge can be acquired, how one knows or does not know, and to what extent knowledge pertinent about someone or something can be acquired. Ancient and medieval Indian texts identify **six pramanas** as correct means of accurate knowledge and truths:[54]

(i) Pratyakṣa (perception);
(ii) Anumāṇa (inference);
(iii) Upamāṇa (comparison and analogy);
(iv) Arthāpatti (postulation, derivation from circumstances);
(v) Anupalabdi (non-perception, negative/cognitive proof);
(vi) Śabda (scriptural testimony/ verbal testimony of past or present reliable experts).

The different schools of Vedanta have historically disagreed as to which of the six are epistemologically valid. For example, while Advaita Vedanta accepts all six pramanas, Vishishtadvaita and Dvaita accept only three pramanas (perception, inference and testimony).

Advaita considers Pratyakṣa (perception) as the most reliable source of knowledge, and Śabda, the scriptural evidence, is considered secondary except for matters related to Brahman, where it is the only evidence. In Vishistadvaita and Dvaita, Śabda, the scriptural testimony, is considered the most authentic means of knowledge instead.

12.5.2 Theories of Cause and Effect

All schools of Vedanta subscribe to the theory of Satkāryavāda, which means that the effect is pre-existent in the cause. But there are two different views on the status of the "effect", that is, the world. Most schools of Vedanta, as well as Samkhya, support Parinamavada, the idea that the world is a real transformation (parinama) of Brahman. The Brahma Sutras espouse the realist Parinamavada position, which appears to have been the view most common among early Vedantins. In contrast to Badarayana, Adi Shankara and Advaita Vedantists hold a different view, Vivartavada, which says that the effect, the world, is merely an unreal (vivarta) transformation of its cause, Brahman.

12.6 Overview of the Main Schools of Vedanta

12.6.1 Shankaracharya

The Upanishads present an associative philosophical inquiry in the form of identifying various doctrines and then presenting arguments for or against them. They form the basic texts and Vedanta interprets them through rigorous philosophical exegesis to defend the point of view of their specific sampradaya. Varying interpretations of the Upanishads and their synthesis, the Brahma Sutras, led to the development of different schools of Vedanta over time.

While Advaita Vedanta is the "most famous" school of Vedanta, and "often, mistakenly, taken to be the only representative of Vedantic thought, and Shankara a Saivite, Vedanta is essentially a Vaisnava theological articulation, a discourse broadly within the parameters of Vaisnavism. Within the Vaishnava traditions four sampradayas have special status, while different scholars have classified the Vedanta schools ranging from three to six as prominent ones.

12.6.2 Bhedabheda, Bhedabheda (difference and non-difference)

Bhedābheda means "difference and non-difference" and is more a tradition than a school of Vedanta. The schools of this tradition emphasise that the individual self (Jīvatman) is both different and not different from Brahman. Notable figures in this school are Bhartriprapancha, Nimbārka (7th century) who founded the Dvaitadvaita school, Bhāskara (8th–9th century), Ramanuja's teacher Yādavaprakāśa, Chaitanya (1486–1534) who founded the Achintya Bheda Abheda school, and Vijñānabhikṣu (16th century).

12.6.3 Dvaitādvaita

Nimbārka (7th century), sometimes identified with Bhāskara, propounded Dvaitādvaita. Brahman (God), souls (chit) and matter or the Universe (achit) are considered as three equally real and co-eternal realities. Brahman is the controller (niyanta), the soul is the enjoyer (bhokta), and the material Universe is the object enjoyed (bhogya). The Brahman is Krishna, the ultimate cause who is omniscient, omnipotent, all-pervading Being. He is the efficient cause of the universe because, as Lord of Karma and internal ruler of souls, He brings about creation so that the souls can reap the consequences of their karma. God is considered to be the material cause of the universe because creation was a manifestation of His powers of soul (chit) and matter (achit); creation is a transformation (parinama) of

God's powers. He can be realised only through a constant effort to merge oneself with His nature through meditation and devotion.

12.6.4 Achintya Bhedabheda

Chaitanya Mahaprabhu (1486 – 1533) was the prime exponent of Achintya-Bheda-Abheda. In Sanskrit achintya means 'inconceivable'. Achintya-Bheda-Abheda represents the philosophy of "inconceivable difference in non-difference", in relation to the non-dual reality of Brahman-Atman which it calls (Krishna), svayam bhagavan. The notion of "inconceivability" (acintyatva) is used to reconcile apparently contradictory notions in Upanishadic teachings. This school asserts that Krishna is Bhagavan of the bhakti yogins, the Brahman of the jnana yogins, and has a divine potency that is inconceivable. He is all-pervading and thus in all parts of the Universe (non-difference), yet he is inconceivable (difference). This school is at the foundation of the Gaudiya Vaishnava religious tradition. The ISKCON or the Hare Krishnas also affiliate to this school of Vedanta Philosophy.

12.6.5 Advaita Vedanta

Advaita Vedanta propounded by Gaudapada (7th century) and Adi Shankara (8th century), espouses non-dualism and monism. Brahman is held to be the sole unchanging metaphysical reality and identical to the individual Atman. The physical world, on the other hand, is always-changing empirical Maya. The absolute and infinite Atman-Brahman is realised by a process of negating everything relative, finite, empirical and changing.

The school accepts no duality, no limited individual souls (Atman / Jivatman), and no separate unlimited cosmic soul. All souls and their existence across space and time are considered to be the same oneness. Spiritual liberation in Advaita is the full comprehension and realisation of oneness, that one's unchanging Atman (soul) is the same as the Atman in everyone else, as well as being identical to Brahman.

12.6.6 Vishishtadvaita (Qualified non-dualism)

Vishishtadvaita, propounded by Ramanuja (11–12th century), asserts that Jivatman (human souls) and Brahman (as Vishnu) are different, a difference that is never transcended. With this qualification, Ramanuja also affirmed monism by saying that there is unity of all souls and that the individual soul has the potential to realise identity with the Brahman. Vishishtadvaita, like Advaita, is a non-dualistic school of Vedanta in a qualified way, and both begin by assuming that all souls can hope for and achieve the state of blissful liberation. On the relation between the Brahman and the world of matter (Prakriti), Vishishtadvaita states both are two different absolutes, both metaphysically true and real, neither is false or illusive, and that saguna Brahman with attributes is also real. Ramanuja states that God, like man, has both soul and body, and the world of matter is the glory of God's body. The path to Brahman (Vishnu), according to Ramanuja, is devotion to godliness and constant remembrance of the beauty and love of the personal god (bhakti of saguna Brahman).

12.6.7 Dvaita (Dualism)

Dvaita, propounded by Madhvacharya (13th century), is based on the premise of dualism. Atman (soul) and Brahman (as Vishnu) are understood as two completely different entities. Brahman is the creator of the universe, perfect in knowledge, perfect in knowing, perfect in its power, and distinct from souls, distinct from matter. In Dvaita Vedanta, an individual soul must feel attraction, love, attachment and complete devotional surrender to Vishnu for salvation, and it is only His grace that leads to redemption and salvation. Madhva believed that some souls are eternally doomed and damned, a view not found in Advaita and Vishishtadvaita Vedanta. While the Vishishtadvaita Vedanta asserted "qualitative monism and quantitative pluralism of souls", Madhva asserted both "qualitative and quantitative pluralism of souls".

12.6.8 Shuddhādvaita (Pure Nondualism)

Shuddhadvaita (pure non-dualism), propounded by Vallabhacharya (1479–1531 CE), states that the entire universe is real and is subtly Brahman only in the form of Krishna. Vallabhacharya agreed with Advaita Vedanta's ontology, but emphasised that prakriti (empirical world, body) is not separate from the Brahman, but just another manifestation of the latter. Everything, everyone, everywhere – soul and body, living and non-living, jiva and matter – is the eternal Krishna. The way to Krishna, in this school, is bhakti. Vallabha opposed renunciation of monistic sannyasa as ineffective and advocates the path of devotion (bhakti) rather than knowledge (jnana). The goal of bhakti is to turn away from ego, self-centered-ness and deception, and to turn towards the eternal Krishna in everything continually offering freedom from samsara.

Each of these Vedanta Philosophies will be discussed in details in the chapters to follow.

Chapter - 13

Bhedabheda Vedanta Philosophy

13.1 Introduction to Bhedabheda Vedanta Philosophy

Bhedābheda Vedānta is a subschool of Vedānta, which teaches that the individual self (jīvātman) is both different and not different from the ultimate reality known as Brahman.

The characteristic position of all the different Bhedābheda Vedānta schools is that the individual self (jīvātman) is both different and not different from the ultimate reality known as Brahman. Each thinker within the Bhedābheda Vedānta tradition has their own particular understanding of the precise meanings of the philosophical terms: "difference" and "non-difference". Bhedābheda Vedāntic ideas can be traced to some of the very oldest Vedāntic texts, including quite possibly Bādarāyaṇa's Brahma Sūtra (c. 4th century CE).

Bhedābheda predates the positions of two other major schools of Vedānta. The Advaita (Non-dual) Vedānta that claims that the individual self is completely identical to Brahman, and the Dvaita (Dualist) Vedānta (13th century) that teaches complete difference between the individual self and Brahman.

Bhedābheda Vedānta is one of the several traditions of Vedānta philosophy in India. characteristic position of all the different Bhedābheda Vedānta schools is that the individual self (jīvātman) is both different and not different from the ultimate reality known as Brahman. Bhedābheda reconciles the positions of two other major schools of Vedānta. The Advaita (Monist) Vedānta that claims the individual self is completely identical to Brahman, and the Dvaita (Dualist) Vedānta that teaches complete difference between the individual self and Brahman. However, each thinker within the Bhedābheda Vedānta tradition has his own particular understanding of the precise meanings of the philosophical terms: "difference" and "non-difference." Bhedābheda Vedāntic ideas can be traced to some of the very oldest Vedāntic texts, including quite possibly Bādarāyaṇa's Brahma Sūtra (app. 4th century CE). Bhedābheda ideas also had an enormous influence on the devotional (bhakti) schools of India's medieval period. Among medieval Bhedābheda thinkers are Vallabha (1479-1531 CE), founder of the Puṣṭimārga devotional sect now centered in Nathdwara, Rajasthan, and Caitanya (1485-1533 CE) the founder of the Gaudīya Vaiṣṇava sect based in the northeastern Indian state of West Bengal.

Bhedābheda is often presented as a school of Vedānta. Vedānta, in turn, is sometimes spoken about as a single philosophy, when in reality "Vedānta" has different uses. Its most inclusive use is as a label for a philosophy that purports to be expressed at length in the latter part of the Vedas, that is, the Upanishads. It is centrally concerned with the inquiry into the nature of an ultimate entity called "Brahman." There are many different accounts of this synoptic philosophy, and the various accounts are often considered schools of philosophy themselves. Unlike the well-known schools of Advaita (Non-Dualist) Vedānta, Viśiṣṭādvaita (Non-Dualism of the Qualified) Vedānta, and Dvaita (Dualist) Vedānta, it makes more sense to refer to Bhedābheda Vedānta as a "tradition" or "family" of philosophies rather than as a single "school." This is because, unlike the three aforementioned schools, Bhedābheda has no single founder who created an institutionalised network of monasteries dedicated to the study, development, and propagation of the founder's teachings.

The history of Bhedābheda in India stretches back at least until the 7th century CE and likely quite earlier, and continues into the present day. Although there are substantial philosophical disagreements among the many Bhedābheda thinkers, their philosophies also show certain characteristic similarities. A few viewpoints that almost all Bhedābheda schools share, include the understanding of the relation between individual self (jīvātman) and Brahman as one of part and whole; the doctrine that the phenomenal world is a real transformation of Brahman (Pariṇāmavāda); and the doctrine that liberation can only be attained by means of a combination of knowledge and ritual action (Jñānakarmasamuccayavāda), not by knowledge alone.

13.1.1 Badarayana and Bhartriprapancha

Numerous scholars have concluded that Bādarāyaṇa's Brahma Sūtra (circa 4th century CE), one of the foundational texts common to all Vedānta schools, was written from a Bhedābheda Vedāntic viewpoint. While that claim is disputed by other schools, there is little doubt that Bhedābheda predates Shankara's Advaita Vedānta. In his commentary on the Bṛhadāraṇyaka Upaniṣad, Shankara (8th century) repeatedly criticises interpretations by an earlier Vedantin named Bhartriprapancha, who characterised the relation between Brahman and individual souls as one of difference and non-difference. One of the central disagreements between the two is that Shankara claims that Brahman's entire creation is a mere appearance (vivarta), while Bhartriprapancha maintains that it is real.

13.1.2 Bhāskara

The first Bhedābhedavādin widely recognised as such by the later tradition is Bhāskara (8th to 9th century). He was either a younger contemporary of Shankara or perhaps lived slightly after Shankara. His only extant work is a commentary on the Brahma Sūtra. That work is expressly written in order to defend the earlier claims of Bhedābhedavādins against Shankara's interpretation of the Brahma Sūtra. Although he never mentions Shankara by name, he makes it clear from the beginning that his primary intention in commenting on the Brahma Sūtra is to oppose some predecessor: "I am writing a commentary on this sūtra in order to obstruct those commentators who have concealed its ideas and replaced them with their own" (Bhāskara 1903: p. 1). Bhāskara is the earliest in a long line of Vedāntic authors concerned to refute Advaita (including Ramanuja and Madhva, not to mention numerous Bhedābhedavādins). Many of the stock arguments used against the Advaita originated with Bhāskara, if indeed he did not borrow them from an even earlier source. He also seems to have been remembered by the collective Advaita tradition as a thorn in its side. So, for instance, in the 14th century hagiography of Shankara, the Śaṅkaradigvijaya, Mādhava depicts one "Bhaṭṭa Bhāskara" as a haughty and famous Bhedābhedavādin whom Shankara defeats in a lengthy debate.

13.1.3 Yādavaprakāśa and Nimbārka

While the Viśiṣṭādvaita philosopher Ramanuja (11th to 12th century) is widely acknowledged as the most influential Vedantin after Shankara, Ramanuja's complicated relationship with Bhedābhedavāda is rarely discussed. Ramanuja's teacher Yādavaprakāśa was a Bhedābhedavādin. Yādavaprakāśa works have been lost, and therefore almost all of what we know of his ideas comes from Ramanuja and one of Ramanuja's commentators, Sudarśanasūri. However, it is possible from these numerous hints to draw a sketch of Yādavaprakāśa's basic views. Ramanuja depicts Yādavaprakāśa as an exponent of Svābhāvika Bhedābhedavāda, the view that Brahman is both different and not different than the world in its very nature, and that difference is not simply due to difference of artificial limiting conditions. Yādavaprakāśa shares this basic viewpoint with Nimbārka (13th century), and disagrees with the Aupādhika Bhedābhedavāda of Bhāskara, who maintains that the difference of the world and Brahman is due to limiting conditions. Another characteristic of Yādavaprakāśa's thought is his repeated insistence that Brahman has the substance of pure existence (sanmātradravya). The relationship between Brahman and the world is not merely one of class and individual, but rather both are existent entities, standing in the relationship of cause and effect.

13.1.4 Vallabha

In the late medieval period, the doctrine of Bhedābheda became increasingly associated with devotional (bhakti) movements in North India. It is largely on the basis of their reputations as the founders of religious sects, and not as philosophers per se, that thinkers such as Vallabha (1479-1531) and Caitanya (1485-1533) became widely known. Among the former's most influential works are a commentary on the Brahma Sūtra entitled the Anubhāṣya, and his commentary on the Bhāgavata Purāṇa, entitled the Subodhinī. Vallabha founded the Vaiṣṇava sect of the Puṣṭimārga ("path of nourishment") now based in Nathdwara, Rajasthan. His philosophical system, called Śuddhādvaita (Pure Non-Dualism), takes its name from his view that there is no dualism whatsoever between a real Brahman and an unreal world. Since both are completely real, he denies that there can be any sort of ontological dualism of real and unreal between the two—therefore it is a "pure" non-dualism. Obviously, this refers to the Advaita school's view that the phenomenal world is not real in an ultimate sense, and is a clever attempt to re-appropriate the valued label "Advaita" for his own school. Yet in this regard all Bhedābhedavādins might claim the name Śuddhādvaita, since they all assert the reality of the phenomenal world.

13.1.5 Caitanya

Caitanya was another medieval Vaiṣṇava philosopher/theologian, famous for a school of thought known as Acintya Bhedābhedavāda (Inconceivable Difference and Non-difference). Although Caitanya never wrote down his teachings, numerous followers authored works based on his philosophy, such as Jīva Gosvāmin, author of a well-known commentary on the Bhāgavata Purāṇa. This system's notion of "inconceivability" (acintyatva) is a central concept used to reconcile apparently contradictory notions, such as the simultaneous oneness and multiplicity of Brahman, or the difference and non-difference of God and his powers. The tradition of Acintya-Bhedābheda, also commonly known as Gaudīya Vaiṣṇavism, thrives to this day in the Indian state of West Bengal. Perhaps the most famous offshoot of this devotional tradition is the International Society for Krishna Consciousness (ISKON), more popularly known in the West by the name the "Hari Krishnas."

13.1.6 Vijñānabhikṣu

The last major Bhedābheda thinker in pre-modern India, Vijñānabhikṣu (16th century), did not follow the path of bhakti. Vijñānabhikṣu sought to show the ultimate unity of the schools of Vedānta, Sāṅkhya, Yoga, and Nyāya, and is most well-known today for commentaries on Sāṅkhya and Yoga texts. In his innovative sub-commentary on Patanjali's Yoga Sūtra, Vijñānabhikṣu argues that yoga is the most effective means to liberation, although he never repudiates the Bhedābheda metaphysical framework of his earliest writings. Vijñānabhikṣu was a theist who considered Viṣṇu the supreme God. In his commentary on the Sāṅkhya Sūtra, he argues that the Sāṅkhya school requires an omnipotent God in order to cause the union of its two fundamental principles, primordial nature (prakṛti) and pure consciousness (purusha). Vijñānabhikṣu grounds his reinterpretations of fundamental concepts in Sāṅkhya-Yoga in Bhedābheda metaphysics. In his earliest works, such as his Bhedābheda Vedāntic commentary on the Brahma Sūtras, he understands the concepts of difference and non-difference in terms of separation and non-separation. Although for him the fundamental relation of the individual self and Brahman is one of non-separation, the Sāṅkhya-Yoga analysis of the individual selves as multiple and separate from one another is correct, as long as it is understood that this state of separation is temporary and adventitious. While Vijñānabhikṣu's acceptance of Sāṅkhya-Yoga philosophical truths puts him at odds with some earlier Bhedābhedavādins, he continues in the tradition of Bhāskara in his trenchant criticism of the Advaita Vedāntins, whom he decries as "crypto-Buddhists" (pracchannabauddha) and "Vedāntins in name alone" (vedāntibruva).

13.2 Ontology

One of the most notable differences between Bhedābheda Vedānta and Advaita (Monistic) Vedānta is their views on the existence of the phenomenal world. While Advaita holds that the phenomenal world is ultimately unreal (mithyā) and that only Brahman truly exists, Bhedābheda thinkers insist that the phenomenal world is real, and not at all illusory. In this basic assertion they are in line with the majority of Indian philosophical schools, including the schools of Qualified Non-Dualist (Viśiṣṭādvaita) Vedānta, Dualist (Dvaita) Vedānta, Nyāya, Sāṅkhya, and Mīmāṃsā. Although Advaitins cite certain passages from the Upanishads as supporting the notion that the world is akin to a mirage or a magical trick, Bhedābhedavādins accuse Advaitins of borrowing this idea from the Mind-only (Cittamātra) school of Buddhism, and frequently employ the epithet of "crypto-Buddhist" (pracchannabauddha) to refer to Advaitins.

13.2.1 Part and Whole

Bhedābhedavādins understand the relation between Brahman and the individual souls to be a relation between a whole and its parts. They frequently employ stock examples to illustrate this relation. Some of the most common are a fire and its sparks, the sun and its rays, a father and his son, and the ocean and its waves. Each of these is an example of a part-whole relation, which is also a variety of difference and non-difference (Bhedābheda). So, to take one example, the sparks that come off of a fire are both the same as that fire and different from it. They are the same insofar as they came from the fire, and are constituted by the same substance as fire. But they are also distinguishable from the original fire, as occupying a separate point in space. Although these four examples each seem to illustrate a different relation (and it may seem to make no sense at all to understand a son as a "part" of his father), Bhedābhedavādins cite these familiar examples from the physical world in order to shed light on the true metaphysical relation between Brahman and the individual selves. While each might capture some aspect of that relation, inevitably they are mere approximations, requiring further commentary and philosophical analysis.

Advaita Vedāntins object to the characterisation of the individual self as a part, and characterise Brahman as partless. All schools of Vedānta understand the Veda as the ultimate epistemic authority, and arguments from scripture play a large part in intra-Vedāntic disputes. Advaitins point out that both the Upanishads and the Brahma Sūtras say that Brahman is partless (niravayava, niṣkala). Furthermore, the assertion that Brahman has parts seems to defy logic. It is inconceivable that Brahman could be made up of parts, for things that are made up of parts are dependent on those parts, and impermanent. Advaitins offer their own stock examples to show that Brahman cannot be divided up, and that any such division is purely an artificial limitation on an indivisible entity. For example, Advaitins commonly liken Brahman to the element called "space" (ākāśa). According to traditional science in India, space is an element that is omnipresent in the world, just as all Vedāntins agree that Brahman is omnipresent. Although we can talk about space as being delimited (the space inside a room, the space inside a pot), such limitations of space are purely accidental, not essential to the element itself. It may appear to an observer that the space inside a pot and the space outside the pot are two different entities, but this is a misunderstanding of the fundamental nature of space.

The Bhedābhedavādins can themselves appeal to textual authority for the idea that the relation between Brahman and the individual self is a relation between a whole and its parts. In Brahma Sūtra 2.3.43, The individual self is referred to as a "part" (aṁśa), and Bhedābhedavādins cite this passage whenever they require a textual support for their views. However, Advaitins take this description of the relation as a figurative, and not literal description of the status of the individual self. Otherwise, this passage will conflict with Brahma Sūtra 2.1.26, which says that Brahman is "partless" (niravayava). For Advaita, the world appears as if to be made of parts. But when it is understood correctly, all of the many entities in the world are seen to be false, and only one entity, a single, partless Brahman remains. Bhedābhedavādins, in their assertion of the world's phenomenal reality, insist that multiplicity is real. Brahman is simultaneously one and many, depending on the perspective from which it is viewed, just as the ocean can be described as one or many, depending on the perspective from which it is described. Bhedābhedavādins maintain that Brahman's being made up of parts in no way diminishes the perfection of Brahman, just as the existence of waves in the ocean in no way diminishes the amount of water therein.

13.2.2 Aupādhika and Svābhāvika Bhedābheda

All Bhedābhedavādins maintain the reality of the phenomenal world and the multiplicity of individual selves. However, some Bhedābheda-thinkers edge closer to the Advaita position by arguing that although multiplicity is real, it is in some way less real than the absolute unity of Brahman. The early Bhedābheda thinker Bhāskara (8th to 9th century CE) exemplifies this tendency to reduce the ontological status of the phenomenal world, while still maintaining its reality. Bhāskara's philosophy is an example of Aupādhika Bhedābhedavāda ("Difference and Non-difference Based on Limiting Conditions"). According to Bhāskara, the one, absolute Brahman becomes finite and multiple by means of limiting conditions (upādhis). Just as a pure diamond appears to be red when it is placed next to a red flower, so too the absolute Brahman appears finite when it is transformed through limiting conditions. This transformation is a real one; the individual self really is finite, subject to ignorance, suffering, and bondage, so long as it is filtered through limiting conditions. Although the individual self is real as differentiated from Brahman, for Bhāskara difference is merely a temporary state. In its natural state, Brahman is one and not many. Although it undergoes limitations to become finite, the ultimate goal of the individual is to realise his or her absolute state. Liberation is precisely the removal of such limiting conditions.

At the other end of the spectrum from Bhāskara's Aupadhika Bhedābhedavāda is Nimbārka's philosophy of Svābhāvika Bhedābheda (Natural Difference and Non-Difference). For Nimbārka (13th century),

Brahman is different and non-different not because of artificial limiting conditions, but contains both difference and non-difference as its essential nature. Along with Yādavaprakāśa (11th century), Nimbārka comes closest to upholding both difference and non-difference as equally real states of Brahman. The tendency among most Bhedābhedavādins, however, is to subordinate difference to non-difference. Although difference is a real state that Brahman undergoes as it transforms into multiple individual selves, Bhāskara in essence makes the state of non-difference "more real" than the state of difference. In this way, school of Bhedābheda Vedānta is often closer to the school of Advaita (Monist) Vedānta than it is to the school of Dvaita (Dualist) Vedānta.

13.3 Causality

13.3.1 Pariṇāmavāda (Theory of real transformation)

Closely related to Bhedābheda Vedānta's ontology is its theory of causality. Bhedābheda Vedāntins subscribe to the theory of Pariṇāmavāda, which states that the phenomenal world is a real transformation (pariṇāma) of the material cause of the world. They share this theory with the Sāṅkhya school of philosophy, as well as with most other schools of Vedānta. The major difference between the Vedāntic theory of Pariṇāmavāda and the Sāṅkhya's Pariṇāmavāda is the understanding of what constitutes the material cause of the world. For Sāṅkhya, primordial nature (prakṛti) transforms itself into the phenomenal world. The principle of primordial nature is completely insentient, and the process of transformation that creates the world is a blind, automatic process. For Bhedābheda Vedāntins, Brahman is both the material and efficient cause of the universe. Brahman, unlike the Sāṅkhya's prakṛti, is sentient. Yet both the sentient (individual souls) and insentient (physical things) have their origin in Brahman, according to Bhedābhedavādins. In spite of their apparent proximity to the Sāṅkhya school on the issue of causality, early Bhedābheda thinkers such as Bhāskara took pains to critique the Sāṅkhya notion of prakṛti, accusing it of being both contrary to scripture and contrary to logic. A few later Bhedābheda thinkers took a softer line on Sāṅkhya. The most notable of these was Vijñānabhikṣu (16th century), who argued for the ultimate unity of Sāṅkhya and Bhedābheda Vedānta doctrines.

13.3.2 Vivartavāda (Theory of unreal manifestation)

Once again, it is useful to contrast the doctrines of the Bhedābheda school with Advaita Vedānta. Advaita Vedānta maintains the doctrine of Vivartavāda, which states that the world is an unreal manifestation (vivarta) of Brahman. Advaita, like other schools of Vedānta, identifies Brahman as both material and efficient cause. But for the Advaitins, Brahman is the cause of an unreal effect. Although the world can be described as conventionally real (vyavahārasat), the Advaitins claim that all of Brahman's effects must ultimately be acknowledged as unreal before the individual self can be liberated. Although the theory of Vivartavāda is traditionally accepted as a theory shared by the entire Advaita school, some recent historians have questioned this, noting passages in the work of Shaṅkara, the founder of the Advaita, that appear to be closer to the theory of pariṇāma. It is likely that the theory of Vivartavāda is a theory that emerged gradually out of the earlier Vedāntic theory of Pariṇāmavāda, rather than one that sprang fully formed out of the head of Shaṅkara. It also bears repeating that some Bhedābheda Vedāntins come perilously close to the Advaita view of the phenomenal world as only conventionally real, as they often emphasise that multiplicity is an unnatural, temporary state.

13.3.3 Satkāryavāda (Theory of pre-existent effect)

Proponents of both Vedāntic theories of causality, Pariṇāmavāda and Vivartavāda, justify each by citing a central passage at Chāndogya Upanishad 6.1.4-5. There, the sage Aruni describes the nature of causality to his son, Śvetaketu, using the example of the relation of clay to a pot:

It is like this, son. By means of just one lump of clay one would perceive everything made of clay—the transformation is a verbal handle, a name—while the reality is just this: 'It's clay.' It is like this, son. By means of just one copper trinket one would perceive everything made of copper—the transformation is a verbal handle, a name—while the reality is just this: 'It's copper.'

This passage uses the examples of an everyday material cause, clay or copper, to shed light on the nature of cause and effect. It expresses the doctrine of Satkāryavāda, which says that the effect preexists in its cause. All Vedāntins subscribe to this theory—the doctrines of real transformation (pariṇāma) and unreal manifestation (Vivartavāda) can be understood as two different versions of the theory of Satkāryavāda. According to Satkāryavāda, the lump of clay does not go out of existence when it is transformed into a pot, a cup, a saucer, or the like, only to be replaced by something entirely new. Although the form of the clay has changed, its essence, its clay-ness, remains. The same logic applies to everything caused by Brahman. The entire world, in all of its many forms, nonetheless shares the same essence, as being Brahman. This view, something like an early Indian theory of the conservation of matter, suggests that nothing ever arrives in the universe completely new, but only as a transformation of some earlier material cause. Nothing can be created ex nihilo. In this belief, the Vedāntins are at odds with the Buddhist and Nyāya schools, who for separate reasons argue that the effect does not preexist in the cause.

Although Bhedābheda Vedāntins and Advaita Vedāntins have the theory of Satkāryavādain common, they part ways when asked to characterise the status of the effect. Is the effect a real transformation (pariṇāma) of the cause, or merely an unreal manifestation (vivarta)? The passage at Chāndogya Upanishad 6.1.4-5 has been interpreted in both ways. Advaitins emphasise the apparent nominalism expressed in this passage: "the transformation is a verbal handle, a name—while the reality is just this: 'It's copper.'" This might suggest that the effect is unreal, and only the cause is truly real. But Bhedābhedavādins see this passage as simply another instantiation of the principle of difference and non-difference, just as it is illustrated by the examples of a fire and its sparks or the sun and its rays. From one perspective, focusing on substance, we can say that all of the various cups, saucers, and plates are one—they are all clay. Yet at the same time, they have been transformed by the pot-maker into different forms, multiple in number, occupying different points in space. From this perspective, the effects are real. Just as the many pots, plates, and saucers are simultaneously different and non-different from the original lump of clay, so too all of the individual selves are both different and non-different from Brahman, the original material cause.

13.4 Theology and Soteriology

13.4.1 God in Bhedābhedavāda

In the medieval period, Bhedābheda Vedānta became closely associated with theism in general, and the movement of bhakti devotionalism in particular. There is a reason that bhaktas such as Vallabha (1479-1531 CE) and Caitanya (1485-1533) built the foundations of their theological systems on centuries-old Bhedābheda concepts. Like the schools of Ramanuja and Madhva, Bhedābhedavāda is a realist school. Whereas in the Advaita school even God has to be understood as ultimately unreal, since He too is merely Brahman limited by the artificial condition of lordliness, certain types of Bhedābheda philosophy can accommodate a God who is real in his qualified (saguṇa) form. Although on a certain level, an Advaitin can profess a belief in God, he or she knows that ultimately God is merely a crutch, a heuristic to enable human beings to go one step closer to that ultimate Brahman devoid of qualities (nirguṇa). Such a God is ultimately unsatisfying for those whose primary interest is devotion—in any system of Advaita, devotion must occupy a lower position than pure knowledge.

On the other hand, many worshippers will also be unsatisfied with the Dvaita school's uncompromising notion that they themselves are completely separate from God, and that ultimate unification with the Godhead is impossible. Both Bhedābhedavāda and Viśiṣṭādvaita offer the possibility to bridge these two alternatives, by offering the alternative of both a real God possessing qualities and the possibility of personal participation in that Godhead.

13.4.2 Knowledge combined with ritual acts leads to liberation

Besides insistence that the phenomenal world is a real transformation (pariṇāma) of Brahman, another view shared by Bhedābhedavādins is the necessity of ritual acts in combination with knowledge (Jñānakarmasamuccayavāda) in order to obtain liberation. Bhāskara devotes much of the beginning of his commentary on the Brahma Sūtra to a critique of Shankara's radical view that knowledge alone is sufficient for the attainment of Brahman, as long as one has fulfilled one's ritual requirements at an earlier stage. Although today polemics between Vedāntins are usually depicted in solely philosophical or theological terms, this suggests that above all, Shankara's new teachings were seen by other Vedāntins in the 8th century as a serious threat to the ritual-social order. Bhāskara's arguments in favour of Brahmanic ritualism are an important reminder of the continuities between early Vedānta and the Pūrva Mīmāṃsā (Prior Exegesis) school of ritual hermeneutics. The two schools are so close that Sanskrit authors in pre-modern India typically refer to Vedānta by the names "Brahma Mīmāṃsā" (Exegesis of Brahman) or "Uttara Mīmāṃsā" (Later Exegesis), emphasising the central importance of Vedic interpretation for all Vedāntic thinkers.

The notion of bhakti finds a home in Bhedābhedavāda, since Bhedābheda takes activity in the world (Karman) seriously, believing that activities in the world are real, and produce real effects. But it should not be thought that all Bhedābhedavādins were proponents of bhakti. The early Bhedābheda of Bhāskara was not concerned at all with bhakti. Instead, Bhāskara uses Bhedābheda conceptual terminology as a conservative apologist, to defend the importance of Brahmanical ritual orthodoxy from Shaṅkara, a radical who rejected the ultimate efficacy of Vedic ritual. It is only with Nimbārka, a Bhedābheda thinker heavily influenced by the bhakti system of Ramanuja, that we first fully see the union of bhakti-worship and Bhedābhedavāda. Even in medieval northern India, where bhakti was influential and widespread, not all Bhedābhedavādins were bhaktas. Vijñānabhikṣu, for example, was more interested in espousing a modified, Bhedābheda Vedāntic form of Patañjali's Yoga than he was to proselytise for the path of devotion. Such flexibility of the Bhedābheda philosophical apparatus has allowed it to survive as a living tradition for over 1500 years in a number of very different historical contexts. Although in the modern period Bhedābheda Vedānta has been eclipsed in popularity by neo-Vedāntic interpretations of Advaita Vedānta philosophy, its lineage continues today among traditional scholars in Puṣṭimārga and Gaudīya Vaiṣṇava religious communities. And, for the first time in its long history, in the early 21st century Bhedābheda Vedānta is beginning to receive the attention it deserves among historians, philosophers, and theologians outside of India.

Chapter - 14

Advaita Vedanta Philosophy

Advaita jñānaṃ manovṛtti mātram.
Non-dual realisation is a mere mental modification.
- Adi Shankaracharya, Upanishad Bhashya

14.1 Biography of Adi Shankaracharya

Adi Shankaracharya was an exponent of the Advaita Vedanta school of philosophy which refers to the recognition that the true Self, Atman, is the same as the highest Reality, Brahman. He was an 8th century Indian Hindu philosopher and theologian whose teachings had a profound influence on the growth of Hinduism. Also known as Shri Adi Bhagavatpada Acharya (the guru at the feet of Lord), he was a religious reformist who critiqued the rituals-oriented schools of Hinduism and cleansed the Vedic religious practices of ritualistic excesses. Adi Shankara is best remembered for his remarkable reinterpretations of Hindu scriptures and his commentaries on the Vedic canon (Brahma Sutras, Principal Upanishads and Bhagavad Gita). His teachings on the philosophy have tremendously influenced various sects of Hinduism and have contributed to the development of the modern Indian thought.

Born in 788 CE in the southern Indian state of Kerala. He was born to Nambudiri Brahmin parents. Rajasekhara, a rich landlord, built a Siva temple in Kaladi and formed an Agrahara for brahmins who were in the service of the temple. Vidyadhiraja was doing Puja (worship) in the temple. He had only one son named Sivaguru. Sivaguru studied the Shastras and married at the proper age. He had no child. He and his wife Aryamba prayed to Lord Siva to bless them with a son. A son was born to them in the vasanta ritu or the spring season at noon, in the auspicious Abhijit Muhurtai and under the constellation Ardhra (nakshatra). This son was Shankara. His father died while Shankara was very young. Shankara's upanayanam, the initiation into student-life, had to be delayed due to the death of his father, and was then performed by his mother. Adi Shankara was inclined towards spirituality and religion from a young age. He mastered all the Vedas and the six Vedangas from his guru and travelled widely, dispersing spiritual knowledge and spreading the tenets of Advaita Vedanta.

It is said that his mother Aryamba had a vision that Lord Shiva himself told her that he would incarnate in the form of her first-born child. Right from childhood he showed a penchant towards spiritual knowledge. He could easily recite the Puranas and the Epics and mastered the Vedas during his early years in Gurukul. Adi Shankara's teachings were thoroughly adopted by his disciples later on.

Shankara's hagiography describes him as someone who was attracted to the life of Sannyasa (hermit) from early childhood. His mother disapproved this. A story, found in all hagiographies, describe Shankara at the age of eight going to a river with his mother, Sivataraka, to bathe, and where he was caught by a crocodile. Shankara called out to his mother to give him permission to become a Sannyasin or else the crocodile would kill him. The mother agreed, Shankara was freed and left his home for education. He reached a Saivite sanctuary along a river in a north-central state of India, and became the disciple of a teacher named Govinda Bhagavatpada. The stories in various hagiographies diverge in details about the first meeting between Shankara and his Guru, where they met, as well as what happened later.

The biographies vary in their description of where he went, who he met and debated and many other details of his life. Most mention Shankara studying the Vedas, Upanishads and Brahmasutra with Govindapada, and Shankara authoring several key works in his youth, while he was studying with his teacher. It is with his teacher Govinda, that Shankara studied Gaudapadiya Karika, as Govinda was himself taught by Gaudapada. Most also mention a meeting with scholars of the Mimamsa school of Hinduism, namely Kumarila and Prabhakara, as well as Mandana and various Buddhists, in Shastrarth (an Indian tradition of public philosophical debates attended by large number of people, sometimes with royalty). Thereafter, the biographies about Shankara vary significantly. Different and widely inconsistent accounts of his life include diverse journeys, pilgrimages, public debates, installation of yantras and lingas, as well as the founding of monastic centres in north, east, west and south India.

Adi Shankara is believed to have died in 820 CE, at the age of 32, at Kedarnath in the northern Indian state of Uttarakhand, a Hindu pilgrimage site in the Himalayas. Texts say that he was last seen by his disciples behind the Kedarnath temple, walking in the Himalayas until he was not traced.

His contribution is beyond imagination; a few of these contributions in the form of commentaries which are treasures to Hindu Sanatana belief. These are Vivekachudamani, Atma Bodha, Aparoksh Anubhuti, Ananda Lahari, Atma-Anatma Vivek, Drig-Drishya Vivek and Upadesa Sahasri. "More than 300 works—commentative, expository, and poetical—written in the Sanskrit language, are attributed to him. His masterpiece is the Brahma-sutra-Bhashya, the commentary on the Brahma-sutra, which is a fundamental text of the Vedanta school.

He wanted to get formally initiated into the sacred order of Sannyasa and thus sought a guru to guide him in this direction. He met Swami Govindapada Acharya in a hermitage in Badrikashram (Badrinath) in the Himalayas. He narrated his life's story to the guru and requested him to accept him as a pupil.

The details regarding the later years of his life are somewhat obscure though it is generally accepted that he travelled widely, participated in public philosophical debates with religious scholars, preached his teachings to his disciples and founded several "matha" (monasteries).

He is regarded as the founder of the Dasanami Sampradaya of Hindu monasticism. He organised the Hindu monks of a section of the Ekadandi monks under four monasteries, with the headquarters at Dwarka in the West, Jagannatha Puri in the East, Sringeri in the South and Badrikashram in the North. He then placed four of his prominent disciples, Sureswara Acharya, Padmapada, Hastamalaka and Trotakacharya, in charge of the mathas.

14.2 Gaudapada, Adi Shankara (Advaita Vedanta) (6th to 9th centuries)

Influenced by Buddhism, Advaita Vedanta departs from the Bhedabheda-philosophy, instead postulating the identity of Atman with the Whole (Brahman),

Gaudapada (c. 6th century CE), was the teacher or a more distant predecessor of Govindapada, the teacher of Adi Shankara. Shankara is widely considered as the apostle of Advaita Vedanta. Gaudapada's treatise, the Karika– also known as the Mandukya Karika or the Agama Śastraṃ– is the earliest surviving complete text on Advaita Vedanta. Gaudapada's Karika relied on the Mandukya, Brihadaranyaka and Chandogya Upanishads.

In the Karika, Advaita (non-dualism) is established on rational grounds upapatti) independent of scriptural revelation; its arguments are devoid of all religious, mystical or scholastic elements. Scholars are divided on a possible influence of Buddhism on Gaudapada's philosophy. The fact that Shankara, in addition to the Brahma Sutras, the principal Upanishads and the Bhagavad Gita, wrote an independent commentary on the Karika proves its importance in Vedāntic literature.

Adi Shankara elaborated on Gaudapada's work and more ancient scholarship to write detailed commentaries on the Prasthanatrayi and the Karika. The Mandukya Upanishad and the Karika have been described by Shankara as containing "the epitome of the substance of the import of Vedanta". It was Shankara who integrated Gaudapada work with the ancient Brahma Sutras, "and give it a locus classicus" alongside the realistic strain of the Brahma Sutras. His interpretation, including works ascribed to him, has become the normative interpretation of Advaita Vedanta. A noted contemporary of Shankara was Mandana Mishra, who regarded Mimamsa and Vedanta as forming a single system and advocated their combination known as Karma-jnana-samuchchaya-vada. The treatise on the differences between the Vedanta school and the Mimamsa school was a contribution of Adi Shankara. Advaita Vedanta rejects rituals in favour of renunciation, for example.

Advaita Vedanta emphasises Jivanmukti, the idea that moksha (freedom, liberation) is achievable in this life in contrast to other Indian philosophies that emphasise Videhamukti, or moksha after death. The school uses concepts such as Brahman, Atman, Maya, Avidya, meditation and others that are found in major Indian religious traditions, but interprets them in its own way for its theories of moksha. Advaita Vedānta is one of the most studied and most influential schools of classical Indian thought. Many scholars describe it as a form of monism, while others describe the Advaita philosophy as non-dualistic. Advaita is considered to be a philosophy or spiritual pathway rather than a religion, as it does not require those who follow it to be of a particular faith or sect.

Correct understanding of Advaita Vedanta is believed to provide knowledge of one's true identity as Ātman, the dispassionate and unchanging witness-consciousness, and the identity of Ātman and Brahman, which results in liberation. This is achieved through what Adi Shankara refers to as anubhava, immediate intuition, a direct awareness which is construction-free, and not construction-filled. It is not an awareness of Brahman, but instead an awareness that is Brahman.

The main question here is the relation between Atman and Brahman, which is solved by regarding them to be identical. This truth is established from the oldest Principal Upanishads and Brahma Sutras, and is also found in parts of the Bhagavad Gita and numerous other Hindu texts, and is regarded to be self-evident. The main aim of the commentaries is to support this nondualistic (of Atman and Brahman) reading of the Sruti. Reason is being used to support revelation, the Sruti, the ultimate source of truth.

Purushartha – the four goals of human life

Advaita, like other schools, accepts Purushartha – the four goals of human life as natural and proper:

- **(i) Dharma:** the right way to life, the "duties and obligations of the individual toward himself and the society as well as those of the society toward the individual";
- **(ii) Artha:** the means to support and sustain one's life;
- **(iii) Kāma**: pleasure and enjoyment;
- **(iv) Moksha:** liberation, release.

Of these, much of the Advaita Vedānta philosophy focuses on the last, gaining liberation in one's current life. The first three are discussed and encouraged by Advaitins, but usually in the context of knowing Brahman and Self-realisation.

14.3 Moksha – Liberation

The primary goal, in Advaita, is to gain self-knowledge and complete understanding of the identity of Atman and Brahman. Correct knowledge of Atman and Brahman leads to dissolution of all dualistic tendencies and to liberation, Moksha is attained by realising one's true identity as Ātman, and the identity of Atman and Brahman, the complete understanding of one's real nature as Brahman in this life.

According to Advaita Vedānta, liberation can be achieved while living, and is called Jivanmukti. The Atman-knowledge, that is the knowledge of true Self and its relationship to Brahman is central to this liberation in Advaita thought. Atman-knowledge, to Advaitins, is that state of full awareness, liberation and freedom which overcomes dualities at all levels, realising the divine within oneself, the divine in others and all beings, the non-dual Oneness, that Brahman is in everything, and everything is Brahman.

In Advaita Vedānta, the interest is not in liberation in after life, but in one's current life. Advaita Vedānta school holds that liberation can be achieved while living, and a person who achieves this is called a Jivanmukta.

14.4 Mahavakyas – The Great Sentences and the Advaitic Theme

Several Mahavakyas, or "the great sentences", have Advaitic theme, that is "the inner immortal self and the great cosmic power are one and the same". Here are these Mahavakyas:

(i) **Aitareya Upanishad, V.3:** Prajnanam brahma, meaning, Prajnanam is brahman.

(ii) **Bṛhadāraṇyaka Upanishad I.4.10:** Aham brahmasmi, meaning, I am Brahman or I am Divine.

(iii) **Chandogya Upanishad Vi.8.7:** Tat tvam asi, meaning, That thou art, or You are that.

(iv) **Mandukya Upanishad II :** Ayam atma brahma, meaning, This Atman is Brahman.

14.5 Need of a Guru

Since the realisation of the Self cannot be had from books or scriptures, Shankara insists on the necessity of instruction by a Self-realised Guru (teacher). The intense desire to liberate and the effort required by the sadhaka (aspirant) is emphasised. If there is no effort, there cannot be a result. Advaita Vedānta school has traditionally had a high reverence for Guru (teacher), and recommends that a competent Guru be sought in one's pursuit of spirituality. However, the Guru is not mandatory in Advaita school. Adi Shankara, states regularly employed compound words "such as Sastracaryopadesa (instruction by way of the scriptures and the teacher) and Vedāntacaryopadesa (instruction by way of the Upanishads and the teacher) to emphasise the importance of Guru". This reflects the Advaita tradition which holds a competent teacher as important and essential to gaining correct knowledge, freeing oneself from false knowledge, and to self-realisation.

A guru is someone more than a teacher, traditionally a reverential figure to the student, with the guru serving as a "counsellor, who helps mould values, shares experiential knowledge as much as literal knowledge, an exemplar in life, an inspirational source and who helps in the spiritual evolution of a student.

14.6 Levels of Reality – Truths

The classical Advaita Vedānta explains all reality and everything in the experienced world to be same as the Brahman. To Advaitins, there is a unity in multiplicity, and there is no dual hierarchy of a Creator and the created universe. All objects, all experiences, all matter, all consciousness, all awareness, in Advaita philosophy is not the property but the very nature of this one fundamental reality Brahman with this premise, the Advaita school states that any ontological effort must presuppose a knowing self, and this effort needs to explain all empirical experiences such as the projected reality while one dreams during sleep, and the observed multiplicity of living beings. This Advaita does by positing its theory of three levels of reality, the theory of two truths, and by developing and integrating these ideas with its theory of errors (anirvacaniya khyati).

Shankara proposes **three levels of reality**, using sublation as the ontological criterion:

(i) **Paramarthika (paramartha, absolute),** the Reality that is metaphysically true and ontologically accurate. It is the state of experiencing that "which is absolutely real and into which both other reality levels can be resolved". This reality is the highest, it can't be sublated (assimilated) by any other.

(ii) **Vyavaharika (vyavahara), or samvriti-saya,** consisting of the empirical or pragmatical reality. It is ever changing over time, thus empirically true at a given time and context but not metaphysically true. It is "our world of experience, the phenomenal world that we handle every day when we are awake". It is the level in which both jiva (living creatures or individual souls) and Ishvara are true; here, the material world is also true but this is incomplete reality and is sublatable.

(iii) **Pratibhasika (Pratibhasika, apparent reality, unreality),** "reality based on imagination alone". It is the level of experience in which the mind constructs its own reality. Well-known examples of Pratibhasika are the imaginary reality such as the "roaring of a lion" fabricated in dreams during one's sleep, and the perception of a rope in the dark as being a snake.

14.7 Three States of Consciousness and Turiya

Advaita posits three states of consciousness, namely waking (jagrit), dreaming (svapna), deep sleep (sushupti), which are empirically experienced by human beings, and correspond to the Three Bodies Doctrine:

(i) The first state is the waking state, in which we are aware of our daily world.[210] This is the gross body.

(ii) The second state is the dreaming mind. This is the subtle body.

(iii) The third state is the state of deep sleep. This is the causal body.

(iv) Advaita also posits the fourth state of **Turiya**, which some describe as pure consciousness, the background that underlies and transcends these three common states of consciousness. Turiya is the state of liberation, where states Advaita school, one experiences the infinite (Ananta) and non-different (advaita/

abheda), that is free from the dualistic experience, the state in which ajativada, non-origination, is apprehended. Turiya state is where the foundational Self is realised, it is measureless, it is measureless, neither cause nor effect, all pervading, without suffering, blissful, changeless, self-luminous, real, immanent in all things and transcendent. Those who have experienced the Turiya stage of self-consciousness have reached the pure awareness of their own non-dual Self as one with everyone and everything, for them the knowledge, the knower, the known becomes one, they are the Jivanmukta.

Identity of Ātman and Brahman

According to Advaita Vedānta, Atman is identical to Brahman. This is expressed in the mahavakya "tat tvam asi", "thou are that." There is "a common ground, viz. consciousness, to the individual and Brahman." Each soul, in Advaita view, is non-different from the infinite. According to Shankara, Ātman and Brahman seem different at the empirical level of reality, but this difference is only an illusion, and at the highest level of reality they are really identical. Moksha is attained by realising the identity of Ātman and Brahman, the complete understanding of one's real nature as Brahman in this life.

According to Advaita Vedānta, Brahman is the sole reality. The status of the phenomenal world is an important question in Advaita Vedānta, and different solutions have been proposed. The perception of the phenomenal world as real is explained by maya (constantly changing reality) and avidya ("ignorance"). Other than Brahman, everything else, including the universe, material objects and individuals, are ever-changing and therefore maya. Brahman is Paramarthika Satyam, "Absolute Truth", and "the true Self, pure consciousness, the only Reality (sat), since It is untinged by difference, the mark of ignorance, and since It is the one thing that is not sublatable".

The doctrine of Maya is used to explain the empirical reality in Advaita. Jiva, when conditioned by the human mind, is subjected to experiences of a subjective nature, states Vedānta school, which leads it to misunderstand Maya and interpret it as the sole and final reality. Advaitins assert that the perceived world, including people and other existence, is not what it appears to be". It is Maya, they assert, which manifests and perpetuates a sense of false duality or divisional plurality. The empirical manifestation is real but changing, but it obfuscates the true nature of metaphysical Reality which is never changing. Advaita school holds that liberation is the unfettered realisation and understanding of the unchanging Reality and truths – the

Self, that the Self (Soul) in oneself is same as the Self in another and the Self in everything (Brahman).

14.8 'Atma Bodha' Book by Adi Shankara

Atma-bodha is a short Sanskrit text attributed to Adi Shankara of Advaita Vedanta school of Hindu philosophy. The text in sixty-eight verses describes the path to Self-knowledge or the awareness of Atman. The Vedanta tradition states that the text was written by Shankara for his disciple, Sanandana, also known as Padmapada. The Atma Bodha or Self-Knowledge, is a short treatise on Advaita Vedanta, the philosophy of Nondualistic Vedanta. the great philosopher of Non-dualism. The text of Atmabodha avoids the technicalities found in the Vedas, but conveys the message of jnana yoga (the path of knowledge) to the layman. Shankara starts with the requirements of the aspirant, and goes on to explain the nature of world -Samsara, the embodiments of the soul, the influence of maya and the superimposition of Atman. He describes the meditation technique based on aphorism 'I am Brahman,' the supreme being, Aham Brahmasmi', and elucidates the fruits of Self-realisation and the state of the jivanmukta (liberated soul).

The treatise of the knowledge of self, Atma bodha, is meant for those whose sins have been destroyed by religious austerities, who are calm, devoid of attachment and are persons desirous of liberation (that is, mumukshus: desirous of moksha). The qualified are those who have the four-fold requisites, 1. discrimination between real and unreal (viveka); 2. non-attachment (i.e., indifferent to the results of one's action); 3. desire for emancipation (mumukshus); and 4. the six-fold qualities: (a) sama (restraint of internal senses); (b) dama (restraint of external senses); (c)uparati (control of senses, without jumping from one object to another); (d) samadhana (mind constantly on the Self); (e) titlkkha (indifferent endurance); and (f) shraddha (faith).

The rest of the sixty-seven verses may be roughly classified into the following subjects, means for emancipation (2-5), samsara (6-12), various shariras

In the third verse of 'Atma Bodha' Shankara says that karma is not opposed to ignorance, though it cannot destroy ignorance. Undoubtedly a great religious reformer and philosopher, Shankara embraces within his fold all pantheism (a doctrine which identifies God with the universe, or regards the universe as a manifestation of God) while maintaining the principle of non-duality.

Some excerpts from Book on "Atma Bodha" by Adi Shankaracharya:

Action cannot destroy ignorance, for it is not in conflict with ignorance. Knowledge alone destroys ignorance, as light destroys dense darkness.

- Verse 3

According to Non-dualistic Vedanta the Ultimate Reality is Brahman, which is One without a second. It alone exists; names and forms are illusory. One sees multiplicity on account of ignorance. Again, under the influence of ignorance one performs action associated with the multiple factors of doer, instrument, and result. By means of action a man fulfils his various desires. Therefore, action is in harmony with ignorance and cannot directly destroy it. But, if a man is firmly established in the Knowledge of Non-duality and if he realises that he is the Absolute, the embodiment of Freedom, Bliss, and Perfection, then the false notion of his self as a finite, physical entity which impels him to various actions disappears. The action performed by a knower of Brahman is free from the notion of duality. The action of an ignorant person is selfish and egocentric. Only a knower of Brahman can perform really unselfish work. According to some Vedantists, even the knower of Brahman retains a trace of ignorance, with the help of which he performs action in the relative world. They contend that complete Self-knowledge is not possible except at the time of death; for the bare maintenance of the body requires certain activities, such as eating and sleeping, which are not possible without a trace of body-consciousness.

It is only because of ignorance that the Self appears to be finite. When ignorance is destroyed, the Self, which does not admit of any multiplicity whatsoever, truly reveals Itself by Itself, like the sun when the cloud is removed.

-Verse 4

According to Non-dualistic Vedanta, Self-Knowledge, which is the goal of man's spiritual endeavour, is not the attainment of something new or foreign; it is a rediscovery of the ever present Self hidden under layers of ignorance. As the true nature of the sun is hidden by a cloud, so the true nature of the eternal Self is hidden by ignorance. On account of this ignorance the all-pervading Spirit seems to be a physical and finite being.

The Soul regarding Itself as a jiva is overcome by fear, just like the man who regards a rope as a snake. The Soul regains fearlessness by realising that It is not a jiva but the Supreme Soul.

- Verse 26

Perception of duality gives rise to fear and expectation, both of which are groundless. The expectation of attaining something in the dual world for the happiness of the Soul brings in its train disappointment and suffering;

for duality itself is based on illusion. No abiding satisfaction from the fulfilment of desires is ever possible in the dual world. The realisation of Non-duality alone brings peace and blessedness.

By negating all the upadhis through the help of the scriptural statement " It is not this, It is not this," realise the oneness of the individual soul and the Supreme Soul by means of the great Vedic aphorisms.

- Verse 29

I alone am the supreme Brahma which is pure, eternal and free and which is indivisible, non-dual and changeless in all the periods of time. It is knowledge itself and is infinite.

- Verse 36

There are no distinctions, such as 'knower', 'knowledge' and the 'object of knowledge' in the Supreme self (Paramatma). As the nature of Paramatma is endless Bliss and Self luminous, there are no such distinctions within itself. At alone shines.

- Verse 41

'Realise that to be Brahman which is Existence-Knowledge-Bliss Absolute, which is non-dual and infinite, eternal and One, and which fills all the quarters-all that is above and below and all that exists between.

- Verse 56

The Supreme Brahman pervades the entire Universe outwardly and inwardly and shines of Itself, like the fire that permeates a red-hot iron ball both inwardly and outwardly shines of itself.

- Verse 62

He who, renouncing all activities, worships in the sacred and stainless shrine of Atman, which is independent of time, place, and distance ; which is present everywhere; which is the destroyer of heat and cold, and the other opposites ; and which is the giver of eternal happiness, becomes all-knowing and all-pervading and attains, hereafter, Immortality.

- Verse 68

14.9 'Aparoksh Anubhuti' (Self-Realisation) Book by Adi Shankara

The Aparokshanubhuti is a famous work attributed to Adi Shankara. It is a popular introductory work (prakran grantha) that expounds Advaita Vedanta philosophy. It describes a method that seekers can follow to directly experience the essential truth of one's one nature. Thus, the work is literally titled Aparokshanubhuti, or Direct Experience. It is the direct cognition of the Atman which is always present in all thought. The central theme of this book is the identity of the Jivatman (individual self) and Paramatman (Universal Self). This identity is realised through the removal of the ignorance that hides the truth, by the light of Vichara or enquiry alone.

Excerpts from this Book are:

7. Turning away completely from all sense objects is the height of Uparati, and patient endurance of all sorrow or pain is known as Titiksha which is conducive to happiness.

Uparati differs very little from Sama and Dama, yet there is a difference. While practising Sama and Dama there is an effort to restrain the mind's outgoing propensities. But in Uparati the equipoise of the mind becomes spontaneous and there is no further striving, to gain it.

I2. Who am I ? How is this (world) created? Who is its creator? Of what material is this (world) made? This is the way of that vichara (enquiry).

Who am I?-We know that we are I but we do not know what our real nature is. In the waking state we think that we are the body, the physical being, and consequently feel ourselves strong or weak, young or old. At another time, in the dream state, regardless of the physical existence we remain only in a mental state, where we are merely thinking beings and feel only the misery or happiness that our thoughts create for us. Again, in deep sleep, we enter into a state where we cannot find the least trace of any such attribute where-by we can either assert or deny our existence. We pass through these states almost daily and yet do not know which of them conforms to our real nature. So, the question, 'Who am I?' is always with us an unsolved riddle. So, it is necessary for us to investigate this.

13. I am neither the body, a combination of the (five) elements (of matter), nor am I an aggregate of the senses; I am something different from these. This is the way of that Vichara.

This body has its origin in insentient matter and as such it is devoid of consciousness. If I be the body, I should be unconscious; but by no means am I so. Therefore, I cannot be the body.

16. As I am also the One, the Subtle, the Knower, I the Witness, the Ever-Existent and the Unchanging, so there is no doubt that I am "That"2 (i.e., Brahman). Such is this enquiry.

21. Atman is eternal, since it is Existence· itself: the body is transient, as it is non-existence in essence.

24. I am verily Brahman, I being equanimous, quiescent and by nature absolute Existence, Knowledge and Bliss. I am not the body, which is non-existence itself. This is called true Knowledge by the wise.

31. The Supreme (Purusha) known as "I" (ego) is but one, whereas the gross bodies are many. So how can this body be Purusha?

33. It is a fact of direct experience that the 'I' (Atman) is without any change/ whereas the body is always undergoing changes. So how can this body be Purusha ?

43. No division in Consciousness is admissible at any time as it is always one and the same. Even the individuality of the Jiva must be known as false, like the delusion of a snake in a rope.

45. There exists no other material cause of this phenomenal universe except Brahman. Hence this whole universe is but Brahman and nothing else.

49. Inasmuch as all beings are born of Brahman, the supreme Atman, they must be understood to be verily Brahman.

56. This world, though an object of our daily experience and serving all practical purposes, is, like the dream world, of the nature of non-existence, inasmuch as it is contradicted the next moment.

62. Just as the appearance of a ghost in an empty place, of a castle in the air, and of a second moon in the sky (is illusory), so is the appearance of the universe in Brahman.

87. Thus, through ignorance arises in Atman the delusion of the body, which, again, through Self-realisation, disappears in the supreme Atman.

101. The Atman that is absolute existence and knowledge cannot be realised without constant practice. So, one seeking after knowledge, should long meditate upon Brahman for the attainment of the desired goal.

129. While thinking of an object the mind verily identifies itself with that, and while thinking of a void it really becomes blank, whereas by the thought of Brahman, it attains to perfection. So, one should constantly think of (Brahman to attain) perfection.

142. Having reduced the visible to the invisible, the wise should think of the universe as one with Brahman. Thus, alone, will he abide in eternal felicity with the mind full of consciousness and bliss.

14.10 Vivekachudamani Book by Adi Shankaracharya

The Vivekachudamani is an introductory treatise within the Advaita Vedanta tradition of Hinduism, traditionally attributed to Adi Shankara of the eighth century. It is in the form of a poem in the Shardula Vikridita meter, and for many centuries has been celebrated as a prakaraṇa grantha (teaching manual) of Advaita.

Vivekachudamani literally means the "Crest-jewel of discrimination". The text discusses key concepts and the viveka or discrimination or discernment between real (unchanging, eternal) and unreal (changing, temporal), Prakriti and Atman, the oneness of Atman and Brahman, and self-knowledge as the central task of the spiritual life and for Moksha. It expounds the Advaita Vedanta philosophy in the form of a self-teaching manual, with many verses in the form of a dialogue between a student and a spiritual teacher.

Vivekachudamani consists of 580 verses in Sanskrit. These cover a range of spiritual topics and their answers according to the Advaita Vedanta tradition of Hinduism.

Following are the excerpts from this book:

3. These are three things which are rare indeed and are due to the grace of God –namely, a human birth, the longing for Liberation, and the protecting care of a perfected sage.

6. Let people quote the Scriptures and sacrifice to the gods, let them perform rituals and worship the deities, but there is no Liberation without the realisation of one's identity with the Atman, no, not even in the lifetime of a hundred Brahmas put together.

10. Let the wise and erudite man, having commenced the practice of the realisation of the Atman give up all works and try to cut loose the bonds of birth and death.

20. A firm conviction of the mind to the effect that Brahman is real and the universe unreal, is designated as discrimination (Viveka) between the Real and the unreal.

33. Who is versed in the Vedas, sinless, unsmitten by desire and a knower of Brahman par excellence, who has withdrawn himself into Brahman; who is calm, like fire that has consumed its fuel, who is a boundless reservoir of mercy that knows no reason, and a friend of all good people who prostrate themselves before him.

56. Neither by Yoga, nor by Sankhya, nor by work, nor by learning, but by the realisation of one's identity with Brahman is Liberation possible, and by no other means.

61. For one who has been bitten by the serpent of Ignorance, the only remedy is the knowledge of Brahman. Of what avail are the Vedas and (other) Scriptures, Mantras (sacred formulae) and medicines to such a one ?

62. A disease does not leave off if one simply utters the name of the medicine, without taking it; (similarly) without direct realisation one cannot be liberated by the mere utterance of the word Brahman.

110. Maya can be destroyed by the realisation of the pure Brahman, the one without a second, just as the mistaken idea of a snake is removed by the discrimination of the rope. She has her Gunas as Rajas, Tamas and Sattva, named after their respective functions.

160. The stupid man thinks he is the body, the book-learned man identifies himself with the mixture of body and soul, while the sage possessed of realisation due to discrimination looks upon the eternal Atman as his Self, and thinks, "I am Brahman".

216. This Atman is a self-cognised entity because It is cognised by Itself. Hence the individual soul is itself and directly the Supreme Brahman, and nothing else.

224. Once having realised Brahman, one no longer returns to the realm of transmigration. Therefore, one must fully realise one's identity with Brahman.

225. Brahman is Existence, Knowledge, Infinity, pure, supreme, self-existent, eternal and indivisible Bliss, not different (in reality) from the individual soul, and devoid of interior or exterior. It is (ever) triumphant.

239. Sages realise the Supreme Truth, Brahman, in which there is no differentiation of knower, knowledge and known, which is infinite, transcendent, and the Essence of Knowledge Absolute.

251. All modifications of clay, such as the jar, which are always accepted by the mind as real, are (in reality) nothing but clay. Similarly, this entire universe which is produced from the real Brahman, is Brahman Itself and nothing but That. Because there is nothing else whatever but Brahman, and That is the only self-existent Reality, our very Self, therefore art thou that serene, pure, Supreme Brahman, the One without a second.

283. Through the realisation of the identity of Brahman and the soul, resulting from such great dicta as "Thou art That", do away with thy superimposition, with a view to strengthening thy identification with Brahman.

318. When the desire for realising Brahman has a marked manifestation, the egoistic desires readily vanish, as the most intense darkness effectively vanishes before the glow of the rising sun.

361. As gold purified by thorough heating on the fire gives up its impurities and attains to its own lustre, so the mind, through meditation, gives up its impurities of Sattva, Rajas and Tamas, and attains to the reality of Brahman.

397. By the elimination of all apparent existences superimposed on the soul, the supreme Brahman, Infinite, the One without a second and beyond action, remains as Itself.

429. He who, even having his mind merged in Brahman, is nevertheless quite alert, but free at the same time from the characteristics of the waking state, and whose realisation is free from desires, is accepted as a man liberated-in-life.

447. Through the realisation of one's identity with Brahman, all the accumulated actions of a hundred crore of cycles come to nought, like the actions of dream-state on awakening.

465. There is only Brahman, the One without a second, the Essence of Existence, Knowledge and Eternal Bliss, and devoid of activity; there is no duality whatsoever in It.

14.11 'Brahma Sūtras Bhashya' book by Adi Shankara

Several commentaries on the Brahma Sūtras are lost to history or yet to be found; of the surviving ones, the most well studied commentaries on the Brahma Sūtras include the Bhashya by Adi Shankara.

Following are some of the excerpts from this book:

1.1. That omniscient and omnipotent source must be Brahman from which occur the birth, continuance and dissolution of this universe that is manifested through name and form, that is associated with diverse agents and experiences, that provides the support for actions and results, having well-regulated space, time and causation and that defies all thoughts about the real nature of this creation.

1.7. Nothing is possible to exist separate from Brahman, as there is no proof. In fact, we are not able to find any proof for the existence of anything else. It has been established that the birth etc. of everything which has origin is from Brahman. The effect is non-different from the cause. And anything which is birthless and which is different from Brahman is not possible. Because it is understood from Sruti "O amiable one, in the beginning, Sat alone was, one without a second." Because of the assertion that when one is known, everything is known, the existence of anything other than Brahman cannot be conceived.

1.16. We speak of that entity as the creator of the universe which is by nature eternal, pure, intelligent and which is greater than and different from the embodied being. With regard to that Brahman, the faults of not doing what is beneficial and the like cannot arise, for there is nothing beneficial to be achieved or harmful to be eschewed by It, which is by nature eternally free. Nor there is anything to debar its knowledge or power since it is omniscient and omnipotent.

2.1. From the Srutis, it is understood that Jiva is eternal; Similarly, the birthlessness, changelessness; it is the unchanging Brahman itself exists as the Self and it is Brahman. What are those Srutis? "The individual self does not die" (Chand.U..6-11-3) "That Self is undecaying, immortal, undying, fearless and Brahman" (Br.U.4-4-25) The intelligent one is not born and does not die; This ancient one is birthless, eternal and unchanging (Kat.U,1-2-18) "Having created that, He entered into that (Tai.U.2-6-1) "Let me manifest myself as name and form entering as the individual self" (Chan.U.6-3-2) "This Self permeates those bodies up to the tips and nails (Br.1-4-7) "Thou art That" (Chan.U.6-8-7) "I am Brahman" (Br. 1-4-10) "This Self, the perceiver of everything, is Brahman" (Br. U.2-5-19) These and other Srutis speak of eternality deny the origin of the individual Self.

2.3. It is only the Supreme Brahman itself which while remaining immutable appears to exist as an individual soul owing to its association with limiting adjuncts. The eternal consciousness of the Supreme Brahman is mentioned in these Srutis "Knowledge, Bliss, Brahman" (Br.3-9-28) "Brahman is Truth, knowledge, Infinite" (Tai,2-1-1) "Without interior or exterior, entire, pure intelligence alone" (4-5-13) If the individual Self is but the Supreme Brahman Itself, then it can be understood that like fire possessing heat and light, the Jiva is also possessed of eternal Consciousness by its very nature.

2.7. During the state of ignorance, when the individual soul is blinded by the darkness of ignorance, Samsara consisting of the agent and the experiencer results from the behest of the Iswara, who presides over all activities, resides in all beings, who is the witness, imparts intelligence and is the Supreme soul. Only by his grace, liberation from knowledge is possible.......Iswara makes the individual soul do according to the efforts of Dharma or adharma already done by him. Therefore, the defects pointed out do not arise. Iswara is only the efficient cause just like the rain in allocating the inequality of the results which depends on the inequality of the Dharma and Adharma done by the individual soul.

3. 8. Just as it is understood that world etc come from Brahman, so also the organs are from the Supreme Brahman, ...In these, it is to be construed that Pranas come from Supreme Brahman just as space.

4.17. And yet the creation of space etc. also has no absolute reality; for under the aphorism "the effect is non-different from the cause since terms like 'origin' etc are met with, we showed that the whole creation is but Maya".

5.2. What is superimposition? It is awareness of what was seen in another locus and is the form of memory. Some say that it is superimposition of the attributes of one thing on another. Some also say that the superimposition on another is an illusion because of its non-discrimination. Some others also say that the superimposition on another is imagination of opposite attributes there itself. In any case there is no straying away from the awareness of one thing as something else. Similar is the worldly experience - shell appears like silver and a single moon appears as two.

5.6. Learned men consider this Superimposition as defined as avidya, nescience. They said that the realisation of the real nature of that entity by discrimination as Vidya. When this is so, the locus on which there is a superimposition, is not connected to the bad or good characteristics of that which is superimposed. With this understanding of the superimposition mutually on the Self and non-Self, known thus as avidya, nescience, all worldly behaviour or valid means of knowledge and objects is engaged in; similarly, all Sastras containing injunctions, prohibitions and liberation.

6.2. This thing, that is avyakta, is sometimes referred to by the word space........Sometimes it is called immutable......sometimes it is called Maya......That Maya is surely unmanifest....for it can neither be ascertained as real nor as unreal.

6.4. This appearance of the supreme Self in identity with the three states is a mere superimposition, as in the case of the rope appearing as a snake etc. With regard to this it is said by teacher Gaudapada versed in the traditional views of Vedanta - "When the individual sleeping under the influence of beginningless Maya is awakened, then he realises the birthless, sleepless, dreamless, nondual.

7.5. The pure knowledge of the seers like Kapila is regarded as unobstructed. There is also the Sruti. Who saw Kapila emerging out in the beginning of creation and filled him with knowledge after birth, Therefore, it is not proper to make their view appear as wrong. Moreover, they establish their interpretation with the help of logic. For that reason also the Vedanta has to be explained with the help of the Smritis.

Vaiseshikas

8. The Vaiseshikas assert that the ultimate atoms stand at the last limit of a process of breaking up of composite things till there can be no further division, that these atoms are of four kinds possessed of colour etc, that they are the constituents of the four elements and the modifications of the elements endowed with the qualities of colour etc. and they are eternal. This tenet of theirs is baseless. For by virtue of possessing colour etc., the atomicity and everlastingness of the atoms stand contradicted; that is to say the atoms become grosser and less eternal than the ultimate cause, a position that is opposite of what the atomists intend.

It has been said that the doctrine of Vaiseshika is not to be relied upon since it is built on wrong logic, it is contrary to Vedas and is not accepted by worthy people. He is a half-nihilist having an affinity with nihilism. It is now explained that the full-nihilists are not to be relied upon all the more. They are of various kinds, depending upon the differences in the doctrine or of the persons who are taught. Among them there are three schools - (i) Sarvastitvavadins (Soutrantikas and Vaibhashikas). (ii) Vijnavadins (Yogacharas) and (iii) Sarvasunyavadins (Madyamakas) The Sarvastit-vavadins, accept both external and internal things. External are the elements and elementals. Internal are the citta and caittas. Elements are earth etc. Elementals are colour etc. and organs of sight etc. The four kinds of ultimate atoms of earth etc., have the characteristics of solidity, fluidity, heat and motion and get massed together in the form of earth. Similarly, there are five skandhas (groups), like, (i) colour, (ii) the idea of "I", (iii) feelings, (iv) conceptual knowledge, and (v) attitude. They also combine to form the basis of internal dealings.

The idea of Brahman Itself is to be superimposed on the sun and the rest. Why? Because of superiority. Thus, the sun etc are seen to be superimposed with a superior idea.

When Brahman becomes realised, subsequent sins become non-attached and earlier ones destroyed. Why? Because it is so declared in the scriptures.

The virtues and vices that have already begun to fructify are exhausted through experiencing the results and then the aspirant becomes Brahman.

Chapter - 15

Vishishtadvaita Vedanta Philosophy

15.1 Introduction to Vishishtadvaita Vedanta Philosophy

Vishishtadvaita (Viśiṣṭādvaita) is one of the most popular schools of the Vedanta school of Hindu philosophy. Vedanta literally means the end of the Vedas. VishishtAdvaita (literally "Advaita with uniqueness; qualifications") is a non-dualistic school of Vedanta philosophy. It is non-dualism of the qualified whole, in which Brahman alone is seen as the Supreme Reality, but is characterised by multiplicity. It can be described as qualified monism or qualified non-dualism or attributive monism. It is a school of Vedanta philosophy which believes in all diversity subsuming to an underlying unity.

Visistadvaita, a Vedanta Darsana, maintains its position in the history of Indian thought by establishing its own siddhanta by a criticism of rival systems. It has, at the same time, a synthetic insight into the essentials of other Darsanas, and accepts whatever in them is consistent with its basic principles. It is neither pure philosophy nor pure religion. It is a true philosophy of religion, which reconciles the opposition between philosophy and religion, and the conflict between monism and pluralism. If it is liberally interpreted in terms of contemporary philosophy and comparative religion without, in any way, sacrificing its foundational principles, it is capable of satisfying the demands of science and philosophy on the one hand, and of ethics and religion on the other.

It is the task of philosophy as an intellectual enquiry into the whole of reality to frame the ultimate problems of life. The three persistent problems of philosophy relate to God, nature and the self. Of them, the enquiry into the nature of God is the most valuable. The existence of God is established by the well-known theistic proofs, and not by revealed theology. Faith and reason belong to different realms. It is impossible to prove the existence of God by logical thinking. On the other hand, mere reason is ill founded and self-contradictory. As free thought leads to atheism, blind faith leads to dogmatism.

Visistadvaita offers a contrast to mere philosophical speculation on the whole of reality on one hand, and to religion in the sense of a faith in revealed theology on the other. Theology insists on dogmatic faith in truths regarded as infallible on account of scriptural authority or divine disclosure. It is by its nature antagonistic to the free exercise of reason on the facts provided by human experience, which is the hallmark of philosophy. Ramanuja's system of Visistadvaita recognises the claims of both faith and reason. It aims at harmonising or reconciling them. It admits a free play of reason as to the data of sense perception and inference. It also accepts spiritual intuition, anubhava of the great seers, and the doctrines or views recorded in the scriptures.

Ramanuja, the 11–12th century philosopher and the main proponent of Vishishtadvaita philosophy contends that the Prasthanatrayi ("The three courses"), namely the Upanishads, the Bhagavad Gita, and the Brahma Sutras are to be interpreted in a way that shows this unity in diversity, for any other way would violate their consistency. Vedanta Desika defines Vishishtadvaita using the statement,

Asesha Chit-Achit Prakaaram Brahmaikameva Tatvam

Brahman, as qualified by the sentient and insentient modes (or attributes), is the only reality.

15.2 Philosophers of Vishishtadveta

The Vishishtadvaitic thought is considered to have existed for a long time, and it is surmised that the earliest works are no longer available. The names of the earliest of these philosophers is only known through **Ramanuja**'s Vedartha Sangraham. Bodhayana, Dramida, Tanka, Guhadeva, Kapardi and Bharuci the prominent ones in the line of the philosophers considered to have expounded the Visishtadvaitic system.

Bodhayana is considered to have written an extensive vritti (commentary) on the Purva and Uttara Mimamsas. **Tanka** is attributed with having written commentaries on Chandogya Upanishad and Brahma Sutras. **Nathamuni** of the ninth century AD, the foremost Acharya of the Vaishnavas, collected the Tamil prabandhas, classified them, made the redaction, set the hymns to music and spread them everywhere. He is said to have received the divine hymns straight from Nammalvar, the foremost of the twelve Alvars, by yogic insight in the temple at Alwar Thirunagari, which is located near Tirunelveli in South India. **Yamunacharya** renounced kingship and spent his last days in the service of the Lord at Srirangam and in laying the fundamentals of the Vishishtadvaita philosophy by writing four basic works on the subject.

Ramanuja is the main proponent of Vishishtadvaita philosophy. The philosophy itself is considered to have existed long before Ramanuja's time. Ramanuja continues along the line of thought of his predecessors while expounding the knowledge expressed in the Upanishads, Brahma Sutras and Bhagavad Gita. Vedanta Desika and Pillai Lokacharya, disciples in the tradition of Ramanuja, had minor disagreements not on the philosophy, but on some aspects of the theology, giving rise to the Vadakalai and Thenkalai schools of thought.

Swaminarayan, the founder of Swaminarayan Sampradaya, propagated a related philosophy, and based the Swaminarayan Sampradaya (original name is Uddhava Sampradaya) partly on these ideals.

15.3 Key Principles of Vishishtadvaita

There are three key principles of Vishishtadvaita:

(i) Tattva: The knowledge of the 3 real entities namely, jiva (living souls; the sentient); ajiva (the non-sentient) and Ishvara (Vishnu-Narayana or Parabrahman, Supreme-self and the cause of all manifestations and in-dwelling giver of grace based on Karma).

(ii) Hita: The means of realisation, as through bhakti (devotion) and prapatti (self-surrender).

Vivishta: most exclusive (not equal / different from rest).

(iii) Purushartha: The goal to be attained, as moksha or liberation from bondage.

Tattvajnaana is the philosophic exposition of the Brahman as the immanent ground of existence, and the inner self of all things. Hita involves the determination of the moral and spiritual means of sadhana for realising the Brahman. Purushartha is the attainment of the Brahman as the summum bonum of life by realising which everything is realised.

15.4 Epistemology

15.4.1 Pramanas

Pramana refers to the correct knowledge, arrived at by thorough reasoning, of any object. Pramana ("sources of knowledge") forms one part of a triputi (trio):

(i) Pramatir, the subject; the knower of the knowledge;

(ii) Pramana, the cause or the means of the knowledge; and

(iii) Prameya, the object of knowledge.

Truth is the knowledge of a thing as it is and as it works, or as it satisfies the practical interests of life. According to Ramanuja, every kind of knowledge is true if it is consistent with experience in its exactitude. He accepts the trustworthiness of the three pramanas, namely, pratyaksa including abhaava, anumana including upamana and arthapatti, and sabda.

(i) Pratyaksa — the knowledge gained by means of perception. Perception refers to knowledge obtained by cognition of external objects based on sensory perception. In modern-day usage this will also include knowledge obtained by means of observation through scientific instruments since they are an extension of perception.

(ii) Anumana (inference) — the knowledge gained by means of inference. Inference refers to knowledge obtained by deductive reasoning and analysis.

(iii) Shabda — the knowledge gained by means of shruti. Shruti refers to knowledge gained from scriptures - primarily the Upanishads, the Brahma Sutras and the Bhagavad Gita.

15.4.2 Rules of epistemology

There are three rules of hierarchy when there is apparent conflict between the three modes of acquiring knowledge:

(i) Shabda or Shruti, Pramana occupies the highest position in matters which cannot be settled or resolved by pratyaksa (perception) or by anumana (inference).

(ii) Anumana occupies the next position. When an issue cannot be settled through sensory perception alone, it is settled based on inference, that is, whichever is the more logical argument.

(iii) When pratyaksa yields a definitive position on a particular issue, such a perception cannot be ignored by interpreting Shabda in a way which violates that perception.

15.5 Metaphysics of Vishishtadveta

15.5.1 Ontology

The ontology in Vishishtadvaita consists of explaining the relationship between Ishvara (Parabrahman), the sentient beings (chit-brahman) and the insentient Universe (achit-brahman). In the broadest sense, Ishvara is the Universal Soul of the pan-organistic body consisting of the Universe and sentient beings. The three ontological entities are described below:

(i) Ishvara: Ishvara (denoted by Vishnu (Narayana)) is the Supreme Cosmic Spirit who maintains complete control over the Universe and all the sentient beings, which together also form the pan-organistic body of Ishvara. The triad of Ishvara along with the universe and the sentient beings is Brahman, which signifies the completeness of existence. Ishvara is Parabrahman endowed with innumerable auspicious qualities (Kalyana Gunas). Ishvara is perfect, omniscient, omnipresent, incorporeal, independent, the creator of the universe, it's active ruler and also its eventual destroyer. He is causeless, eternal and unchangeable — and is yet the material and the efficient cause of the universe and sentient beings. He is both immanent (like whiteness in milk) and transcendent (like a watch-maker independent of a watch). He is the subject of worship. He is the basis of morality and giver of the fruits of one's Karma. He rules the world with His Maya — His divine power.

Ishvara is considered to have a 2-fold characteristic: he is the indweller of all beings and all beings dwell in Ishvara.

(ii) Antarvyapi: When Ishvara is thought of as the indweller of all beings, he is referred to as the Paramatman, or the innermost self of all beings.

He who inhabits water, yet is within water, whom water does not know, whose body water is and who controls water from within — He is your Self, the Inner Controller, the Immortal. He who inhabits the sun, yet is within the sun, whom the sun does not know, whose body the sun is and who controls the sun from within — He is your Self, the Inner Controller, the Immortal.

- Brihadaranyaka Upanishad 3.7.4-14

(iii) Bahuvyapi: When Ishvara is thought of as the all-encompassing and the residence of all beings that is, all beings reside in Ishvara, he is referred to as the parama-purusha. The sentient beings and the insentient universe which form part of the pan-organistic body of Ishvara are encapsulated by Ishvara.

15.5.2 Chit

Chit is the world of sentient beings, or of entities possessing consciousness. It is similar to the Purusha of Samkhya system. The sentient beings are called Jīvās and they are possessors of individual consciousness as denoted by "I". The scope of Chit refers to all beings with an "I" consciousness, or more specifically self-awareness. Therefore, all entities which are aware of their own individual existence are denoted as chit. This is called Dharmi-jnana or substantive consciousness. The sentient beings also possess varying levels of Dharma-bhuta-jnana or attributive consciousness.

The jivas possess **three** different types of existence:

(i) Nityas, or the eternally free Jivas who were never in Samsara;

(ii) Muktas, or the Jivas that were once in Samsara but are free; and

(iii) Baddhas, or the Jivas which are still in Samsara.

15.5.3 Achit

Achit is the world of insentient entities as denoted by matter or more specifically the non-conscious Universe. It is similar to the Prakriti of Samkhya system.

15.5.4 Brahman

There is a subtle difference between Ishvara and Brahman. Ishvara is the substantive part of Brahman, while jivas and jagat are its modes (also secondary attributes), and kalyanagunas (auspicious attributes) are the primary attributes. The secondary attributes become manifested in the effect state when the world is differentiated by name and form. The kalyanagunas are eternally manifest.

Brahman is the description of Ishvara when comprehended in fullness–that is, a simultaneous vision of Ishvara with all his modes and attributes.

The relationship between Brahman and Jivas, Jagat is expressed by Ramanuja in numerous ways. He calls this relationship as one of:

- sharira/Sharir- (body/indweller);
- prakara/prakari (attribute or mode/substance);
- shesha/sheshi (Owned/owner);
- amsha/amshi (part/whole);
- Adharadeya/sambandha (supporter/supported);
- niyamya/niyanta (controlled/controller);
- rashksya/rakshaka (redeemed/redeemer).

These relationships can be experienced holding Brahman as the father, son, mother, sister, wife, husband, friend, lover and lord. Hence, Brahman is a personal being.

What does **Nirguna Brahman** mean?

Ramanuja argues vehemently against understanding Brahman as one without attributes. Brahman is Nirguna in the sense that impure qualities do not touch it. He provides three valid reasons for staking such a claim:

- **Shruti/Shabda Pramana:** All shrutis and shabdas denoting Brahman always list either attributes inherent to Brahman or not inherent to Brahman. The shrutis only seek to deny Brahman from possessing impure and defective qualities which affect the world of beings. There is evidence in the shrutis to this regard. The shrutis proclaim Brahman to be beyond the tri-gunas which are observed. However, Brahman possesses an infinite number of transcendental attributes, the evidence of which is given in vakyas like "satyam jnanam anantam Brahma" (Taittiriya Upanishad).

- **Pratyaksha Pramana:** Ramanuja states that "a contentless cognition is impossible". And all cognition must necessarily involve knowing Brahman through the attributes of Brahman.
- **Anumana Pramana:** Ramanuja states that "Nirgunatva" itself becomes an attribute of Brahman on account of the uniqueness of no other entity being Nirguna. Ramanuja had simplified relationship between Brahma and Soul. According to him, though soul is integral part of Brahma it has independent existence.

15.6 Theory of Existence in Vishishtadveta

The three ontological entities i.e. Ishvara, Chit and Achit are fundamentally real. It upholds the doctrine of Satkaryavada as against Asatkaryavada.

Briefly,

- **Satkaryavada** is pre-existence of the effect in the cause. It maintains that karya (effect) is sat or real. It is present in the karana (cause) in a potential form, even before its manifestation.
- **Asatkaryavada** is non-existence of the effect in the cause. It maintains that karya (effect) is asat or unreal until it comes into being. Every effect, then, is a new beginning and is not born out of cause.

More specifically, the effect is a modification of what exists in the cause and does not involve new entities coming into existence. This is called as parinamavada or evolution of effect from the cause. This doctrine is common to the Samkhya system and Vishishtadvaita system. The Samkhya system adheres to Prakriti-Parinama vada whereas Vishishtadvaita is a modified form of Brahma-Parinama vada.

15.6.1 Kārya and kārana

The kārana (cause) and kārya (effect) in Vishishtadvaita is different from other systems of Indian philosophy. Brahman is both the kārana (cause) and the kārya (effect). Brahman as the cause does not become the Universe as the effect.

Brahman is assigned two kāranatvas (ways of being the cause):

- **Nimitta kāranatva** — Being the Efficient/ Instrumental cause. For example, a goldsmith is assigned Nimitta kāranatva as he acts as the maker of jewellery and thus becomes the jewellery's Instrumental cause.
- **Upādāna kāranatva** — Being the material cause. For example, the gold is assigned Upādāna kāranatva as it acts as the material of the jewellery and thus becomes the jewellery's material cause.

According to Vishishtadvaita, the Universe and Sentients always exist. However, they begin from a subtle state and undergo transformation. The subtle state is called a causal state, while the transformed state is called the effect state. The causal state is when Brahman is internally not distinguishable by name and form.

It can be said that Vishishtadvaita follows Brahma-Prakara-Parinama Vada. That is to say, it is the modes (Jivas and Jagat) of Brahman which is under evolution. The cause and effect only refer to the pan-organistic body transformation. Brahman as the Universal Self is unchanging and eternal.

Brahman having the subtle (sūkshma) chit and achit entities as his Sariram / Prakaaram (body/mode) before manifestation is the same Brahman having the expanded (stūla) chit and achit entities as Sariram / Prakaaram (body/mode) after manifestation.

The essential feature is that the underlying entity is the same, the changes are in the description of that entity.

For example Jack was a baby. Jack was a small kid. Jack was a middle-aged person. Jack was an old man. Jack is dead. The body of a single personality named Jack is described as continuously changing. Jack does not become "James" because of the change.

15.7 Interpretation of Mahāvākyas

1. sarvam khalv idam brahma from Chandogya Upanishad 3.14.1

Translated literally, this means All this is Brahman. The ontology of Vishishtadvaita system consists of:

(a) Ishvara is Para-brahman with infinite superlative qualities, whose substantive nature imparts the existence to the modes.

(b) Jivas are chit-brahman or sentient beings (which possess consciousness). They are the modes of Brahman which show consciousness.

(c) Jagat is achit-brahman or matter/Universe (which are non-conscious). They are the mode of Brahman which are not conscious.

Brahman is the composite whole of the triad consisting of Ishvara along with his modes i.e. Jivas and Jagat.

2. ayam ātmā brahma from Mandukya Upanishad 1.2

Translated literally, this means the Self is Brahman. From the earlier statement, it follows that on account of everything being Brahman, the self is not different from Brahman.

3. Tat tvam asi from Chandogya Upanishad 6.8.7

Translated literally, it means Thou art that that here refers to Brahman and thou refers to jiva.

Ramanuja chooses to take the position of universal identity. He interprets this passage to mean the subsistence of all attributes in a common underlying substratum. This is referred to as samānādhikaranya. Thus, Ramanuja says the purport of the passage is to show the unity of all beings in a common base. Ishvara (Parabrahman) who is the Cosmic Spirit for the pan-organistic body consisting of the Universe and sentient beings, is also simultaneously the innermost self (Atman) for each individual sentient being (Jīvā). All the bodies, the Cosmic and the individual, are held in an adjectival relationship (aprthak-siddhi) in the one Isvara.

Tat Tvam Asi declares that oneness of Isvara.

When multiple entities point to a single object, the relationship is established as one of substance and its attributes.

For example in a statement:

Jack is a tall and intelligent boy.

The descriptors tall-ness, intelligence and boy-ness all refer to a common underlying Jack.

Similarly, when the Upanishads declare Brahman is the Universe, Purusha, Self, Prana, Vayu, and so on, the entities are attributes or modes of Brahman.

If the statement *tat tvam asi* is taken to mean as only the self is brahman, then sarvam khalv idam brahma will not make sense.

15.8 Truth, Error and Avidya

15.8.1 Truth

Visistadvaita accepts the integrity of experience in all its levels as noticed in pratyaksa (perception), anumana (inference) and sastra (scripture).

This is on the ground that jnana is self-valid and true, that the sat (real) alone is cognised and that there is no knowledge of asat (unreal). If the Brahman alone is satya (real) and the world of experience is tuccha (futile, false) and mithya (non-existent) on the ground of the self-contradictions of dualistic knowledge, no knowledge is possible or desirable. Meticulous monistic logic does not admit the coexistence of the Brahman and maya or different degrees of reality.

Maya is non-existence, as opposed to sat. It cannot, therefore, coexist with the Brahman. If maya refers to the world of illusion, then it contradicts the theory of degrees of reality, and the truth of two standpoints as the vyavahaarika (the world of practical life) and the paramaarthika, which is absolutely real. If truth is self-existent, and the false non-existent, there is no need for a theory of truth or a test of truth based on abaadha (the principle of non-contradiction). Absolutism recognises the distinction between reality and existence. But this distinction is not an opposition. To Ramanuja, the Brahman is the sat or supreme reality that is the pervading essence of the universe, and its indwelling self and it is, therefore, true. The universe is not the Brahman enveloped by maya or avidya. It is Brahma maya, pervaded by the Brahman. Its radiant light illumines it. It exists in the Brahman, and not as the Brahman. Nor does it exhaust its content.

Reality exists as the Brahman as cit and acit. Acit is matter, which is ever-changing and may be called asatya. Cit is the eternal self with a uniform nature or intelligence, which is realised as distinct from the ever-changing prakrti or matter. It is, therefore, called satya or the true, and the inner self of the existent prakriti. The Brahman may be called satyasyasatyam, the real of all real, the true of the true, Vaasudeva. Reality and value coexist. Matter has an extrinsic and ephemeral value, while the self has intrinsic value. The self is, therefore, satya and matter is asatya. The Brahman is the true of the true, and gives value to both. This view repudiates realism, idealism and monism as one-sided and abstract. It recognises the reality and value of nature, the individual self and the Brahman.

Truth is the knowledge of a thing as it is and as it works, or as it satisfies the practical interests of life. According to Ramanuja, every kind of knowledge is true if it is consistent with experience in its exactitude. He accepts the trustworthiness of the three pramanas, namely, pratyaksa including abhaava, anumana including upamana and arthapatti, and sabda. All the three pramanas are coherent, and they are not contradictory. Pratyaksa is the foundation of knowledge. Reasoning is based on it and does not supersede it. Sruti is the consummation of all knowledge. But it cannot be at variance with pratyaksa. Truth is an immanent criterion. It includes the more of itself. The three pramanas, in their integral unity and perfection, enable the truth-seeker to know the whole of reality.

15.8.2 Error

According to Ramanuja, truth is revelatory, svatahpramana, and cognition is real. Therefore, strictly speaking, there is no need for a theory of truth. Consequently, any theory of error becomes meaningless. Truth is, in fact, the natural and normal feature of knowledge in the state of spiritual freedom where there is no distinction between prama, truth and bhrama, error. While the jnana of the self is eternally pure and perfect, and free from avidya, the intelligence of the finite self is subject to self-contradictions, and contradictions of avidya-karman which deprive it of its pure and all-pervasive character. This privation is called error.

Jnana is normally true cognition. Even a false cognition like the bent stick is perspective and is real. Its extent and variety are determined by the logical and moral development of the self. If error is traced to the fissure between knowing and being, and the self-contradictions of relational experience, and if avidya is the obscuring principle of reality, it is not possible for us to go from degrees of truth to the Absolute. Indeed, the Absolute would itself be infected by illusion. The Advaita theory of non-contradiction is no theory at all, for it says that error is abhava or non-existent, and reality is beyond prama and bhrama.

Ramanuja's theory of error saves the Absolute from its self-deceptive maya or avidya, and its illogical appearances. It attributes error to the finite self, which has inexplicably allowed itself to be obscured by avidya. According to this theory, every empirical experience is incomplete or partial knowledge. Even prama is only partial truth. The distinction between prama and bhrama is one of degree, and vanishes when jnana is freed from the moral determinations of karma.

Visistadvaita utilises every theory of error, which fits in with its central idea and accepts the tests of pragmatism and realism so far as they go in harmonising experience. The experience of an object as having gray colour owing to colour-blindness is a psychic fact, and is real. The shade of colouration is an aspect of the spatial order.

The criterion of truth comprises the three theories of coherence, correspondence and workability in so far as they conform to the method of Visistadvaita. There is coherence if the given judgment is consistent with all other judgments and with the whole of knowledge. There is correspondence if there is exact conformity between the object as it is, and its perception by the senses. Knowledge is true if it satisfies the ends of life by its workability.

Correspondence thus follows coherence, and verification results from the inner value of truth. Thus, pragmatism, realism and idealism are interrelated in the Visistadvaita epistemology. Falsity is abnormal and pathological as in mental disorders. Each case has to be judged on merits. Error, too, is difficult of classification. But it can be of different types like hallucination, illusion or dream, which may be explained psychologically and by the criteria furnished by pragmatism and realism.

15.8.3 Avidya

The Advaita theory of avidya holds that avidya is neither real nor unreal, nor both, and is, therefore, inexplicable. For example, in the illusion caused by mistaking the shell for silver, there is a misunderstanding, which is indeterminable. It is first felt to be real and then rejected as unreal when there is true knowledge of the thing. It cannot be both real and unreal. It is adhyāsa (false superimposition), for the silver cognition is superimposed on the shell cognition.

The Mimamsa theory of akhyati (non-apprehension) accepts the reality of the cognitions, the perceived shell and the conceived silver. It traces the mistake to a defect in the tools of knowledge on account of which we fail to notice that silver is a recollected element. In the Naiyyayika theory of anyatha-khyati, both shell and silver are real things. Shell is wrongly perceived as another real object, namely silver. The non-existence of shell means the existence of another object, silver and this error is subjective.

In this regard, Ramanuja's method of verification is pragmatic, but is not consistent. Truth may work, but what works is not necessarily true. Avidya, according to Advaita, is the innate obscuration of pure consciousness, which, somehow, divides the Absolute to distort it into the world of difference. It is an innate error without a beginning, positive and indeterminable. However, jnana can remove it. The universal experience 'I do not know' refers to ignorance and is indefinite. In sleep where there is a temporary cessation of consciousness of duality and difference, ignorance remains in its causal state, karana-Sarira. It is owing to avidya that the Brahman, which is sat, cit and ananda, is confused with the empirical self, which is anrta (transient), jada (inert) and duhkha (miserable). This state is called adhyasa, which is the cause of all the evils of samsara.

Avidya is thus, according to Advaita, the root of error in philosophy, original confusion or misconception. It is the basis of the baseless world of space-time-cause like the snake in the rope illusion. The Brahman alone is. What is not the Brahman is false as it is different from It as in the snake in the rope illusion. Difference cannot exist by itself. It is only a distortion of reality. To trace the cause of avidya is illegitimate as the concept of causality itself has its origin in avidya. Pure consciousness is the locus (asraya) of avidya, and also its object. It is ever self-effulgent. Avidya cannot conceal it. The pure consciousness does not reside in the jiva, as the jiva itself is its creation. Like the sun that shines unaffected by the mist, the atman is self-effulgent, and is not affected by avidya.

Avidya is somehow there in the Brahman and we do not know why. We do not know it as the thought cannot go beyond thought. Avidya is, therefore, indefinable and inexplicable, as it is neither real nor unreal nor both. It is not real as it is dissolved in the state of liberation. It is real, as it now exists. It cannot be both, too. It is a frank admission of the self-contradictions of life, though the Absolute is beyond such discrepancy.

Chapter - 16

Dvaita Vedanta Philosophy

16.1 Introduction to Dvaita Vedanta

Tattvavāda (also popularly known as Dvaita Vedanta) is a sub-school in the Vedanta tradition of Hindu philosophy. Alternatively known as Bhedavāda, Bimbapratibimbavāda, Pūrnabrahmavāda and Svatantra-Advitiya-Brahmavāda, the Dvaita Vedanta sub-school was founded by the 13th century scholar **Madhvacharya**, also called Anandatirtha (c. 1199–1278), who came from the area of modern Karnataka state, where he still has many followers. Already during his lifetime, Madhva was regarded by his followers as an incarnation of the wind god Vayu, who was sent to earth by the god Vishnu to save the good, after the powers of evil had sent the philosopher Shankara, an important proponent of the Advaita ("Nondualist") school, whose teaching of monism ran counter to Madhva's.

In his expositions, Madhva shows the influence of the Nyaya philosophical school. He maintains that Vishnu is the supreme God, thus identifying the Brahman, or absolute reality, of the Upanishads with a personal god, as Ramanuja (c. 1050–1137) had done before him. There are in Madhva's system three eternal, ontological orders: that of God, that of soul, and that of inanimate nature. The existence of God is demonstrable by logical proof, though only scripture teaches his nature. He is the epitome of all perfections and possesses a nonmaterial body, which consists of saccidananda (being, spirit, and bliss). God is the efficient cause of the universe, but Madhva denies that he is the material cause, for God cannot have created the world by splitting himself nor in any other way, since that militates against the doctrine that God is unalterable; in addition, it is blasphemous to accept that a perfect God changes himself into an imperfect world.

The individual souls are countless in number and are of atomic proportions. They are a "portion" of God and exist completely by the grace of God; in their actions they are totally subject to God. It is God too that allows the soul, to a limited extent, freedom of action in a way commensurate with one's past acts (karma).

The Dvaita Vedanta school believes that God and the individual souls (jīvātman) exist as independent realities, and these are distinct, being said that Vishnu (Narayana) is independent, and souls are dependent on him. The Dvaita school contrasts with the other two major sub-schools of Vedanta, the Advaita Vedanta of Adi Shankara which posits nondualism – that ultimate reality (Brahman) and human soul (Ātman) are identical and all reality is interconnected oneness, and Vishishtadvaita of Ramanuja which posits qualified nondualism – that ultimate reality (Brahman) and human soul are different but with the potential to be identical.

Dvaita is one of the living systems of Vedantic thought in India, having its own well-defined community of followers, religious institutions and extensive philosophical literature in Sanskrit, and a substantial body of devotional literature in Kannada. Dvaita system has been the chief rival in thought to the Advaita of Shankara, in the history of Indian Philosophy. It stood up for realism in Indian thought against all forces of idealism and acosmism. The followers of Madhva, especially Jayatirtha and Vyasatirtha, present the logical skill and depth of acute dialectic thinking almost unrivalled in the whole range of Indian thought. Madhva derives his philosophical tenets from the three authoritative prasthanas (the Upanishads, the Bhagavadgita, and the Brahma Sutras), from the puranas and Mahabharata. The quintessence of Madhva's philosophy is that Vishnu (Hari) is the supreme God, the world is real and the difference between God and soul does actually exist. All the living beings are dependent upon Vishnu, and they are divided into higher and lower classes; liberation consists in the enjoyment of bliss that is inherent in oneself; pure devotion is the means of attaining it.

Pluralism is its dominant constituent. The Dvaita system (Dualism) derives its name from its antagonism to the Advaita system (Non-dualism). It stands for recognition of the distinction between the finite self and the Supreme Being. The extension of this principle is the assertion of similar distinction between the finite self and the nature on one hand, and that between nature and the Supreme Being on the other. Similarly, the selves are to be distinguished among themselves, and objects constitutive of nature are to be considered a plurality. This five-fold difference, pancha-bheda is a fundamental verity. It is held to be the meaning of the term pra-pancha signifying the universe as a whole. Madhva's pluralism relates to inalienable uniqueness as a basic characteristic of all that exists in the realms of nature and beyond.

16.2 Madhvacharya

Madhvacarya of 12th century AD is the founder of the Dvaita Vedanta. Traditionally he is also known as Anandatirtha and Purnaprajna. His birthplace is said to be the village of Pajaka near Udupi in Karnataka. Madhva proclaims himself as the third incarnation of Vayu after Hanuman and Bhima. Madhva was a many-sided personality. He had a stupendous memory and he was a splendid debater. Although he accepted Sannyasa at the hands of Acyutapreksacarya, a renowned Advaita teacher, he opposed Shankara's monistic tenets and interpretations. He was convinced that the sacred texts don't propagate the mayavada, but the realistic theism. Madhvacarya installed the idol of Lord Krishna at Udupi which has become a centre of the Dvaita Vedanta with the tradition of ashtamaths, with his eight disciples. Madhva was a prolific writer in Sanskrit both in prose and in verse. He quoted profusely from Vedic, Buddhist, Jaina and other systems of philosophy and religion of India. In short, he was scholar, saint, philosopher and mystic. The works of Madhva are thirty-seven in number. Some of his major works are his commentaries on Prasthanatraya (Gita, Brahmasutra and Upanishads), commentaries on Vedas, Epics and puranas, and his Ten prakarnas (other writings). In his tradition, there have been commentaries (tikkas) on Madhva's works written by Jayatirtha and Vyasatirtha.

16.3 Philosophy of Dvaita Vedanta

Dvaita Vedanta is a dualistic interpretation of the Vedas which espouses dualism by theorising the existence of two separate realities. The first and the only independent reality (svatantra-tattva), states the Dvaita school, is that of Vishnu as Brahman. Vishnu is the supreme Self, in a manner similar to the monotheistic God in other major religions. He is believed to be almighty, eternal, always existing, everlasting, all-knowing, and compassionate. The second reality is that of dependent (asvatantra-tattva) but equally real universe that exists with its own separate essence. Everything that is composed of the second reality, such as individual soul, matter, and the like exist with their own separate reality. The distinguishing factor of this philosophy, as opposed to monistic Advaita Vedanta, is that God takes on a personal role and is seen as a real eternal entity that governs and controls the universe.

Like Ramanuja, Madhvacharya also embraced Vaishnavism. Madhvacharya posits God as being personal and saguna, that is endowed with attributes and qualities (in human terms, which are not believed to be able to fully describe God). To Madhvacharya, the metaphysical concept of Brahman in the Vedas was Vishnu. He stated "brahmaśabdaśca Viṣṇaveva", that Brahman can only refer to Vishnu. Scriptures which say different are declared as non-authoritative by him. To him, Vishnu was not just any other deva, but rather the one and only Supreme Being. According to him, the devas are souls of deceased persons who were rewarded for good deeds by being reincarnated into the heavenly worlds and becoming following organs of God's will, which would also be the case with Vayu and Lakshmi. He also believes that they are mortal, and that some of them could sink into lower stages of existence after death. Therefore, he believes that only God shall be worshipped through them, and that worshipping them on their own behalf is an apostasy which emerged during Treta Yuga, and did not yet exist during Satya Yuga. According to him, this must also be noticed regarding murtis.

Dvaita Vedanta acknowledges two principles; however, it holds one of them (the sentient) as being eternally dependent on the other. The individual souls are depicted as reflections, images or shadows of the divine, but never in any way identical with the divine. Moksha (liberation), therefore, is described as the realisation that all finite reality is essentially dependent on the Supreme. God is believed to have shown the way to attain moksha through several avatars.

The theism of Dvaita is based on scriptural revelation. Madhva declares that the God he adores is to be known only through sound scriptural authority, sadaagama. For him, the sound scriptures are 'the Vedas beginning with the Rigveda, the Mahabharata, the whole of Pancaratra Agama, the original Ramayana, the Puranas in accordance with these, and all other sacred works in conformity to them'. Of these, only the Veda shakhas are considered impersonal and eternal. The rest are personal compositions of divine personalities in augmentation of their teachings. Madhva holds that the above scriptures are venerable authorities in their entirety. The Ramayana mentioned in the list is original Ramayana by Valmiki. Jayatirtha includes even Manu-dharma-sastra among the later conforming texts. This body of revelation literature is considered in the Dvaita system as furnishing sound theism which is the ultimate philosophy.

Five fundamental, eternal and real differences are described in Dvaita school:

(i) Between the individual souls (or jīvātman) and God (paramathma or Vishnu).
(ii) Between matter (inanimate, insentient) and God.
(iii) Between individual souls (jīvātman).

(iv) Between matter and jīvātman.
(v) Between various types of matter.

These five differences are said to explain the nature of the universe. The world is called prapañca (pañca "five") by the Dvaita school for this reason.

Madhva differed significantly from traditional Hindu beliefs owing to his concept of eternal damnation. According to him, there are three different classes of souls: (i) One class, Mukti-yogyas, which would qualify for liberation, (ii) another, the Nitya-samsarins, which would be subject to eternal rebirth or eternal transmigration and (iii) a third class, Tamo-yogyas, which would be condemned to eternal hell (Andhatamisra). No other Hindu philosopher or school of Hinduism holds such beliefs. In contrast, most Hindus believe in universal salvation, that all souls will eventually obtain Moksha, even if after millions of rebirths.

16.4 Metaphysics of Dvaita Vedanta

16.4.1 Concept of God

As we have seen earlier, Madhva recognises two kinds of reality, independent (svatantra) and dependent (paratantra). God is the independent reality. Individual souls and the world are dependent realities. He speaks of God as a personal God. God is the supreme person called Isvara. He is completely independent, perfect, absolute and pure consciousness. He is savisesa. He possesses infinite qualities. He assumes various manifestations. The supreme Lord is Vishnu. Lakshmi, the consort of Vishnu, is eternally blessed and absolutely accomplished. She eternally contemplates Vishnu. Lakshmi is dependent on Vishnu. She is intelligent Prakriti. Prakriti is the material cause of the world. The Lord enters into Prakriti and makes Himself into many. The Lord's will is Prakriti.

Dvaita system considers that the Vedic revelation is about Vaishnavism, identifying the supreme Reality propounded in the Veda as Vishnu, Vaasudeva or Narayana. It is true that the Veda shakhas contain adoration of many deities but, for him, they leave us in no doubt as to which deity is the God of gods, the supreme divine Reality according to them. Madhva quotes a significant passage from the Rigveda, among others, wherein it is stated that the other gods derive their limited prowess from the worship of Vishnu. It is interesting to note that Sayana explains the passage in almost the same spirit. Among the Upanishads, the fourth chapter of the Taittiriya abounds in the glorification of Narayana as the supreme God in the section called Narayana-anuvaka. Madhva also quotes from Harivamsa that enunciates the pervasive Vaishnavism of the Vedic literature. The Vedic literature speaks nowhere of the nonexistence of Vishnu before creation, as it does in reference to other gods. Nowhere are any deficiencies ascribed to Him as is done with regard to other gods. The names of all gods are applied to Vishnu Himself indicative of His omnipresence in and through all gods. Madhva argues that a detailed scrutiny of the Vedic literature reveals the supremacy of Vishnu among the Vedic gods, and not to accept it would be against evidence.

The understanding of God in Dvaita Vedanta is theistic. It is his 'theology', so to say. This is described as uncompromising theism. For Madhva, Vishnu is the Supreme God. The purpose and goal of all the scriptures (sadagamas) is revealing and making that Supreme known to people. That is to say the prime import (mahatatparya) of the sacred texts is Vishnu. Not only the scriptures, even Madhva asserts that every word in the language primarily signifies Vishnu and refers only secondarily to other objects. The language of people is only to signify God.

With regard to the attributes and qualities of the Supreme God, Vishnu, Madhva is a great theologian. Vishnu possesses all auspicious, blessed, infinite and eternal attributes. The relation between God and His attributes is governed by the principle of visesa, by virtue of which a thing is distinguished from its permanent attributes though they are identical in essence. There is no fundamental distinction between God and His attributes. He is the Supreme Reality possessing all excellences like infinite knowledge, bliss, power, etc. He manifests in various forms, incarnates as avataras and is present in the Sacred images. He is apprehensible through the Vedas (shruti) though not fully comprehensible.

As any theistic understanding would go, the Supreme God is everything in relation to the world. For him, Vishnu is the efficient cause (nimitta-karana) of the universe. He is the cause of creation (srishti), preservation (sthiti) and destruction (pralaya). In His relation to the souls, He is the liberator. As He himself is the primary cause of, the bondage of samsara (chain of existence) for the soul. The so-called apparent causes of bondage such as ignorance (avidya), action (karma) and the subtle body (linga-sarira) are only the secondary causes of the chain of existence. Ultimately God's grace is needed for removal of bondage though the efforts are fruitful initially from the part of the jiva. For Madhva, it is Vishnu's grace (prasada) alone which can give salvation (mukti) to the Jiva.

16.4.2 Concept of Jiva

Jiva, by essence, is spiritual consciousness that is partless. This Jiva possesses knowledge and bliss. In this possession Jiva is similar to God but is dependent on God. For Madhva, God is the perfect Jiva, and the individual Jivas are only images of God. Madhva defended the distinction and plurality among the jivas. This becomes also a feature of his realism. He classifies Jivas. Some are not liable to pain; some are liable to pain as they are on their way to purification. Yet some others are eternally punished. These are the evil souls who become so weighed down by karma that they are not able to rise.

Accordingly, each jiva is distinct and unique because of its Yogyatā. Each Jiva resembles and reflects God. It becomes a pratibimba, reflection of the bimba, Vishnu in accordance with its svarupa. This distinction (taratamya) of the Jivas remains a foundation for his theory of gradation among the Jivas, starting from Laksmi and coming down to those bound for hell. In agreement to each one's svarupa, according to Madhva, there are three kinds of Jivas. The first kind of jivas are those who are fit for liberation (muktiyogyas). The second ones are those that are caught in the cycle of birth and rebirth (nithyasamsarins) and travel endlessly in their journey. In the third category, there are souls that are eternally condemned to hell (tamoyogya). By making such a distinction, taratamya among the Jivas Madhva tries to give an original solution to the problem of evil, and to lift God (Vishnu) above all blame for evil in the world.

16.4.3 Concept of World

The world is Prakriti and is not created by God as it has eternal existence. The external world is affirmed to be ultimately real (satya) and continues to exist at all times. The world process is beginningless and eternal (anadi and nitya). All the material products originate from prakriti or primal matter. Sattva, rajas and tamas are its three gụnas. The Dvaita conception of causation differs from the well-known views of Advaita and Visịstadvaitạ. It is known as Sad-asat-karya vada, that is, the effect is considered as neither existent only nor non-existent. It exists as the cause, but not as the effect.

In his metaphysical thought the unique contribution of Madhva is the notion of 'bheda' and 'visesa'. Madhva accepts five-fold difference or bheda in reality, namely, the difference between God and soul (Isvara and Jiva), between soul and soul (Jiva and Jiva), between God and matter, between soul and matter, and between different material objects. Difference doesn't mean independence. God (Vishnu) alone is independent reality (svatantra-tattva), and all other beings are dependent on God (Paratantra-tattva). The system of Madhva accepts ten categories: Substance (Dravya), attribute (guna), action (karma), universals (samanya), specialty ('visesa'), the specified ('visista'), the whole (amsin), potency (sakti), similarity (sadrsya) and non-existence (abhava). Substances are twenty in number. Of these, Brahman, and souls are sentient (chetana). The rest are insentient (achetana). The twenty substances are: Brahman, Lakshmi, Jivas, space (akasa), Time (kala), primal matter (Prakrti), and its eight evolutes, the cosmic egg (Brahmanda), ignorance (avidya), speech sounds (varna), Darkness (timira), mental impressions (vasana) and reflection (pratibimba).

16.5 Purushartha

Purushartha is the supreme value or ideal to be pursued and realised by the finite self. Dvaita conceives of moksha, liberation as the ultimate perfection of life, the final goal to be attained. It advocates the renunciation of lower ends such as kama, artha and even dharma. Moksha signifies emancipation from all the afflictions of life. Dvaita upholds the continuance of conscious individuality as necessary for the attainment of supreme self-consummation that moksha is. According to it, moksha must be the fulfillment of conscious individuality in the attainment of the positive experience of eternal joy. All the schools of Vedanta contend that joy, infinite and eternal, is to be found only in the Brahman. To make possible this positive aspect of moksha, the finite self must integrate with the Brahman, the sole repository of bliss. In a way this integration is there as an eternal metaphysical fact, but the finite self must attune itself in its consciousness and life to the Brahman. What is required is integration in consciousness.

For Dvaita, the integration cannot mean the merger of the individual self into the universal self, shedding its specific personality. It can only mean its absorption in the experience of the Brahman with full recognition of its utter dependence on that Soul of souls. It is union without self-extinction, by way of experience, conformity in will and a life of blissful subordination. Ultimate surrender to the Supreme is the highest exultation and the pinnacle of joy. It is an enfoldment of the inherent nature of the individual in the commanding presence of God, and that constitutes to the bliss.

16.6 Sadhana, Means of Attainment

Dvaita outlines the means, sadhana for realisation of the supreme end, moksha. Sadhana is a progressive endeavour and it mobilises all the resources of personality. Madhva assimilates into his scheme of sadhana the entire heritage of the Upanishadic thought, the bhakti literature such as the Puranas, the Agamas, and the Epics including the Bhagavad-Gita. The foremost and the ultimate factor that brings about man's liberation, attainment of moksha, is the grace, prasada of Narayana. 'Without Narayana's prasada, moksha is not possible' says Madhva.

There are several levels of grace that confers this boon. 'The grace that responds to karma is the lowest, that, which is in answer to disciplines such as sravana, is of the middle level, and that which rewards the precious possession of knowledge is the highest'. This prasada is an ever-existent reality. All that is required of human effort is to actuate it towards the granting of moksha. It is ultimately God Himself through His grace, which is indistinguishable from His essence because of the principle of Visesa, that effectuates this grace to the man, moved towards that end, by the spiritual endeavour of the aspirant.

The works of grace of Narayana are manifold. The Vishnu-tattva-vinirnaya lays down that 'Vishnu grants knowledge to the ignorant, grants liberation to the man of knowledge, and grants ananda to the liberated individual.' Grace is a continuously operative factor in spiritual life, and does not cease to be required even when the goal is accomplished. What brings grace to operational manifestation is bhakti of the aspirant. Dvaita tradition defines bhakti thus:

Mahatmya-jnana pursvastu sudrdhah sarvatodhikah; sneho
bhaktriti proktahtaya muktih nacanyatha.

The two constituents of bhakti are knowledge of the greatness of God and love towards Him. This love must be steadfast and surpass in its intensity all other love including self-love. It is that height of bhakti that could invoke the necessary grace of Narayana for the purpose of moksha. There are different levels of bhakti, four levels stated in the Gita. Only the highest bhakti is what brings about the prasada for moksha.

16.7 Adi Shankaracharya, Ramanuja and Madhvacharya in Vedanta Philosophy

Hinduism discusses all aspects of life and living, giving followers practical and workable tips on living a peaceful, joyful and prosperous life, without putting in too much effort into it all. According to the philosophy, self-realisation is the key to understanding the secrets of life and, ultimately, living a life full of peace and joy.

This concept of self-realisation; the understanding of reality and decoding the "I" factor, gave rise to three main streams of philosophy, which now make up the entire fabric of Hindu thought as a whole. These three sub-schools of Vedanta or Vedantic thought constitute Advaita, Visishtadvaita and Dvaita. Simply put; the basic difference between the three Vedantas lies in the way they define the concept of reality and nature.

All Vedantic philosophies are based on Prasthaanatrayi, or the three axioms of Vedanta, as follows:

1. The Upanishads, known as Upadesha Prasthana and the Shruti Prasthana;
2. The Brahma Sutras, also known as Nyasa Prasthana or Yukti Prasthana; and
3. The Bhagavad Gita, also known as Sadhana Prasthana and the Smriti Prasthana.

All the three Vedantas rely on these Prasthanas. The scriptures deal in detail with the relationship between Brahma (the Ultimate Reality), Atman (the Individual Soul) and Jagat (the World). They also advise the followers on the path to be taken in order to attain moksha (salvation) from Samsara (bondage from this material world). The main difference between these schools of thought arises because the Prasthanatrayi talks about both the Brahman with attributes (Saguna) and the Brahman without attributes (Nirguna).

Three great Hindu saints and seers were primarily responsible for propagating these schools of Vedanta. They were as follows:

- Adi Shankaracharya for Advaita;
- Ramanujacharya for Visishtadvaita;
- Madhvacharya for Dvaita.

16.7.1 Adi Shankaracharya

Shankara is most known for his Bhashyas (systematic reviews and commentaries) on ancient Indian treatises. The Brahmasutrabhashya was his foremost work and went on to become a fundamental text of the Vedanta school of Hinduisṃ. His commentaries on ten Mukhya Upanishads are also considered to be important. Other works include commentaries on the Bhagavad Gita and his Vivarana on the commentary by Vedavyasa on Yogasutras and the Apasthamba-Dharma sutras.

In the Stotra (poetic works) category, Adi Shankara is attributed as the author of Daksinamurti Stotra, the Bhajagovinda Stotra, the Sivanandalahari, the Carpata-panjarika, the Visnu-satpadi, the Harimide, the Dasa-shloki, and the Krishnashtaka. Shankaracharya also authored Upadesasahasri, which is his most important work. Other than the original Prakaranas, seventy-six works were attributed to the Shankaracharya.

Shankara's stotras include hymns dedicated to both Krishna (Vaishnavism) and Shiva (Shaivism). These two are usually considered as two entirely different sects within Hinduism. However, the Advaitic nature of his philosophy tried to propagate a universal, unified view of Vedanta.

16.7.1.1 Advaita Vedanta

Adi Shankara systematised the works of his predecessors. His Advaita (non-dualism) philosophy postulates that the Atman is but one with the Brahman. According to him, the Atman is unchanging, while other changing realities are not absolute. Advaita Vedanta is based on shastra (scriptures), yukti (reasoning) and anubhava (experience). Shankaracharya's thinking was that a Jivanmukta (one liberated during the course of his lifetime) would be self-realised and would be aware of Oneness of Self and the Universal Spirit. The Acharya averred that, while the practice of Yoga would be helpful, it would not be able to gaining moksha. The followers would have to deeply study the Upanishads and delve into their real meaning. To Shankara, the study of the Upanishads was the necessary and sufficient means to attain moksha. He also stressed on the presence of the Guru to impart the necessary knowledge.

The world, though not unreal, is illusory once the perception of the highest Brahman is attained. This knowledge can be attained by following the four-fold path of Viveka (discrimination); Vairagya (detachment); Sama, Dama and Shraddha (calmness, self-control and patience) and Mumukshutva (constant yearning to attain liberation). Bhakti or Devotion is only one step to attain the grace of God. This would be the first step to understand the non-dualistic nature of the Jeevatma and the Paramatma.

While Shankara's Vedanta is similar to Mahayana Buddhism, the main difference is that Hinduism believes in the existence of Atman - something that is completely absent in the latter.

16.7.1.2 Influence on Hinduism

Shankara's philosophy and teachings form the basis of Smartism and have influence Sant Mat lineages. He introduced the Panchayatana path of worship - the worship of five deities, namely, Ganesha, Surya, Vishnu, Shiva and Devi. He explained that all these deities were but forms of the One Eternal Brahman. Though many seers had tried to propagate Advaita earlier, it was only after Adi Shankaracharya that it became the systematised Vedanta that it is today. Shankaracharya reformed Smartas and revived the tradition. He not only fought to wipe out the orthodoxy and the varnasrama dharma theory they had followed till then; but he also encouraged them to follow the practice of panchayatanapuja, in order to unify the entire system as a whole. Adi Shankaracharya's teachings have shaped much of the

Hindu psyche and continue to be as relevant even in today's modern world.

16.7.2 Ramanuja - Visishtadvaita Vedanta

Ramanujacharya was yet another important exponent of the tradition of Vaishnavism. He was born into a Tamil Brahmin family in the village of Sriperumbudur, Tamil Nadu. His philosophy highly influenced the Bhakti movement. He is also known by names such as Sri Ramanujacharya, Udaiyavar, Ethiraajar, Bhashyakarar, Godaagrajar, Thiruppavai Jeeyar, Emberumaanaar and Lakshmana Muni.

Ramanuja's most important contribution to Hinduism was his establishment of the Visishtadvaita (qualified monism) Vedanta. According to this school of philosophy, there exists plurality and distinction between Atman and Brahman. However, he also asserted that there is a unity of all souls and that each individual soul has the potential to become one with the Supreme Brahman.

Ramanuja established the Visishtadvaita Vedanta school of philosophical thought; the foundation of which, was qualified monism.

He accepted that Vedas are a reliable source of knowledge and critiqued the other two schools of Vedanta, namely, Advaita Vedanta and Dvaita Vedanta, as having misinterpreted the Vedic texts. He strongly stated that the purvapaksin (previous schools) only selectively support the Upanishadic passages and ignore those that support the concept of pluralism.

He said that the scriptures should always be considered in their totality and not in parts. According to Ramanujacharya, the Vedas mention both oneness and plurality and so on, the truth must incorporate both monism and pluralism. He called this qualified monism or Visishatadvaita Vedanta.

Similarities and Dissimilarities with the Other Vedantas

Ramanuja's Visishtadvaita agrees with the theistic devotional aspect of Madhvacharya's Dvaita Vedanta. Both schools state that Jiva and Brahman are totally different from each other and that this difference can never be transcended. Both schools are of the view that Vishnu alone is the independent reality and that all other Gods and beings are dependent on him. In contrast to Dvaita Vedanta, though, Ramanuja's "qualified non-dualism" states that souls share the same essential nature of the Brahman; that all souls are the same; and that it is possible for every soul to reach the bliss state of the Brahman himself. In sharp contrast, Madhvacharya believed that souls would never ever be able to reach the state of the Brahman.

Visishtadvaita and Advaita schools both believe in non-dualism. Both systems state that all souls can hope to achieve the blissful state of the Brahman. Advaita posits that only the Brahman is the unchanging reality, while everything else is relative, illusory and ever-changing. Shankara states that the Atman can attain the Brahman once it comprehends the truth and its actual nature of oneness with the Universal Power. In contrast, Ramanuja states that both Brahman and the material world are two different absolutes, both metaphysically real. According to him, neither is false of illusory. All of the world matter constitutes God's form and the path to the nirguna Brahman is through devotion and maintaining constant love towards the personal God; the saguna Brahman; no other than Vishnu Himself.

16.7.2.1 Influence on Hinduism

Ramanujacharya was highly influential, as he developed a different approach to Vedanta by giving the concept of bhakti an intellectual basis. His Visishtadvaita Vedanta made bhakti the central aspect of Hindu philosophy. Ramanuja undertook major tours and travels around India and tirelessly propagated his philosophy, thereby far extending the reach of his organisation. He not only developed theories, but also published philosophical texts and set up centers for the study of Vedanta, during the time between the 11th and 12th centuries.

Ramanuja reformed the Ranganathaswamy Temple complex at Srirangam and also organised a network of temples dedicated to Vishnu-Lakshmi worship. His philosophy influenced several generations of poet saints to further the Bhakti movement. The birthplace of Ramanujacharya houses a temple and an active Visishtadvaita school as well. His monastery and temple traditions are still followed the same way in the largest and most important Vaishnava centers, namely, the Ranganathaswamy Temple in Srirangam and the Venkateswara Temple in Tirumala, Tirupati.

16.7.3 Madhva - Dvaita Vedanta

Madhvacharya, also known as Purnaprajna and Ananda Teertha, was the main proponent of the Dvaita (dualism) school of Vedanta. He referred to his philosophy as Tattva vada, meaning, "arguments from a realistic point of view".

16.7.3.1 Philosophy of Dvaita Vedanta

Madhva was a severe critic of Adi Shankara's Advaita Vedanta (based on non-dualism) and Ramanuja's Vishishtadvaita Vedanta (based on qualified non-dualism). His teachings are based on the premise that there is a fundamental difference between the Atman and the Brahman. According to him, the two are different unchanging realities, which can never be identical. The individual soul, he stated, was dependent on the Brahman. Moksha could be attained only and only by the grace of God. Madhava's Dvaita Vedanta influenced Vaishnavism and the Bhakti movement in medieval India.

16.7.3.2 Literary Works

Madhva is credited with the creation of thirty-seven Dvaita texts. Of these, thirteen are Bhashyas on the Principal Upanishads, Brahma Sutras, the Bhagavad Gita, a commentary on forty hymns of the Rigveda, a review of the Mahabharata in poetic style and a commentary called Bhagavata-Tatparya-Nirnaya, on the Bhagavata Purana. Madhvacharya restricted outsiders, who were not from the Dvaita school, from accessing any of his work.

16.7.3.3 Influence on Hinduism

- Madhvacharya's influence led to the formation of the Haridasa sect of Vaishnavism in Karnataka, which is also referred to as Vyasakuta, Dasakuta or Dasa Dasapantha. They made a great contribution to the Bhakti movement, with their beautiful and meaningful devotional songs.
- The Acharya's influence is most prominently seen on the Chaitanya school of Bengal Vaishnavism and in Assam as well. A subsect of Gaudiya Vaishnavas from Orissa and West Bengal proclaim themselves to be followers of Madhvacharya.
- The Acharya established eight Mutts in Udupi. They are called the Madhva Mutts or Udupi Ashta Mutts. They are laid out in a rectangle and surround the Anantheshwara Krishna temple. Incidentally, the monks' studies and their course of succession (Paryaya system) were also established by Madhva. There are twenty-four other Madhva Mutts set up all over India. All of them follow the procedures as stipulated by the Acharya in his Tantrasara.

16.7.4 Common Features of All Schools of Vedanta

In spite of the obvious differences that exist between all the schools of Vedanta, there are fundamental similarities and common features between them. They are as follows:

- Brahman is the eternal, unchanging reality and the cause of the material world.

- The Upanishads are a reliable source of knowledge. Vedanta is the pursuit of that knowledge, in order to understand Brahman.
- Rebirth is a fact and being steeped in Vedanta is a way to attain jivan mukti.
- The Atman is responsible for its own acts and has to experience karma as a result of these acts.
- The Advaita, Dvaita and Visishtadvaita schools of Vedanta rejected Buddhism, Jainism and many other Vedantic schools as well.

Chapter - 17

Shuddhadvaita Vedanta Philosophy

17.1 Introduction to Shuddhadvaita Vedanta

Shuddadvaita (śuddhādvaita "pure non-dualism") is the "purely non-dual" philosophy propounded by **Vallabhacharya** (1479-1531 CE), the founding philosopher and guru of the Vallabha sampradāya ("tradition of Vallabha") or Pushimārga ("The path of grace"), a Hindu Vaishnava tradition focused on the worship of Krishna. Shuddhadvaita Vedanta is also known as the Rudrasampradhaaya of Vaishnavism. Vallabhacharya's pure form (nondualist) philosophy is different from Advaita. The Shrinathji temple at Nathdwara, and compositions of eight poets (ashtachap), including **Surdas**, are central to the worship by the followers of the sect.

Though the tradition originated near Vrindavana in the current Indian state of Uttar Pradesh, in modern times followers of Shuddadvaita are concentrated in the states of Rajasthan and Gujarat.

Vallabhacharya was a devotional philosopher, who founded the Pushti sect in India. He won the title of Jagadguru by travelling and debating scholars from a young age.

In 1493-94, Vallabhacharya is said to have identified an image of Krishna at the Govardhan hill at Braj. This image, now called Shrinathji and located at Nathdwara, Rajasthan, is central to the worship by Vallabha followers.

Vallabha's son Vitthalanaatha has written Vidvanmandana. The commentary on the Anubhaashya is the Bhaashyaprakaasha by Purushottama, which itself has been commented on by Gopeshvara in his Rashmi. Gopeshvara has also commented on the Subhodini and Vidvanmandana in his Suvarnasutra. Giridhara's Shuddhadvaitamaartaanda and Balakrishnabhatta's Prameyaratnaarnava are other important works of this school.

17.1.1 Surdas

Surdas (Sūr) was a 16th century blind Hindu devotional poet and singer, who was known for his works written in praise of Krishna, the supreme lord. He was a great Vaishnava (devotee of Lord Krishna) and is respected and revered by all the Vaishnava traditions. They are usually written in Braj Bhasha, one of the two literary dialects of Hindi.

Surdas is usually regarded as having taken his inspiration from the teachings of, whom he is supposed to have met in 1510. There are many stories about him, but most consideringly he is said to have been blind from birth. He is said to have become foremost among the poets, the Sampradaya designates as its Ashtachāp (eight seals), following the convention that each poet affixes his oral signature called chap at the end of each composition.

The book *Sur Sagar* (Sur's Ocean) is traditionally attributed to Surdas. However, many of the poems in the book seem to be written by later poets in Sur's name. The Sur Sagar in its present form focuses on descriptions of Krishna as the lovely child of Gokul and Vraj, written from the gopis' perspective. Surdas was a great religious singer.

Surdas was a part of the Bhakti movement spreading across the Indian subcontinent. This movement represented spiritual empowerment of the masses. The corresponding spiritual movement of the masses first happened in South India in the seventh century and spread to North India in the 14th-17th centuries.

17.1.2 Initiating Mantra of Shuddhadvaita Vedanta

According to Vallabha tradition, one night in 1494, Vallabhacharya received the Brahmasambandha mantra (the mantra that binds one with Brahman, or Krishna) from Krishna himself (hence the name, mukhāvatāra) at Gokula. The eight-syllable mantra, *Shri* ***krishṇaḥ sharaṇaṃ mama*** (Lord Krishna is my refuge), was passed onto new initiates in Vallabh sampradaya, and the divine name is said to rid the recipient of all impurities of the soul (doshas).

17.2 Philosophy of Shuddhadvaita Vedanta

Shuddhadwait is defined more thoroughly in verse 27-28 from Shuddhadwait Martand:

> "It is Karmadharaya samaasa : Shuddham cha tat adwaitam (The Pure and its non-dualism). Or, it is the Shashti Tatpurusha samaasa Shuddhyoh adwaitam (The Non-dual is pure). In this system, the combination of Maya with Brahman is done away with; therefore the cause of this world is not Brahman covered by Maya. But the pure Brahman and only pure Brahman is the effect and cause of this world."

The Shuddhadvaita philosophy has also been explained by various scholars of the sect, such as Devarshi Ramanath Shastri, who has enunciated the tenets of this philosophy in his books 'Shuddhadvait Siddhantasaar' and Shuddhadvaita Darshan.

According to Shuddhadvaita Vedanta, Krishna is:

- The Supreme Person;
- The indwelling spirit in all beings (antaryami);
- His form called akshara (indestructible) is the cause of the world, including all matters (parkriti) and selver. However, the world and selves are not different from Krishna, the Brahman.

17.2.1 Supreme Divinity

According to Shuddhadvaita, Brahman is equated to only Sri Krishna, who is the absolute and supreme reality, Purushottama. Vallabha rejects the idea that Purushottama Brahman is impersonal but rather asserts Sri Krishna to be the embodiment of Sachidananda whilst elaborating that everything in essence is a manifestation of Sri Krishna and any attempt to qualify Brahman to be attribute-less in the scriptures is to establish that he has no material qualities.

However, accepting the above, Vallabha does recognise another aspect of Brahman as Akshara Brahman. Here he admits that though lower in nature but consisting of Sachidananda it manifests itself according to the eligibility of the devotee as the abode of Purushottama Brahman, impersonal Brahman, the abodes of other demi-gods, whilst its primary role is to be the womb of creation and source for both individual souls and material creation. Thus, concluding, Purushottama Brahman Sri Krsna is both the creator and the created.

Although Vallabha does quote shruti texts, to establish the superiority of Sri Krishna, he mainly relies on the inferred supremacy of the Srimad Bhagavat Purana to gain much of his inspiration, quoting verses which directly correlate to his belief system.

17.2.2 Individual Soul

Vallabha explains that the individual soul is identical with and an atomic entity of Brahman. He states that although the individual soul shares all three aspects of Purushottama, Sri Krishna however conceals the bliss aspect of the soul which in turn leads the soul to come into contact with ignorance thus binding the soul to the material world. Vallabha defines the soul being in one of three states:

(i) Pure – when the jiva is separated from Brahman and though the attribute of bliss is concealed yet the jiva is not touched by ignorance.

(ii) Bound – when the jiva is separated from Brahman with the attribute of bliss concealed and it being affected by ignorance.

(iii) Liberated – when the jiva though separated from Brahman with the attribute of bliss concealed but now not affect by ignorance as the realisation of his true nature has been graced upon them.

Vallabha defines ignorance as the individual misidentifying his true nature with the body, the internal and external organs, the vital breath, the faculty of cognition and the complete ignorance of his true nature.

Vallabha further elaborates that as the soul in essence is a particle of Brahman, the particle is dependent on the supreme, and hence in reality the nature and role of the soul is that of a servant to his master, thus providing the explanation that the individual soul should serve Brahman ceaselessly.

Furthermore he states the soul though divine, belongs to a certain nature, of which it is predetermined and in **a category of three:**

(i) **Pushti jivas** – The souls of grace – These souls according to Vallabha are the exalted souls who are blessed by Sri Krishna and have been conferred His grace. These souls neither care for the Vedic injunctions ordained in Vedic literature as they have already been given the grace which the scriptures promote as the fruit. These souls again by the grace of Sri Krishna have been revealed their true nature of bliss which exists in their inherent nature. Vallabha further clarifies two categories within Pushti souls, those that are pure pushti souls and those that are mixed with other natures.

(ii) **Maryada jivas** – The souls of Vedic injunctions – These souls bound by the limited world follow the path ordained in the injunctions of the Vedic scriptures. They share pure qualities as described in the scriptures whilst following the path of knowledge, action and devotion to God, here the soul does eventually reach liberation but not given the pure grace of God as the pushti jivas.

(iii) **Pravaha jivas** – The souls of worldly flow – These souls are bound in the circle of birth and death whilst disregarding the scriptural injunctions. Their outlook is purely materialistic with no desire for spiritual life.

Additional to the categories above, Vallabha does say, however, that each category can show characteristics of another, however, this is temporal whilst their true nature remains the same.

17.2.3 Reality

Vallabha asserts that both sentient and insentient entities are fundamentally Brahman, hence real in nature and only a modification of Brahman rather than a product of Brahman. His logic is based on scriptural evidence which state that 'he is all this' and in the beginning only Brahman existed.

Furthermore, Vallabha goes on to explain that creation and dissolution of the multitude of beings and the material worlds is by the mere sport and will of Sri Krishna. Vallabha clarifies that as all sentient and insentient matter is none other than Brahman in reality, Brahman uses the facilities of concealment and revelation for objects to appear as they are. Similar to the individual soul which has the attribute of bliss concealed, insentient matter fundamentally having the attributes of Brahman has the attributes of consciousness and bliss concealed, thus only revealing the attribute of truth.

17.2.4 Liberation

According to Vallabha, liberation has a two-pronged approach, both though inspired in the culmination of devotion. As Pushti marga recognises the path of maryada, the instruction of following Vedic injunctions, they do appreciate that the followers of those respective paths do attain liberation. Nonetheless the clause is such that they do not enter the higher realm which is designated to the souls of Pushti.

In Pushti marga the means is the end itself, for Pushti marga devotees, to attend and serve the Lord with the initiation of brahma sambandha is the pivotal point of where the devotee does not desire liberation but rather the grace of God to keep serving Sri Krishna with the instruction described by Vallabhacharya and his son Vithalnathji, popularly known as Gosainji.

However, the Pushti philosophy makes a marked difference regarding after death liberation compared to that of the maryada path. Unlike maryada souls, Pushti souls receive the privilege with the grace of Sri Krishna to enter Goloka Dham, the abode of Sri Krishna. Here the soul, dependent on the individual's actions and the type of Pushti jiva, receive the grace of either being an attendant of Sri Krishna, union with Sri Krishna or a conscious object in the abode of Goloka witnessing the past times of Sri Krishna.

17.3 Tattvarth Deep Nibandha

Tattvarth Deep Nibandha is one of the works of Vallabhacharya, the exponent of the Shuddha-advaita system of Philosophy in India.

His Philosophy of Shuddha-advaita is explained at great length in his work Anubhasya, which is a commentary on the Brahma Sutras of Bada-rayan Vyas. In his Subodhini commentary on the Bhagawat, he has explained this philosophy also. His son Vitthaleshji and his descendents, Shri Purushottamji, Yogi Gopeshwarji, Girdharji, Murlidharji etc. also have explained this philosophy both by their learned commentaries on his works and also by their independent works. In all these works, has been discussed the problem of ultimate reality of the world and the summum bonum (ultimate truth) of life.

Various ways are suggested for liberation from pain by different schools. Vallabhacharya, the author of *Tattva Deep* Nibandha undertakes here to offer solution from his own point of view. For the sake of convenience, he divides his work into **three chapters:**

1. Shastrarth
2. Sarvanirnaya
3. Bhagwatarth

In the first chapter, Vallabhacharya gives the interpretation of the scriptures; in the second, his verdict, on the character of the various scriptures, and in the third his exposition of the underlying meaning of Bhagawat.

The first chapter contains 104 verses. On each of these verses, he has written his own commentary called '**Prakasha**'. This elucidates in an explanatory manner, what he has stated concisely and pithily in the verse-part. To make clear the 'Prakasha' portion, Purushottamji has written a scholarly commentary called 'Avran-bhang' which means breaking or removing of the veil. The obscurity of the thought in Vallabhacharya's Prakasha is the veil, which he has removed by his commentary.

The first verse of the first chapter, he devotes to the salutation of Lord Krishna, whom he regards as the Supreme Lord. In the second Verse he states the problem of this work. It is as he says, 'emancipation.' Only the Satvik and the votaries of God are entitled to it. It is for them that he undertakes to consider that problem in this work.

Every philosophical problem should be approached from the following four points of view:

1. Pramana
2. Pramey
3. Sadhan
4. Fal

Here emancipation is the fruit. Its real character should first of all be known by means of proofs. That will come under the Pramana section. Then the question of the main objects of knowledge, worth knowing are discussed in Prameya Section. Then the various means for the realisation of ultimate fruit are explained under the Sadhana section. In the fruit section, the real nature of fruit are explained. The first chapter that is, Shastrath Prakaran deals with the Pramana.

17.3.1 Pramana Chapter

Pramana means 'Proofs of knowledge.' Pramana is defined as 'Pramakaran' – an instrument of knowledge. 'Prama' is explained as 'Yathartha Anubhav', that is, it must be direct cognition, free from doubt, perversion of facts or false reasoning.

The 'Yatharthatva' of 'Anubhav' is explained as 'Tadvati Tatprakaaratvam' for instance 'Rajat' (Silver) has Rajatva 'Silverness'. So, when we say 'Rajat' is 'Rajatva', it is 'Yatharth' (exact) cognition. The work 'Karan' means 'Sadhaktam Kaaran', that is, the cause that is most essential in producing a certain result. So anything that is most essential in exact cognition of the object is called 'Pramana.' Here the question to be decided is what should be our 'Pramana' in the right appreciation of our problem of emancipation and understanding the ultimate reality of the world viz. Brahman. In V. 7 Shree Vallabhacharya mentions only 'Sabda Pramana' as valid, ("Sabda Eva Pramanam"). Vallabhacharya rules out all except 'Shabda', because except 'Pratyaksh' and 'Anumaan', others are included under any of the first three. For instance, 'Sambhav' means probability. This is included in inference. The fact of probability depends upon the statement, to be understood by inference. What is called 'Chesta' is humour.

17.3.2 Pramey Chapter

But what is this highest entity called God or Brahman? The author answers the question first by giving the Karya Lakshana of God and then by Swaroop Lakshana. By Karya Lakshana we mean, the concept of 'God' as expressed in the term of Karya i.e. effect viz world. The author says that if you put a question 'What is God?' then, I say that He is the creator of the world and the souls. The author of the Brahman Sutras also pursues this method of describing Brahman, in his second aphorism *'Janmandhasya Yato'* i.e. God is one from which the world originates in which it exists and into which it finally is absorbed. So in the opinion of the author, the world and the souls are creations of Brahman. He is the material cause as well as the efficient cause. In order to understand the relation subsisting between the cause 'Brahman' and its effect 'the World' let us understand what is meant by cause.

A cause is that which preceding its effect is invariably concomitant with it and at the same time is not proved to be an essential and accidental circumstance i.e. three essentials constitute our notion of a cause :

1. Priority to effect
2. Invariability with it
3. Its Non-accidentality.

17.4 Avikrataparinaamavaada

According to the Upanishads, Brahman made the world out of itself. Advaita interprets this as there's no real modification (parinaama) of Brahman into the universe and that the manifestation of Brahman as the universe is only an appearance (vivarta). Vallabha on the other hand holds that the manifestation is real. But again it is not parinaama as this manifestation doesn't involve any change or transformation in Brahman. This view of Vallabha which is takes a middle place between vivarta and parinaama is called avikrtaparinaamavaada.

Vallabha rejects the relation of samavaaya between substance and attribute and advocates tadaatmaya or identity. Attributes are identical to the substance and effects are identical to the cause. The substance really appears as the attributes and the cause really appears as the effect. As Brahman is the inherent material cause of this world, he is identical with the effect (the universe) but still as far as Brahman is concerned the manifestation doesn't involve any change in him.

Brahman is also the efficient cause. He manifests Himself as the universe without undergoing any change. Creation basically means manifestation of Brahman into the universe without involving any change in Brahman and dissolution means withdrawal of this manifestation by Brahman into himself. Like sparks spring forth from fire, the universe springs forth from Brahman. Just like cotton spreads itself as threads, Brahman spreads himself as this universe.

17.5 God, Souls and Matter

Brahman is Shri Krishna and his essence is sat-chit-ananda - existence, knowledge and bliss. Matter and souls are his parts and real manifestations. He is the abode of all good qualities and includes even seemingly contrary ones - He is smaller than the smallest, greater than the greatest, one as well as many. It is by His power or maya that He manifests Himself as this diverse universe revealing His natures of existence, knowledge and bliss in different proportions. From His nature as existence springs forth life (prana), senses and bodies. From His nature of knowledge springs forth infinite atomic souls which are the subjects of bondage. And from His nature as bliss spring forth the antaryaamins (inner controllers) who are the presiding deities of the souls and are as many in number as the souls.

God is the supreme antaryaamin - the inner ruler of the universe. In the material world only the existence aspect of God is manifested while knowledge and bliss are obscured. In the souls, existence and knowledge are manifested while bliss is obscured. In the antaryaamins all the three aspects are manifested. All the three forms - jagat, jiva and antaryaamins - are essentially identical with God. While jagat is dissimilar from him (vijaatiya), the jivas are similar to him (sajaatiya) and the antaryaamins are inside him (svagata). He pervades all the forms which are non-different from him. There's no difference either homogeneous or heterogeneous or internal in God.

Jagat is different from samsara. Jagat is the real manifestation of God, while samsara is the cycle of births and deaths imagined by the soul due to ignorance which is five-fold : 1. ignorance of its real nature, 2. false identification with the body, 3. false identification with the senses, 4. false identification with the vital breaths, and 5. with the mind. With the dawn of knowledge ignorance vanishes and with it vanishes samsara. But jagat being a real manifestation of God, endures.

The soul as it is a part of God is identical with him and only appears as different due to the limited manifestations of some divine aspects and obscuration of others.

17.6 Pushtimaarga

Bhakti as a firm and all surpassing affection (sneha) for God with a full sense of his greatness is the only means to liberation. It is the loving service of God which means attachment to God and detachment from all other things. It is neither worship nor knowledge, but prema (affection). In Pushtimaarga, bhakti is attained without any individual effort simply by the grace of God who destroys all sins forthwith. Pleased with devotion, God either takes the devotee within himself and keeps him near Himself to enjoy the sweetness of service.

Chapter - 18

Neo-Vedanta Philosophy

18.1 Neo-Vedanta

Neo-Vedanta, also called Hindu modernism, neo-Hinduism, Global Hinduism and Hindu Universalism, are terms to characterise interpretations of Hinduism that developed in the 19th century. The term "Neo-Vedanta" was coined by German Indologist Paul Hacker to distinguish modern developments from "traditional" Advaita Vedanta. Scholars have repeatedly argued that these modern interpretations incorporate western ideas into traditional Indian religions, especially Advaita Vedanta, which is asserted as central or fundamental to Hindu culture. Other scholars have described a Greater Advaita Vedanta, which developed since the medieval period. Drawing on this broad pool of sources, after Muslim rule in India was replaced by British rule, Hindu religious and political leaders and thinkers responded to western colonialism and orientalism, contributing to the Indian freedom struggle and the modern national and religious identity of Hindus in the Republic of India. This societal aspect is covered under the term of Hindu reform movements. Prominent in Neo-Vedanta is **Vivekananda,** who's theology is often characterised in earlier scholarship as "a rupture from 'traditional' or 'classical' Hinduism, particularly the 'orthodox' Advaita Vedanta of the eighth century of Shankara.

Neo-Vedanta has been influential in the perception of Hinduism, both in the West and in the higher educated classes in India. It has received appraisal for its "solution of synthesis", but has also been criticised for its Universalism. The terms "Neo-Hindu" or "Neo-Vedanta" themselves have also been criticised for its refix "Neo-" then intended to imply that these modern interpretations of Hinduism are "inauthentic" or in other ways problematic. The terms "Neo-Vedanta" and "Neo-Hinduism" refer to "the adoption of Western concepts and standards and the readiness to reinterpret traditional ideas in the light of these new, imported and imposed modes of thought".

The term "Neo-Vedanta" appears to have arisen in Bengal in the 19th century, where it was used by both Indians and Europeans. The term neo-Vedanta was first coined by Christian commentators, some of whom were first-hand observers of developments in Brahmo theology, engaged in open, sometimes acrimonious debates with the Brahmos, whom they partly admired for their courage in abandoning traditions of polytheism and image worship but whom they also scorned for having proffered to other Hindus. It seems likely that the term "Neo-Hinduism" was invented by a Bengali, Brajendra Nath Seal (1864–1938), who used the term to characterise the literary work of Bankim Chandra Chatterjee (1838–1894).

18.2 Swami Vivekananda (1863–1902) and Ramakrishna Mission

Vivekananda was born Narendranath Datta (shortened to Narendra or Naren) in a Bengali family at his ancestral home at 3, Gourmohan Mukherjee Street in Calcutta, the capital of British India, on 12 January 1863 during the Makar Sankranti festival. He belonged to a traditional family and was one of nine siblings. His father, Vishwanath Datta, was an attorney at the Calcutta High Court. Durgacharan Datta, Narendra's grandfather was a Sanskrit and Persian scholar, who left his family and became a monk at age twenty-five. His mother, Bhubaneswari Devi, was a devout housewife. The progressive, rational attitude of Narendra's father and the religious temperament of his mother helped shape his thinking and personality.

Narendranath was interested in spirituality from a young age and used to meditate before the images of deities such as Shiva, Rama, Sita, and Mahavir Hanuman. He was fascinated by wandering ascetics and monks. Narendra was naughty and restless as a child, and his parents often had difficulty controlling him. His mother said, "I prayed to Shiva for a son and he has sent me one of his demons".

18.2.1 Education of Narendra

In 1871, at the age of eight, Narendranath enrolled at Ishwar Chandra Vidyasagar's Metropolitan Institution, where he went to school until his family moved to Raipur in 1877. In 1879, after his family's return to Calcutta, he was the only student to receive first-division marks in the Presidency College entrance examination. He was an avid reader in a wide range of subjects, including philosophy, religion, history, social science, art and literature. He was also interested in Hindu scriptures, including the Vedas, the Upanishads, the Bhagavad Gita, the Ramayana, the Mahabharata and the Puranas. Narendra was trained in Indian classical music, and regularly participated in physical exercise, sports and organised activities. Narendra studied Western logic, Western philosophy and European history at the General Assembly's Institution (now known as the Scottish Church

College). In 1881, he passed the Fine Arts examination, and completed a Bachelor of Arts degree in 1884. Narendra studied the works of David Hume, Immanuel Kant, Johann Gottlieb Fichte, Baruch Spinoza, Georg W. F. Hegel, Arthur Schopenhauer, Auguste Comte, John Stuart Mill and Charles Darwin. He became fascinated with the evolutionism of Herbert Spencer and corresponded with him, translating Herbert Spencer's book Education (1861) into Bengali. While studying Western philosophers, he also learned Sanskrit scriptures and Bengali literature.

William Hastie (principal of Christian College, Calcutta, from where Narendra graduated) wrote, "Narendra is really a genius. I have travelled far and wide but I have never come across a lad of his talents and possibilities, even in German universities, among philosophical students. He is bound to make his mark in life".

Narendra was known for his prodigious memory and the ability at speed reading. Several incidents have been given as examples. In a talk, he once quoted verbatim, two or three pages from Pickwick Papers. Another incident that is given is his argument with a Swedish national where he gave reference to some details on Swedish history that the Swede originally disagreed with but later conceded. In another incident with Dr. Paul Deussen's at Kiel in Germany, Vivekananda was going over some poetical work and did not reply when the professor spoke to him. Later, he apologised to Dr. Deussen explaining that he was too absorbed in reading and hence did not hear him. The professor was not satisfied with this explanation but Vivekananda quoted and interpreted verses from the text leaving the professor dumbfounded about his feat of memory. Once, he requested some books written by Sir John Lubbock from a library and returned them the very next day claiming that he had read them. The librarian refused to believe him until cross-examination about the contents convinced him that Vivekananda was being truthful.

18.2.2 Early Life of Narendra

Some accounts have called Narendra a shruti-dhara (a person with a prodigious memory).

In 1880, Vivekananda joined Keshub Chandra Sen's Nava Vidhan, which was established by Sen after meeting Ramakrishna and reconverting from Christianity to Hinduism. Narendranath (a.k.a. Narendra) became a member of a Freemasonry lodge "at some point before 1884" and of the Sadharan Brahmo Samaj in his twenties, a breakaway faction of the Brahmo Samaj led by Keshub Chandra Sen and Debendranath Tagore. From 1881 to 1884 he was also active in Sen's Band of Hope, which tried to discourage the youth from smoking and drinking. It was in this cultic milieu that Narendra became acquainted with western esotericism. His initial beliefs were shaped by Brahmo concepts, which included belief in a formless God and the deprecation of idolatry, and a "streamlined, rationalised, monotheistic theology strongly coloured by a selective and modernistic reading of the Upanishads and of the Vedanta". He propagated the idea that "the divine, the absolute, exists within all human beings regardless of social status", and that "seeing the divine as the essence of others will promote love and social harmony".

During this period, he came in contact with **Ramakrishna**, who eventually became his guru. Ramakrishna gradually brought Narendra to a Vedanta-based worldview that "provides the ontological basis for the spiritual practice of serving human beings as actual manifestations of God." On one occasion in 1884, Sri Ramakrishna was explaining... that one of the main religious practices of Vaishnavas is 'showing compassion to all beings' and that Ramakrishna then asserted It must not be compassion, but service to all. Serve them, knowing that they are all manifestations of God. Ramakrishna's teachings that day affected the young Naren so deeply that he took his friends aside afterward and explained its profound ethical significance to them.

One can bring Vedanta from the forest to the home and practice it in daily life. Let people continue with whatever they are doing; there's no harm in this. People must first fully believe and be convinced that God has manifested Himself before them as the world and its creatures.... If people consider everyone to be God, how can they consider themselves to be superior to others and harbour attachment, hatred, arrogance—or even compassion [Daya]—toward them? Their minds will become pure as they serve all beings as God, and soon they will experience themselves as parts of the blissful God. They will realise that their true nature is pure, illumined, and free.

18.2.3 Vivekananda's Speech at the Parliament of Religions

Vivekananda's acquaintance with western esotericism made him very successful in western esoteric circles, beginning with his speech in 1893 at the Parliament of Religions. Vivekananda adapted traditional Hindu ideas and religiosity to suit the needs and understandings of his western audiences, who were especially attracted by and familiar with western esoteric traditions and movements like Transcendentalism and New Thought. An important element in his adaptation of Hindu religiosity was the introduction of his four yoga's model, which includes Raja yoga, his interpretation of Patanjali's Yoga sutras, which offered a practical means to realise the divine force within which is central to modern western esotericism. In 1896, his book *Raja Yoga* was published, which became an instant success and was highly influential in the western understanding of Yoga.

18.3 Neo-Vedanta Philosophy as proposed by Swami Vivekananda

Neo-Vedanta is closer to Ramanuja's qualified non-dualism than it is to Shankara's Advaita Vedanta. Neo-Vedanta does not regard the world to be illusionary, in contrast to Shankara's Advaita Vedanta. The basis of the Neo-Vedanta philosophy was laid by Sri Ramakrishna (1836-1886) and its superstructure was built by his ardent disciple Swami Vivekananda (1863-1902). They both emphasised the practical nature of Vedanta. By the Neo-Vedanta of Swami Vivekananda is meant the New Vedanta as distinguished from the old traditional Vedanta developed by Shankaracharya (c. 788-820 AD). Shankara's Vedanta is known as Advaita or non-dualism, pure and simple. Hence it is sometimes referred to as Kevala-Advaita or unqualified monism. It may also be called abstract monism in so far as Brahman, the Ultimate Reality, is, according to it, devoid of all qualities and distinctions, nirguna and nirvisheṣha.

Neo-Vedantism is a re-establishment and re-statement, reconstruction and revaluation, reorientation and reinterpretation of the Advaita Vedanta of Shankara with modern arguments, in modern language, suited to modern man, adjusting itself with all the modern challenges. The Neo-Vedanta is also Advaitic in as much as it holds that Brahman, the Ultimate Reality, is one without a second, *ekamevadvitiyam*. But as distinguished from the traditional Advaita of Shankara, it is a synthetic Vedanta, which reconciles Dvaita or dualism and Advaita or non-dualism and also other theories of reality. In this sense it may also be called concrete monism in so far as it holds that Brahman is both qualified, *saguṇa* and qualityless, *nirguna*.

The germs of Neo-Vedantism as also the rationale and beginning of its practical application are to be found in the life and teachings of Sri Ramakrishna. It was left to Swami Vivekananda to develop them into the philosophy of Neo-Vedanta and lay the foundation of practical Vedanta. The fundamental principles on which Neo-Vedanta and its practical application rest, may be traced to the Vedas and Upanishads. But it was Sri Ramakrishna, who demonstrated and synthesised the teachings through his manifold spiritual experiences. Neo-Vedanta philosophy of Swami Vivekananda is characterised by his teachings and works, and as currently embodied by the Ramakrishna Movement internationally.

Following are the salient features of Neo-Vedanta:

18.3.1 Brahman

For Swami Vivekananda, Brahman as Infinite Existence, Infinite Knowledge and Infinite Bliss, (sat-cit-ananda), is the ultimate reality and the only reality. These are the only attributes that can be ascribed to Brahman, and they are one. It is without a name, without a form or stain, being beyond space, time and causation. It is one without a second. It is all in all. None else exists. "There is neither nature, nor God, nor the universe, only that One Infinite Existence, out of which, through name and form all these are manufactures" Swami Vivekananda maintains that the Advaita clearly postulates one reality only, that is, Brahman; everything else is "unreal", manifested and manufactured out of Brahman by the power of Maya. To reach back to that Brahman is our goal. We are, each one of us, that Brahman, that Reality, plus this Maya. Brahman is an indeterminate, impersonal Being without qualities and distinctions, without any relation to any object or the world of objects. This means that Swami Vivekananda's Brahman is perfectly formless, quality-less and distinction-less, nirguna and nirvisheṣha, like Shankara's Absolute and that there is no difference between them on this point. However, this is only one aspect of Brahman as viewed by Swami Vivekananda. For, in Swami Vivekananda's Vedantic thought there are two movements, a negative and a positive. The description of Brahman given above is the result of the negative movement of his thought. It is the traditional approach to Brahman by the path of negation, *neti-neti*. But as a complementary to the negative path, he also follows a positive path and reaffirms all that was at first negated in a new light and with a new meaning.

To understand Brahman, Swami Vivekananda states, "We have to go through the negation, and then the positive side will begin. We have to give up ignorance and all that is false, and then truth will begin to reveal itself to us. When we have grasped the truth, things which we give up at first will take new shape and form, will appear to us in a new light, and become deified. They would have become sublimated, and then we shall understand them in their true light. But to understand them we have first to get a glimpse of truth; we must give them up at-first, and then we get them back again, deified.

For Swami Vivekananda, the aspect of the Absolute as Ishvara, the Personal God, is none other than the relative aspect of Brahman. He points out that it is the same -sat-chit-ananda who is also the God of love, the Impersonal and Personal is one. The Personal God worshipped by the bhakta (devotee) is not separate or different from Brahman. All is Brahman, the One without a second; only Brahman, as unity or absolute, is too much of an abstraction to be loved and worshipped; so, the bhakti chooses the relative aspect of Brahman, that is Ishvara, the Supreme Ruler.

The Personal God as we conceive of Him is in fact a phenomenon. The very idea of causation exists only in the phenomenal world, and God as the cause of this universe must naturally be thought of as limited, and yet He is the same Impersonal God. The Impersonal instead of doing away with the Personal, the Absolute instead of pulling down the relative, only explains it to the full satisfaction of our reason and heart. The Personal God and all that exists in the universe are the same Impersonal Being seen through our minds.

Swami Vivekananda maintains that the world of objects is not totally negated in Brahman. It is not, as is the case with Shankara's Advaita, that Brahman alone is real and the world is false or illusory, *Brahman satyam, jaganmithya*, but that in a sense the world is also real. Swami Vivekananda states that the Vedanta does not in reality denounce the world. What it seeks to teach is the deification of the world and not its annihilation - giving up the world as we ordinarily think of it, as it appears to us and to know what it really is. As Swami Vivekananda states: "Deify it (the world), it is God alone"; and he cites the opening verse of the Isa Upanishad, which says:

"Isavasyam idam sarvam yat kim ca jagatyamjagat"

"All this - whatsoever moves on the earth -should be covered by the Lord."

He further explains: "You can have your wife; it does not mean that you are to abandon her but that you are to see God in the wife". So also, you are to "see God in your children. So, in everything. In life and in death, in happiness and in misery the Lord is equally present. The whole world is full of the Lord. Open your eyes and see Him. This is what Vedanta teaches."

As further evidence of Swami Vivekananda's affirmation of the world in God, we may consider what he says with regard to the way and the attitude with which we are to work in the world. This, he says, is the Vedantic way and the Vedantic attitude. We are to work by giving up the apparent, that is, the illusive world. This means that we are to work by seeing God everywhere. The sum total of all souls, which, as he put it, is "the only God I believe in, and above all my God the wicked, my God the miserable, my God the poor of all races". Desire to live a hundred years, he says, have all earthly desires, if you wish, only deify them, convert them into heaven. Thus, working, you will find the way out. There is no other way. If a man plunges headlong into the foolish luxuries of the world without knowing the truth, he has missed his footing, he cannot reach the goal. And if a man curses the world, goes into a forest, mortifies his flesh, and kills himself little by little by starvation, makes his heart a barren waste, kills out all feelings, and becomes harsh, stern and dried up, that man also has missed the way. These are the two extremes, the two mistakes at either end. Both have lost the way; both have missed the goal. So work, says the Vedanta, putting God in everything and knowing Him to be in everything.

Swami Vivekananda's Neo-Vedanta makes no difference between the sacred and the secular life. As world is Brahman, worldly activity too is sacred and all selfless work is worship. Therefore, selfless activity is not only social but also spiritual. As long as man lives in the world, he must perform worldly activity in the spirit of detachment. Thus, Neo-Vedanta encourages individual freedom and selfless activity on the part of the individual, and social equality and oneness in society.

18.3.2 The Universe

We may now consider Swami Vivekananda's affirmation of the world from the orientation of Brahman. "The Absolute", he says "has become the universe by coming through space, time and causation. The universe is the reflection of that One Eternal Being on the screen of Maya - the triad of space, time and causation. These are only ideas or concepts of our mind and have no place in Brahman. The world is a creation of name and form, of Maya. We are looking upon the One existence in different forms and under different names, and 'creating' all these images of objects upon it.

There is neither time, space, nor causation in the Absolute, it is beyond them all. They have no real existence, yet they are not non-existent, since it is through them that all things are manifesting as this universe. Further, they sometimes vanish. Swami Vivekananda illustrates this in terms of the wave and the ocean. The wave is the same as the ocean, and yet we know it as a wave, and as such different from the ocean. What makes it different from the ocean are its names and forms. If the wave subsides, the form vanishes in a moment, and yet the form was not a delusion. So long as the wave existed the form was there, and you are bound to see the form. This, for Swami Vivekananda is Maya. The differentiation is in the form, not in the substance. You may destroy the form and it disappears for ever; but the substance remains the same.

Swami Vivekananda explains that Maya is not illusion as it is popularly interpreted. He states "Maya is real, yet it is not real". It is real in that the Real is behind it and gives it its appearance of reality. That which is real in Maya is the Reality in and through Maya. Yet the Reality is never seen; and hence that which is seen is unreal, and it has no real independent existence of itself, but is dependent upon the Real for its existence. Maya then is a paradox - real, yet not real; an illusion, yet not an illusion. He who knows the Real sees in Maya not illusion, but reality. He who knows not the Real sees in Maya the illusion and thinks it real. Hence the Absolute is manifesting itself as many, through the veil of time, space and causation. Swami Vivekananda states: "We now see that all the various forms of cosmic energy, such as matter, thought, force, intelligence, and so forth, are simply the manifestations of that cosmic intelligence, or, the Supreme Lord. Everything that you see, feel, or hear, the whole universe, is His creation; or to be a little more accurate is His projection."

Swami Vivekananda's view of the relation between substance and quality, noumenon (he thing-in-itself the thing as it appears to an observer) and phenomenon lends further evidence in support of the contention that for him the universe is a real manifestation of the Absolute in various forms. By substance is meant the unchanging ground and support of changing qualities. So also, by noumenon is meant the immutable reality (i.e., the Absolute), underlying the world of mutation and change (i.e., the world of changing objects) which is called phenomenon. Swami Vivekananda was of the view that we cannot think of the substance as separate from the qualities; we cannot think of change and not-change at the same time; it would be impossible. But the very thing which is the substance is the quality; substance and quality are not two things. It is the unchangeable that is appearing as the changeable. The unchangeable substance of the universe, (the Absolute), is not something separate from it. The noumenon is not something different from the phenomenon, but it is the very noumenon (the Absolute) which has become the phenomena From the above it is evident that Swami Vivekananda gives a philosophical exposition of Sri Ramakrishna's teaching that Brahman and Shakti are non-different, *'abheda'*. What Swami Vivekananda calls the unchangeable substance of the universe or the noumenon is the same as Brahman, and what he calls the qualities or the phenomena are just the contents of the universe as a play of energies, powers and forces, in a word, Shakti. The Shakti is sometimes called Mahlimliyii as the manifest universe of space, time and causation. Thus, we may say that for Swami Vivekananda the universe as such is really a manifestation of Brahman. However, the fact remains that at times his thoughts switch off to the other pole from which he says that the universe is an apparent manifestation of Brahman. These seemingly conflicting statements are reconciled by Swami Vivekananda himself in his treatment of Advaita, Dvaita and other schools of thought.

18.3.3 Advaita, Vishishtadvaita, Dvaita

Like Sri Ramakrishna, Swami Vivekananda was of the view that Advaita, Dvaita and Vishishtadvaita are all true and that 'descriptions' of Brahman given by them relate to the same reality. In Advaita, Brahman is *nirguna*, that is, devoid of quality and form. It is indeterminate and impersonal. But for Dvaita and Vishishtadvaita, Brahman has all good qualities. He is *saguṇa*, that is, with qualities. He is a Personal Being and as the omnipotent and omniscient creator, sustainer and destroyer of the world. So also, there are different conceptions of the world and of the soul and its liberation in Advaita, Vishishtadvaita and Dvaita. In Advaita, the world is the product of maya, an illusory creation of God's magical power. The individual self as a limited person is also unreal. But the real self of man, the Atman in him is ever pure, free, infinite and immortal; it is the same sat-chit-ananda that Brahman is, and as such. It is Brahman itself. Its false association with the body through ignorance, avidya, is the root cause of bondage. Therefore, moksha, liberation, is to be attained only through knowledge, jnana, of the self as identical with Brahman. The performance of religious works (karma), or devotion to and worship of God (bhakti) do not lead to liberation. Of course, karma and bhakti are important in so far as they purify the mind and generate in us the desire to know Brahman. But after that, ignorance can be removed and liberation attained only through knowledge of the Self or of Brahman.

According to Dvaita and Vishishtadvaita, the world is a real creation of Brahman by his wonderful, but real creative power. The world is, therefore. as real as Brahman. The individual soul, according to Dvaita and Vishishtadvaita, is a limited, finite being, though it is essentially conscious and eternal. It is not identical with, but different from Brahman and is completely dependent on Him. When, through ignorance, it identifies itself with the body and forgets God, it comes under bondage. Liberation from bondage cannot be attained through mere knowledge of God, self and the world. However, we must have true knowledge of them. But after we have the requisite knowledge, we must constantly remember God and love and worship Him. It is through such steadfast devotion to God, (karma and bhakti), that man receives God's grace; and it is God's grace that liberates man from bondage. Hence it is bhakti or devotion, combined with jnana and karma (knowledge and work), what leads to liberation.

Swami Vivekananda in his Neo-Vedanta philosophy has brought about a reconciliation of Advaita, Vishishtadvaita and Dvaita. According to him, God is personal and impersonal at the same time. Even man may be said to be both personal and impersonal. We are personalised impersonal beings.

If we use the word in the absolute sense, we are impersonal; but if we use it in a relative meaning, we are personal. The Impersonal according to Swami Vivekananda, is a living God, a principle. The difference between personal and impersonal is that the personal is only a man, and the impersonal idea is that He is the angel, the man, the animal, and yet something more, because Impersonality includes all personalities, is the sum total of everything in the universe and infinitely more besides.

18.3.4 Practical Vedanta (Neo-Vedanta)

One of the greatest contributions of Swami Vivekananda is his emphasis on the practical nature of Vedanta. In his numerous lectures he clearly shows how Vedanta was a practical philosophy in the past and that many of the Vedantic thoughts emanated from persons who lived the busiest lives in the world, namely, the ruling monarchs of ancient India. He also points out that the Bhagavad Gita, which is the quintessence of Vedanta philosophy, was taught to Arjuna by Sri Krishna on the battlefield of Kurukshetra. Swami Vivekananda maintained that the Vedanta, as a religion must be intensely practical. "We must be able to carry it out in every part of our lives. And not only this, the fictitious differentiation between religion and the life of the world must vanish, for the Vedanta teaches oneness - one life throughout".

The central ideal of Vedanta is oneness. There are no two in anything, no two lives. There is but one life, one world, one existence. Everything is that One, the difference is in degree and not in kind. It is the same life that pulsates through all beings, from Brahman to the amoeba, the difference is only in the degree of manifestation. We must not look down with contempt on others. All of us are going towards the same goal. We have no right to look down with contempt upon those who are not developed exactly in the same degree as we are. Condemn none, if you can stretch out a helping hand, do so. If you cannot, fold your hands, bless your brothers and let them go their own way.

18.3.5 The Self (Atman)

The Vedanta declares that it is through the Self that you know everything, therefore "know thy self". Swami Vivekananda maintains that this is not impossible and impracticable, but quite a feasible and practical proposition. Your real Self is the abiding and constant consciousness, the standing witness in you, which observes all changes in your body and mind, but is not involved in them, rather, it stands above them. It is the pure immutable, unflickering light of consciousness in you which is also pure existence and is ever free and blissful. You are that sat-cit-ananda, not the small miserable being that you ignorantly think yourself to be. Your self is the universal self that is one with all things and beings, that shines in the sun, the moon and the stars and illumines them all.

18.3.6 Humanism

Another vital practical side of Swami Vivekananda's Neo-Vedantism is the call for us to be first Gods, and then help others to be Gods. We should look upon every man, woman and everyone as God. As a Vedantin Swami Vivekananda firmly believes that all life is one. The life and existence of an individual is not separate, distinct and independent from that of others. As all individuals are sparks of the same Divine Force or Entity, all are free and equal and one.

18.3.7 Vedantic Universalism

An important practical aspect of Swami Vivekananda's Neo-Vedanta is acceptance, not mere tolerance of other forms of worship. According to it, other forms of worship, including the worship of God through ceremonials and forms, are not in error. It is the journey from truth to truth, from lower truth to higher truth. Truth is nobody's property, no race, no individual can lay any exclusive claim to it. Truth is the nature of all souls. Swami Vivekananda, like his Master Sri Ramakrishna, stated that we should see others with eyes of love, with sympathy, knowing that they are going along the same path that we have trod. The Neo-Vedanta not only tolerates but accepts and respects other religions of the world as but different paths that lead to the same goal - God. Swami Vivekananda says "all religions are different forces in the economy of God, working for the good of mankind. We Hindus do not merely tolerate, we unite ourselves with every religion, praying in the mosque of the Muslim, worshipping before the fire of the Zoroastrian, and kneeling to the cross of the Christian. We know that all religions alike, from the lowest fetishism to the highest absolutism, are but so many attempts of the human soul to grasp and realise the Infinite.

Chapter - 19

Kashmir Shaivism Philosophy

19.1 Introduction to Kashmir Shaivism

No account of the philosophical systems of India would be complete without Kashmir Shaivism, for its analysis of Nature is more comprehensive than any of the six Darshanas; therefore, it must be included. It is a system of Ideal Monism founded by Vasugupta in the ninth century. Its central position is that there is only one Ultimate Principle, but that this principle has two aspects, one transcendental and the other immanent. Its analysis of the process of cosmic evolution postulates thirty-six categories (tattvas). What the other systems assume, Kashmir Shaivism explains, for it shows the origin of Spirit and Matter; it discusses the nature of the Ultimate Principle; and it explains the cause of the initial impulse in Nature. Kashmir Shaivism is a philosophical system based on the Siva sutra, which is one of the texts of that vast body of Indian literature called the Tantras. There is probably no body of traditional literature that has suffered such widespread criticism, from Western and Eastern scholars alike, as the Tantras, due mainly to their esoteric character which made it impossible for scholars to obtain adequate information of their true content. The ban on their investigation was finally removed by the fruitful labours of the late Sir John Woodroffe, the first to defend the outraged Tantras, and now the field of Tantrik literature can be intelligently investigated. For a correct and complete understanding of Indian culture, it is imperative that this body of traditional literature is properly understood; therefore, a brief outline of their position in the history of Hindu thought will be helpful.

Kashmir Shaivism, or Trika Shaivism, is as nondualist tradition of Shaiva-Shakta Tantra which originated sometime after 850 CE. Though this tradition was very influential in Kashmir and is thus often called Kashmir Shaivism, it was actually a pan-Indian movement termed "Trika" by its great exegete, Abhinavagupta, which also flourished in Orissa and Maharashtra. Defining features of the Trika tradition are its idealistic and monistic Pratyabhijna ("Recognition") philosophical system, propounded by Utpaladeva (c. 925–975 CE) and Abhinavagupta (c. 975–1025 CE), and the centrality of the three goddesses Para, Parapara, and Apara.

While Trika draws from numerous Shaiva texts, such as the Shaiva Agamas and the Shaiva and Shakta Tantras, its major scriptural authorities are the Mālinīvijayottara Tantra, the Siddhayogeśvarīmata and the Anāmaka-tantra. Its main exegetical works are those of Abhinavagupta, such as the Tantraloka, Mālinīślokavārttika, and Tantrasāra which are formally an exegesis of the Mālinīvijayottara Tantra, although they also drew heavily on the Kali-based Krama subcategory of the Kulamārga. Another important text of this tradition is the Vijñāna-bhairava-tantra, which focuses on outlining numerous yogic practices.

Kashmir Shaivism claimed to supersede Shaiva Siddhanta, a dualistic tradition which scholars consider normative tantric Shaivism. The Shaiva Siddhanta goal of becoming an ontologically distinct Shiva (through Shiva's grace) was replaced by recognising oneself as Shiva who, in Kashmir Shaivism's monism, is the entirety of the universe.

19.1.1 History of Kashmir Shaivism

It is said that Lord Shiva Himself felt the need to resolve conflicting interpretations of the Agamas and counter the encroachment of dualism on the ancient monistic doctrines. In the early 800s, Shri Vasugupta was living on Mahadeva Mountain near Srinagar. Tradition states that one night Lord Siva appeared to him in a dream and told him of the whereabouts of a great scripture carved in rock. Upon awakening, Vasugupta rushed to the spot and found seventy-seven terse sutras etched in stone, which he named the Siva Sutras. Vasugupta expounded the Sutras to his followers, and gradually the philosophy spread. On this scriptural foundation arose the school known as Kashmir Shaivism, Northern Shaivism, Pratyabhijna Darshana ("recognition school"), or Trikashasana ("Trika system"). Trika, "three," refers to the school's three-fold treatment of the Divine: Shiva, Shakti and Soul, as well as to the three sets of scriptures and a number of other triads.

Kashmir Shaivism is a system of idealistic monism based on the Shiva sutra. It derives its name from the tradition that the Shiva sutra was supposedly revealed in Kashmir by Shiva himself. Because this system deals with the three-fold principle of God, Soul, and Matter, it is also called Triksiisana, Trikasastra or simply Trika. The terms Kashmir Shaivism and Trika may be used interchangeably.

The Father of Kashmir Shaivism was Vasugupta to whom the Shiva sutra is assigned. There are several accounts relating how the Shiva sutra was revealed to Vasugupta, but in no instance is it to be understood that Shiva materialised and whispered it into the ear of Vasugupta; instead, it means that Vasugupta received the sutras by inspiration rather than by intellectual analysis. That is, after a lifetime devoted to study and meditation, he finally awakened the inner depths of consciousness through the practice of Yoga and saw reality in all its fullness. Afterwards he recorded his experience much in the same way as a traveller returning from a foreign land leaves a written account of his journey.

Little is known of the life of Vasugupta aside from the fact that he lived during the end of the 8th century and the beginning of the 9th century. His retirement was spent in a small hermitage below the holy Mahadeva peak in the lovely valley of the Harwan stream behind the Shalimar garden near Srinagar, the capital of Kashmir.

Kashmir Shaivism, with its potent stress on man's recognition of an already existing oneness with Shiva, is the most single-mindedly monistic of the six schools. It arose in the ninth century in Northern India, then a tapestry of small feudal kingdoms. Maharajas patronised the various religions. Dating from around 850–900 CE, the Shiva Sutras and Spanda karika were the first attempt from the Śākta Śaiva domain to present a non-dualistic metaphysics and gnostic soteriology in opposition to the dualistic exegesis of the Shaiva Siddhanta. The Shiva Sutras appeared to Vasugupta in a dream, according to tradition. The Spanda karika was either composed by Vasugupta or his student Bhatta Kallata. Somananda, the first theologian of monistic Shaivism, was the teacher of Utpaladeva, who was the grand-teacher of Abhinavagupta, who in turn was the teacher of Kshemaraja.

19.1.2 Abhinavagupta

Abhinavagupta (c. 950 – 1016 CE) was a philosopher, mystic and aesthetician from Kashmir. He was also considered as an influential musician, poet, dramatist, exegete, theologian, and logician – a polymathic personality who exercised strong influences on Indian culture.

Abhinavagupta was born in a Kashmiri Brahmin family of scholars and mystics and studied all the schools of philosophy and art of his time under the guidance of as many as fifteen (or more) teachers and gurus. In his long life he completed over 35 works, the largest and most famous of which is Tantraloka, an encyclopaedic treatise on all the philosophical and practical aspects of Kaula and Trika (known today as Kashmir Shaivism). Another one of his very important contributions was in the field of philosophy of aesthetics with his famous Abhinavabhāratī commentary of Nāṭyaśāstra of Bharata Mun.

The Tantrāloka, Mālinīślokavārttika, and Tantrasāra of the Kashmirian Abhinavagupta (975–1025 CE) are formally an exegesis (critical explanation or interpretation of a text) on the Mālinīvijayottara Tantra, although they also drew heavily on the Kali-based Krama tradition of the Kulamārga. Jayaratha (1150–1200 CE) wrote a commentary on the Tantrāloka.

19.1.3 20th century revival of Kashmir Shaivism (Swami Lakshman Joo)

There were no major writers or publications after approximately the 14th century. In the 20th century **Swami Lakshman Joo**, a Kashmiri Hindu, helped revive both the scholarly and yogic streams of Kashmir Shaivism. His contribution is enormous. He inspired a generation of scholars who made Kashmir Shaivism a legitimate field of inquiry within the academy.

Lakshman Joo was born in the city of Srinagar in Kashmir. He was the fifth child in a household of four boys and five girls. His father, Narayandas ("Nav Narayan") Raina, was the first person to have introduced houseboats in the Kashmir Valley. His mother's name was Arnyamali Raina. At the age of five he was introduced to the path of spirituality by his elder brother Maheshvaranath. Up to the age of eight his spiritual progress in the lineage of Kashmiri Shaivism was monitored by his family priest, Pandit Swami Ram Joo (1854-1915), and later by his chief disciple Swami Mehatab Kak (1870-1942). At the age of 19, it is said, he experienced a clear taste of Self-realisation. Shortly afterwards he left home, as he wrote, "in search of the Supreme" and moved to the famous ashram of Sadhamalyun (Sadhuganga) in Handwara. Persuaded by his father to return to Srinagar, he continued to study Sanskrit and Shaiva philosophy under the guidance of a scholar named Maheshwar Razdan.

In 1934-35, he moved to an isolated place above the village of Gupta Ganga near Nishat suburb of Srinagar where his parents built him a house. This was a place where Abhinavagupta had lived nine centuries before. In 1962, he moved down the hill to a place closer to the famous Dal Lake a few hundred meters from the Nishat Gardens. Around the age of 30 he travelled in India, spending time on a Mumbai beach and a short time with Mahatma Gandhi at Sevagram and then with Sri Aurobindo at Pondicherry. From there he found his way to Tiruvannamalai to meet Ramana Maharshi. There he spent some weeks and later commented; "I felt those golden days were indeed divine".

Little was known about Swami Lakshman Joo for almost three decades (1930-1960), as it was his habit to spend the winter months in silence and seclusion. Still, in the summer he had occasional visits from both scholars and saints. The Indian Spiritual Master Meher Baba visited his ashram in 1944. In 1948, Lilian Silburn from the National Centre for Scientific Research, Paris, visited the Swami. She would return regularly for the next ten years, during which time she studied the major texts of Kashmir Shaiva philosophy, all of which were published in French. It was through Silburn that André Padoux, another prolific scholar of Kashmir Shaivism came to meet the Swami. Paul Reps, the American artist, author and poet stumbled across the Ashram in 1957. With Swami Lakshman Joo he studied the ancient text of Vijnana Bhairava Tantra, and later published the 112 practices of transcending in the fourth chapter of his book *Zen Flesh, Zen Bones*. This teaching also influenced Osho, and formed the basis of '*The Book of Secrets*'. It was a few years later, in 1965, after attending a Sanskrit conference in Varanasi, chaired by the renowned Sanskrit Tantra scholar Gopinath Kaviraj, that the word quickly spread that the tradition of Kashmir Shaivism was alive and well, and fully embodied in the person of Swami Lakshman Joo. Maharishi Mahesh Yogi visited the Swami each summer from 1966 to 1969. The two saints formed a lasting relationship. Baba Muktananda, of Siddha Yoga also visited on two occasions. Until his death in 1991, Swami Lakshman Joo freely taught, giving weekly lectures on the mystical and philosophical texts of Kashmir Shaivism. Many of these lectures were audio recorded by John Hughes and later published. Lakshman Joo's interpretation of Kashmir Shaivism attracted the attention of both Indian of western Indologists. The Swami has had correspondence with Professor Giuseppe Tucci of the University of Rome La Sapienza, and his regular visitors included scholars, such as, Jaideva Singh, Professor Nilkanth Gurtoo, Acharya Rameshwar Jha, Jankinath Kaul "Kamal", Raniero Gnoli, Alexis Sanderson and Mark Dyczkowski.

In 1991, the Swami travelled to the United States and established the Universal Shaiva Fellowship where he designated John Hughes and his wife Denise to continue publishing his teachings of Kashmir Shaivism. In India the teachings of Lakshman Joo are carried on by Ishwar Ashram Trust, an organisation founded shortly after his death.

Acharya Rameshwar Jha, a disciple of Lakshman Joo, is often credited with establishing the roots of Kashmir Shaivism in the learned community of Varanasi. Rameshwar Jha with his creativity, familiarity with the ancient texts and personal experiences, provided access to concepts of non-dualistic Kashmir Shaivism. His writings of Sanskrit verses have been published as the books '*Purnta Pratyabhijna*' and '*Samit Swatantram*'.

Swami Muktananda, although not belonging to the direct lineage of Kashmir Shaivism, felt an affinity for the teachings, validated by his own direct experience. He encouraged Motilal Banarsidass to publish Jaideva Singh's translations of Shiva Sutras, Pratyabhijnahrdayam, Spanda Karikas and Vijnana Bhairava, all of which Singh studied in-depth with Lakshman Joo. He also introduced Kashmir Shaivism to a wide audience of western meditators through his writings and lectures on the subject.

The **Vijnana Bhairava Tantra**, a chapter from the Rudrayamala Tantra, was introduced to the West by Paul Reps, a student of Lakshman Joo, by including an English translation in his book Zen Flesh, Zen Bones. Cast as a discourse between the God Shiva and his consort Devi or Shakti, it presents 112 meditation methods or centring techniques (dharanas).

19.1.4 Practice of Kashmir Shaivism

(i) Prerequisites: Since it is a Tantric tradition, a necessary prerequisite for Trika yogic practice is tantric initiation or diksha. The Mālinīvijayottara Tantra, a major source for the tradition, states: "Without initiation there is no qualification for Shaiva yoga." Although domesticated into a householder tradition, Kashmir Shaivism recommended a secret performance of Kaula practices in keeping with its tantric heritage. This was to be done in seclusion from public eyes, therefore allowing one to maintain the appearance of a typical householder. The Mālinīvijayottara Tantra outlines several major preconditions conferring the authority to practice Yoga:

The Yogin who has mastered posture [and] the mind, controlled the vital energy, subdued the senses, conquered sleep, overcome anger and agitation and who is free from deceit, should practise Yoga in a quiet, pleasant cave or earthen hut free from all obstructions.

(ii) Six Lakshyas: Numerous texts such as the Mālinīvijayottara Tantra also outline six "varieties of the goal" or "targets" (Lakshyas) of yogic practices, mainly:

(a) Contemplation of void (vyoman), which bestows all Perfections and Liberation.

(b) Contemplation of body (vigraha), which bestows the coercion of deities like Vishnu or Rudra.

(c) Contemplation of drop (bindu), which bestows sovereignty over Yogins.

(d) Contemplation of phoneme (varna), which bestows the Perfection of Mantra.

(e) Contemplation of world (bhuvana), which bestows regency of a world.

(f) Contemplation of resonance (dhvani), which leads to isolation and liberation.

Each of the goals is given specific practices. For example, in the Mālinīvijayottara Tantra, perfecting the Void is said to be reached by moving the mind and vital energy (through the use of mantric resonance) through two groups of three voids located along the central channel (which are also correlated with a system of six cakras), reaching to the region above the head. Different scriptures outline different lists of voids and their location in the body. The practice of resonance deals with various sounds, and how the yogin is to focus on a specific sound and its resonance within the central channel.

Regarding mantra, different Shaiva tantras and texts teach different mantras and bija (seed) mantras. These mantras are generally intoned (uccara) at different positions in the body along the central channel (such as at the heart, throat, forehead, etc). The Diksottara tantra for example, teaches the intonation of the 'hamsah' mantra, beginning in the heart region. Some texts teach "a lineal ascent through the heart, the throat, the palate, and the forehead, culminating with the transcendence of sonic experience as the 'Limit of Resonance' [nadanta] in the cranium is pierced." Other texts have the mantric energy follow the breath through the nose outside the body.

19.1.5 Yogas

Since Trika Shaivism is a synthesis of various traditions, its texts, like the Mālinīvijayottara Tantra, distinguishes **four different types** of Shaiva yoga. According to Somadev Vasudeva:

Two of these have been assimilated from the Tantras of the Siddhanta, the conquest of the reality-levels (tattvajaya), which has been transformed into a radically new type of yoga based on the fifteen levels of the apperceptive process, and, the yoga of six ancillaries (shaḍaṅgayoga), which is taken over with only minor variations. The third is Kaula yoga with its system of four immersions (pindastha, padastha, rupastha and rupatita) and as a fourth may be counted as the three types of possession (avesa) taught in the Trika (anava, sakta and sambhava), which are innovatively presented as three meta-categories under which all yogic exercises can be subsumed.

19.1.6 The conquest of the Tattvas

In Trika texts as well as those of other Shaiva schools, it is common to formulate the process of yogic conquest of the realities (tattvas) as a series of Dhāraṇās. Dhāraṇās ("introspections") are "complex sequences of meditative practices" which focus on a series of contemplations on a "hierarchy of apperceptive states designed to bring him ever closer to the level of the highest perceiver, Shiva". This hierarchy of meditations and visualisations is based on the Shaiva schema of the 36 tattvas. According to Somadev Vasudeva, the procedure can be described thus:

The Yogin starts by disengaging the mind from external stimuli and then fixes it upon a tattva [such as earth, water, etc] with ever-deepening absorption. He attains an internalised vision of the reality, and compares it with his authoritative, scriptural knowledge of the highest level. By means of Tarka [reasoning], an ontological value judgement, he discerns that it is different from Shiva and thus transcends it. The Yogin's ascension inevitably brings him to the reality which is Shiva at the zenith of all paths.

One example of the meditation on the tattva of buddhi (intellect) from the Mālinīvijayottara Tantra is as follows:

Contemplating in the heart, a lotus with colour of the rising sun, with eight petals containing the [eight bhavas] of dharma etc., and a pericarp, [the Yogin's] intellect becomes steady within a month. Within six, he becomes a knower of the Shruti (scripture). Within three years he himself becomes an author of scriptures. Contemplating his own [physical] form there (in the heart), he perceives the principle of intellect.

19.1.7 Yoga with six ancillaries (ṣaḍangayoga)

Trika yoga generally uses a system of six "limbs" or ancillaries (aṅgas) which are seen as subsidiary to the principal conquest of the tattvas. This system was adopted from the dualistic Saiva Siddhanta as well as in Pāñcarātra scriptures such as the Jayakhyasamhita. According to Somadeva Vasudeva, in Trika, ṣaḍaṅgayoga "is to be understood as a collection of helpful or even indispensable yogic techniques which enable the prospective Yogin to achieve the required "coalescence" or "identification" (tanmayata, lit. the "consisting-of-that-ness") with the object of contemplation."

These **six subsidiaries** as outlined by the Mālinīvijayottara Tantra, are:

(i) **Prāṇāyāma**, control of the "breath" or "vital energy" (prana), includes various forms of inhalation, exhalation, kumbhaka, as well as proper posture (asana), defined as either lotus or some other seated posture. The practice of udgatha (eruption) is also taught, which is a "process whereby the retained air is propelled or launched upwards from the navel-region so that it strikes the head."

(ii) **Dhāranā** (fixations or concentrations). Four dharanas are taught: Fire, Water, Sovereign (defined as bindu and nada) and Nectar (fixating upon a lunar disc above the cranium which drops divine nectar into the central channel, filling the body).

(iii) **Tarka** (judgment or reasoning), defined as "the ascertainment of what is to be cultivated and what is to be rejected."

(iv) **Dhyāna** (meditation), defined as "attentive contemplation on Shiva" or "a focused stream of awareness directed towards the judged and thus accepted reality".

(v) **Samādhi**, a deep absorption that arises from prolonged (the text states 48 minutes) and "firmly established" meditation, in which the yogin "becomes as though non-existent. He reaches a state where he becomes as though dead, from which even intense sounds and other such [sense data] cannot rouse him."

(vi) **Pratyāhāra**, complete withdrawal of the mind.

In the Mālinīvijayottara Tantra (chapter 17), these are seen as six progressive steps leading to complete identification with the object of meditation. It is important to note that different Shaiva tantras outline different forms of the six ancillaries, and "there is no consensus as to their order, their definition or even their subdivisions" among the different tantras.

19.1.8 Yogic suicide

The practice of utkranti, also called "yogic suicide", is also taught in nondual Shaiva Tantras like the Mālinīvijayottara Tantra, which uses the vital energy rising through the central channel to end one's life and proceed to union with Shiva. The text says that this abandonment of the body can be done at the end of one's life, after one has mastered all that one has set out to achieve.

19.1.9 Four Upayas

To attain moksha, sādhana or spiritual practice is necessary. Kashmir Shaivism describes four major methods (upāyas):

(i) āṇavopāya, the method of the body,

(ii) śāktopāya, the method of the mind,

(iii) śāmbhavopāya, the method of consciousness,

(iv) anupāya the 'methodless' method.

Āṇavopāya - purification of the body

While most other paths observe offering incense and external objects to the deity, this path takes on to offering breaths. The individual controls his heart and pulse by reducing it significantly. The final stage is renouncing consumption of food and water. As a result, he/she connects the state of the supreme in the form of Shiva which results in purification of the body and generation of ojas.

19.1.10 Influences and major exponents

The philosophy of Trika Shaivism is called Pratyabhijñā (Recognition) and it is mainly a nondual idealistic and monistic theism. It is influenced by the works of the Shaiva monist Vasugupta (c. 800–850 CE) and numerous Shaiva scriptures such as the Agamas and Shaiva-Shakta Tantras. The Trika philosophical system of Pratyabhijñā is presented in the works of Somānanda (c. 900–950 CE), Utpaladeva (c. 925–975 CE), Abhinavagupta (c. 975–1025 CE) and his disciple Kshemarāja (c. 1000–1050).

The philosophy of Pratyabhijñā (Recognition), as outlined by thinkers like Utpaladeva, teaches that though the identity of all souls is one with God (Isvara) or Shiva (which is the single reality, Being and absolute consciousness), they have forgotten this due to Maya or ignorance. However, through knowledge one can recognise one's authentic divine nature and become a liberated being. Another important element of Trika theology is the active and dynamic nature of consciousness, which is described as the spontaneous vibration or pulsation (spanda) of universal consciousness, which is an expression of its freedom (svātāntrya) and power (Shakti). Because of this, though this philosophy is idealist, it affirms the reality of the world and everyday life, as a real transformation (parinama), manifestation or appearance (ābhāsa) of the absolute consciousness. The Absolute is also explained through the metaphor of light (prakasha) and reflective awareness (vimarsha).

19.1.11 Non-duality in Kashmir (Trika) Shaivism

All that exists, throughout all time and beyond, is one infinite divine Consciousness, free and blissful, which projects within the field of its awareness a vast multiplicity of apparently differentiated subjects and objects: each object, an actualisation of a timeless potentiality inherent in the Light of Consciousness, and each subject the same plus a contracted locus of self-awareness. This creation, a divine play, is the result of the natural impulse within Consciousness to express the totality of its self-knowledge in action, an impulse arising from love. The unbounded Light of Consciousness contracts into finite embodied loci of awareness out of its own free will. When those finite subjects identify with the limited and circumscribed cognitions and circumstances that make up this phase of their existence, instead of identifying with the transindividual overarching pulsation of pure Awareness that is their true nature, they experience what they call "suffering." To rectify this, some feel an inner urge to take up the path of spiritual gnosis and yogic practice, the purpose of which is to undermine their misidentification and directly reveal within the immediacy of awareness the fact that the divine powers of Consciousness, Bliss, Willing, Knowing, and Acting comprise the totality of individual experience as well—thereby triggering a recognition that one's real identity is that of the highest Divinity, the Whole in every part. This experiential gnosis is repeated and reinforced through various means until it becomes the nonconceptual ground of every moment of experience, and one's contracted sense of self and separation from the Whole is finally annihilated in the incandescent radiance of the complete expansion into perfect wholeness. Then one's perception fully encompasses the reality of a universe dancing ecstatically in the animation of its completely perfect divinity.

This single supreme reality is also sometimes referred to as Aham (the heart). It is considered to be a non-dual interior space of Śiva, support for the entire manifestation, supreme mantra and identical to Śakti. In Kashmir Shivaism the highest form of Kali is Kalasankarshini who is Nirguna, formless and is often show as a flame above the head of Guhya Kali the highest gross form of Kali. In Nepali Newar arts, both form and formless attributes of Kali is often envisioned in a single art form showing the hierarchy of goddesses in their tradition. In it Guhya Kali image culminates in flame, with Kalasankarshini, the highest deity in the sequence, who consumes time within herself and is envisioned solely as a flame representing Para Brahman.

19.2 Three Broad Divisions: Agama, Spanda and Pratyabhijna Shastra

Kashmir (Trika) Shaivite literature is divided in three broad divisions: Agama Shastra, Spanda Shastra and Pratyabhijna Shastra. Agama Shastra includes works of divine origin: specifically, the Shaiva Agama literature, but also including Vasugupta's Shiva Sutras. The Spanda Shastra, or Spanda Karikas (of which only two sutras are left), are both attributed to Vasugupta's disciple Kallata (ca 850-900). These elaborate the principles of the Shiva Sutras. The Pratyabhijna Shastra's principal components are the Shiva Drishti by Vasugupta's disciple, Somananda, and the Pratyabhijna Sutras by Somananda's pupil, Utpaladeva (ca 900-950). Abhinavagupta (ca 950-1000) wrote some forty works, including Tantraloka, "Light on Tantra," a comprehensive text on Agamic Shaiva philosophy and ritual. It was Abhinavagupta, whose brilliant and encyclopaedic works established Kashmir Shaivism as an important philosophical school.

19.2.1 Agama Shastra

Agama Shastra is believed to be of divine origin. To this class chiefly belong the following works : Malini, Vijya or Vijayettara, Svacchanda Tuntram, Vijnana Bhairava, Ananda Bhairava (lost), Mrgendra, Matahga, Netra, Naishvasa, Svayambhuva, Rudra-yamala, Vidyarnava, etc. Shiva-sutras which were revealed later by the Sage Vasugupta are said to be the most important part of the Agama Shastra. The next two divisions of the Shaiva Shastra emerged as a result of development of human thought concerning the main Shastra of divine origin (Agama Shastra). The line of thought was developed by two acharyas Bhatta Kallata (9th century) and Somananda, contemporary of Vasugupta (850-900 AD), in two different directions while Kallata handed down the doctrine as a system of religion, Somananda supplied the logical reasoning in their support and thus founded a system of Advaita philosophy of the Shaivas on the basis of what was at first, taught as a system of faith. Thus, there appeared the other two Shastras.

19.2.2 Spanda Shastra

The original text belonging to this Shastra (Spanda-karika) and the literature that subsequently developed on it, have already been seen to be the work of Kallata. The Spanda-shastra lays down the main principles, as enumerated in the Shiva-sutras, in a greater detail and in a more amplified form, without giving philosophical reasonings in their support. In fact, the Spanda system owes its origin to the Shiva Sutras and concerns itself with their elucidation and popularisation. The author describes Spanda as that power of consciousness which infuses life into the physical senses. An object when sensed has no basis apart from consciousness. Spanda Karikas (verses) are 51 in number in which the fundamental principles of Shaivism, as aphoristically given in the Shiva Sutras, are epitomised. The basic idea underlying the Spanda-Shastra is that Shiva's Spanda (energy) out of its own nature manifests on the background of its own pure self the whole universe comprising the thirty-six tattvas (principles or categories of objective reality) from the earth up to Parama Shiva. According to this doctrine, the world is a play of energy force or vibration, which appears to be in conformity with the modern science. It is not an illusion, the result of error in perception (avidya) as the Vedantins suppose. Their doctrine that 'vishva yan-na tad eva brahma' (what is not the world, that is Brahman) is rejected by the Spanda school.

19.2.3 Pratybhijna Shastra

Kashmir was then a meeting ground of the various philosophical currents. It is from the concourse of the then prevailing thought-currents flowing from various schools of Buddhists, Vaidikas, the Shaivas and Shaktas, the Vaiyakaranas (Grammarians) the Samkhyas, the Naiyayikas, the Vedantins and the expounders of the Yoga system, that a monistic school of philosophy, distinctly known as Pratyabhijna Shastra emerged in the valley among the followers of Shaiva cult. The Kashmir Shaivas, the originators of the Pratyabhijna system, have incorporated in it most of the ideas from the said systems and have propounded their various doctrines in a technique of their own derived from the Shaivagamas, which distinguish the system from the other systems.

Somananda was indeed the founder of the Pratyabhijna School which takes its name from the 'Pratyabhijna karika' by Utpaladeva, the disciple of the former. The credit of being the founder of the school goes to Somananda, for the reason that it is he who, for the first time wrote a treatise (prakarana) on Shaiva philosophy. Utpaladeva was in fact the systematiser of Somananda's thought. Like Shankaracharya, a commentator of Badarayana's School of Vedanta, Abhinavagupta (another luminary among the celebrities of Kashluir Shaivism) gets the credit of being the expounder of Pratyabhijna system. His two commentaries: one short namely 'Vimarshini' and the other long (Vivrti-vimarshini), are on the 'Pratyabhijana Karika' of Utpaladeva. Somananda flourished in the later part of the ninth century AD, Utpaladeva in the first part of the tenth century and Abhinavagupta in the last part of the tenth and the first part of the eleventh century.

Notwithstanding his devotion to the secret doctrine of monistic Shaivagamas handed down to him traditionally from his ancestors, Somananda revolted against the prevailing schools of thought, including certain sections of Shaivas themselves. He summarily criticised the various schools of Buddhism, the Jainism, the Samkhya, the Nyaya and Vaiseshika, the Vaivakarana and the monistic Vedanta. It appears that Somananda was against the traditional ideas about the Divinity, the meaning and purpose of life, the human activities and behaviours on earth, the real significance of 'moksha' (salvation or liberation) and the like. Somananda seems to have conceived of re-interpreting religio-philosophic thought in vogue in his day and laid the foundation of a new school in its pristine purity, eclectic in its essence and containing the noble truths and glorious spiritual and humanistic values of ancient Vedantic thought. This new school came later to be known as 'Pratyabhijna School' (the doctrine of Recognition) after the title of the main treatise on the system, composed by Somananda's disciple Utpaladeva. The doctrine propounded in this school is indeed a reform and revaluation or reappraisal of Indian religio-philosophical thought.

The strict sense of the term 'Pratyabhijna' is recognition, but in the system, it comprehends the sense of awareness, consciousness, realisation, 'knowledge in practice' or practical use of knowledge. Pratyabhijna school thinks that man is ignorant (unaware) of the very nature of one's own Self (Shiva-Atman), viz. his inner being, the profounder faculty within him, and its power of 'Iccha' (Will), 'Jnana' (knowledge, Thought) and 'Kriya' (Action), viz., man's abilities with which he is endowed by Providence.

The school believes that the powers (Shaktis) or abilities with which man is born in this world, comprise his supreme (Divine) inheritance. It is only then, when he becomes aware of his Divine inheritance, that he can make the best use of it in making his life successful and felicitous.

Pratyabhijna is, in its essence, a deep and systematic study of man as microcosm and the world he lives in as macrocosm. In it, there is a perfectly scientific analysis of all the human faculties, man's entire physical, mental and spiritual organisms and that of the One Objective Reality (Parama Shiva) into thirty-six primary realities indispensable for the constitution of the universe and processes of creation, etc. The system being broad-based, tackles all the problems of human interest and lays great stress on the spiritual values of life. It is thus a school of 'Spiritual Pragmatism'.

Utpala, the second teacher of the system, tells us that the Pratyabhijna philosophy is revealed to him by the grace of the Lord (katham cit asadhya maheshvarasya dasyam), and it is for the good of humanity (janasya upakaram icchan) that he expounds the doctrine. He says with emphasis that man should recognise himself, viz., be aware of his inner being (Self) and his deeper faculties of 'knowledge' and 'action' (drkkriyatmika Sakti), if he desires to make his life all prosperous and blissful (samasta sampat samavapti hetum tat pratyabhijnam upapadayami). Our profounder faculties remain hidden from us due to lack of knowlege or experience and owing to innate forgetfulness (moha) on our part. The Prityabhijna is directed to removing the veil of ignorance from us and turning our attention towards the deeper faculties within us. The teacher believes that the faculties of thought and action comprise the very life of man (jnanam kriya hi bhutanam jivatam jivanam matam). In the real sense of the term, knowledge in that which is transformed into action, or practical use of which is made in one's life. Pratyabhijna says (hints) with emphasis that knowledge put into action or practice is really meaningful.

Conception of the macrocosm in the Pratyabhijna system is based on a very deep study of the microcosm. The system believes that 'Maheshvara', the Great Lord or Divine Father of all this creation, endowed with 'Mahesvarya' or 'Svatantrya-Shakti' (Sovereignty or Thought and Action) with which he executed the acts of creation, etc. of this orderly world. This 'Svatantrya-Shakti' or creative power of the Lord is two-fold, comprising 'Prakasha' and 'Vimarsha', viz. power of manifestation and power of perception or concretisation, functioning respectively as Universal Consciousness (Psychical Power) and Universal Energy (Physical Power or Objective Reality), technically called 'Shiva' and 'Shakti'. The former, i. e. Universal Consciousness assumes three forms: Power of Remembrance (Smrti-shakti), Power of Knowledge (Jnana-shakti) and Power of

Differentiation (Apohana-shakti). The latter, i.e. Universal Energy functions as Power of Action (Kriya- Shakti) of the Lord. This is governed by three universal laws of Nature - the law of Division (Bhedabheda), the law of Perception (Mana-tat-phala meya), and the law of Causation (Karsna karya). The Transcendental Lord (Vishvottirna) thus concretises or materialises Himself into this created world (becomes Vishvamaya, the cosmos) by evolving thirty-six 'Tattvas' or primary realities from the One Objective Reality, the primordial natural force principle or Prima Materia of all things. As the Lord is conceived to be endowed with Svatantrya-shakti, viz. Sovereignty of will and psychical and physical powers to make Him potent to execute all creative activity which accounts for the emanation of macrocosm with ever-new creations of infinite sentient and insentient beings from His Own Self or Being, so is every individual created being (as microcosm) endowed with its potential powers (faculties) of will, cognition and action, including psychical powers of remembrance, knowledge and differentiation (Smriti-shakti; Jnana-shakti and Apohana-shakti) and its physical powers (Kriya-shakti) as supreme inheritence from his Divine Father-Maheshvara to make him potent to perform all creative activity in his life time. It is 'recognition' or awareness and right use of one's divine faculties (supreme inheritence) with which man is born in this world that make his life felicitous and blissful (evam atmanam estasya samyag jnana - kriye tatha, janan yathepsitan pashyan janati ca karati ca). The fact is that the Self (being a spark of the divine) is the pivot of one's life and Self-recognition is the means of achieving one's all fortunes and success in life (samasta-sampat samavapti-hetum; janasya-ayatna siddhyartham).

Pratyabhijna is one of the greatest humanistic movements of Kashmir, which might well be called the 'Philosophy of Humanism'. It is a wonderful synthesis of nearly all earlier systems of India's philosophic thinking, and is completely free from 'negativism' and 'escapism' of certain schools of Vedantins and from the 'nihilism' of some Buddhist schools. It is most realistic in its attitude to life. It is a most dynamic system in which emphasis is laid on what is called Svatantrya, the complete autonomy of thought and action as the goal of life. It may also be called a school of Spiritual Pragmatism, because its doctrines have a practical bearing upon human interests, besides having its main direction to the spiritual elevation of humanity.

19.3 Tattvas in Kashmir Shaivism

The subject and object must be considered separately for the purpose of explanation, but it must always be borne in mind that they are both present, only one is more evident in the same way that a picture has two sides, a front and a back, but only one side can be seen at a time. These two factors are the first two tattvas in the process of cosmic evolution, and are technically called the Shiva Tattva and the Shakti Tattva.

19.3.1 Shiva Tattva

The first factor in the process of cosmic evolution is called the Shiva Tattva. The term Shiva is used to deify the ultimate condition of consciousness in its Immanent aspect for the purpose of worship. Consciousness in this condition is technically called Chit, the static aspect of consciousness in the manifest world. Consciousness must be considered here in the broadest possible sense of the term, as the power to know, to feel, and to act. Actually, there is no English equivalent for Chit. Only study and reflection will reveal its full connotation. By definition a manifestation necessitates a subject and object.

The Shiva Tattva is postulated to account for the Subject (Aham) of the dual relationship of universal manifestation. In this condition, consciousness is the subject, knower, experiencer; it is the static centre of all things; it is the static support of all things; it is the substratum of all change, as is the bed of a river. It can never be seen, but it can be known by its effects. In this condition the emphasis is on the Aham (I) without any awareness of the existence of Idam (This). It is pure consciousness; the ideal universe of perfect equilibrium has vanished, and consciousness has begun to stir. The Shiva Tattva is the Chit aspect of the universal condition of Sat-Chit-Ananda.

Since the Shiva Tattva represents the passive aspect of pure consciousness, it is dependent upon the active aspect of consciousness to bring it into being. To account for this aspect of consciousness, the next category is Postulated.

19.3.2 Shakti Tattva

The second factor in the process of cosmic evolution is called the Shakti Tattva. The term Shakti is derived from the root sak, “to be able, to be capable of”; therefore, the power of consciousness to act. It is the kinetic aspect of consciousness. By logical necessity the Shakti Tattva is postulated to account for the Object (Idam) of the dual relationship of universal manifestation. It accounts for the universal cause of all motion and change observed throughout the manifest world. Shakti is the universal stream of consciousness that brings all things into being and destroys all things at the end of each cycle of time. As Shiva is the Chit-aspect of the universal condition of Sat-Cit-Ananda, Shakti is the Ananda-aspect. When this condition is predominant, a condition of supreme bliss is experienced.

The Shakti Tattva represents the force that negates universal consciousness by producing a strain on the surface of consciousness. It polarises consciousness into the positive and negative, the Aham and Idam, the Subject and Object. It is the universal energy that brings all things into being, and, as such, it is considered as the feminine aspect of Nature, the Mother of the Universe.

The first two tattvas, Shiva Tattva and Shakti Tattva, are unproduced, and therefore, eternal. During the period of Pralaya, universal dissolution, they exist in the universal sea of pure consciousness in a state of equilibrium, ever ready to manifest once the balance is upset. Since they are unproduced, they are not considered as stages in the process of the evolution of consciousness. They are merely an appearance on the surface of consciousness as a swell on the surface of the ocean before the manifestation of a wave.

Shakti, Cosmic Energy, is said to have three principal modes to account for the three fundamental psychological steps that precede the determination of every action. They are technically called Iccha, the power of Will; Jnana, the power of Knowledge; and Kriya, the power of Action. One follows the other in logical succession; and with the predominance of each respective mode in the process of the evolution of consciousness, the first three tattvas produced come into being.

19.3.3 Sadashiva Tattva

The third stage in the process of cosmic evolution is called the Sadashiva Tattva. This term is compounded of sada, "always," and shiva, "happy or prosperous"; therefore, "always happy or prosperous." This stage is also called the Sadakhya Tattva, the state in which there is the first notion of Being.

By logical necessity, in any manifestation there must be a first step forward. The Sadashiva Tattva is postulated to account for that phenomenon in universal manifestation. It is, therefore, the first evolute of consciousness. As a produced thing, it must, by definition, have parts; those parts are the dual relationship of I am This. Here the emphasis is on the Aham (I). The subject (Aham) is said to become aware of itself in relation to its object (Idam). In the universal condition the entire experience is subjective, for there is no inner and outer, as in the world known to us.

This category accounts for the power of Universal Desire, technically called the Iccha Shakti, the Will-aspect of Shakti, or consciousness. It manifests itself as a vague and indistinct feeling, an undefined and unformulated idea that eludes the mind. It is the condition that precedes any determinate action. It is referred to as the state of Divine Wonder. As produced tattva, it is destructible, and, therefore, not eternal. As the first evolute produced in the process of the evolution of consciousness, it is the last evolute dissolved in the involution of consciousness at the time of universal reabsorption.

19.3.4 Ishvara Tattva

The fourth stage in the process of cosmic evolution is called the Ishvara Tattva. The term Ishvara means "Lord." It is used to deify that condition in Nature when all is recognised as One. This tattva is postulated to account for that condition when the subject (Aham) recognises the object (Idam). Here the relationship is This am I, with the emphasis on the This (Idam). It is the stage of complete self-identification, as when one awakens from a sound sleep. Here This (Idam) is said to emerge into full view, and the Divine Glory of his being is recognised. This category accounts for the power of Universal Knowledge, technically called the Jnana Shakti, the Knowledge-aspect of Shakti, or consciousness. It is knowledge as such without reference to any emotion; it is pure awareness without reaction. There is no desire to go toward or away. It is the knowledge that precedes ultimate action.

19.3.5 Sadvidya Tattva

The fifth stage of cosmic evolution is called the Sadvidya Tattva. This term is compounded of sat, "true," and vid, "to know," and means to have true knowledge. It is also called Buddha Vidya Tattva, meaning the tattva of pure knowledge. This tattva is postulated to account for the complete unity in the dual relationship of I am This. It is, therefore, the condition of complete recognition without emphasis either on the subject (Aham) or on the object (Idam). This category accounts for power of universal action, technically called Kriya Shakti, the Action-aspect of Shakti, or consciousness. In the preceding tattvas, action has been absent. In the Sadashiva Tattva, consciousness was lost in the ecstasy of divine wonder while embracing Itself as the subject (Aham); in the Ishvara Tattva, consciousness was overcome by exaltation while gazing at Itself as the object (Idam). In the Sadvidya Tattva, consciousness looks first at Aham (I) and then at ldam (This), which necessitates movement; therefore, this tattva is said to manifest that aspect of universal consciousness that creates all things.

The first five tattvas, from Shiva Tattva to Sadvidya Tattva, are classified for the purpose of worship as the Pure category (Shuddha Tattva). They represent the manifestation of the universal aspect of consciousness in contrast to the limited aspect to follow. They are called Pure because the dual relationship of subject and object is a single unit, that is, the object is seen as a part of the subject. In the condition to follow, the subject and object are separated, so that the object is seen as something separate and apart from the subject. The force that separates them is another mode of Shakti, the active aspect of consciousness. This force is technically called Maya Shakti, the power of consciousness to separate and divide.

19.3.6 Maya Tattva and its Evolutes

The sixth category in the process of cosmic evolution is called the Maya Tattva. The term Maya means "delusion." Here it is used to mean the veiling, obscuring force of Nature. As such, it displays universal consciousness as a duality. The category of Maya is postulated to account for the manifestation of form out of the formless, the finite out of the infinite. The same principle was postulated in the Vedanta system, but there it was said to be not real or not unreal, that is, not part of the Ultimate, yet not something else. In this doctrine, Kashmir Shaivism, Maya is considered not as a separate reality, but as the gross power of consciousness, and is referred to as Maya Shakti. During the period of universal dissolution (Pralaya), it is in its subtle aspect. At no time is it ever non-existent; it is merely non-active, that is, dormant; therefore, it is eternal and unproduced.

Maya is defined as the finitising principle, that which limits the universal conditions of consciousness and produces the states of limited experience. It is said to cast asunder the Divine Unity of the Godhead and brings Mind and Matter into being. The reason why Maya exerts its influence at this stage is found in the law of Nature that every period of action is followed by a period of rest, as witnessed by the fact that sleep always follows action. When Nature goes to sleep after the experience of universal manifestation, the five evolutes of Maya appear; therefore, the world of limited experience is the cosmic dream of nature.

The five evolutes of Maya are Kaala, Niyati, Raga, Vidya, and Kala.

19.4 Advaita Vedanta of Adi Shankara vs Kashmir Shaivism

Both, Advaita Vedanta of Adi Shankara and Kashmir Shaivism, advocate monism. Fundamentally, they have a single conception, but each develops it individually to suit particular minds. The physical reason for their individual development, apart from that of the mental, may be due to the historical background and geographical situation of each.

Badarayana, probably, founded Vedanta in the plains of India while Durvasa expounded Kashmir (Trika) Shaivism in the Himalayan ranges, the two being sober and sentimental respectively. Vedanta is an enquiry into the nature of the Ultimate Reality while Shaivism discusses the nature of this Ultimate Reality and explains the cause of the initial impulse in nature. The sources of Vedanta are Vedas and those of Shaivism are the Tantras, which give supplementary explanations to Vedic thought. Both are said to be of divine authorship. No doubt, they are the revelations favoured to great sages and seers of this ancient land. But neither objects the postulates of either of these.

Both of these evolved philosophies seem to have had prevailed in this beautiful land of Kashmir since the very early times, that is, the first century AD or earlier. This is evident from a keen observation of the performances of daily and occasional rites and rituals by the Kashmiri Pandits even up to this day. Hymns from the Vedas and recitations from the Tantras are included in all kinds of such performances, simultaneously. Even later hymns like Mukundamala- a hymn to Lord Vishnu, and Sivamahimnastotram- a hymn to Lord Siva - the supreme deities of the two philosophies, are recited and worship offered simultaneously by devotees in traditional way. By this we understand that people in this land of Kashyap have from the very early times been accommodating perhaps because of their gift of intelligence from Nature. They always assimilated what came their way. Thus, the old religion here seems to have been polytheistic, of course, with special inclination towards ritualistic Shaivism.

Kula system of Shaivism, advocating the highest form of Shiva had been introduced here in the fourth century AD Krama system of Shaivism, connected with Raja-Yoga, and Kundalini Yoga, which stress that vital air and mind are interdependent, also had been introduced here early.

Then, Shankaracharya (788-820 AD) visited this valley in the first two decades of the ninth century. He only re-established the true faith of Upanishads called the Vedanta. To check further deterioration caused by the split in Buddhism, he explained the Upanishads in a system on the basis of Brahma Sutras in its commentary. He gave Vedanta Philosophy the right footing when he wrote his valuable commentaries on the ten principal Upanishads and the Bhagavad-Gita. He composed a number of hymns to different deities like Saraswati. Krishna, Skanda and so on, to give the unilateral direction to multifarious faiths in the whole country. He gave practical instructions that worship of different deities leads to the same goal, the Ultimate Truth on realisation.

SECTION - 3: BUDDHIST PHILOSOPHY

Chapter - 20

Introduction to Buddhist Philosophy

Buddhism

Buddhism is a religion originated from India, which is based on a series of original teachings attributed to Gautama Buddha. It originated in ancient India as a Sramana tradition sometime between the 6th and 4th centuries BCE, spreading through much of Asia. It is the world's fourth-largest religion with over 520 million followers, or over 7% of the global population, known as Buddhists. Buddhism encompasses a variety of traditions, beliefs and spiritual practices largely based on the Buddha's teachings (born Siddhārtha Gautama in the 5th or 4th century BCE) and resulting interpreted philosophies.

As expressed in the Buddha's Four Noble Truths, the goal of Buddhism is to overcome suffering (dhukha) caused by desire and ignorance of reality's true nature, including impermanence (anicca) and the non-existence of the self (anatta). Most Buddhist traditions emphasise transcending the individual self through the attainment of Nirvana or by following the path of Buddhahood, ending the cycle of death and rebirth. Buddhist schools vary in their interpretation of the path to liberation, the relative importance and canonicity assigned to the various Buddhist texts, and their specific teachings and practices. Widely observed practices include meditation, observance of moral precepts, monasticism, taking refuge in the Buddha, the Dharma and the Sangha, and the cultivation of the Paramitas (perfections, or virtues).

Two major extant branches of Buddhism are generally recognised by scholars: Theravāda (Pali: "The School of the Elders") and Mahāyāna (Sanskrit: "The Great Vehicle"). Theravada has a widespread following in Sri Lanka and Southeast Asia such as Cambodia, Laos, Myanmar and Thailand. Mahayana, which includes the traditions of Zen, Pure Land, Nichiren Buddhism, Tiantai Buddhism (Tendai), and Shingon, is practiced prominently in Nepal, Malaysia, Bhutan, China, Japan, Korea, Vietnam, and Taiwan. Vajrayana, a body of teachings attributed to Indian adepts, may be viewed as a separate branch or as an aspect of Mahayana Buddhism. Tibetan Buddhism, which preserves the Vajrayana teachings of eighth-century India, is practiced in the countries of the Himalayan region, Mongolia, and Kalmykia. Historically, until the early 2nd millennium, Buddhism was also widely practiced in Afghanistan and Pakistan; it also had a foothold to some extent in other places including the Philippines, the Maldives, and Uzbekistan.

20.1 Gautama Buddha

Gautama Buddha, popularly known as the Buddha (also known as Siddhattha Gotama or Siddhārtha Gautama or Buddha Shakyamuni), was a Śramaṇa who lived in ancient India (c. 5th to 4th century BCE). He is regarded as the founder of the world religion of Buddhism, and revered by most Buddhist schools as a savior, the Enlightened One who rediscovered an ancient path to release clinging and craving and escape the cycle of birth and rebirth. He taught for around 45 years and built a large following, both monastic and lay. His teaching is based on his insight into the arising of duḥkha (the unsatisfactoriness of clinging to impermanent states and things) and the ending of duhkha—the state called Nibbāna or Nirvana (extinguishing of the three fires). He was born 480 BCE in Lumbini, Shakya Republic (present-day Nepal) (according to Buddhist tradition) and died in 400 BCE (aged 80) in Kushinagar, Malla Republic (present-day India) (according to Buddhist tradition). Name of his spouse was Yasodharā, and Child Rāhula; Parents Śuddhodana (father), Maya Devi (mother).

The Buddha was born into an aristocratic family in the Shakya clan but eventually renounced lay life. According to Buddhist tradition, after several years of mendicancy, meditation, and asceticism, he awakened to understand the mechanism which keeps people trapped in the cycle of rebirth. The Buddha then travelled throughout the Ganges plain teaching and building a religious community. The Buddha taught a middle path between sensual indulgence and the severe asceticism found in the Indian śramaṇa movement. He taught a training of the mind that included ethical training, self-restraint, and meditative practices such as jnana and mindfulness. The Buddha also critiqued the practices of Brahmin priests, such as animal sacrifice and the caste system.

A couple of centuries after his death he came to be known by the title Buddha, which means "Awakened One" or "Enlightened One". Gautama's teachings were compiled by the Buddhist community in the Vinaya, his codes for monastic practice, and the Suttas, texts based on his discourses. These were passed down in Middle-Indo Aryan dialects through an oral tradition. Later generations composed additional texts, such as systematic treatises known as Abhidharma, biographies of the Buddha, collections of stories about the Buddha's past lives known as Jataka tales, and additional discourses, i.e. the Mahayana sutras.

Besides "Buddha" and the name Siddhārtha Gautama (Pali: Siddhattha Gotama), he was also known by other names and titles, such as Shakyamuni ("Sage of the Shakyas").

In the early texts, the Buddha also often refers to himself as Tathāgata. the term is often thought to mean either "one who has thus gone" (tathā-gata) or "one who has thus come" (tathā-āgata), possibly referring to the transcendental nature of the Buddha's spiritual attainment.

A common list of epithets are commonly seen together in the canonical texts, and depict some of his spiritual qualities:

- Sammasambuddho – Perfectly self-awakened.
- Vijja-carana-sampano – Endowed with higher knowledge and ideal conduct.
- Sugata – Well-gone or Well-spoken.
- Lokavidu – Knower of the many worlds.
- Anuttaro Purisa-damma-sarathi – Unexcelled trainer of untrained people.
- Satthadeva-Manussanam – Teacher of gods and humans.
- Bhagavato – The Blessed one.
- Araham – Worthy of homage. An Arahant is "one with taints destroyed, who has lived the holy life, done what had to be done, laid down the burden, reached the true goal, destroyed the fetters of being, and is completely liberated through final knowledge."
- Jina – Conqueror. Although the term is more commonly used to name an individual who has attained liberation in the religion Jainism, it is also an alternative title for the Buddha.

The Pali Canon also contains numerous other titles and epithets for the Buddha, including: All-seeing, All-transcending sage, Bull among men, The Caravan leader, Dispeller of darkness, The Eye, Foremost of charioteers, Foremost of those who can cross, King of the Dharma (Dharmaraja), Kinsman of the Sun, Helper of the World (Lokanatha), Lion (Siha), Lord of the Dhamma, Of excellent wisdom (Varapañña), Radiant One, Torchbearer of mankind, Unsurpassed doctor and surgeon, Victor in battle, and Wielder of power.

While the earliest sources merely depict Gotama seeking a higher spiritual goal and becoming an ascetic or sramana after being disillusioned with lay life, the later legendary biographies tell a more elaborate dramatic story about how he became a mendicant. The earliest accounts of the Buddha's spiritual quest is found in texts such as the Pali Ariyapariyesanā-sutta ("The discourse on the noble quest." These texts report that what led to Gautama's renunciation was the thought that his life was subject to old age, disease and death and that there might be something better (i.e. liberation, nirvana). The early texts also depict the Buddha's explanation for becoming a sramana as follows: "The household life, this place of impurity, is narrow - the samana life is the free open air. It is not easy for a householder to lead the perfected, utterly pure and perfect holy life." Dharmaguptaka Vinaya and the Mahāvastu all agree that his mother and father opposed his decision and wept with tearful faces when he decided to leave.

Immediately after his awakening, the Buddha hesitated on whether or not he should teach the Dharma to others. He was concerned that humans were overpowered by ignorance, greed, and hatred that it would be difficult for them to recognise the path, which is "subtle, deep and hard to grasp." However, the god Brahmā Sahampati convinced him, arguing that at least some "with little dust in their eyes" will understand it. The Buddha relented and agreed to teach. According to Anālayo, it does not contain this story, but this event does appear in other parallel texts, such as in an Ekottarika-āgama discourse, in the Catusparisat-sūtra, and in the Lalitavistara.

After deciding to teach, the Buddha initially intended to visit his former teachers, Alara Kalama and Udaka Ramaputta, to teach them his insights, but they had already died, so he decided to visit his five former companions, on his way to Vārānasī (Benares), he met another wanderer, called Ājīvika Upaka. The Buddha proclaimed that he had achieved full awakening, but Upaka was not convinced and "took a different path".

The story continues with the Buddha reaching the Deer Park (Sarnath) (Mrigadāva, also called Rishipatana, "site where the ashes of the ascetics fell") near Vārānasī, where he met the group of five ascetics and was able to convince them that he had indeed reached full awakening.

20.2 Four Noble Truths – Dukkha and its Ending in Buddhism

The truth of dukkha is the basic insight that life in this mundane world, with its clinging and craving to impermanent states and things is dukkha, and unsatisfactory. Dukkha can be translated as "incapable of satisfying", "the unsatisfactory nature and the general insecurity of all conditioned phenomena"; or "painful." Dukkha is most commonly translated as "suffering," but this is inaccurate, since it refers not to episodic suffering, but to the intrinsically unsatisfactory nature of temporary states and things, including pleasant but temporary experiences. We expect happiness from states and things which are impermanent, and therefore cannot attain real happiness.

In Buddhism, dukkha is one of the three marks of existence, along with impermanence and anatta (non-self). Buddhism, like other major Indian religions, asserts that everything is impermanent (anicca), but, unlike them, also asserts that there is no permanent self or soul in living beings (anatta). The ignorance or misperception (avijjā) that anything is permanent or that there is self in any being is considered a wrong understanding, and the primary source of clinging and dukkha.

Dukkha arises when we crave (Pali: taṇhā) and cling to these changing phenomena. The clinging and craving produces karma, which ties us to samsara, the cycle of death and rebirth. Craving includes kama-tanha, craving for sense-pleasures; bhava-tanha, craving to continue the cycle of life and death, including rebirth; and vibhava-tanha, craving to not experience the world and painful feelings.

Dukkha ceases, or can be confined, when craving and clinging cease or are confined. This also means that no more karma is being produced, and rebirth ends. Cessation is nirvana, "blowing out," and peace of mind.

By following the Buddhist path to moksha, liberation, one starts to disengage from craving and clinging to impermanent states and things. The term "path" is usually taken to mean the Noble Eightfold Path, but other versions of "the path" can also be found in the Nikayas. The Theravada tradition regards insight into the four truths as liberating in itself.

20.3 The Cycle of Rebirth in Buddhism

20.3.1 Saṃsāra in Buddhism

Saṃsāra means "wandering" or "world", with the connotation of cyclic, circuitous change. It refers to the theory of rebirth and "cyclicality of all life, matter, existence", a fundamental assumption of Buddhism, as with all major Indian religions. Samsara in Buddhism is considered to be dukkha, unsatisfactory and painful, perpetuated by desire and avidya (ignorance), and the resulting karma. Liberation from this cycle of existence, nirvana, has been the foundation and the most important historical justification of Buddhism.

Buddhist texts assert that rebirth can occur in six realms of existence, namely three good realms (heavenly, demi-god, human) and three evil realms (animal, hungry ghosts, hellish). Samsara ends if a person attains nirvana, the "blowing out" of the afflictions through insight into impermanence and non-self.

20.3.2 Rebirth in Buddhism

Rebirth refers to a process whereby beings go through a succession of lifetimes as one of the many possible forms of sentient life, each running from conception to death. In Buddhist thought, this rebirth does not involve a soul or any fixed substance. This is because the Buddhist doctrine of anatta (Sanskrit: Anātman, no-self doctrine) rejects the concepts of a permanent self or an unchanging, eternal soul found in other religions.

The Buddhist traditions have traditionally disagreed on what it is in a person that is reborn, as well as how quickly the rebirth occurs after death. Some Buddhist traditions assert that "no-self" doctrine means that there is no enduring self, but there is avacya (inexpressible) personality (pudgala) which migrates from one life to another.

The majority of Buddhist traditions, in contrast, assert that vijñāna (a person's consciousness) though evolving, exists as a continuum and is the mechanistic basis of what undergoes the rebirth process. The quality of one's rebirth depends on the merit or demerit gained by one's karma (i.e. actions), as well as that accrued on one's behalf by a family member. Buddhism also developed a complex cosmology to explain the various realms or planes of rebirth.

Each individual rebirth takes place within one of the five realms according to Theravadins, or six according to other schools – heavenly, demi-gods, humans, animals, hungry ghosts and hellish.

In East Asian and Tibetan Buddhism, rebirth is not instantaneous, and there is an intermediate state (Tibetan "bardo") between one life and the next. The orthodox Theravada position rejects the intermediate state, and asserts that rebirth of a being is immediate. However, there are passages in the Samyutta Nikaya of the Pali Canon that seem to lend support to the idea that the Buddha taught about an intermediate stage between one life and the next.

20.3.3 Karma in Buddhism

In Buddhism, karma (from Sanskrit: "action, work") drives saṃāra – the endless cycle of suffering and rebirth for each being. Good, skillful deeds (Pāli: kushala) and bad, unskillful deeds (Pāli: akushala) produce "seeds" in the unconscious receptacle (ālaya) that mature later either in this life or in a subsequent rebirth. The existence of karma is a core belief in Buddhism, as with all major Indian religions, and it implies neither fatalism nor that everything that happens to a person is caused by karma.

A central aspect of Buddhist theory of karma is that intent (cetanā) matters and is essential to bring about a consequence or phala "fruit" or vipāka "result". However, good or bad karma accumulates even if there is no physical action, and just having ill or good thoughts creates karmic seeds; thus, actions of body, speech or mind all lead to karmic seeds. In the Buddhist traditions, life aspects affected by the law of karma in past and current births of a being include the form of rebirth, realm of rebirth, social class, character and major circumstances of a lifetime. It operates like the laws of physics, without external intervention, on every being in all six realms of existence including human beings and gods.

A notable aspect of the karma theory in Buddhism is merit transfer. A person accumulates merit not only through intentions and ethical living, but also is able to gain merit from others by exchanging goods and services, such as through dāna (charity to monks or nuns). Further, a person can transfer one's own good karma to living family members and ancestors.

20.4 Moksha and Nirvana in Buddhism

The cessation of the kleshas and the attainment of nirvana (nibbāna), with which the cycle of rebirth ends, has been the primary and the soteriological goal of the Buddhist path for monastic life since the time of the Buddha. The term "path" is usually taken to mean the Noble Eightfold Path, but other versions of "the path" can also be found in the Nikayas. In some passages in the Pali Canon, a distinction is being made between right knowledge or insight (sammā-ñāṇa), and right liberation or release (sammā-vimutti), as the means to attain cessation and liberation.

Nirvana literally means "blowing out, quenching, becoming extinguished". In early Buddhist texts, it is the state of restraint and self-control that leads to the "blowing out" and the ending of the cycles of sufferings associated with rebirths and re-deaths. Many later Buddhist texts describe nirvana as identical with anatta with complete "emptiness, nothingness". In some texts, the state is described with greater detail, such as passing through the gate of emptiness (sunyata) – realising that there is no soul or self in any living being, then passing through the gate of signlessness (animitta) – realising that nirvana cannot be perceived, and finally passing through the gate of wishlessness (apranihita) – realising that nirvana is the state of not even wishing for nirvana.

The nirvana state has been described in Buddhist texts partly in a manner similar to other Indian religions, as the state of complete liberation, enlightenment, highest happiness, bliss, fearlessness, freedom, permanence, non-dependent origination, unfathomable, and indescribable. It has also been described in part differently, as a state of spiritual release marked by "emptiness" and realisation of non-self.

While Buddhism considers the liberation from saṃsāra as the ultimate spiritual goal, in traditional practice, the primary focus of a vast majority of lay Buddhists has been to seek and accumulate merit through good deeds, donations to monks and various Buddhist rituals in order to gain better rebirths rather than nirvana.

20.5 Pratītyasamutpāda and Twelve Nidānas in Buddhism

Pratityasamutpada, also called "dependent arising, or dependent origination", is the Buddhist theory to explain the nature and relations of being, becoming, existence and ultimate reality. Buddhism asserts that there is nothing independent, except the state of nirvana. All physical and mental states depend on and arise from other pre-existing states, and in turn from them arise other dependent states while they cease.

The 'dependent arisings' have a causal conditioning, and thus Pratityasamutpada is the Buddhist belief that causality is the basis of ontology, not a creator God nor the ontological Vedic concept called universal Self (Brahman) nor any other 'transcendent creative principle'. However, Buddhist thought does not understand causality in terms of Newtonian mechanics, rather it understands it as conditioned arising. In Buddhism, dependent arising refers to conditions created by a plurality of causes that necessarily co-originate a phenomenon within and across lifetimes, such as karma in one life creating conditions that lead to rebirth in one of the realms of existence for another lifetime.

Buddhism applies the theory of dependent arising to explain origination of endless cycles of dukkha and rebirth, through Twelve Nidānas or "twelve links". It states that because Avidyā (ignorance) exists Saṃskāras (karmic formations) exists, because Saṃskāras exists therefore Vijñāna (consciousness) exists, and in a similar manner it links Nāmarūpa (sentient body), Ṣaḍāyatana (six senses), Sparśa (sensory stimulation), Vedanā (feeling), Taṇhā (craving), Upādāna (grasping), Bhava (becoming), Jāti (birth), and Jarāmaraṇa (old age, death, sorrow, pain). By breaking the circuitous links of the Twelve Nidanas, Buddhism asserts that liberation from these endless cycles of rebirth and dukkha can be attained.

20.6 Anātman and Śūnyatā in Buddhism

A related doctrine in Buddhism is that of anatta (Pali) or Anātman

(Sanskrit). It is the view that there is no unchanging, permanent self, soul or essence in phenomena. The Buddha and Buddhist philosophers who follow him such as Vasubandhu and Buddhaghosa, generally argue for this view by analyzing the person through the schema of the five aggregates, and then attempting to show that none of these five components of personality can be permanent or absolute. This can be seen in Buddhist discourses such as the Anattalakkhana Sutta.

"Emptiness" or "voidness" (Skt: Śūnyatā, Pali: Suññatā), is a related concept with many different interpretations throughout the various Buddhisms. In early Buddhism, it was commonly stated that all five aggregates are void (rittaka), hollow (tucchaka), coreless (asāraka), for example, as in the Pheṇapiṇḍūpama Sutta (SN 22:95). Similarly, in Theravada Buddhism, it often simply means that the five aggregates are empty of a Self.

Emptiness is a central concept in Mahāyāna Buddhism, especially in Nagarjuna's Madhyamaka school, and in the Prajñāpāramitā sutras. In Madhyamaka philosophy, emptiness is the view which holds that all phenomena (dharmas) are without any svabhava (literally "own-nature" or "self-nature"), and are thus without any underlying essence, and so are "empty" of being independent. This doctrine sought to refute the heterodox theories of svabhava circulating at the time.

20.7 The Three Jewels in Buddhism

All forms of Buddhism revere and take spiritual refuge in the "three jewels" (triratna): Buddha, Dharma and Sangha.

20.7.1 Buddhahood

While all varieties of Buddhism revere "Buddha" and "buddhahood", they have different views on what these are. Whatever that may be, "Buddha" is still central to all forms of Buddhism.

In Theravada Buddhism, a Buddha are someone who have become awake through their own efforts and insight. They have put an end to their cycle of rebirths and have ended all unwholesome mental states which lead to bad action and thus are morally perfected. While subject to the limitations of the human body in certain ways (for example, in the early texts, the Buddha suffers from backaches), a Buddha is said to be "deep, immeasurable, hard-to-fathom as is the great ocean," and also has immense psychic powers (abhijñā).

Theravada generally sees Gautama Buddha (the historical Buddha Sakyamuni) as the only Buddha of the current era. While he is no longer in this world, he has left us the Dharma (Teaching), the Vinaya (Discipline) and the Sangha (Community). There are also said to be two types of Buddhas, a sammasambuddha is also said to teach the Dharma to others, while a paccekabuddha (solitary buddha) does not teach.

Mahāyāna Buddhism meanwhile, has a vastly expanded cosmology, with various Buddhas and other holy beings (aryas) residing in different realms. Mahāyāna texts not only revere numerous Buddhas besides Sakyamuni, such as Amitabha and Vairocana, but also see them as transcendental or supramundane (lokuttara) beings. Mahāyāna Buddhism holds that these other Buddhas in other realms can be contacted and are able to benefit beings in this world. In Mahāyāna, a Buddha is a kind of "spiritual king", a "protector of all creatures" with a lifetime that is countless of eons long, rather than just a human teacher who has transcended the world after death. Buddha Sakyamuni's life and death on earth is then usually understood as a "mere appearance" or "a manifestation skillfully projected into earthly life by a long-enlightened transcendent being, who is still available to teach the faithful through visionary experiences."

20.7.2 Dharma

"Dharma" (Pali: Dhamma) in Buddhism refers to the Buddha's teaching, which includes all of the main ideas outlined above. While this teaching reflects the true nature of reality, it is not a belief to be clung to, but a pragmatic teaching to be put into practice. It is likened to a raft which is "for crossing over" (to nirvana) not for holding on to.

It also refers to the universal law and cosmic order which that teaching both reveals and relies upon. It is an everlasting principle which applies to all beings and worlds. In that sense it is also the ultimate truth and reality about the universe, it is thus "the way that things really are."

The Dharma is the second of the three jewels which all Buddhists take refuge in. All Buddhas in all worlds, in the past, present and in the future, are believed by Buddhists to understand and teach the Dharma. Indeed, it is part of what makes them a Buddha that they do so.

20.7.3 Sangha, Bodhisattva, and Arhat

The third "jewel" which Buddhists take refuge in is the "Sangha", which refers to the monastic community of monks and nuns who follow Gautama Buddha's monastic discipline which was "designed to shape the Sangha as an ideal community, with the optimum conditions for spiritual growth." The Sangha consists of those who have chosen to follow the Buddha's ideal way of life, which is one of celibate monastic renunciation with minimal material possessions (such as an alms bowl and robes).

The Sangha is seen as important because they preserve and pass down Buddha Dharma. The Sangha lives the teaching, preserves the teaching as Scriptures and teaches the wider community. Without the Sangha there is no Buddhism.

The Sangha also acts as a "field of merit" for laypersons, allowing them to make spiritual merit or goodness by donating to the Sangha and supporting them. In return, they keep their duty to preserve and spread the Dharma everywhere for the good of the world.

The Sangha is also supposed to follow the Vinaya (monastic rule) of the Buddha, thereby serving as a spiritual example for the world and future generations. The Vinaya rules also force the Sangha to live in dependence on the rest of the lay community (they must beg for food etc.) and thus draw the Sangha into a relationship with the lay community.

There is also a separate definition of Sangha, referring to those who have attained any stage of awakening, whether or not they are monastics. This sangha is called the āryasaṅgha "noble Sangha". All forms of Buddhism generally reveres these āryas (Pali: ariya, "noble ones" or "holy ones") who are spiritually attained beings. Aryas have attained the fruits of the Buddhist path. Becoming an arya is a goal in most forms of Buddhism. The āryasaṅgha includes holy beings such as bodhisattvas, arhats and stream-enterers.

In early Buddhism and in Theravada Buddhism, an arhat (literally meaning "worthy") is someone who reached the same awakening (bodhi) of a Buddha by following the teaching of a Buddha. They are seen as having ended rebirth and all the mental defilements. A Bodhisattva ("a being bound for awakening") meanwhile, is simply a name for someone who is working towards awakening (bodhi) as a Buddha. According to all the early Buddhist schools as well as Theravada, to be considered a Bodhisattva one has to have made a vow in front of a living Buddha and also has to have received a confirmation of one's future Buddhahood. In Theravada, the future Buddha is called Metteyya (Maitreya) and he is revered as a Bodhisatta currently working for future Buddhahood.

Mahāyāna Buddhism generally sees the attainment of the arhat as an inferior one, since it is seen as being done only for the sake of individual liberation. It, thus, promotes the Bodhisattva path as the highest and most worthwhile. While in Mahāyāna, anyone who has given rise to Bodhicitta (the wish to become a Buddha that arises from a sense of compassion for all beings) is considered a Bodhisattva, some of these holy beings (such as Maitreya and Avalokiteshvara) have reached very high levels of spiritual attainment and are seen as being very powerful supramundane beings who provide aid to countless beings through their advanced powers.

20.8 Four Noble Truths and Eightfold Path to Liberation in Buddhism

Even if we have never heard of the Buddha, at some level we already know the foundation of his teachings, which we call the Dharma: that in this life, there is suffering. The Buddha also taught the way to free ourselves from this suffering. The heart of these teachings is the Four Noble Truths and the corresponding commitments, which are:

Four Noble Truths:

1. There is suffering. We commit to understanding the truth of suffering.
2. There is a cause of suffering. We commit to understanding that craving leads to suffering.
3. There is an end to suffering. We commit to understanding and experiencing that less craving leads to less suffering.
4. There is a path that leads to the end of suffering. We commit to cultivating the path.

The Buddha taught that by living ethically, practicing meditation, and developing wisdom and compassion, we can end the suffering that is created by resisting, running from, and misunderstanding reality. We have found that these practices and principles can end the suffering of addiction.

The **Eightfold Path** helps us find our way in recovery and consists of the following:

1. Wise Understanding;
2. Wise Intention;
3. Wise Speech;
4. Wise Action;
5. Wise Livelihood;
6. Wise Effort;
7. Wise Mindfulness; and
8. Wise Concentration.

While the Noble Eightfold Path is best-known in Buddhism, a wide variety of paths and models of progress have been used and described in the different Buddhist traditions. However, they generally share basic practices such as sila (ethics), samadhi (meditation, dhyana) and prajña (wisdom), which are known as the three trainings. An important additional practice is a kind and compassionate attitude toward every living being and the world. Devotion is also important in some Buddhist traditions, and in the Tibetan traditions visualisations of deities and mandalas are important. The value of textual study is regarded differently in the various Buddhist traditions. It is central to Theravada and highly important to Tibetan Buddhism, while the Zen tradition takes an ambiguous stance.

An important guiding principle of Buddhist practice is the Middle Way (madhyamapratipad). It was a part of Buddha's first sermon, where he presented the Noble Eightfold Path that was a 'middle way' between the extremes of asceticism and hedonistic sense pleasures. In Buddhism, the doctrine of "dependent arising" (conditioned arising, pratītyasamutpāda) to explain rebirth is viewed as the 'middle way' between the doctrines that a being has a "permanent soul" involved in rebirth (eternalism) and "death is final and there is no rebirth" (annihilationism).

20.9 Theravada Path in Buddhism

Theravada Buddhism is a diverse tradition and thus includes different explanations of the path to awakening. However, the teachings of the Buddha are often encapsulated by Theravadins in the basic framework of the Four Noble Truths and the Eighthfold Path.

Some Theravada Buddhists also follow the presentation of the path laid out in Buddhaghosa's Visuddhimagga. This presentation is known as the "Seven Purifications" (satta-visuddhi). This schema and its accompanying outline of "insight knowledges" (vipassanā-ñāṇa) is used by modern influential Theravadin scholars, such Mahasi Sayadaw (in his "The Progress of Insight") and Nyanatiloka Thera (in "The Buddha's Path to Deliverance").

20.10 Mahayana Path in Buddhism

Mahāyāna Buddhism is based principally upon the path of a Bodhisattva. A Bodhisattva refers to one who is on the path to buddhahood. The term Mahāyāna was originally a synonym for Bodhisattvayāna or "Bodhisattva Vehicle."

In the earliest texts of Mahāyāna Buddhism, the path of a bodhisattva was to awaken the bodhicitta. Between the 1st and 3rd century CE, this tradition introduced the Ten Bhumi doctrine, which means ten levels or stages of awakening. This development was followed by the acceptance that it is impossible to achieve Buddhahood in one (current) lifetime, and the best goal is not nirvana for oneself, but Buddhahood after climbing through the ten levels during multiple rebirths. Mahāyāna scholars then outlined an elaborate path, for monks and laypeople, and the path includes the vow to help teach Buddhist knowledge to other beings, so as to help them cross samsara and liberate themselves, once one reaches the Buddhahood in a future rebirth. One part of this path are the pāramitā (perfections, to cross over), derived from the Jatakas tales of Buddha's numerous rebirths.

The doctrine of the bodhisattva bhūmis was also eventually merged with the Sarvāstivāda Vaibhāṣika schema of the "five paths" by the Yogacara school. This Mahāyāna "five paths" presentation can be seen in Asanga's Mahāyānasaṃgraha.

The Mahāyāna texts are inconsistent in their discussion of the pāramitās, and some texts include lists of two, others four, six, ten and fifty-two. The six paramitas have been most studied, and these are:

(i) **Dāna pāramitā:** perfection of giving; primarily to monks, nuns and the Buddhist monastic establishment dependent on the alms and gifts of the lay householders, in return for generating religious merit; some texts recommend ritually transferring the merit so accumulated for better rebirth to someone else.

(ii) **Śīla pāramitā:** perfection of morality; it outlines ethical behaviour for both the laity and the Mahayana monastic community; this list is similar to Śīla in the Eightfold Path (i.e. Right Speech, Right Action, Right Livelihood).

(iii) **Kṣānti pāramitā:** perfection of patience, willingness to endure hardship.

(iv) **Vīrya pāramitā:** perfection of vigour; this is similar to Right Effort in the Eightfold Path.

(v) **Dhyāna pāramitā:** perfection of meditation; this is similar to Right Concentration in the Eightfold Path.

(vi) **Prajñā pāramitā:** perfection of insight (wisdom), awakening to the characteristics of existence such as karma, rebirths, impermanence, no-self, dependent origination and emptiness; this is complete acceptance of the Buddha teaching, then conviction, followed by ultimate realisation that "dharmas are non-arising".

In Mahāyāna Sutras that include ten pāramitā, the additional four perfections are "skillful means, vow, power and knowledge". The most discussed pāramitā and the highest rated perfection in Mahayana texts is the "Prajna-paramita", or the "perfection of insight". This insight in the Mahāyāna tradition, states Shōhei Ichimura, has been the "insight of non-duality or the absence of reality in all things".

20.11 Common Buddhist Practices

20.11.1 Hearing and learning the Dharma

In various suttas which present the graduated path taught by the Buddha, such as the Samaññaphala Sutta and the Cula-Hatthipadopama Sutta, the first step on the path is hearing the Buddha teach the Dharma. This then said to lead to the acquiring of confidence or faith in the Buddha's teachings.

Mahayana Buddhist teachers such as Yin Shun also state that hearing the Dharma and study of the Buddhist discourses is necessary "if one wants to learn and practice the Buddha Dharma." Likewise, in Indo-Tibetan Buddhism, the "Stages of the Path" (Lamrim) texts generally place the activity of listening to the Buddhist teachings as an important early practice.

20.11.2 Refuge

Traditionally, the first step in most Buddhist schools requires taking of the "Three Refuges", also called the Three Jewels (Sanskrit: triratna, Pali: tiratana) as the foundation of one's religious practice. This practice may have been influenced by the Brahmanical motif of the triple refuge, found in the Rigveda 9.97.47, Rigveda 6.46.9 and Chandogya Upanishad 2.22.3–4. Tibetan Buddhism sometimes adds a fourth refuge, in the lama. The three refuges are believed by Buddhists to be protective and a form of reverence.

The ancient formula which is repeated for taking refuge affirms that "I go to the Buddha as refuge, I go to the Dhamma as refuge, I go to the Sangha as refuge." Reciting the three refuges, is considered not as a place to hide, rather a thought that "purifies, uplifts and strengthens the heart".

20.11.3 Śīla – Buddhist ethics

Śīla (Sanskrit) or sīla (Pāli) is the concept of "moral virtues", that is the second group and an integral part of the Noble Eightfold Path. It generally consists of right speech, right action and right livelihood.

One of the most basic forms of ethics in Buddhism is the taking of "precepts". This includes the Five Precepts for laypeople, Eight or Ten Precepts for monastic life, as well as rules of Dhamma (Vinaya or Patimokkha) adopted by a monastery.

Other important elements of Buddhist ethics include giving or charity (dāna), Mettā (Good-Will), Heedfulness (Appamada), 'self-respect' (Hri) and 'regard for consequences' (Apatrapya).

20.11.4 Five precepts in Buddhism

Buddhist scriptures explain the five precepts (Pali: pañcasīla; Sanskrit: pañcaśīla) as the minimal standard of Buddhist morality. It is the most important system of morality in Buddhism, together with the monastic rules.

The five precepts are seen as a basic training applicable to all Buddhists. They are:

(i) "I undertake the training-precept (sikkha-padam) to abstain from onslaught on breathing beings." This includes ordering or causing someone else to kill. The Pali suttas also say one should not "approve of others killing" and that one should be "scrupulous, compassionate, trembling for the welfare of all living beings."

(ii) "I undertake the training-precept to abstain from taking what is not given." This also covers fraud, cheating, forgery as well as "falsely denying that one is in debt to someone."

(iii) "I undertake the training-precept to abstain from misconduct concerning sense-pleasures." This generally refers to adultery, as well as rape and incest. It also applies to sex with those who are legally under the protection of a guardian. It is also interpreted in different ways in the varying Buddhist cultures.

(iv) "I undertake the training-precept to abstain from false speech." This includes "any form of lying, deception or exaggeration... even non-verbal deception by gesture or other indication... or misleading statements." The precept is often also seen as including other forms of wrong speech such as "divisive speech, harsh, abusive, angry words, and even idle chatter."

(v) "I undertake the training-precept to abstain from alcoholic drink or drugs that are an opportunity for heedlessness." Intoxication is seen as a way to mask rather than face the sufferings of life. It is seen as damaging to one's mental clarity, mindfulness and ability to keep the other four precepts.

Undertaking and upholding the five precepts is based on the principle of non-harming (Pāli and Sanskrit: ahiṃsa). The Pali Canon recommends one to compare oneself with others, and on the basis of that, not to hurt others. Compassion and a belief in karmic retribution form the foundation of the precepts. Undertaking the five precepts is part of regular lay devotional practice, both at home and at the local temple. However, the extent to which people keep them differs as per region and time. They are sometimes referred to as the śrāvakayāna precepts in the Mahāyāna tradition, contrasting them with the bodhisattva precepts.

The five precepts are not commandments and transgressions do not invite religious sanctions, but their power has been based on the Buddhist belief in karmic consequences and their impact in the afterlife. Killing in Buddhist belief leads to rebirth in the hell realms, and for a longer time in more severe conditions if the murder victim was a monk. Adultery, similarly, invites a rebirth as prostitute or in hell, depending on whether the partner was unmarried or married. These moral precepts have been voluntarily self-enforced in lay Buddhist culture through the associated belief in karma and rebirth. Within the Buddhist doctrine, these precepts are meant to develop mind and character to make progress on the path to enlightenment.

The monastic life in Buddhism has additional precepts as part of patimokkha, and unlike lay people, transgressions by monks do invite sanctions. Full expulsion from sangha follows any instance of killing, engaging in sexual intercourse, theft or false claims about one's knowledge. Temporary expulsion follows a lesser offence. The sanctions vary as per monastic fraternity (nikaya).

Lay people and novices in many Buddhist fraternities also uphold eight (asta shila) or ten (das shila) from time to time. Four of these are same as for the lay devotee: no killing, no stealing, no lying, and no intoxicants. **The other four precepts are:**

- No sexual activity;
- Abstain from eating at the wrong time (e.g., only eat solid food before noon);
- Abstain from jewellery, perfume, adornment, entertainment;
- Abstain from sleeping on high bed i.e. to sleep on a mat on the ground.

All eight precepts are sometimes observed by lay people on uposatha days: full moon, new moon, the first and last quarter following the lunar calendar. The ten precepts also include to abstain from accepting money.

In addition to these precepts, Buddhist monasteries have hundreds of rules of conduct, which are a part of its patimokkha.

20.11.5 Vinaya

Vinaya is the specific code of conduct for a sangha of monks or nuns. It includes the Patimokkha, a set of 227 offences including 75 rules of decorum for monks, along with penalties for transgression, in the

Theravadin tradition. The precise content of the Vinaya Pitaka (scriptures on the Vinaya) differs in different schools and tradition, and different monasteries set their own standards on its implementation. The list of pattimokkha is recited every fortnight in a ritual gathering of all monks. Buddhist text with vinaya rules for monasteries have been traced in all Buddhist traditions, with the oldest surviving being the ancient Chinese translations.

Monastic communities in the Buddhist tradition cut normal social ties to family and community, and live as "islands unto themselves". Within a monastic fraternity, a sangha has its own rules. A monk abides by these institutionalised rules, and living life as the vinaya prescribes it is not merely a means, but very nearly the end in itself. Transgressions by a monk on Sangha vinaya rules invites enforcement, which can include temporary or permanent expulsion.

20.12 Restraint and Renunciation

Another important practice taught by the Buddha is the restraint of the senses (indriyasamvara). In the various graduated paths, this is usually presented as a practice which is taught prior to formal sitting meditation, and which supports meditation by weakening sense desires that are a hindrance to meditation. The sense restraint is when one, "guards the sense doors in order to prevent sense impressions from leading to desires and discontent." This is not an avoidance of sense impression, but a kind of mindful attention towards the sense impressions which does not dwell on their main features or signs (nimitta). This is said to prevent harmful influences from entering the mind. This practice is said to give rise to an inner peace and happiness which forms a basis for concentration and insight.

A related Buddhist virtue and practice is renunciation, or the intent for desirelessness (nekkhamma). Generally, renunciation is the giving up of actions and desires that are seen as unwholesome on the path, such as lust for sensuality and worldly things. Renunciation can be cultivated in different ways. The practice of giving, for example, is one form of cultivating renunciation. Another one is the giving up of lay life and becoming a monastic (bhiksu or bhiksuni). Practicing celibacy (whether for life as a monk, or temporarily) is also a form of renunciation. Many Jataka stories such as the focus on how the Buddha practiced renunciation in past lives.

One way of cultivating renunciation taught by the Buddha is the contemplation (anupassana) of the "dangers" (or "negative consequences") of sensual pleasure (kāmānaṃ ādīnava). As part of the graduated discourse, this contemplation is taught after the practice of giving and morality.

Another related practice to renunciation and sense restraint taught by the Buddha is "restraint in eating" or moderation with food, which for monks generally means not eating after noon. Devout laypersons also follow this rule during special days of religious observance (uposatha). Observing the Uposatha also includes other practices dealing with renunciation, mainly the eight precepts.

For Buddhist monastics, renunciation can also be trained through several optional ascetic practices called dhutaṅga.

In different Buddhist traditions, other related practices which focus on fasting are followed.

20.13 Mindfulness and Clear Comprehension

The training of the faculty called "mindfulness" (Pali: sati, Sanskrit: smṛti, literally meaning "recollection, remembering") is central in Buddhism. Mindfulness is a full awareness of the present moment which enhances and strengthens memory. The Indian Buddhist philosopher Asanga defined mindfulness thus: "It is non-forgetting by the mind with regard to the object experienced. Its function is non-distraction." Sati is also an awareness of things in relation to things, and hence an awareness of their relative value.

There are different practices and exercises for training mindfulness in the early discourses, such as the four Satipaṭṭhānas (Sanskrit: smṛtyupasthāna, "establishments of mindfulness") and Ānāpānasati (Sanskrit: ānāpānasmṛti, "mindfulness of breathing").

A closely related mental faculty, which is often mentioned side by side with mindfulness, is sampajañña ("clear comprehension"). This faculty is the ability to comprehend what one is doing and is happening in the mind, and whether it is being influenced by unwholesome states or wholesome ones.

20.14 Meditation – Samādhi and Dhyāna

A wide range of meditation practices has developed in the Buddhist traditions, but "meditation" primarily refers to the attainment of samādhi and the practice of dhyāna (Pali: jhāna). Samādhi is a calm, undistracted, unified and concentrated state of consciousness. It is defined by Asanga as "one-pointedness of mind on the object to be investigated. Its function consists of giving a basis to knowledge (jñāna)." Dhyāna is "state of perfect equanimity and awareness (upekkhā-sati-parisuddhi)," reached through focused mental training.

The practice of dhyāna aids in maintaining a calm mind, and avoiding disturbance of this calm mind by mindfulness of disturbing thoughts and feelings.

20.14.1 Origins

The earliest evidence of yogis and their meditative tradition, states, is found in the Keśin hymn 10.136 of the Rigveda. While evidence suggests meditation was practiced in the centuries preceding the Buddha, the meditative methodologies described in the Buddhist texts are some of the earliest among texts that have survived into the modern era. These methodologies likely incorporate what existed before the Buddha as well as those first developed within Buddhism.

There is no scholarly agreement on the origin and source of the practice of dhyāna. Some scholars see the four dhyānas as a Buddhist invention. It is further argued by others that the Buddha learned dhyāna from brahmanical teachers.

Whatever the case, the Buddha taught meditation with a new focus and interpretation, particularly through the four dhyānas methodology, in which mindfulness is maintained. Further, the focus of meditation and the underlying theory of liberation guiding the meditation has been different in Buddhism. For example, the verse 4.4.23 of the Brihadaranyaka Upanishad with its "become calm, subdued, quiet, patiently enduring, concentrated, one sees soul in oneself" is most probably a meditative state. The Buddhist discussion of meditation is without the concept of soul and the discussion criticizes both the ascetic meditation of Jainism and the "real self, soul" meditation of Hinduism.

20.14.2 Four rupa-jhāna

Buddhist texts teach various meditation schemas. One of the most prominent is that of the four rupa-jhānas (four meditations in the realm of form), which are "stages of progressively deepening concentration". They are states of "perfect mindfulness, stillness and lucidity." They are described in the Pali Canon as trance-like states without desire. In the early texts, the Buddha is depicted as entering jhāna both before his awakening under the bodhi tree and also before his final nirvana.

The four rupa-jhānas are:

(i) **First jhāna:** The first dhyana can be entered when one is secluded from sensuality and unskillful qualities, due to withdrawal and right effort. There is pīti ("rapture") and non-sensual sukha ("pleasure") as the result of seclusion, while vitarka-vicara (thought and examination) continues.

(ii) Second jhāna: There is pīti ("rapture") and non-sensual sukha ("pleasure") as the result of concentration (samadhi-ji, "born of samadhi"); ekaggata (unification of awareness) free from vitarka-vicara ("discursive thought"); sampasadana ("inner tranquility").

(iii) Third jhāna: Here pīti drops away, and there is upekkhā (equanimous; "affective detachment"), and one is mindful, alert, and senses pleasure (sukha) with the body.

(iv) Fourth jhāna: A stage of "pure equanimity and mindfulness" (upekkhāsatipārisuddhi), without any pleasure or pain, happiness or sadness.

There is a wide variety of scholarly opinions (both from modern scholars and from traditional Buddhists) on the interpretation of these meditative states as well as varying opinions on how to practice them.

20.14.3 The Formless Attainments

Often grouped into the jhāna-scheme are four other meditative states, referred to in the early texts as arupa samāpattis (formless attainments). These are also referred to in commentarial literature as immaterial/formless jhānas (arūpajhānas). The first formless attainment is a place or realm of infinite space (ākāsānañcāyatana) without form or colour or shape. The second is termed the realm of infinite consciousness (viññāṇañcāyatana); the third is the realm of nothingness (ākiñcaññāyatana), while the fourth is the realm of "neither perception nor non-perception". The four rupa-jhānas in Buddhist practice, lead to rebirth in successfully better rupa Brahma heavenly realms, while arupa-jhānas lead into arupa heavens.

20.14.4 Meditation and insight

In the Pali canon, the Buddha outlines two meditative qualities which are mutually supportive: samatha (Pāli; Sanskrit: śamatha; "calm") and vipassanā (Sanskrit: vipaśyanā, insight). The Buddha compares these mental qualities to a "swift pair of messengers" who together help deliver the message of nibbana (SN 35.245).

The various Buddhist traditions generally see Buddhist meditation as being divided into those two main types. Samatha is also called "calming meditation", and focuses on stilling and concentrating the mind i.e. developing samadhi and the four dhyānas. Vipassanā, focuses on "the generation of penetrating and critical insight (paññā)".

There are numerous doctrinal positions and disagreements within the different Buddhist traditions regarding these qualities or forms of meditation. For example, in the Pali Four Ways to Arahantship Sutta (AN 4.170), it is said that one can develop calm and then insight, or insight and then calm, or both at the same time. Meanwhile, in Vasubandhu's Abhidharmakośakārikā, vipaśyanā is said to be practiced once one has reached samadhi by cultivating the four foundations of mindfulness (smṛtyupasthānas).

Scholars have argued that these two meditation types reflect a tension between two different ancient Buddhist traditions regarding the use of dhyāna, one which focused on insight-based practice and the other which focused purely on dhyāna. However, other scholars have disagreed with this "two paths" thesis, instead seeing both of these practices as complementary.

20.14.5 The Brahma-viharas

The four immeasurables or four abodes, also called Brahma-viharas, which are virtues or directions for meditation in Buddhist traditions, which helps a person be reborn in the heavenly (Brahma) realm. These are traditionally believed to be a characteristic of the deity Brahma and the heavenly abode he resides in.

The **four Brahma-vihara are:**

- **(i)** **Loving-kindness** (Pāli: mettā, Sanskrit**: maitrī**) is active good will towards all;
- **(ii)** **Compassion** (Pāli and Sanskrit: **karuṇā**) results from metta; it is identifying the suffering of others as one's own;
- **(iii)** **Empathetic joy** (Pāli and Sanskrit: **muditā**): is the feeling of joy because others are happy, even if one did not contribute to it; it is a form of sympathetic joy; and
- **(iv)** **Equanimity** (Pāli: upekkhā, Sanskrit: **upekṣā**): is even-mindedness and serenity, treating everyone impartially.

The Buddhist scriptures acknowledge that the four Brahmavihara meditation practices "did not originate within the Buddhist tradition". The Brahmavihara (sometimes as Brahmaloka), along with the tradition of meditation and the above four immeasurables are found in pre-Buddha and post-Buddha Vedic and Sramanic literature. Aspects of the Brahmavihara practice for rebirths into the heavenly realm have been an important part of Buddhist meditation tradition.

The Buddhist usage of the brahma-vihāra originally referred to an awakened state of mind, and a concrete attitude toward other beings which was equal to "living with Brahman" here and now. The later tradition took those descriptions too literally, linking them to cosmology and understanding them as "living with Brahman" by rebirth in the Brahma-world. The Buddha taught that "kindness – what Christians tend to call love – was a way to salvation."

20.15 Tibetan Tantric Practice and Vajrayana & Tantra Techniques

Some Buddhist traditions, especially those associated with Tantric Buddhism (also known as Vajrayana and Secret Mantra) use images and symbols of deities and Buddhas in meditation. This is generally done by mentally visualising a Buddha image (or some other mental image, like a symbol, a mandala, a syllable, etc.), and using that image to cultivate calm and insight. One may also visualise and identify oneself with the imagined deity. While visualisation practices have been particularly popular in Vajrayana, they may also found in Mahayana and Theravada traditions.

In Tibetan Buddhism, unique tantric techniques which include visualisation (but also mantra recitation, mandalas, and other elements) are considered to be much more effective than non-tantric meditations and they are one of the most popular meditation methods. The methods of Unsurpassable Yoga Tantra, (Anuttarayogatantra) are in turn seen as the highest and most advanced. Anuttarayoga practice is divided into two stages, the Generation Stage and the Completion Stage. In the Generation Stage, one meditates on emptiness and visualises oneself as a deity as well as visualising its mandala. The focus is on developing clear appearance and divine pride (the understanding that oneself and the deity are one). This method is also known as deity yoga (devata yoga). There are numerous meditation deities (yidam) used, each with a mandala, a circular symbolic map used in meditation.

In the Completion Stage, one meditates on ultimate reality based on the image that has been generated. Completion Stage practices also include techniques such as tummo and phowa. These are said to work with subtle body elements, like the energy channels (nadi), vital essences (bindu), "vital winds" (vayu), and chakras. The subtle body energies are seen as influencing consciousness in powerful ways, and are thus used in order to generate the 'great bliss' (maha-sukha) which is used to attain the luminous nature of the mind and realisation of the empty and illusory nature of all phenomena ("the illusory body"), which leads to enlightenment.

Completion practices are often grouped into different systems, such as the six dharmas of Naropa, and the six yogas of Kalachakra. In Tibetan Buddhism, there are also practices and methods which are sometimes seen as being outside of the two tantric stages, mainly Mahamudra and Dzogchen (Atiyoga).

20.16 Practice: Monks, Laity

Buddhism has been healthy, not only ordained but also more committed lay people have practiced formal meditation. Loud devotional chanting however, has been the most prevalent Buddhist practice and considered a form of meditation that produces "energy, joy, lovingkindness and calm", purifies mind and benefits the chanter.

Throughout most of Buddhist history, meditation has been primarily practiced in Buddhist monastic tradition, and historical evidence suggests that serious meditation by lay people has been an exception. In recent history, sustained meditation has been pursued by a minority of monks in Buddhist monasteries. Western interest in meditation has led to a revival where ancient Buddhist ideas and precepts are adapted to Western mores and interpreted liberally, presenting Buddhism as a meditation-based form of spirituality.

20.17 Prajñā, Bodhi, Kenshō, Satori, Subitism and Vipassana

Prajñā (Sanskrit) or paññā (Pāli) is wisdom, or knowledge of the true nature of existence. Another term which is associated with prajñā and sometimes is equivalent to it is vipassanā (Pāli) or vipaśyanā (Sanskrit), which is often translated as "insight". In Buddhist texts, the faculty of insight is often said to be cultivated through the four establishments of mindfulness.

In the early texts, Paññā is included as one of the "five faculties" (indriya) which are commonly listed as important spiritual elements to be cultivated. Paññā along with samadhi, is also listed as one of the "trainings in the higher states of mind" (adhicittasikkha).

The Buddhist tradition regards ignorance (avidyā), a fundamental ignorance, misunderstanding or mis-perception of the nature of reality, as one of the basic causes of dukkha and samsara. Overcoming this ignorance is part of the path to awakening. This overcoming includes the contemplation of impermanence and the non-self-nature of reality, and this develops dispassion for the objects of clinging, and liberates a being from dukkha and saṃsāra.

Prajñā is important in all Buddhist traditions. It is variously described as wisdom regarding the impermanent and not-self nature of dharmas (phenomena), the functioning of karma and rebirth, and knowledge of dependent origination. Likewise, vipaśyanā is described in a similar way, such as in the Paṭisambhidāmagga, where it is said to be the contemplation of things as impermanent, unsatisfactory and not-self.

Some scholars have argued that the idea that insight leads to liberation was a later development in Buddhism and that there are inconsistencies with the early Buddhist presentation of samadhi and insight. However, others have argued that insight is a key aspect of the early Buddhist process of liberation, which cooperates with samadhi to remove the obstacles to enlightenment (i.e., the āsavas).

In Theravāda Buddhism, the focus of vipassanā meditation is to continuously and thoroughly know how phenomena (dhammas) are impermanent (annica), not-Self (anatta) and dukkha. The most widely used method in modern Theravāda for the practice of vipassanā is that found in the Satipatthana Sutta. There is some disagreement in contemporary Theravāda regarding samatha and vipassanā. Some in the Vipassana Movement strongly emphasise the practice of insight over samatha, and other Theravadins disagree with this.

In Mahāyāna Buddhism, the development of insight (vipaśyanā) and tranquility (śamatha) are also taught and practiced. The many different schools of Mahāyāna Buddhism have a large repertoire of meditation techniques to cultivate these qualities. These include visualisation of various Buddhas, recitation of a Buddha's name, the use of tantric Buddhist mantras and dharanis. Insight in Mahāyāna Buddhism also includes gaining a direct understanding of certain Mahāyāna philosophical views, such as the emptiness view and the consciousness-only view. This can be seen in meditation texts such as Kamalaśīla's Bhāvanākrama ("Stages of Meditation", 9th century), which teaches insight (vipaśyanā) from the Yogācāra-Madhyamaka perspective.

20.18 Devotion in Buddhism

Most forms of Buddhism "consider saddhā (Skt: śraddhā), 'trustful confidence' or 'faith', as a quality which must be balanced by wisdom, and as a preparation for, or accompaniment of, meditation." Because of this, devotion (Skt. bhakti; Pali: bhatti) is an important part of the practice of most Buddhists. Devotional practices include ritual prayer, prostration, offerings, pilgrimage, and chanting. Buddhist devotion is usually focused on some object, image or location that is seen as holy or spiritually influential. Examples of objects of devotion include paintings or statues of Buddhas and bodhisattvas, stupas, and bodhi trees. Public group chanting for devotional and ceremonial is common to all Buddhist traditions and goes back to ancient India where chanting aided in the memorisation of the orally transmitted teachings. Rosaries called malas are used in all Buddhist traditions to count repeated chanting of common formulas or mantras.

Chanting is, thus, a type of devotional group meditation which leads to tranquility and communicates the Buddhist teachings.

In East Asian Pure Land Buddhism, devotion to the Buddha Amitabha is the main practice. In Nichiren Buddhism, devotion to the Lotus Sutra is the main practice. Devotional practices such as pujas have been a common practice in Theravada Buddhism, where offerings and group prayers are made to deities and particularly images of Buddha. Devotional worship has been a significant practice in Theravada Buddhism, and deep devotion is part of Buddhist traditions starting from the earliest days.

Guru devotion is a central practice of Tibetan Buddhism. The guru is considered essential and to the Buddhist devotee, the guru is the "enlightened teacher and ritual master" in Vajrayana spiritual pursuits. For someone seeking Buddhahood, the guru is the Buddha, the Dharma and the Sangha, wrote the 12th-century Buddhist scholar Sadhanamala. The veneration of and obedience to teachers is also important in Theravada and Zen Buddhism.

Chapter - 21

The Four Noble Truths and Eightfold Path

Of the three yanas in Buddhism, the first is the **Theravada path** which is often called the 'Hinayana.' 'Hinayana' literally means 'lesser vehicle' but this term should in no way be a reproach or be construed to in any way diminish the importance of these teachings. In fact, the teachings of the Hinayana are very important because they suit the capacities and development of a great number of students. If it weren't for these teachings, which are particularly appropriate for those with limited wisdom or diligence, many persons would never reach the Mahayana path. Without the Theravada teachings there would be no way for practitioners to enter the dharma because they would not have had a way to enter the Buddhist path. This path is similar to a staircase: the lower step is the first step. This doesn't mean it is not important or should be ignored because without these essential steps one can never gain access to the upper stories. It should be very clear that this term 'lesser' vehicle is in no way a pejorative term. It provides the necessary foundation on which to build. The fundamental teachings of the Theravada are the main subject matter of the first turning of the wheel of dharma. These teachings were given mainly in India in the town of Sarnath which is near the Indian city of Varanasi which is also called Benares. The main subject matter of these teachings were **the Four Noble Truths.**

21.1 The Four Noble Truths

The Four Noble Truths are the very foundation of the Buddhist teaching, and that is why they are so important. In fact, if you don't understand the Four Noble Truths, and if you have not experienced the truth of this teaching personally, it is impossible to practice Buddha Dharma. In Buddhism, the Four Noble Truths ("The four Arya Satyas") are "the truths of the Noble Ones", the truths or realities for the "spiritually worthy ones".

The truths are:

(i) **Dukkha** (suffering, incapable of satisfying, painful) is an innate characteristic of existence in the realm of samsara;

(ii) **Samudaya** (origin, arising) of this dukkha, which arises or "comes together" with taṇhā ("craving, desire or attachment");

(iii) **Nirodha** (cessation, ending) of this dukkha can be attained by the renouncement or letting go of this taṇhā;

(iv) **Marga** (path, Noble Eightfold Path) is the path leading to renouncement of tanha and cessation of dukkha.

They are traditionally identified as the first teaching given by the Buddha, and considered one of the most important teachings in Buddhism.

In the Uttaratantra, Maitreya states that there are four stages to curing an illness. Just as the disease need be diagnosed, its cause eliminated, a healthy state achieved and the remedy implemented, so also should suffering, its causes, its cessation and the path be known, removed, attained and undertaken.

Maitreya uses the analogy of a sick person to explain the way in which realisations based on the Four Noble Truths can be attained. In order for a sick person to get well, the first step is that he or she must know that he is ill, otherwise the desire to be cured will not arise. Once you have acknowledged that you are sick, then naturally you will try to find about what led to it and what makes your condition even worse. When you have identified these, you will gain an understanding of whether or not the illness can be cured, and a wish to be free from the illness will arise in you. In fact, this is not is not just a mere wish, because once you have recognised the conditions that led to your illness, your desire to be free of it will be much stronger since that knowledge will give you a confidence and conviction that you can overcome the illness. With that conviction, you will want to take all the medications and remedies necessary. In the same way, unless you know that you are suffering, your desire to be free from suffering will not arise in the first place. So the first step we must take as practicing is to recognise our present state as duhkha or suffering, frustration and unsatisfactoriness. Only then will we wish to look into the causes and conditions that give rise to suffering. It is very important to understand the context of the Buddhist emphasis on recognising that we are all in a state of suffering, otherwise there is a danger we could misunderstand the Buddhist outlook, and think that it involves rather morbid thinking, a basic pessimism and almost an obsessiveness about the reality of suffering. The reason why Buddha laid so much emphasis on developing insight into the nature of suffering is because there is an alternative - there is a way out, it is actually possible to free oneself from it.

This is why it is so crucial to realise the nature of suffering, because the stronger and deeper your insight into suffering is, the stronger your aspiration to gain freedom from it becomes. So the Buddhist emphasis on the nature of suffering should be seen within this wider perspective, where there is an appreciation of the possibility of complete freedom from suffering. If we had no concept of liberation, then to spend so much time reflecting on suffering would be utterly pointless.

The four truths appear in many grammatical forms in the ancient Buddhist texts, and they have both a symbolic and a propositional function. Symbolically, they represent the awakening and liberation of the Buddha, and of the potential for his followers to reach the same spiritual experience as him. As propositions, the Four Truths are a conceptual framework that appear in the Pali canon and early Hybrid Sanskrit Buddhist scriptures. They are a part of the broader "network of teachings" (the "dhamma matrix"), which have to be taken together. They provide a conceptual framework for introducing and explaining Buddhist thought, which has to be personally understood or "experienced".

As a proposition, the four truths defy an exact definition, but refer to and express the basic orientation of Buddhism: unguarded sensory contact gives rise to craving and clinging to impermanent states and things, which are dukkha, "incapable of satisfying" and painful. This craving keeps us caught in samsara, "wandering," usually interpreted as the endless cycle of repeated rebirth, and the continued dukkha that comes with it. There is a way to end this cycle, namely by attaining nirvana, cessation of craving, whereafter rebirth and the accompanying dukkha will no longer arise again. This can be accomplished by following **the eightfold path**, confining our automatic responses to sensory contact by restraining oneself, cultivating discipline and wholesome states, and practicing mindfulness and dhyana (meditation).

The function of the four truths, and their importance, developed over time and the Buddhist tradition slowly recognised them as the Buddha's first teaching. This tradition was established when prajna, or "liberating insight", came to be regarded as liberating in itself, instead of or in addition to the practice of dhyana. This "liberating insight" gained a prominent place in the sutras, and the four truths came to represent this liberating insight, as a part of the enlightenment story of the Buddha.

The four truths grew to be of central importance in the Theravada tradition of Buddhism by about the 5th-century CE, which holds that the insight into the four truths is liberating in itself. They are less prominent in the Mahayana tradition, which sees the higher aims of insight into sunyata, emptiness, and following the Bodhisattva path as central elements in their teachings and practice. The Mahayana tradition reinterpreted the four truths to explain how a liberated being can still be "pervasively operative in this world".

We could say that the two sets of causes and effects on the one hand, to the process of an unenlightened existence, which relates to the causal chain between suffering and its origins, and, on the other hand, to the process of an enlightened existence which pertains to the causal links between the path and true cessation. When the Buddha elaborated on these two processes, he taught what is called the doctrine of the Twelve Links of Dependent Origination, or Twelve 'Nidanas.'

The nidanas are the Twelve Links in the cycle of existence, which goes from ignorance, to volition, to consciousness, and so on, all the way to old age and death. When the causal process of an unenlightened existence is described in detail - that is, a life which is led within the framework of suffering and its origin - then the sequence of the Twelve Links begins with ignorance, and proceeds with volition, consciousness and so on. This sequence describes how an individual sentient being, as a result of certain causes and conditions, enters into the process of unenlightened existence.

However, if that same individual engages in certain spiritual practices, he or she can reverse this process, and the alternative sequence is that of the process which leads to enlightenment. For example, if the continuum of ignorance comes to an end then the continuum of volitional actions will cease. If that ceases, then the consciousness that serves as the support for such actions will cease; and so on. You can see that the teachings on the Twelve Links of Dependent Origination are in some sense an elaboration on the two sets of causes and conditions described by the Four Noble Truths.

The Truth of Suffering

The first of the Four Noble Truths is the Truth of Suffering. The various philosophical schools of Buddhism interpret the word 'truth' in different ways. For example, there is a fundamental difference between the Prasangika-Madhyamaka school and the Shravakayana schools is the way they distinguish ordinary beings from Arya or superior beings. The Shravakayana makes the distinction on the basis of whether or not a person has gained direct intuitive insight into the Four Noble Truths. The Prasangika-Madhyamikas do not accept this criterion, because they hold that even ordinary beings can have direct intuitive realisations of the Four Noble Truths.

We will turn straightaway to the meaning of duhkha or suffering. In this context, duhkha is the ground or basis of painful experience, and refers generally to our state of existence as conditioned by karma, delusions and afflictive emotions. As Asanga states in the Compendium of Knowledge, the concept of duhkha must embrace both the environment where we live and the individual beings living within it.

The three Realms of Suffering

In order to understand the environment in which unenlightened beings live, we must look briefly at Buddhist cosmology. According to the Buddhist teachings, there are Three Realms of existence: the Desire Realm, the Form Realm, and the Formless Realm.' The difficulty here, for most of us, is how to understand these Three Realms. In particular, how should we conceive of form realms and formless realms? It is not enough to simply say that Buddha talked about these in the scriptures- that alone is not a sufficient reason for a Buddhist to accept their existence. Perhaps the most helpful approach is to understand these realms in terms of different levels of consciousness. For example, according to Buddhism, the very distinction between enlightened existence and unenlightened existence is made on the basis of the respective levels of consciousness. A person whose mind is undisciplined and untamed is in the state of samsara or suffering; whereas someone whose mind is disciplined and tamed is in the state of nirvana, or ultimate peace. We also find that the Buddhist distinction between ordinary and Arya beings is made on the basis of their respective levels of consciousness or realisation. Anyone who has gained direct intuitive realisation of emptiness, or the ultimate nature of reality, is said to be an Arya according to Mahayana, and anyone who has not gained that realisation is called an ordinary being. In relation to the Three Realms, the subtler the level of consciousness an individual attains, the subtler the realm of existence he can inhabit.

For example, if a person's ordinary mode of being is very much within the context of desire and attachment- that is to say that he tends to develop attachment to whatever he perceives, like desirable forms or pleasant sensations and so on - then such attachment to physical objects, thought processes and sensory experiences leads to a form of existence which is confined within the Desire Realm, both now and in the future. At the same time, there are people who have transcended attachment to objects of immediate perception and to physical sensations, but who are attached to the inner states of joy or bliss. That type of person creates causes that will lead him or her to future rebirths where physical existence has a much more refined form. Furthermore, there are those who have transcended attachment not only to physical sensations but to pleasurable inner sensations of joy and bliss, too. They tend more towards a state of equanimity. Their level of consciousness is much subtler than the other two, but they are still attached to a particular mode of being. The grosser levels of their mind can lead to the Fourth Level of the Form Realm, while the subtler attachment towards equanimity leads to the Formless Realms. So, this is the way we relate the Three Realms to levels of consciousness. On the basis of this cosmology, Buddhism talks about the infinite process of the universe, coming into being and going through a process of dissolution before again coming into being. This process has to be understood in relation to the Three Realms of existence. According to the Sarvastivadin Abhidharma literature' (the Buddhist discourses on meta-physics and psychology which serve as a reference in Tibetan Buddhism), it is from the Third Level of the Form Realm downwards that the world is subject to the continuous process of arising and dissolution. From the Fourth Level of the Form Realm upwards, which includes the Formless Realm, the world is beyond this process which we could call the evolution of the physical universe. This infinite process of evolution is very similar to the modern scientific notion of the Big Bang. If the scientific cosmological theory of the Big Bang accepts only one Big Bang as the beginning of everything, then of course that would not fit with basic Buddhist cosmology. In this case, Buddhists would have to bite their nails and come up with some way of explaining how the Big Bang does not contradict the Buddhist idea of the evolutionary process of the universe. However, if the Big Bang theory does not entail only one Big Bang at the beginning, but accepts a multiplicity of Big Bangs, then that would correspond very well to the Buddhist understanding of the evolutionary process.

21.2 Full Set - Dhammacakkappavattana Sutta

The four truths are best known from their presentation in the Dhammacakkappavattana Sutta text, which contains two sets of the four truths, while various other sets can be found in the Pāli Canon, a collection of scriptures in the Theravada Buddhist tradition. The full set, which is most commonly used in modern expositions, contains grammatical errors, pointing to multiple sources for this set and translation problems within the ancient Buddhist community. Nevertheless, they were considered correct by the Pali tradition, which did not correct them.

According to the Buddhist tradition, the Dhammacakkappavattana Sutta, "Setting the Wheel of Dhamma in Motion", contains the first teachings that the Buddha gave after attaining full awakening, and liberation from rebirth. This discourse was identified as the first sermon of the Buddha only at a later date," and the four truths may originally not have been part of this sutta, but were later added in some versions. Within this discourse, the four noble truths are given as follows ("bhikkus" is normally translated as "Buddhist monks"):

(i) Now this, bhikkhus, is the noble truth of suffering: birth is suffering, aging is suffering, illness is suffering, death is suffering; union with what is displeasing is suffering; separation from what is pleasing is suffering; not to get what one wants is suffering; in brief, the five aggregates subject to clinging are suffering.

(ii) Now this, bhikkhus, is the noble truth of the origin of suffering: it is this craving [taṇhā, "thirst"] which leads to re-becoming, accompanied by delight and lust, seeking delight here and there; that is, craving for sensual pleasures, craving for becoming, craving for dis-becoming.

(iii) Now this, bhikkhus, is the noble truth of the cessation of suffering: it is the remainder-less fading away and cessation of that same craving, the giving up and relinquishing of it, freedom from it, non-reliance on it.

(iv) Now this, bhikkhus, is the noble truth of the way leading to the cessation of suffering: it is this noble eightfold path; that is, right view, right intention, right speech, right action, right livelihood, right effort, right mindfulness, right concentration.

According to this sutra, with the complete comprehension of these four truths release from samsara, the cycle of rebirth, was attained:

Knowledge and vision arose in me: 'Unprovoked is my release. This is the last birth. There is now no further becoming.

The comprehension of these four truths by his audience leads to the opening of the Dhamma Eye, that is, the attainment of right vision:

Whatever is subject to origination is subject to cessation.

21.2.1 Basic Set

The basic set is as follows:

- idam dukkham, "this is pain";
- ayam dukkha-samudayo, "this is the origin of pain";
- ayam dukkha-nirodha, "this is the cessation of pain";

- ayam dukkha-nirodha-gamini patipada, "this is the path leading to the cessation of pain."

The key terms in the longer version of this expression, dukkha-nirodha-gamini Patipada, can be translated as follows:

Gamini: leading to, making for Patipada: road, path, way; the means of reaching a goal or destination.

21.2.2 Mnemonic set

The Pali canon contains various shortened forms of the four truths, the "mnemonic set", which were "intended to remind the hearer of the full form of the NTs." The earliest form of the mnemonic set was "dukkham samudayo nirodho magga", without the reference to the Pali terms sacca or arya, which were later added to the formula. The four mnemonic terms can be translated as follows:

(i) **Dukkha** – "incapable of satisfying", "the unsatisfactory nature and the general insecurity of all conditioned phenomena"; "painful". Dukkha is most commonly translated as "suffering". This is an incorrect translation, since it refers to the ultimately unsatisfactory nature of temporary states and things, including pleasant but temporary experiences. Dukkha is the opposite of sukha, "pleasure", and it is better translated as "pain".

(ii) **Samudaya** – "origin", "source", "arising", "coming to existence"; "aggregate of the constituent elements or factors of any being or existence", "cluster", "coming together", "combination", "producing cause", "combination", "rising".

(iii) **Nirodha** – cessation; release; to confine; "prevention, suppression, enclosing, restraint".

(iv) **Marga** – "path".

21.3 Explanation of the Four Truths

21.3.1 Dukha and its Ending

As a proposition, the four truths defy an exact definition, but refer to and express the basic orientation of Buddhism: sensory contact gives rise to clinging and craving to temporary states and things, which is ultimately unsatisfactory and painful, dukkha, and sustains samsara, the repeated cycle of bhava (becoming, habitual tendencies) and jāti ("birth", interpreted as either rebirth, the coming to be of a new existence; or as the arising of the sense of self as a mental phenomenon. By following the Buddhist path, craving and clinging can be confined, peace of mind and real happiness can be attained, and the repeated cycle of repeated becoming and birth will be stopped.

The truth of **dukkha**, "incapable of satisfying", "painful", is the basic insight that samsara, life in this "mundane world", with its clinging and craving to impermanent states and things" is dukkha, unsatisfactory and painful. We expect happiness from states and things which are impermanent, and therefore cannot attain real happiness.

The truth of **samudaya**, "arising", "coming together", or dukkha-samudaya, the origination or arising of dukkha, is the truth that repeated life in this world, and its associated dukkha arises, or continues, with taṇhā, "thirst", craving for and clinging to these impermanent states and things. This clinging and craving produces karma, which leads to renewed becoming, keeping us trapped in rebirth and renewed dissatisfaction. Craving includes kama-tanha, craving for sense-pleasures; bhava-tanha, craving to continue the cycle of life and death, including rebirth; and vibhava-tanha, craving to not experience the world and painful feelings. While dukkha-samudaya, the term in the basic set of the four truths, is traditionally translated and explained is "the origin (or cause) of suffering", giving a causal explanation of dukkha, the wider connotations of the term samudaya, "coming into existence together": together with dukkha arises tanha, thirst. Craving does not cause dukkha, but comes into existence together with dukkha, or the five skandhas. It is this craving which is to be confined, as understood at the end of the Dhammacakkappavattana Sutta: "whatever arises ceases".

The truth of **nirodha**, "cessation," "suppression," "renouncing," "letting go", or dukkha-nirodha, the cessation of dukkha, is the truth that dukkha ceases, or can be confined, when one renounces or confines craving and clinging, and nirvana is attained. Nirvana refers to the moment of attainment itself, and the resulting peace of mind and happiness (khlesa-nirvana), but also to the final dissolution of the five skandhas at the time of death (skandha-nirvana or parinirvana); in the Theravada-tradition, it also refers to a transcendental reality which is "known at the moment of awakening". Modern Buddhist usage tends to restrict 'nirvāṇa' to the awakening experience and reserve 'parinirvāṇa' for the death experience. When nirvana is attained, no more karma is being produced, and rebirth and dissatisfaction will no longer arise again. Cessation is nirvana, "blowing out", and peace of mind.

When village people in India were cooking rice and waiting for it to cool, they might remark, "Wait a little for the rice to become nibbana". So here, nibbana means the cool state of mind, free from the fires of the defilements. The cooler the mind, the more Nibbana in that moment. We can notice for ourselves relative states of coolness in our own minds as we go through the day.

The truth of **magga**, refers to the path to the cessation of, or liberation from dukkha. The **fourth noble truth** is called 'the truth of the path' because the path leads us to the ultimate goal. We do this step by step, stage by stage, progressively completing our journey. The Buddha's teaching are called 'the dharma,' and the symbol of these teachings is the wheel that you see on the roofs of temples and monasteries. This is the symbol of the Enlightened One's teachings. For instance, if you go to Samye Ling, you will see on the roof of the temple the wheel of the dharma supported by two deer. 'Why a wheel' Wheels take you somewhere, and the dharma wheel is the path that takes us to the very best place along the finest road. This wheel of the Buddha's teaching has eight spokes because the path that Buddhists follow has eight major aspects known as 'the eight-fold path of realised beings' or 'the noble eight-fold path.' We need to follow this eight-fold path and it is essential that we know what this path is and how to practice on this path. These eight aspects to the noble eight-fold path can be grouped into three areas: superior conduct, superior concentration, and superior wisdom which make up seven of the eight spokes with the eighth spoke, superior effort which is the quality that supports the other seven. Superior effort is needed for achieving correct conduct, correct concentration, and the development of correct wisdom.

By following the Noble **Eightfold Path**, to moksha, liberation, restraining oneself, cultivating discipline, and practicing mindfulness and meditation, one starts to disengage from craving and clinging to impermanent states and things, and rebirth and dissatisfaction will be ended. The term "path" is usually taken to mean the Noble Eightfold Path, but other versions of "the path" can also be found in the Nikayas. The Theravada tradition regards insight into the four truths as liberating in itself.

The well-known eightfold path consists of the understanding that this world is fleeting and unsatisfying, and how craving keeps us tied to this fleeting world; a friendly and compassionate attitude to others; a correct way of behaving; mind-control, which means not feeding on negative thoughts, and nurturing positive thoughts; constant awareness of the feelings and responses which arise; and the practice of dhyana, meditation. The tenfold path adds the right (liberating) insight, and liberation from rebirth.

The four truths are to be internalised, and understood or "experienced" personally, to turn them into a lived reality.

The four truths describe dukkha and its ending as a means to reach peace of mind in this life, but also as a **means to end rebirth**.

The Four Noble Truths describe the knowledge needed to set out on the path to liberation from rebirth. By understanding the four truths, one can stop this clinging and craving, attain a pacified mind, and be freed from this cycle of rebirth and re-death. The moksha is a central concept in Indian religions, and "literally means freedom from samsara. The desire is the cause of suffering because desire is the cause of rebirth. When desire ceases, rebirth and its accompanying suffering ceases.

Once birth has arisen, "ageing and death", and various other dukkha states follow. While saying that birth is the cause of death may sound rather simplistic, in Buddhism it is a very significant statement; for there is an alternative to being born. This is to attain Nirvāna, so bringing an end to the process of rebirth and re-death. Nirvāna is not subject to time and change, and so is known as the 'unborn'; as it is not born it cannot die, and so it is also known as the "deathless". To attain this state, all phenomena subject to birth – the khandhas and nidānas – must be transcended by means of non-attachment.

The last sermon, the Maha-parinibbana Sutta (Last Days of the Buddha, Digha Nikaya 16), states it as follows:

[...] it is through not realising, through not penetrating the Four Noble Truths that this long course of birth and death has been passed through and undergone by me as well as by you [...] But now, bhikkhus, that these have been realised and penetrated, cut off is the craving for existence, destroyed is that which leads to renewed becoming [rebirth], and there is no fresh becoming.

21.4 Taṇhā

Taṇhā is an important concept in Buddhism, referring to "thirst, desire, longing, craving, greed", either physical or mental. It is typically translated as craving, and is of three types: kāma-taṇhā (craving for sensual pleasures), bhava-taṇhā (craving for existence), and vibhava-taṇhā (craving for non-existence).

In the second of the Four Noble Truths, the Buddha identified taṇhā as a principal cause in the arising of dukkha (suffering, pain, unsatisfactoriness).

The taṇhā is what manifests as suffering and rebirths. However, it is not the first cause nor the only cause of dukkha or samsara, because the origination of everything is relative and dependent on something else. The Pali canons of Buddhism assert other defilements and impurities (kilesā, sāsavā dhammā), in addition to taṇhā, as the cause of Dukkha. Taṇhā nevertheless, is always listed first, and considered the principal, all-pervading and "the most palpable and immediate cause" of dukkha.

Taṇhā is the key origin of dukkha in Buddhism. It reflects a mental state of craving. Greater the craving, more is the frustration because the world is always changing and innately unsatisfactory; craving also brings about pain through conflict and quarrels between individuals, which are all a state of Dukkha. It is such taṇhā that leads to rebirth and endless Samsara, stated Buddha as the second reality, and it is marked by three types of craving: sensory, being or non-existence. In Buddhist philosophy, there are right view and wrong view. The wrong views, it ultimately traces to Taṇhā, but it also asserts that "ordinary right view" such as giving and donations to monks, is also a form of clinging. The end of Taṇhā occurs when the person has accepted the "transcendent right view" through the insight into impermanence and non-self.

Both appropriate and inappropriate tendencies are linked to the fires of Taṇhā, and these produce fruits of kamma thereby rebirths. Quenching and blowing out these fires completely, is the path to final release from dukkha and samsara, in Buddhism. The Pali texts repeatedly recommend that one must destroy Taṇhā completely, and this destruction is a necessary for nirvana.

21.4.1 Three Types of Taṇhā

(i) **Kāma-taṇhā** (sensual pleasures craving): craving for sense objects which provide pleasant feeling, or craving for sensory pleasures. This includes not only desire for sense-pleasures, wealth and power, but also "desire for, and attachment to, ideas and ideals, views, opinions, theories, conceptions and beliefs (dhamma-taṇhā)."

(ii) **Bhava-taṇhā** (craving for being): craving to be something, to unite with an experience. This is ego-related, seeking of certain identity and desire for certain type of rebirth eternally. This type of craving is driven by the wrong view of eternalism (eternal life) and about permanence.

(iii) **Vibhava-taṇhā** (craving for non-existence): craving to not experience unpleasant things in the current or future life, such as unpleasant people or situations. This sort of craving may include attempts at suicide and self-annihilation, and this only results in further rebirth in a worse realm of existence. This type of craving is driven by the wrong view of annihilationism, that there is no rebirth.

21.4.2 Cessation of Taṇhā

The third noble truth teaches that the cessation of taṇhā is possible. The Dhammacakkappavattana Sutta states:

Bhikkhus, there is a noble truth about the cessation of suffering. It is the complete fading away and cessation of this craving [taṇhā]; its abandonment and relinquishment; getting free from and being independent of it.

Cessation of taṇhā can be obtained by following the Noble Eightfold Path. In Theravada Buddhism, the cessation results from the gaining of true insight into impermanence and non-self. The 'insight meditation' practice of Buddhism focuses on gaining "right mindfulness" which entails understanding three marks of existence - dukkha (suffering), anicca (impermanence) and anatta (non-self). The understanding of the reality of non-self, promotes non-attachment because if there is no soul, then there is no locus for clinging. Once one comprehends and accepts the non-self-doctrine, there are no more desires, i.e. taṇhā ceases.

21.4.3 Tanha versus Chanda

Relation to the three poisons

Taṇhā and avidya (ignorance) can be related to the three poisons:

(i) **Avidya or Moha** (ignorance), the root of the three poisons, is also the basis for taṇhā.

(ii) **Raga** (attachment) is equivalent to bhava-taṇhā (craving to be) and kāma-taṇhā (sense-craving).

(iii) **Dosha (Dvesha)** (aversion) is equivalent to vibhava-taṇhā (craving not to be).

Taṇhā is related to aversion and ignorance. Craving leads to aversion, anger, cruelty and violence which are unpleasant states and cause suffering to one who craves. Craving is based on misjudgement that the world is permanent, unchanging, stable, and reliable.

For example, in the first discourse of the Buddha, the Buddha identified taṇhā as the principal cause of suffering. However, his third discourse, the Fire Sermon, and other suttas, the Buddha identifies the causes of suffering as the "fires" of raga, dosha (dvesha), and moha; in the Fire Sermon, the Buddha states that nirvana is obtained by extinguishing these fires.

21.5 The Noble Eightfold Path

The Noble Eightfold Path (Sanskrit: āryāṣṭāgamārga) is an early summary of the path of Buddhist practices leading to liberation from samsara, the painful cycle of rebirth, in the form of nirvana.

The Eightfold Path is the fourth of the Buddha's Noble Truths, and he described it as the way that leads to the uprooting of the causes of suffering, and thus to increasingly stable and profound peacefulness, wisdom, virtue, and happiness. Each of the eight elements of this Path is described by a word that is typically translated as "right" or "wise." Both meanings are useful to reflect upon regarding your own suffering and yearning for its end. Each element of the Path is right, in the sense of being correct, moral, and a pointed instruction about how to live. Each element is also wise, in the sense of resulting from deep understanding and leading to good results. In keeping with the weight of tradition and the value of the sharp edge of the word, "right," that's what is used in this summary.

While the eight elements of the Path are presented here in their traditional sequence, they are not something you develop in order. They are all important, all the time. Yet some may become more prominent aspects of your practice at one time or another. The heart of each element of the Path is non-clinging, the essence of the Third Noble Truth: the cause of the end of suffering.

The Eightfold Path consists of eight practices: (i) right view, (ii) right resolve, (iii) right speech, (iv) right conduct, (v) right livelihood, (vi) right effort, (vii) right mindfulness, and (viii) right samadhi ('meditative absorption or union'). In early Buddhism, these practices started with understanding that the body-mind works in a corrupted way (right view), followed by entering the Buddhist path of self-observance, self-restraint, and cultivating kindness and compassion; and culminating in dhyana or samadhi, which reinforces these practices for the development of the body-mind. In later Buddhism, insight (prajñā) became the central soteriological instrument, leading to a different concept and structure of the path, in which the "goal" of the Buddhist path came to be specified as ending ignorance and rebirth.

The Noble Eightfold Path is one of the principal teachings of Buddhism, taught to lead to Arhatship. In the Theravada tradition, this path is also summarised as sila (morality), samadhi (meditation) and prajna (insight). In Mahayana Buddhism, this path is contrasted with the Bodhisattva path, which is believed to go beyond Arhatship to full Buddhahood.

In Buddhist symbolism, the Noble Eightfold Path is often represented by means of the dharma wheel (dharmachakra), in which its eight spokes represent the eight elements of the path.

Origin of the Noble Eightfold Path

The description of the Buddhist path may initially have been as simple as the term the middle way. In time, this short description was elaborated, resulting in the description of the eightfold path. The longer descriptions of "the path" can be found in the early texts, which can be condensed into the eightfold path.

The Eight Divisions

The eight Buddhist practices in the Noble Eightfold Path are:

1. **Right Resolve or Intention**: the giving up of home and adopting the life of a religious mendicant in order to follow the path; this concept aims at peaceful renunciation, into an environment of non-sensuality, non-ill-will (to loving kindness), away from cruelty (to compassion). Such an environment aids contemplation of impermanence, suffering, and non-self.
2. **Right Speech:** no lying, no rude speech, no telling one person what another says about him to cause discord or harm their relationship.
3. **Right Conduct or Action**: no killing or injuring, no taking what is not given, no sexual acts, no material desires.
4. **Right Livelihood**: beg to feed, only possessing what is essential to sustain life;
5. **Right Effort**: preventing the arising of unwholesome states, and generating wholesome states, the bojjhagā (seven factors of awakening). This includes indriya-samvara, "guarding the sense-doors", restraint of the sense faculties.
6. **Right Mindfulness** (sati; Satipatthana; Sampajañña): "retention", being mindful of the dhammas ("teachings", "elements") that are beneficial to the Buddhist path. In the vipassana movement, sati is interpreted as "bare attention": never be absent minded, being conscious of what one is doing; this encourages the awareness of the impermanence of body, feeling and mind, as well as to experience the five aggregates (skandhas), the five hindrances, the four True Realities and seven factors of awakening.
7. **Right samadhi** (passaddhi; ekaggata; sampasadana): practicing four stages of dhyāna ("meditation"), which includes samadhi proper in the second stage, and reinforces the development of the bojjhagā, culminating into upekkha (equanimity) and mindfulness. In the Theravada tradition and the Vipassana movement, this is interpreted as ekaggata, concentration or one-pointedness of the mind, and supplemented with Vipassana-meditation, which aims at insight.

8. **Right View**: our actions have consequences, death is not the end, and our actions and beliefs have consequences after death. The Buddha followed and taught a successful path out of this world and the other world (heaven and underworld/hell). Later on, right view came to explicitly include karma and rebirth, and the importance of the Four Noble Truths, when "insight" became central to Buddhist soteriology.

21.6 Explanation of the Noble Eightfold Path

21.6.1 Right View

"Right view" (samyak-dṛṣṭi / sammā-diṭṭhi) or "right understanding" states that our actions have consequences, that death is not the end, that our actions and beliefs also have consequences after death, and that the Buddha followed and taught a successful path out of this world and the other world (heaven and underworld or hell). Majjhima Nikaya 117, Mahācattārīsaka Sutta, a text from the Pāli Canon, describes the first seven practices as requisites of right samadhi, starting with right view:

Of those, right view is the forerunner [...] And what is the right view with effluents, siding with merit, resulting in acquisitions? 'There is what is given, what is offered, what is sacrificed. There are fruits, and results of good and bad actions. There is this world and the next world. There is mother and father. There are spontaneously reborn beings; there are contemplatives and brahmans who faring rightly and practicing rightly, proclaim this world and the next after having directly known and realised it for themselves.' This is the right view with effluents, siding with merit, resulting in acquisitions.

Later on, right view came to explicitly include karma and rebirth, and the importance of the Four Noble Truths, when "insight" became central to Buddhist soteriology. This presentation of right view still plays an essential role in Theravada Buddhism.

The purpose of right view is to clear one's path from confusion, misunderstanding, and deluded thinking. It is a means to gain right understanding of reality. In the interpretation of some Buddhist movements, right view is non-view: as the enlightened become aware that nothing can be expressed in fixed conceptual terms and rigid, dogmatic clinging to concepts is discarded.

Theravada

Right view can be further subdivided, states translator Bhikkhu Bodhi, into mundane right view and superior or supramundane right view:

Mundane right view, knowledge of the fruits of good behaviour. Having this type of view will bring merit and will support the favourable rebirth of the sentient being in the realm of samsara.

Supramundane (world-transcending) right view, the understanding of karma and rebirth, as implicated in the Four Noble Truths, leading to awakening and liberation from rebirths and associated dukkha in the realms of samsara.

According to Theravada Buddhism, mundane right view is a teaching that is suitable for lay followers, while supramundane right view, which requires a deeper understanding, is suitable for monastics. Mundane and supramundane right view involve accepting the following doctrines of Buddhism:

Karma: Every action of body, speech, and mind has karmic results, and influences the kind of future rebirths and realms a being enters into.

Three marks of existence: everything, whether physical or mental, is impermanent (anicca), a source of suffering (dukkha), and lacks a self (anatta).

The Four Noble Truths are a means to gaining insights and ending dukkha.

21.6.2 Right Intention

Right Intention (samyak-saṃkalpa / sammā-saṅkappa) can also be known as "right thought", "right aspiration", or "right motivation". In this factor, the practitioner resolves to leave home, renounce the worldly life and dedicate himself to an ascetic pursuit. In section III.248, the Majjhima Nikaya states,

And what is right resolve? Being resolved on renunciation, on freedom from ill will, on harmlessness: This is called right resolve.

Like right view, this factor has two levels. At the mundane level, the resolve includes being harmless (ahimsa) and refraining from ill will (avyabadha) to any being, as this accrues karma and leads to rebirth. At the supramundane level, the factor includes a resolve to consider everything and everyone as impermanent, a source of suffering and without a Self.

21.6.3 Right Speech

Right speech (samyag-vāc / sammā-vācā) in most Buddhist texts is presented as four abstentions, such as in the Pali Canon thus:

And what is right speech? Abstaining from lying, from divisive speech, from abusive speech, and from idle chatter: This is called right speech.

Instead of the usual "abstention and refraining from wrong" terminology, a few texts such as the Samaññaphala Sutta and Kevata Sutta in Digha Nikaya explain this virtue in an active sense, after stating it in the form of an abstention. For example, Samaññaphala Sutta states that a part of a monk's virtue is that "he abstains from false speech. He speaks the truth, holds to the truth, is firm, reliable, no deceiver of the world." Similarly, the virtue of abstaining from divisive speech is explained as delighting in creating concord. The virtue of abstaining from abusive speech is explained in this Sutta to include affectionate and polite speech that is pleasing to people. The virtue of abstaining from idle chatter is explained as speaking what is connected with the Dhamma goal of his liberation.

In the Abhaya-raja-kumara Sutta, the Buddha explains the virtue of right speech in different scenarios, based on its truth value, utility value and emotive content. The Tathagata, states Abhaya Sutta, never speaks anything that is unfactual or factual, untrue or true, disagreeable or agreeable, if that is unbeneficial and unconnected to his goals. Further, adds Abhaya Sutta, the Tathagata speaks the factual, the true, if in case it is disagreeable and unendearing, only if it is beneficial to his goals, but with a sense of proper time. Additionally, adds Abhaya Sutta, the Tathagata, only speaks with a sense of proper time even when what he speaks is the factual, the true, the agreeable, the endearing and what is beneficial to his goals.

The Buddha thus explains right speech in the Pali Canon as never speaking something that is not beneficial; and, only speaking what is true and beneficial, "when the circumstances are right, whether they are welcome or not".

21.6.4 Right Action

Right action (samyak-karmānta / sammā-kammanta) is like right speech, expressed as abstentions but in terms of bodily action. In the Pali Canon, this path factor is stated as:

And what is right action? Abstaining from killing, abstaining from stealing, abstaining from sexual misconduct. This is called right action.

The prohibition on killing precept in Buddhist scriptures applies to all living beings, not just human beings. Bhikkhu Bodhi agrees, clarifying that the more accurate rendering of the Pali canon is a prohibition on "taking life of any sentient being", which includes human beings, animals, birds, insects but excludes plants because they are not considered sentient beings. Further, adds Bodhi, this precept refers to intentional killing, as well as any form of intentional harming or torturing any sentient being. This moral virtue in early Buddhist texts, both in context of harm or killing of animals and human beings, is similar to ahimsa precepts found in the texts particularly of Jainism as well as of Hinduism, and has been a subject of significant debate in various Buddhist traditions.

21.6.5 Right Livelihood

Right livelihood (samyag-ājīva / sammā-ājīva) precept is mentioned in many early Buddhist texts, such as the Mahācattārīsaka Sutta in Majjhima Nikaya as follows:

"And what is right livelihood? Right livelihood, I tell you, is of two sorts: There is right livelihood with effluents, siding with merit, resulting in acquisitions; there is right livelihood that is noble, without effluents, transcendent, a factor of the path.

"And what is the right livelihood with effluents, siding with merit, resulting in acquisitions? There is the case where a disciple of the noble ones abandons wrong livelihood and maintains his life with right livelihood. This is the right livelihood with effluents, siding with merit, resulting in acquisitions.

"And what is the right livelihood that is noble, without effluents, transcendent, a factor of the path? The abstaining, desisting, abstinence, avoidance of wrong livelihood in one developing the noble path whose mind is noble, whose mind is without effluents, who is fully possessed of the noble path. (...)

The early canonical texts state right livelihood as avoiding and abstaining from wrong livelihood. This virtue is further explained in Buddhist texts as "living from begging, but not accepting everything and not possessing more than is strictly necessary". For lay Buddhists, this precept requires that the livelihood avoid causing suffering to sentient beings by cheating them, or harming or killing them in any way.

The Anguttara Nikaya III.208 asserts that the right livelihood does not trade in weapons, living beings, meat, alcoholic drink or poison. The same text, in section V.177, asserts that this applies to lay Buddhists. This has meant that raising and trading cattle livestock for slaughter is a breach of "right livelihood" precept in the Buddhist tradition, and Buddhist countries lack the mass slaughter houses found in Western countries.

The prohibition on stealing in the Pali Canon is an abstention from intentionally taking what is not voluntarily offered by the person to whom that property belongs. This includes taking by stealth, by force, by fraud or by deceit. Both the intention and the act matters, as this precept is grounded on the impact on one's karma.

The prohibition on sexual misconduct in the Noble Eightfold Path refers to "not performing sexual acts". This virtue is more generically explained in the Cunda Kammaraputta Sutta, which teaches that one must abstain from all sensual misconduct, including getting sexually involved with someone unmarried (anyone protected by parents or by guardians or by siblings), and someone married (protected by husband), and someone betrothed to another person, and female convicts or by dhamma.

For monastics, the abstention from sensual misconduct means strict celibacy while for lay Buddhists this prohibits adultery as well as other forms of sensual misconduct. Later Buddhist texts state that the prohibition on sexual conduct for lay Buddhists includes any sexual involvement with someone married, a girl or woman protected by her parents or relatives, and someone prohibited by dhamma conventions (such as relatives, nuns and others).

21.6.6 Right Effort

Right effort (samyag-vyāyāma / sammā-vāyāma) is preventing the arising of unwholesome states, and the generation of wholesome states. This includes indriya-samvara, "guarding the sense-doors", restraint of the sense faculties. Right effort is presented in the Pali Canon, such as the Sacca-vibhanga Sutta, as follows:

And what is right effort?

Here the monk arouses his will, puts forth effort, generates energy, exerts his mind, and strives to prevent the arising of evil and unwholesome mental states that have not yet arisen.

He arouses his will... and strives to eliminate evil and unwholesome mental states that have already arisen. He arouses his will... and strives to generate wholesome mental states that have not yet arisen.

He arouses his will, puts forth effort, generates energy, exerts his mind, and strives to maintain wholesome mental states that have already arisen, to keep them free of delusion, to develop, increase, cultivate, and perfect them.

This is called right effort.

The unwholesome states (akusala) are described in the Buddhist texts, as those relating to thoughts, emotions, intentions, and these include pancanivarana (five hindrances) – (i) sensual thoughts, (ii) doubts about the path, (iii) restlessness, (iv) drowsiness, and (v) ill will of any kind. Of these, the Buddhist traditions consider sensual thoughts and ill will needing more right effort. Sensual desire that must be eliminated by effort includes anything related to sights, sounds, smells, tastes and touch. This is to be done by restraint of the sense faculties (indriya-samvara). Ill will that must be eliminated by effort includes any form of aversion including hatred, anger, resentment towards anything or anyone.

21.6.7 Right Mindfulness

In the vipassana movement, mindfulness (samyak-smṛti / sammā-sati) is interpreted as "bare attention": never be absent minded, being conscious of what one is doing. While originally, in Yogic practice, sati may have meant to remember the meditation object, to cultivate a deeply absorbed, secluded state of mind, in the oldest Buddhism it has the meaning of "retention", being mindful of the dhammas ("teachings", "elements") that are beneficial to the Buddhist path. Mindfulness was a means to prevent the arising of craving, which resulted simply from contact between the senses and their objects. This may have been the Buddha's original idea. Mindfulness aids one not to crave and cling to any transitory state or thing, by complete and constant awareness of phenomena as impermanent, suffering and without self.

The Satipatthana Sutta describes the contemplation of four domains, namely (i) body, (ii) feelings, (iii) mind, and (iv) phenomena. The Satipatthana Sutta is regarded by the Vipassana movement as the quintessential text on Buddhist meditation, taking cues from it on "bare attention" and the contemplation on the observed phenomena as dukkha, anatta and anicca. The four upassanā have been misunderstood by the developing Buddhist tradition, including Theravada, to refer to four different foundations. The four upassanā do not refer to four different foundations of which one should be aware, but are an alternate description of the jhanas, describing how the samskharas are tranquilized:

(i) the six sense-bases which one needs to be aware of (kāyānupassanā);
(ii) contemplation on vedanās, which arise with the contact between the senses and their objects (vedanānupassanā);
(iii) the altered states of mind to which this practice leads (cittānupassanā); and
(iv) the development from the five hindrances to the seven factors of enlightenment (dhammānupassanā).

The contemporary Vipassana movement interprets the Satipatthana Sutta as "describing a pure form of insight (vipassanā) meditation" for which samatha (calm) and jhāna are not necessary. Yet, in pre-sectarian Buddhism, the establishment of mindfulness was placed before the practice of the jhanas, and associated with the abandonment of the five hindrances and the entry into the first jhana.

The dhyāna-scheme describes mindfulness also as appearing in the third and fourth dhyana, after initial concentration of the mind. While the second jhana denotes a state of absorption, in the third and fourth jhana one comes out of this absorption, being mindfully awareness of objects while being indifferent to them. The later tradition has falsified the jhana by classifying them as the quintessence of the concentrated, calming kind of meditation, ignoring the other – and indeed higher – element".

21.6.8 Right Concentration (Samadhi)

Samadhi (samyak-samādhi / sammā-samādhi) is a common practice in Indian religions. The term samadhi derives from the root sam-a-dha, which means 'to collect' or 'bring together', and thus it is often translated as 'concentration' or 'unification of mind'. In the early Buddhist texts, samadhi was also associated with the term "samatha" (calm abiding). In the suttas, samadhi is defined as one-pointedness of mind (Cittass'ekaggatā). Buddhagosa defines samadhi as "the centering of consciousness and consciousness concomitants evenly and rightly on a single object...the state in virtue of which consciousness and its concomitants remain evenly and rightly on a single object, undistracted and unscattered."

According to Bhikkhu Bodhi, the right concentration factor is reaching a one-pointedness of mind and unifying all mental factors, but it is not the same as "a gourmet sitting down to a meal, or a soldier on the battlefield" who also experience one-pointed concentration. The difference is that the latter have a one-pointed object in focus with complete awareness directed to that object – the meal or the target, respectively. In contrast, right concentration meditative factor in Buddhism is a state of awareness without any object or subject, and ultimately unto no-thingness and emptiness, as articulated in apophatic discourse.

Practice

Neither the Four Noble Truths nor the Noble Eightfold Path discourse provide details of right samadhi. The explanation is to be found in the Canonical texts of Buddhism, in several Suttas, such as the following in Saccavibhanga Sutta:

And what is right concentration?

(i) Here, the monk, detached from sense-desires, detached from unwholesome states, enters and remains in the first jhana (level of concentration, Sanskrit: dhyāna), in which there is applied and sustained thinking, together with joy and pleasure born of detachment;

(ii) And through the subsiding of applied and sustained thinking, with the gaining of inner stillness and oneness of mind, he enters and remains in the second jhana, which is without applied and sustained thinking, and in which there are joy and pleasure born of concentration;

(iii) And through the fading of joy, he remains equanimous, mindful and aware, and he experiences in his body the pleasure of which the Noble Ones say: "equanimous, mindful and dwelling in pleasure", and thus he enters and remains in the third jhana;

(iv) And through the giving up of pleasure and pain, and through the previous disappearance of happiness and sadness, he enters and remains in the fourth jhana, which is without pleasure and pain, and in which there is pure equanimity and mindfulness.

This is called right concentration.

Mindfulness

Although often translated as "concentration", as in the limiting of the attention of the mind on one object, in the fourth dhyana "equanimity and mindfulness remain", and the practice of concentration-meditation may well have been incorporated from non-Buddhist traditions. Samadhi consists of the four stages of dhyana meditation, but ...to put it more accurately, the first dhyana seems to provide, after some time, a state of strong concentration, from which the other stages come forth; the second stage is called samadhija.

While the second jhana denotes a state of absorption, in the third and fourth jhana one comes out of this absorption, being mindfully awareness of objects while being indifferent to it. The later tradition has falsified the jhana by classifying them as the quintessence of the concentrated, calming kind of meditation, ignoring the other – and indeed higher – element."

Order of Practice

Originally the path culminated in the practice of dhyana/samadhi as the core soteriological practice. According to the Pali and Chinese canon, the samadhi state (right concentration) is dependent on the development of preceding path factors:

The Blessed One said: "Now what, monks, is noble right concentration with its supports and requisite conditions? Any singleness of mind equipped with these seven factors – right view, right resolve, right speech, right action, right livelihood, right effort, and right mindfulness – is called noble right concentration with its supports and requisite conditions.

—Maha-cattarisaka Sutta

According to the discourses, right view, right resolve, right speech, right action, right livelihood, right effort, and right mindfulness are used as the support and requisite conditions for the practice of right concentration. Understanding of the right view is the preliminary role, and is also the forerunner of the entire Noble Eightfold Path.

Chapter - 22

Theravada Philosophy

Theravāda ("School of the Elders") is the most commonly accepted name of Buddhism's oldest existing school. The school's adherents, termed Theravādins, have preserved their version of Gautama Buddha's teaching or Buddha Dhamma in the Pāli Canon for over a millennium.

Note: Pali canon, also called Tipitaka (Pali: "Triple Basket") or Tripitaka (Sanskrit), the complete canon, first recorded in Pali, of the Theravada ("Way of the Elders") branch of Buddhism. The schools of the Mahayana ("Greater Vehicle") branch also revere it yet hold as scripture additional writings (in Sanskrit, Chinese, Tibetan, and other languages) that are not accepted as canonical by Theravada Buddhists. It is thought to be the oldest complete canon within Buddhism.

The Pāli Canon is the most complete Buddhist canon surviving in a classical Indian language, Pāli, which serves as the school's sacred language and lingua franca. In contrast to Mahāyāna and Vajrayāna, Theravāda tends to be conservative in matters of doctrine (pariyatti) and monastic discipline (vinaya). One element of this conservatism is the fact that Theravāda rejects the authenticity of the Mahayana sutras (which appeared c. 1st century BCE onwards).

Modern Theravāda derives from the Mahāvihāra order, a Sri Lankan branch of the Vibhajjavāda tradition, who are in turn a sect of the Indian Sthavira Nikaya. This tradition began to establish itself in Sri Lanka from the 3rd century BCE onwards. It was in Sri Lanka that the Pāli Canon was written down and the school's commentary literature developed. From Sri Lanka, the Theravāda Mahāvihāra tradition subsequently spread to the rest of Southeast Asia. It is the dominant religion in Cambodia, Laos, Myanmar, Sri Lanka, and Thailand and is practiced by minorities in India, Bangladesh, China, Nepal, and Vietnam. The diaspora of all of these groups, as well as converts around the world, also embrace and practice Theravāda Buddhism.

During the modern era, new developments have included Buddhist modernism, the Vipassana movement which reinvigorated Theravāda meditation practice, the growth of the Thai Forest Tradition which reemphasised forest monasticism and the spread of Theravāda to other Asian and western countries such as India, Nepal, several European countries and the United States by immigrants and converts.

22.1 History of Theravada Philosophy

22.1.1 Pre-Modern

As far as the histories go, it seems that, in its initial form, the Theravada school began about 100 years after the Buddha's time. A few months after the Parinibbana, a great council of elders was held to formalise and establish the Teachings. A hundred years later they had a second council, again to go over all the Teachings (the discourses and the monastic rules), in the attempt to keep everyone on the same page. However, as it transpired, it was at this time that the first major split in the Sangha occurred.

The Theravāda school descends from the Vibhajjavāda, a division within the Sthāvira nikāya, one of the two major orders that arose after the first schism in the Indian Buddhist community. Theravāda sources trace their tradition to the Third Buddhist council, when elder Moggaliputta-Tissa is said to have compiled the Kathavatthu, an important work which lays out the Vibhajjavāda doctrinal position.

One of the reasons why the Theravada tradition has been sustained pretty much in its original form ever since then is because of the Emperor Ashoka. He was a warrior-noble king about whom it was said, in typical mythical fashion, that he killed 99 of his brothers in order to take over the throne. He then proceeded to work on the rest of India, conquering the vast majority of the Indian subcontinent. After a particularly gruesome battle with the Kalingans, where there were about 60,000 dead, he looked out over the sea of groaning, weeping, bleeding, and dismembered bodies and was suddenly struck by the folly of his ways. He realised, "This really is a terrible track that I've got myself onto." But of course by then he'd conquered the whole of India so he could afford to give himself some breathing space. He also realised, "I've got to do something about my spiritual life because if I don't do something quickly, I'm in bad, bad trouble." He invited different teachers from different sects — not just Buddhist — to come and explain their teachings to him. One after another, different people came, but nobody was very convincing to him. Then one day, from the window of his palace, he saw a young Buddhist novice walking down the street. He was so struck by the demeanor of this child (only seven years old) that he thought,

"How could such a young child have such a noble bearing and look so serene?" So he told his people to bring the child into the palace.

The king invited him in and said, "Please take a seat." The novice, knowing the protocol that a member of the Sangha should never sit lower than a lay person, and seeing that the only high chair in the place was the throne, climbed up onto the king's throne. Even if Ashoka hadn't killed 99 of his brothers and conquered all India, this would have raised a few hairs on the back of his neck. So he said to the novice, "What do you think you're doing climbing on the throne?" The novice said something like, "The Dhamma is that which is supreme in the world. Having given my life to the realisation of that Truth, it is my obligation to put myself in a seat which represents that."

The Emperor then started asking him questions. He was so impressed with the answers the novice gave, he thought, "I've got to find out whom this child's teachers are." It turned out that the boy was from the Theravada school of the Buddha's disciples. Eventually that was the school that Ashoka espoused, and since he was by then in charge of India, he decided India would become a Buddhist nation. Primarily he patronised the Theravada tradition, although he also gave support to other Buddhist lineages as well as to various non-Buddhist sects. Later his son and daughter, Mahinda and Sanghamitta, went to Sri Lanka — Sanghamitta was a bhikkhuni, a Buddhist nun, and Mahinda was a monk. They took the Theravada tradition to Sri Lanka and established it there in about 240 BCE.

Aided by patronage of Mauryan kings like Ashoka, this school spread throughout India and reached Sri Lanka through the efforts of missionary monks like Mahinda. In Sri Lanka, it became known as the Tambapaṇṇiya (and later as Mahāvihāravāsins) which was based at the Great Vihara (Mahavihara) in Anuradhapura (the ancient Sri Lankan capital). According to Theravāda sources, another one of the Ashokan missions was also sent to Suvaṇṇabhūmi ("The Golden Land"), which is also referred to as Southeast Asia.

It was through this circumstance that Sri Lanka later became a stronghold of Theravada Buddhism. It has sustained itself there for many, many centuries particularly because Sri Lanka is an island and therefore protected by its isolation. In India empires came and went, civilisations arose and departed, and many different Buddhist schools came into being and dissolved or fragmented. They eventually spread through the north into Afghanistan, Tibet, and China — later on to Korea and Japan. Theravada largely disappeared on the mainland of India in later times and completely so along with all other Buddhist schools with the advent of the Muslim invasions. Despite this, there on Sri Lanka (which was called Tambapanni in those days) the little cluster of Theravadans were hanging on, pretty much unbothered by anybody else. There were, of course, wars and famines over time, as well as other Buddhist schools operating there, however Theravada Buddhism was continually restored and maintained as the main religion.

Theravada Buddhism eventually spread throughout South-east Asia (there was a lot of traffic between India and that region) as at different times missionaries were invited from Sri Lanka and went out to Burma and later on to Thailand, Cambodia, and Laos. Because, particularly in those countries, they had no strong, uniting cultural forms, Theravada Buddhism and the Indian culture that backed it up became the defining influence. When it arrived in Thailand, Laos, and Burma, their societies shaped themselves around it. In most Buddhist countries, the features of the Buddha images resemble the features of the people of that country. However, what is found in Southeast Asia is that the Buddhas often have Indian features. The Thai Buddha images usually don't look like Thais at all, they have Indian features, large noses, and an Indian cast to their forms.

By the first century BCE, Theravāda Buddhism was well established in the main settlements of the Kingdom of Anuradhapura. The Pali Canon, which contains the main scriptures of the Theravāda, was committed to writing in the first century BCE. Throughout the history of ancient and medieval Sri Lanka, Theravāda was the main religion of the Sinhalese people and its temples and monasteries were patronised by the Sri Lankan kings, who saw themselves as the protectors of the religion.

Over time, two other sects split off from the Mahāvihāra tradition, the Abhayagiri and Jetavana. While the Abhayagiri sect became known for the syncretic study of Mahayana and Vajrayana texts as well as the Theravāda canon, the Mahāvihāra tradition did not accept these new created scriptures. Instead, Mahāvihāra scholars like Buddhaghosa focused on the exegesis of the Pali scriptures and on the Abhidhamma. These Theravāda sub-sects often came into conflict with each other over royal patronage. The reign of Parākramabāhu I (1153–1186) saw an extensive reform of the Sri Lankan sangha after years of warfare on the island. Parākramabāhu created a single unified sangha which came to be dominated by the Mahāvihāra sect.

Epigraphical evidence has established that Theravāda Buddhism became a dominant religion in the Southeast Asian kingdoms of Sri Ksetra and Dvaravati from about the 5th century CE onwards. The oldest surviving Buddhist texts in the Pāli language are gold plates found at Sri Ksetra dated circa 5th to 6th century. Before the Theravāda tradition became the dominant religion in Southeast Asia, Mahāyāna, Vajrayana and Hinduism were also prominent.

Starting at around the 11th century, Sinhalese Theravāda monks and Southeast Asian elites led a widespread conversion of most of mainland Southeast Asia to the Theravādin Mahavihara school. The patronage of monarchs such as the Burmese king Anawrahta (Pali: Aniruddha, 1044–1077) and the Thai king Ram Khamhaeng (flourit. late 13th century) was instrumental in the rise of Theravāda Buddhism as the predominant religion of Burma and Thailand.

Burmese and Thai kings saw themselves as Dhamma Kings and as protectors of the Theravāda faith. They promoted the building of new temples, patronised scholarship, monastic ordinations and missionary works as well as attempted to eliminate certain non-Buddhist practices like animal sacrifices. During the 15th and 16th centuries, Theravāda also became established as the state religion in Cambodia and Laos. In Cambodia, numerous Hindu and Mahayana temples, most famously Angkor Wat and Angkor Thom, were transformed into Theravādin monasteries.

22.1.2 Modern History

In the 19th and 20th centuries, Theravāda Buddhists came into direct contact with western ideologies, religions and modern science. The various responses to this encounter have been called "Buddhist modernism". In the British colonies of Ceylon (modern Sri Lanka) and Burma (Myanmar), Buddhist institutions lost their traditional role as the prime providers of education (a role that was often filled by Christian schools). In response to this, Buddhist organisations were founded which sought to preserve Buddhist scholarship and provide a Buddhist education. Anagarika Dhammapala, Migettuwatte Gunananda Thera, Hikkaduwe Sri Sumangala Thera and Henry Steel Olcott (one of the first American western converts to Buddhism) were some of the main figures of the Sri Lankan Buddhist revival. Two new monastic orders were formed in the 19th century, the Amarapura Nikāya and the Rāmañña Nikāya.

In Burma, an influential modernist figure was king Mindon Min (1808–1878), known for his patronage of the Fifth Buddhist council (1871) and the Tripiṭaka tablets at Kuthodaw Pagoda (still the world's largest book) with the intention of preserving the Buddha Dhamma. Burma also saw the growth of the "**Vipassana movement**", which focused on reviving Buddhist meditation and doctrinal learning. Ledi Sayadaw (1846–1923) was one of the key figures in this movement. After independence, Myanmar held the Sixth Buddhist council (Vesak, 1954 to Vesak, 1956) to create a new redaction of the Pāli Canon, which was then published by the government in 40 volumes. The Vipassana movement continued to grow after independence, becoming an international movement with centers around the world. Influential meditation teachers of the post-independence era include U Narada, Mahasi Sayadaw, Sayadaw U Pandita, Nyanaponika Thera, Webu Sayadaw, **U Ba Khin and his student S.N. Goenka.**

Meanwhile, in Thailand (the only Theravāda nation to retain its independence throughout the colonial era), the religion became much more centralised, bureaucratised and controlled by the state after a series of reforms promoted by Thai kings of the Chakri dynasty. King Mongkut (c. 1851–1868) and his successor Chulalongkorn (1868–1910) were especially involved in centralising sangha reforms. Under these kings, the sangha was organised into a hierarchical bureaucracy led by the Sangha Council of Elders (Pali: Mahāthera Samāgama), the highest body of the Thai sangha. Mongkut also led the creation of a new monastic order, the Dhammayuttika Nikaya, which kept a stricter monastic discipline than the rest of the Thai sangha (this included not using money, not storing up food and not taking milk in the evening). The Dhammayuttika movement was characterised by an emphasis on the original Pali Canon and a rejection of Thai folk beliefs which were seen as irrational. Under the leadership of Prince Wachirayan Warorot, a new education and examination system was introduced for Thai monks.

The 20th century also saw the growth of "forest traditions" which focused on forest living and strict monastic discipline. The main forest movements of this era are the Sri Lankan Forest Tradition and the Thai Forest Tradition, founded by Ajahn Mun (1870–1949) and his students.

Theravāda Buddhism in Cambodia and Laos went through similar experiences in the modern era. Both had to endure French colonialism, destructive civil wars and oppressive communist governments. Under French Rule, French Indologists of the École française d'Extrême-Orient became involved in the reform of Buddhism, setting up institutions for the training of Cambodian and Lao monks, such as the Ecole de Pali which was founded in Phnom Penh in 1914. While the Khmer Rouge effectively destroyed Cambodia's Buddhist institutions, after the end of the communist regime the Cambodian Sangha was re-established by monks who had returned from exile. In contrast, communist rule in Laos was less destructive since the Pathet Lao sought to make use of the sangha for political ends by imposing direct state control. During the late 1980s and 1990s, the official attitudes towards Buddhism began to liberalise in Laos and there was a resurgence of traditional Buddhist activity such as merit making and doctrinal study.

The modern era also saw the spread of Theravāda Buddhism around the world and the revival of the religion in places where it remains a minority faith. Some of the major events of the spread of modern Theravāda include:

- The 20th century Nepalese Theravāda movement which introduced Theravāda Buddhism to Nepal and was led by prominent figures such as Dharmaditya Dharmacharya, Mahapragya, Pragyananda and Dhammalok Mahasthavir.
- The establishment of some of the first Theravāda Viharas in the Western world, such as the London Buddhist Vihara (1926), Das Buddhistische Haus in Berlin (1957) and the Washington Buddhist Vihara in Washington, DC (1965).
- The founding of the Bengal Buddhist Association (1892) and the Dharmankur Vihar (1900) in Calcutta by the Bengali monk Kripasaran Mahasthavir, which were key events in the Bengali Theravāda revival.
- The founding of the Maha Bodhi Society in 1891 by Anagarika Dharmapala which focused on the conservation and restoration of important Indian Buddhist sites, such as Bodh Gaya and Sarnath.
- The introduction of Theravāda to other Southeast Asian nations like Singapore, Indonesia and Malaysia. Especially with Ven. K. Sri Dhammananda missionary efforts among English-speaking Chinese communities.
- The return of Western Theravādin monks trained in the Thai Forest Tradition to western countries and the subsequent founding of monasteries led by western monastics, such as Abhayagiri Buddhist Monastery, Chithurst Buddhist Monastery, Metta Forest Monastery, Amaravati Buddhist Monastery, Birken Forest Buddhist Monastery, Bodhinyana Monastery and Santacittarama.
- The spread of the **Vipassana movement around the world by the efforts of people like S.N. Goenka**, Anagarika Munindra, Joseph Goldstein, Jack Kornfield, Sharon Salzberg, Dipa Ma, and Ruth Denison.
- The Vietnamese Theravāda movement, led by figures such as Ven. Hộ-Tông (Vansarakkhita).

22.2 Texts in Theravada

22.2.1 Pāli Tipiṭaka

In Theravāda, the Pāli Tipiṭaka, also known as the Pāli Canon is "the highest authority on what constitutes the Dhamma (the truth or teaching of the Buddha) and the organisation of the Sangha (the community of monks and nuns)."

The language of the Tipiṭaka, Pāli, is a middle-Indic language which is the main religious and scholarly language in Theravāda. This language may have evolved out of various Indian dialects, and is related to, but not the same as, the ancient language of Magadha.

An early form of the Tipiṭaka may have been transmitted to Sri Lanka during the reign of Ashoka, which saw a period of Buddhist missionary activity. After being orally transmitted (as was the custom for religious texts in those days) for some centuries, the texts were finally committed to writing in the 1st century BCE. Theravāda is one of the first Buddhist schools to commit its Tipiṭaka to writing. The recension of the Tipiṭaka which survives today is that of the Sri Lankan Mahavihara sect.

The oldest manuscripts of the Tipiṭaka from Sri Lanka and Southeast Asia date to the 15th century, and they are incomplete. Complete manuscripts of the four Nikayas are only available from the 17th century onwards. However, fragments of the Tipiṭaka have been found in inscriptions from Southeast Asia, the earliest of which have been dated to the 3rd or 4th century. The Pāli Tipiṭaka has been transmitted with a high degree of accuracy for well over 1,500 years.

The Pāli Tipitaka consists of three parts: the Vinaya Pitaka, Sutta Pitaka and Abhidhamma Pitaka. Of these, the Abhidhamma Pitaka is believed to be a later addition to the collection, its composition dating from around the 3rd century BCE onwards. The Pāli Abhidhamma was not recognised outside the Theravāda school. There are also some texts which were late additions that are included in the fifth Nikaya, the Khuddaka Nikāya ('Minor Collection'), such as the Paṭisambhidāmagga (possibly c. 3rd to 1st century BCE) and the Buddhavaṃsa (c. 1st and 2nd century BCE).

The main parts of the Sutta Pitaka and some portions of the Vinaya shows considerable overlap in content to the Agamas, the parallel collections used by non-Theravāda schools in India which are preserved in Chinese and partially in Sanskrit, Prakrit, and Tibetan, as well as the various non-Theravāda Vinayas. On this basis, these Early Buddhist texts (i.e. the Nikayas and parts of the Vinaya) are generally believed to be some of the oldest and most authoritative sources on the doctrines of pre-sectarian Buddhism by modern scholars.

Much of the material in the earlier portions is not specifically "Theravādan", but the collection of teachings that this school's adherents preserved from the early, non-sectarian body of teachings. While the Theravādans may have added texts to their Tipiṭaka (such as the Abhidhamma texts and so on), they generally did not tamper with the earlier material.

The historically later parts of the canon, mainly the Abhidhamma and some parts of the Vinaya, contain some distinctive elements and teachings which are unique to the Theravāda school and often differ with the Abhidharmas or Vinayas of other early Buddhist schools. For example, while the Theravāda Vinaya contains a total of 227 monastic rules for bhikkhus, the Dharmaguptaka Vinaya (used in East Asian Buddhism) has a total of 253 rules for bhikkhus (though the overall structure is the same). These differences arose from the systematisation and historical development of doctrines and monasticism in the centuries after the death of the Buddha.

The Abhidhamma-pitaka contains "a restatement of the doctrine of the Buddha in strictly formalised language." Its texts present a new method, the Abhidhamma method, which attempts to build a single consistent philosophical system (in contrast with the suttas, which present numerous teachings given by the Buddha to particular individuals according to their need). Because the Abhidhamma focuses on analysing the internal lived experience of beings and the intentional structure of consciousness, it has often been compared to a kind of phenomenological psychology by numerous modern scholars such as Nyanaponika, Bhikkhu Bodhi and Alexander Piatigorsky.

The Theravāda school has traditionally held the doctrinal position that the canonical Abhidhamma Pitaka was actually taught by the Buddha himself. Modern scholarship in contrast, has generally held that the Abhidhamma texts date from the 3rd century BCE onwards. However, some scholars also hold that the early Abhidhamma texts developed out of exegetical and catechetical work which made use of doctrinal lists which can be seen in the suttas, called matikas.

22.2.2 Non-canonical Literature

There are numerous Theravāda works which are important for the tradition even though they are not part of the Tipiṭaka. Perhaps the most important texts apart from the Tipiṭaka are the works of the influential scholar Buddhaghosa (4th–5th century CE), known for his Pāli commentaries (which were based on older Sri Lankan commentaries of the Mahavihara tradition). He is also the author of a very important compendium of Theravāda doctrine, the Visuddhimagga. Other figures like Dhammapala and Buddhadatta also wrote Theravāda commentaries and other works in Pali during the time of Buddhaghosa. While these texts do not have the same scriptural authority in Theravāda as the Tipiṭaka, they remain influential works for the exegesis of the Tipiṭaka.

An important genre of Theravādin literature is shorter handbooks and summaries, which serve as introductions and study guides for the larger commentaries. Two of the more influential summaries are Sariputta Thera's Pālimuttakavinayavinicchayasaṅgaha, a summary of Buddhaghosa's Vinaya commentary and Anuruddha's Abhidhammaṭṭhasaṅgaha (a "Manual of Abhidhamma").

Throughout the history of Theravāda, Theravāda monks also produced other works of Pāli literature such as historical chronicles (like the Dipavamsa and the Mahavamsa), hagiographies, poetry, Pāli grammars, and "sub-commentaries" (that is, commentaries on the commentaries).

While Pāli texts are symbolically and ritually important for many Theravādins, most people are likely to access Buddhist teachings though vernacular literature, oral teachings, sermons, art and performance as well as films and Internet media. There is a far greater volume of Theravāda literature in vernacular languages than in Pāli.

An important genre of Theravādin literature, in both Pāli and vernacular languages are the Jataka tales, stories of the Buddha's past lives. They are very popular among all classes and are rendered in a wide variety of media formats, from cartoons to high literature. The Vessantara Jātaka is one of the most popular of these.

Most Theravāda Buddhists generally consider Mahāyāna Buddhist scriptures to be apocryphal, meaning that they are not authentic words of the Buddha.

22.3 Core Teachings of Theravada

The core of Theravāda Buddhist doctrine is contained in the Pāli Canon, the only complete collection of Early Buddhist Texts surviving in a classical Indic language. These basic Buddhist ideas are shared by the other Early Buddhist schools as well as by Mahayana traditions. They include central concepts such as:

- A doctrine of Karma (action), which is based on intention (cetana) and a related doctrine of rebirth which holds that after death, sentient beings which are not fully awakened will transmigrate to another body, possibly in another realm of existence. The type of realm one will be reborn in, is determined by the beings past karma. This cyclical universe filled with birth and death is named samsara.

- A rejection of other doctrines and practices found in Brahmanical Hinduism, including the idea that the Vedas are a divine authority. Any form of sacrifices to the gods (including animal sacrifices) and ritual purification by bathing are considered useless and spiritually corrupted. The Pāli texts also reject the idea that castes are divinely ordained.
- A set of major teachings called the bodhipakkhiyādhammā (factors conducive to awakening).
- Descriptions of various meditative practices or states, namely the four jhanas (meditative absorptions) and the formless dimensions (arupāyatana).
- Ethical training (sila) including the ten courses of wholesome action and the five precepts.
- Nirvana (Pali: nibbana), the highest good and final goal in Theravāda Buddhism. It is the complete and final end of suffering, a state of perfection. It is also the end of all rebirth, but it is not an annihilation (uccheda).
- The corruptions or influxes (āsavas), such as the corruption of sensual pleasures (kāmāsava), existence-corruption (bhavāsava), and ignorance-corruption (avijjāsava).
- The doctrine of impermanence (anicca), which holds that all physical and mental phenomena are transient, unstable and inconstant.
- The doctrine of not-self (anatta), which holds that all the constituents of a person, namely, the five aggregates (physical form, feelings, perceptions, intentions and consciousness), are empty of a self (atta), since they are impermanent and not always under our control. Therefore, there is no unchanging substance, permanent self, soul, or essence.
- The Five hindrances (pañca nīvaraṇāni), which are obstacles to meditation: (1) sense desire, (2) hostility, (3) sloth and torpor, (4) restlessness and worry and (5) doubt.
- The Four Divine Abodes (brahmavihārā), also known as the four immeasurables (appamaññā).
- The Four Noble Truths, which state, in brief: (1) There is dukkha (suffering, unease); (2) There is a cause of dukkha, mainly craving (tanha); (3) The removal of craving leads to the end (nirodha) of suffering, and (4) there is a path (magga) to follow to bring this about.

- The framework of Dependent Arising (paṭiccasamuppāda), which explains how suffering arises (beginning with ignorance and ending in birth, old age and death) and how suffering can be brought to an end.
- The Middle Way, which is seen as having two major facets. First, it is a middle path between extreme asceticism and sensual indulgence. It is also seen as a middle view between the idea that at death beings are annihilated and the idea that there is an eternal self (Pali: atta).
- The Noble Eightfold Path, one of the main outlines of the Buddhist path to awakening. The eight factors are: Right View, Right Intention, Right Speech, Right Conduct, Right Livelihood, Right Effort, Right Mindfulness, and Right Samadhi.
- The practice of taking refuge in the "Triple Gems": the Buddha, the Dhamma and the Saṅgha.
- The Seven Aids to Awakening (satta bojjhaṅgā): mindfulness (sati), investigation (dhamma vicaya), energy (viriya), bliss (pīti), relaxation (passaddhi), samādhi, and equanimity (upekkha).
- The six sense bases (saḷāyatana) and a corresponding theory of Sense impression (phassa) and consciousness (viññana).
- Various frameworks for the practice of mindfulness (sati), mainly, the four satipatthanas (establishments of mindfulness) and the 16 elements of anapanasati (mindfulness of breathing).

Oftentimes when we chant The Buddha's Teaching on Loving Kindness, people find that it all sounds wonderful, and then come the last four lines:

By not holding to fixed views,
The pure-hearted one, having clarity of vision,
Being freed from all sense-desires,
Is not born again into this world.

22.4 Abhidhamma Philosophy

Theravāda scholars developed a systematic exposition of the Buddhist doctrine called the Abhidhamma. In the Pāli Nikayas, the Buddha teaches through an analytical method in which experience is explained using various conceptual groupings of physical and mental processes, which are called "dhammas". Examples of lists of dhammas taught by the Buddha include the twelve sense 'spheres' or ayatanas, the five aggregates or khanda and the eighteen elements of cognition or dhatus.

Theravāda traditionally promotes itself as the Vibhajjavāda "teaching of analysis" and as the heirs to the Buddha's analytical method. Expanding this model, Theravāda Abhidhamma scholasticism concerned itself with analyzing "ultimate truth" (paramattha-sacca) which it sees as being composed of all possible dhammas and their relationships. The central theory of the Abhidhamma is thus known as the "dhamma theory". "Dhamma" has been translated as "factors", "psychic characteristics", "psycho-physical events" and "phenomena".

Dhammas ("principles" or "elements") are "those items that result when the process of analysis is taken to its ultimate limits". However, this does not mean that they have an independent existence, for it is "only for the purposes of description" that they are postulated. Dhammas are defined as "the constituents of sentient experience; the irreducible 'building blocks' that make up one's world, albeit they are not static mental contents and certainly not substances." Thus, while in Theravāda Abhidhamma, dhammas are the ultimate constituents of experience, they are not seen as substances, essences or independent particulars, since they are empty (suñña) of a self (attā) and conditioned. This is spelled out in the Patisambhidhamagga, which states that dhammas are empty of svabhava (sabhavena suññam).

The canonical Pāli Abhidhamma remains pragmatic and psychological, and "does not take much interest in ontology" in contrast with the Sarvastivada tradition. The Abhidhamma remains focused on the practicalities of insight meditation and leaves ontology "relatively unexplored". However, the later Theravāda sub-commentaries (ṭīkā) do show a doctrinal shift towards ontological realism from the earlier epistemic and practical concerns.

The Theravāda Abhidhamma holds that there is a total of 82 possible types of dhammas, 81 of these are conditioned (sankhata), while one is unconditioned, which is nibbana. The 81 conditioned dhammas are divided into three broad categories: consciousness (citta), associated mentality (cetasika) and materiality, or physical phenomena (rupa). Since no dhamma exists independently, every single dhamma of consciousness, known as a citta, arises associated (sampayutta) with at least seven mental factors (cetasikas). In Abhidhamma, all awareness events are thus seen as being characterised by intentionality and never exist in isolation. Much of Abhidhamma philosophy deals with categorising the different consciousnesses and their accompanying mental factors as well as their conditioned relationships (paccaya).

22.5 Cosmology

The Pāli Tipiṭaka outlines a hierarchical cosmological system with various planes existence (bhava) into which sentient beings may be reborn depending on their past actions. Good actions lead one to the higher realms, bad actions lead to the lower realms. However, even for the gods (devas) in the higher realms like Indra and Vishnu, there is still death, loss and suffering.

The main **categories of the planes of existence** are:

(i) **Arūpa**-bhava, the formless or incorporeal plane. These are associated with the four formless meditations, that is: infinite space, infinite consciousness, infinite nothingness and neither perception nor non-perception. Beings in these realms live extremely long lives (thousands of kappas).

(ii) **Kāma-bhava**, the plane of desires. This includes numerous realms of existence such as: various hells (niraya) which are devoid of happiness, the realms of animals, the hungry ghosts (peta), the realm of humans, and various heaven realms where the devas live (such as Tavatimsa and Tusita).

(iii) **Rūpa-bhava**, the plane of form. The realms in this plane are associated with the four meditative absorptions (jhanas) and those who attain these meditations are reborn in these divine realms.

These various planes of existence can be found in countless world systems (loka-dhatu), which are born, expand, contract and are destroyed in a cyclical nature across vast expanses of time (measures in kappas). This cosmology is similar to other ancient Indian systems, such as the Jain cosmology. This entire cyclical multiverse of constant birth and death is called samsara. Outside of this system of samsara is nibbana (lit. "vanishing, quenching, blowing out"), a deathless (amata) and transcendent reality, which is a total and final release (vimutti) from all suffering (dukkha) and rebirth.

22.6 Soteriology and Buddhology

According to Theravāda doctrine, release from suffering (i.e. nibbana) is attained in four stages of awakening (bodhi):

1. **Stream-Enterers**: Those who have destroyed the first three fetters (the false view of self, doubt/indecision, and clinging to ethics and vows);
2. **Once-Returners**: Those who have destroyed the first three fetters and have weakened the fetters of desire and ill-will;

3. **Non-Returners**: Those who have destroyed the five lower fetters, which bind beings to the world of the senses;
4. **Arahants** (lit. "honorable" or "worthies"): Those who have realised Nibbana and are free from all defilements. They have abandoned all ignorance, craving for existence, restlessness (uddhacca) and subtle pride (māna).

In Theravāda Buddhism, a Buddha is a sentient being who has discovered the path out of samsara by themselves, has reached Nibbana and then makes the path available to others by teaching (known as "turning the wheel of the Dhamma"). A Buddha is also believed to have extraordinary powers and abilities (abhiññā), such as the ability to read minds and fly through the air.

The Theravāda canon depicts Gautama Buddha as being the most recent Buddha in a line of previous Buddhas stretching back for aeons. They also mention the future Buddha, named Metteya. Traditionally, the Theravāda school also rejects the idea that there can be numerous Buddhas active in the world at the same time.

Regarding the question of how a sentient being becomes a Buddha, the Theravāda school also includes a presentation of this path. Indeed, according to Buddhaghosa, there are three main soteriological paths: the path of the Buddhas (buddhayāna); the way of the individual Buddhas (paccekabuddhayāna); and the way of the disciples (sāvakayāna).

However, unlike in Mahayana Buddhism, the Theravāda holds that the Buddha path is not for everyone and that beings on the Buddha path (bodhisattas) are quite rare. While in Mahayana, bodhisattas refers to beings who have developed the wish to become Buddhas, Theravāda (like other early Buddhist schools), defines a bodhisatta as someone who has made a resolution (abhinīhāra) to become a Buddha in front of a living Buddha, and has also received a confirmation from that Buddha that they will reach Buddhahood. Dhammapala's Cariyāpiṭaka is a Theravāda text which focuses on the path of the Buddhas, while the Nidānakathā and the Buddhavaṃsa are also Theravāda texts which discuss the Buddha path.

22.7 Main Doctrinal Differences with Other Buddhist Traditions

The orthodox standpoints of Theravāda in comparison to other Buddhist schools are presented in the Kathāvatthu ("Points of Controversy"), as well as in other works by later commentators like Buddhaghosa.

Traditionally, the Theravāda maintains the following key doctrinal positions, though not all Theravādins agree with the traditional point of view:

- On the philosophy of time, the Theravāda tradition follows philosophical presentism, the view that only present moment phenomena (dhamma) exist, against the eternalist view of the Sarvāstivādin tradition, which held that dhammas exist in all three times – past, present, future.
- The arahant is never a layperson, for they have abandoned the fetters of a layperson, including married life, using money, etc.
- The power (bala) of a Buddha is unique and not common to the disciples (savaka) or arahants.
- Theravāda Abhidhamma holds that a single thought (citta) cannot last as long as a day.
- Theravāda Abhidhamma holds that insight into the four noble truths happens in one moment (khaṇa), rather than gradually (anupubba), as was held by Sarvastivada. The defilements (kilesa) are also abandoned in a single moment, not gradually.
- Theravāda Abhidhamma traditionally rejects the view that there is an intermediate or transitional state (antarabhāva) between rebirths, they hold that rebirth happens instantaneously (in one mind moment). However, as has been noted by various modern scholars like Bhikkhu Sujato, there are canonical passages which support the idea of an intermediate state (such as the Kutuhalasāla Sutta). Some Theravāda scholars have defended the idea of an intermediate state and it is also a very common belief among some monks and laypersons in the Theravāda world (where it is commonly referred to as the gandhabba or antarabhāva).
- Theravāda also does not accept the Mahayana notion that there are two forms of nibbana, an inferior "localised" or "abiding" (pratiṣṭhita) nirvana and a non-abiding (apratiṣṭhita) nirvana. Such a dual nirvana theory is absent in the suttas. According to the Kathāvatthu, there can be no divining line separating the unconditioned element and there is no superiority or inferiority in the unity of nibbana.
- Theravāda exegetical works consider nibbana to be a real existent, instead of just a conceptual or nominal existent (prajñapti) referring to the mere destruction (khayamatta) of the defilements or non-existence of the five aggregates, as was held by some in

the Sautrantika school for example. In Theravāda scholasticism, nibbana is defined as the cessation (nirodha) consisting in non-arising and exists separately from the mere destruction of passion, hatred and delusion.

- Theravāda exegetical works, mental phenomena last for a very short moment or instant (khaṇa), but physical phenomena do not.
- Theravāda holds that the Buddha resided in the human realm (manussa-loka). It rejects the docetic view found in Mahayana, which says that the Buddha's physical body was a mere manifestation, emanation or magical creation (nirmāṇa) of a transcendental being, and thus, that his birth and death a mere show and unreal. Also, the Theravāda school rejects the view that there are currently numerous Buddhas in all directions.
- Theravāda holds that there is a ground level of consciousness called the bhavaṅga, which conditions the rebirth consciousness.
- Theravāda rejects the Pudgalavada doctrine of the pudgala ("person" or "personal entity") as being more than a conceptual designation imputed on the five aggregates.
- Theravāda rejects the view of the Lokottaravada schools which held that the all acts done by the Buddha (including all speech, defecation and urination, etc.) were supramundane or transcendental (lokuttara). Also, for Theravāda, a Buddha does not have the power to stop something that has arisen from ceasing, they cannot stop a being from getting old, sick or dying, and they cannot create a permanent thing (like a flower that doesn't die).
- Theravāda traditionally defends the idea that the Buddha himself taught the Abhidhamma Pitaka. This is now being questioned by some modern Theravādins in light of modern Buddhist studies scholarship.
- Theravāda, nibbana is the only unconstructed phenomenon (asankhata-dhamma, asankhatadhatu). Unlike in the Sarvāstivāda school, space (akasa), is seen as a constructed dhamma in Theravāda. Even the four noble truths are not unconstructed phenomena, neither is the domain of cessation (nirodhasamapatti). "Tness" (tathatā) is also a constructed phenomenon. According to the Dhammasangani, nibbana, the unconstructed element, is 'without condition' (appaccaya) and is different from the five aggregates which are 'with condition' (sappaccaya).

- Theravāda, the bodhisatta path is suitable only for a few exceptional people (like Sakyamuni and Metteya). Theravāda also defines a bodhisatta as someone who has made a vow in front of a living Buddha.
- Theravāda, there is a physical sensory organ (indriya) that conditions the mental consciousness (manovinñāna) and is the material support for consciousness. Some later Theravāda works like the Visuddhimagga locate this physical basis for consciousness at the heart (hadaya-vatthu), the Pali Canon itself is silent on this issue. Some modern Theravāda scholars propose alternative notions. For example, the basis for consciousness.
- Theravādins generally reject the Mahayana sutras as Buddhavacana (word of the Buddha), and do not study or see these texts (or Mahayana doctrines) as reliable sources. They reject the view that the Tipitaka is incomplete or inferior (i.e. "Hinayana") and that Mahayana texts are somehow more advanced.
- Theravādins traditionally believe that an awakened arahant has an "incorruptible nature" and is thus morally perfect. He has no ignorance or doubts. According to Theravāda doctrine, arahants (as well as the other three lesser ariyas: stream enterers etc.) cannot fall back or regress from their state.

22.8 Lay and Monastic Life

Traditionally, Theravāda Buddhism has observed a distinction between the practices suitable for a lay person and the practices undertaken by ordained monks (in ancient times, there was a separate body of practices for nuns). While the possibility of significant attainment by laymen is not entirely disregarded by the Theravāda, it generally occupies a position of less prominence than in the Mahāyāna and Vajrayāna traditions, with monastic life being hailed as a superior method of achieving Nirvana. The view that Theravāda, unlike other Buddhist schools, is primarily a monastic tradition has, however, been disputed.

Both Mahāyāna and Theravāda have as their foundation strong monastic communities, which are almost identical in their regulations. Schools of Mahāyāna Buddhism without monastic communities of fully ordained monks and nuns are relatively recent and atypical developments, usually based on cultural and historical considerations rather than differences in fundamental doctrine. Both Mahāyāna and Theravāda also provided a clear and important place for lay followers.

The role of lay people has traditionally been primarily occupied with activities that are commonly termed merit-making (falling under the category of kammatic Buddhism). Merit-making activities include offering food and other basic necessities to monks, making donations to temples and monasteries, burning incense or lighting candles before images of the Buddha, chanting protective or scriptural verses from the Pali Canon, building roads and bridges, charity to the needy and providing drinking water to strangers along roadside. Some lay practitioners have always chosen to take a more active role in religious affairs, while still maintaining their lay status. Dedicated lay men and women sometimes act as trustees or custodians for their temples, taking part in the financial planning and management of the temple. Others may volunteer significant time in tending to the mundane needs of local monks (by cooking, cleaning, maintaining temple facilities, etc.). Study of the Pāli scriptures and the practice of meditation are less common among the lay community in the past, though in the 20th century these areas have become more popular to the lay community, especially in Thailand.

It is also possible for a lay disciple to become enlightened. As Bhikkhu Bodhi notes, "The Suttas and commentaries do record a few cases of lay disciples attaining the final goal of Nirvana. However, such disciples either attain Arahantship on the brink of death or enter the monastic order soon after their attainment. They do not continue to dwell at home as Arahant householders, for dwelling at home is incompatible with the state of one who has severed all craving."

In the modern era, it is now common for lay disciples to practice meditation, attend lay meditation centers and even aim for awakening. The impetus for this trend began in Myanmar and was supported by prime minister U Nu who himself established the International Meditation Center (IMC) in Yangon. Modern lay teachers such as U Ba Khin (who was also the Accountant General of the Union of Burma) promoted meditation as part of a layperson's daily routine. Another development in modern Theravāda is "the formation of lay Buddhist associations that have partially assumed the social service responsibilities formerly associated with the monastery".

Theravāda sources dating back to medieval Sri Lanka (2nd century BCE to 10th century CE) such as the Mahavamsa show that monastic roles in the tradition were often seen as being in a polarity between urban monks (Sinhala: khaamawaasii, Pāli: gamavasi) on one end and rural forest monks (Sinhala: aranyawaasii, Pali: araññavasi, nagaravasi, also known as Tapassin) on the other. The ascetic focused monks were known by the names Pamsukulikas (rag robe wearers) and Araññikas (forest dwellers).

The Mahavamsa mentions forest monks associated with the Mahavihara. The Pāli Dhammapada Commentary mentions another split based on the "duty of study" and the "duty of contemplation". This second division has traditionally been seen as corresponding with the city – forest split, with the city monks focusing on the vocation of books (ganthadhura) or learning (pariyatti) while the forest monks leaning more towards meditation (vipassanadhura) and practice (patipatti). However, this opposition is not consistent, and urban monasteries have often promoted meditation while forest communities have also produced excellent scholars, such as the Island Hermitage of Nyanatiloka.

Scholar monks generally undertake the path of studying and preserving Theravāda's Pāli literature. Forest monks tend to be the minority among Theravāda sanghas and also tend to focus on asceticism (dhutanga) and meditative praxis. They view themselves as living closer to the ideal set forth by the Buddha, and are often perceived as such by lay folk, while at the same time often being on the margins of the Buddhist establishment and on the periphery of the social order.

While this divide seems to have been in existence for some time in the Theravāda school, only in the 10th century is a specifically forest monk monastery, mentioned as existing near Anuradhapura, called "Tapavana". This division was then carried over into the rest of Southeast Asia as Theravāda spread.

Today there are forest-based traditions in most Theravāda countries, including the Sri Lankan Forest Tradition, the Thai Forest Tradition as well as lesser-known forest-based traditions in Burma and Laos, such as the Burmese forest-based monasteries of the Pa Auk Sayadaw. In Thailand, forest monks are known as phra thudong (ascetic wandering monks) or phra thudong kammathan (wandering ascetic meditator).

22.9 The Goal

There was an occasion when a wanderer, named Vacchagotta, came to ask the Buddha the question, "Where do enlightened beings go when they die?"

The Buddha said, "If we had a little fire burning in front of us and let it go out, then I asked you, 'Where did the fire go, north, south, east, or west? What would you say?'"

Vacchagotta furrowed his brow and said, "It didn't go anywhere. It just went out. The question doesn't apply."

The Buddha said, "Exactly so, Vacchagotta. The way you phrased the question presumes a reality that does not exist." We cannot say an enlightened being goes anywhere. The state of an enlightened one at the breaking up of the body is indescribable.

There is another exchange that the Buddha had, with a wanderer called Upasiva in the Sutta Nipata, in The Way to the Beyond. Upasiva has asked the Buddha a similar question, to which he replies:

"Like a flame struck by a sudden gust of wind,
in a flash it has gone out,
and nothing more can be known about it.
It is the same with a wise person
freed from mind and body —
in a flash they have gone,
and nothing more can be known about them;
designation applies to them no more."
"Please explain this clearly to me, Sir," said Upasiva,
"for it's a state that you have understood:
one who has reached the end —
do they not exist,
or are they made immortal, perfectly free?"
"One who has reached the end
has no criterion
by which they can be measured.
That by which they could be talked of
is no more.
You cannot say, 'They do not exist.'
When all modes of being,
all phenomena are removed,
then all means of description
have gone too."

Chapter - 23

Mahayana Philosophy

23.1 Introduction to Mahayana

Mahāyāna (Great Vehicle) is a term for a broad group of Buddhist traditions, texts, philosophies, and practices. Mahāyāna Buddhism developed in India (c. 1st century BCE onwards) and is considered one of the two main existing branches of Buddhism (the other being Theravāda). Mahāyāna accepts the main scriptures and teachings of early Buddhism, but also adds various new doctrines and texts such as the Mahāyāna Sūtras and its emphasis on the bodhisattva path and Prajñāpāramitā. Vajrayāna or Mantra traditions are a subset of Mahāyāna, which make use of numerous tantric methods considered to be faster and more powerful at achieving Buddhahood by Vajrayānists.

"Mahāyāna" also refers to the path of the bodhisattva striving to become a fully awakened Buddha (samyaksaṃbuddha) for the benefit of all sentient beings, and is thus also called the "Bodhisattva Vehicle" (Bodhisattvayāna). Mahāyāna Buddhism generally sees the goal of becoming a Buddha through the bodhisattva path as being available to all and sees the state of the arhat as incomplete. Mahāyāna also includes numerous Buddhas and bodhisattvas that are not found in Theravada (such as Amitābha and Vairocana). Mahāyāna Buddhist philosophy also promotes unique theories, such as the Madhyamaka theory of emptiness (śūnyatā), the Vijñānavāda doctrine and the Buddha-nature teaching.

Although it was initially a small movement in India, Mahāyāna eventually grew to become an influential force in Indian Buddhism. Large scholastic centers associated with Mahāyāna such as Nalanda and Vikramashila thrived between the seventh and twelfth centuries. In the course of its history, Mahāyāna Buddhism spread throughout South Asia, Central Asia, East Asia, and Southeast Asia. It remains influential today in China, Taiwan, Mongolia, Korea, Japan, Vietnam, Nepal, Malaysia, and Bhutan. The Mahāyāna tradition is the largest major tradition of Buddhism existing today.

The term Mahāyāna ("Great Vehicle") was originally an honorary synonym for Bodhisattvayāna ("Bodhisattva Vehicle"), the vehicle of a bodhisattva seeking buddhahood for the benefit of all sentient beings. The term Mahāyāna (which had earlier been used simply as an epithet for Buddhism itself) was therefore adopted at an early date as a synonym for the path and the teachings of the bodhisattvas. Since it was simply an honorary term for Bodhisattvayāna, the adoption of the term Mahāyāna and its application to Bodhisattvayāna did not represent a significant turning point in the development of a Mahāyāna tradition.

The earliest Mahāyāna texts, such as the Lotus Sūtra, often use the term Mahāyāna as a synonym for Bodhisattvayāna, but the term Hīnayāna is comparatively rare in the earliest sources. The presumed dichotomy between Mahāyāna and Hīnayāna can be deceptive, as the two terms were not actually formed in relation to one another in the same era.

Among the earliest and most important references to Mahāyāna are those that occur in the Lotus Sūtra (Skt. Saddharma Puṇḍarīka Sūtra) dating between the 1st century BCE and the 1st century CE. The term first used in an earlier Gandhāri Prakrit version of the Lotus Sūtra was not the term mahāyāna but the Prakrit word mahāyāna in the sense of mahājñāna (great knowing). At a later stage when the early Prakrit word was converted into Sanskrit, this mahājāna, being phonetically ambivalent, may have been converted into mahāyāna, possibly because of what may have been a double meaning in the famous Parable of the Burning House, which talks of three vehicles or carts (yāna).

23.2 Origins of Mahāyāna

The origins of Mahāyāna are still not completely understood and there are numerous competing theories. The earliest views of Mahāyāna assumed that it existed as a separate school in competition with the so-called "Hīnayāna" schools. Some of the major theories about the origins of Mahāyāna include the following:

The Lay view states that laypersons were particularly important in the development of Mahāyāna. This view is partly based on some texts like the Vimalakirti Sūtra, which praise lay figures at the expense of monastics. This theory is no longer widely accepted since numerous early Mahāyāna works promote monasticism and asceticism.

The Mahāsāṃghika origin theory, which argues that Mahāyāna developed within the Mahāsāṃghika tradition. This is defended by many scholars such who argue that at least some Mahāyāna elements developed among Mahāsāṃghika communities (from the 1st century BCE onwards), possibly in the area along the Kṛṣṇa River in the Āndhra region of southern India. The Mahāsāṃghika doctrine of the supramundane (lokottara) nature of the Buddha is sometimes seen as a precursor to Mahāyāna views of the Buddha. Some scholars also see Mahāyāna figures like Nāgārjuna, Dignaga, Candrakīrti, Āryadeva, and Bhavaviveka as having ties to the Mahāsāṃghika tradition of Āndhra. However, other scholars have also pointed to different regions as being important, such as Gandhara and northwest India.

The Mahāsāṃghika origins theory has also slowly been shown to be problematic by scholarship that revealed how certain Mahāyāna sutras show traces of having developed among other nikāyas or monastic orders (such as the Dharmaguptaka).Because of such evidence, some scholars argue that the movement was not sectarian and was possibly pan-buddhist. There is no evidence that Mahāyāna ever referred to a separate formal school or sect of Buddhism, but rather that it existed as a certain set of ideals, and later doctrines, for aspiring bodhisattvas.

The "forest hypothesis" meanwhile states that Mahāyāna arose mainly among "hard-core ascetics, members of the forest dwelling (aranyavasin) wing of the Buddhist Order", who were attempting to imitate the Buddha's forest living. This theory is based on certain sutras like the Ugraparipṛcchā Sūtra and the Mahāyāna Rāṣṭrapālapaṛiprcchā which promote ascetic practice in the wilderness as a superior and elite path. These texts criticise monks who live in cities and denigrate the forest life. The Ugraparipṛccha Sūtra represents the earliest form of Mahāyāna, which presents the bodhisattva path as a 'supremely difficult enterprise' of elite monastic forest asceticism. Mahāyāna was primarily a textual movement, focused on the revelation, preaching, and dissemination of Mahāyāna sutras, that developed within, and never really departed from, traditional Buddhist social and institutional structures.

23.3 Early Mahāyāna

The earliest textual evidence of "Mahāyāna" comes from sūtras ("discourses", scriptures) originating around the beginning of the common era. Jan Nattier has noted that some of the earliest Mahāyāna texts, such as the Ugraparipṛccha Sūtra use the term "Mahāyāna", yet there is no doctrinal difference between Mahāyāna in this context and the early schools. Instead, Nattier writes that in the earliest sources, "Mahāyāna" referred to the rigorous emulation of Gautama Buddha's path to Buddhahood.[17]

Some important evidence for early Mahāyāna Buddhism comes from the texts translated by the Indoscythian monk Lokakṣema in the 2nd century

CE, who came to China from the kingdom of Gandhāra. These are some of the earliest known Mahāyāna texts. Study of these texts show that they strongly promote monasticism (contra the lay origin theory), acknowledge the legitimacy of arhatship, do not recommend devotion towards 'celestial' bodhisattvas and do not show any attempt to establish a new sect or order. A few of these texts often emphasise ascetic practices, forest dwelling, and deep states of meditative concentration (samadhi).

Indian Mahāyāna never had nor ever attempted to have a separate Vinaya or ordination lineage from the early schools of Buddhism, and therefore each bhikṣu or bhikṣuṇī adhering to the Mahāyāna formally belonged to one of the early Buddhist schools. Membership in these nikāyas, or monastic orders, continues today, with the Dharmaguptaka nikāya being used in East Asia, and the Mūlasarvāstivāda nikāya being used in Tibetan Buddhism. Therefore, Mahāyāna was never a separate monastic sect outside of the early schools.

While monastic Mahāyānists belonged to a nikāya, not all members of a nikāya were Mahāyānists. From Chinese monks visiting India, we now know that both Mahāyāna and non-Mahāyāna monks in India often lived in the same monasteries side by side. It is also possible that, formally, Mahāyāna would have been understood as a group of monks or nuns within a larger monastery taking a vow together (known as a "kriyākarma") to memorise and study a Mahāyāna texts.

The earliest stone inscription containing a recognizably Mahāyāna formulation and a mention of the Buddha Amitābha (an important Mahāyāna figure) was found in the Indian subcontinent in Mathura, and dated to around 180 CE. Remains of a statue of a Buddha bear the Brāhmī inscription: "Made in the year 28 of the reign of King Huviṣka, ... for the Blessed One, the Buddha Amitābha." There is also some evidence that the Kushan Emperor Huviṣka himself was a follower of Mahāyāna. A Sanskrit manuscript fragment in the Schøyen Collection describes Huviṣka as having "set forth in the Mahāyāna." Evidence of the name "Mahāyāna" in Indian inscriptions in the period before the 5th century is very limited in comparison to the multiplicity of Mahāyāna writings transmitted from Central Asia to China at that time.

Based on archeological evidence the Indian Mahāyāna remained an extremely limited minority movement – if it remained at all – that attracted absolutely no documented public or popular support for at least two more centuries. Likewise, Mahāyāna's virtual invisibility in the archaeological record until the fifth century. These communities were probably not a single unified movement, but scattered groups based on different practices and sutras. One reason for this view is that Mahāyāna sources are extremely diverse, advocating many different, often conflicting doctrines and positions.

We find one scripture (the Aksobhya-vyuha) that advocates both srávaka and bodhisattva practices, propounds the possibility of rebirth in a pure land, and enthusiastically recommends the cult of the book, yet seems to know nothing of emptiness theory, the ten bhumis, or the trikaya, while another (the P'u-sa pen-yeh ching) propounds the ten bhumis and focuses exclusively on the path of the bodhisattva, but never discusses the paramitas. A Madhyamika treatise (Nagarjuna's Mulamadhyamika-karikas) may enthusiastically deploy the rhetoric of emptiness without ever mentioning the bodhisattva path, while a Yogacara treatise (Vasubandhu's Madhyanta-vibhaga-bhasya) may delve into the particulars of the trikaya doctrine while eschewing the doctrine of ekayana. We must be prepared, in other words, to encounter a multiplicity of Mahayanas flourishing even in India, not to mention those that developed in East Asia and Tibet.

In spite of being a minority in India, Indian Mahāyāna was an intellectually vibrant movement, which developed various schools of thought during what The Golden Age of Indian Buddhist Philosophy (from the beginning of the first millennium CE up to the 7th century). Some major Mahāyāna traditions are Prajñāpāramitā, Mādhyamaka, Yogācāra, Buddha-nature (Tathāgatagarbha), and the school of Dignaga and Dharmakirti as the last and most recent. Major early figures include Nagarjuna, Āryadeva, Aśvaghoṣa, Asanga, Vasubandhu, and Dignaga. Mahāyāna Buddhists seem to have been active in the Kushan Empire (30–375 CE), a period which saw great missionary and literary activities by Buddhists.

23.4 Growth of Mahāyāna Movement

The Mahāyāna movement (or movements) remained quite small until it experienced much growth in the fifth century. Very few manuscripts have been found before the fifth century (the exceptions are from Bamiyan). The fifth and sixth centuries appear to have been a watershed for the production of Mahāyāna manuscripts. Likewise it is only in the 4th and 5th centuries CE that epigraphic evidence shows some kind of popular support for Mahāyāna, including some possible royal support at the kingdom of Shan as well as in Bamiyan and Mathura.

Still, even after the 5th century, the epigraphic evidence which use the term Mahāyāna is still quite small and is notably mainly monastic, not lay. By this time, Chinese pilgrims, such as Faxian (337–422 CE), Xuanzang (602–664), Yijing (635–713 CE) were travelling to India, and their writings do describe monasteries which they label 'Mahāyāna' as well as monasteries where both Mahāyāna monks and non-Mahāyāna monks lived together.

After the fifth century, Mahāyāna Buddhism and its institutions slowly grew in influence. Some of the most influential institutions became massive monastic university complexes such as Nalanda (established by the 5th-century CE Gupta emperor, Kumaragupta I) and Vikramashila (established under Dharmapala c. 783 to 820) which were centers of various branches of scholarship, including Mahāyāna philosophy. The Nalanda complex eventually became the largest and most influential Buddhist centre in India for centuries. Even so it seems that fewer than 50 percent of the monks encountered by Xuanzang (Hsüan-tsang; c. 600–664) on his visit to India actually were Mahāyānists.

23.5 Expansion of Mahāyāna Movement Outside India

Over time Indian Mahāyāna texts and philosophy reached Central Asia and China through trade routes like the Silk Road, afterwards spreading throughout East Asia. Over time, Central Asian Buddhism became heavily influenced by Mahāyāna and it was a major source for Chinese Buddhism. Mahāyāna works have also been found in Gandhāra, indicating the importance of this region for the spread of Mahāyāna. Central Asian Mahāyāna scholars were very important in the Silk Road Transmission of Buddhism. They include translators like Lokakṣema (c. 167–186), Dharmarakṣa (c. 265–313), Kumārajīva (c. 401) and Dharmakṣema (385–433). The site of Dunhuang seems to have been a particularly important place for the study of Mahāyāna Buddhism.

By the fourth century, Chinese monks like Faxian (c. 337–422 CE) had also begun to travel to India (now dominated by the Guptas) to bring back Buddhist teachings, especially Mahāyāna works. These figures also wrote about their experiences in India and their work remains invaluable for understanding Indian Buddhism. In some cases Indian Mahāyāna traditions were directly transplanted, as with the case of the East Asian Madhymaka (by Kumārajīva) and East Asian Yogacara (especially by Xuanzang). Later, new developments in Chinese Mahāyāna led to new Chinese Buddhist traditions like Tiantai, Huayen, Pure Land and Chan Buddhism (Zen). These traditions would then spread to Korea, Vietnam and Japan.

Forms of Mahāyāna Buddhism which are mainly based on the doctrines of Indian Mahāyāna sutras are still popular in East Asian Buddhism, which is mostly dominated by various branches of Mahāyāna Buddhism. In this tradition in the Far East, primacy has always been given to study of the Mahāyāna sūtras.

23.6 Later Developments in Mahāyāna

Beginning during the Gupta (c. 3rd century CE–575 CE) period a new movement began to develop which drew on previous Mahāyāna doctrine as well as new Pan-Indian tantric ideas. This came to be known by various names such as **Vajrayāna** (Tibetan: rdo rje theg pa), **Mantrayāna**, and Esoteric Buddhism or "Secret Mantra" (Guhyamantra). This new movement continued into the Pala era (8th century–12th century CE), during which it grew to dominate Indian Buddhism. Possibly led by groups of wandering tantric yogis named mahasiddhas, this movement developed new tantric spiritual practices and also promoted new texts called the Buddhist Tantras. Philosophically, Vajrayāna Buddhist thought remained grounded in the Mahāyāna Buddhist ideas of Madhymaka, Yogacara and Buddha-nature. Tantric Buddhism generally deals with new forms of meditation and ritual which often makes use of the visualisation of Buddhist ḍeities (including Buddhas, bodhisattvas, dakinis, and fierce deities) and the use of mantras. Most of these practices are esoteric and require ritual initiation or introduction by a tantric master (vajracarya) or guru.

The source and early origins of Vajrayāna remains a subject of debate among scholars. Some scholars argue that Vajrayāna derives its tantric content from Shaivism and that it developed as a result of royal courts sponsoring both Buddhism and Saivism. Vajrayāna works like the Samvara and Guhyasamaja texts show direct borrowing from Shaiva tantric literature. However, other scholars question the idea that Indian tantrism developed in Shaivism first and that it was then adopted into Buddhism. It is difficult to a chronology for the Shaiva tantric literature that both traditions developed side by side, drawing on each other as well as on local Indian tribal religion.

Whatever the case, this new tantric form of Mahāyāna Buddhism became extremely influential in India, especially in Kashmir and in the lands of the Pala Empire. It eventually also spread north into Central Asia, the Tibetan plateau and to East Asia. **Vajrayāna remains the dominant form of Buddhism in Tibet**, in surrounding regions like Bhutan and in Mongolia. Esoteric elements are also an important part of East Asian Buddhism where it is referred to by various terms. These include: Zhēnyán, Mìjiao, Mìzōng, or Tángmì. in Chinese and Shingon, Tomitsu, Mikkyo, and Taimitsu in Japanese.

23.7 Worldview about Mahāyāna Buddhism

Few things can be said with certainty about Mahāyāna Buddhism in general other than that the Buddhism practiced in China, Indonesia,

Vietnam, Korea, Tibet, and Japan is Mahāyāna Buddhism. Mahāyāna can be described as a loosely bound collection of many teachings and practices (some of which are seemingly contradictory). Mahāyāna constitutes an inclusive and broad set of traditions characterised by plurality and the adoption of a vast number of new sutras, ideas and philosophical treatises in addition to the earlier Buddhist texts.

Broadly speaking, Mahāyāna Buddhists accept the classic Buddhist doctrines found in early Buddhism (i.e. the Nikāya and Āgamas), such as the Middle Way, Dependent origination, the Four Noble Truths, the Noble Eightfold Path, the Three Jewels, the Three marks of existence and the bodhipakṣadharmas (aids to awakening). Mahāyāna Buddhism further accepts some of the ideas found in Buddhist Abhidharma thought. However, Mahāyāna also adds numerous Mahāyāna texts and doctrines, which are seen as definitive and in some cases superior teachings. The broad range and doctrinal liberality of Mahāyāna as "a vast ocean where all kinds of living beings are allowed to thrive in a most generous manner, almost verging on a chaos."

The main impulse behind Mahāyāna is the vision which sees the motivation to achieve Buddhahood for the sake of other beings as being the supreme religious motivation. This is way that Mahāyāna is defined in his Bodhipathapradipa. Mahāyāna is not as such an institutional identity. Rather, it is an inner motivation and vision, and this inner vision can be found in anyone regardless of their institutional position. Thus, instead of a specific school or sect, Mahāyāna is a "family term" or a religious tendency, which is united by "a vision of the ultimate goal of attaining full Buddhahood for the benefit of all sentient beings (the 'bodhisattva ideal') and also (or eventually) a belief that Buddhas are still around and can be contacted (hence the possibility of an ongoing revelation)."

23.8 The Buddhas and Bodhisattvas

Buddhas and Bodhisattvas (beings on their way to Buddhahood) are central elements of Mahāyāna. Mahāyāna has a vastly expanded cosmology and theology, with various Buddhas and powerful bodhisattvas residing in different worlds and buddha-fields (buddha ksetra). Buddhas, unique to Mahāyāna, include the Buddhas **Amitābha** ("Infinite Light"), Akṣobhya ("the Imperturbable"), **Bhaiṣajyaguru** ("Medicine guru") and Vairocana ("the Illuminator"). In Mahāyāna, a Buddha is seen as a being that has achieved the highest kind of awakening due to his superior compassion and wish to help all beings.

An important feature of Mahāyāna is the way that it understands the nature of a Buddha, which differs from non-Mahāyāna understandings.

Mahāyāna texts not only often depict numerous Buddhas besides Sakyamuni, but see them as transcendental or supramundane (lokuttara) beings with great powers and huge lifetimes. The White Lotus Sutra famously describes the lifespan of the Buddha as immeasurable and states that he actually achieved Buddhahood countless of aeons (kalpas) ago and has been teaching the Dharma through his numerous avatars for an unimaginable period of time.

Furthermore, Buddhas are active in the world, constantly devising ways to teach and help all sentient beings. In Mahāyāna, a Buddha is often seen as "a spiritual king, relating to and caring for the world", rather than simply a teacher who after his death "has completely 'gone beyond' the world and its cares". Buddha Sakyamuni's life and death on earth is then usually understood docetically as a "mere appearance", his death is a show, while in actuality he remains out of compassion to help all sentient beings. The Buddha in Mahāyāna is an omnipotent and almighty divinity "endowed with numerous supernatural attributes and qualities."

The idea that Buddhas remain accessible is extremely influential in Mahāyāna and also allows for the possibility of having a reciprocal relationship with a Buddha through prayer, visions, devotion and revelations. Through the use of various practices, a Mahāyāna devotee can aspire to be reborn in a (**buddhakṣetra, Buddha's pure land or buddhafield**), where they can strive towards buddhahood in the best possible conditions. Depending on the sect, liberation into a buddhafield can be obtained by faith, meditation, or sometimes even by the repetition of Buddha's name. Faith based devotional practices focused on rebirth in pure lands are common in East Asian Pure Land Buddhism.

The influential Mahāyāna concept of the three bodies (trikāya) of a Buddha developed to make sense of the transcendental nature of the Buddha. This doctrine holds that the "bodies of magical transformation" (nirmāṇakāyas) and the "enjoyment bodies" (saṃbhogakāya) are emanations from the ultimate Buddha body, the Dharmakaya, which is none other than the ultimate reality itself, i.e. emptiness or Thusness.

The influential Mahāyāna concept of the three bodies (trikāya) of a Buddha developed to make sense of the transcendental nature of the Buddha. This doctrine holds that the "bodies of magical transformation" (nirmāṇakāyas) and the "enjoyment bodies" (saṃbhogakāya) are emanations from the ultimate Buddha body, the Dharmakaya, which is none other than the ultimate reality itself, i.e. emptiness or Thusness.

The Mahāyāna **bodhisattva** path (mārga) or vehicle (yāna) is seen as being the superior spiritual path by Mahāyānists, over and above the paths of those who seek arhatship or "solitary buddhahood" for their own sake (Śrāvakayāna and Pratyekabuddhayāna). Mahāyāna Buddhists generally hold that pursuing only the personal release from suffering i.e. nirvāṇa is a smaller or inferior aspiration (called "hinayana"), because it lacks the wish and resolve to liberate all other sentient beings from saṃsāra (the round of rebirth) by becoming a Buddha.

This wish to help others is called bodhicitta. One who engages in this path to complete buddhahood is called a bodhisattva. High level bodhisattvas are seen as extremely powerful supramundane beings which are objects of devotion and prayer throughout Mahāyāna lands. Popular bodhisattvas which are revered across Mahāyāna include Avalokiteshvara, Manjushri, Tara and Maitreya. Bodhisattvas could reach the personal nirvana of the arhats, but they reject this goal and remain in saṃsāra to help others out of compassion.

According to eighth century Mahāyāna philosopher Haribhadra, the term "bodhisattva" can technically refer to those who follow any of the three vehicles, since all are working towards bodhi (awakening) and hence the technical term for a Mahāyāna bodhisattva is a mahāsattva (great being) bodhisattva. A Mahāyāna bodhisattva is best defined as: that being who has taken the vow to be reborn, no matter how many times this may be necessary, in order to attain the highest possible goal, that of Complete and Perfect Buddhahood. This is for the benefit of all sentient beings.

There are two models for the nature of bodhisattvas which are seen in the various Mahāyāna texts. One is the idea that a bodhisattva must postpone their awakening until Buddhahood is attained. This could take aeons and in the meantime they will be helping countless beings. After reaching Buddhahood, they do pass on to nirvāṇa. The second model is the idea that there are two kinds of nirvāṇa, the nirvāṇa of an arhat and a superior type of nirvāṇa called apratiṣṭhita (non-abiding, not-established) that allows a Buddha to remain forever engaged in the world, The idea of apratiṣṭhita nirvāṇa may have taken some time to develop and is not obvious in some of the early Mahāyāna literature.

23.9 The Bodhisattva Path

In most classic Mahāyāna sources (as well as in non-Mahāyāna sources on the topic), the bodhisattva path is said to take three or four asaṃkheyyas ("incalculable aeons"), requiring a huge number of lifetimes of practice. However, certain practices are sometimes held to provide shortcuts to Buddhahood (these vary widely by tradition). According to the Bodhipathapradīpa (A Lamp for the Path to Awakening) by the Indian master Atiśa, the central defining feature of a bodhisattva's path is the universal aspiration to end suffering for themselves and all other beings, i.e. bodhicitta.

The bodhisattva's spiritual path is traditionally held to begin with the revolutionary event called the "arising of the Awakening Mind" (bodhicittotpāda), which is the wish to become a Buddha in order to help all beings. This is achieved in different ways, such as the meditation taught by the Indian master Shantideva in his Bodhicaryavatara called "equalising self and others and exchanging self and others." Other Indian masters like Atisha and Kamalashila also teach a meditation in which we contemplate how all beings have been our close relatives or friends in past lives. This contemplation leads to the arising of deep love (maitrī) and compassion (karuṇā) for others, and thus bodhicitta is generated. According to the Indian philosopher Shantideva, when great compassion and bodhicitta arises in a person's heart, they cease to be an ordinary person and become a "son or daughter of the Buddhas".

The idea of the bodhisattva is not unique to Mahāyāna Buddhism and it is found in Theravada and other early Buddhist schools. However, these schools held that becoming a bodhisattva required a prediction of one's future Buddhahood in the presence of a living Buddha. In Mahāyāna a bodhisattva is applicable to any person from the moment they intend to become a Buddha (i.e. the arising of bodhicitta) and without the requirement of a living Buddha. Some Mahāyāna sūtras like the Lotus Sutra, promote the bodhisattva path as being universal and open to everyone.

The generation of bodhicitta may then be followed by the taking of the bodhisattva vows to "lead to Nirvana the whole immeasurable world of beings" as the Prajñaparamita sutras state. This compassionate commitment to help others is the central characteristic of the Mahāyāna bodhisattva. These vows may be accompanied by certain ethical guidelines or bodhisattva precepts. Numerous sutras also state that a key part of the bodhisattva path is the practice of a set of virtues called pāramitās (transcendent or supreme virtues). Sometimes six are outlined: giving, ethical discipline, patient endurance, diligence, meditation and transcendent wisdom. Other sutras (like the Daśabhūmika) give a list of ten, with the addition of upāya (skillful means), praṇidhāna (vow, resolution), Bala (spiritual power) and Jñāna (knowledge). Prajñā (transcendent knowledge or wisdom) is arguably the most important virtue of the bodhisattva. This refers to an understanding of the emptiness of all phenomena, arising from study, deep consideration and meditation.

23.9.1 The Lotus Sutra

The development of the doctrine can also be associated with the Lotus Sūtra and its influence on later sūtras. One of the unique themes in the Lotus Sūtra, particularly in the tenth chapter titled "Teachers of the Dharma", is that everyone has the ability to become a Búddha. In other words, this ability is not limited to monks, nuns, laypeople, śrāvakas, or bodhisattvas, but the chapter insists that other beings such as non-human creatures, dragon kings, centaurs, etc., also have this ability. It also insists that all living being not only have the ability to become a Buddha, but can be a 'teacher of the Dharma' here and now. A connotation to Buddha-nature is also found within the twelfth chapter of the Lotus Sūtra titled 'Devadatta'. It gives no information about the historical Devadatta, but gives the encouragement to understand that just as Devadatta, known everywhere to be evil, has the potential to become a buddha, so too with everyone else. The story of Devadatta is followed by another story about adragon princess who is both a nāga and a female whom the bodhisattva Mañjuśrī proclaims will reach enlightenment immediately, despite her being what she is. This goes contrary to common prejudices and informed opinion.

23.9.2 Bodhisattva Levels

Various texts associate the beginning of the bodhisattva practice with what is called the "path of accumulation" or equipment (saṃbhāra-mārga), which is the first path of the classic five paths schema.

The Daśabhūmika Sūtra as well as other texts also outline a series bodhisattva levels or spiritual stages (bhūmis) on the path to buddhahood. The various texts disagree on the number of stages however, the Daśabhūmika giving ten, for example (and mapping each one to the ten paramitas), the Bodhisattvabhūmi giving seven and thirteen and the Avatamsaka outlining 40 stages.

In later Mahāyāna scholasticism, such as in the work of Kamalashila and Atiśa, the five paths and ten bhūmi systems are merged and this is the progressive path model that is used in Tibetan Buddhism. In these systems, the first bhūmi is reached once one attains "direct, nonconceptual and nondual insight into emptiness in meditative absorption", which is associated with the path of seeing (darśana-mārga). At this point, a bodhisattva is considered an ārya (a noble being).

23.10 Skillful means and the One Vehicle

Skillful means or Expedient techniques (Skt. upāya) is another important virtue and doctrine in Mahāyāna Buddhism. The idea is most famously expounded in the White Lotus Sutra, and refers to any effective method or technique that is conducive to spiritual growth and leads beings to awakening and nirvana. This doctrine states that the Buddha adapts his teaching to whoever he is teaching to out of compassion. Because of this, it's possible that the Buddha may teach seemingly contradictory things to different people. This idea is also used to explain the vast textual corpus found in Mahāyāna.

A closely related teaching is the doctrine of the One Vehicle (ekayāna). This teaching states that even though the Buddha is said to have taught three vehicles (the disciples' vehicle, the vehicle of solitary Buddhas and the bodhicattva vehicle, which are accepted by all early Buddhist schools), these actually are all skillful means which lead to the same place: buddhahood. Therefore, there really aren't three vehicles in an ultimate sense, but one vehicle, the supreme vehicle of the Buddhas, which is taught in different ways depending on the faculties of individuals. Even those beings who think they have finished the path (i.e. the arhats) are actually not done, and they will eventually reach buddhahood.

This doctrine was not accepted in full by all Mahāyāna traditions. The Yogācāra school famously defended an alternative theory which held that not all beings could become Buddhas. This became a subject of much debate throughout Mahāyāna Buddhist history.

23.11 Prajñāpāramitā (Transcendental Knowledge)

Some of the key Mahāyāna teachings are found in the Prajñāpāramitā ("Transcendent Knowledge" or "Perfection of Wisdom") texts, which are some of the earliest Mahāyāna works. Prajñāpāramitā is a deep knowledge of reality which Buddhas and bodhisattvas attain. It is a transcendent, non-conceptual and non-dual kind of knowledge into the true nature of things. This wisdom is also associated with insight into the emptiness (śūnyatā) of dharmas (phenomena) and their illusory nature (māyā). This amounts to the idea that all phenomena (dharmas) without exception have "no essential unchanging core" (i.e. they lack svabhāva, an essence or inherent nature), and therefore have "no fundamentally real existence." These empty phenomena are also said to be conceptual constructions.

Because of this, all dharmas (things, phenomena), even the Buddha's Teaching, the Buddha himself, Nirvāṇa and all living beings, are like "illusions" or "magic" (māyā) and "dreams" (svapna). This emptiness or lack of real existence applies even to the apparent arising and ceasing of phenomena. Because of this, all phenomena are also described as unarisen (anutpāda), unborn (ajata), "beyond coming and going" in the

Prajñāpāramitā literature. Most famously, the Heart Sutra states that "all phenomena are empty, that is, without characteristic, unproduced, unceased, stainless, not stainless, undiminished, unfilled." The Prajñāpāramitā texts also use various metaphors to describe the nature of things, for example, the Diamond Sutra compares phenomena to: "A shooting star, a clouding of the sight, a lamp, an illusion, a drop of dew, a bubble, a dream, a lightning's flash, a thunder cloud."

Prajñāpāramitā is also associated with not grasping, not taking a stand on or "not taking up" (aparigṛhīta) anything in the world. The Aṣṭasāhasrikā Prajñāpāramitā Sūtra explains it as "not grasping at form, not grasping at sensation, perception, volitions and cognition." This includes not grasping or taking up even correct Buddhist ideas or mental signs (such as "not-self", "emptiness", bodhicitta, vows), since these things are ultimately all empty concepts as well.

Attaining a state of fearless receptivity (ksanti) through the insight into the true nature of reality (Dharmatā) in an intuitive, non-conceptual manner is said to be the prajñāpāramitā, the highest spiritual wisdom. The "patient acceptance of the non-arising of dharmas" (anutpattika-dharmakshanti) is "one of the most distinctive virtues of the Mahāyānistic saint." The Prajñāpāramitā texts also claim that this training is not just for Mahāyānists, but for all Buddhists following any of the three vehicles.

23.12 Madhyamaka (Centrism)

The Mahāyāna philosophical school termed Madhyamaka (Middle theory or Centrism, also known as śūnyavāda, 'the emptiness theory') was founded by the second century figure of Nagarjuna. This philosophical tradition focuses on refuting all theories which posit any kind of substance, inherent existence or intrinsic nature (svabhāva).

In his writings, Nagarjuna attempts to show that any theory of intrinsic nature is contradicted by the Buddha's theory of dependent origination, since anything that has an independent existence cannot be dependently originated. The śūnyavāda philosophers were adamant that their denial of svabhāva is not a kind of nihilism (against protestations to the contrary by their opponents).

Using the two truths theory, Madhyamaka claims that while one can speak of things existing in a conventional, relative sense, they do not exist inherently in an ultimate sense. Madhyamaka also argues that emptiness itself is also "empty", it does not have an absolute inherent existence of its own. It is also not to be understood as a transcendental absolute reality. Instead, the emptiness theory is merely a useful concept which should not be clung to. In fact, for Madhyamaka, since everything is empty of true existence, all things are just conceptualisations (prajñapti-matra), including the theory of emptiness, and all concepts must ultimately be abandoned in order to truly understand the nature of things.

23.13 Vijñānavāda (The Consciousness Doctrine)

Vijñānavāda ("the doctrine of consciousness", a.k.a. vijñapti-mātra, "perceptions only" and citta-mātra "mind only") is another important doctrine promoted by some Mahāyāna sutras which later became the central theory of a major philosophical movement which arose during the Gupta period called Yogācāra. The primary sutra associated with this school of thought is the Saṃdhinirmocana Sūtra, which claims that śūnyavāda is not the final definitive teaching (nītārtha) of the Buddha. Instead, the ultimate truth (paramārtha-satya) is said to be the view that all things (dharmas) are only mind (citta), consciousness (vijñāna) or perceptions (vijñapti) and that seemingly "external" objects (or "internal" subjects) do not really exist apart from the dependently originated flow of mental experiences.

When this flow of mentality is seen as being empty of the subject-object duality we impose upon it, one reaches the non-dual cognition of "Thusness" (tathatā), which is nirvana. This doctrine is developed through various theories, the most important being the eight consciousnesses and the three natures. The Saṃdhinirmocana calls its doctrine the 'third turning of the dharma wheel'. The Pratyutpanna sutra also mentions this doctrine, stating: "whatever belongs to this triple world is nothing but thought [citta-mātra]. Why is that? It is because however I imagine things, that is how they appear".

The most influential thinkers in this tradition were the Indian brothers Asanga and Vasubandhu, along with an obscure figure termed Maitreyanātha. Yogācāra philosophers developed their own interpretation of the doctrine of emptiness which also criticised Madhyamaka for falling into nihilism.

23.14 Buddha-Nature

The doctrine ofTathāgata embryo or Tathāgata womb (Tathāgatagarbha), also known as Buddha nature, matrix or principle (Skt: Buddha-dhātu) is important in all modern Mahāyāna traditions, though it is interpreted in many different ways. Broadly speaking, Buddha-nature is concerned with explaining what allows sentient beings to become Buddhas. The earliest sources for this idea may include the Tathāgatagarbha Sūtra and the Mahāyāna Mahāparinirvāṇa Sūtra. The Mahāyāna Mahāparinirvāṇa refers to "a sacred nature that is the basis for [beings] becoming buddhas", and it also describes it as the 'Self' (atman).

This concept is the base or support for the practice of the path, and thus it is the "cause" (hetu) for the fruit of buddhahood. The Tathāgatagarbha Sūtra states that within the defilements is found "the tathagata's wisdom, the tathagata's vision, and the tathagata's body...eternally unsullied, and... replete with virtues no different from my own...the tathagatagarbhas of all beings are eternal and unchanging".

The ideas found in the Buddha nature literature is a source of much debate and disagreement among Mahāyāna Buddhist philosophers as well as modern academics. Some scholars have seen this as an influence from Brahmanic Hinduism, and some of these sutras admit that the use of the term 'Self' is partly done in order to win over non-Buddhist ascetics (in other words, it is a skillful means). The Buddha nature discussed in some Mahāyāna sūtras does not represent a substantial self (ātman) which the Buddha critiqued; rather, it is a positive expression of emptiness (śūnyatā) and represents the potentiality to realise Buddhahood through Buddhist practices. Similarly, this doctrine was not originally dealing with ontological issues, but with "religious issues of realising one's spiritual potential, exhortation, and encouragement."

The Buddha nature genre of sūtras can be seen as an attempt to state Buddhist teachings using positive language while also maintaining the middle way, to prevent people from being turned away from Buddhism by a false impression of nihilism. This is the position taken by the Laṅkāvatāra Sūtra, which states that the Buddhas teach the doctrine of tathāgatagarbha (which sounds similar to an atman) in order to help those beings who are attached to the idea of an atman. However, the sutra goes on to say that the tathāgatagarbha is empty and is not actually a substantial self.

A different view is the idea that Buddha-nature sutras such as the Mahāparinirvāṇa and the Tathāgatagarbha Sūtra teach an affirmative vision of an eternal, indestructible Buddhic Self. A western scholar and lama sees Buddha nature as a true Self that is real and permanent.

23.15 Arguments for Authenticity

Indian Mahāyāna Buddhists faced various criticisms from non-Mahāyānists regarding the authenticity of their teachings. The main critique they faced was that Mahāyāna teachings had not been taught by the Buddha, but were invented by later figures. Numerous Mahāyāna texts discuss this issue and attempt to defend the truth and authenticity of Mahāyāna in various ways.

One idea that Mahāyāna texts put forth is that Mahāyāna teachings were taught later because most people were unable to understand the Mahāyāna sūtras at the time of the Buddha and that people were ready to hear the Mahāyāna only in later times. Certain traditional accounts state that Mahāyāna sutras were hidden away or kept safe by divine beings like Nagas or bodhisattvas until the time came for their dissemination.

Similarly, some sources also state that Mahāyāna teachings were revealed by other Buddhas, bodhisattvas and devas to a select number of individuals (often through visions or dreams). Some scholars have seen a connection with this idea and Mahāyāna meditation practices which involve the visualisation of Buddhas and their Buddha lands.

Another argument that Indian Buddhists used in favour of the Mahāyāna is that its teachings are true and lead to awakening since they are in line with the Dharma. Because of this, they can be said to be "well said" (subhasita), and therefore, they can be said to be the word of the Buddha in this sense. This idea that whatever is "well spoken" is the Buddha's word can be traced to the earliest Buddhist texts, but it is interpreted more widely in Mahāyāna. From the Mahāyāna point of view, a teaching is the "word of the Buddha" because it is in accord with the Dharma, not because it was spoken by a specific individual (i.e. Gautama). This idea can be seen in the writings of Shantideva (8th century), who argues that an "inspired utterance" is the Buddha word if it is "connected with the truth", "connected with the Dharma", "brings about renunciation of kleshas, not their increase" and "it shows the laudable qualities of nirvana, not those of samsara."

The modern Japanese Zen Buddhist scholar D. T. Suzuki similarly argued that while the Mahāyāna sūtras may not have been directly taught by the historical Buddha, the "spirit and central ideas" of Mahāyāna derive from the Buddha. According to Suzuki, Mahāyāna evolved and adapted itself to suit the times by developing new teachings and texts, while maintaining the spirit of the Buddha.

23.16 Mahayana Practice

Mahāyāna Buddhist practice is quite varied. A common set of virtues and practices which is shared by all Mahāyāna traditions are the six perfections or transcendent virtues (pāramitā).

A central practice advocated by numerous Mahāyāna sources is focused around "the acquisition of merit, the universal currency of the Buddhist world, a vast quantity of which was believed to be necessary for the attainment of Buddhahood". Another important class of Mahāyāna

Buddhist practice are textual practices that deal with listening to, memorising, reciting, preaching, worshipping and copying Mahāyāna sūtras.

23.16.1 Pāramitā

Mahāyāna sūtras, especially those of the Prajñāpāramitā genre, teach the practice of the six transcendent virtues or perfections (pāramitā) as part of the path to Buddhahood. Special attention is given to transcendent knowledge (prajñāpāramitā), which is seen as a primary virtue. The term pāramitā can mean "excellence" or "perfection" as well as "that which has gone beyond" or "transcendence".

The Prajñapāramitā sūtras, and a large number of other Mahāyāna texts list six perfections:

1. Dāna pāramitā: generosity, charity, giving.
2. Śīla pāramitā: virtue, discipline, proper conduct (see also: Bodhisattva precepts).
3. Kṣānti pāramitā: patience, tolerance, forbearance, acceptance, endurance.
4. Vīrya pāramitā: energy, diligence, vigour, effort.
5. Dhyāna pāramitā: one-pointed concentration, contemplation, meditation.
6. Prajñā pāramitā: transcendent wisdom, spiritual knowledge.

   This list is also mentioned by the Theravāda commentator Dhammapala, who describes it as a categorisation of the same ten perfections of Theravada Buddhism. According to Dhammapala, Sacca is classified as both Śīla and Prajñā, Mettā and Upekkhā are classified as Dhyāna, and Adhiṭṭhāna falls under all six. Bhikkhu Bodhi states that the correlations between the two sets shows there was a shared core before the Theravada and Mahayana schools split.

   In the Ten Stages Sutra and the Mahāratnakūṭa Sūtra, four more pāramitās are listed:[177]

7. Upāya pāramitā: skillful means.
8. Praṇidhāna pāramitā: vow, resolution, aspiration, determination, this related to the bodhisattva vows.
9. Bala pāramitā: spiritual power.
10. Jñāna pāramitā: knowledge.

23.16.2 Meditation

Mahāyāna Buddhism teaches a vast array of meditation practices. These include meditations which are shared with the early Buddhist traditions, including mindfulness of breathing; mindfulness of the unattractivenes of the body; loving-kindness; the contemplation of dependent origination; and mindfulness of the Buddha. In Chinese Buddhism, these five practices are known as the "five methods for stilling or pacifying the mind" and support the development of the stages of dhyana.

The Yogācārabhūmi-Śāstra (compiled c. 4th century), which is the most comprehensive Indian treatise on Mahāyāna practice, discusses classic Buddhist numerous meditation methods and topics, including the four dhyānas, the different kinds of samādhi, the development of insight (vipaśyanā) and tranquility (śamatha), the four foundations of mindfulness (smṛtyupasthāna), the five hindrances (nivaraṇa), and classic Buddhist meditations such as the contemplation of unattractiveness, impermanence (anitya), suffering (duḥkha), and contemplation death (maraṇasaṃjñā).

Other works of the Yogācāra school, such as Asaṅga's Abhidharmasamuccaya, and Vasubandhu's Madhyāntavibhāga-bhāsya also discuss meditation topics such as mindfulness, smṛtyupasthāna, the 37 wings to awakening, and samadhi.

A very popular Mahāyāna practice from very early times involved the visualisation of a Buddha while practicing mindfulness of a Buddha (buddhānusmṛti) along with their Pure Land. This practice could lead the meditator to feel that they were in the presence of the Buddha and in some cases it was held that it could lead to visions of the Buddhas, through which one could receive teachings from them.

This meditation is taught in numerous Mahāyāna sūtras such as the Pure Land sutras, the Akṣobhya-vyūha and the Pratyutpanna Samādhi. The Pratyutpanna states that through mindfulness of the Buddha meditation one may be able to meet this Buddha in a vision or a dream and learn from them.

Similarly, the Samādhirāja Sūtra for states that:

Those who, while walking, sitting, standing, or sleeping, recollect the moon-like Buddha, will always be in Buddha's presence and will attain the vast nirvāṇa. His pure body is the colour of gold, beautiful is the Protector of the World. Whoever visualises him like this practices the meditation of the bodhisattvas.

In the case of Pure Land Buddhism, it is widely held that the practice of reciting the Buddha's name (called nianfo in Chinese and nembutsu in Japanese) can lead to rebirth in a Buddha's Pure Land, as well as other positive outcomes. In East Asian Buddhism, the most popular Buddha used for this practice is Amitabha.

East Asian Mahāyāna Buddhism also developed numerous unique meditation methods, including the Chan (Zen) practices of huatou, koan meditation, and silent illumination (Jp. shikantaza). Tibetan Buddhism also includes numerous unique forms of contemplation, such as tonglen ("sending and receiving") and lojong ("mind training").

There also numerous meditative practices which are generally considered to be part of a separate category than general or mainstream Mahāyāna meditation. These are the various practices associated with Vajrayāna (also termed Mantrayāna, Secret Mantra, Buddhist Tantra, and Esoteric Buddhism). This family of practices, which include such varied forms as Deity Yoga, Dzogchen, Mahamudra, the Six Dharmas of Nāropa, the recitation of mantras and dharanis, and the use of mudras and mandalas, are very important in Tibetan Buddhism as well as in some forms of East Asian Buddhism (like Shingon and Tendai).

23.17 Mahayana Scriptures

Mahāyāna Buddhism takes the basic teachings of the Buddha as recorded in early scriptures as the starting point of its teachings, such as those concerning karma and rebirth, anātman, emptiness, dependent origination, and the Four Noble Truths. Mahāyāna Buddhists in East Asia have traditionally studied these teachings in the Āgamas preserved in the Chinese Buddhist canon. "Āgama" is the term used by those traditional Buddhist schools in India who employed Sanskrit for their basic canon. These correspond to the Nikāyas used by the Theravāda school. The surviving Āgamas in Chinese translation belong to at least two schools. Most of the Āgamas were never translated into the Tibetan canon, which only contains a few translations of early sutras corresponding to the Nikāyas or Āgamas. However, these basic doctrines are contained in Tibetan translations of later works such as the Abhidharmakośa and the Yogācārabhūmi-Śāstra.

23.17.1 Mahāyāna sutras

In addition to accepting the essential scriptures of the early Buddhist schools as valid, Mahāyāna Buddhism maintains large collections of sūtras that are not recognised as authentic by the modern Theravāda school. The earliest of these sutras do not call themselves 'Mahāyāna,' but use the terms vaipulya (extensive) sutras, or gambhira (profound) sutras. These were also not recognised by some individuals in the early Buddhist schools. In other cases, Buddhist communities such as the Mahāsāṃghika school were divided along these doctrinal lines. In Mahāyāna Buddhism, the Mahāyāna sūtras are often given greater authority than the Āgamas.

The first of these Mahāyāna-specific writings were written probably around the 1st century BCE or 1st century CE. Some influential Mahāyāna sutras are the Prajñaparamita sutras such as the Aṣṭasāhasrikā Prajñāpāramitā Sūtra, the Lotus Sutra, the Pure Land sutras, the Vimalakirti Sutra, the Golden Light Sutra, the Avatamsaka Sutra, the Sandhinirmocana Sutra and the Tathāgatagarbha sūtras.

Mahāyāna sutras contain several elements besides the promotion of the bodhisattva ideal, including "expanded cosmologies and mythical histories, ideas of purelands and great, 'celestial' Buddhas and bodhisattvas, descriptions of powerful new religious practices, new ideas on the nature of the Buddha, and a range of new philosophical perspectives." These texts present stories of revelation in which the Buddha teaches Mahāyāna sutras to certain bodhisattvas who vow to teach and spread these sutras after the Buddha's death. Regarding religious praxis, the most commonly promoted practices in Mahāyāna sutras were seen as means to achieve Buddhahood quickly and easily and included "hearing the names of certain Buddhas or bodhisattvas, maintaining Buddhist precepts, and listening to, memorising, and copying sutras, that they claim can enable rebirth in the pure lands Abhirati and Sukhavati, where it is said to be possible to easily acquire the merit and knowledge necessary to become a Buddha in as little as one lifetime." Another widely recommended practice is anumodana, or rejoicing in the good deeds of Buddhas and Bodhisattvas.

The practice of meditation and visualisation of Buddhas has been seen by some scholars as a possible explanation for the source of certain Mahāyāna sutras which are seen traditionally as direct visionary revelations from the Buddhas in their pure lands. The importance of dream revelations in certain Mahāyāna sutras such as the Arya-svapna-nirdesa lists and interprets 108 dream signs.

One feature of Mahāyāna sutras (especially earlier ones) is "the phenomenon of laudatory self-reference – the lengthy praise of the sutra itself, the immense merits to be obtained from treating even a verse of it with reverence, and the nasty penalties which will accrue in accordance with karma to those who denigrate the scripture." Some Mahāyāna sutras also warn against the accusation that they are not the word of the Buddha (buddhavacana), such as the Astasāhasrikā (8,000 verse) Prajñāpāramitā, which states that such claims come from Mara (the evil tempter). Some of these Mahāyāna sutras also warn those who would denigrate Mahāyāna sutras or those who preach it (i.e. the dharmabhanaka) that this action can lead to rebirth in hell.

Another feature of some Mahāyāna sutras, especially later ones, is increasing sectarianism and animosity towards non-Mahāyāna practitioners (sometimes called sravakas, "hearers") which are sometimes depicted as being part of the 'hīnayāna' (the 'inferior way') who refuse to accept the 'superior way' of the Mahāyāna. The earlier Mahāyāna sutras like the Ugraparipṛcchā Sūtra and the Ajitasena sutra do not present any antagonism towards the hearers or the ideal of arhatship like later sutras do. Regarding the bodhisattva path, some Mahāyāna sutras promote it as a universal path for everyone, while others like the Ugraparipṛcchā see it as something for a small elite of hardcore ascetics.

In the 4th century Mahāyāna abhidharma work Abhidharmasamuccaya, Asaṅga refers to the collection which contains the āgamas as the Śrāvakapiṭaka and associates it with the śrāvakas and pratyekabuddhas. Asaṅga classifies the Mahāyāna sūtras as belonging to the Bodhisattvapiṭaka, which is designated as the collection of teachings for bodhisattvas.

23.17.2 Other Literature

Mahāyāna Buddhism also developed a massive commentarial and exegetical literature, many of which are called śāstra (treatises) or vrittis (commentaries). Philosophical texts were also written in verse form (karikās), such as in the case of the famous Mūlamadhyamika-karikā (Root Verses on the Middle Way) by Nagarjuna, the foundational text of Madhyamika philosophy. Numerous later Madhyamika philosophers like Candrakirti wrote commentaries on this work as well as their own verse works.

Mahāyāna Buddhist tradition also relies on numerous non-Mahayana commentaries (śāstra), a very influential one being the Abhidharmakosha of Vasubandhu, which is written from a non-Mahayana Sarvastivada–Sautrantika perspective.

Vasubandhu is also the author of various Mahāyāna Yogacara texts on the philosophical theory known as vijñapti-matra (conscious construction only). The Yogacara school philosopher Asanga is also credited with numerous highly influential commentaries. In East Asia, the Satyasiddhi śāstra was also influential.

Another influential tradition is that of Dignāga's Buddhist logic whose work focused on epistemology. He produced the Pramānasamuccaya, and later Dharmakirti wrote the Pramānavārttikā, which was a commentary and reworking of the Dignaga text.

Later, Tibetan and Chinese Buddhists continued the tradition of writing commentaries.

23.18 Classifications

Dating back at least to the Saṃdhinirmocana Sūtra is a classification of the corpus of Buddhism into three categories, based on ways of understanding the nature of reality, known as the "Three Turnings of the Dharma Wheel". According to this view, there were three such "turnings":

(i) In the first turning, the Buddha taught the Four Noble Truths at Varanasi for those in the śravaka vehicle. It is described as marvelous and wonderful, but requiring interpretation and occasioning controversy. The doctrines of the first turning are exemplified in the Dharmacakra Pravartana Sūtra. This turning represents the earliest phase of the Buddhist teachings and the earliest period in the history of Buddhism.

(ii) In the second turning, the Buddha taught the Mahāyāna teachings to the bodhisattvas, teaching that all phenomena have no-essence, no arising, no passing away, are originally quiescent, and essentially in cessation. This turning is also described as marvelous and wonderful, but requiring interpretation and occasioning controversy. Doctrine of the second turning is established in the Prajñāpāramitā teachings, first put into writing around 100 BCE. In Indian philosophical schools, it is exemplified by the Mādhyamaka school of Nāgārjuna.

(iii) In the third turning, the Buddha taught similar teachings to the second turning, but for everyone in the three vehicles, including all the śravakas, pratyekabuddhas, and bodhisattvas. These were meant to be completely explicit teachings in their entire detail, for which interpretations would not be necessary, and controversy would not occur. These teachings were established by the Saṃdhinirmocana Sūtra as early as the 1st or 2nd century CE. In the Indian philosophical schools, the third turning is exemplified by the Yogācāra school of Asaṅga and Vasubandhu.

Some traditions of Tibetan Buddhism consider the teachings of Esoteric Buddhism and Vajrayāna to be the third turning of the Dharma Wheel. Tibetan teachers, particularly of the Gelugpa school, regard the second turning as the highest teaching, because of their particular interpretation of Yogācāra doctrine. The Buddha Nature teachings are normally included in the third turning of the wheel.

The different Chinese Buddhist traditions have different schemes of doctrinal periodisation called panjiao which they use to organise sometimes bewildering array of texts.

23.19 Relationship with the Early Texts

Scholars have noted that many key Mahāyāna ideas are closely connected to the earliest texts of Buddhism. The seminal work of Mahāyāna philosophy, Nāgārjuna's Mūlamadhyamakakārikā, mentions the canon's Katyāyana Sūtra (SA 301) by name, and may be an extended commentary on that work. Nāgārjuna systematised the Mādhyamaka school of Mahāyāna philosophy. He may have arrived at his positions from a desire to achieve a consistent exegesis of the Buddha's doctrine as recorded in the canon. In his eyes the Buddha was not merely a forerunner, but the very founder of the Mādhyamaka system. Nāgārjuna also referred to a passage in the canon regarding "nirvanic consciousness" in two different works.

Yogācāra, the other prominent Mahāyāna school in dialectic with the Mādhyamaka school, gave a special significance to the canon's Lesser Discourse on Emptiness. A passage there (which the discourse itself emphasises) is often quoted in later Yogācāra texts as a true definition of emptiness. The thought presented in the Yogācāra school's Abhidharma-samuccaya is undeniably closer to that of the Pali Nikayas than is that of the Theravadin Abhidhamma.

Both the Mādhyamikas and the Yogācārins saw themselves as preserving the Buddhist Middle Way between the extremes of nihilism (everything as unreal) and substantialism (substantial entities existing). The Yogācārins criticised the Mādhyamikas for tending towards nihilism, while the Mādhyamikas criticised the Yogācārins for tending towards substantialism.

Key Mahāyāna texts introducing the concepts of bodhicitta and Buddha nature also use language parallel to passages in the canon containing the Buddha's description of "luminous mind" and appear to have evolved from this idea.

23.20 Contemporary Mahāyāna Buddhism

The main contemporary traditions of Mahāyāna in Asia are:

The East Asian Mahāyāna traditions of China, Korea, Japan and Vietnam, also known as "Eastern Buddhism". There are about 360 million Eastern Buddhists in Asia. In the Indo-Tibetan tradition (mainly found in Tibet, Mongolia, Bhutan, parts of India and Nepal), also known as "Northern Buddhism", the number of people belonging to "Northern Buddhism totals only around 18.2 million."

There are also some minor Mahāyāna traditions practiced by minority groups, such as Newar Buddhism practiced by the Newar people (Nepal) and Azhaliism practiced by the Bai people (Yunnan).

Lastly, some religious traditions such as Bon and Shugendo are strongly influenced by Mahāyāna Buddhism, though they may not considered as being "Buddhist" per se.

Most of the major forms of contemporary Mahāyāna Buddhism are also practiced by Asian immigrant populations in the West and also by western convert Buddhists.

23.20.1 Chinese

Contemporary Chinese Mahāyāna Buddhism (also known as Han Buddhism) is practiced through many varied forms, such as Chan, Pure land and mantra practices. This group is the largest population of Buddhists in the world. There are between 228 and 239 million Mahāyāna Buddhists in the People's Republic of China (this does not include the Tibetan and Mongolian Buddhists who practice Tibetan Buddhism).

The East Asian Mahāyāna Buddhist population in other nations as follows: Taiwanese Buddhists, 8 million; Malaysian Buddhists, 5.5 million; Singaporean Buddhists, 1.5 million; Hong Kong, 0.7 million; Indonesian Buddhists, 4 million, The Philippines: 2.3 million. Most of these are Han Chinese populations.

The modern development of an ideology called Humanistic Buddhism (Chinese: pinyin: rénjiān fójiào, more literally "Buddhism for the Human World") has also been influential on Chinese Buddhist leaders and institutions. Chinese Buddhists may also practice some form of religious syncretism with other Chinese religions. Chinese Buddhism is practice in mainland China, as well as in Taiwan and wherever there are Chinese diaspora communities.

23.20.2 Korean

Korean Buddhism consists mostly of the Korean Seon school (i.e. Zen), primarily represented by the Jogye Order and the Taego Order. Korean Seon also includes some Pure Land practice. It is mainly practiced in South Korea, with a rough population of about 10.9 million Buddhists. There are also some minor schools, such as the Cheontae (i.e. Korean Tiantai), and the esoteric Jingak and Chinŏn schools.

While North Korea's totalitarian government remains repressive and ambivalent towards religion, at least 11 percent of the population is considered to be Buddhist.

23.20.3 Japanese

Japanese Buddhism is divided into numerous traditions which include various sects of Pure Land Buddhism, Tendai, Nichiren Buddhism, Shingon and Zen. There are also various Mahāyāna oriented Japanese new religions that arose in the post-war period. Many of these new religions are lay movements like Sōka Gakkai and Agon Shū.

An estimate of the Japanese Mahāyāna Buddhist population is 52 million and a recent 2018 survey puts the number at 84 million. It should also be noted that many Japanese Buddhists also participate in Shinto practices, such as visiting shrines, collecting amulets and attending festivals.

23.20.4 Vietnamese

Vietnamese Buddhism is strongly influenced by the Chinese tradition. It is a synthesis of numerous practices and ideas. Vietnamese Mahāyāna draws practices from Vietnamese Thiền (Chan/Zen), Tịnh độ (Pure Land), and Mật Tông (Mantrayana) and its philosophy from Hoa Nghiêm (Huayan) and Thiên Thai (Tiantai). New Mahāyāna movements have also developed in the modern era, perhaps the most influential of which has been Thích Nhất Hạnh's Plum Village Tradition, which also draws from Theravada Buddhism.

Though Vietnamese Buddhism suffered extensively during the Vietnam war (1955-1975) and during subsequent communist takeover of the south, there has been a revival of the religion since the liberalisation period following 1986. There are about 43 million Vietnamese Mahāyāna Buddhists.

23.20.5 Northern Buddhism

Indo-Tibetan Buddhism, Tibetan Buddhism or "Northern" Buddhism derives from the Indian Vajrayana Buddhism that was adopted in medieval Tibet. Though it includes numerous tantric Buddhist practices not found in East Asian Mahāyāna, Northern Buddhism still considers itself as part of Mahāyāna Buddhism (albeit as one which also contains a more effective and distinct vehicle or yana).

Contemporary Northern Buddhism is traditionally practiced mainly in the Himalayan regions and in some regions of Central Asia, including:

- The Tibet autonomous region (PRC): 5.4 million;
- North and North-east India (Sikkhim, Ladakh, West Bengal, Jammu and Kashmir): 0.4 million;
- Pakistan: 0.16 million;
- Nepal: 2.9 million;
- Bhutan: 0.49 million;

- Mongolia: 2.7 million;
- Inner Mongolia (PRC): 5 million;
- Buryatia, Tuva and Kalmykia (Russian Federation): 0.7 million.

As with Eastern Buddhism, the practice of northern Buddhism declined in Tibet, China and Mongolia during the communist takeover of these regions (Mongolia: 1924, Tibet: 1959). Tibetan Buddhism continued to be practiced among the Tibetan diaspora population, as well as by other Himalayan peoples in Bhutan, Ladakh and Nepal. Post 1980s though, Northern Buddhism has seen a revival in both Tibet and Mongolia due to more liberal government policies towards religious freedom. Northern Buddhism is also now practiced in the Western world by western convert Buddhists.

23.21 Ten Disputed Practices in Mahayana

According to Pāli sources the ten disputed practices and the rules they violated were as follows:

1. Carrying salt in an animal horn-violated a rule against the storing of Food;
2. Taking food when the shadow on the sundial is two fingers past noon—violated a rule against eating after noon;
3. After eating, travelling to another village to eat another meal the same day—violating the rule against overeating;
4. Holding several fortnightly assemblies within the same boundaries (sīmā)—violated procedures requiring all monks within the sīmā to attend the same fortnightly assembly;
5. Confirming an ecclesiastical in an incomplete assembly and obtaining approval from absent monks afterward—violated the rules of procedure at monastic meetings;
6. Citing habitual practice as the authority for violations of monastic procedures—violated the rules of procedure;
7. Drinking milk whey after meals—violated the rule against eating special food when one was not sick;
8. Drinking unfermented wine—violated the rule against drinking intoxicating beverages;
9. Using a mat with fringes—violated the rule concerning the measurements of rugs; and
10. Accepting gold and silver—violated the rule prohibiting monks from receiving gold and silver.

23.22 Mahāyāna and Hinayāna

The term "Mahāyāna" is usually translated as "Great Vehicle" and the term "Hinayāna" as "Small Vehicle". The appellation "Hinayāna" thus was a deprecatory term used by Mahāyāna practitioners to refer to Nikāya Buddhism. No Buddhist groups ever refer to themselves as Hinayanists.

It is unclear whether Mahayanists referred to the whole Nikāya Buddhism as Hinayāna or only to a specific group. The arguments of the Mahāprajñāpāramitopadeśa (Ta-zhi-tu-lun T1509) are primarily directed against the Vaibhāsikas of the Sarvāstivādin School. The Sarvāstivādins were viewed as Hinayanists in this and many other Mahāyāna texts. Unfortunately, it is not known whether the term "Hinayāna" in Mahāyāna scriptures also referred to the Theravāda and Mahāsanghikas.

A comparison of Fa-hsien's travel diary to that of another Chinese pilgrim, Hsuan-tsang (pinyin: Xuanzang 600-664), Hsi-yu chi (A Record of Travels to Western Regions, T2087), clearly indicates that Fa-hsien used the term "Hinayāna" to refer to all of the schools of Nikāya Buddhism in approximately the same manner. Hsuan-tsang understood Indian Buddhism in approximately the same manner. Hsuan-tsang placed the epithet "Hinayāna" in front of the names of certain schools, such as the Sarvāstivādin, Sammatīya, and Lokuttaravādin Hsuan-tsang referred to the Sri Lankan Theravāda School as "the Mahāyāna Theravāda School". Thus, Hsuan-tsang did not regard all sects of Nikāya Buddhism as Hinayāna. However, he regarded the Lokuttaravādin sect, which is of Mahāsanghika lineage, as Hinayāna despite the many Mahāyāna element found in the Lokuttaravādin biography of the Buddha, the Mahāvastu.

Hinayāna and Mahāyāna Buddhism are not so clearly distinguished in Iching (635-713) travel diary, A Record of Buddhism in India and the Malay Archipelago (Nan-hai- chi-kuei-nei-fa chuan, T 2125). I-ching observed no significant differences in the life styles of Hinayāna and Mahāyāna monks. Both follow the vinaya, were expected to use three robes and a begging bowl, and based their practice on the Four Noble Truths. I-ching noted that "those who paid homage to bodhisattvas and read Mahāyāna sūtras" were Mahāyāna practitioners, while those who did not do were Hinayāna. Only the Mādhyamika and Yogācāra schools were consistently referred to as Mahāyāna. I-ching spent most of his time at the large monastery at Nālandā in central India. His use of the terms "Hinayāna" and "Mahāyāna" may indicate that the divisions between the two types of Buddhism were not very clearly observed at Nālandā in the seventh century.

Hsuan-tsang and I-ching travelled to India when Mahāyāna Buddhism was in its middle period. Their writings, consequently, do not describe

Early Mahāyāna Buddhism. However, in general, the term "Hinayāna" was most often applied to the Sarvāstivādin School. The term "Śrāvakayāna" (vehicle of the listener) and "Bodhisattvayāna" (vehicle of the bodhisattva) are seen older than the terms "Hinayāna" and "Mahāyāna". Hinayāna was eventually substituted for Śrāvakayāna and Mahāyāna for Bodhisattvayāna. Śrāvakayāna was probably used to refer to Nikāya Buddhism in general.

23.22.1 The Doctrinal Differences between Hinayāna and Mahāyāna

The element yāna in the term's "Hinayāna" and "Mahāyāna" literally means "vehicle," and it refers to Buddhist doctrine. By practicing in accordance with doctrine, a person could across the river of cycle existence, travelling from the shore that represented the realm of delusion to the other shore, which represented the realm of enlightenment. Doctrine was compared to a vehicle that would take the practitioner to salvation. The differences between Hinayāna and Mahāyāna doctrine are many. But the major difference, at least according to the Mahāyāna tradition, lies in the attitudes of each toward the salvation of others. The Mahāyāna tradition maintains that a person must save himself by saving others. The Mahāyāna descriptions of religious practice as the six perfections (pāramitā) illustrate how a person could benefit himself only by helping others. These doctrines reflected a view of the world based on the teaching of Dependent Origination.

In contrast, according to Sarvāstivādin and Theravādin doctrine, the goal of practice was to attain salvation for oneself by cutting off all defilements. Once salvation had been attained, the practitioner had accomplished all that was to be done and entered nirvāṇa. Saving others was not a necessary requirement for the completion of practice. Even after enlightenment had been attained, helping others was not required. Śrāvakayāna Buddhism was sometimes called "Buddhism for disciples" because it could be mastered by practicing under qualified teachers. The practitioner was not required to progress from being student to teacher. The term "śrāvaka", which means "listener" or "one who studies", also reflects these qualities. This lack of social concern is probably related to the understanding of the doctrine of Dependent Origination professed by many of the schools of Nikāya Buddhism. For them, Dependent Origination referred to the integration of discrete entities, each with its own nature.

Within the Śrāvakayāna tradition, teachings were transmitted from teacher to disciple. Preaching the Dharma and teaching were practices performed by monks. Because Śrāvakayāna doctrines did not require monks to help others as an integral part of their practice, however, these doctrines were considered "Hinayāna" by Mahāyāna advocates. While

Mahayanists called the Hinayāna tradition "Buddhism for disciples," they conceived of the Mahāyāna tradition as a form of Buddhism that would allow them to become teachers. It was a teaching that would enable them to become Buddhas, to become equal to the Buddha, the teacher of the śrāvakas. Mahāyāna Buddhism encouraged the practitioner to teach even while he was studying, an attitude based on the premise that the practitioner already possessed the potential necessary to realise Buddhahood. A person who knew that he had this potential was called a bodhisattva.

The Mahāyāna conception of the bodhisattva was modeled on the accounts of Śākyamuni Buddha's former lives, which were related in Buddhist literature. Thus, Mahāyāna Buddhism was a teaching or vehicle for bodhisattvas, a bodhisattvayāna. Some Mahāyāna practitioners believed that all people, not only themselves, possessed the potential to become Buddhas. These practitioners wished to help all other people realise that they too had this potential and consequently stressed the importance of helping others. Their beliefs eventually developed into the doctrine that all sentient beings possess the Buddha-nature. Thus, Mahāyāna Buddhism was concerned with lay people and this world while Hinayāna Buddhism was a monastic form of Buddhism characterised by withdrawal from the everyday world.

These differences in attitudes between Hinayāna and Mahāyāna Buddhism resulted in a variety of divergent doctrines. For Hinayāna Buddhists, nirvāṇa was the final goal, characterised by some Mahayanists as the extinction of body and mind. In contrast, Mahāyāna Buddhists argued that the practitioner was to attain "active nirvāṇa" (apratisthita-nirvāṇa) in which he did not remain quiescent. Bodhisattvas such as Manjuśrī, Samantabhadra, and Avalokiteśvara had more powers than Buddhas, but continued to devote themselves to saving sentient beings instead of attaining Buddhahood. Buddhas such as Amitabha or Śakyamuni (as an eternal Buddha) never entered extinction (parinirvāṇa). They continued to help sentient beings. Entering nirvāṇa was seen as nothing more than an expedient means to help save sentient beings. Nobody actually entered nirvāṇa as an ultimate state, according to this Mahāyāna view.

Chapter - 24

Vajrayana Philosophy

Vajrayāna along with Mantrayāna, Guhyamantrayāna, Tantrayāna, Tantric Buddhism and Esoteric Buddhism are names referring to Buddhist traditions associated with Tantra and "Secret Mantra", which developed in the medieval Indian subcontinent and spread to Tibet, East Asia, Mongolia and other Himalayan states.

King Songtsen Gampo (reigned from 617-650 CE)– had 5 wives, two of which were Buddhist - Tritsun was Nepalese and Wenzheng was Chinese. He built the Jokhang, Tibet's first Buddhist temple to honour the practices of his wives. King Trisong Detsen – a Buddhist who in an effort to quell hostile priests and nobles followed the indigenous religion of Tibet. Bon – invited Mahayana Buddhist teacher, Padmasambhava to his court. Padmasambhava found a way to accommodate both Buddhist dharma and Bon traditions so that both could be seen as compatible.

Vajrayāna practices are connected to specific lineages in Buddhism, through the teachings of lineage holders. Others might generally refer to texts as the Buddhist Tantras. It includes practices that make use of mantras, dharanis, mudras, mandalas and the visualisation of deities and Buddhas.

Tibetan Buddhism is a syncretic result of three major influences: (i) Mahayana Buddhism – via Padmasambhava – carrying the core doctrines of historical Buddhism with a heavy emphasis on Karuna and the role of the Bodisattvas; (ii) Tantrayana Buddhism/Tantric Hindu Darshana, which emphasises the role that one's body and senses can play in the awakening of the mind (yes, it is Tantric traditions that bring us the Kama Sutra); and (iii) Bon – the indigenous religious tradition of Tibet –which emphasises the mystical and animistic nature of the world.

Traditional Vajrayāna sources claim that the tantras and the lineage of Vajrayāna was taught by the Buddha Shakyamuni and other figures such as the bodhisattva Vajrapani and Padmasambhava. Contemporary historians of Buddhist studies meanwhile argue that this movement dates to the tantric era of medieval India (c. 5th century CE onwards).

According to Vajrayāna scriptures, the term Vajrayāna refers to one of three vehicles or routes to enlightenment, the other two being the Śrāvakayāna (also known pejoratively as the Hīnayāna) and Mahāyāna (a.k.a Pāramitāyāna).

There are several Buddhist tantric traditions that are currently practiced, including Indo-Tibetan Buddhism, Chinese Esoteric Buddhism, Shingon Buddhism and Newar Buddhism.

24.1 Introduction to Vajrayana

Vajrayana is practiced in Tibetan Buddhism practiced, the Himalayan regions of India, Nepal, and Bhutan, Buddhist Tantra is most often termed Vajrayāna and Secret mantra (Skt. Guhyamantra, gsang sngags). The vajra is a mythical weapon associated with Indra which was said to be indestructible and unbreakable (like a diamond) and extremely powerful (like thunder). Thus, the term is variously translated as Diamond Vehicle, Thunderbolt Vehicle, Indestructible Vehicle and so on.

In Chinese Esoteric Buddhism it is generally known by various terms such as Zhēnyán (Chinese: "true word", referring to mantra), Tángmì or Hanmì "Tang Esotericism" or "Han Esotericism"), Mìzōng ("Esoteric Sect") or Mìjiao (Chinese: Esoteric Teaching). The Chinese term mì ("secret, esoteric") is a translation of the Sanskrit term Guhya ("secret, hidden, profound, abstruse").

In Japan Buddhist esotericism it is known as Mikkyō ("secret teachings") or by the term Shingon (a Japanese rendering of Zhēnyán), which also refers to a specific school of Shingon-shū.

24.2 History of Vajrayana

24,2,1 Mahasiddhas and the Tantric Movement

Tantric Buddhism is associated with groups of wandering yogis called mahasiddhas in medieval India. These tantric figures thrived during the latter half of the first millennium CE. The mahasiddhas date back to the medieval period in North India and used methods that were radically different from those used in Buddhist monasteries, including practicing in charnel grounds.

Since the practice of Tantra focuses on the transformation of poisons into wisdom, the yogic circles came together in tantric feasts, often in sacred sites (pitha) and places (ksetra) which included dancing, singing, consort practices and the ingestion of taboo substances like alcohol, urine, and meat. At least two of the mahasiddhas cited in the Buddhist literature are comparable with the Shaiva Nath saints (Gorakshanath and Matsyendranath) who practiced Hatha Yoga.

A movement called Sahaja-siddhi developed in the 8th century in Bengal. It was dominated by long-haired, wandering mahasiddhas who openly challenged and ridiculed the Buddhist establishment. The mahasiddhas pursued siddhis, magical powers such as flight and extrasensory perception as well as spiritual liberation.

Buddhist siddhas demonstrated the appropriation of an older sociological form—the independent sage/magician, who lived in a liminal zone on the borders between fields and forests. Their rites involved the conjunction of sexual practices and Buddhist mandala visualisation with ritual accoutrements made from parts of the human body, so that control may be exercised over the forces hindering the natural abilities of the siddha to manipulate the cosmos at will. At their most extreme, siddhas also represented a defensive position within the Buddhist tradition, adopted and sustained for the purpose of aggressive engagement with the medieval culture of public violence. They reinforced their reputations for personal sanctity with rumors of the magical manipulation of various flavours of demonic females (dakini, yaksi, yogini), cemetery ghouls (vetala), and other things that go bump in the night. Operating on the margins of both monasteries and polite society, some adopted the behaviours associated with ghosts (preta, pisaca), not only as a religious praxis but also as an extension of their implied threats.

24.3 Tantras in Buddhism

Many of the elements found in Buddhist tantric literature are not wholly new. Earlier Mahāyāna sutras already contained some elements which are emphasised in the Tantras, such as mantras and dharani. The use of protective verses or phrases actually dates back to the Vedic period and can be seen in the early Buddhist texts, where they are termed paritta. The practice of visualisation of Buddhas such as Amitābha is also seen in pre-tantric texts like the Longer Sukhāvatīvyūha Sūtra.

There are other Mahāyāna sutras which contain "proto-tantric" material such as the Gandavyuha and the Dasabhumika which might have served as a central source of visual imagery for Tantric texts. Later Mahāyāna texts like the Kāraṇḍavyūha Sūtra (c. 4th-5th century CE) expounded the use of mantras such as ***Om mani padme hum***, associated with vastly powerful beings like Avalokiteshvara. The popular Heart Sutra also includes a mantra.

Vajrayāna Buddhists developed a large corpus of texts called the Buddhist Tantras, some of which can be traced to at least the 7th century CE but might be older.

Some of the earliest of these texts, Kriya tantras such as the Mañjuśrī-mūla-kalpa (c. 6th century), teach the use of mantras and dharanis for mostly worldly ends including curing illness, controlling the weather and generating wealth. The Tattvasaṃgraha Tantra (Compendium of Principles), classed as a "Yoga tantra", is one of the first Buddhist tantras which focuses on liberation as opposed to worldly goals. In another early tantra, the Vajrasekhara (Vajra Peak), the influential schema of the five Buddha families is developed. Other early tantras include the Mahāvairocana Abhisaṃbodhi and the Guhyasamāja (Gathering of Secrets).

The Guhyasamāja is a Mahayoga class of Tantra, which features forms of ritual practice considered "left-hand" (vamachara) such as the use of taboo substances like alcohol, consort practices, and charnel ground practices which evoke wrathful deities. It divides the tantras into those which were "a development of Mahāyānist thought" and those "formed in a rather popular mold toward the end of the eighth century and declining into the esoterism of the left", this "left esoterism" mainly refers to the Yogini tantras and later works associated with wandering yogis. This practice survives in Tibetan Buddhism, but it is rare for this to be done with an actual person. It is more common for a yogi or yogini to use an imagined consort (a buddhist tantric deity, i.e. a yidam).

These later tantras such as the Hevajra Tantra and the Chakrasamvara are classed as "Yogini tantras" and represent the final form of development of Indian Buddhist tantras in the ninth and tenth centuries. The Kalachakra tantra was developed in the 10th century. It is farthest removed from the earlier Buddhist traditions, and incorporates concepts of messianism and astrology not present elsewhere in Buddhist literature.

The rise of Tantric Buddhism was a response to the feudal structure of Indian society in the early medieval period (ca. 500-1200 CE) which saw kings being divinised as manifestations of gods. Likewise, tantric yogis reconfigured their practice through the metaphor of being consecrated (abhiśeka) as the overlord (rājādhirāja) of a mandala palace of divine vassals, an imperial metaphor symbolising kingly fortresses and their political power.

24.4 Relationship to Shaivism

The question of the origins of early Vajrayāna has been taken up by various scholars. The Buddhist tantra employed various elements of a "pan-Indian religious substrate" which is not specifically Buddhist, Shaiva or Vaishnava.

Various classes of Vajrayāna literature developed as a result of royal courts sponsoring both Buddhism and Shaivism. The relationship between the two systems can be seen in texts like the Mañjusrimulakalpa, which later came to be classified under Kriya tantra, and states that mantras taught in the Shaiva, Garuda and Vaishnava tantras will be effective if applied by Buddhists since they were all taught originally by Manjushri.

The Vajrayāna Yogini tantras draw extensively from the material also present in Shaiva Bhairava tantras classified as Vidyapitha. The comparison of them shows similarity in ritual procedures, style of observance, deities, mantras, mandalas, ritual dress, Kapalika accouterments like skull bowls, specialised terminology, secret gestures, and secret jargons. There is even direct borrowing of passages from Shaiva texts. There are numerous examples such as the Guhyasiddhi of Padmavajra, a work associated with the Guhyasamaja tradition, which prescribes acting as a Shaiva guru and initiating members into Shaiva Siddhanta scriptures and mandalas. The Samvara tantra texts adopted the pitha list from the Shaiva text Tantrasadbhava, introducing a copying error where a deity was mistaken for a place.

The claims for direct influence from Shaiva Vidyapitha texts are problematic because "the chronology of the Vidyapitha tantras is by no means so well established and that the available evidence suggests that received Shaiva tantras come into evidence sometime in the ninth to tenth centuries with their affirmation by scholars like Abhinavagupta (c. 1000 C E). The list of pithas or sacred places are certainly not particularly Buddhist, nor are they uniquely Kapalika venues, despite their presence in lists employed by both traditions. like the Buddhists, the Shaiva tradition was also involved in the appropriation of Hindu and non-Hindu deities, texts and traditions, an example being "village or tribal divinities like Tumburu".

The Buddhists and Kapalikas as well as other ascetics (possibly Pasupatas) mingled and discussed their paths at various pilgrimage places and that there were conversions between the different groups:

The Buddhist-Kapalika connection is more complex than a simple process of religious imitation and textual appropriation. There can be no question that the Buddhist tantras were heavily influenced by Kapalika and other Saiva movements, but the influence was apparently mutual. Perhaps a more nuanced model would be that the various lines of transmission were locally flourishing and that in some areas they interacted, while in others they maintained concerted hostility. Thus, the influence was both sustained and reciprocal, even in those places where Buddhist and Kapalika siddhas were in extreme antagonism.

24.4.1 Traditional Legends

According to several Buddhist tantras as well as traditional Tibetan Buddhist sources, the tantras and the Vajrayana was taught by the Buddha Shakyamuni, but only to some individuals. There are several stories and versions of how the tantras were disseminated. The Jñana Tilaka Tantra, for example, has the Buddha state that the tantras will be explained by the bodhisattva Vajrapani. One of the most famous legends is that of king Indrabhuti (also known as King Ja) of Oddiyana (a figure related to Vajrapani, in some cases said to be an emanation of him).

Other accounts attribute the revelation of Buddhist tantras to Padmasambhava, claiming that he was an emanation of Amitaba and Avaloketishvara and that his arrival was predicted by the Buddha. Some accounts also maintain Padmasambhava is a direct reincarnation of Buddha Shakyamuni.

24.5 Philosophical Background

The philosophical view of the Vajrayana is based on Mahayana Buddhist philosophy, mainly the Madhyamaka and Yogacara schools. The major difference seen by Vajrayana thinkers is the superiority of Tantric methods, which provide a faster vehicle to liberation and contain many more skillful means (upaya).

The importance of the theory of emptiness is central to the Tantric Buddhist view and practice. The Buddhist emptiness view sees the world as being fluid, without an ontological foundation or inherent existence, but ultimately a fabric of constructions. Because of this, tantric practice such as self-visualisation as the deity is seen as being no less real than everyday reality, but a process of transforming reality itself, including the practitioner's identity as the deity. In a universe where all events dissolve ontologically into Emptiness, the touching of Emptiness in the ritual is the re-creation of the world in actuality.

The doctrine of Buddha-nature, as outlined in the Ratnagotravibhāga of Asanga, was also an important theory which became the basis for Tantric views. This intrinsic secret (behind) diverse manifestation is the utmost secret and aim of Tantra. This "Buddha embryo" (tathāgatagarbha) is a "non-dual, self-originated Wisdom (jnana), an effortless fount of good qualities" that resides in the mindstream but is "obscured by discursive thought." This doctrine is often associated with the idea of the inherent or natural luminosity (Skt: prakṛti-prabhāsvara-citta) or purity of the mind (prakrti-parisuddha).

Another fundamental theory of Tantric practice is that of transformation. In Vajrayāna, negative mental factors such as desire, hatred, greed, pride are used as part of the path. The tantric doctrine is an attempt to place kama, desire, in every meaning of the word, in the service of liberation. This view is outlined in the following quote from the Hevajra tantra:

Those things by which evil men are bound, others turn into means and gain thereby release from the bonds of existence. By passion the world is bound, by passion too it is released, but by heretical Buddhists this practice of reversals is not known.

The Hevajra further states that "one knowing the nature of poison may dispel poison with poison." This idea is already present in Asanga's Mahayana-sutra-alamkara-karika and therefore it is possible that he was aware of Tantric techniques, including sexual yoga.

According to Buddhist Tantra, there is no strict separation of the profane or samsara and the sacred or nirvana, rather they exist in a continuum. All individuals are seen as containing the seed of enlightenment within, which is covered over by defilements. The Vajrayana sees Buddhahood not as something outside or an event in the future, but as immanently present.

Indian Tantric Buddhist philosophers such as Buddhaguhya, Vimalamitra, Ratnākaraśānti and Abhayakaragupta continued the tradition of Buddhist philosophy and adapted it to their commentaries on the major Tantras. Abhayakaragupta's Vajravali is a key source in the theory and practice of tantric rituals. After monks such as Vajrabodhi and Śubhakarasiṃha brought Tantra to Tang China (716 to 720), tantric philosophy continued to be developed in Chinese and Japanese by thinkers such as Yi Xing and Kūkai.

Likewise in Tibet, Sakya Pandita (1182-28 - 1251), as well as later thinkers like Longchenpa (1308–1364) expanded on these philosophies in their tantric commentaries and treatises. The status of the tantric view continued to be debated in medieval Tibet. Tibetan Buddhist Rongzom Chokyi Zangpo (1012–1088) held that the views of sutra such as Madhyamaka were inferior to that of tantra, which was based on basic purity of ultimate reality. Tsongkhapa (1357–1419) on the other hand, held that there is no difference between Vajrayāna and other forms of Mahayana in terms of prajnaparamita (perfection of insight) itself, only that Vajrayāna is a method which works faster.

24.6 Place within Buddhist Tradition

Various classifications are possible when distinguishing Vajrayāna from the other Buddhist traditions. Vajrayāna can be seen as a third yana, next to Śrāvakayāna and Mahayana. Vajrayāna can be distinguished from the Sutrayana. The Sutrayana is the method of perfecting good qualities, where the Vajrayāna is the method of taking the intended outcome of Buddhahood as the path. Vajrayāna can also be distinguished from the paramitayana. According to this schema, Indian Mahayana revealed two vehicles (yana) or methods for attaining enlightenment: the method of the perfections (Paramitayana) and the method of mantra (Mantrayana).

The Paramitayana consists of the six or ten paramitas, of which the scriptures say that it takes three incalculable aeons (yugas) to lead one to Buddhahood. The tantra literature, however, claims that the Mantrayana leads one to Buddhahood in a single lifetime. According to the literature, the mantra is an easy path without the difficulties innate to the Paramitayana. Mantrayana is sometimes portrayed as a method for those of inferior abilities. However, the practitioner of the mantra still has to adhere to the vows of the Bodhisattva.

24.7 Characteristics of Vajrayana

24.7.1 Goal

The goal of spiritual practice within the Mahayana and Vajrayāna traditions is to become a Sammāsambuddha (fully awakened Buddha), those on this path are termed Bodhisattvas. As with the Mahayana, motivation is a vital component of Vajrayāna practice. The Bodhisattva-path is an integral part of the Vajrayāna, which teaches that all practices are to be undertaken with the motivation to achieve Buddhahood for the benefit of all sentient beings.

In the vehicle of Sutra Mahayana the "path of the cause" is taken, whereby a practitioner starts with his or her potential Buddha-nature and nurtures it to produce the fruit of Buddhahood. In the Vajrayāna the "path of the fruit" is taken whereby the practitioner takes his or her innate Buddha-nature as the means of practice. The premise is that since we innately have an enlightened mind, practicing seeing the world in terms of ultimate truth can help us to attain our full Buddha-nature. Experiencing ultimate truth is said to be the purpose of all the various tantric techniques practiced in the Vajrayana.

24.7.2 Esoteric Transmission

Vajrayāna Buddhism is esoteric in the sense that the transmission of certain teachings only occurs directly from teacher to student during an empowerment (abhiṣeka) and their practice requires initiation in a ritual space containing the mandala of the deity. Many techniques are also commonly said to be secret, but some Vajrayana teachers have responded that secrecy itself is not important and only a side-effect of the reality that the techniques have no validity outside the teacher-student lineage.

The secrecy of teachings was often protected through the use of allusive, indirect, symbolic and metaphorical language (twilight language) which required interpretation and guidance from a teacher. The teachings may also be considered "self-secret", meaning that even if they were to be told directly to a person, that person would not necessarily understand the teachings without proper context. In this way, the teachings are "secret" to the minds of those who are not following the path with more than a simple sense of curiosity.

Because of their role in giving access to the practices and guiding the student through them, the role of the Vajracharya Lama is indispensable in Vajrayāna.

24.7.3 Affirmation of the Feminine, Antinomian and Taboo

Some Vajrayāna rituals traditionally included the use of certain taboo substances, such as blood, semen, alcohol and urine, as ritual offerings and sacraments, though some of these are often replaced with less taboo substances such as yogurt. Tantric feasts and initiations sometimes employed substances like human flesh.

The use of these substances is related to the non-dual (advaya) nature of a Buddha's wisdom (buddhajñana). Since the ultimate state is in some sense non-dual, a practitioner can approach that state by "transcending attachment to dual categories such as pure and impure, permitted and forbidden". As the Guhyasamaja Tantra states "the wise man who does not discriminate achieves Buddhahood".

Vajrayāna rituals also include sexual yoga, union with a physical consort as part of advanced practices. Some tantras go further, the Hevajra tantra states 'You should kill living beings, speak lying words, take what is not given, consort with the others' women. While some of these statements were taken literally as part of ritual practice, others such as killing were interpreted in a metaphorical sense. In the Hevajra, "killing" is defined as developing concentration by killing the life-breath of discursive thoughts. Likewise, while actual sexual union with a physical consort is practiced, it is also common to use a visualised mental consort.

The symbolic meaning of tantric sexuality is ultimately rooted in bodhicitta and the bodhisattva's quest for enlightenment is likened to a lover seeking union with the mind of the Buddha. The importance of the psycho-physical experiences arising in sexual yoga, termed "great bliss" (mahasukha): "Bliss melts the conceptual mind, heightens sensory awareness, and opens the practitioner to the naked experience of the nature of mind. This tantric experience is not the same as ordinary self-gratifying sexual passion since it relies on tantric meditative methods using the subtle body and visualisations as well as the motivation for enlightenment. As the Hevajra tantra says:

This practice [of sexual union with a consort] is not taught for the sake of enjoyment, but for the examination of one's own thought, whether the mind is steady or waving.

Feminine deities and forces are also increasingly prominent in Vajrayāna. In the Yogini tantras in particular, women and female yoginis are given high status as the embodiment of female deities such as the wild and nude Vajrayogini. The Candamaharosana Tantra (viii:29–30) states:

- Women are heaven, women are the teaching (dharma);
- Women indeed are the highest austerity (tapas);
- Women are the Buddha; women are the Sangha; and
- Women are the Perfection of Wisdom.

In India, there is evidence to show that women participated in tantric practice alongside men and were also teachers, adepts and authors of tantric texts.

24.7.4 Vows and Behaviour

Practitioners of Vajrayāna need to abide by various tantric vows or pledges called samaya. These are extensions of the rules of the Prātimokṣa and Bodhisattva vows for the lower levels of tantra, and are taken during initiations into the empowerment for a particular Unsurpassed Yoga Tantra. The special tantric vows vary depending on the specific mandala practice for which the initiation is received and also depending on the level of initiation. Ngagpas of the Nyingma school keep a special non-celibate ordination.

A tantric guru, or teacher is expected to keep his or her samaya vows in the same way as his students. Proper conduct is considered especially necessary for a qualified Vajrayana guru. For example, the Ornament for the Essence of Manjushrikirti states:

- Distance yourself from Vajra Masters who are not keeping the three vows;

- who keep on with a root downfall, who are miserly with the Dharma;
- and who engage in actions that should be forsaken;
- Those who worship them go to hell and so on as a result.

24.8 Tantra Techniques

While all the Vajrayāna Buddhist traditions include all of the traditional practices used in Mahayana Buddhism such as developing bodhicitta, practicing the paramitas, and meditations, they also make use of unique tantric methods and Dzogchen meditation which are seen as more advanced. These include mantras, mudras, deity yoga, other visualisation-based meditations, subtle body yogas like tummo and rituals like the goma fire ritual. Vajrayana teaches that these techniques provide faster path to Buddhahood.

A central feature of tantric practice is the use of mantras, and seed syllables (bijas). Mantras are words, phrases or a collection of syllables used for a variety of meditative, magical and ritual ends. Mantras are usually associated with specific deities or Buddhas, and are seen as their manifestations in sonic form. They are traditionally believed to have spiritual power, which can lead to enlightenment as well as supramundane abilities (siddhis).

Buddhist esotericism is centered on what is known as "the three mysteries" or "secrets": the tantric adept affiliates his body, speech, and mind with the body, speech, and mind of a Buddha through mudra, mantras and samadhi respectively. Padmavajra (c 7th century) explains in his Tantrarthavatara Commentary, the secret Body, Speech, and Mind of the Buddhas are:

- **Secret of Body:** Whatever form is necessary to tame the living beings.
- **Secret of Speech:** Speech exactly appropriate to the lineage of the creature, as in the language of the yaksas, etc.
- **Secret of Mind:** Knowing all things as they really are.

These elements are brought together in the practice of tantric deity yoga, which involves visualising the deity's body and mandala, reciting the deity's mantra and gaining insight into the nature of things based on this contemplation. Advanced tantric practices such as deity yoga are taught in the context of an initiation ceremony by tantric gurus or vajracharyas (vajra-masters) to the tantric initiate, who also takes on formal commitments or vows (samaya). In Tibetan Buddhism, advanced practices like deity yoga are usually preceded by or coupled with "preliminary practices" called ngondro, consisting of five-to-seven accumulation practices and includes prostrations and recitations of the 100-syllable mantra.

Vajrayana is a system of tantric lineages, and thus only those who receive an empowerment or initiation (abhiseka) are allowed to practice the more advanced esoteric methods. In tantric deity yoga, mantras or bijas are used during the ritual evocation of deities which are said to arise out of the uttered and visualised mantric syllables. After the deity's image and mandala has been established, heart mantras are visualised as part of the contemplation in different points of the deity's body.

24.8.1 Deity Yoga

The fundamental practice of Buddhist Tantra is "deity yoga" (devatayoga), meditation on a chosen deity or "cherished divinity" (Skt. Iṣṭa-devatā,), which involves the recitation of mantras, prayers and visualisation of the deity, the associated mandala of the deity's Buddha field, along with consorts and attendant Buddhas and bodhisattvas. According to the Tibetan scholar Tsongkhapa, deity yoga is what separates Tantra from Sutra practice.

In the Unsurpassed Yoga Tantras, the most widespread tantric form in Indo-Tibetan Buddhism, this method is divided into two stages, the generation stage (utpatti-krama) and the completion stage (nispanna-krama). In the generation stage, one dissolves one's reality into emptiness and meditates on the deity-mandala, resulting in identification with this divine reality. In the completion stage, the divine image along with the subtle body is applied to the realisation of luminous emptiness.

This dissolution into emptiness is then followed by the visualisation of the deity and re-emergence of the yogi as the deity. During the process of deity visualisation, the deity is to be imaged as not solid or tangible, as "empty yet apparent", with the character of a mirage or a rainbow. This visualisation is to be combined with "divine pride", which is "the thought that one is oneself the deity being visualised." Divine pride is different from common pride because it is based on compassion for others and on an understanding of emptiness.

A Tibetologist outlines two main types of completion practice: a formless and image-less contemplation on the ultimate empty nature of the mind and various yogas that make use of the subtle body to produce energetic sensations of bliss and warmth.

The subtle body yogas systems like the Six Dharmas of Naropa and the Six Yogas of Kalachakra make use of energetic schemas of human psycho-physiology composed of "energy channels" (Skt. nadi), "winds" or currents (Skt. vayu), "drops" or charged particles (Skt. bindu) and chakras ("wheels"). These subtle energies are seen as "mounts" for consciousness, the physical component of awareness. They are engaged by various means such as pranayama (breath control) to produce blissful experiences that are then applied to the realisation of ultimate reality.

Other methods which are associated with the completion stage in Tibetan Buddhism include dream yoga (which relies on lucid dreaming), practices associated with the bardo (the interim state between death and rebirth), transference of consciousness (phowa) and Chöd, in which the yogi ceremonially offers their body to be eaten by tantric deities in a ritual feast.

24.9 Other Practices

Another form of Vajrayana practice are certain meditative techniques associated with Mahāmudrā and Dzogchen, often termed "formless practices" or the path of self-liberation. These techniques do not rely on deity visualisation per se but on direct pointing-out instruction from a master and are often seen as the most advanced and direct methods.

Another distinctive feature of Tantric Buddhism is its unique and often elaborate rituals. They include pujas (worship rituals), prayer festivals, protection rituals, death rituals, tantric feasts (ganachakra), tantric initiations (abhiseka) and the goma fire ritual (common in East Asian Esotericism).

An important element in some of these rituals (particularly initiations and tantric feasts) seems to have been the practice of ritual sex or sexual yoga (karmamudra, "desire seal", also referred to as "consort observance", vidyavrata, and euphemistically as "puja"), as well as the sacramental ingestion of "power substances" such as the mingled sexual fluids and uterine blood (often performed by licking these substances off the vulva, a practice termed yonipuja).

The practice of ingestion of sexual fluids is mentioned by numerous tantric commentators, sometimes euphemistically referring to the penis as the "vajra" and the vagina as the "lotus". The Cakrasamvara Tantra commentator Kambala, writing about this practice, states:

The seats are well-known on earth to be spots within the lotus mandala; by abiding within it there is great bliss, the royal nature of nondual joy. Therefore, the lotus seat is supreme: filled with a mixture of semen and uterine blood, one should especially kiss it, and lolling with the tongue take it up. Unite the vajra and lotus, with the rapture of drinking [this] liquor.

These sexual practices probably originated in a non-monastic context, but were later adopted by monastic establishments (such as Nalanda and Vikramashila). The anxiety of figures like Atisa towards these practices, and the stories of Virūpa and Maitripa being expelled from their monasteries for performing them, shows that supposedly celibate monastics were undertaking these sexual rites.

Because of its adoption by the monastic tradition, the practice of sexual yoga was slowly transformed into one which was either done with an imaginary consort visualised by the yogi instead of an actual person, or reserved to a small group of the "highest" or elite practitioners. Likewise, the drinking of sexual fluids was also reinterpreted by later commentators to refer subtle body anatomy of the perfection stage practices.

24.10 Texts

There is an extended body of texts associated with Buddhist Tantra, including the "tantras" themselves, tantric commentaries and shastras, sadhanas (liturgical texts), ritual manuals, dharanis, poems or songs (dohas), termas and so on. Though we do not know precisely at present just how many Indian tantric Buddhist texts survive today in the language in which they were written, their number is certainly over one thousand five hundred. A large part of this body of texts has also been translated into Tibetan, and a smaller part into Chinese. Aside from these, there are perhaps another two thousand or more works that are known today only from such translations. We can be certain as well that many others are lost to us forever, in whatever form. Of the texts that survive a very small proportion has been published; an almost insignificant percentage has been edited or translated reliably.

Vajrayāna texts exhibit a wide range of literary characteristics—usually a mix of verse and prose, almost always in a Sanskrit that "transgresses frequently against classical norms of grammar and usage," although also occasionally in various Middle Indic dialects or elegant classical Sanskrit. In Chinese Mantrayana (Zhenyan), and Japanese Shingon, the most influential esoteric texts are the Mahavairocana Tantra and the Vajraśekhara Sūtra. In Tibetan Buddhism, a large number of tantric works are widely studied and different schools focus on the study and practice of different cycles of texts. The Sakyapa specialise in the Hevajra Tantra, the Nyingmapa specialise in the various so-called Old Tantras and terma cycles, and the most important Kagyudpa and Gelugpa tantras are Guhyasamāja, Cakrasaṃvara and Kālacakra.

Chapter - 25

Concept of Karma and Rebirth in Buddhism

25.1 Buddhist Understanding of Karma

Karma (Sanskrit, also karman, Pāli: kamma) is a Sanskrit term that literally means "action" or "doing". In the Buddhist tradition, karma refers to action driven by intention (cetanā) which leads to future consequences. Those intentions are considered to be the determining factor in the kind of rebirth in samsara, the cycle of rebirth.

Karmaphala is the "fruit", "effect" or "result" of karma. A similar term is karmavipaka, the "maturation" or "cooking" of karma. The remote effects of karmic choices are referred to as the 'maturation' (vipāka) or 'fruit' (phala) of the karmic act.

Karma and karmaphala are fundamental concepts in Buddhism. The concepts of karma and karmaphala explain how our intentional actions keep us tied to rebirth in samsara, whereas the Buddhist path, as exemplified in the Noble Eightfold Path, shows us the way out of samsara.

25.1.1 Rebirth

Rebirth is a common belief in all Buddhist traditions. It says that birth and death in the six realms occur in successive cycles driven by ignorance (avidyā), desire (trsnā), and hatred (dvesa). The cycle of rebirth is called samsāra. It is a beginningless and ever-ongoing process. Liberation from samsāra can be attained by following the Buddhist Path. This path leads to vidyā, and the stilling of trsnā and dvesa. Hereby the ongoing process of rebirth is stopped.

25.1.2 Karma

The cycle of rebirth is determined by karma, literally "action". In the Buddhist tradition, karma refers to actions driven by intention (cetanā), a deed done deliberately through body, speech or mind, which leads to future consequences. According to the Nibbedhika Sutta, Anguttara Nikaya 6.63:

Intention (cetana), I tell you, is kamma. Intending, one does kamma by way of body, speech and intellect.

It is the psychological impulse behind an action that is 'karma', that which sets going a chain of causes culminating in karmic fruit. Actions, then, must be intentional if they are to generate karmic fruits.

The Buddha defined karma as intention; whether the intention manifested itself in physical, vocal or mental form, it was the intention alone which had a moral character: good, bad or neutral [...] The focus of interest shifted from physical action, involving people and objects in the real world, to psychological process.

This was a great innovation, which overturns brahmanical, caste-bound ethics. It is a rejection of caste-bound differences, giving the same possibility to reach liberation to all people, not just Brahmanins. Not by birth is one a brahmin or an outcaste, but by deeds (kamma).

It is the doctrine of Karma that explains the difference among living beings.

Once a young man named Subbha went to Lord Buddha and put this question: Ven'ble Gotama, I see so many differences among living beings, and human beings for that matter- some are born in rich conditions and others in poor conditions, some are intelligent and others. are dull, some are lovely and others are repulsive, some live long and others die quite young. So what could be the reason for all these differences? Lord Buddha said that these differences are due to differences in actions. Similarly Majjhima Nikaya III, 204 says that it is Karmas which divide people into high and low. It is through a difference in their Karma that men are not alike; some lived long, some lived short, some are healthy and some are weak, some wise and some foolish. Karma allots to beings, meanness and greatness".

25.1.3 Karmaphala

Karma leads to future consequences, karma-phala, "fruit of action". Any given action may cause all sorts of results, but the karmic results are only those results which are a consequence of both the moral quality of the action, and of the intention behind the action. The consequences envisioned by the law of karma encompass more (as well as less) than the observed natural or physical results which follow upon the performance of an action.

The "law of karma" applies specifically to the moral sphere. It is not concerned with the general relation between actions and their consequences, but rather with the moral quality of actions and their consequences, such as the pain and pleasure and good or bad experiences for the doer of the act.

Good moral actions lead to wholesome rebirths, and bad moral actions lead to unwholesome rebirths. The main factor is how they contribute to the well-being of others in a positive or negative sense. Especially dāna, giving to the Buddhist order, became an increasingly important source of positive karma.

How these intentional actions lead to rebirth, and how the idea of rebirth is to be reconciled with the doctrines of impermanence and no-self, is a matter of philosophical inquiry in the Buddhist traditions, for which several solutions have been proposed. In early Buddhism no explicit theory of rebirth and karma was worked out, and "the karma doctrine may have been incidental to early Buddhist soteriology." In early Buddhism, rebirth was ascribed to craving or ignorance.

In later Buddhism, the basic idea is that intentional actions, driven by kleshas ("disturbing emotions"), cetanā ("volition"), or taṇhā ("thirst", "craving") create impressions, tendencies or "seeds" in the mind. These impressions, or "seeds", will ripen into a future result or fruition. If we can overcome our kleshas, then we break the chain of causal effects that leads to rebirth in the six realms. The twelve links of dependent origination provides a theoretical framework, explaining how the disturbing emotions lead to rebirth in samsara.

However, the theory of Karma should not be mistaken for fatalism. It does not regard the stock of past Karma as a dead weight lying on the shoulders of man, hindering his work and implying complete pre-determination as what the individual will be so. Instead it views the individuals as free agent who are not only supposed to have a capacity to distinguish between right and wrong but also have a capacity of a free choice. In fact, if the doctrine of Karma were to advocate complete determinism it would have gone against the very spirit of the scriptures, which enjoin certain prescriptions and prohibitions, because if one is bound to do what one does all prescriptions and prohibitions would be rendered useless. Far from advocating determinism, this doctrine highlights our free agency but in doing so it also makes us aware of our responsibilities and enlightens us towards our duties. Thus, it links freedom with responsibilities.

We may sum up our analysis of the theory of Karma by restating that neither it stands for the denial of human freedom nor for discouragement in moral effort. It implies that we are at every moment making our character and shaping our destiny. As the Buddha said, "action is the field, consciousness the seed, and craving the moisture which led to the rebirth of a being.

25.1.4 Complex Process

The Buddha's teaching of karma is not strictly deterministic, but incorporated circumstantial factors, unlike that of the Jains. It is not a rigid and mechanical process, but a flexible, fluid and dynamic process, and not all present conditions can be ascribed to karma. There is no set linear relationship between a particular action and its results. The karmic effect of a deed is not determined solely by the deed itself, but also by the nature of the person who commits the deed, and by the circumstances in which it is committed.

Karma is also not the same as "fate" or "predestination". Karmic results are not a "judgement" imposed by a God or other all-powerful being, but rather the results of a natural process. Certain experiences in life are the results of previous actions, but our responses to those experiences are not predetermined, although they bear their own fruit in the future. Unjust behaviour may lead to unfavourable circumstances which make it easier to commit more unjust behaviour, but nevertheless the freedom not to commit unjust behaviour remains.

25.1.5 Liberation from Samsāra

The real importance of the doctrine of karma and its fruits lies in the recognition of the urgency to put a stop to the whole process. The Acintita Sutta warns that "the results of kamma" is one of the four incomprehensible subjects, subjects that are beyond all conceptualisation and cannot be understood with logical thought or reason.

This sutra may have been a warning against the tendency, "probably from the Buddha's day until now", to understand the doctrine of karma "backwards", to explain unfavourable conditions in this life when no other explanations are available. Gaining a better rebirth may have been, and still is, the central goal for many people. The adoption, by laity, of Buddhist beliefs and practices is seen as a good thing, which brings merit and good rebirth, but does not result in Nirvana, and liberation from samsāra, the ultimate goal of the Buddha.

25.2 Karma in the Pali Suttas

According to the Buddhist tradition, the lord Buddha gained full and complete insight into the workings of karma at the time of his enlightenment.

According to these knowledges were later additions to the story, just like the notion of "liberating insight" itself.

The lord Buddha asserted that it is not possible to avoid experiencing the result of a karmic deed once it has been committed.

In the Anguttara Nikaya, it is stated that karmic results are experienced either in this life or in future lives. The former may involve a readily observable connection between action and karmic consequence, such as when a thief is captured and tortured by the authorities, but the connection need not necessarily be that obvious and in fact usually is not observable.

The Sammyutta Nikaya makes a basic distinction between past karma (P. purānakamma) which has already been incurred, and karma being created in the present (P. navakamma). Therefore, in the present one both create new karma (P. navakamma) and encounters the result of past karma (P. kammavipāka). Karma in the early canon is also threefold: Mental action (S. manaḥkarman), bodily action (S. kāyakarman) and vocal action (S. vākkarman).

25.3 Karma within Buddhist Traditions

Various Buddhist philosophical schools developed within Buddhism, giving various interpretations regarding more refined points of karma. A major problem is the relation between the doctrine of no-self, and the "storage" of the traces of one's deeds, for which various solutions have been offered.

25.3.1 Karma in Early Indian Buddhism

Origins:

The concept of karma originated in the Vedic religion, where it was related to the performance of rituals or the investment in good deeds to ensure the entrance to heaven after death, while other persons go to the underworld.

Pre-sectarian Buddhism:

The concept of karma may have been of minor importance in early Buddhism. It has been questioned whether karma already played a role in the theory of rebirth of earliest Buddhism, noting that "the karma doctrine may have been incidental to early Buddhist soteriology." Originally, karma may have been only one of several concepts connected with rebirth. In early Buddhism rebirth was ascribed to craving or ignorance. Early Buddhism does not identify bodily and mental motion, but desire (or thirst, trsna), as the cause of karmic consequences. There is no single major systematic exposition on the subject of karma and an account has to be put together from the dozens of places where karma is mentioned in the texts, which may mean that the doctrine was incidental to the main perspective of early Buddhist soteriology.

The Buddha at first sought, and realised, "the deathless" (amata/amrta), which is concerned with the here and now. Only after this realisation did he become acquainted with the doctrine of rebirth. The Buddha introduced a concept of karma that differed considerably from the commonly held views of his time. Not physical and mental activities as such were seen as responsible for rebirth, but also intentions and desire.

The doctrine of karma may have been especially important for common people, for whom it was more important to cope with life's immediate demands, such as the problems of pain, injustice, and death. The doctrine of karma met these exigencies, and in time it became an important soteriological aim in its own right.

25.3.2 Karma in Vaibhāṣika-Sarvāstivādin Tradition

The Vaibhāśika-Sarvāstivāda was widely influential in India and beyond. Their understanding of karma in the Sarvāstivāda became normative for Buddhism in India and other countries.

Sarvastivadins argued that there exists a dharma of "possession" (prapti), which functions with all karmic acts, so that each act or thought, though immediately passing away, creates the "possession" of that act in the continuum of instants we experience as a person. This possession itself is momentary, but continually reproduces a similar possession in the succeeding instant, even though the original act lies in the past. Through such continual regeneration, the act is "possessed" until the actualisation of the result. The Abhidharmahṛdaya by Dharmaśrī was the first systematic exposition of Vaibhāśika-Sarvāstivāda doctrine, and the third chapter, the Karma-varga, deals with the concept of karma systematically.

Another important exposition, the Mahāvibhāṣa, gives three definitions of karma:

(i) action; karma is here supplanted in the text by the synonyms kriya or karitra, both of which mean "activity";
(ii) formal vinaya conduct;
(iii) human action as the agent of various effects; karma as that which links certain actions with certain effects, is the primary concern of the exposition.

The 4th century philosopher Vasubandhu compiled the Abhidharma-kośa, an extensive compendium which elaborated the positions of the

Vaibhāṣika-Sarvāstivādin school on a wide range of issues raised by the early sutras. Chapter four of the Kośa is devoted to a study of karma, and chapters two and five contain formulations as to the mechanism of fruition and retribution. This became the main source of understanding of the perspective of early Buddhism for later Mahāyāna philosophers.

25.3.3 Karma in Dārṣṭāntika-Sautrāntika

The Dārṣṭāntika-Sautrāntika school pioneered the idea of karmic seeds (S. Bīja) and "the special modification of the psycho-physical series" (S. saṃtatipaṇāmaviśeṣa) to explain the workings of karma.

The Sautrantikas insisted that each act exists only in the present instant and perishes immediately. To explain causation, they taught that with each karmic act a "perfuming" occurs which, though not a dharma or existent factor itself, leaves a residual impression in the succeeding series of mental instants, causing it to undergo a process of subtle evolution eventually leading to the act's result. Good and bad deeds performed are thus said to leave "seeds" or traces of disposition that will come to fruition.

25.4 Karma in Theravādin Tradition

25.4.1 Canonical Texts

In the Theravāda Abhidhamma and commentarial traditions, karma is taken up at length. The Abhidhamma Sangaha of Anuruddhācariya offers a treatment of the topic, with an exhaustive treatment in book five (5.3.7).

The Kathāvatthu discusses a number of controverted points related either directly or indirectly to the notion of kamma. This involved debate with the Pudgalavādin school, which postulated the provisional existence of the person (S. pudgala, P. puggala) to account for the ripening of karmic effects over time. The Kathāvatthu also records debate by the Theravādins with the Andhakas (who may have been Mahāsāṃghikas) regarding whether or not old age and death are the result (vipāka) of karma. The Theravāda maintained that they are not—not, apparently because there is no causal relation between the two, but because they wished to reserve the term vipāka strictly for mental results, subjective phenomena arising through the effects of kamma.

In the canonical Theravāda view of kamma, "the belief that deeds done or ideas seized at the moment of death are particularly significant.

25.4.2 Transfer of Merit

The Milindapañha, a paracanonical Theravāda text, offers some interpretations of karma theory at variance with the orthodox position. In particular, Nāgasena allows for the possibility of the transfer of merit to humans and one of the four classes of petas, perhaps in deference to folk belief. Nāgasena makes it clear that demerit cannot be transferred. One scholar asserts that the sharing of merit "can be linked to the Vedic śrāddha, for it was Buddhist practice not to upset existing traditions when well-established custom was not antithetic to Buddhist teaching."

The Petavatthu, which is fully canonical, endorses the transfer of merit even more widely, including the possibility of sharing merit with all petas.

25.5 Karma in Mahayana Tradition

25.5.1 Indian Yogācāra Tradition

In the Yogācāra philosophical tradition, one of the two principal Mahāyāna schools, the principle of karma was extended considerably. In the Yogācāra formulation, all experience without exception is said to result from the ripening of karma. Karmic seeds (S. bija) are said to be stored in the "storehouse consciousness" (S. ālayavijñāna) until such time as they ripen into experience. The term vāsāna ("perfuming") is also used, and Yogācārins debated whether vāsāna and bija were essentially the same, the seeds were the effect of the perfuming, or whether the perfuming simply affected the seeds. The seemingly external world is merely a "by-product" (adhipati-phala) of karma. The conditioning of the mind resulting from karma is called saṃskāra.

The Treatise on Action (Karmasiddhiprakaraṇa), also by Vasubandhu, treats the subject of karma in detail from the Yogācāra perspective.

Vasubandhu's Viṃśatikā (Twenty Verses) repeatedly emphasises in a variety of ways that karma is intersubjective and that the course of each and every stream of consciousness (vijñāna-santāna, i.e., the changing individual) is profoundly influenced by its relations with other consciousness streams.

Whereas in earlier systems it "was not clear how a series of completely mental events (the deed and its traces) could give rise to non-mental, material effects," with the (purported) idealism of the Yogācāra system this is not an issue.

In Mahāyāna traditions, karma is not the sole basis of rebirth. The rebirths of bodhisattvas after the seventh stage (S. bhūmi) are said to be consciously directed for the benefit of others still trapped in saṃsāra. Thus, theirs are not uncontrolled rebirths.

25.5.2 Karma in Mādhyamaka Philosophy

Nāgārjuna articulated the difficulty in forming a karma theory in his most prominent work, the Mūlamadhyamakakārikā (Fundamental Verses on the Middle Way):

If (the act) lasted till the time of ripening, (the act) would be eternal. If (the act) were terminated, how could the terminated produce a fruit?

The Mūlamadhyamakavṛtty-Akutobhayā, also generally attributed to Nāgārjuna, concludes that it is impossible both for the act to persist somehow and also for it to perish immediately and still have efficacy at a later time.

25.5.3 Karma in Tibetan Buddhism

In Tibetan Buddhism, the teachings on karma belong to the preliminary teachings, that turn the mind towards the Buddhist dharma.

In the Vajrayana tradition, negative past karma may be "purified" through such practices as meditation on Vajrasattva because they both are the mind's psychological phenomenon. The performer of the action, after having purified the karma, does not experience the negative results he or she otherwise would have.[Engaging in the ten negative actions out of selfishness and delusions hurts all involved. Otherwise, loving others, receives love; whereas; people with closed hearts may be prevented from happiness. One good thing about karma is that it can be purified through confession, if the thoughts become positive. Within Guru Yoga seven branch offerings practice, confession is the antidote to aversion.

25.5.4 Karma in East Asian traditions

Zen

Dōgen Kigen argued in his Shobogenzo that karmic latencies are emphatically not empty, going so far as to claim that belief in the emptiness of karma should be characterised as "non-Buddhist," although he also states that the "law of karman has no concrete existence.

Zen's most famous koan about karma is called Baizhang's Wild Fox. The story of the koan is about an ancient Zen teacher whose answer to a question presents a wrong view about karma by saying that the person who has a foundation in cultivating the great practice "does not fall into cause and effect." Because of his unskillful answer the teacher reaps the result of living 500 lives as a wild fox. He is then able to appear as a human and ask the same question to Zen teacher Baizhang, who answers, "He is not in the dark about cause and effect." Hearing this answer, the old teacher is freed from the life of a wild fox. The Zen perspective avoids the duality of asserting that an enlightened person is either subject to or free from the law of karma and that the key is not being ignorant about karma.

Tendai

The Japanese Tendai/Pure Land teacher Genshin taught a series of ten reflections for a dying person that emphasised reflecting on the Amida Buddha as a means to purify vast amounts of karma.

Nichiren Buddhism

Nichiren Buddhism teaches that transformation and change through faith and practice changes adverse karma—negative causes made in the past that result in negative results in the present and future—to positive causes for benefits in the future.

25.6 Concept of Rebirth in Buddhism

Rebirth in Buddhism refers to the teaching that the actions of a person lead to a new existence after death, in an endless cycle called saṃsāra. This cycle is considered to be dukkha, unsatisfactory and painful. The cycle stops only if moksha (liberation) is achieved by insight and the extinguishing of craving. Rebirth is one of the foundational doctrines of Buddhism, along with karma, Nirvana and moksha.

The rebirth doctrine, sometimes referred to as reincarnation or transmigration, asserts that rebirth does not necessarily take place as another human being, but can also lead to an existence in one of the six realms of existence, which also include heaven realms, the animal realm, the ghost realm and hell realms. Rebirth, as stated by various Buddhist traditions, is determined by karma, with good realms favoured by kushala (good or skilful karma), while a rebirth in evil realms is a consequence of akushala (bad karma). While nirvana is the ultimate goal of Buddhist teaching, much of traditional Buddhist practice has been centred on gaining merit and merit transfer, whereby one gains rebirth in the good realms and avoids rebirth in the evil realms.

The rebirth doctrine has been a subject of scholarly studies within Buddhism since ancient times, particularly in reconciling the rebirth doctrine with its anti-essentialist anatman (not-self) doctrine. The various Buddhist traditions throughout history have disagreed on what it is in a person that is reborn, as well as how quickly the rebirth occurs after each death.

Some Buddhist traditions assert that vijñana (consciousness), though constantly changing, exists as a continuum or stream (santana) and is what undergoes rebirth. Some traditions like Theravada assert that rebirth occurs immediately and that no "thing" (not even consciousness) moves across lives to be reborn (though there is a causal link, like when a seal is imprinted on wax). Other Buddhist traditions such as Tibetan Buddhism posit an interim existence (bardo) between death and rebirth, which may last as many as 49 days. This belief drives Tibetan funerary rituals. A now defunct Buddhist tradition called Pudgalavada asserted there was an inexpressible personal entity (pudgala) which migrates from one life to another.

There is no word corresponding exactly to the English terms "rebirth", "metempsychosis", "transmigration" or "reincarnation" in the traditional Buddhist languages of Pāli and Sanskrit. Rebirth is referred to by various terms, representing an essential step in the endless cycle of samsara, terms such as "re-becoming" or "becoming again" (Sanskrit: punarbhava, Pali: punabbhava), re-born (punarjanman), re-death (punarmrityu), or sometimes just "becoming" (Pali/Sanskrit: bhava), while the state one is born into, the individual process of being born or coming into the world in any way, is referred to simply as "birth" (Pali/Sanskrit: jāti). The entire universal process of beings being reborn again and again is called "wandering about" (Pali/Sanskrit: saṃsāra).

Some English-speaking Buddhists prefer the term "rebirth" or "re-becoming" (Sanskrit: punarbhava; Pali: punabbhava) to "reincarnation" as they take the latter to imply an entity (soul) that is reborn. Buddhism denies there is any such soul or self in a living being, but does assert that there is a cycle of transmigration consisting of rebirth and redeath as the fundamental nature of existence.

25.7 Historical Context of Rebirth

Before the time of the Buddha, many ideas on the nature of existence, birth and death were in vogue. The ancient Indian Vedic and Sramana schools affirmed the idea of soul, karma and cycle of rebirth. The competing Indian materialist schools denied the idea of soul, karma and rebirth, asserting instead that there is just one life, there is no rebirth, and death marks complete annihilation. From these diverse views, Buddha accepted the premises and concepts related to rebirth, but introduced innovations. Buddha believed in other worlds, that there actually is another world (any world other than the present human one, that is, different rebirth realms), one who holds the view 'there is no other world' has wrong view...

—Buddha, Majjhima Nikaya i.402, Apannaka Sutta

Buddha also asserted that there is karma, which influences the future suffering through the cycle of rebirth, but added that there is a way to end the cycle of karmic rebirths through nirvana. The Buddha introduced the concept that there is no soul (self) tying the cycle of rebirths, in contrast to themes asserted by various Hindu and Jaina traditions, and this central concept in Buddhism is called anattā; Buddha also affirmed the idea that all compounded things are subject to dissolution at death or anicca. The Buddha's detailed conception of the connections between action (karma), rebirth and causality is set out in the twelve links of dependent origination.

In Early Buddhism

There are many references to rebirth in the **Early Buddhist Texts** (henceforth EBTs). Some key suttas which discuss rebirth include Mahakammavibhanga Sutta (Majjhima Nikaya "MN"); Upali Sutta ; Kukkuravatika Sutta; Moliyasivaka Sutta (Samyutta Nikaya); and Sankha Sutta.

There are various terms which refer to the rebirth process, such as Āgati-gati, Punarbhava and others. The term Āgati literally means 'coming back, return', while Gati means 'going away' and Punarbhava means 're-becoming'. Numerous other terms for rebirths are found in the Buddhist scriptures, such as Punagamana, Punavasa, Punanivattati, Abhinibbatti, and words with roots of *jati and *rupa.

The EBTs state that on the night of his awakening, the Buddha attained the ability to recall a vast number of past lives along with numerous details about them. These early scriptures also state that he could remember "as far as ninety-one eons" (Majjhima Nikaya i.483).

Bhikkhu Sujato notes that there are three main principles of rebirth in early Buddhism:

- Rebirth is regarded as an ongoing process to be escaped from in the search for liberation.
- Rebirth is determined by one's own mind, particularly one's ethical choices.
- The practice of Buddhism aims at ending rebirth.

According to Bhikkhu Anālayo, the Buddhist teaching of Dependent Origination is closely connected with the doctrine of rebirth. One of the 12 elements of Dependent Origination is "birth" (jati), which according to Anālayo refers to the rebirth of living beings. He cites SN 12.2 and its parallel in Samyukta Agama "SA" 298 as evidence.: SN 12.2 defines "birth" in the context of Dependent Origination as "the birth of the various beings into the various orders of beings, their being born, descent into the womb, production, the manifestation of the aggregates, the obtaining of the sense bases."

The early Buddhist conception of rebirth is one in which consciousness is always dependent on other factors, mainly name and form (nama-rupa) which refers to the physical body and various cognitive elements (such as feeling, perception and volition). Because of this, consciousness (viññana) is seen as supported by the body and its cognitive apparatus and cannot exist without it (and vice versa). However, consciousness can jump from one body to another (this is compared to how a spark from a hot iron can travel through the air in AN 7.52). This process applies to the very moment of conception, which requires a consciousness to enter the womb. This is indicated by Dirgha Agama "DA" 13 and its parallels (DN 15, Madhyama Agama "MA" 97). DA 13 states.

[The Buddha said]: Ananda, in dependence on consciousness there is name and form. What is the meaning of this? If consciousness did not enter the mother's womb, would there be name and form? [Ananda] replied: No.

The same sutra states that if consciousness were to depart from the womb, the fetus could not continue to grow. Drawing on these sutras and others (such as SN 22.8 and SA 1265) Anālayo concludes that "consciousness appears to be what provides the transition from one body to another". However, according to Sujato, the EBTs indicate that it is not just consciousness which undergoes rebirth, but some form of all the five aggregates.

The EBTs also seem to indicate that there is an in-between state (antarābhava) between death and rebirth. According to Bhikkhu Sujato, the most explicit passage supporting this can be found in the Kutuhalasāla Sutta, which states that "when a being has laid down this body, but has not yet been reborn in another body, it is fuelled by craving."

Another term which is used to describe what gets reborn in the EBTs is gandhabba ("spirit"). According to the Assalayana Sutta (and its parallel at MA 151), for conception to be successful, a gandhabba must be present (as well as other physiological factors).

According to the EBTs, this rebirth consciousness is not a tabula rasa (blank slate), but contains certain underlying tendencies (anusaya) which in turn "form an object for the establishment of consciousness" (SA 359, SN 13.39). These subliminal inclinations are thus a condition for continued rebirth and also carry imprints from past lives.

According to the EBTs, past life memories can be retrieved through the cultivation of deep meditative states (samadhi). The Buddha himself is depicted has having developed the ability to recollect his past lives as well as to access the past life memories of other conscious beings in texts like the Bhayabherava Sutta (MN 4, the parallel Agama text is at Ekottara

Agama 31.1) and the Mahapadana Sutta (DN 14, parallel at DA 1). Another key point affirmed by the EBTs is that the series of past lives stretches so far back into the past that a beginning point cannot be found (see e.g. SN 15.3 and SA 938).

25.8 Life after Death According to Buddhism

All life is in a cycle of death and rebirth called samsara. This cycle is something to escape from. When someone dies his energy passes into another form.

Buddhist believe in karma or 'intentional action'.

Through good actions, such as ethical conduct, and by developing concentration and wisdom, Buddhists hope to either gain enlightenment or to ensure a better future for themselves. These good actions are set out in the Eightfold Path, which includes right speech, right livelihood, and right concentration. Good actions will result in a better rebirth, while bad actions will have the opposite effect.

Depending on the actions performed in previous lives, rebirth could be as a human or animal or even ghosts, demi-gods, or gods. Being born as a human is seen by Buddhists as a rare opportunity to work towards escaping this cycle of samsara. The escape from samsara is called **Nirvana** or **enlightenment**.

Once Nirvana is achieved, and the enlightened individual physically dies, Buddhists believe that they will no longer be reborn.

The Buddha taught that when Nirvana is achieved, Buddhists are able to see the world as it really is. Nirvana means realising and accepting the Four Noble Truths and being awake to reality.

Some Buddhists believe that enlightened individuals can choose to be reborn in order to help others become enlightened. Others believe that, when Nirvana is achieved, the cycle of samsara, all suffering and further existence for that individual itself ends.

Why don't Buddhists believe in souls or an eternal creator God?

Anicca - Buddhists believe that nothing is permanent. Everything changes. So, this means that things like everlasting souls or eternal gods *cannot* exist. Buddhism, unlike other religions, does not believe in a creator God or an eternal or everlasting soul.

Anatta - Buddhists believe that there is no permanent self or soul. Because there is no unchanging permanent essence or soul, Buddhists sometimes talk about energy being reborn, rather than souls.

Why do Buddhists believe in life after death?

Buddhists believe in life after death because the Buddha taught that human beings are each born an infinite number of times, unless they achieve Nirvana. In the Dhammapada the Buddha states:

> Long is the cycle of birth and death to the fool who does not know the true path.
>
> *- Dhammapada*

The Dhammapada contains many other teachings about samsara, enlightenment, and Nirvana:

> One road leads to wealth; another road leads to nirvana. Let the mendicant, the disciple of Buddha, learn this and not strive for honour but seek wisdom
>
> *- Dhammapada*

The Buddha taught his disciples not to fear death. This has been interpreted by Buddhists as suggesting that if they live well, their rebirth will be good.

After his enlightenment, the Buddha could remember his previous lives. Some of these previous lives are recorded in the Buddhist scripture, the Jataka.

In **Tibetan Buddhism** there are many writings about life after death including the 'Tibetan Book of the Dead'. This is a guide telling the dying person how to react and try to ensure a positive outcome of the experiences. It includes descriptions of the bardo states. These are states between dying and being reborn.

Mahayana Buddhism also uses images to teach about life after death. The Wheel of Existence shows the different realms Buddhists believe you can be reborn into.

Belief in life after death may be influenced by the meaning and purpose it gives to the lives of Buddhists.

25.9 Saṃsāra

Saṃsāra is a Sanskrit/Pali word that means "world". It is also the concept of rebirth and "cyclicality of all life, matter, existence", a fundamental belief of most Indian religions. Popularly, it is the cycle of death and rebirth. Saṃsāra is sometimes referred to with terms or phrases such as transmigration, karmic cycle, reincarnation or Punarjanman, and "cycle of aimless drifting, wandering or mundane existence".

The concept of Saṃsāra has roots in the post-Vedic literature; the theory is not discussed in the Vedas themselves. It appears in developed form, but without mechanistic details, in the early Upanishads. The full exposition of the Saṃsāra doctrine is found in Sramanic religions such as Buddhism and Jainism, as well as various schools of Hindu philosophy after about the mid-1st millennium BC. The Saṃsāra doctrine is tied to the karma theory of Hinduism, and the liberation from Saṃsāra has been at the core of the spiritual quest of Indian traditions, as well as their internal disagreements. The liberation from Saṃsāra is called Moksha, Nirvana, Mukti or Kaivalya.

Saṃsāra in Buddhism is the "suffering-laden cycle of life, death, and rebirth, without beginning or end". Also referred to as the wheel of existence (Bhavacakra), it is often mentioned in Buddhist texts with the term punarbhava (rebirth, re-becoming); the liberation from this cycle of existence, Nirvana, is the foundation and the most important purpose of Buddhism.

Samsara is considered permanent in Buddhism, just like other Indian religions. Karma drives this permanent Samsara in Buddhist thought and "short of attaining enlightenment, in each rebirth, one is born and dies, to be reborn elsewhere in accordance with the completely impersonal causal nature of one's own karma; This endless cycle of birth, rebirth, and redeath is Saṃsāra". The Four Noble Truths, accepted by all Buddhist traditions, are aimed at ending this Samsara-related re-becoming (rebirth) and associated cycles of suffering.

Like Jainism, Buddhism developed its own Samsara theory, that evolved over time the mechanistic details on how the wheel of mundane existence works over the endless cycles of rebirth and redeath. In early Buddhist traditions, Saṃsāra cosmology consisted of five realms through which wheel of existence recycled. This included hells (niraya), hungry ghosts (pretas), animals (tiryak), humans (manushya), and gods (devas, heavenly). In latter traditions, this list grew to a list of six realms of rebirth, adding demi-gods (asuras),which were included in gods realm in earlier traditions. The "hungry ghost, heavenly, hellish realms" respectively formulate the ritual, literary and moral spheres of many contemporary Buddhist traditions.

The Saṃsāra concept, in Buddhism, envisions that these six realms are interconnected, and everyone cycles life after life, and death is just a state for an afterlife, through these realms, because of a combination of ignorance, desires and purposeful karma, or ethical and unethical actions. Nirvana is typically described as the freedom from rebirth and the only alternative to suffering of Samsara, in Buddhism. However, the Buddhist texts developed a more comprehensive theory of rebirth from fears of redeath, called amata (death-free), a state which is considered synonymous with nirvana.

Chapter - 26

Pure Land Buddhism

26.1 Introduction to Pure Land Buddhism

Pure Land Buddhism, also referred to as Amidism in English, is a broad branch of Mahayana Buddhism and one of the most widely practiced traditions of Buddhism in East Asia. Pure Land is a tradition of Buddhist teachings that are focused on the Buddha Amitābha. The three primary texts of the tradition, known as the "Three Pure Land Sutras", are the Longer Sukhāvatīvyūha Sūtra (Infinite Life Sutra), Amitayurdhyana Sutra (Contemplation Sutra) and the Shorter Sukhāvatīvyūha Sūtra (Amitabha Sutra).

Pure Land oriented practices and concepts are found within basic Mahāyāna Buddhist cosmology, and form an important component of the Mahāyāna Buddhist traditions of China, Japan, Korea, Tibet and Vietnam. The term "Pure Land Buddhism" is used to describe both the Pure Land soteriology of Mahayana Buddhism, which may be better understood as "Pure Land traditions" or "Pure Land teachings," and the separate Pure Land sects that developed in Japan from the work of Hōnen. Pure Land Buddhism is built on the belief that there will never be a world which is not corrupt, so the rebirth in another plane, referred to as the "Pure Land" is the goal.

26.2 Early History of Pure Land Buddhism

26.2.1 History in India

The Pure Land teachings were first developed in India, and were very popular in Kashmir and Central Asia, where they may have originated. Pure Land sutras were brought from the Gandhāra region to China as early as 147 CE, when the Kushan monk Lokakṣema began translating the first Buddhist sūtras into Chinese. The earliest of these translations show evidence of having been translated from the Gāndhārī language, a Prakrit. There are also images of Amitābha with the bodhisattvas

Avalokiteśvara and Mahāsthāmaprāpta which were made in Gandhāra during the Kushan era.

In the Buddhist traditions of India, Pure Land doctrines and practices were disseminated by well-known exponents of the Mahāyāna teachings, including Nāgārjuna and Vasubandhu. Pure Land schools arose because of the belief that humans were becoming incapable of Dharma, emphasising that humans needed help from another power; that power being Amitābha Buddha. Although Amitābha is honoured and venerated in Pure Land traditions, this was clearly distinguished from worship of the Hindu gods, as Pure Land practice has its roots in the Buddhist ideal of the bodhisattva.

26.2.2 Pure Land Sutras

The three principal Pure Land sūtras are the Longer Sukhāvatīvyūha Sūtra, Amitayurdhyana Sutra and the Shorter Sukhāvatīvyūha Sūtra. These sutras describe Amitābha and his Pure Land of Bliss, called Sukhavati. Also related to the Pure Land tradition is the Pratyutpanna Samādhi Sūtra, which gives an early description of the practice of reciting the name of Amitābha as a meditation method, although it does not enumerate any vows of Amitābha or the qualities of Sukhāvatī.

Bodhisattvas hear about the Buddha Amitābha and call him to mind again and again in this land. Because of this calling to mind, they see the Buddha Amitābha. Having seen him they ask him what dharmas it takes to be born in the realm of the Buddha Amitābha. Then the Buddha Amitābha says to these bodhisattvas: "If you wish to come and be born in my realm, you must always call me to mind again and again, you must always keep this thought in mind without letting up, and thus you will succeed in coming to be born in my realm."

In addition to these sutras, many other Mahāyāna texts also feature Amitābha, and a total of 290 such works have been identified in the Taishō Tripiṭaka.

The long and short Sukhāvatīvyūha sūtras were composed during the 1st and 2nd centuries CE, though the smaller Sukhāvatīvyūha are considered to be earlier.

The descriptions of Sukhāvatī given in the Sukhāvatīvyūha sūtras suggests that these descriptions were originally used for meditation: "This land, called Sukhāvatī or "blissful," is described in great detail, in a way that suggests that the sūtras were to be used as guides to visualisation meditation, and also gives an impression of a magical world of intense visual and sonorous delight."

In the Infinite Life Sutra, Gautama Buddha begins by describing to his attendant Ānanda a past life of the buddha Amitābha. He states that in a past life, Amitābha was once a king who renounced his kingdom, and became a monastic bodhisattva named Dharmākara ("Dharma Storehouse"). Under the guidance of the buddha Lokeśvararāja ("World Sovereign King"), innumerable buddha-lands throughout the ten directions were revealed to him. After meditating for five eons as a bodhisattva, he then made a great series of vows to save all sentient beings, and through his great merit, created the realm of Sukhāvatī ("Ultimate Bliss"). This land of Sukhāvatī would later come to be known as the Pure Land in Chinese translation.

Contemporary Pure Land traditions see Amitābha expounding the Dharma in his buddha-field (Skt. buddhakṣetra), or "pure land", a region offering respite from karmic transmigration. Amitābha's pure land of Sukhāvatī is described in the Longer Sukhāvatīvyūha Sūtra as a land of beauty that surpasses all other realms. It is said to be inhabited by many gods, men, flowers, fruits, and adorned with wish-granting trees where rare birds come to rest. In Pure Land traditions, entering the Pure Land is popularly perceived as equivalent to the attainment of enlightenment. Upon entry into the Pure Land, the practitioner is then instructed by Amitābha Buddha and numerous bodhisattvas until full and complete enlightenment is reached. This person then has the choice of returning at any time as a bodhisattva to any of the six realms of existence in order to help all sentient beings in saṃsāra, or to stay the whole duration, reach buddhahood, and subsequently deliver beings to the shore of liberation.

In Mahāyāna Buddhism, there are many buddhas, and each buddha has a pure land. Amitābha's pure land of Sukhāvatī is understood to be in the western direction, whereas Akṣobhya's pure land of Abhirati is to the east. Though there are other traditions devoted to various Pure Lands, each of Pure Lands except Amitābha's is called by the different name without calling it pure land, and Amitabha's is by far the most popular. Few Pure Land buddhists have practiced the harder Pratyutpanna samadhi.

Sutras of Pure Land Buddhism preach that Dharma brings effects equally without distinction of saints or the imperial family. This is one of the reasons that became most popular among the populace. In addition, it references that, benevolences expecting the reward do not have good deeds, and suggests that good and evil may be interchanged in the difference of one's situation. Hence, it was thought that menial persons could be released from the underworld like Hell and arrive at Pure Land easily depending on their good deeds in one's lifetime. However, because this teaching includes extremely difficult subject matter, various denominations or sects appeared over the interpretation.

26.2.3 Early History in China

The Pure Land teachings first became prominent in China with the founding of Donglin Temple at Mount Lu by Huiyuan in 402. As a young man, Huiyuan practiced Daoism, but felt the theories of immortality to be vague and unreliable, and unrepresentative of the ultimate truth. Instead, he turned to Buddhism and became a monk learning under Dao'an. Later he founded a monastery at the top of Mount Lu and invited well-known literati to study and practice Buddhism there, where they formed the White Lotus Society. They accepted the Shorter Sukhāvatīvyūha Sūtra and the Longer Sukhāvatīvyūha Sūtra as their standards among the Buddhist sūtras, and they advocated the practice of reciting the name of Amitābha Buddha in order to attain rebirth in the western pure land of Sukhāvatī. Mount Lu is regarded as being among the most sacred religious sites of the Pure Land Buddhist tradition, and the site of the first Pure Land gathering.

The Pure Land teachings and meditation methods quickly spread throughout China and were systematised by a series of elite monastic thinkers, namely Tanluan, Daochuo, Shandao, and others. The main teaching of the Chinese Pure Land tradition is based on focusing the mind with Mindfulness of the Buddha through recitation of the name of Amitābha Buddha, so as to attain rebirth in his pure land of Sukhāvatī. Early Pure Land as practiced in China by Tanluan is described as follows:

> [Tanluan] describes the visualisation of Amitābha and Sukhāvatī in minute detail, he regards the invocation of the Buddha's name as a spell working in the inconceivable realm (acintya-dhātu), and he describes how the realised Pure Land devotee manifests human (nirmita) bodies in all times and places. His knowledge of Buddhism is deep. He uses over twenty sūtras and more than a dozen śāstras to argue his case. There are eighty-one references to the Mahāprajñāpāramitāupadeśa alone, and twenty-one references to the Chinese Mādhyamaka Master Sengchao, none of them trivial or out of place.

At a later date, the Pure Land teachings spread to Japan and slowly grew in prominence. Genshin (942–1017) caused Fujiwara no Michinaga (966-1028) to accept the Pure Land teachings. Hōnen (1133–1212) established Pure Land Buddhism as an independent sect in Japan known as Jōdo-shū. Today Pure Land is an important form of Buddhism in Japan, China, Korea, and Vietnam. Pure Land schools make up almost 40 percent of Japanese Buddhism practitioners with the most temples, second to Chan schools. These schools were influenced by the thought that humans could no longer understand the dharma by themselves.

26.3 Meditation

26.3.1 Mindfulness of Amitābha Buddha

Repeating the name of Amitābha is traditionally a form of mindfulness of the Buddha. This term was translated into Chinese as nianfo, by which it is popularly known in English. The practice is described as calling the buddha to mind by repeating his name, to enable the practitioner to bring all his or her attention upon that Buddha. This may be done vocally or mentally, and with or without the use of Buddhist prayer beads. Those who practice this method often commit to a fixed set of repetitions per day. According to tradition, the second patriarch of the Pure Land school, Shandao is said to have practiced this day and night without interruption, each time emitting light from his mouth. Therefore, he was bestowed with the title "Great Master of Light" by Emperor Gaozong of Tang.

In Chinese Buddhism, there is a related practice called the "dual path of Chan and Pure Land cultivation", which is also called the "dual path of emptiness and existence." As taught by Nan Huai-Chin, the name of Amitābha is recited slowly, and the mind is emptied out after each repetition. When idle thoughts arise, the name is repeated again to clear them. With constant practice, the mind is able to remain peacefully in emptiness, culminating in the attainment of samādhi.

26.3.2 Pure Land Rebirth Dhāraṇī

Repeating the Pure Land Rebirth dhāraṇī is another method in Pure Land Buddhism. Similar to the mindfulness practice of repeating the name of Amitābha, this dhāraṇī is another method of meditation and recitation in Pure Land Buddhism. The repetition of this dhāraṇī is said to be very popular among traditional Chinese Buddhists. It is traditionally preserved in Sanskrit, and it is said that when a devotee succeeds in realising singleness of mind by repeating a mantra, its true and profound meaning will be clearly revealed.

namo amitābhāya tathāgatāya tadyathā
amṛt[od]bhave amṛta[siddhambhave]
amṛtavikrānte amṛtavikrāntagāmini
gagana kīrtī[kare] svāhā

The Chinese use a version of this dhāraṇī that was transliterated from Sanskrit into Chinese characters, called the "Amitabha Pure Land Rebirth Mantra", "Mantra for Birth in the Pure Land", also known as the Pure Land Rebirth Dhāraṇī. The full name is "the dhāraṇī for pulling out karmic obstructions and obtaining rebirth in the Pure Lands". The translation exists in various forms and this is one commonly used.

26.3.3 Visualisation methods

Another practice found in Pure Land Buddhism is meditative contemplation and visualisation of Amitābha, his attendant bodhisattvas, and the Pure Land. The basis of this is found in the Amitayurdhyana Sutra, in which the Gautama Buddha describes to Queen Vaidehi the practices of sixteen progressive visualisation methods, corresponding to the attainment of various levels of rebirth in the Pure Land. The first of these steps is contemplation of a setting sun, until the visualisation is clear whether the eyes are open or closed. Each progressive step adds complexity to the visualisation of Sukhāvatī, with the final contemplation being an expansive visual which includes Amitābha and his attendant bodhisattvas. This progressive visualisation method was widely followed in the past for the purpose of developing samādhi. Visualisation practices for Amitābha are also popular in Shingon Buddhism as well as other schools of Vajrayana.

26.4 Going to the Pure Land

Practitioners believe that there is evidence of dying people going to the pure land, such as:

- Knowing the time of death: some prepare by bathing and nianfo.
- The "Three Saints of the West": Amitābha and the two bodhisattvas, Avalokiteśvara on his right and Mahāsthāmaprāpta, appear and welcome the dying person. Visions of other buddhas or bodhisattvas are disregarded as they may be bad spirits disguising themselves, attempting to stop the person from entering the Pure Land.
- Records of practicing Pure Land Buddhists who have died have been known to leave śarīra, or relics, after cremation.

The last part of the body to become cold is the top of the head (posterior fontanelle). In Buddhist teaching, souls who enter the Pure Land leave the body through the fontanelle at the top of the skull. Hence, this part of the body stays warmer longer than the rest of the body. The Verses on the Structure of the Eight Consciousnesses reads: "to birth in saints the last body temperature in top of head, to deva in eyes, to human in heart, to hungry ghosts in belly, to animals in knee cap, to the hells-realm in sole of feet."

The dying person may demonstrate some, but not necessarily all, of these evidences. For example, his facial expression may be happy, but he may not demonstrate other signs, such as sharira and dreams.

When a person dies, at first "good luck at the underworld" is prayed for the dead person. The family remains in mourning for 49 days till the dead person's reincarnation (Pure Land sects may say "till achieving Pure Land"). It is thought that the great sinner transmigrates to a beast or a hungry ogre without being able to go to the Pure Land.

26.5 Variance Between Traditions

In Tibet, which has a Tantric culture, the original Indic general orientation of seeking rebirth in the Pure Land of any deity was retained. Tibetan practitioners may also visualise themselves as a Buddha. By contrast, the Chinese traditions are oriented towards seeking assistance from an "other-Amitabha Buddha" which is outside the self, and may consider the Western Pure Land to exist only in the mind.

26.5.1 Indian Buddhism

Regarding Pure Land practice in Indian Buddhism, as described in the Pure Land sūtras from India, Mindfulness of the Buddha is the essential practice. These forms of mindfulness are essentially methods of meditating upon Amitābha Buddha. There is an intermingling of Mahāyāna teachings with Buddhist meditation schools in Kashmir for the rise of Mahāyāna practices related to buddhānusmṛti, mindfulness of the Buddha.

Great innovations undoubtedly arose from the intermingling of early Buddhism and the Mahāyāna in Kashmir. Under the guidance of Sarvāstivādin teachers in the region, a number of influential meditation schools evolved which took as their inspiration the Bodhisattva Maitreya. [...] The Kashmiri meditation schools were undoubtably highly influential in the arising of the buddhānusmṛti practices, concerned with the 'recollection of the Buddha(s)', which were later to become characteristic of Mahāyāna Buddhism and the Tantra.

26.5.2 Chinese Buddhism

Pure Land cosmology, soteriology, and ritual were always part-and-parcel of Chinese Buddhism in general and Chan monasticism in particular. The modern conception of an independent and self-conscious Chinese Pure Land school in History with its own patriarchate and teachings, and the associated notion of Chan/Pure Land syncretism, are inordinately influence by the Japanisation of buddhist studies and the enduring legacy of Japanese sectarian disputes over Chinese Patriarchs. In reality, Pure Land and Zen practice are often seen as being mutually compatible, and no strong distinctions are made. Chinese Buddhists have traditionally viewed the practice of meditation and the practice of reciting Amitābha Buddha's name, as complementary and even analogous methods for achieving enlightenment. This is because they view recitation as a meditation method used to concentrate the mind and purify thoughts. Chinese Buddhists widely consider this form of recitation as a very effective form of meditation practice.

Historically, many Buddhist teachers in China have also taught both Chan and Pure Land together. For example, in the Ming dynasty, Hanshan Deqing and many of his contemporaries advocated the dual practice of the Chan and Pure Land methods, advocating mindfulness of Amitābha to purify the mind for the attainment of self-realisation.

26.5.3 Tibetan Buddhism

Tibetan Pure Land Buddhism has a long and innovative history dating from the 8th-9th centuries, the era of the Tibetan Empire, with the translation and canonisation of the Sanskrit Sukhāvatīvyūha sūtras in Tibetan. Tibetan compositions of pure-land prayers and artistic renditions of Sukhāvatī in Central Asia date to that time. Tibetan pure-land literature forms a distinct genre and encompasses a wide range of scriptures, "aspiration prayers to be born in Sukhāvatī", commentaries on the prayers and the sūtras, and meditations and rituals belonging to the Vajrayāna tradition. The incorporation of phowa (mind transference techniques) in pure-land meditations is textually attested in the 14th century, in The Standing Blade of Grass, a terma text allegedly dating to the time of the Tibetan Empire. A good number of Buddhist treasure texts are dedicated to Amitābha and to rituals associated with his pure-land, while the wide acceptance of phowa in Tibetan death rituals may owe its popularity to Pure Land Buddhism promoted by all schools of Tibetan Buddhism.

There are many treasure texts associated with Tibetan Pure Land Buddhism and tertön Longsal Nyingpo (1625–1682/92 or 1685–1752) of Katok Monastery revealed a terma on the pure land.

It is important to apply our knowledge internally. The Buddha attained enlightenment in this way. The pure lands are internal; the mental afflictions are internal. The crucial factor is to recognise the mental afflictions. Only by recognising their nature can we attain Buddhahood.

26.5.4 Japanese Buddhism

In Japanese Buddhism, Pure Land teachings developed into independent institutional sects, as can be seen in the Jōdo-shū, Jōdo Shinshū, Yūzū-nembutsu-shū, and Ji-shū.

The majority of the important schools of Japanese Buddhism developed in the Middle Ages, between the twelfth and fourteenth centuries. However, they were mostly influenced by the Tendai school in the sixth century as their founding monks were all trained originally in the school. The Tendai school's teachings were based on the Lotus Sūtra and Mahāyāna Nirvāṇa Sūtra, encompassing a wide range of teachings and eclectic practices of austerities.

Strong institutional boundaries exist between sects which serve to clearly separate the Japanese Pure Land schools from the Japanese Zen schools. One notable exception to this is found in the Ōbaku Zen school, which was founded in Japan during the 17th century by the Chinese Buddhist monk Ingen (Chinese Yinyuan Longqi). The Ōbaku school of Zen retains many Chinese features such as mindfulness of Amitābha through recitation and recitation of the Pure Land sūtras.

26.6 Synopses of the Three Sutras

26.6.1.1 The Larger Sutra: Part One

Amitāyus, as Bodhisattva Dharmākara, awakened aspiration for enlightenment, made the Forty-eight Vows, attained buddhahood, and established his glorious buddha land.

1. Time and place of the assembly and its audience.
2. Distinguished virtues of the bodhisattvas in the audience.
3. The Buddha's unusually majestic appearance.
4. The fifty-three past buddhas.
5. The fifty-fourth buddha, Lokeśvararāja, and his disciple Dharmākara.

   Dharmākara praises the Buddha in verses.
6. Dharmākara sees many buddha lands and resolves to establish his own.
7. The Forty-eight Vows.
8. The verses confirming Dharmākara's resolution.
9. His bodhisattva practice.
10. His attainment of buddhahood and a general discussion of the Pure Land.
11. The light of Amitāyus.
12. The lifespan of Amitāyus and the inhabitants of his Pure Land.
13. Number of śrāvakas at the first teaching assembly.
14. The jewelled trees.
15. The bodhi tree and music.

16. Glorious and blissful aspects of the Pure Land.
17. Bodily appearance of the inhabitants and their enjoyment of pleasures.
18. Comparison between the karmic rewards of a beggar and a king.
19. Comparisons between different heavens and between the glories of heavenly beings and those in the Pure Land.
20. Further pleasures to be enjoyed in the Pure Land.
21. Flowers and their innumerable rays of light.

26.6.1.2 The Larger Sutra: Part Two

Methods of attainment of birth in the Pure Land; the virtues of the bodhisattvas born there; moral teachings based on karma; reality of evil acts and suffering; admonitions against doubt; visits of bodhisattvas to the Pure Land from other worlds; and the benefits gained by the audience.

22. Praise of the Name of Amitāyus by other buddhas and attainment of birth by faith.
23. The highest grade of aspirants.
24. The middle grade of aspirants.
25. The lowest grade of aspirants.
26. Visits of bodhisattvas to the Pure Land from other worlds.
27. Verses on the same.
28. Activity of the bodhisattvas born there with a special mention of Avalokiteśvara and Mahāsthāmaprāpta.
29. Teaching of the Dharma by Amitāyus and exquisite sounds produced by the trees, etc.
30. Virtues of the bodhisattvas in the Pure Land.
31. Three kinds of evil acts and their retributions.
32. Śākyamuni's encouragement to do good and aspire to birth, and Maitreya's appreciation of the Buddha's benevolence.
33. Śākyamuni's further admonition against evil acts and encouragement to do good and aspire to birth in the Pure Land.
34. Introduction to the five kinds of evils and their retributions.
35. The first evil.
36. The second evil.
37. The third evil.
38. The fourth evil.
39. The fifth evil.

40. His admonition against the five kinds of evil and encouragement to do good.
41. Amitāyus and the Pure Land seen by the audience.
42. Two types of birth in the Pure Land.
43. The causes of the two types of birth.
44. Śākyamuni's encouragement of faith.
45. Birth within the lotus blossom compared to the king's prison for princes who have committed offenses.
46. Visits of bodhisattvas to the Pure Land from fourteen other buddha lands.
47. Śākyamuni's encouragement to hear and practice this sutra, his promise to keep it in the world for another hundred years after the extinction of all other Buddhist teachings, and the difficulty of encountering this sutra, etc.
48. Benefits gained by the audience.

26.6.2 The Contemplation Sutra

A tragedy in the royal family of Magadha leads to the Buddha's revelation of the Pure Land Way. Thirteen meditations and the recitation of the Name of Amitāyus are presented as the cause of birth there.

1. Time and place of the assembly and its audience.
2. King Bimbisāra's imprisonment by his son Ajātaśatru.
3. Queen Vaidehī's imprisonment.
4. The Buddha's visit to Vaidehī.
5. Vaidehī's desire to be born in the land of Amitāyus in response to the Buddha's revelation of many buddha lands.
6. The light of the Buddha's smile shining upon Bimbisāra's head.
7. The three acts of merit for attaining birth in the land of Amitāyus.
8. Vaidehī's request that the Buddha teach her how to visualise the land of Amitāyus.
9. The first meditation, on the setting sun.
10. The second meditation, on the water.
11. The third meditation, on the ground.
12. The fourth meditation, on the jewelled trees.
13. The fifth meditation, on the water in the ponds.
14. The sixth meditation, on various objects.

15. The appearance of Amitāyus with the two bodhisattvas and the seventh meditation, on the lotus throne.
16. The eighth meditation, on the image of Amitāyus.
17. The ninth meditation, on the glory of Amitāyus.
18. The tenth meditation, on Avalokiteśvara.
19. The eleventh meditation, on Mahāsthāmaprāpta.
20. The twelfth meditation, on the aspirants themselves as they are born in the land of Amitāyus.
21. The thirteenth meditation, on images of Amitāyus and the two bodhisattvas.
22. On the nine grades of birth: first, the highest level of the highest grade.
23. Second, the middle level of the highest grade.
24. Third, the lowest level of the highest grade.
25. Fourth, the highest level of the middle grade.
26. Fifth, the middle level of the middle grade.
27. Sixth, the lowest level of the middle grade.
28. Seventh, the highest level of the lowest grade.
29. Eighth, the middle level of the lowest grade.
30. Ninth, the lowest level of the lowest grade.
31. The benefits gained by the audience.
32. The Buddha's explanation of the names of this sutra and his admonition to Ānanda.
33. The Buddha's return to Vulture Peak; Ānanda's explanation to the audience of what has happened.

26.6.3 The Smaller Sutra

The glorious features of the land of Amitāyus are explained, and the Dharma through which he saves beings is praised by the buddhas of the six directions.

1. Time and place of the assembly and its audience.
2. The Land of Utmost Bliss and Amitāyus introduced.
3. Magnificent aspects of the Land of Utmost Bliss.
4. The reason why this buddha is called "Amitābha" and "Amitāyus."
5. The virtues and number of the bodhisattvas in that land and the practice required for the attainment of birth there.

6. Praise of the virtue of Amitāyus by the buddhas **in the east**.
7. Praise of the same by the buddhas **in the south**.
8. Praise of the same by the buddhas **in the west.**
9. Praise of the same by the buddhas **in the north**.
10. Praise of the same by the buddhas **in the zenith**.
11. Praise of the same by the buddhas **in the nadir.**
12. The reason why this sutra is called "Praise of the Inconceivable Virtue and Protection by All Buddhas," and Śākyamuni's urging aspiration for birth in that land.
13. Praise of Śākyamuni's virtue by all the buddhas.
14. End of the sutra with a description of the audience's joy.

Chapter - 27

Taking Refuge in the Three Jewels in Buddhism

27.1 What is Taking Refuge in the Three Jewels?

The Three Jewels are: (i) The Buddha, the fully enlightened one; (ii) The Dharma, the teachings expounded by the Buddha. (iii) The Sangha, the monastic order of Buddhism that practice Dharmas.

Taking refuge means returning, taking shelter, relying on, trusting. Any action that involves returning, depending, taking shelter, and trusting is considered taking refuge. Trying to learn Buddhism without taking refuge is to be a bystander and not a participant. If we feel constrained by taking refuge, then Buddhism is no path to liberation.

Self-proclaimed Buddhists are not real Buddhists. They are like people who are fond of another country, emigrate there, pretend to be citizens, but never apply for citizenship. Those who refrain from taking refuge, but insist upon calling themselves Buddhists, may glean some benefit from the teachings, but the essence of Buddhism will always elude them. Taking refuge is a required process, not an option. The sutras or Buddhist scriptures tell us that even people who perform good deeds will not be able to eradicate bad karma unless they take refuge in the Three Jewels. In taking refuge in the Three Jewels, we recognise the Buddha for discovering the Dharma and our own Buddha within—our potential to liberation. We also recognise the transmitters of Dharma, the Sangha members throughout the ages. Through them we realise the Dharma.

Why are the Buddha, Dharma, and Sangha called Jewels? It is because they generate an inexhaustible amount of merit and wisdom that they are considered genuine "jewels." Gold, silver, and precious gems are rare and valuable. That is why they are called "treasures"; the merit and wisdom of the Buddha, Dharma, and Sangha can bring us benefits in the world and beyond it. They are more precious than ordinary jewels because they bring peace to the world and help us thoroughly transcend our negative emotions, sufferings, and achieve awakening. The Three Jewels are the best of all jewels.

We are originally buddhas, and we are intrinsically connected with the Three Jewels. Because we misunderstand our original nature; we wander the cycle of birth and death without finding the way home. Taking refuge is to start the journey homeward.

Since early Buddhism, devotees expressed their faith through the act of taking refuge, which is threefold. In this, it centres on the authority of a Buddha as a supremely awakened being, by assenting to a role for a Buddha as a teacher of both humans and devās (heavenly beings). This often includes other Buddhas from the past, and Buddhas who have not yet arisen. Secondly, the taking of refuge honours the truth and efficacy of the Buddha's spiritual doctrine, which includes the characteristics of phenomenon (Pali: saṅkhāra) such as their impermanence (Pali: anicca), and the path to liberation. The taking of refuge ends with the acceptance of worthiness of the community of spiritually developed followers (the saṅgha), which is mostly defined as the monastic community, but may also include lay people and even devās provided they are nearly or completely enlightened. Early Buddhism did not include bodhisattvas in the Three Refuges, because they were considered to still be on the path to enlightenment.

Early texts describe the saṅgha as a "field of merit", because early Buddhists regarded offerings to them as particularly karmically fruitful. Lay devotees support and revere the saṅgha, of which they believe it will render them merit and bring them closer to enlightenment. At the same time, the Buddhist monk is given a significant role in promoting and upholding faith among laypeople. Although many examples in the canon are mentioned of well-behaved monks, there are also cases of monks misbehaving. In such cases, the texts describe that the Buddha responds with great sensitivity to the perceptions of the lay community. When the Buddha sets out new rules in the monastic code to deal with the wrongdoings of his monastics, he usually states that such behaviour should be curbed, because it would not "persuade non-believers" and "believers will turn away". He expects monks, nuns and novices to not only to lead the spiritual life for their own benefit, but also to uphold the faith of the people. On the other hand, they are not to take the task of inspiring faith to the extent of hypocrisy or inappropriateness, for example, by taking on other professions apart from being a monastic, or by courting favours by giving items to the laypeople.

Thus, taking refuge is a form of aspiration to lead a life with the Triple Gem at its core. Taking refuge is done by a short formula in which one names the Buddha, the dharma and the saṅgha as refuges. In early Buddhist scriptures, taking refuge is an expression of determination to follow the Buddha's path, but not a relinquishing of responsibility. Refuge is common to all major schools of Buddhism.

27.2 Different Levels of the Three Jewels

The Three Jewels may be understood on different levels and in many ways. We will first divide them into two groups, that of the Phenomenal and the Fundamental. These two groupings can be understood in the context of the teachings of "two truths" in Buddhism. These refer to the "absolute" truth and the "conventional" truth. The absolute or fundamental truth is the view of reality as experienced by the enlightened. Since it transcends dualistic logic, it cannot exactly be expressed in words and conceptual constructs. The relative truth is reality on a phenomenal level; it is what ordinary people experience, and is expressed readily in dualistic concepts and words. For a deeply enlightened person who has realised the absolute truth, the two truths are inseparable. But for a person who only understands the conventional truth, absolute truth remains an abstract concept.

These two truths provide a framework to understanding the different levels of taking refuge in the Three Jewels. We start by taking refuge in the Phenomenal Three Jewels; that is, a true refuge in this world that provides insight and guidance toward awakening and liberation. The Phenomenal Three Jewels are tangible, so they are easily understood by ordinary people. Once nirvana is realised—that is, you are fully awakened to the inseparability of the two truths—you embody the Fundamental Three Jewels. At this point, to speak of a refuge outside of you becomes irrelevant; the Fundamental Three Jewels are inseparable from you. This is abstract to most people, but quite clear to someone who has already actualised the true suchness of self-nature. It is important to know that all sentient beings have buddha-nature, the potentiality for buddhahood. It is only because of the vexations and confusion of karma that we cannot perceive this truth. The reason we take refuge in the Phenomenal Three Jewels is to find and manifest our buddha-nature in the Fundamental Three Jewels.

27.3 Recitation in Pali

The most used recitation in the Pali language goes:

Buddham saranam gacchami.
I take refuge in the Buddha.

Dhammam saranam gacchami.
I take refuge in the Dharma.

Sangham saranam gacchami.
I take refuge in the Sangha.

Dutiyampi Buddham saranam gacchami.
For the second time, I take refuge in the Buddha.

Dutiyampi Dhammam saranam gacchami.
For the second time, I take refuge in the Dharma.

Dutiyampi Sangham saranam gacchami.
For the second time, I take refuge in the Sangha.

Tatiyampi Buddham saranam gacchami.
For the third time, I take refuge in the Buddha.

Tatiyampi Dhammam saranam gacchami.
For the third time, I take refuge in the Dharma.

Tatiyampi Sangham saranam gacchami.
For the third time, I take refuge in the Sangha.

Except this, there are various recitations mentioned in Pali literature for taking refuge in the Three Jewels. Pali texts may employ the Brahmanical motif of a group of three refuges, as found in Rig Veda 9.97.47, Rig Veda 6.46.9 and Chandogya Upanishad 2.22.3-4.

27.4 Faith

Faith is an important teaching element in both Theravada and Mahayana traditions. Faith in Buddhism arises from accumulated experience and reasoning.

In the Kalama Sutra, the Buddha explicitly argues against simply following authority or tradition, particularly those of religions contemporary to the Buddha's time. There remains value for a degree of trusting confidence and belief in Buddhism, primarily in the spiritual attainment and salvation or enlightenment. Faith in Buddhism centres on belief in the Three Jewels.

27.5 Five Precepts

Lay followers often undertake five precepts in the same ceremony as they take the refuges. Monks administer the precepts to the laypeople, which creates an additional psychological effect. The five precepts are:

(i) to refrain from killing;

(ii) to refrain from stealing;

(iii) to refrain from lying;

(iv) to refrain from improper sexual conduct;

(v) to refrain from consuming intoxicants.

In Early Buddhist Texts, the role of the five precepts gradually developed. First of all, the precepts were combined with a declaration of faith in the triple gem (the Buddha, his teaching and the monastic community). Next, the precepts developed to become the foundation of lay practice. The precepts were seen as a preliminary condition for the higher development of the mind. At a third stage in the texts, the precepts were actually mentioned together with the triple gem, as though they were part of it. Lastly, the precepts, together with the triple gem, became a required condition for the practice of Buddhism, as lay people had to undergo a formal initiation to become a member of the Buddhist religion. When Buddhism spread to different places and people, the role of the precepts began to vary. In countries in which Buddhism was adopted as the main religion without much competition from other religious disciplines, such as Thailand, the relation between the initiation of a lay person and the five precepts has been virtually non-existent, and the taking of the precepts has become a sort of ritual cleansing ceremony. In such countries, people are presumed Buddhist from birth without much of an initiation. The precepts are often committed to by new followers as part of their installment, yet this is not very pronounced. However, in some countries like China, where Buddhism was not the only religion, the precepts became an ordination ceremony to initiate lay people into the Buddhist religion. A layperson who upholds the precepts is described in the texts as a "jewel among laymen".

27.6 Three Jewels and Three Roots

In Tibetan Buddhism there are three refuge formulations, the Outer, Inner, and Secret forms of the Three Jewels. The 'Outer' form is the 'Triple Gem', (Sanskrit: triratna), the 'Inner' is the Three Roots and the 'Secret' form is the 'Three Bodies' or trikaya of a Buddha. These alternative refuge formulations are employed by those undertaking deity yoga and other tantric practices within the Tibetan Buddhist Vajrayana tradition as a means of recognising Buddha Nature.

SECTION - 4: JAIN PHILOSOPHY

Chapter - 28

Introduction to Jain Philosophy

28.1 Introduction to Jainism

Jainism, Indian religion teaching a path to spiritual purity and enlightenment through disciplined nonviolence (ahimsa, literally "non-injury") to all living creatures.

Along with Hinduism and Buddhism, Jainism is one of the three most ancient Indian religious traditions still in existence and an integral part of South Asian religious belief and practice. While often employing concepts shared with Hinduism and Buddhism, the result of a common cultural and linguistic background, the Jain tradition must be regarded as an independent phenomenon rather than as a Hindu sect or a Buddhist heresy, as some earlier Western scholars believed.

The name Jainism derives from the Sanskrit verb ji, "to conquer." It refers to the ascetic battle that, it is believed, Jain renunciants (monks and nuns) must fight against the passions and bodily senses to gain enlightenment, or omniscience and purity of soul. The most illustrious of those few individuals who have achieved enlightenment are called Jina (literally, "Conqueror"), and the tradition's monastic and lay adherents are called Jain ("Follower of the Conquerors"), or Jaina. This term came to replace a more ancient designation, Nirgrantha ("Bondless"), originally applied to renunciants only.

Jainism has been confined largely to India, although the recent migration of Indians to other, predominantly English-speaking countries has spread its practice to many Commonwealth nations and to the United States. Precise statistics are not available, but it is estimated that there are more than six million Jains, the vast majority of whom live in India.

The three main pillars of Jainism are ahiṃsā (non-violence), anekāntavāda (non-absolutism), and aparigraha (non-attachment).

Jains take five main vows: ahiṃsā (non-violence), satya (truth), asteya (not stealing), brahmacharya (sexual continence), and aparigraha (non-possessiveness). These principles have affected Jain culture in many ways, such as leading to a predominantly vegetarian lifestyle. Parasparopagraho jīvānām (the function of souls is to help one another) is the faith's motto and the Ṇamōkāra mantra is its most common and basic prayer.

Jainism traces its spiritual ideas and history through a succession of twenty-four leaders or Tirthankaras, with the first in the current time cycle being Rishabhadeva, whom the tradition holds to have lived millions of years ago; the twenty-third tirthankara Parshvanatha, whom historians date to 9th century BCE; and the **twenty-fourth tirthankara, Mahavira** around 600 BCE. Jainism is considered to be an eternal dharma with the tirthankaras guiding every time the cycle of the cosmology.

Jainism is one of the world's oldest continuously-practiced religions. It has two major ancient sub-traditions, Digambaras and Śvētāmbaras, with different views on ascetic practices, gender and which texts can be considered canonical; both have mendicants supported by laypersons (śrāvakas and śrāvikas). The Śvētāmbara tradition in turn has three subtraditions: Mandirvāsī, Terapanthi and Sthānakavasī. The religion has between four and five million followers, known as Jains, who reside mostly in India. Outside India, some of the largest communities are in Canada, Europe, and the United States, with Japan hosting a fast-growing community of converts. Major festivals include Paryushana and Das Lakshana, Ashtanika, Mahavir Janma Kalyanak, Akshaya Tritiya, and Dipawali.

28.2 History of Jainism

28.2.1 Early history (7th century BCE–c. 5th century CE)

Scholars of religion generally hold that Jainism originated in the 7th–5th century BCE in the Ganges basin of eastern India, the scene of intense religious speculation and activity at that time. Buddhism also appeared in this region, as did other belief systems that renounced the world and opposed the ritualistic Brahmanic schools whose prestige derived from their claim of purity and their ability to perform the traditional rituals and sacrifices and to interpret their meaning. These new religious perspectives promoted asceticism, the abandonment of ritual, domestic and social action, and the attainment of spiritual illumination in an attempt to win, through one's own efforts, freedom from repeated rebirth (samsara).

Jains believe that their tradition does not have a historical founder. The first Jain figure for whom there is reasonable historical evidence is

Parshvanatha (or Parshva), a renunciant teacher who may have lived in the 7th century BCE and founded a community based upon the abandonment of worldly concerns. Jain tradition regards him as the 23rd Tirthankara (literally, "Ford Maker"; i.e., one who leads the way across the stream of rebirths to salvation) of the current age (kalpa). The 24th and last Tirthankara of that age was Vardhamana, who is known by the epithet Mahavira ("Great Hero") and is believed to have been the last teacher of "right" knowledge, faith, and practice. Although traditionally dated to 599–527 BCE, Mahavira must be regarded as a close contemporary of the Buddha (traditionally believed to have lived in 563–483 BCE but who probably flourished about a century later). The legendary accounts of Mahavira's life preserved by the Jain scriptures provide the basis for his biography and enable some conclusions to be formulated about the nature of the early community he founded.

Mahavira, like the Buddha, was the son of a chieftain of the Kshatriya (warrior) class. At the age of 30, he renounced his princely status to take up the ascetic life. Although he was accompanied for a time by the eventual founder of the Ajivika sect, Goshala Maskariputra, Mahavira spent the next 12-1/2 years following a path of solitary and intense asceticism. He then converted 11 disciples (called ganadharas), all of whom were originally Brahmans. Two of these disciples, Indrabhuti Gautama and Sudharman, both of whom survived Mahavira, are regarded as the founders of the historical Jain monastic community, and a third, Jambu, is believed to be the last person of the current age to gain enlightenment. Mahavira is believed to have died at Pavapuri, near modern Patna.

The community appears to have grown quickly. According to Jain tradition, it numbered 14,000 monks and 36,000 nuns at the time of Mahavira's death. From the beginning the community was subject to schisms (strong disagreement among members of an organisation or group that makes them divide into separate groups) over technicalities of doctrine; however, these were easily resolved. The only schism to have a lasting effect concerned a dispute over proper monastic practice, with the Shvetambara ("White-Robed") sect arguing that monks and nuns should wear white robes and the Digambara ("Sky-Clad"; i.e., naked) sect claiming that a true monk (but not a nun) should be naked. This controversy gave rise to a further dispute as to whether or not a soul can attain liberation (moksha) from a female body (a possibility the Digambaras deny).

This sectarian division, still existent today, probably took time to assume formal shape. Its exact origins remain unclear, in part because the stories describing the origins of the schism were designed to justify each sect's authority and denigrate the other. These accounts were written centuries after the fact and are valueless as genuine historical testimony. The consolidation of the Shvetambara-Digambara division was probably the result of a series of councils held to codify and preserve the Jain scriptures, which had existed as oral tradition long after Mahavira's death. Of the councils recorded in Jain history, the last one, held at Valabhi in Saurashtra (in modern Gujarat) in either 453 or 456 CE, without Digambara participation, codified the Shvetambara canon that is still in use. The Digambara monastic community denounced the codification, and the schism between the two communities became irrevocable.

During this period, Jainism spread westward to Ujjain, where it apparently enjoyed royal patronage. Later, in the 1st century BCE, according to tradition, a monk named Kalakacharya apparently overthrew King Gardabhilla of Ujjain and orchestrated his replacement with the Shahi kings (who were probably of Scythian or Persian origin). During the reign of the Gupta dynasty (320–c. 600 CE), a time of Hindu self-assertion, the bulk of the Jain community migrated to central and western India, becoming stronger there than it had been in its original home in the Ganges basin.

28.2.2 Early medieval developments (500–1100)

There is archaeological evidence of the presence of Jain monks in southern India from before the Common Era, and the Digambara sect has had a significant presence in what is now the state of Karnataka for almost 2,000 years. The early medieval period was the time of Digambara Jainism's greatest flowering. Enjoying success in modern-day Karnataka and in neighbouring Tamil Nadu state, the Digambaras gained the patronage of prominent monarchs of three major dynasties in the early medieval period—the Gangas in Karnataka (3rd–11th century); the Rashtrakutas, whose kingdom was just north of the Ganga realm (8th–12th century); and the Hoysalas in Karnataka (11th–14th century). Digambara monks are reputed to have engineered the succession of the Ganga and the Hoysala dynasties, thus stabilising uncertain political situations and guaranteeing Jain political protection and support.

The Digambaras' involvement in politics allowed Jainism to prosper in Karnataka and the Deccan. Many political and aristocratic figures had Jain monks as spiritual teachers and advisers. Epigraphical evidence reveals an elaborate patronage system through which kings, queens, state ministers, and military generals endowed the Jain community with tax revenues and with direct grants for the construction and upkeep of temples. Most famously, in the 10th century the Ganga general Chamundaraya oversaw the creation of a colossal statue of Bahubali (locally called Gommateshvara; son of Rishabhanatha, the first Tirthankara) at Shravanabelagola.

During this period Digambara writers produced numerous philosophical treatises, commentaries, and poems, which were written in Prakrit, Kannada, and Sanskrit. A number of kings provided patronage for this literary activity, and some wrote various works of literature themselves. The monk Jinasena, for example, wrote Sanskrit philosophical treatises and poetry with the support of the Rashtrakuta king Amoghavarsha I. An author in Kannada and Sanskrit, Amoghavarsha apparently renounced his throne and became a disciple of Jinasena in the early 9th century.

The Shvetambaras in the north were less prominently embroiled in dynastic politics than their southern counterparts, though there is evidence of such activity in Gujarat and Rajasthan. They supported the accession of kings such as Vanaraja in the 8th century and Kumarapala, whose accession was masterminded by Hemachandra, the great Shvetambara scholar and minister of state, in the 12th century. The Shvetambaras were no less productive than their Digambara contemporaries in the amount and variety of literature they produced during this period.

While Mahavira had rejected the claims of the caste system that privileged Brahman authority on the basis of innate purity, a formalised caste system nonetheless gradually appeared among the Digambara laity in the south. This hierarchy was depicted and sanctioned by Jinasena in his Adipurana, a legendary biography of the Tirthankara Rishabhanatha and his two sons Bahubali and Bharata. The hierarchy differed from the Hindu system in that the Kshatriyas were assigned a place of prominence over the Brahmans and in its connection of purity, at least theoretically, with a moral rather than a ritual source. In addition, Jinasena did not see the caste system as an inherent part of the universe, as did Hindu theologians and lawgivers.

28.2.3 Late medieval–early modern developments (1100–1800)

In the period of their greatest influence (6th–late 12th century), Jain monks of both sects, perhaps influenced by intense lay patronage, turned from living as wandering ascetics to permanent residence in temples or monasteries. A legacy of this transformation is the contemporary Digambara practice of the bhattaraka, through which a cleric takes monastic initiation but, rather than assuming a life of naked ascetic wandering, becomes an orange-robed administrator and guardian of holy places and temples. Some medieval Jain writers saw this compromise with ancient scriptural requirements as both a cause of and evidence for the religion's inexorable decline. However, Jainism's marginalisation in India can best be ascribed to sociopolitical factors.

The Shvetambara Jain community's eclipse was greatly accelerated by the successful invasion of western and northern India by Muslim forces in the 12th century. Although it faced persecution and the destruction of important shrines, the Jain community perhaps suffered most from the sudden shift of political control from indigenous to foreign hands and the loss of direct access to sources of power. While some Jain laymen and monks served Muslim rulers as political advisers or teachers—including Hiravijaya, who taught the Moghul emperor Akbar—the Shvetambara community was gradually compelled to redefine itself and today thrives as a mercantile group.

At roughly the same time, various Shvetambara monastic subsects (gaccha) appeared, forming on the basis of both regional and teacher associations. Some of the most important of these subsects still exist, such as the Gaccha Kharatara (founded 11th century) and the Tapa Gaccha (founded 13th century). The gacchas included lay followers, often differed markedly from one another over issues of lineage, ritual, and the sacred calendar, and claimed to represent the true Jainism. According to tradition, their leading teachers sought to reform lax monastic practice and participated in the conversion of Hindu Rajput clans in western India that subsequently became Shvetambara Jain caste groups.

Although most gacchas accepted the practice of image worship, the Lumpaka, or Lonka Gaccha, did not. Founded by the mid-15th-century layman Lonka Shah, the Lonka Gaccha denied the scriptural warranty of image worship and in the 17th century emerged as the non-image-worshipping Sthanakavasi sect. At the end of the 18th century, the Sthanakavasi underwent a schism when Acharya Bhikshu founded the Terapanthi ("Following the 13 Tenets") sect, which claims to have avoided heresy and laxity throughout its history by investing authority in a single teacher.

In the south, Digambara Jainism, for all its prominence in aristocratic circles, was attacked by Hindu devotional movements that arose in Tamil Nadu as early as the 6th century. One of the most vigorous of these Hindu movements was that of the Lingayats, or Virashaivas, which appeared in full force in the 12th century in northern Karnataka, a stronghold of Digambara Jainism. The Lingayats gained royal support, and many Jains themselves became Lingayats in the ensuing centuries. With the advent of the Vijayanagar empire in the 14th century, the Digambara Jains lost much of their royal support and survived only in peripheral areas of the southwest and in pockets of the north.

As with the Shvetambaras, the Digambara laity were among the most strident critics of their community's deteriorating situation. The most significant Digambara reform movement occurred in the early 17th century, led by the layman and poet Banarsidas. This movement stressed the mystical elements of the Jain path and attacked what it saw as the emptiness of Digambara temple ritual and the profligacy of the community's clerical leaders.

28.2.4 Jain history since the 19th century

By the middle of the 19th century, image-venerating Shvetambara monks had virtually disappeared, and control of temples and ritual passed into the hands of quasi-monastic clerics known as yati. Monastic life, however, experienced a revival under the auspices of charismatic monks such as Atmaramji (1837–96), and the number of Shvetambara image-worshipping renunciants grew to approximately 1,500 monks and 4,500 nuns in the 20th century. The Tapa Gaccha is the largest subsect; the non-image-worshipping Shvetambara sects (the Sthanakavasis and Terapanthis) are smaller in number. The Digambara monastic community also experienced a revival of its ideals in the early 20th century with the ascendance of the great monk Acharya Shantisagar, from whom virtually all the 120 or so contemporary Digambara monks claim lineal descent.

In modern times the Shvetambara and Digambara communities in India have devoted much energy to preserving temples and publishing their religious texts. The Jains also have been involved in general welfare work, such as drought relief in Gujarat in the 1980s, support for Jain widows and the poor, and, as part of their practice of noninjury (ahimsa) and vegetarianism, maintaining shelters to save old animals from slaughter.

During the 20th century, Jainism evolved into a worldwide faith. As a result of age-old trading links, many Jains from western India settled in eastern African countries, most notably Kenya and Uganda. Political unrest in the 1960s compelled many of them to relocate to the United Kingdom, where the first Jain temple outside India was consecrated in Leicester, and then increasingly to the United States and Canada, where they successfully assumed their traditional mercantile and professional occupations. A desire to preserve their religious identity has led expatriate Jains to form trans-sectarian organisations such as the Jain Samaj, founded in Europe in 1970, and the Federation of Jain Associations in North America (also known as JAINA), founded in 1981. English-language publications such as Jain Digest and Jain Spirit have presented Jain ideals, such as nonviolence, vegetarianism, and, most recently, environmentalism, to members of the Jain diaspora and the wider world. In the 21st century, online resources for Jains and those interested in learning about Jainism also were made available.

28.3 Important Figures of Jain Legend

The Jains developed their own legendary history, the Deeds of the 63 Illustrious Men, which Western scholars call the Universal History. The most important figures in this history are the 24 Tirthankaras, perfected human beings who appear from time to time to preach and embody the faith. Other important figures in the history are from the Hindu tradition, most notably Krishna—regarded by the Jains as a cousin of the 22nd Tirthankara, Arishtanemi—and the hero Rama, who is treated as a pious, nonviolent Jain. By incorporating yet redefining such important Hindu figures, the Jains were able to both remain part of and separate from the surrounding Hindu world.

28.4 Doctrines of Jainism

Even though Jain doctrine holds that no one can achieve liberation in this corrupt time, the Jain religious goal is the complete perfection and purification of the soul. This, they believe, occurs only when the soul is in a state of eternal liberation (moksha) from corporeal bodies. Liberation of the soul is impeded by the accumulation of karmas—bits of material, generated by a person's actions, that attach themselves to the soul and consequently bind it to physical bodies through many births. This has the effect of thwarting the full self-realisation and freedom of the soul. As a result, Jain renunciants do not seek immediate enlightenment; instead, through disciplined and meritorious practice of nonviolence, they pursue a human rebirth that will bring them nearer to that state. To understand how the Jains address this problem, it is first necessary to consider the Jain conception of reality.

28.4.1 Time and the Universe

Time, according to the Jains, is eternal and formless. It is understood as a wheel with 12 spokes (ara), the equivalent of ages, six of which form an ascending arc and six a descending one. In the ascending arc (utsarpini) humans progress in knowledge, age, stature, and happiness, while in the descending arc (avasarpini) they deteriorate. The two cycles joined together make one rotation of the wheel of time, which is called a kalpa. These kalpas repeat themselves without beginning or end.

The Jain world is eternal and uncreated. Its constituent elements, the five basics of reality (astikayas), are soul, matter, space, the principles of motion, and the arrest of motion; for the Digambaras there is a sixth substance, time. These elements are eternal and indestructible, but their conditions change constantly, manifesting three characteristics: arising, stability, and falling away. On this basis, Jainism claims to provide a more realistic analysis of the world and its complexities than Hinduism or Buddhism.

Jains divide the inhabited universe into five parts. The lower world (adholoka) is subdivided into seven tiers of hells, each one darker and more painful than the one above it. The middle world (madhyaloka) comprises a vast number of concentric continents separated by seas. At the centre is the continent of Jambudvipa. Human beings occupy Jambudvipa, the second continent contiguous to it, and half of the third. The focus of Jain activity, however, is Jambudvipa, the only continent on which it is possible for the soul to achieve liberation. The celestial world (urdhvaloka) consists of two categories of heaven: one for the souls of those who may or may not have entered the Jain path and another for those who are far along on the path, close to their emancipation. At the apex of the occupied universe is the siddhashila, the crescent-shaped abode of liberated souls (siddhas). Finally, there are some areas inhabited solely by ekendriyas, single-sense organisms that permeate the occupied universe.

28.4.2 Jiva and ajiva

Jain reality comprises two components, jiva ("soul," or "living substance") and ajiva ("nonsoul," or "inanimate substance"). Ajiva is further divided into two categories: nonsentient material entities and nonsentient nonmaterial entities.

The essential characteristics of jiva are consciousness (chetana), bliss (sukha), and energy (virya). In its pure state, jiva possesses these qualities limitlessly. The souls, infinite in number, are divisible in their embodied state into two main classes, immobile and mobile, according to the number of sense organs possessed by the body they inhabit. The first group consists of souls inhabiting immeasurably small particles of earth, water, fire, and air, along with the vegetable kingdom, which possess only the sense of touch. The second group comprises souls that inhabit bodies that have between two and five sense organs. Moreover, the universe is populated with an infinite number of minute beings, nigodas, some of which are slowly evolving while the rest have no chance of emerging from their hapless state.

Formless and genderless, jiva cannot be directly perceived by the senses. Like the universe, it is without a point of ultimate origin or end. While not all-pervasive, it can, by contraction or expansion, occupy various amounts of space. Like the light of a lamp in a small or a large room, jiva can fill both the smaller and the larger bodies it occupies. The soul assumes the exact dimensions of the body it occupies, but it is not identical with that body. On death it assumes the shape of the last physical body that housed it.

Matter (pudgala) has the characteristics of touch, taste, smell, and colour; however, its essential characteristic is lack of consciousness. The smallest unit of matter is the atom (paramanu). Heat, light, and shade are all forms of fine matter.

The nonsentient nonmaterial substances are space, time, and the principles of motion and its arrest. They are always pure and are not subject to defilement. The principles of motion and its arrest permeate the universe; they do not exist independently but rather form a necessary precondition for any object's movement or coming to rest.

28.4.3 Karma

The fundamental tenet of Jain doctrine is that all phenomena are linked in a universal chain of cause and effect. Every event has a definite cause. By nature, each soul is pure, possessing infinite knowledge, bliss, and power; however, these faculties are restricted throughout time by the soul's contact with matter. This matter, which produces the chain of cause and effect, of birth and death, is karma, an atomic substance and not a process, as it is in Hinduism and Buddhism. To be free from the shackles of karma, a person must stop the influx of new karmas and eliminate the acquired ones.

Karmic particles are acquired as the result of intentional "passionate" action, though the very earliest Jain teachings on this subject claimed that any action, even if unintentional, attracted karma. Acquired karmas can be annihilated through a process called nirjara ("wearing away"), which includes fasting, restricting diet, controlling taste, retreating to lonely places, along with mortifications of the body, atonement and expiation for sins, modesty, service, study, meditation, and renunciation of the ego. Nirjara is, thus, the calculated cessation of passionate action.

Because of karma a soul is imprisoned in a succession of bodies and passes through various stages of spiritual development before becoming free from all karmic bondage. These stages of development (gunasthanas) involve progressive manifestations of the innate faculties of knowledge and power and are accompanied by decreasing sinfulness and increasing purity.

28.4.4 Theories of knowledge as applied to Liberation

In Jain thought, four stages of perception—observation, will to recognize, determination, and impression—lead to subjective cognition (matijnana), the first of five kinds of knowledge (jnana). The second kind, shrutajnana, derives from the scriptures and general information. Both are mediated cognition, based on external conditions perceived by the senses. In addition, there are three kinds of immediate knowledge—avadhi (supersensory perception), manahparyaya (reading the thoughts of others), and kevala (omniscience). Kevala is necessarily accompanied by freedom from karmic obstruction and by direct experience of the soul's pure form unblemished by attachment to matter. Omniscience, the foremost attribute of a liberated jiva, is the emblem of its purity; thus, a liberated soul, such as a Tirthankara, is called a kevalin ("possessor of omniscience"). However, not all kevalins are Tirthankaras: becoming a Tirthankara requires the development of a particular type of karmic destiny.

For the Jains all knowledge short of omniscience is flawed. Because reality is characterised by arising, change, and decay, as opposed to simple permanence (for the Hindus) and impermanence (for the Buddhists), the Jains developed an epistemological system based on seven perspectives (naya). This system, anekantavada, "the many-pointed doctrine," takes into account the provisional nature of mundane knowledge. To gain some approximation to reality, a judgment must ideally be framed in accord with all seven perspectives.

According to Jainism, yoga, the ascetic physical and meditative discipline of the monk, is the means to attain omniscience and thus liberation (moksha). Yoga is the cultivation of true knowledge of reality, faith in the teachings of the Tirthankaras, and pure conduct; it is thus intimately connected to the Three Jewels (ratnatraya) of right knowledge, right faith, and right practice (respectively, samyagjnana, samyagdarshana, and samyakcharitra).

28.4.5 Jain ethics

The **Three Jewels** constitute the basis of the Jain doctrinal and ethical stance. Right knowledge, faith, and practice must be cultivated together because none of them can be achieved in the absence of the others. Right faith leads to calmness or tranquillity, detachment, kindness, and the renunciation of pride of birth, beauty of form, wealth, scholarship, prowess, and fame. Right faith leads to perfection only when followed by right practice. Yet, there can be no virtuous conduct without right knowledge, the clear distinction between the self and the nonself. Knowledge without faith and conduct is futile. Without purification of mind, all austerities are mere bodily torture. Right practice is thus spontaneous, not a forced mechanical quality. Attainment of right practice is a gradual process, and a layperson can observe only partial self-control; a renunciant, however, is able to observe more comprehensive rules of conduct.

Two separate courses of conduct are laid down for the ascetics and the laity. In both cases the code of morals is based on the doctrine of nonviolence (ahimsa). Because thought gives rise to action, violence in thought merely precedes violent behaviour.

Violence in thought, then, is the greater and subtler form of violence because it arises from ideas of attachment and aversion, grounded in passionate states, which result from negligence or lack of care in behaviour. Jainism enjoins avoidance of all forms of injury—whether committed by body, mind, or speech—and subscribes emphatically to the teaching that "nonviolence is the highest form of religious practice." For Jains, this principle, which manifests itself most obviously in the form of vegetarianism, is the single most important component of their tradition's message. Notable in this connection is the friendship between the Jain layman Raychandrabhai Mehta and Mohandas Gandhi, who considered his interactions with Mehta to have been important in formulating his own ideas on the use of nonviolence as a political tactic.

28.4.6 Monks, nuns, and their Practices

Shvetambara monks are allowed to retain a few possessions such as a robe, an alms bowl, a whisk broom, and a mukhavastrika (a piece of cloth held over the mouth to protect against the ingestion of small insects), which are presented by a senior monk at the time of initiation. For the non-image-worshipping Sthanakavasis and the Terapanthis, the mukhavastrika must be worn at all times. After initiation a monk must adhere to the "great vows" (mahavratas) to avoid injuring any life-form, lying, stealing, having sexual intercourse, or accepting personal possessions. To help him keep his vows, a monk's life is carefully regulated in all details by specific ordinances and by the oversight of his superiors. For example, to help him observe the vow of nonviolence, a monk may not take his simple, vegetarian meals after dark, because to do so would increase the possibility of harming insects that might be attracted to the food. In addition, drinking water must first be boiled to ensure that there are no life-forms in it. Monks are expected to suffer with equanimity hardships imposed by the weather, geographic terrain, travel, or physical abuse; however, exceptions are allowed in emergencies, since a monk who survives a calamity can purify himself by confession and by practicing even more rigorous austerities.

Digambara monks take the same "great vows" as do the Shvetambara, but, in acknowledgment of a much more intense interpretation of the vow of nonpossession, full-fledged Digambara monks remain naked, while lower-grade Digambara monks wear a loincloth and keep with them one piece of cloth not more than 1.5 yards (1.4 metres) long. Digambara monks use a peacock-feather duster to sweep the ground where they walk to avoid injuring any life-forms and drink water from a gourd. They beg for their only meal of the day using the cupped palms of their hand as an alms bowl. They regard their interpretation of the Jain monastic vocation as more in accord with the ancient model than that followed by the Shvetambaras.

28.5 Monasticism: Jainism

All Jain renunciants must exercise the three guptis (care in thought, speech, and action) and the five samitis (types of vigilance over conduct). Essential to regular monastic ritual are the six "obligatory actions" (avashyaka), practiced daily and at important times of the ritual calendar: equanimity (samayika, a form of contemplative activity, which, in theory operates throughout the monk's entire career); praise of the Tirthankaras; obeisance to the Tirthankaras, teachers, and scriptures; confession; resolution to avoid sinful activities; and "abandonment of the body" (standing or sitting in a meditative posture).

The type of austerities in which a monk engages, the length of time he practices them, and their severity are carefully regulated by his preceptor, who takes into account the monk's spiritual development, his capacity to withstand the austerities, and his ability to understand how they help further his spiritual progress. The theoretical culmination of a monk's ascetic rigours is the act of sallekhana, in which he lies on one side on a bed of thorny grass and ceases to move or eat. This act of ritual starvation is the monk's ultimate act of nonattendance, by which he lets go of the body for the sake of his soul. Jain ideology views this as the ultimate act of self-control and triumph over the passions, rather than simply as suicide. While widely followed in ancient and medieval times, sallekhana is much less common today.

Both the Shvetambaras and Digambaras allow the initiation of nuns, and among the Shvetambaras nuns outnumber monks by a ratio of approximately 3 to 1. Nevertheless, the status of Jain nuns is less prestigious than that of monks, to whom they are obliged by convention and textual stipulation to defer, despite the fact that these nuns are often women of great learning and spiritual attainment. In Digambara Jainism, nuns, who wear robes, accept the necessity of being reborn as men before they can advance significantly on the ascetic path.

28.6 Religious Activity of the Laity (lay people, as distinct from the clergy)

While Jain literature from earliest times emphasises the place of the monk and his concerns, it is clear that almost from the religion's outset the majority of Jains have been laypersons who support the community of renunciants. The medieval period was a time of particularly intense reflection by both Shvetambara and Digambara monks on the role of the laity. Many treatises discussing the layman's religious behaviour and vows were produced between the 5th and 17th century. According to these writings, lay behaviour should mirror the ascetic "great vows." Jain doctrine, however, holds that while the ascetic path can lead to the destruction (nirjara) of karma, the lay path allows only for the warding off (samvara) of new karma and thus does not radically alter an individual's karmic status.

The layman (Jainism's focus is invariably upon the male) is enjoined to observe eight basic rules of behaviour, which vary but usually include the avoidance of night eating, as well as a diet that excludes meat, wine, honey, and types of fruits and roots deemed to harbour life-forms. There are also 12 vows to be taken: five anuvratas ("little vows"), three gunavratas, and four shikshavratas. The anuvratas are vows to abstain from violence, falsehood, and stealing; to be content with one's own wife; and to limit one's possessions. The other vows are supplementary and meant to strengthen and protect the anuvratas. They involve avoidance of unnecessary travel, of harmful activities, and of the pursuit of pleasure; fasting and control of diet; offering gifts and service to monks, the poor, and fellow believers; and voluntary death if the observance of the major vows proves impossible.

Lay people are further enjoined to perform the six "obligatory actions" at regular intervals, especially the samayika, a meditative and renunciatory ritual of limited duration. This ritual is intended to strengthen the resolve to pursue the spiritual discipline of Jain dharma (moral virtue) and is thought to bring the lay votary close to the demands required of an ascetic. It may be performed at home, in a temple, in a fasting hall, or before a monk.

Dating from early in the history of Jainism are 11 stages of a layman's spiritual progress, or pratima ("statue"). Medieval writers conceived pratima as a ladder leading to higher stages of spiritual development. The last two stages lead logically to renunciation of the world and assumption of the ascetic life.

It was natural for monastic legislators to portray the careers of idealised lay people as a preparatory stage to the rigours of ascetic life, but for Jain lay life to have meaning it need not necessarily culminate in initiation as a monk. With its careful rules about food, its regular ceremonies and cultural traditions, Jainism provides the laity a rounded social world. Typically, Jain lay life is characterised by strict vegetarianism, disciplined business or professional activity, and responsible conduct of family affairs with a view to establishing a sound social reputation. Lay Jains believe that pious activity—including fasting and almsgiving, and especially the practice of nonviolence—enables an individual not only to advance a little further along the path to final liberation but to improve his current material situation. As a result, there is a stark contrast between the great prosperity of the Jain lay community and the austere self-denial of the monks and nuns it supports.

Until very recently Jainism had not developed any distinctive life-cycle rituals for events such as birth and marriage, although in the 9th century the Digambara monk Jinasena attempted to legislate in this area. In general, practice has tended to conform to prevailing local custom, provided this does not infringe on basic Jain principles.

28.7 Image Veneration

Temple worship is mentioned in early texts that describe gods paying homage to images and relics of Tirthankaras in heavenly eternal shrines. While Mahavira himself appears to have made no statement regarding image veneration, it quickly became a vital part of the Jain tradition. Numerous images of Tirthankaras in the sitting and standing postures dating from the early Common Era have been uncovered in excavations of a Jain stupa, or funerary monument, at Mathura in Uttar Pradesh. The earliest images of Tirthankaras are all nude and distinguished by carved inscriptions of their names on the pedestals. By the 5th century, symbols specific to each Tirthankara (e.g., a lion for Mahavira) began to appear. The practice of associating one of the 24 shasanadevatas ("doctrine goddesses") with images of individual Tirthankaras began in the 9th century. Some of these goddesses, such as Ambika ("Little Mother"), who is associated with the Tirthankara Arishtanemi, continue to have great importance for the Jain devotee. The images are generally located near the entrance to Jain temples and can be propitiated for aid in worldly matters.

Closely associated with the obligatory rites of the laity, worship (puja) can be made to all liberated souls, to monks, and to the scriptures. The focus for most image-venerating Jains (murtipujaka) is the icon of the Tirthankara located in the central shrine room of the temple or, alternatively, in a domestic shrine. Temples also house subsidiary Tirthankara images. Although Tirthankaras remain unaffected by offerings and worship and cannot, as individuals who are liberated from rebirth, respond in any way, such devotional actions serve as a form of meditative discipline. Daily worship includes hymns of praise and prayers, the recitation of sacred formulas and the names of the Tirthankaras, and idol veneration—bathing the image and making offerings to it of flowers, fruit, and rice. Shvetambaras also decorate images with clothing and ornaments. A long-standing debate within both Jain communities concerns the relative value of external acts of worship and internalised acts of mental discipline and meditation. Monks and nuns of all sects are prohibited from displays of physical worship.

28.8 Festivals

Important days in the Jain calendar are called parvan, and on these days religious observances, such as structured periods of fasting and festivals, take place. The principal Jain festivals can generally be connected with the five major events in the life of each Tirthankara: descent into his mother's womb, birth, renunciation, attainment of omniscience, and final emancipation.

The Jain calendar includes many festivals. Among them is the Shvetambara fasting ceremony, oli, which is celebrated for nine days twice a year (in March–April and September–October) and which corresponds to the mythical celestial worship of the images of the Tirthankaras. The most significant time of the Jain ritual year, however, is the four-month period, generally running from late July to early November, when monks and nuns abandon the wandering life and live in the midst of lay communities. For Shvetambaras, the single most important festival, Paryushana, occurs in the month of Bhadrapada (August–September). Paryushana ("Abiding") designates, on the one hand, pacification by forgiving and service with wholehearted effort and devotion and, on the other, staying at one place for the monsoon season. The festival is characterised by fasting, preaching, and scriptural recitation. On its last day, Samvatsari ("Annual"), alms are distributed to the poor, and a Jina image is ceremonially paraded through the streets. A communal confession is performed by the laity, and letters are sent asking for forgiveness and the removal of all ill feelings about conscious or unconscious misdeeds during the past year. The equivalent Digambara festival is called Dashalakshanaparvan ("Observance Day of the 10 Religious Qualities") and centres on the public display of an important text, the Tattvartha-sutra.

On the full-moon day of the month of Kartika (October–November), at the same time that Hindus celebrate Diwali (the festival of lights), Jains commemorate the nirvana (final liberation; literally "becoming extinguished") of Mahavira by lighting lamps. Another important

Shvetambara ceremony, Jnanapanchami (literally "Knowledge Fifth," where "Fifth" signifies a date), occurs five days later and is celebrated with temple worship and with reverence of the scriptures. The equivalent Digambara festival takes place in May–June. Mahavira Jayanti, the birthday of Mahavira, is celebrated by both sects in early April with public processions.

The most famous of all Jain festivals, Mastakabhisheka ("Head Anointment"), is performed every 12 years at the Digambara sacred complex at Shravanabelagola ("White Lake of the Ascetics") in Karnataka state. In this ceremony the 57-foot (17-metre-) high statue of Bahubali is anointed from above with a variety of substances (water, milk, flowers, etc.) in the presence of an audience that can approach one million.

Pilgrimage, viewed as a particularly meritorious activity, is popular among renunciants and laity alike. Places of pilgrimage were created during the medieval period at sites marking the principal events in the lives of Tirthankaras, some of which were destroyed during the Muslim invasions, which started in the 8th century. Parasnath Hill and Rajgir in Bihar state and Shatrunjaya and Girnar hills on the Kathiawar Peninsula are among such important ancient pilgrimage sites. Other shrines that have become pilgrimage destinations are Shravanabelagola in Karnataka state, Mounts Abu and Kesariaji in Rajasthan state, and Antariksha Parshvanatha in Akola district of Maharashtra. For those unable to go on pilgrimage to the most famous sites, it is possible to worship their depictions in local temples. Small regional networks of shrines are also regarded as simulacra of the great pilgrimage sites.

28.9 Jain Literature

28.9.1 Canonical and commentarial literature

Jain canonical scriptures do not belong to a single period, nor is any text free from later revision or additions. The sacred literature, transmitted orally, was first systematised in a council at Patna about the end of the 4th century BCE, of which little can be said, and again in two later councils at Mathura (early 3rd century CE) and Valabhi. The fourth and last council, at Valabhi in the mid-5th century, is considered the source of the existing Shvetambara canon, though some commentators insist that the present version comes from the Mathura council.

The original, unadulterated teachings of the Tirthankaras, the Purvas, are said to have been contained in 14 ancient or "prior" (purva) texts, which are now lost. Shvetambaras and Digambaras agree that a time will come when the teachings of the Tirthankaras will be completely lost; Jainism will then disappear from the earth and reappear at an appropriate point in the next time cycle (kalpa). The two sects disagree, however, about the extent to which the corruption and loss of the Tirthankaras' teachings has already occurred. Consequently, the texts for each sect differ.

The Shvetambaras embrace an extensive agama (Sanskrit: "tradition," or "received teachings"; i.e., collection of canonical texts) as the repository of their tradition. Based upon what are believed to be discourses by Mahavira that were compiled by his disciples, this canon preserves his teachings in an imperfect way, since it has been subject to both interpolation and loss throughout the ages. The number of texts considered to make up the Shvetambara canon has varied over time and by monastic group. Largely through the influence of the 19th-century Austrian scholar Johann Georg Bühler, however, Western scholars have fixed the number of texts in this canon at 45, divided into six groups: the 11 Angas ("Parts"; originally there were 12, but one, the Drishtivada, has been lost), 12 Upangas (subsidiary texts), 4 Mula-sutras (basic texts), 6 Cheda-sutras (concerned with discipline), 2 Chulika-sutras (appendix texts), and 10 Prakirnakas (mixed, assorted texts). The Angas contain several dialogues, mainly between Mahavira and his disciple Indrabhuti Gautama, presumably recorded by the disciple Sudharman, who transmitted the teachings to his own disciples.

According to modern scholars, the Acharanga (first chapter) and the Sutrakritanga, among the Angas, and sections of the Uttaradhyayana, among the Mula-sutras, represent the oldest parts of the canon. The fifth Anga, the Bhagavati, is an extensive repository of early Jain teachings. The Cheda-sutra text Dashashrutaskandha concludes with the ritually important Kalpa-sutra, which recounts the lives of the Jinas and includes an appendix of rules for monastic life and a list of eminent monks.

Bhadrabahu, traditionally recognised as the last Jain sage to know the contents of the Purvas, is thought to be the author of the Niryuktis, the earliest commentaries on the Jain canonical texts. These concise, metrical commentaries, written in Prakrit, gave rise to an expanded corpus of texts called Bhashyas and Churnis. Composed between the 4th and the 7th century, these texts contain many ancient Jain legends and historical traditions and a large number of popular stories that support Jain doctrine. The Bhashyas and Churnis, in turn, gave rise in the medieval period to a large collection of Sanskrit commentaries. Haribhadra, Shilanka, Abhayadeva, and Malayagiri are the best-known authors of such commentaries.

Digambaras give canonical status to two works in Prakrit: the also called Shatkhandagama ("Scripture of Six Sections"), and the Kashayaprabhrita ("Chapters on the Kashayas"). The Karmaprabhrita, allegedly based on the lost Drishtivada text, deals with the doctrine of karma and was redacted by Pushpadanta and Bhutabalin in the mid-2nd century; the Kashayaprabhrita, compiled by Gunadhara from the same source about the same time, deals with the passions (kashaya) that defile and bind the soul. Later commentaries by Virasena (in the 8th century) and his disciple Jinasena (in the 9th century) on the Kashayaprabhrita are also highly respected by Digambaras.

The religious merit that accrues from hearing and reading Jain texts encouraged the careful and loving preservation of manuscripts. The Jains have traditionally maintained important libraries throughout India, among the most significant of which are those for the Shvetambaras at Chambay (or Khambhat), Patan (both in Gujarat state), and Jaisalmer (Rajasthan) and those for the Digambaras at Karanja (Maharashtra) and Mudbidri (Karnataka). The miniatures on palm-leaf and paper manuscripts and on wooden book covers preserved in the Jain monastic libraries provide a continuous history of the art of painting in western India from the 11th century to the present.

28.9.2 Philosophical and other literature

In addition to their canons and commentaries, the Shvetambara and Digambara traditions have produced a voluminous body of literature, written in several languages, in the areas of philosophy, poetry, drama, grammar, music, mathematics, medicine, astronomy, astrology, and architecture. In Tamil the epics Chilappatikaram and Jivikachintamani, which are written from a Jain perspective, are important works of early postclassical Tamil literature. Jain authors were also an important formative influence on Kannada literature. The Jain lay poet Pampa's Adipurana (another text dealing with the lives of Rishabha, Bahubali, and Bharata) is the earliest extant piece of mahakavya ("high poetic") Kannada literature. Jains were similarly influential in the Prakrit languages, Apabhramsha, Old Gujarati, and, later, Sanskrit. A particular forte of Jain writers was narrative, through which they promoted the religion's ideals. The most remarkable example of this is the huge Sanskrit novel *The Story of Upamiti's Series of Existences* by the 10th-century Shvetambara monk Siddharshi.

Of particular importance, both as a systemisation of the early Jain worldview and as an authoritative basis of later philosophical commentary, is the Tattvartha-sutra of Umasvati, whose work is claimed by both the Digambara and Umasvamin communities. Composed early in the Common Era, the Tattvartha-sutra was the first Jain philosophical work in Sanskrit to address logic, epistemology, ontology, ethics, cosmography, and cosmogony.

Digambaras also value the Prakrit works of Kundakunda (c. 2nd century, though perhaps later), including the Pravachanasara (on ethics), the Samayasara (on the essence of doctrine), the Niyamasara (on Jain monastic discipline), and the six Prabhritas ("Chapters"; on various religious topics). Kundakunda's writings are distinguished by their deployment of a two-perspective (naya) model, according to which all outward aspects of Jain practice are subordinated to an inner, spiritual interpretation.

The details of Jain doctrine did not change much throughout history, and no major philosophical disagreements exercised Jain intellectuals. The main concerns of the medieval period were to ensure that scriptural statements were compatible with logic and to controvert the rival claims of the Hindus and the Buddhists.

Chapter - 29

Svetambara and Digambara Sects in Jainism

29.1 Two Schools of Thought in Jainism

Broadly, Jainism is divided into two major schools of thought: Svetambara and Digambara. These are further divided into different sub-sects and traditions. While there are differences in practices, the core philosophy and main principles of each sect is the same.

Traditionally, the original doctrine of Jainism was contained in scriptures called Purva. There were fourteen Purva. These are believed to have originated from Rishabhanatha, the first tirthankara. There was a twelve-year famine around fourth century BCE. At that time, Chandragupta Maurya was the ruler of Magadha and Bhadrabahu was the head of Jain community. Bhadrabahu went south to Karnataka with his adherents and Sthulabhadra, another Jain leader remained behind. During this time the knowledge of the doctrine was getting lost. A council was formed at Pataliputra where eleven scriptures called Angas were compiled and the remnant of fourteen purvas were written down in 12th Anga, Ditthivaya by the adherents of Sthulbhadra. When followers of Bhadrabahu returned, there was a dispute between them regarding the authenticity of the Angas. Also, those who stayed at Magadha started wearing white clothes which was unacceptable to the other who remain naked. This is how the Digambara and Svetambara sect came about. The Digambara being the naked ones where as Svetambara being the white clothed. According to Digambara, the purvas and the angas were lost. In course of time, the cannons of Svetambara were also getting lost. About 980 to 993 years after the Nirvana of Mahavira, a Vallabhi council was held at Vallabhi (now in Gujarat). This was headed by Devardhi Ksamashramana. It was found that the 12th Anga, the Ditthivaya, was lost too. The other Angas were written down. This is a traditional account of schism. According to Svetambara, there were eight schisms (Nihvana).

According to Digambara tradition, Ganadhara knew fourteen Purva and eleven Anga. Knowledge of Purva was lost around 436 years after Mahavira and Anga were lost around 683 years after Mahavira. The texts which do not belong to Anga are called Angabahyas. There were fourteen Angabahyas. The first four Angabahyas, Samayika, Chaturvimasvika, Vandana and Pratikramana corresponds to sections of second Mulasutra of Svetambara. The only texts of angabahyas which occurs in Svetambara texts are Dasavaikalika, Uttaradhyayana and Kalpavyavahara.

29.2 Śvētāmbara

The Śvētāmbara (śvētapaṭa; also spelled Shwethambara, Svetambar, Shvetambara or Swetambar) is one of the two main branches of Jainism, the other being the Digambara. Śvētāmbara means "white-clad", and refers to its ascetics' practice of wearing white clothes, which sets it apart from the Digambara "sky-clad" Jains, whose ascetic practitioners go naked. Śvētāmbaras, unlike Digambaras, do not believe that ascetics must practice nudity.

The Svetambara and Digambara traditions have had historical differences ranging from their dress code, their temples and iconography, attitude towards Jain nuns, their legends and the texts they consider as important. Svetambara Jain communities are currently found mainly in Gujarat, Rajasthan and coastal regions of Maharashtra. About four-fifths of all Jains in India are Svetambaras.

29.3 History of Svetambaras and Digambaras

The Svetambaras and Digambaras disagree on how the Svetambaras sub-tradition started in Jainism. According to Svetambaras, they are the original followers of God Mahavira, and Digambaras arose 609 years after the death of Mahavira (about 1st-century CE) because of an arrogant man named Sivabhuti who became a Jain monk in a fit of pique after a fight at home. He is accused of starting the Digambara Jain tradition with what Svetambara refer to as "eight concealments" of rejecting Jain texts preserved by the Svetambara tradition, and misunderstanding the Jain ideology including those related to nuns and clothing. In contrast, according to Digambaras, they are the original followers of god Mahavira and Svetambaras branched off later in the time of Bhadrabahu when their forecasted twelve-year famine triggered their migration from central India. One group of Jain monks headed west and north towards Rajasthan, while the second group headed south towards Karnataka. The former became Svetambaras and retained their "heretic" beliefs and practices such as wearing "white clothes" they adopted there, say the Digambaras. Neither of these explanations can be found in early Jain or non-Jain texts. The earliest version of this Digambara story appears in the 10th-century CE, while the earliest version of the Svetambara story appears in the 5th-century CE.

The Svetambaras have subtraditions. A majority of the Svetambaras are murtipujakas, that is they actively offer devotional puja in temples, worship before the images or idols of Tirthankaras and important Jain goddesses. Others are split into various subtraditions where either Jain temples and halls are built but puja is minor, or where all construction and use of temples, images and idols is actively discouraged and avoided. These subtraditions began around 14th-century through 18th-century. One of the key Jain scholars who opposed devotional temples, images and idols was Lonka Shah (c. 1476 CE). These later subtraditions are primarily Sthānakavāsī and Terapanth orders. Early colonial era observers and some early 20th-century Jain writers such as Malvaniya hypothesised that this movement against idol worship may be the impact of Islam on Jainism, but later scholarship states that the subtraditions arose from an internal dispute and debate on the principles of Ahimsa (non-violence). The new movements argued that the construction of temples or buildings of any kind, idols and images, as well as the puja rituals hurt and kill small creatures and microscopic life forms in soil, wood and other materials involved, and is thus against their core principle of non-violence.

The newer Śvētāmbara subtraditions cover their mouth with a white cloth or muhapatti to practice ahimsa even when they talk. By doing so they minimise the possibility of inhaling small organisms. The terapanthi order is strongly aniconic and has lakhs of followers in many parts of the world.

29.4 Digambara

Digambara (sky-clad) is one of the two major schools of Jainism, the other being Śvētāmbara (white-clad). The Sanskrit word Digambara means "sky-clad", referring to their traditional monastic practice of neither possessing nor wearing any clothes.

Digambara and Śvētāmbara traditions have had historical differences ranging from their dress code, their temples and iconography, attitude towards female monastics, their legends, and the texts they consider as important.

Digambara monks cherish the virtue of non-attachment and non-possession of any material goods. Monks carry a community-owned picchi, which is a broom made of fallen peacock feathers for removing and thus saving the life of insects in their path or before they sit.

The Digambara literature can be traced only to the first millennium, with its oldest surviving sacred text being the mid-second century Ṣaṭkhaṅḍāgama "Scripture in Six Parts" of Dharasena (the Moodabidri manuscripts). One of the most important scholar-monks of the Digambara tradition was Kundakunda.

Digambara Jain communities are currently found mainly in Jain temples of Karnataka, parts of south Maharashtra and Madhya Pradesh. Less than one-fifth of all Jains in India have a Digambara heritage.

29.5 History of Digambaras

The Greek records of 4th-century BC mention gymnosophists (naked philosophers) which may have links to the tradition of "nude ascetics" claimed by the Digambaras. The context in which the Greek records mention gymnosophists include ritual suicide by cremation traceable to ancient Brahmanism, rather than the traditional Jain ritual of suicide by starvation (sallekhana). The archeological evidences indicate that Jain monks moved from the practice of total nudity towards wearing clothes in later period. Tirthankara statues found in Mathura and dated to 2nd-century or after are naked. The oldest Tirthankara statue wearing a cloth is dated in 5th century. Digamabara statues of tirthankara belonging to Gupta period has half-closed eyes.

In 17th-century, adhyatma movement in Agra led to rise of terapanthi and bisapanthi sub-sects based on the differences over acceptance of authority of bhattarakas. King Jai Singh II (1688-1743) of Amer kingdom built separate temples for the two sub-sects in his newly established capital of Jaipur. Terapanthis, led by scholars like Pandit Todarmal and Banarasidas, rejected the authority of bhattarakas.

29.6 Lineage of Digambaras

According to Digambara texts, after liberation of the Lord Mahavira, three Anubaddha Kevalīs attained Kevalajñāna (omniscience) sequentially – Gautama Gaṇadhara, Acharya Sudharma, and Jambusvami in next 62 years. During the next hundred years, five Āchāryas had complete knowledge of the scriptures, as such, called Śruta Kevalīs, the last of them being Āchārya Bhadrabahu. Spiritual lineage of heads of monastic orders is known as Pattavali. Digambara tradition consider Dharasena to be the 33rd teacher in succession of Gautama, 683 years after the nirvana of Mahavira.

In the Digambara tradition, the following lineage of teachers are revered: Mahavira, Gautama, Kundakunda, Bhadrabahu, Umaswami,

Samantabhadra, Siddhasena Divakara, Pujyapada, Manatunga, Virasena, Jinasena and Nemichandra. Kundakunda is considered the most significant scholar monk of the Digambara tradition of Jainism. He authored Prakrit texts such as the Samayasāra and the Pravacanasāra. Other prominent Acharyas of this tradition were, Virasena (author of a commentary on the Dhavala), Samantabhadra and Siddhasena Divakara. The Satkhandagama and Kasayapahuda have major significance in the Digambara tradition.

There have been several Digambara monastic lineages that all trace their descent to Lord Mahavira. The historical linages included Mula Sangha (further divided into Nandi, Sena, Simha and Deva Sanghas) and now largely extinct Kashtha Sangha (which included Mathura sangha, "Lat-Vagad" etc.), Dravida Sangh. The text Darshana-Sara of Devasena discusses the supposed differences among the orders. The Mula sangha orders include Deshiya Gana (Bhattarakas of Shravanabelgola etc.) and Balatkara Gana (Bhattarakas of Humcha, and numerous linages of North/ Central India) traditions. The Bhattarakas of Shravanabelagola and Mudbidri belong to Deshiya Gana and the Bhattaraka of Humbaj belongs to the Balatkara Gana.

29.7 Scripture and Literature of Digambaras

he Digambara sect of Jainism rejects the texts and canonical literature of the Svetambara sect. They believe that the words of Mahavira neither survive nor could be recorded. The original teachings went through a rapid period of decline, state the Digambaras, and Svetambara claims of preserving the sacred knowledge and ancient angas is false.

According to the Digambaras, their 33rd achārya was Dharasena who knew one anga, and he taught these to Pushpadanta and Bhutabali, 683 years after the moksha of Mahavira. That anga was also lost with the death of those two. Dharasena's teachings that have survived are Ṣaṭkhaṅḍāgama (Scripture of Six Parts) and Kasayapahuda (Treatise on the Passions), which were written on palm leaves near a cave in Mount Girnar (Gujarat) and a copy of which with a 12th-century commentary came to Tulu Nadu (south Karnataka). This has survived as the Mudbidri manuscripts, which were used by regional Jains not for reading and study, but as an object of devotional worship for centuries. In the 19th century, the fragile and decaying manuscript was copied and portions of it leaked to scholars between 1896 and 1922 despite objections of Digambara monks. It is considered to be the oldest known Digambara text ultimately traceable to the 2nd-century.

These two oldest known Digambara tradition texts – Satkhandagama and Kasayapahuda – are predominantly a treatise about the soul and Karma theory, written in Prakrit language. Philologically, the text belongs to about the 2nd century, and has nothing that suggests it is of "immemorial antiquity". In details, the text is quite similar in its teachings to those found in Prajnapana – the 4th upanga – of Svetambaras. Between the two, the poetic meter of Satkhandagama suggests it was composed after the Svetambara text.

Digambaras, unlike Svetambaras, do not have a canon. They do have a quasi-canonical literature grouped into four literary categories called anuyoga (exposition) since the time of the Digambara scholar Rakshita. The prathmanuyoga (first exposition) contains the universal history, the karananuyoga (calculation exposition) contains works on cosmology, the charananuyoga (behaviour exposition) includes texts about proper behaviour for monks and lay people, while the dravyanuyoga (entity exposition) contains metaphysical discussions. In the Digambara tradition, it is not the oldest texts that have survived in its temples and monasteries that attract the most study or reverence, rather it is the late 9th-century Mahapurana (universal history) of Jinasena that is the most revered and cherished. The Mahapurana includes not only religious history, but also the mythical sociological history of the Jaina people – including the Jain caste system and its origins as formulated by Rishabhanatha – from the Digambara Jaina perspective. The Digamabara tradition maintains a long list of revered teachers, and this list includes Kundakunda, Samantabhadra, Pujyapada, Jinasena, Akalanka, Vidyanandi, Somadeva and Asadhara.

29.8 Monks and Nuns of Digambaras

The lifestyle and behavioural conduct of a Digambara monk is guided by a code called mulacara (mulachara). This includes 28 mūla guṇas (primary attributes) for the monk. The oldest text containing these norms is the 2nd-century Mulachara attributed to Vattekara, that probably originated in the Mathura region.

28 mūla guṇas are: 5 mahāvratas (great vows); 5 samitis (restraints); 5 indriya nirodha (control of the five senses); 6 āvaśyakas (essential observations); and 7 niyamas (rules).

Digambara monks do not wear any clothes as it is considered to be parigraha (possession), which ultimately leads to attachment. The monks carry picchi, a broom made up of fallen peacock feathers for removing small insects to avoid causing injury and Kamandalu (the gourd for carrying pure, sterilised water). The head of all monastics is called Āchārya, while the saintly preceptor of saints is the upādhyāya. The Āchārya has 36 primary attributes (mūla guṇa) in addition to the 28 mentioned above.

The monks perform kayotsarga daily, in a rigid and immobile posture, with the arms held stiffly down, knees straight, and toes directed forward.

Female monastics in Digambara tradition are known as aryikas. Digambara nuns, unlike the monks in their tradition, wear clothes. Given their beliefs such as non-attachment and non-possession, the Digambara tradition has held that women cannot achieve salvation (moksha) as men can, and the best a nun can achieve is to be reborn as a man in the next rebirth. The monks are held to be of higher status than nuns in Digambara monasteries, states from the Digambara monk's perspective, both Digambara nuns and Svetambara monastic community are simply more pious Jain layperson, who do not or are unable to fully practice the Jain monastic vows.

Digambara nuns are relatively rare in comparison to the nuns found in Svetambara traditions. According to a 1970s and 1980s survey of Jain subtraditions, there were about 125 Digambara monks in India and 50 Digambara nuns. This compared to 3,400 nuns and 1,200 monks in the Svetambara tradition.

29.9 Difference Between Svetambara and Digambara

29.9.1 Liberation of Woman

This is one of the main differences between Svetambara and Digambara.

Digambara believes that women cannot achieve nirvana or liberation directly. They first have to reborn as a man for this. They give two reasons for this:

Digambara monks are completely naked. This is not possible for women as they have to possess clothes. It is impractical for women in this society to live naked. Due to this they cannot lead the life of a true monk and hence cannot achieve liberation.

Digambaras also believe that women are inherently himsic (which is best translated as harmful). It is due to the belief that menstrual blood kills micro-organisms living in the female body. Though there is no scientific evidence and this view is not found in modern Jain thinking.

Svetambara, on the other hand, have a different opinion. According to them, women are equally capable of achieving liberation as a man. They believe in Sabastra Mukti.

They believe that anybody can achieve salvation, be it a householder or a monk.

29.9.2 Dress

Digambara believes that in order to achieve nirvana or liberation, one must renounce everything including clothes. Therefore, Digambara monks are completely naked.

Svetambara, on the contrary, believes that practice of nudity is not essential to attain liberation. Therefore, they wear white clothes.

29.9.3 Possessions

Digambara monks are not allowed to have any kind of possessions. They believe that it is necessary to renounce everything to lead the life of a true monk. However, they usually carry three things with them:

(i) **Picchi** – broom made up of fallen feathers of a peacock. They use this broom to remove small insects without harming them.

(ii) **Kamandalu** – oblong water pot used for carrying pure and sterilised drinking water.

(iii) **Shastra** – scriptures.

Svetambara monks are allowed to possess 14 specified things, which include:

- White clothes
- Rajoharaṇa – broom made up of soft white wool attached to a wooden handle. Using this they remove small insects from their path without harming them.
- Begging Bowl.
- Books etc.

29.9.4 Birth of Mahavira

Svetambara Jains believe that Mahavira's embryo was first formed in Brahmin lady, Devanand. But the change of embryo happens because of God Indra's army commander, Hari-Naigamesin (also known as Kartikeya) on the 83rd day after conception.

The embryo is transferred to a Kshatriya lady, Trisala, who is the wife of King Siddhartha.

Digambara Jains do not accept this story.

Also, Svetambara Jains believe that Mahavira's mother had 14 auspicious dreams before his birth. However, Digambara Jains believe that she had 16 dreams instead of 14.

29.9.5 Marriage of Mahavira

Svetambaras believe that before renouncing the worldly life, Mahavira was married to princess Yasoda. Also, he had a daughter named Priyadarsana (also known as Anojja) through her.

Digambaras do not believe in this. According to them, Mahavira's parents wanted him to marry Yasoda, but he refused this proposal. Thus, they believe that Mahavira is Bal Brahmachari i.e. he never married and remain celibate during his lifetime.

29.9.6 Idols

Svetambara idols of Tirthankars are decorated with jewels, wearing loincloth with prominent staring eyes. However, Digambara idols are naked, undecorated with downcast eyes.

29.9.7 Scriptures

In Jainism, the discourse delivered by Tirthankaras is known as Śhrut Jnāna. It comprises of 11 Angas and 14 Purvas.

Digambara holds the opinion that original texts of Jainism were lost long time ago.

Svetambara believes that they have the original Jain scriptures. However, they also accept that their collection is also incomplete.

Tattvartha Sutra is the probably the most authoritative text in Jainism, accepted by both Svetambara and Digambara.

29.9.8 Food

29.9.8.1 For Ascetics (Monks):

Svetambara monks collect their food in a bowl. They can seek and collect food freely given to them, from more than one household. Also, they can eat more than once in a day.

Digambara monks are strict in the sense that they eat food only once in a day. They cannot use a bowl to collect food. So they collect it using their hands and then eat it from their hands only. They only collect food from one household, only where their Sankalpa (preconceived idea) is fulfilled.

29.9.8.2 For Kevali (Omniscient):

This is one of the important differences between Svetambara and Digambara.

Digambara believes that once a monk attains omniscience (Kevala Jnana), then he does not need food to survive.

Svetambara Jains have a different opinion on this. They consider that until Kevali (or omniscient), male or female has not abandoned the body, they need food for the nourishment of the body.

29.9.9 19th Tirthankara Mallinatha

Digambara Jains believe that Mallinatha was a male.

On the contrary, Svetambara Jains believe that Mallinatha was a female by the name Malli.

29.9.10 Time of Birth and Death of Mahavira

Birth of Mahavira according to:

- Digambara Jains – 582 BC,
- Svetambara Jains – 599 BC.

Death of Mahavira according to:

- Digambara Jains – 510 BC,
- Svetambara Jains – 527 BC.

29.9.11 Namokar Mantra

It is probably the most important prayer in Jainism.

Digambara Jains believe that one should recite only the first five lines of the Mantra.

However, Svetambara Jains hold that one should recite all the nine lines.

(i) NAMO ARIHANTÄNAM
I bow down to Arihants

(ii) NAMO SIDDHÄNAM
I bow down to Siddhas

(iii) NAMO ÄYARIYÄNAM
I bow down to Acharyas

(iv) NAMO UVAJJHÄYÄNAM
I bow down to Upadhyayas

(v) NAMO LOE SAVVASÄHUNAM
I bow down to all Jain Sadhus

29.9.12 Other Differences

Svetambara recognises Sabastra Guru but Digambaras do not.

Svetambara believes that in Kaivalya condition, Mahavira was suffering from illness. However, Digambara holds the view that he was not suffering from any kind of illness.

Chapter - 30

Anekantavada Philosophy in Jainism

30.1 Introduction to Anekantavada

Anekāntavāda (many-sidedness) is the Jain doctrine about metaphysical truths that emerged in ancient India. It states that the ultimate truth and reality is complex and has multiple aspects. Anekantavada has also been interpreted to mean non-absolutism, "intellectual Ahimsa", religious pluralism, as well as a rejection of fanaticism that leads to terror attacks and mass violence. Some scholars state that modern revisionism has attempted to reinterpret anekantavada with religious tolerance, openmindedness and pluralism. The word may be literally translated as "non-one-sidedness doctrine," or "the doctrine of not-one-side."

According to Jainism, no single, specific statement can describe the nature of existence and the absolute truth. This knowledge (Kevala Jnana), it adds, is comprehended only by the Arihants. Other beings and their statements about absolute truth are incomplete, and at best a partial truth. All knowledge claims, according to the anekāntavāda doctrine must be qualified in many ways, including being affirmed and denied. Anekāntavāda is a fundamental doctrine of Jainism.

Jain philosophy is based on the nature of reality, which is considered through Non-absolutism or Many-fold Aspects (Anekantavada). According to this view, reality possesses infinite characteristics, which cannot be perceived or known at once by any ordinary man. Different people think about different aspects of the same reality and therefore their partial findings are contradictory to one another. Hence they indulge in debates claiming that each of them was completely true. The Jain philosophers thought over this conflict and tried to reveal the whole truth. They established the theory of Non-absolutistic standpoint (Anekantavada) with its two wings, Nayavada and Syadvada. Proper understanding of the co-existence of mutually opposing groups through these principles rescues one from conflicts. Mutual co-operation is the Law of Nature.

The origins of anekāntavāda can be traced back to the teachings of Mahāvīra (599–527 BCE), the 24th Jain Tīrthankara. The dialectical concepts of syādvāda "conditioned viewpoints" and nayavāda "partial viewpoints" arose from anekāntavāda in the medieval era, providing Jainism with more detailed logical structure and expression. The details of the doctrine emerged in Jainism in the 1st millennium CE, from debates between scholars of Jain, Buddhist and vedic schools of philosophies.

30.2 Philosophical Overview of Anekāntatva

Things are visible and invisible as well. We stand by visible objects and accept them as they surely are but do not recognise their invisible characteristics. Until and unless one does not recognise both these characters of an object, he cannot reach to the truth and justice. None is absolutely similar or dissimilar, friend or enemy, good or bad. As a matter of fact, every entity hides in itself the innumerable possibilities. Coal can be converted into the state of the diamond or coal is the first stage of diamond. This is the conception of Anekantavada. It should be remembered here that total impossibility of becoming is very rare. Rational cannot be irrational and irrational cannot be rational. On the contrary, it can be converted into something else. One becomes desperate, as he does not understand the theory of relativity. He forgets that the modes are not imperishable. They are to be changed. Sorrow can be converted into pleasure. Absoluteness has no meaning in any field. Substance cannot be fully explained without the assistance of Anekantavada. Life itself cannot be properly understood without this philosophical notion. Pluralism, monotheism existence and nonexistence, eternality and non-eternality and so on go together. These characters of an entity can be comprehended with the help of real standpoint (Niscayanaya) and Practical standpoint (Vyavaharanaya).

In fact, the Jain doctrine of anekantavada emerges to be a social attempt at equality and respect to all diverse views and ideologies through the philosophical elucidation of the truth or reality. The idea of reality gets enrichment in Jainism as it proposes that the reality cannot be the one and ultimate, it can have multi-dimensional form. So, what is reality for one individual may not be the reality for others. Anekantavada brings forth a synthesis, a happy blend and proposes that reality has many forms as seen by various individuals and all must respect the reality perceived by one-another. This is the way the society can progress and this is the way to resolve conflicts and to aim at peace in society. The Jain doctrine of anekāntavāda, also known as anekāntatva, states that truth and reality is complex and always has multiple aspects. Reality can be experienced, but it is not possible to totally express it with language. Human attempts to communicate is naya, or "partial expression of the truth". Language is not Truth, but a means and attempt to express truth. From truth, according to Māhavira, language returns and not the other way around. One can experience the truth of a taste, but cannot fully express that taste through language. Any attempts to express the experience is syāt, or valid "in some respect" but it still remains a "perhaps, just one perspective, incomplete". In the same way, spiritual truths are complex, they have multiple aspects, language cannot express their plurality, yet through effort and appropriate karma they can be experienced.

The anekāntavāda premises of the Jains is ancient, as evidenced by its mention in Buddhist texts such as the Samaññaphala Sutta. The Jain āgamas suggest that Māhavira's approach to answering all metaphysical philosophical questions was a "qualified yes" (syāt). These texts identify anekāntavāda doctrine to be one of the key differences between the teachings of the Māhavira and those of the Buddha. The Buddha taught the Middle Way, rejecting extremes of the answer "it is" or "it is not" to metaphysical questions. The Māhavira, in contrast, taught his followers to accept both "it is" and "it is not", with "perhaps" qualification and with reconciliation to understand the absolute reality. Syādvāda (predication logic) and Nayavāda (perspective epistemology) of Jainism expand on the concept of anekāntavāda. Syādvāda recommends the expression of anekānta by prefixing the epithet syād to every phrase or expression describing the nature of existence.

The Jain doctrine of anekāntavāda states that "no philosophic or metaphysical proposition can be true if it is asserted without any condition or limitation". For a metaphysical proposition to be true, according to Jainism, it must include one or more conditions (syadvada) or limitations (nayavada, standpoints).

30.2.1 Syādvāda

Syādvāda is the theory of conditioned predication, the first part of which is derived from thc Sanskrit word syāt, which is the third person singular of the optative tense of the Sanskrit verb 'as', 'to be', and which becomes syād when followed by a vowel or a voiced consonant, in accordance with sandhi. The optative tense in Sanskrit (formerly known as the 'potential') has the same meaning as the present tense of the subjunctive mood in most Indo-European languages, including Hindi, Latin, Russian, French, etc. It is used when there is uncertainty in a statement; not 'it is', but 'it may be', 'one might', etc. The subjunctive is very commonly used in Hindi, for example, in 'kya kahun?', 'what to say?'.

Syat can be translated into English as meaning "perchance, may be, perhaps" (it is). The use of the verb 'as' in the optative tense is found in the more ancient Vedic era literature in a similar sense. For example, sutra 1.4.96 of Panini's Astadhyayi explains it as signifying "a chance, maybe, probable".

In Jainism, however, syadvada and anekanta is not a theory of uncertainty, doubt or relative probabilities. Rather, it is "conditional yes or conditional approval" of any proposition. This usage has historic precedents in classical Sanskrit literature, and particularly in other ancient Indian religions (Buddhism and Hinduism) with the phrase syad etat, meaning "let it be so, but", or "an answer that is 'neither yes nor no', provisionally accepting an opponent's viewpoint for a certain premise". This would be expressed in archaic English with the subjunctive: 'be it so', a direct translation of syad etat. Traditionally, this debate methodology was used by Indian scholars to acknowledge the opponent's viewpoint, but disarm and bound its applicability to certain context and persuade the opponent of aspects not considered.

In Jain context syadvada does not mean a doctrine of doubt or skepticism, rather it means "multiplicity or multiple possibilities". Syat in Jainism connotes something different from what the term means in Buddhism and Hinduism. In Jainism, it does not connote an answer that is "neither yes nor no", but it connotes a "many sidedness" to any proposition with a sevenfold predication.

Syādvāda is a theory of qualified predication. It states that all knowledge claims must be qualified in many ways, because reality is many-sided. It is done so systematically in later Jain texts through saptibhaṅgīnaya or "the theory of sevenfold scheme". These saptibhaṅgī seem to be have been first formulated in Jainism by the 5th or 6th century CE Svetambara scholar Mallavadin, and they are:

- Affirmation: syād-asti—in some ways, it is,
- Denial: syān-nāsti—in some ways, it is not,
- Joint but successive affirmation and denial: syād-asti-nāsti—in some ways, it is, and it is not,
- Joint and simultaneous affirmation and denial: syāt-asti-avaktavyaḥ—in some ways, it is, and it is indescribable,
- Joint and simultaneous affirmation and denial: syān-nāsti-avaktavyaḥ—in some ways, it is not, and it is indescribable,
- Joint and simultaneous affirmation and denial: syād-asti-nāsti-avaktavyaḥ—in some ways, it is, it is not, and it is indescribable,

- Joint and simultaneous affirmation and denial: syād-avaktavyaḥ—in some ways, it is indescribable.

Each of these seven predicates state the Jain viewpoint of a multifaceted reality from the perspective of time, space, substance and mode. The phrase syāt declares the standpoint of expression – affirmation with regard to own substance (dravya), place (ksetra), time (kāla), and being (bhava), and negation with regard to other substance (dravya), place (ksetra), time (kāla), and being (bhava). Thus, for a 'jar', in regard to substance (dravya) – earthen, it simply is; wooden, it simply is not. In regard to place (ksetra) – room, it simply is; terrace, it simply is not. In regard to time (kāla) – summer, it simply is; winter, it simply is not. In regard to being (bhava) – brown, it simply is; white, it simply is not. And the word 'simply' has been inserted for the purpose of excluding a sense not approved by the 'nuance'; for avoidance of a meaning not intended.

According to Samantabhadra's text Āptamīmāṁsā (Verse 105), "Syādvāda, the doctrine of conditional predications, and kevalajñāna (omniscience), are both illuminators of the substances of reality. The difference between the two is that while kevalajñāna illumines directly, syādvāda illumines indirectly". Syadvada is indispensable and helps establish the truth, according to Samantabhadra.

30.2.2 Nayavāda

Nayavāda is the theory of standpoints or viewpoints. Nayavāda is a compound of two Sanskrit words—naya ("standpoint, viewpoint, interpretation") and vāda ("doctrine, thesis"). Nayas are philosophical perspective about a particular topic, and how to make proper conclusions about that topic.

According to Jainism, there are seven nayas or viewpoints through which one can make complete judgments about absolute reality using syadvada. These seven nayas are:

- Naigama-naya: common sense or a universal view;
- Samgraha-naya: generic or class view that classifies it;
- Vyavahara-naya: pragmatic or a particular view assesses its utility;
- Rijusutra-naya: linear view considers it in present time;
- Sabda-naya: verbal view that names it;
- Samabhirudha-naya: etymological view uses the name and establishes it nature; and
- Evambhuta-naya: actuality view considers its concrete particulars.

The naya theory emerged after about the 5th century CE, and underwent extensive development in Jainism. There are many variants of nayavada concept in later Jain texts.

A particular viewpoint is called a naya or a partial viewpoint. Nayavada does not deny the attributes, qualities, modes and other aspects; but qualifies them to be from a particular perspective. A naya reveals only a part of the totality, and should not be mistaken for the whole. A synthesis of different viewpoints is said to be achieved by the doctrine of conditional predications (syādvāda).

30.3 Jiva, the changing soul views in Jainism

Ancient India, particularly the centuries in which the Mahavira and the Buddha lived, was a ground of intense intellectual debates, especially on the nature of reality and self or soul. Jain view of soul differs from those found in ancient Buddhist and Hindu texts, and Jain view about jiva and ajiva (self, matter) utilises anekantavada.

The Upanishadic thought (Hindu) postulated the impermanence of matter and body, but the existence of an unchanging, eternal metaphysical reality of Brahman and Ātman (soul, self). The Buddhist thought also postulated impermanence, but denied the existence of any unchanging, eternal soul or self and instead posited the concept of anatta (no-self). According to the vedāntin (Upanishadic) conceptual scheme, the Buddhists were wrong in denying permanence and absolutism, and within the Buddhist conceptual scheme, the vedāntins were wrong in denying the reality of impermanence. The two positions were contradictory and mutually exclusive from each other's point of view. The Jains managed a synthesis of the two uncompromising positions with anekāntavāda. From the perspective of a higher, inclusive level made possible by the ontology and epistemology of anekāntavāda and syādvāda, Jains do not see such claims as contradictory or mutually exclusive; instead, they are seen as ekantika or only partially true. The Jain breadth of vision embraces the perspectives of both Vedānta which, according to Jainism, "recognises substances but not process", and Buddhism, which "recognises process but not substance". Jainism, on the other hand, pays equal attention to both substance (dravya) and process (paryaya).

This philosophical syncretisation of paradox of change through anekānta has been acknowledged by modern scholars who wrote:

Our experience of the world presents a profound paradox which we can ignore existentially, but not philosophically. This paradox is the paradox of change. Something – 'A' changes and therefore it cannot be permanent.

On the other hand, if 'A' is not permanent, then what changes? In this debate between the "permanence" and "change", Hinduism seems more inclined to grasp the first horn of the dilemma and Buddhism the second. It is Jainism that has the philosophical courage to grasp both horns fearlessly and simultaneously, and the philosophical skill not to be gored by either.

30.4 Inclusivist or Exclusivist

Some Indian writers state that Anekantavada is an inclusivist doctrine positing that Jainism accepts "non-Jain teachings as partial versions of truth", a form of sectarian tolerance. Other scholars state this is incorrect and a reconstruction of Jain history because Jainism has consistently seen itself in "exclusivist term as the one true path". Classical Jain scholars saw their premises and models of reality as superior than the competing spiritual traditions of Buddhism and Hinduism, both of which Jainism considered inadequate. For instance, the Jain text Uttaradhyayana Sutra in section 23.63 calls the competing Indian thought to be "heterodox and heretics" and that they "have chosen a wrong path, the right path is that taught by the Jinas". Similarly, the early Jain scholar Haribhadra, who likely lived between the 6th and 8th century, states that those who do not follow the teachings of Jainism cannot be "approved or accommodated".

Anekāntavāda to be epistemological respect for view of others" about the nature of existence whether it is "inherently enduring or constantly changing", but "not relativism; it does not mean conceding that all arguments and all views are equal.

In contemporary times, the Anekantavada doctrine has been interpreted by some Jains as intending to "promote a universal religious tolerance", and a teaching of "plurality" and "benign attitude to other [ethical, religious] positions". This is problematic and a misreading of Jain historical texts and Mahavira's teachings. The "many pointedness, multiple perspective" teachings of the Mahavira is a doctrine about the nature of Absolute Reality and human existence, and it is sometimes called "non-absolutism" doctrine. However, it is not a doctrine about tolerating or condoning activities such as sacrificing or killing animals for food, violence against disbelievers or any other living being as "perhaps right". The Five vows for Jain monks and nuns, for example, are strict requirements and there is no "perhaps, just one perspective". Similarly, since ancient times, Jainism co-existed with Buddhism and Hinduism but Jainism was highly critical of the knowledge systems and ideologies of its rivals, and vice versa.

30.5 History and Development

The principle of anekāntavāda is the foundational Jain philosophical concept. The development of anekāntavāda also encouraged the development of the dialectics of syādvāda (conditioned viewpoints) and nayavāda (partial viewpoints).

The Jain anekāntavāda doctrine emerged in a milieu that included Buddhists and Hindus in ancient and medieval India. The diverse Hindu schools such as Nyaya-Vaisheshika, Samkhya-Yoga and Mimamsa-Vedanta, all accepted the premise of Atman that "unchanging permanent soul, self exists and is self-evident", while various schools of early Buddhism denied it and substituted it with Anatta (no-self, no-soul). Further, for causation theories, Vedanta schools and Madhyamika Buddhists had similar ideas, while Nyaya-Vaisheshika and non-Madhyamika Buddhists generally agreed on the other side. Jainism, using its anekāntavāda doctrine occupied the centre of this theological divide on soul-self (jiva) and causation theories, between the various schools of Buddhist and Hindu thought.

30.5.1 Origins of Anekāntavāda

The origins of anekāntavāda are traceable in the teachings of Mahāvīra, who used it effectively to show the relativity of truth and reality. Taking a relativistic viewpoint, Mahāvīra is said to have explained the nature of the soul as both permanent, from the point of view of underlying substance, and temporary, from the point of view of its modes and modification.

30.5.2 Early History of Anekāntavāda

Early Jain texts were not composed in Vedic or classical Sanskrit, but in Ardhamagadhi Prakrit language. The earliest Jain literature that presented a developing form of a substantial anekantavada doctrine is found in Sanskrit texts, and after Jaina scholars had adopted Sanskrit to debate their ideas with Buddhists and Hindus of their era. These texts show a synthetic development, the existence and borrowing of terminology, ideas and concepts from rival schools of Indian thought but with innovation and original thought that disagreed with their peers.

The early Svetambara canons and teachings do not use the terms anekāntavāda and syādvāda, but contain teachings in rudimentary form without giving it proper structure or establishing it as a separate doctrine. Śvētāmbara text, Sutrakritanga contains references to Vibhagyavāda, which, is the same as syādvāda and saptibhaṅgī. Vibhagyavada was interpreted as syadvada, the former mentioned in the Svetambara Jain canonical text Sutrakritanga. However, the Digambara Jains dispute this text is canonical or even authentic.

A monk should be modest, though he be of a fearless mind; he should expound the syādvāda, he should use the two permitted kinds of speech, living among virtuous men, impartial and wise.

—Sūtrakritānga, 14:22, A Svetambara text disputed by the Digambaras

The Bhagvatisūtra (also called Vyākhyāprajñapti) mentions three primary predications of the saptibhaṅgīnaya. This too is a Svetambara text, and considered by Digambara Jains as unauthentic.

The earliest comprehensive teachings of anekāntavāda doctrine is found in the Tattvarthasutra of Umasvati, considered to be authoritative by all Jain sects including Svetambara and Digambara. The century in which Umaswati lived is unclear, but variously placed by contemporary scholars to sometime between 2nd and 5th century.

The Digambara scholar Kundakunda, in his mystical Jain texts, expounded on the doctrine of syādvāda and saptibhaṅgī in Pravacanasāra and Pancastikayasāra. Kundakunda also used nayas to discuss the essence of the self in Samayasāra. Kundakunda is believed in the Digambara tradition to have lived about the 1st-century CE, but has been placed by early modern era scholars to 2nd or 3rd century CE. In contrast, the earliest available secondary literature on Kundakunda appears in about the 10th century, which has led recent scholarship to suggest that he may have lived in or after 8th-century. This radical reassessment in Kundakunda chronology, if accurate, would place his comprehensive theories on anekantavada to the late 1st millennium CE.

30.5.3 Parable of the blind men and elephant

The Jain texts explain the anekāntvāda concept using the parable of blind men and elephant, in a manner similar to those found in both Buddhist and Hindu texts about limits of perception and the importance of complete context. The parable has several Indian variations, but broadly goes as follows:

A group of blind men heard that a strange animal, called an elephant, had been brought to the town, but none of them were aware of its shape and form. Out of curiosity, they said: "We must inspect and know it by touch, of which we are capable". So, they sought it out, and when they found it they groped about it. In the case of the first person, whose hand landed on the trunk, said "This being is like a thick snake". For another one whose hand reached its ear, it seemed like a kind of fan. As for another person, whose hand was upon its leg, said, the elephant is a pillar like a tree-trunk. The blind man who placed his hand upon its side said, "elephant is a wall"

Another who felt its tail, described it as a rope. The last felt its tusk, stating the elephant is that which is hard, smooth and like a spear.

This parable is called Andha-gaja-nyaya maxim in Jain texts.

Two of the Jain references to this parable are found in Tattvarthaslokavatika of Vidyanandi (9th century) and it appears twice in the Syādvādamanjari of Ācārya Mallisena (13th century). Whenever anyone takes a partial, unconditional view of the ultimate reality, and denies the possibility of another aspect of that reality, it is an instance of the above parable and a defective view. The above parable and states that all reality has infinite aspects and attributes, all assertions can only be relatively true. This does not mean skepticism or doubt is the right path to knowledge but that any philosophical assertion is only conditionally, partially true. Any and all viewpoints that do not admit an exception are false views.

While the same parable is found in Buddhist and Hindu texts to emphasise the need to be watchful for partial viewpoints of a complex reality, the Jain text apply it to isolated topic and all subjects. For example, the syadvada principle states that all the following seven predicates must be accepted as true for a cooking pot:

- from a certain point of view, or in a certain sense, the pot exists;
- from a certain point of view, the pot does not exist;
- from a certain point of view, the pot exists and does not exist;
- from a certain point of view, the pot is inexpressible;
- from a certain point of view, the pot both exists and is inexpressible;
- from a certain point of view, the pot both does not exist and is inexpressible; and
- from a certain point of view, the pot exists, does not exist, and is also inexpressible.

30.5.4 Medieval developments

Ācārya Haribhadra (8th century CE) was one of the leading proponents of anekāntavāda. He wrote a doxography, a compendium of a variety of intellectual views. This attempted to contextualise Jain thoughts within the broad framework, rather than espouse narrow partisan views. It interacted with the many possible intellectual orientations available to Indian thinkers around the 8th century.

Ācārya Amrtacandra starts his famous 10th century CE work of Purusathasiddhiupaya with strong praise for anekāntavāda: "I bow down to the principle of anekānta, the source and foundation of the highest scriptures, the dispeller of wrong one-sided notions, that which takes into account all aspects of truth, reconciling diverse and even contradictory traits of all objects or entity."

Ācārya Vidyānandi (11th century CE) provides the analogy of the ocean to explain the nature of truth in Tattvarthaslokavārtikka.

Yaśovijaya Gaṇi, a 17th-century Jain monk, went beyond anekāntavāda by advocating madhāyastha, meaning "standing in the middle" or "equidistance". This position allowed him to praise qualities in others even though the people were non-Jain and belonged to other faiths. There was a period of stagnation after Yasovijayaji, as there were no new contributions to the development of Jain philosophy.

30.6 More on Anekāntavāda

The Jainism believes, unlike Buddhism, that the substance is dynamic (Parinami) in character. It means the thing is eternal from real standpoint and momentary from practical standpoint. Causal efficiency, according to them, is possible neither in the thing which is of the static nature (Kutasthanitya) nor in the thing, that is incongruous with the doctrine of momentary (Ksanikavada), but it is possible only in the thing, which is permanent-in-change. (Parinamanasilata).

The controversial point in the philosophical system is mainly related with the nature of reality. Some systems of thought accept only the Universal (Samanya) character of reality. Advaitavadins and the Sankhyas are the typical representatives of this view. Some other schools led by the Buddhists recognise only particular (Visesa) character of reality. The third school of thought belongs to Nyaya-Vaisesikas, who treat Universal and Particular as absolutely distinctive entities.

According to Jainism, an entity has infinite characteristics, which are divided into two categories, viz. Universal and Particular. Just as different colours can exist in the lustrous gem without conflicting with each other, so the universal and particular elements could abide in the reality. Thus, each and every reality in universalised- cum-particularised along with substance with modes (Dravyaparyayatmaka). Here Dravya represents the Universal character and Paryaya represents the particular character of the thing. For example, the jar is made of gold, which can be changed into several modes, while preserving gold as the permanent substance. They are mutually interdependent, identical and separate from each other.

The nature of reality, according to this theory, is permanent-in-change. It possesses three common characteristics, such as Utpada (origination), Vyaya (destruction) and Dhrauvya (permanence through birth and decay). It also possesses the attributes (Gunas) called Anvayi, which coexist with substance (Dravya) and modifications (Paryaya) called Vyatireki, which succeed each other. Productivity and destructivity constitute the dynamic aspect of an entity and permanence is its enduring factor.

Nayavada (the theory of partial truth) is an integral part of the conception of Anekantavada, which is essential to conceive the sole nature of reality. It provides the scope for acceptance of different viewpoints on the basis that each reveals the partial truth about and object. It is, as the matter of fact, the way of approach and observation which is an imperative necessity to understand of one's different interests and inclinations in different lights on the basis that there could be the valid truth in each of them, and therefore requires their proper value and impartial estimation. Naya investigates analytically the particular standpoint of the problem in all respects in the context of the entire reality. But if anything is treated as the complete truth, it is not Naya, but Durnaya or Nayabhasa or Kunaya. For instance, "It is" is Naya, and "It is and is only" is Durnaya, while "It is relatively (Syat)" is an example of Syadvada.

Syadvada investigates them into the constant and comprehensive synthesis. The prefix "Syat" in the Syadvada is an indeclinable and stands for multiplicity or multiple characters (Anekanta). It reveals certainly regarding any problem and not merely the possibility or probability. It is unique contribution of Jainism to Indian philosophy. There is the word Kathancit in Sanskrit literature, which is used as the substitute for "Syat" by Jainism as well as non-Jain philosophers. In English it may be translated with the word "relatively".

Syatï is connected with relative expression about the nature of reality. It makes an effort to respect other doctrines by warning us against allowing the use of "Eva" or "only" to proceed beyond its prescribed limits and penetrates the truth patiently and non-violently. It is a humble attitude of tolerance and justice and to pay respect for other's views. This view can be understood through the use of Saptabhangi or the theory of seven-fold prediction, which is the method of cognition to comprehend the correct nature of reality through the sevenfold relative dialectic method. It is treated as complementary to the Syadvada doctrine. Akalanka thinks of it as the way, which considers reality in the positive (Vidhimukhena) and the negative (Nisedhamukhena) manner without incompatibility in the certain context. There is no violation of the Law of Contradiction here as dual character of entities exists in respect of its own individuality and does not exist apart from and outside this nature (Sarvamasti svarupena pararupena nasti ca). In relativistic standpoint, both being and non-being can exist together. The theory of Relativity, which is also supported by

Einstein, is practically accepted by all as the perfect mathematical theory in the scientific world.

This Anekantavada guards us from holding opinions that are based on views that are one-sided and extreme and that under the cloak of Anekanta reality maintain one-sided views. Every person ventilates his views about the given object according to his attitude and capacity. His limited knowledge is inadequate to throw the flood of light on the entire object. Out of some of the many facts, he deals with only one or some. This partial knowledge and partial success is dangerous especially when he feels that his knowledge is complete and correct. It is, therefore, imperative that we should study other's opinions logically and impartially, even though we belong to the certain brand of faith to try to understand others and accommodate other's views others. This is the real humanitarian outlook. Samantabhadra said it is the "Sarvodayatirtha". Haribhadra's quotation points out in the same direction. He means that we must think objectively irrespective of our religion and ideology:

Agrahi vata ninisati yuktam, tatra yatra matires nivista.
Paksapatarahitasya tu yuktir yatra tatra matiresa nivesam.

Acarya Hemacamndra also opines that we must not swallow uncritically any idea simply because it comes from the great man. The validity of that idea must be tested on the touchstone of logic.

Paksapato na me Vire, na dvesah Kapiladisu.
Yukti madvacanam yasya tasya karyah parigrahah.Dravyas or Tattvas

Reality or substance in Jainism is distinguished from Dravya. Dravya means that which exists and possesses three fundamental characteristics, viz. (i) origin (Utpada), (ii) Destruction (Vyaya), and (iii) permanence (Dhrauvya). It maintains its identity through its several qualities and modes. The Dravya in its reality can neither be created nor destroyed; it has only permanent substantiality. But through its modes, it secures the triple qualities. There is neither quality without substance nor substance without quality. Hence these two are not incompatible in their nature.

Dravya in Jainism is of six kinds, namely, Jiva (soul), Ajiva (non-soul), Dharma (principle of motion), Adharma (principle of rest), Akasa (space), and Kala (time). The first five types of Dravyas are called Astikayas (those exist and have different pradesas or areas like the body) and the last is named Anastikaya. According to another classification it is of three kinds, viz. Sakriya (active), Niskriya (inactive) and Sakriya-Niskriya. The Sakriya Dravya, which have the capacity of moving from place to place, are Pudgalas and Jivas. Contrary to this, the Niskriya Dravyas are space and Kala; Sakriya-Niskriya Dravyas are those realities, which move about without themselves undergoing changes or motion. Dharma and Adharma are Sakriya and Niskriya Dravyas respectively. Pudgala alone is Murta (having forms), which possesses the sense qualities of contact, taste, smell, sound and colour. In another classification, the Dravyas or Tattvas are divided into seven categories, viz. Jiva (Soul), Ajiva (non-soul) Asrava (inflow of Karmic matter) into the soul, Bandha (bondage of soul by Karmic matter), Samvara (stoppage of the inflow of the Karmic matter), Nirjara (shedding of Karmic matter), and Moksha (liberation of soul from Karmic matter).

Chapter - 31

Agamas and Purvas in Jainism

31.1 Agamas in Jainism

Agamas are canonical texts of Jainism based on Mahavira's teachings. Mahavira's preaching were orally compiled by his disciples into various Sutras (texts) which were collectively called Jain canonical or Agamic literature. Traditionally these sutras were orally passed on from teachers (acaryas or gurus) to the disciples for several centuries. The scholars date the composition of Jain agamas at around 6th to 3rd century BCE. Agam Literature consists of original scriptures complied by Gandharas and Srut-kevalis. They are written in the Prakrit language.

31.2 History of Agamas in Jainism

31.2.1 Date of Composition

While some authors date the composition of Jain Agamas starting from 6th century BCE, some other scholars feel that the composition of the Jaina canon would fall somewhere about the end of the fourth or the beginning of the third century BCE. The general consensus amongst scholars is that the earliest portions of Jain canons were composed around 4th or 3rd century BCE. This is also in agreement with Jain tradition according to which the agamic literature and the Purvas were passed from one heads of the order to his disciples for around 170 years after the Nirvana (Jainism) of Mahavira. However, with time, it became difficult to keep the entire Jain literature committed to memory. According to tradition, there occurred twelve years of famine around 350 BC where it was extremely difficult for the Jain ascetics to survive during this time. Under such circumstances they could not preserve the entire canonical literature. The Purvas or the ancient texts were already forgotten and lost after the famine. According to Svetambara tradition, the agamas were collected on the basis of collective memory of the ascetics in the first council of Pataliputra under the stewardship of Acarya Sthulibhadra in around to 463–367 BCE. However, the Digambara

Jain sect maintains that after the famine, the entire Jain canonical literature became extinct.

31.2.2 Final redaction

The Agamas were composed of the following **forty-five** texts:

Eleven Agāmas:

1. *Ācāranga sūtra (Aayarang):* This agama describes the conduct and behaviour of ascetic life and the description of the penance of Lord Mahavira. This is the oldest agama from a linguistic point of view.
2. *Sūtrakrtanga Sutra (Suyagdang):* This agama describes nonviolence, Jain metaphysics, and the refutation of other religious theories such as Kriyavada, Akriyavada, Ajnanavada, and Vinayavada.
3. *Sthānānga Sutra (Thanang):* This agama defines and catalogues the main substances of the Jain religion (defines Jain metaphysics).
4. *Samavāyānga Sutra:* This agama defines and catalogues the main substances of the Jain religion from a different perspective than the Sthananga Sutra.
5. *Vyākhyāprajñapti or Bhagavati sūtra (Viyah Pannati):* This agama explains the subtle knowledge of soul, matter, and other related subjects. 36000 questions and answers are presented in discussion form. It is the largest of the eleven Angagams.
6. *Jnata Dharma Kathanga Sutra (Nayadhammakahao):* This agama explains Jain principles through examples and stories. This text is very useful in understanding the mode of Lord Mahavira's religious preaching.
7. *Upasaka Dashanga Sutra (Uvasagdasao):* This agama explains the code of conduct of the ten lay followers (Shravaks) of Lord Mahavira. This agama is very useful for understanding the code and conduct of ordinary people (Shravaka Dharma) in the Jain religion.
8. *Antakrddaaśāh Antah Kradashanga Sutra (Anatagaddasao):* This agama tells the stories of ten sacred monks attaining liberation (Moksha) by destroying their karmas.
9. *Anuttaroupa Patika Dashanga Sutra (Anuttarov Vaiya Dasao):* This agama contains the stories of an additional ten sacred monks who attained the topmost heaven, known as Anuttara heaven.

10. *Prashna Vyakrana Sutra (Panha Vagarnai):* This agama describes the five great vows (mahavratas) and the five worst sins defined in the Jain religion.
11. *Vipaka Sutra (Vivagsuyam):* This agama explains the results of good and bad karmas through several stories.

Twelve Upanga āgamas (Texts that provide further explanation of Angās):

1. *Aupa Patika Sutra (Ovavaiya):* This agama describes the splendid procession (view) of King Konika when he visited Lord Mahavira. It also explains how a person can attain heaven in the next life.
2. *Raja Prashniya Sutra (Raya Pasen Ijja):* This agama describes the story of Monk Keshi. Monk Keshi was the Ganadhara of Lord Parshvanath. He removed the doubts of King Pradeshi regarding the existence and attributes of the soul. Monk Keshi made the king a follower of the Jain religion. After his death, the king was born as a deva in heaven. He appeared from heaven to shower Lord Mahavira with unprecedented pomp and splendor. The thirty-two dramas (plays) described in this agama throw light upon the ancient dramatic art of India.
3. *Jivabhigama Sutra:* This agama describes the universe and the subtle description of all living beings (souls) of the universe. It gives very important information to the scholars of biology and botany.
4. *Prajnapana Sutra (Pannavana):* This agama describes the form and attributes of souls from a different perspective.
5. *Surya Prajnapti Sutra (Surya Pannti):* This agama describes the Sun, the planets and the associated mathematics regarding their motion.
6. *Jambudveepa Prajnapti Sutra:* This agama provides a description of Jambudveepa. Jambudeepa is a place explained in Jain geography. It also provides information on ancient kings.
7. Chandra Prajnapti Sutra: This agama describes the Moon, the planets and the associated, mathematics regarding their motion. Both of these upangas, the Chandra Prajnapti and Surya Prajnapati, sutras are very important in understanding the astrology of olden times.
8. *Nirayarvali Sutra:* This agama describes the story of ten princes. All ten princes fought with King Chetaka of Vaishali in cooperation with king Konika. King Chetaka was the son of the

10 princes' step-mother. In the end, all ten princes went to hell after dying in war.

9. *Kalpa Vatansika Sutra (Kappavadamsiao):* This agama describes the story of King Konika's children. They did not fight with King Chetaka in the war. They renounced the world and became monks. After their death, they went to heaven.
10. *Pushpika Sutra (Puspiao):* This agama describes the previous lives of certain devas (angels) who worshiped Lord Mahavira.
11. *Pushpa Chulika Sutra:* This agama describes stories similar to those in the Pushpika.
12. *Vrashnidasha Sutra (Vanhidasao):* This agam explains how Lord Neminath convinced ten kings in the Vrashni region to follow the Jain religion.

Six Chedasūtras (Texts relating to the conduct and behaviour of monks and nuns):

1. *Dasha Shruta Skandha Sutra (Achardasha):* There are ten chapters in this Sutra. It contains the following information:
   (a) 20 places of Asamadhi
   (b) 21 powerful faults bringing weakness in conduct
   (c) 33 Ashatanas of Guru
   (d) 8 Sampadas of Acharyas and their kinds
   (e) 10 places of Chitta Samadhi
   (f) 11 Pratimas of Sravaka
   (g) Bhiksu Pratimas
   (h) Kalpasutra - recited during the Paryushanas
   (i) 30 places of Maha Mohaniya karma bandhana
   (j) 9 Nidanas (Niyane)
2. *Brhatkalpa*
3. *Vyavahara Sutra:* This agama describes the system of confession for monks and nuns who fall from proper conduct. It explains the qualifications of the listening monk or nun and with what sort of feeling the confession should be made. It also explains what sort of repentance (Prayashchitta) the monk should perform. There are several other indications of the limits of ascetic life.
4. *Nisheetha Sutra (Nisiha):* This agama explains the procedure of repentance (Prayashchitta) in the form of punishment for the monks and nuns who have conducted themselves badly.

5. *Mahanisheetha Sutra:* This agama explains the process of confession and repentance (Prayashchitta) for monks and nuns. It explains the magnitude of pain one has to suffer if he or she breaks the fourth vow (chastity). It also describes and explains the conduct of good and bad monks.
6. *Jītakalpa*

Four Mūlasūtras (Scriptures which provide a base in the earlier stages of the monkhood):

1. *Uttaradhyayana Sutra:* This agama has the same place in Jain literature as the Dhammapada in Buddhism and the Geeta in the Hindu religion. It contains preaching regarding religious principles and practices, and many stories, dialogues, and examples based on such principles and practices.
2. *Avashyaka Sutra:* The daily rituals or routines which it is necessary to perform during the day and night for the purification of soul are called Avashyaka. A description of the six routines (Avashyakas) are explained in this agam. The six routines are; Samayika, Chaturvinshatistava, Vandanaka, Pratikramana, Kayotsarga, and Pratyakhyana.
3. *Dasha Vaikalika Sutra:* This agama briefly describes and explains the conduct of ascetic life.
4. *Ogha Niryukti or Pinda Niryukti Sutra:* This agama explains certain rules and procedures for monks with respect to travelling, staying, accepting food and other necessities from lay people.

Ten Prakīrnaka sūtras (Texts on Independent or miscellaneous subjects):

1. *Chatuh Sharana:* This agama contains prayers to the **four** benevolent beings:
   (i) Lord Arihant- God in the form of human being
   (ii) Lord Siddha - God in the form of pure consciousness
   (iii) Sadhu - All monks
   (iv) Dharma – Religion
2. *Aatur Pratyakhyana (Aayur-Pachakhana):* This agama explains differences in the death of children, youths, adults, and old people. It also describes the types of vows a wise person should take during various states of illness and how he should beg the pardon of all living beings in the universe.

3. *Bhakti Parijna (Bhatta-parinna):* This agama describes the process of fasting and how one should strive to feel at the time of death.
4. *Sanstaraka (Santharag):* This agama describes the process of dying by one's own desire (Santhara) and its glory.
5. *Tandulavaitalika:* This agama describes the state of pregnancy and provides knowledge about the human body.
6. *Chandra-Vedhyaka:* This agama describes the method of concentrated meditation (Dhyana) that one should observe through the description of Radhavedha.
7. *Devendra-Stava:* This agama describes the names, positions, and residences of Devas (angels) who live in heaven. It also provides a description of the moon, sun, planets, and stars.
8. *Ganita Vidya:* This agama describes palmistry and how it is used to predict the future (Nimitta).
9. *Mahapratyakhyana:* This agama explains how to completely give up the worst sins and how to repent these sins.
10. *Veerastava:* This agama is considered lost. However, it appears from literature referencing this agama that it contained prayers of Lord Mahavira.

Two Cūlikasūtras (The scriptures which further enhance or decorate the meaning of Angas):

1. *Nandi Sutra:* This agama contains an elaborate description of Tirthankaras, Ganadharas, and five types of Knowledge (Jnan); Mati, Shrut, Avadhi, Manaparyay, and Keval-Jnan.
2. *Anuyogadvara Sutra:* This agama provides the description of many rights regarding the mode of preaching.

31.3 Fourteen Purvas

1. *Utpada-purva:* describes the origination, destruction, and permanance nature of substances.
2. *Agraya-niya:* describes seven tattvas, and six dravyas.
3. *Viryanu-vad:* describes the power and qualities of living and nonliving substances.
4. *Asti-nasti-pravad:* Seven ways (saydvad) of considering things and their usage.
5. *Jnana-pravad:* Eight types of knowledge (Jnana).

6. *Satya-pravad:* Description of truth, silence, speakers.
7. *Atma-pravad:* Description of soul (Atma) from Nischaya and Vyavahar point of view.
8. *Karma-pravad:* Bondage and its modification of karma to the soul.
9. *Pratya-khyan:* Description of vows, penances, repentances, and renounciation of bad things.
10. *Vidyanu-vad:* Acquiring special power by learning various Mantras and other knowledge.
11. *Kalyan-vad:* Description of the grand celebrations of great events (Kalyanak).
12. *Prana-vad:* knowledge about removal of pains caused by spirit, ghost, snake etc.
13. *Kriya-visal:* Description 72 arts of man and 64 arts of woman.
14. *Triloka-bindu-sara:* Way of attaining Moksha and glory and happiness from it.

Chapter - 32

Ratnatrya (Three Jewels) in Jainism

32.1 Ratnatraya (Three Jewels) in Jainism

Jainism emphasises that ratnatraya (triple gems of Jainism) — (i) Samyak darśana (Right View), meaning faith, acceptance of the truth of soul (jīva); (ii) Samyak jnana (Right Knowledge), meaning undoubting knowledge of the tattvas; and (iii) Samyak charitra (Right Conduct), meaning behaviour consistent with the Five vows. These are known as the triple gems (or jewels) of Jainism and hence also known as Ratnatraya.

Jain texts often add samyak tap (Right Asceticism) as a fourth jewel, emphasising belief in ascetic practices as the means to liberation (moksha). The four jewels are called moksha marg. According to Jain texts, the liberated pure soul (Siddha) goes up to the summit of universe (Siddhashila) and dwells there in eternal bliss.

The very first sloka (aphorism) of the Sacred Jain text, Tattvartha sutra reads:

Right faith, right knowledge, and right conduct (together) constitute the path to liberation.

—Tattvārthasūtra (1-1)

Ācārya Pujyapada writes in Sarvārthasiddhi:

Perfect release from all karmas is liberation. The path to liberation is the method by which it can be attained. The singular 'path' is used in order to indicate that all the three together constitute the path to liberation. This controverts the views that each of these singly constitutes a path. Hence it must be understood that these three— right faith, right knowledge and right conduct — together constitute the direct path to liberation.

32.1.1 Right Faith

Believe in the seven aspects of Reality (Tattvas) as described by Jina or Arihanta is right faith. So, Jainas believe in Supreme Soul- Arihanta and Siddha (Deva), in their teaching (Sastras) and towards thosc Munics who practice the teachings of Jaina religion (Gurus) as a cause of right faith. In simple words, right faith is a spiritual awakening of one's self.

If we attain right faith, abstain from misconception and refrain from pride, equality of our lives would improve considerably. The main cause of a soul wandering in this world is the lack of right faith. So, the right faith is the first step on the path of salvation. Right faith gives us a proper attitude by which our knowledge and life style acquire the quality of righteousness.

Cultivation of right perception requires a great deal of inner discipline and assiduous practice which demands the following requirements:

1. Faith without doubts,
2. Complete renunciation of desire for worldly comforts,
3. Respect for believers on the path,
4. Absence of likes and dislikes,
5. Disinterest in wrong paths,
6. Bringing non-believers to the path,
7. Cultivation of right faith, and
8. Spreading the knowledge Jainism.

32.1.2 Right Knowledge

The right knowledge is one by which the person becomes free from attachment and his soul is purified. We can achieve the Right knowledge by strong faith in the teaching of arihantas and through the study of their scriptures.

Knowledge that is gained through external agencies is liable to error whereas knowledge gained directly through the faculties of the soul cannot be wrong. The true test of right knowledge lies in its ability to help us in getting what is good for us and in avoiding what is sinful. Right knowledge is useful and reliable because it is a true representation of what is.

Jainism acknowledges eight types of knowledge. Of them, five constitute right knowledge. They are mati (mental knowledge), sruti (acquired knowledge), avadhi (distant knowledge), manahparyaya (paranormal knowledge) and kevala (absolute knowledge). The remaining three types of knowledge constitute false knowledge (mithya gyan). They are invalid knowledge, erroneous knowledge and wrong knowledge.

Mati gyan (mental knowledge) is ordinary perception obtained through the normal faculties of the mind such as perception, cognition, analysis and memory. It is further divided into smriti (remembrance), Pratyabhijna or samana (recognition), tarka (inductive logic) and abhinibodha or anumana (deductive logic). According to another classification, it is divided into upalabdhi (end result), bhavana (feelings and emotion) and upayoga (usefulness). Matigyan comes to us mainly through the sense organs (indriyas). So sensory knowledge always precedes mental knowledge.

Sruti gyan is verbal and non-verbal knowledge acquired through signs, symbols and words. Study and hearing are the usual methods of obtaining srutigyan. While matigyan is acquired through primary contact, srutigyan is acquired through secondary contact or another source. Srutigyan is of four types depending upon how it is acquired: labdhi (contact), bhavana (attention), upayoga (utility) and naya (perspective). The difference between sruti and mati is very subtle because in case of srutigyan also perception, cognition and understanding play an important role.

Matigyan is the raw material from which comes srutigyan as a finished product. The former is based on personal experiences and perceptions while the latter is based on other people's knowledge and experiences that have been borrowed through communication.

Avadhi gyan is clairvoyance or knowledge of distant and remote things acquired through higher faculties, without the use of the senses or study. It comes either from birth (bhava) because of previous karma or from virtues (gunas) acquired by doing good karma and destroying bad karma.

Manahparyaya gyan is the knowledge acquired psychically through other people's minds using the paranormal faculty of mind reading or telepathy. People endowed with this faculty have the ability to actually see the thought forms and mental impressions of other people and know instantly what they are thinking.

Manahparyaya gyan is acquired because of previous good karma or virtue acquired in the present life by removing impure karma. Manahparyaya is a kind of avadhigyan but it is limited to the extent of other people's minds and what is going on in them. In comparison, avadhigyan extends to everything and everywhere.

Secondly, both human beings and others can acquire avadhigyan, but manahparyaya is possible only in case of humans.

Kevala gyan is the "Only" knowledge or the absolute knowledge. It is also described as the perfect knowledge and the ultimate knowledge. Kevala gyan is not subject to standpoints or perspectives because it contains all viewpoints and perspectives simultaneously. It is omniscient, omnipresent, indescribable, unlimited, eternal and transcendental to which the limitations of space and time do not apply. It is acquired only when a person has achieved nirvana.

Knowledge obtained by these five means is divided into both direct knowledge (pratyaksha) and indirect knowledge (paroksha). Direct knowledge is that knowledge which is acquired directly without the intervention of an external agency. Of the five types of knowledge, the first two is considered indirect and hence less reliable while the last three are direct and more reliable. Indirect knowledge is susceptible to error, invalid conclusions, and falsehood, whereas direct knowledge is perfect.

From right perception comes right knowledge. From right knowledge comes right conduct and the power of discrimination. As karma is gradually removed from the embodied self, it begins to acquire different types of right knowledge. First comes perceptual knowledge. From it arises the desire to study and acquire the sruti knowledge. From the study of the doctrine and its practice comes clairvoyance or knowledge of distant objects and telepathy. These extraordinary powers enable the jiva to come into contact with higher beings from whom it gains more knowledge leading to its further purification. As the Jiva becomes adept in different types of knowledge, it gradually moves on the path of liberation and achieves keval gyan or the highest knowledge. Ultimately, in the transcendental state, the Jiva gains perfect knowledge and becomes complete.

32.1.3 Right Conduct

Withdrawal from the immoral conduct and devoting one's self to the moral conduct is the right faith. Without moral observance, the spiritual practices cannot be sustained. The practice of right conduct has been described as of two kinds- the partial and the complete. House holders (sravakas) start practicing the right conduct partially and in due course of time, if they become monks, they practice it completely. The right conduct is based on the practice of Ahimsa, Satya, Acaurya, Brahmcarya and Aparigraha. It should be emphasised that the Right Conduct also includes all religious and spiritual practices like worship, prayer, charity and so on. Thus, we can achieve salvation only through the three jewels of Right Faith, Right Knowledge and Right Conduct.

32.2 Coupling of the Three Jewels

The three jewels are interconnected and work in tandem. One cannot have right conduct without right knowledge and one cannot have right knowledge without right perception. Right conduct comes from the awareness of what is right and what is wrong and by doing what is right. It is practicing right knowledge as revealed by the Tirthankaras and the jinas. At the core of their teachings is the practice of non-violence as a solution to the problem of karma. However, ahimsa has to be practiced in conjunction with other teachings. A follower of Jainism should not have any doubt about the teachings of the Jinas. From faith comes the conviction and the resolve to remain committed to the path. Faith in the doctrine is therefore the first commitment expected of each follower. The conviction is further cemented by the 12 vows or vratas, which each initiate into Jainism has to undertake to begin his or her journey on the path. Of the 12 vows, five are main vows or maha-vratas and the rest are supplementary vows or anuvratas. Jain scriptures provide ancillary information on how to practice each of the main vows.

32.2.1 Right Faith and Right Knowledge

Right view and right knowledge are inter-dependent. For instance, when the clouds disappear, both the heat and the light of the sun are manifested simultaneously. Similarly, when right faith is attained by the soul owing to the subsidence, destruction or destruction- cum-subsidence of faith-deluding karmas, right sensory knowledge and right scriptural knowledge are attained by the soul at the same time by the removal of wrong sensory and wrong scriptural knowledge.

32.2.2 Right Knowledge and Right Conduct

Right knowledge must be accompanied by Right conduct which is necessary for the destruction of karmic bonds. Without this, there is no release from the cycle of transmigration, i.e., repeated births and deaths. Just like the light from millions of lamps is of no value to a blind person, studying scriptures alone is of no use to a person who does not apply them.

32.3 Stages on the Path to Liberation (Gunasthana)

Jainism acknowledges that the soul advances to its liberated stage in various steps, called Gunasthana. Jain literature describes these states in detail. The following provides a concise summary on the various statuses of soul on its journey to spiritual advancement.

32.3.1 Awakening - Developing right view

(i) Lowest stage with ignorance, delusion, and with intense attachments and aversions. This is the normal condition of all souls involved in the samsara, and is the starting point of spiritual evolution.

(ii) Indifference to reality with occasional vague memory of spiritual insight.

(iii) Fleeting moments of curiosity towards understanding reality.

(iv) Awareness of reality with trust developed in the right view, combined with willingness to practice self-discipline. The soul may be able to subdue the four passions, namely anger, pride, deceit and greed.

32.3.2 Developing right view and discipline

(v) The soul now begins to observe some of the rules of right conduct with a view to perfecting itself. With the discipline of introductory or minor vows, the soul starts on the process of climbing the spiritual ladder.

(vi) Major vows taken up with firm resolve to control passions. There may be failures due to lack of full control over passions or carelessness.

32.3.3 Developing self-discipline and knowledge

(vii) Intense practice of vows assisted in better self-control and virtually replaced carelessness with spiritual vigilance and vigour.

(viii) Closer to perfect self-control over actions, higher control over mind, thought and passions with the soul ready for reduction of the effects of conduct-deluding karma.

(ix) Higher control over removal of passions, and elimination of conduct-deluding karma begins.

(x) Complete elimination of all passions except for subtle degree of attachment.

32.3.4 Gaining absolute knowledge and bliss

(xi) Suppressed passions and lingering conduct-deluding karma may rise to drag the soul to lower stages; fleeting experiences of equanimity.

(xii) This is the point of no return. All passions as well as conduct-deluding karma are eliminated. Permanent internal peace achieved. No new bondage from this point onwards.

(xiii) All inimical karma destroyed. Omniscience achieved and Arihant stage reached. However, the perfected soul is still trapped in the physical body (with right knowledge attained).

(xiv) This is the last stage on the Path, and is followed by the soul's destruction of the aghātiā karmas. Those who pass this stage are called siddha and become fully established in Right Faith, Right Knowledge and Right Conduct.

Chapter - 33

Mahvratas and Vratas in Jainism

33.1 The Five Maha-vratas (Great Vows) for Ascetics

Vows or vratas are very important elements of Jainism, for both mendicant (ascetics) and lay Jains. These vows may be 'vows of restraint', meaning that the Jain makes a solemn resolution to not do something, or may involve doing something in particular. Right knowledge, right faith, and right conduct are the three most essentials for attaining liberation in Jainism.

Jains take vows in order to make spiritual progress. The eventual goal of Jainism is the soul's liberation from the cycle of rebirth. Most souls remain trapped in the cycle of birth for numerous lifetimes because of the karma bound to them. A soul that is perfect – without any karma – is liberated and can ascend to the top of the universe. Keeping vows eliminates karma because it is a kind of asceticism – tapas. The five fundamental vows are the hardest to live by, especially the absolute mendicant vows. The path to spiritual emancipation is accepted as being very arduous, so Jains admire and honour those who make vows, particularly those who become monks and nuns.

Following are the five Maha-vratas (Great Vows) for Ascetics:

1. Non-violence – Ahimsa
2. Truth – Satya
3. Non-stealing - Achaurya or Asteya
4. Celibacy/Chastity – Brahmacharya
5. Non-attachment/Non-possession - Aparigraha

33.1.1 Non-violence (Ahimsa)

Among these five vows, non-violence (Ahimsa) is the cardinal principle of Jainism and hence it is known as the cornerstone of Jainism. Non-violence is the supreme religion (Ahimsa parmo dharma). It is repeatedly said in Jain literature; "Do not injure, abuse, oppress, enslave, insult, torment, torture, or kill any creature or living being."

According to Jainism all living beings, irrespective of their size, shape, or different spiritual developments are equal. No living being has a right to harm, injure, or kill any other living being, including animals, insects, and plants. Every living being has a right to exist and it is necessary to live with every other living being in perfect harmony and peace.

Nonviolence in Jainism is not a negative virtue. It is based upon the positive quality of universal love and compassion. One who is actuated by this ideal cannot be indifferent to the suffering of others.

Violence of every type should be completely forbidden. Mental tortures by way of harsh words, actions, and any type of bodily injuries should also be avoided. Even thinking evil of someone is considered violence in Jainism.

Practically, it is impossible to survive without killing or injuring some of the smallest living beings. Some lives are killed even when we breathe, drink water, or eat food. Therefore, Jainism says that minimum killing of the lowest form of life should be our ideal for survival.

In the universe, there are different forms of life, such as, human beings, animals, insects, plants, bacteria, and even smaller lives, which cannot be seen even through the most powerful microscopes. Jainism has classified all the living beings according to their senses.

The five senses are touch, taste, smell, sight, and hearing.

It is more painful if a life of the higher forms (more than one sense) is killed. Hence Jainism allows laypeople to use only vegetables as a food for survival. All non-vegetarian food is made by killing living beings. Therefore, Jainism preaches strict vegetarianism, and prohibits non-vegetarian foods.

Jainism explains that violence is not defined by actual harm, for this may be unintentional. It is the intention to harm, the absence of compassion, unawareness, and the ignorance that makes an action violent. Without violent thought there can be no violent actions. Non-violence is to be observed in action, speech, and thought. One should not be violent, ask others to do so, or approve of such an activity.

33.1.2 Truth (Satya)

Anger, greed, fear, and jokes are the breeding grounds of untruth. To speak the truth requires moral courage. Only those who have conquered greed, fear, anger, jealousy, ego, and frivolity can speak the truth.

Jainism insists that one should not only refrain from falsehood, but should always speak the truth, which should be wholesome and pleasant. One should remain silent if the truth causes pain, hurt, anger, or death of any living being.

Truth is to be observed in speech, mind, and deed. One should not utter an untruth, ask others to do so, or approve of such activities.

33.1.3 Non-stealing (Achaurya or Asteya)

Stealing consists of taking another's property without his consent, or by unjust or immoral methods. Further, one should not take anything which does not belong to him. It does not entitle one to take away a thing, which may be lying, unattended or unclaimed. One should observe this vow very strictly, and should not touch even a worthless thing, which does not belong to him. When accepting alms, help, or aid one should not take more than what is minimum needed. To take more than one's need is also considered theft in Jainism.

The vow of non-stealing insists that one should be totally honest in action, thought, and speech. One should not steal, ask others to do so, or approve of such activities.

33.1.4 Celibacy/Chastity (Brahmacharya)

Total abstinence from sensual pleasure and the pleasure of all five senses are called celibacy. Sensual pleasure is an infatuating force, which sets aside all virtues and reason at the time of indulgence. This vow of controlling sensuality is very difficult to observe in its subtle form. One may refrain from physical indulgence but may still think of the pleasures of sensualism, which is prohibited in Jainism.

Monks are required to observe this vow strictly and completely. They should not enjoy sensual pleasures and pleasure of all five senses, ask others to do the same, nor approve of it. There are several rules laid down for observing this vow for householders. They should not have any physical relationship other than own spouse. The relationship with your own spouse should be of limited nature.

33.1.5 Non-attachment/Non-possession (Aparigraha)

Jainism believes that the more worldly wealth a person possesses, the more he is likely to commit sin to acquire and maintain the possession, and in a long run he may be unhappy. The worldly wealth creates attachments, which will continuously result in greed, jealousy, end, and only the sky is the limit for them. Lord Mahavira has said that wants and desires have no end, and only the sky is the limit for them.

An attachment to worldly objects results in the bondage to the cycle of birth and death. Therefore, one who desires of spiritual liberation should withdraw from all attachments to pleasing objects of all the five senses.

Monks observe this vow by giving up attachments to all things such as:

- Material things: wealth, property, grains, house, books, clothes, etc.
- Relationships: father, mother, spouse, children, friends, enemies, other monks, disciples, etc.
- Pleasure of Five Senses: touch, taste, smell, sight, and hearing.
- Feelings: pleasure and painful feelings towards any objects.

They have the equanimity towards music and noise, good and bad smells, soft and hard objects for touch, beautiful and dirty sights, etc. They do not eat food for taste but for survival with the intention to continue to progress spiritually and ultimately to attain liberation. Non-possession and non-attachment are to be observed in speech, mind, and deed. One should not possess, ask others to do so, or approve of such activities.

Jainism has laid down and described in much detail these five great vows for the path of liberation. These are to be observed strictly and entirely by the monks and nuns. Partial observance is laid down for the householders with additional seven vows.

33.2 Twelve Vows of Lay People (Shrävaks and Shrävikäs)

The renouncers' vows are called the Mahavratas (Great Vows) and the vows of the laity, which are modelled after the Great Vows, are called Anuvratas (Lesser Vows). Jain ethics outlines the following twelve vows of limited nature to be carried out by lay people. Every Jain should adopt these vows according to one's individual capacity and circumstances with the intent to ultimately adopt the 5 Mahävratas (great vows). These vows are to be followed in thought, action, and speech, and others should be encouraged to follow them as well. During the Pratikraman (a ritual during which Jains repent for their sins and non-meritorious activities committed knowingly or inadvertently during their daily life through thought, speech or action), lay people reflect on minor violations (Atichär) that occurred in the past of these vows. One would ask for forgiveness for his/her past minor violations, which may have occurred knowingly or unknowingly. He/she would reflect on each of these violations so that in the future they would not repeat the same errors and be more aware if such circumstances arise.

Five Main Vows of Limited Nature (Anuvratas):

1. Ahimsa Anuvrata Limited Vow of Non-violence;
2. Satya Anuvrata Limited Vow of Truthfulness;
3. Achaurya Anuvrata Limited Vow of Non-stealing;
4. Brahmacharya Anuvrata Limited Vow of Chastity; and
5. Aparigraha Anuvrata Limited Vow of Non-attachment.

Three Merit Vows (Guna-vratas):

1. Dik Vrata Vow of Limited Area of Activity;
2. Bhoga Upbhoga Vrata Vow of Limited Use of Consumable and Non-consumable items;
3. Anartha-danda Vrata Vow of Avoidance of Purposeless Sins.

Four Disciplinary Vows (Shikshä-vratas):

1. Sämäyika Vrata Vow of Equanimity and Meditation for Limited duration;
2. Desävakäsika Vrata Vow of Activity within Limited Space and duration;
3. Paushadha Vrata Vow of Ascetic's life for a Limited Duration; and
4. Atithi Samvibhäg Vrata Vow of Charity.

Of these twelve vows, the first five are the main vows of limited nature (Anuvratas). They are more lenient than the great vows (Mahä-vratas). The great vows are for Jain ascetics.

The next three vows are known as merit vows (Guna-vratas), so called because they enhance and purify the effects of the five main vows. They also govern the external conduct of an individual.

The man who incessantly observes all the supplementary vows and sallekhanâ (together, these are called śeelas) for the sake of safeguarding his vows (vratas), gets fervently garlanded (a gesture to indicate her choice for a husband) by the maiden called 'liberation'.

—Puruşārthasiddhyupāya[1

The last four are called disciplinary vows (Shikshä-vratas). They are intended to encourage a person to perform religious duties. They reflect the purity of one's heart. They govern one's internal life and are expressed in a life marked by charity. They are preparatory to the discipline of an ascetic's life. The three merit vows (Gunavrata) and four disciplinary vows (Shikshä vratas) together are known as the seven vows of virtuous conduct (Shilä).

The layperson should be very careful while observing and following these vows. Since these vows are of limited nature, they still leave room for the commitment of necessary sins and possession of property.

Five Main Vows of Limited Nature (Anuvratas)

1. Limited Vow of Nonviolence (Ahimsa Anuvrata): In this vow, a person must not intentionally hurt any living beings (human, animals, birds, insects, plants etc.) physically or emotionally either by thoughts, words or actions, himself or by approving such an act committed by somebody else. Intention in this case applies to selfish motive, sheer pleasure and even avoidable negligence. One may use force, if necessary, in the defence of country, society, family, life, property, and religious institution. Most agricultural, industrial, and occupational activities do involve violence to life, but it should be kept at a minimum, through carefulness and due precaution.

Premeditated violence is prohibited for all. A householder is to partake in necessary violence defensively and vocationally provided he is aware of these Atichärs. Common violence is accepted for survival, but even here one should be careful in preparing food, cleaning one's house, etc. in order to minimize violence. This explains the Jain practices of filtering drinking water, vegetarianism, not eating meals at night, and abstinence from alcohol. Nonviolence is the foundation of Jain ethics.

Lord Mahävira says:

> "One should not injure, subjugate, enslave, torture or kill any living being including animals, insects, plants, and vegetables."

This is the essence of the Jain religion. It embraces the welfare of all animals and it protects the environment. It is the basis of all stages of knowledge and the source of all rules of conduct.

2. Limited Vow of Truthfulness (Satya Anuvrata): Truthfulness is more than abstaining from falsehood. It is seeing the world in its real form and adapting to that reality. The vow of truth puts a person in touch with his inner strength and inner capacities. In this vow, a person avoids gross lies, such as giving false evidence, denying the property of others entrusted to him, and cheating others. If the truth has the potential to harm others or hurt their feelings, it is better to remain silent. A householder should minimize the minor violations to this vow related to self-defence, protection of his family and country, business, and job-related circumstances, and the survival of his life and livelihood. A ritual during which Jains repent (prayaschit) for their sins and non-meritorious activities committed knowingly or inadvertently during their daily life through thought, speech or action.

According to Jain text, Puruṣārthasiddhyupāya:

> All these subdivisions (injury, falsehood, stealing, unchastity, and attachment) are hiṃsā as indulgence in these sullies the pure nature of the soul. Falsehood etc. have been mentioned separately only to make the disciple understand through illustrations.
>
> —Puruṣārthasiddhyupāya

3. Limited Vow of Non-stealing (Achaurya / Asteya): In this vow, a person must not steal, rob, or embezzle others' valuable goods and property. One also must not cheat and use illegal means to acquire worldly assets beyond their minimum needs.

4. Limited Vow of Chastity (Brahmacharya): The basic intent of this vow is to conquer passion and to prevent the waste of energy. Positively stated, the vow is meant to impart a sense of serenity to the soul. In this vow, the householder must not have a sensual relationship with anybody but one's own wedded spouse. Even with one's own spouse, excessive indulgence in sensual pleasure should be avoided. Giving in to sensual pleasure ensnares the mind, which may falter one's efforts towards spiritual progress. This, in turn, can be expounded to include other mind-altering substances such as illicit drugs, certain prescription drugs, smoking and alcohol.

5. Limited Vow of Non-possession / Non-attachment (Aparigraha): Non-possession is the fifth limited vow. As long as a person does not know the richness of joy and peace that comes from within, he tries to fill his empty and insecure existence with the clutter of material acquisitions.

Three Merit Vows (Guna-vratas)

6. Vow of Limited Area of Activity (Dik Vrata): This vow limits one's worldly activities to certain areas in all ten directions: north, south, east, west, north-east, north-west, south-east, south-west, upwards and downwards. A person gives up committing sins in any place outside the limited area of his worldly activity. This vow provides a space limit to the commitment of sins of common violence not restricted by the limited vow of non-violence. Thus, outside the limited area, the limited vows assume the status of full vows (Mahā-vratas).

7. Vow of Limited use of Consumable / Non-consumable items (Bhoga-Upbhoga Vrata): Generally, sins are committed by using or enjoying consumable (Bhoga) and non-consumable (Upbhoga) objects. Consumable (Bhoga) objects include those things that can only be used once, such as food and drink. Non-consumable (Upabhoga) objects include those that can be used several times, such as furniture, clothes, and ornaments. One should limit the use of these two types of items according to one's need and capacity by taking these vows. This vow limits the quantity of items to the commitment of sins not restricted by Aparigraha Anuvrata.

8. Vow of Avoidance of Purposeless Sins (Anartha-danda Vrata): One must not commit unnecessary or purposeless sins or moral offense as defined below:

- Thinking, talking, or preaching evil or ill of others;
- Being inconsiderate; for example, walking on grass unnecessarily or leaving the water running while brushing your teeth;
- Manufacturing or supplying arms for war.
- Reading or listening to immoral literature, or showing carelessness in ordinary behaviour.

Four Disciplinary Vows (Shikshä vratas)

1. Vow of Equanimous State for Limited Duration (Sämäyika Vrata): This vow consists of remaining in equanimous state and sitting down at one place for at least 48 minutes. During this time one concentrates on spiritual activities like reading religious books, praying, or meditating. This vow may be repeated many times in a day. It is to be observed by mind, body, and speech. The equanimous state of 48 minutes makes a person realize the importance of a life-long vow to avoid all sinful activities and is a stepping stone to a life of full renunciation. During Sämäyika, one also meditates on the soul and its relationship with karma. One should practice the vow of Sämäyika by giving up affection and aversion (Rag and Dvesha), observing equanimity towards all objects, thinking evil of no one, and being at peace with the world.

2. Vow of Activity of Limited Space (Desävakäsika Vrata): This vow sets a new limit within the limitations already set by Dik Vrata and Bhoga-Upbhoga Vrata. The general life-long limitation of doing business in certain areas and the use of articles are further restricted for particular days and times of the week. This means that one shall not, during a certain period of time, perform any activity or make any business dealings, or travel beyond a certain city, street, or house.

3. Vow of Ascetic's Life for Limited Duration (Paushadha Vrata): This vow requires a person to live the life of an ascetic for a period of time. During this time one should retire to a secluded place, renounce all sinful activities, abstain from seeking pleasure from all objects of the senses, and observe restraint of body, speech and mind. A person follows the five great vows (Mahä-vratas) completely during this time. This time should be spent in spiritual contemplation, meditation (Sämäyika), self-study, study of the scriptures, and worship of the supreme beings (Arihantas and Siddhas). This vow promotes and nourishes one's religious life and provides training for an ascetic life.

4. Vow of Charity (Atithi Samvibhäg Vrata): One should give food, clothes, medicine, and other articles of one's own possession to monks, nuns, pious and needy people. Food should be pure and offered with reverence. One should not prepare separate food especially for ascetics (monks or nuns) as they are not allowed to receive such food. Donation of one's own food and articles to monks and other needy people provides an inner satisfaction and raises one's consciousness to a higher level. It also saves them from acquiring more sins if they would have used the same for their nourishment, comfort and pleasure.

Peaceful Death (Sanlekhanä): In the final days of life, a householder can attain a peaceful death if he/she truly follows the above twelve vows. A peaceful death is characterised by non-attachment to worldly objects and by suppression of passions at the time of death. The last thought should be of a calm renunciation of the body, and this thought should be present long before death. It should be noted that Sanlekhanä is not a form of suicide or assisted death. It is usually performed by those who have led a very spiritual life and is undertaken in the presence of a guru.

Chapter - 34

Mula Sutras in Jainism

34.1 Mūla-sūtras

The 'Fundamental texts' – mūla-sūtra in Sanskrit – is the generic term that has come to be applied to certain writings in the Śvetāmbara canon. Meant to teach the basics of Jain doctrine and practice to mendicants, these form a set of works, all written in Ardhamāgadhī Prakrit. New monks and nuns begin to study these texts immediately after their initiations. The works are considered to contain the basic elements that must be understood to lead the mendicant life and therefore make up the first stage in the Śvetāmbara monastic curriculum.

Although the Mūla-sūtras deal with subjects that are partly treated in other writings in the Śvetāmbara canon, they can be viewed as being more suitable teaching texts. Among these topics are the mendicant's way of life, his interactions with other mendicants in the context of religious hierarchy or his interactions with lay people while seeking alms. This is a recurring topic in several of the Mūla-sūtras.

Basic teaching means rules, but it also includes parables and legends. These literary forms have a prominent place in one of the Mūla-sūtras, the Uttarādhyayana-sūtra. All the Mūla-sūtras contain passages in both prose and verse. Besides the usual prescriptive style of 'one should...', some of the works also employ the first-person 'I' style, which directly involves the reader. Some passages are markedly similar or even the same as sections found in other Śvetāmbara holy texts. The last work is a set of two specialised verse commentaries relating to daily monastic life, especially alms-gathering.

The last writing has been integrated into the category of 'fundamental texts' by the Śvetāmbara Mūrtipūjaks, but not by the other Śvetāmbara sects. The Sthānaka-vāsins and Śvetāmbara Terāpanthins thus consider there are three Mūla-sūtras while the image-worshipping Śvetāmbaras hold there are four.

This chapter examines the first text – the Daśavaikālika-sūtra – in some detail and discusses the fourth Mūla-sūtra – the Piṇḍa-niryukti and Ogha-niryukti. The other two scriptures are summarised here and explored in depth in separate articles called Uttarādhyayana-sūtra and Āvaśyaka-niryukti.

Following are the four Mūla-sūtras:

1. Daśavaikālika-sūtra
2. Uttarādhyayana-sūtra
3. Āvaśyaka-sūtra
4. Piṇḍa-niryukti and Ogha-niryukti

The first and third scriptures have a prominent place in monastic life. These two works belong to the few canonical texts, in the strict sense, that are part of the modern monastic curriculum as defined by the Jain Mūrtipūjaka Tapāgaccha Conference of 1988.

The first Mūla-sūtra, the Daśavaikālika-sūtra, deals with proper monastic conduct. Therefore, monks and nuns begin memorising it just after initiation – dīkṣā. Memorisation of the whole text is achieved in stages.

The Āvaśyaka-sūtra, the third Mūla-sūtra, is concerned with the six obligatory duties of the mendicant, in particular repentance – pratikramaṇa. New mendicants also start committing this scripture to memory immediately after their initiation.

Furthermore, Mūrtipūjaka mendicants study the second and fourth Mūla-sūtras later in their monastic training.

34.2 Mūla-sūtra-1: Daśa-vaikālika-sūtra: Fundamental Teachings

Contemporary observation as well as various historical reports and accounts show that the Daśa-vaikālika-sūtra is the one learnt first by newly ordained Śvetāmbara mendicants. They learn it by heart before studying its meaning.

The composition of the first Mūla-sūtra is described in a legend that stresses a link with the 24th Jina Mahāvīra and the earliest summaries of his teachings, the Pūrvas. The reason given in the story for the Daśa-vaikālika-sūtra's creation is to pass on the teachings quickly. These two legendary elements have long bestowed authority on the scripture's status as the initial text from which to learn basic Jain beliefs and practices.

Mendicants often recite the first stanzas because they embody the core of Jain teaching, for instance when pouring sandalwood powder on the heads of lay followers as a form of blessing.

34.2.1 Traditional authorship

The authorship of the Daśa-vaikālika-sūtra is inscribed within the traditional history of Śvetāmbara lineages of teachers. It is regarded as having been written by Śayyambhava, also known by his Prakrit name of Seyyambhava. He was the pupil of the teacher Prabhava, who was himself the pupil of Jambū, the elder. In the traditional dating Śayyambhava became head of the monastic community Mahāvīra founded in the 75th year after Mahāvīra's nirvāṇa, thus in 452 BCE.

Śayyambhava is said to have written the Daśa-vaikālika-sūtra for his son Maṇaka. The tale of how he came to compose it is told in the commentaries to the work and in narrative books recounting the 'lives of the Jain elders'. Hemacandra's version of the 12th century can be viewed as a convenient reference.

The Brahmin Śayyambhava was about to perform an animal sacrifice. The Jain teacher Prabhava sent two monks to convert him, who raised doubts in his mind as to the truth of the Veda. Śayyambhava finally recognised the truth of the Jain doctrine and practices, with non-violence at their centre. He was so convinced that he turned to the life of a Jain monk.

At the time of his decision to become a monk, Śayyambhava's young wife was pregnant and duly gave birth to his son. As the boy Maṇaka grew up, he enquired about his father. Without his mother's knowledge, Maṇaka went in search of him.

When he saw the boy for the first time Śayyambhava immediately recognised his son, but talked to him without disclosing his identity. As Maṇaka had said that he would be ordained as a Jain monk if he found his father, Śayyambhava introduced him to the teaching. But through the powers his great spiritual knowledge gave him, Śayyambhava realised that Maṇaka would die in six months' time.

The great monk Śayyambhava thought, 'This child's life will be extremely short'. "How will he learn the teachings? The last Teacher who knows just ten of the fourteen Original Collections of Teachings is permitted to make an epitome of their doctrine, but for what reason may one who knows all fourteen? The reason has arisen: it's to enlighten Maṇaka! I'll prepare a compilation of the topics of the Original Collections of Teachings." When the spiritual leader Śayyambhava had finished his compilation of the Teachings, he named it the 'Ten Evening Chapters'. The treatise is called the Ten Evening Chapters because he composed the ten chapters in an evening. Holy Śayyambhava, the excellent Teacher, the leader of the monastic order, most eminent of the compassionate, recited the treatise to Maṇaka.

As his father had foreseen, Maṇaka died after six months. In a later life he reached final liberation, which was said to have resulted from his learning this treatise.

Śayyambhava then expressed the wish to conceal this compilation, as he had first intended, but was then convinced by his own pupils not to do so.

The monastic community joyfully requested the religious Teacher, 'Let this treatise which was prepared for Maṇaka, be of benefit to the whole world. Then beings who have the capacity for enlightenment, even those of little understanding, will perform their religious duty. "Let them enjoy the benefits of your kindness, in the same way as Maṇaka." Like homeless bees, may they delight in continually resorting to the Ten Evening Chapters, the flower of the lotus plant of religious teaching'. Thus, the, monastic congregation prevented the noble religious teacher Śayyambhava from suppressing the Ten Evening Chapters.

34.2.2 Title of the 'Daśavaikālika-sūtra'

The legendary account of the scripture's creation gives the title of the work as meaning the 'Ten Evening Chapters' and explains it with reference to the time it was written. Another understanding of the title refers to the time when it should be read, because it may mean 'Ten [lectures] beyond [the prescribed study hours]'. This interpretation underlines that this work can be read any time. Mention of the 'time' prescribed for reading refers to a method of grouping scriptures, but is not easy to interpret.

34.2.3 Compendium

The legendary account of its composition emphasises the fact that the Daśa-vaikālika-sūtra is an abridgment of the 14 Pūrvas. Some commentators have developed this idea by making specific connections between certain chapters and given Pūrvas.

Others, however, consider that this work is an epitome of the 12 Aṅgas. Similarly, they establish a systematic connection between given chapters of the Daśa-vaikālika-sūtra and particular Aṅgas. The fact is that most of the topics the Daśa-vaikālika-sūtra covers, are also dealt with in other parts of the canon, especially in the first Aṅga, the Ācārānga-sūtra, the oldest book on monastic conduct. In a number of cases these connections go beyond the contents and relate to points of detail, such as metaphors or phrases.

A number of traditionally famous striking formulas or aphorisms believed to capture the essence of Jainism comes from this work.

34.2.4 Contents of the 'Daśavaikālika-sūtra'

The subject matter of the Daśa-vaikālika-sūtra is mendicant conduct, with several key aspects reiterated and expanded on throughout the chapters and appendices. These key elements of mendicant life are related to food, behaviour towards others, especially superiors and lay people, and knowledge crucial for a monk's proper conduct and spiritual progress. Several passages are identical or very similar to other Śvetāmbara scriptures that deal with these topics.

Chapter 1

The first chapter of the first Mūla-sūtra is brief. It underlines the idea prevailing in the whole book that a monk should live in a way that does not harm those on whom he depends, especially during his search for alms. This is expressed through a famous comparison, also found in similar terms in Buddhist scriptures. It states that the monk should be like the bee which sucks pollen from flowers without hurting them.

Chapter 2

The Daśa-vaikālika-sūtra does not contain any narrative chapter. But the famous story featuring Rājimāti's lesson to Rathanemi is recalled in chapter 2. In this tale, Rathanemi is so beguiled by Rājimāti's beauty that he is about to give up life as a monk until she reminds him of his vows. The purpose of the second chapter is to strongly encourage monks to remain firm on the path of celibacy and not to indulge in desire. The story and verses here are identical to the same episode told in chapter 22 of another Mūla-sūtra, the Uttarādhyayana.

Chapter 3

A condensed description of proper monastic conduct is the subject of chapter 3. Like several other chapters, the emphasis is on the proper way for monks to behave when in contact with lay people. Self-control and endurance are also the themes.

Chapter 4

The fourth chapter of the Daśa-vaikālika-sūtra is extremely important. It starts with an extensive description of the six kinds of life forms:

(i) earth-bodies – puḍhavi;

(ii) water-bodies – āu;

(iii) fire-bodies – teu;

(iv) wind-bodies – vāu;

(v) plant-bodies - vaṇassai; and

(vi) mobile bodies – tasa.

Exact knowledge of this topic is a prerequisite for proper monastic conduct. Such behaviour is characterised by self-control and its consequence, which is non-aggression towards living beings and non-violence. These notions are expressed by the Sanskrit terms ahiṃsā and saṃyama, which occur right at the beginning of the work.

Thus, the monk is told:

- not to harm living beings;
- not to cause others to harm them;
- allow others to harm them in mind, speech or action.

Then comes the exposition of the **five major vows** – mahā-vratas – which define the fundamentals of monastic conduct. They are not formulated as general rules, but phrased in the first person singular as a resolution expressed in the presence of one's teacher. This is a way to involve the reader or vow-taker directly in the process:

(i) I take the first great vow – abstinence from harming any living being in any way;

(ii) I take the second great vow – abstinence from wrong speech;

(iii) I take the third great vow – abstinence from taking what has not been given;

(iv) I take the fourth great vow – abstinence from sexual intercourse; and

(v) I take the fifth great vow – abstinence from keeping any possession.

To the set of the five vows is added a sixth. This vow relates to the prohibition on eating at night – that is, after sunset. This vow is not recorded in the great vows as expressed in the first Aṅga of the Śvetāmbara canon, the Ācārānga-sūtra.

This chapter ends with a set of stanzas emphasising the need for knowledge and the ability to discriminate between good and bad. The verses stress how necessary these two elements are before the monk can begin proper behaviour.

Chapter 5

In two sections, chapter 5 deals extensively with 'the begging-tour' or search for alms which Śvetāmbara mendicants undertake twice a day. The text stresses how precautions have to be taken regarding the:

- origin and nature of the food offered as alms;
- procedure when accepting the food;
- procedure when consuming it.

As the rituals surrounding the seeking, accepting and eating of food as alms are highly complex, numerous faults can be committed easily. Whereas other specialised texts on alms give technical designations and definitions, here the emphasis is on practical aspects, such as:

- what should the mendicant avoid?
- what should he do in a given circumstance?

The text refers to the circumstances where a mendicant interacts with the lay donor – the lady who cooks and provides the food.

The interpretation of particular terms used here has been highly controversial. It is said that the monk should avoid bahu-aṭṭhiyaṃ puggalaṃ aṇimisaṣvā bahu-kaṇṭayaṃ. In the standard Jain understanding, this means to avoid 'fruits with many seeds, scales, thorns'. But the parallel of the phrase found in the first Aṅga, the Ācārāṅga-sūtra, raises difficulties with the usual interpretation. The phrase bahu-y-aṭṭhiyaṃ vā maṃsaṃ macchaṃ vā bahu-kaṇṭagaṃ is used, where the words for 'meat' – maṃsaṃ – and 'fish' – macchaṃ – are straightforward. This suggests that the meaning is 'lump of flesh with many bone pieces' and 'fish with many scales and spikes'. This is one of the traces found in scriptures that indicate that non-vegetarianism was not excluded in earlier times and that ancient Jain ascetics could have eaten meat. These traces can be found even though they are extremely disturbing to Jain orthodoxy and thus tend to be suppressed.

Chapter 6

An elaborate exposition of dharma and conduct, the sixth chapter can be viewed as a longer version of what is summarised in chapter 3. It is presented in the form of a sermon given by a teacher in answer to questions about the nature of his conduct.

Some of the topics are common to other chapters, such as references to the six life forms, the great vows and searching for alms. The expounding teacher often refers to Mahāvīra as the source of his exposition and provides a strong argument in favour of saintly behaviour, which leads to perfect calmness and final liberation.

Chapter 7

The Daśa-vaikālika-sūtra's seventh chapter is on right speech and is derived from a section on the same topic in the Ācārānga-sūtra (II. 4). Purity in speech does not just mean not lying. There is much more to it, which is detailed here.

Rough speech is also included as a type of improper speech. Examples are provided of phrases that should not be uttered because they could hurt or be misleading. Insults are one form of wrong speech, but also sentences that imply violence or could encourage it. For instance, a monk should not say of a man, a quadruped, a bird, or a snake: "He / it is big and fat and fit to be killed and cooked". He should say: "He / it is of increased bulk, his / its body is well grown, he / it has attained a sizeable shape."

The main idea is that the mendicant should:

- think before speaking;
- avoid speaking if it is better not to talk; and
- phrase his statements extremely carefully.

Chapter 8

The topic of the eighth chapter is again the rules of conduct for all circumstances of monastic life. This chapter phrases these rules as either 'the monk should…' or 'he should not…'.

Some rules relate to topics already dealt with in the preceding chapters, such as food or speech. The emphasis is on restraint, detachment and protection from inclinations or passions that prevent the mendicant from reaching the goal of spiritual progression to salvation. The conclusion is:

Such a monk who bears all pains, has subdued his senses, possesses knowledge of tradition, is without egotism and property, shines forth, when the cloud of Karman has disappeared, like the moon at the definitive removal of the cloudy veil.

Chapter 9

There are four sections in Chapter 9, all discussing the relationship between the mendicant and his superiors, between the student and his teacher. In order to be able to learn and progress, a mendicant must behave with modesty, humility and respect. All these notions are conveyed in one term – vinaya – which is also the topic of the first chapter of another Mūla-sūtra, the Uttarādhyayana-sūtra.

Thus, a disciple should not offend or mock his teacher – guru – as the first section explains. This may have unwished for and dangerous consequences: 'after an offence against the Guru there is no Salvation'. The second section starts with the vigorous statement that 'humble behaviour is the root of dharma'. The attitudes of respectful and arrogant monks are described and their respective results contrasted. The third section has a positive approach, concentrating on the one who is humble and well behaved. All the stanzas of this section end with the same motto, which gives the section a formal unity. The motto is: 'he is worthy of respect'.

In the final section, four points regarding the general concept of vinaya are examined in turn, which are:

- devotion to discipline;
- devotion to the sacred texts;
- devotion in fasting; and
- devotion to good conduct.

Chapter 10

Each stanza of chapter 10 of the Daśa-vaikālika-sūtra is also characterised by a concluding refrain. This time it is: 'he is a true monk'. Here is a description of the ideal conduct of the wandering mendicant. It is written in a number of different metres. This poetical piece is similar to the 15th chapter of the Uttarādhyayana-sūtra, which has the same refrain and also uses various metres.

34.3 Mūla-sūtra-2: Uttarādhyayana-sūtra: Basic concepts and Legends

The second Mūla-sūtra is called Uttarajjhayaṇa-sutta in Prakrit, Uttarādhyayana-sūtra in Sanskrit. The term uttara can be understood as meaning 'last', 'additional' or 'excellent'. This scripture deals with all aspects of Jain doctrine and monastic practice, such as:

- detachment,
- proper conduct,
- karma,
- colours of the soul, and
- detailed exposition of living beings.

These fundamental concepts are considered in 36 lessons, all characterised by forceful statements.

34.4 Mūla-sūtra-3: Āvaśyaka-sūtra: Six Obligatory Duties

Called Āvassaya-sutta in Prakrit and Āvaśyaka-sūtra in Sanskrit, the third Mūla-sūtra is also the shortest. In its full form the Āvaśyaka-sūtra is not considered to be extremely old, but it is very important because of its subject. It deals successively with the six obligatory duties of a mendicant, centring around the idea of confession and repentance – pratikramaṇa. It is a liturgical text, containing the formulas a monk must recite in the presence of a teacher to express his wish to adopt proper conduct or to repent for transgressions. In five sections out of six, the formulas are in the first-person singular, with the 'I', a mendicant. Examples include:

'Venerable teacher, I perform the rite of equanimity';

'O teacher, I wish to pay homage / repent and so on'.

Each covering one of the obligatory duties, the six sections are in prose but contain hymns of praise in verse. These devotional songs are also part of the formalised ritual that the Āvaśyaka-sūtra unfolds. This scripture is examined in more depth in the article on the Āvaśyaka-sūtra and its commentary, the Āvaśyaka-niryukti.

34.5 Mūla-sūtra-4: 1. Piṇḍa-niryukti and Ogha-niryukti: Collecting Alms

This Mūla-sūtra is different from the other three works in this class of scripture in several ways.

Firstly, the Śvetāmbarasects of the Sthānaka-vāsins and Terāpanthins do not recognise this text as a Mūla-sūtra. However, Śvetāmbara Mūrtipūjak Jains class it as the fourth Mūla-sūtra. This is a way to give it more prominence, partly due to the fact that it deals at length with all issues regarding the search for alms. Secondly, it is made up of two texts. These are known as the Piṇḍa-nijjutti and Ogha-nijjutti in Prakrit, Piṇḍa-niryukti and the Ogha-niryukti in Sanskrit.

Next, technically its constituent texts belong to another category of Jain writings – that of the niryukti. This generic name is given to a group of ten Prakrit verse-commentaries where scholastic methods of analysis are applied to understand words and concepts. The other existing texts in this category are based on a specific work – a sūtra. This is not the case with these two works, which have arisen independently of any sūtra. They are ascribed to 'Bhadrabāhu' or 'Bhadrabāhu II', who could have lived in the 1st century CE or, according to some, in the 5th century CE.

More generally, the two works are related in their contents, dealing in highly technical and sophisticated ways with daily mendicant life. The Ogha-niryukti deals with various aspects, taking its title from ogha, meaning 'general, global'. This includes the practice of gathering alms, which Śvetāmbara monks and nuns collect twice a day. The second text concentrates on the issue of alms-gathering, with piṇḍa meaning 'rice-ball'. These complementary works also cover matters relating to the alms bowl, with the Ogha-niryukti also treating other monastic implements. They provide a lot of information about material culture; however difficult it may be to grasp.

Hence the Ogha-niryukti and the Piṇḍa-niryukti function as specialised supplements to matters that are especially detailed in another of the 'Fundamental Texts'. This is the Daśa-vaikālika-sūtra, the fifth chapter of which deals with seeking, receiving and consuming alms.

Chapter - 35

Moksha (Liberation) in Jainism

The concept of Moksha or liberation is an ancient Indian tradition. According to Upanishadic teaching without seeing Brahman nobody can attain the liberation {moksha). "When a man knows Brahman, he is free". If one sees that Atman and Brahman are different, he will be in samsara. If he sees these two as one, he will be no more in Samsara. In Upanishadic teaching the highest knowledge is Brahmavidya which is open to all castes.

According to Jainism, the ultimate goal of the soul is to achieve liberation through understanding and realisation. This is accomplished through the supreme ideals of nonviolence, kindness, reverence for all forms of life, non-possessiveness, conquering all passions such as attachments and aversions, and through the philosophy of non-absolutism (Anekäntaväda). Above all, these ideals translate into a religion of universal love and compassion not only towards human beings but also towards all forms of life and environment.

35.1 Moksha in Jainism

Sanskrit moksha or Prakrit mokkha refers to the liberation or salvation of a soul from saṃsāra, the cycle of birth and death. It is a blissful state of existence of a soul, attained after the destruction of all karmic bonds. A liberated soul is said to have attained its true and pristine nature of infinite bliss, infinite knowledge and infinite perception. Such a soul is called siddha and is revered in Jainism.

In Jainism, moksha is the highest and the noblest objective that a soul should strive to achieve. In fact, it is the only objective that a person should have; other objectives are contrary to the true nature of soul. With the right view, knowledge and efforts all souls can attain this state. That is why Jainism is also known as mokṣamārga or the "path to liberation".

According to the Sacred Jain Text, Tattvartha sutra:

> Owing to the absence of the cause of bondage and with the functioning of the dissociation of karmas, the annihilation of all karmas is liberation.
>
> —Tattvārthsūtra (10-2)

In Jainism liberation can come only through true discrimination between soul and matter. The bondage of the soul is its association with matter; liberation must mean the complete dissociation of the soul from matter. This can be attained by complete elimination of the matter with which the soul has become already mingled. Right faith, knowledge and conduct are the three Jewels (tri-ratna) of Jainism. They are inseparably bound up and perfection of one goes with the perfection of the other two.

Moksha in Jainism differs from nibbana in Buddhism. Jainism, holding soul theory, expounds moksha while Buddhism, rejecting the eternal existence of soul, expounds nibbana.

35.2 Bhavyata

According to Jainism, there are two kinds of bondage or bandha:

(i) Bhava bandha

(ii) Dravya bandha

Internal or ideal bondage, i.e. the soul's bondage to bad disposition (bhava bondage). And material bondage, i.e. the soul's actual association with matter (dravya-bondage).

Bondage, in Jaina philosophy, comes, therefore, to mean the fact that jiva, infected with passions, takes up matter in accordance with its karma. As passion or bad disposition of the soul is the internal and primary cause of bondage, and the influx of matter into the soul is only the effect of it. The state when karmic particles actually infiltrate into the soul and bind it is called Bandha or Bondage. In bondage, the karmic matter unites with the soul by intimate interpenetration, just as water unites with milk or fire unites with the red-hot iron ball.

From the point of view of potentiality of moksha, Jain texts bifurcates the souls in two categories–bhavya and abhavya. Bhavya souls are those souls who have faith in moksha and hence will make some efforts to achieve liberation. This potentiality or quality is called bhavyata. However, bhavyata itself does not guarantee moksha, as the soul needs to expend necessary efforts to attain it. On the other hand, abhavya souls are those souls who cannot attain liberation as they do not have faith in moksha and hence never make any efforts to attain it.

35.3 The Path to Liberation

According to Jaina Philosophy, the escape of the jiva from matter is liberation. Liberation can come only through true discrimination between soul and matter. It is setting the self, free from the material superstructure. If the bondage of the soul is its association with matter, liberation must mean the complete dissociation of the soul from matter. This can be attained by stopping complete elimination of the matter with which the soul has become already mingled. The first process is called samvara (i.e. the stoppage of influx) and the second nirjara (i.e. exhaustation or wearing out of karma in the soul).

According to Jainism, the Ratnatraya or "three Gems", samyagdarśana (correct perception), samyagjñāna (right knowledge) and samyakchāritra (right conduct), together constitute the moksha marga or the path to liberation. According to Acharya KundaKunda's Samayasara:

Belief in the nine substances as they are is right faith (samyagdarśana). Knowledge of these substances without doubt, delusion or misapprehension, is right knowledge (samyagjñāna). Being free from attachment etc. is right conduct (samyakcāritra). These three, together, constitute the path to liberation.

Samyak Darshana or rational perception is the rational faith in the true nature of every substance of the universe.

Samyak Caritra or rational conduct is the natural conduct of a (soul) living being. It consists in following austerities, engaging in right activities and observance of vows, carefulness and controls. Once a soul secures samyaktva, mokṣa is assured within a few lifetimes.

Samvara element

In this way the Jainas hold that samvar and nirjara are the means to moksha. Samvar element stops astrava and bandha. With it Jiva is freed attachment, hatred and love and obtains equanimity for pleasure and pain and becomes free of distortions with the result that material particles do not enter it to cause any limitations.

Initially, in samvara distortions like love, hatred and attachment are negative, the state being called 'bhava samvara'. Following this entry of matter is stopped. This is called 'dravya samvara'. Once the entry of karma particles has been stopped, it cannot be started afresh. When all the karma matter of the Jiva has been destroyed he attains moksha.

The Jainas have suggested the following ways of obstructing the entry of karma:

(i) Samitian

(ii) Guptian.

According to Jainism, purification of soul and liberation can be achieved through the path of three jewels: Samyak darśana (Correct View), meaning faith, acceptance of the truth of soul (jīva); Samyak jnana (Correct

Knowledge), meaning undoubting knowledge of the tattvas; and Samyak charitra (Correct Conduct), meaning behaviour consistent with the Five vows. Jain texts often add samyak tap (Correct Asceticism) as a fourth jewel, emphasising belief in ascetic practices as the means to liberation (moksha). The four jewels are called moksha marg. According to Jain texts, the liberated pure soul (Siddha) goes up to the summit of universe (Siddhashila) and dwells there in eternal bliss.

The fourteen stages on the path to liberation are called Gunasthāna. These are:

Gunasthāna (Stages on the Path)	**Meaning**
1. Mithyātva:	The stage of wrong believer (Gross ignorance)
2. Sasādana:	Downfall from right faith
3. Misradrsti:	Mixed right and wrong belief
4. Avirata samyagdrsti:	Vowless right belief
5. Deśavirata:	The stage of partial self-control
6. Pramattasamyata:	Slightly imperfect vows
7. Apramatta samyata:	Perfect vows (Mahavratas)
8. Apūrvakaraṇa:	New thought-activity
9. Anivāttibādara-sāmparāya:	Advanced thought-activity (Passions are still occurring)
10. Sukshma samparaya:	Slightest delusion
11. Upaśānta-kasāya:	Subsided delusion
12. Ksīna kaṣāya:	Destroyed delusion
13. Sayoga kevali:	Omniscience with vibration (destruction of all inimical karmas)
14. Ayoga kevali:	The stage of omniscience without any activity.

Those who pass the last stage are called siddha and become fully established in Right Faith, Right Knowledge and Right Conduct.

35.4 Nirvāna

Nirvāna means final release from the karmic bondage. When an enlightened human, such as an Arihant or a Tirthankara, extinguishes his remaining aghatiya karmas and thus ends his worldly existence, it is called nirvāna. Technically, the death of an Arhat is called their nirvāṇa, as he has ended his worldly existence and attained liberation. ***Moksha (liberation) follows nirvāṇa.*** **However, the terms moksha and nirvana are often**

used interchangeably in the Jain texts. An Arhat becomes a siddha, the liberated one, after attaining nirvana.

In that night in which the Venerable Ascetic Mahavira, died, freed from all pains, the eighteen confederate kings of Kasi and Kosala, the nine Mallakis and nine Licchavis, on the day of new moon, instituted an illumination on the Poshadha, which was a fasting day; for they said: 'Since the light of intelligence is gone, let us make an illumination of material matter!'

35.5 Liberated Soul

A liberated soul dwells in Siddhashila with infinite faith, infinite knowledge, infinite perception, and infinite perfection.

According to the Jain text, Puruṣārthasiddhyupāya:

> Having achieved the ultimate goal, knowing everything that needs to be known, and enjoying eternal and supreme bliss, the Omniscient, Effulgent Soul, rests permanently in the Highest State (of liberation).
>
> —Puruṣārthasiddhyupāya

35.6 Difference between Moksha in Jainism and Nirbana in Buddhism

- Moksha in Jainism is to be attained after death while nibbana in Buddhism is to be attained in this very life.
- Moksha in Jainism is to be attained by cutting off karmic bondage while nibbana in Buddhism is to be attained by eradicating mental defilements through attainment of Noble Path.
- Moksha in Jainism is a place where liberated soul remains forever. Nibbana in Buddhism, however, is where there none of conditioned things remains.

35.7 Two Categories of Moksha in Jainism

To understand the moksha in Jainism we should know first the main teachings of Jainism. Jainism teaches the two categories which are covering the whole universe, uncreated, everlasting, eternal and coexistent. The two categories are jiva and ajiva. Jiva is soul that is conscious while ajiva is non-soul that is unconscious.

According to Jainism the two types of tapas (austerities) should be practiced to destroy the karma that was acquired by love and hatred. If a sage truly performs these two kinds of austerities, he will soon by thoroughly released from the circle of births.

At the third stage moksha comes into being. It is moksha when the partnership between soul and matter is dissolved and its ideal character is restored to the soul. It then transcends samsara and flies up to its permanent abode at the summit of lokakasa. The final condition is one of inactivity, but it is characterised by complete knowledge and absolute bliss. The soul in its pure state is endowed with infinite with infinite perception, infinite knowledge, infinite bliss, and infinite power. The liberated soul transcends samsara. It goes straight to the top of the world and dwells there forever. The freed soul has a beginning but has no end. These free souls enjoy a kind of interpenetrating existence on account of their oneness of statues their oneness of statues.

35.8 Karma Philosophy: Nine Tattvas

The doctrine of karma is the single most important subject of Jain philosophy. It provides a rational explanation to the apparently inexplicable phenomena of cycles of birth and death, happiness and misery, inequalities in mental and physical attainments and the existence of different species of living beings. Jainism believes that from eternity, every soul is ignorant and delusional of its true nature, but nonetheless is bound by karma. The ignorant and deluded soul, while remaining in bondage, continues to attract and bind new karma. It is due to karma that the soul migrates from one life cycle to another, and passes through many pleasures and painful situations. The karma that bind our soul are due not only to the actions of our body, mind, and speech but more importantly, to the intentions behind our actions. Jainism strives for the realisation of the highest perfection of the soul, which in its original purity is free from all pain, suffering, desire, and bondage of the cycle of birth and death. This way it provides the basis for the path of liberation.

Karma philosophy deals with many aspects of our life such as our past karma, our current life, and our future state. These aspects are easily explained in the group of nine Tattvas or fundamentals. The proper knowledge of these Tattvas is essential for spiritual progress and ultimate liberation.

Nine Tattvas (Nine Fundamentals)

(i) Jiva Soul or living being (Consciousness),

(ii) Ajiva: Non-living substances which include all the remaining five substances,

(iii) Äsrava: Causes of the Bondage of karma,

(iv) Bandha: Characteristics of Bondage of karma,

(v) Punya: Merit or karma of good deeds,

(vi) Päp: Sin or Transgression or karma of bad deeds,
(vii) Samvar Stoppage of attachment of new karma,
(viii) Nirjarä Exhaustion of the accumulated karma, and
(ix) Moksha State of total liberation from all karma.

Jiva and Ajiva (Soul and Nonliving Substances)

The first two Tattvas, Jiva and Ajiva, comprise the physical reality of the universe. Jiva Tattva refers to the soul and Ajiva tattva refers to the other five substances which are Matter, Dharma, Adharma, Space, and Time. However, in reference to the Theory of Karma, Ajiva Tattva refers to karma or karmic matter only. The remaining seven or five tattvas explain the relationships between the soul and karma.

Äsrava (Causes of Bondage of Karma)

The primary causes of the attachment or bondage of karma to the soul (known as Äsrava) are as follows:

- Mithyätva A person's illusion, which includes wrong conviction and wrong knowledge of reality,
- Avirati Lack of self-restraint or vowlessness,
- Pramäda Spiritual laziness or unawareness,
- Kashäya Passions like anger, ego, deceit, greed, and lust,
- Yoga Activities of body, speech, and mind.

These causes convert the karma particles or karma Varganä into karma attaching to the soul. Äsrava is in fact defined as any vibration in the soul caused by the activities of body, speech, and thought which bind karma particles to the soul. The soul has had this karmic matter attached to it from eternity. This karmic matter is known as the Kärman body or causal body or karma. The soul, which is covered by karmic matter, continues to acquire new karma from the universe through the abovementioned causes at every moment. Also the old karma after producing their result, are shred or leave the soul when it is time for them to do so. Because of this continuous process of binding and exhausting karma particles, the soul passes through the cycles of birth and death and experiences pleasure and pain. Therefore, under normal circumstances the soul cannot attain freedom from karma and hence cannot attain liberation.

Bandha (Characteristics of Bondage of Karma)

Äsrava causes karma particles to attach to the soul. When karma particles attach to the soul caused by Asrava, its quality of bondage (Bandha) to the soul is explained in the following four forms. These forms are determined at the time of the bondage:

- Prakriti bandha, Type or category of karma bondage;
- Sthiti bandha, Duration of attachment of karma bondage before they produce the result and then separate from the soul;
- Anubhäga or Rasa bandha, The intensity of the attachment of karma bondage;
- Pradesha bandha, Quantity of karma particles attached to the soul.

(a) Prakriti Bandha (Type of Karma Bondage): When karmic matter attaches to the soul, it obscures the soul's essential nature of infinite knowledge, infinite perception, bliss, perfect power, eternal existence, formlessness, and equanimity. The different types of karma obscure different qualities or attributes of the soul. The Jain literature has classified it into eight categories according to the particular attribute of the soul that it obscures. This is known as Prakriti bandha.

(b) Sthiti Bandha (Duration of Attachment of Karma): When karmic matter attaches to the soul, it remains attached for a certain duration till it produces the complete result. The duration of the attachment is determined according to the intensity or dullness of the soul's passions when the karma was originally attached to the soul. After producing the result, the karma will separate or detach from the soul.

(c) Anubhäga Bandha or Rasa Bandha (Intensity of Attachment of Karma): When karma produce the result, the intensity of the result is determined by the severity of the Leshyäs (any one of six Leshyä) along with passions of the soul when the karma were originally attached to it. This phenomenon is called Anubhäga or Rasa bandha.

(d) Pradesha Bandha (Quantity of Karma): The quantity of karma particles that are attached to the soul by our activity of body, mind, and speech (known as Yoga) is called Pradesha Bandha.

Samvar (Stoppage of New Karma)

The process that stops new karma from attaching to the soul is called Samvar. This process is the opposite of Äsrava. It can be accomplished by the constant practice of:

- Samyaktva, Right conviction and Right Knowledge of Reality;
- Vratas, Observance of Vows;
- Apramäda, Awareness or Spiritual-alertness;.
- Akashäya, Being Passionless;
- Ayoga Peacefulness of Mental, Verbal and Physical activities.

Fifty Seven Practical Ways of Samvar

Jain literature defines 57 practical ways, by which one can stop the attachment of karma. These ways are described mainly for monks and nuns but it is strongly recommended to be practiced by Shrävikäs and Shrävikäs as far as possible.

Nirjarä (Removal of Old Karma)

The process which removes the previously accumulated karma is called Nirjarä. This happens naturally when karma produce their result at the time of their maturity. This is known as Sakäm Nirjarä. However, at that time a person reacts to the situation that was created by karma and hence he acquires new karma. So, under normal circumstances a person will not be able to get rid of his/her karma because at every moment he/she removes some old karma and acquires some new karma.

Jainism explains that on a path of spiritual progress a person should remove the previously acquired karma before their maturity. This type of Nirjarä is called Akäm Nirjarä. This is achieved by the observance of rigorous penance and austerities known as Tapa. There are twelve types of Tapas defined in the Jain literature. They are divided into two groups; External Austerities (Bähya Tapa) and Internal Austerities (Abhyantar Tapa). External austerities help to discipline the human body and mind to control and minimise passions and desires. Internal austerities help to purify the soul. The external austerities are essential to help prepare the human body and mind such that the internal austerities will raise the person's spirituality and remove the past karma before they mature. The internal austerities are true austerities because they exhaust the attached karma before they produce the resultant effects of good or bad and thus purify the soul.

(a) External Austerities (Bähya Tapa):

Anashan (Fasting)

Complete abstinence from eating any food and/or drinking liquid. Sometimes one can drink only achit (previously boiled) water for a predetermined period of time, such as for a day or more. This spares our digestive energy to focus on spiritual uplift. This is known as Upaväs.

Alpähära or Unodari (Eat less than Hunger)

Eating at least 10% less than one's appetite at a given time.

Ichhänirodha or Vritti-sankshepa (Limit on Foods and Possessions)

Limiting the number of food items while eating and limiting the possession of material things.

Rasatyäg (Elimination of Tasty Food)

Complete abstinence from eating or drinking juicy and tasty foods such as butter, milk, tea, sweets, fried food, snacks, spicy food, and juices. Also one should eliminate junk food which has little or no nutrition value. In other words, there is no attachment to the taste of the food. We need to eat a minimum quantity of food to live a healthy life but we do not need to eat food for taste and enjoyment.

Käya-klesha (Voluntarily enduring sufferings)

One willfully subject to the sufferings of a body even when one does not have to and remaining undisturbed while experiencing sufferings. This is the general term for all types of penances (Tapa). Activities include travelling bare foot in severe heat or cold weather and removal of hair by hand as practiced by Jain monks and nuns.

Sanlinatä (Giving up Pleasures of Five Senses)

Sitting in a lonely place in various postures, with all the senses and mind withdrawn inwardly and giving up the pleasures of the five senses and the mind.

(b) Internal Austerities (Abhyantar Tapa):

Präyashchitta (Repentance for Bad Deeds)

For the spiritual purification, one truly repents for bad deeds and the breach of vows that occurred in the past and truly commits not to repeat them in future.

Vinay

Humility and proper behaviour towards all living beings such as Sädhus, Sädhvis, teachers, elders, co-workers, and poor.

Vaiyävruttya

One renders selfless service to Sädhus and Sädhvis, elderly, needy people, and to those who are suffering.

Swädhyäy

One studies the religious literature and listens to religious discourses and scriptures on the nature and quality of soul, karma, their relationship, and other elements of universe.

Dhyäna

After acquiring the above virtues, one contemplates and meditates on the nature of the soul.

Käyotsarga or Vyutsarga

Käyotsarga is the ultimate internal austerity, where the activities of the body, speech, and mind are withdrawn. This process involves making the body and mind as steady or still as possible to contemplate that the soul is separate from our human body. This austerity in its highest state destroys all four Ghäti Karma.

Moksha (Stage of Total Liberation from Karma)

A person who has destroyed all the Ghäti karmas by doing meditation and Käyotsarga is known as an omniscient or Kevali. However at the time of his/her death, one destroys the remaining four Aghäti karmas, and achieves nirvana, liberation, or Moksha. A liberated soul totally realizes its true attributes of infinite knowledge, infinite perception, infinite power or unlimited energy, and total bliss. The soul does not possess any physical body and is untouched by all kinds of miseries of the world forever. Now the soul exists in a state of pure consciousness. It reaches the top of Lokäkäsh and remains there forever in its blissful existence. It never returns to the cycles of birth, life, miseries, and death. This state of the soul is the liberated or perfect state, and is called "Nirvana".

SECTION - 5: COMPARISON BETWEEN HINDU, BUDDHIST AND JAIN PHILOSOPHIES

Chapter - 36

Similarities between Hindu, Buddhist and Jain Philosophies

36.1 Universal 'OM' Mantra in Hinduism, Buddhism and Jainism

Om itīdaṃ sarvam (Taittirīya Upaniṣad 1.8) "This whole world is OM". The syllable OM, also known as Aum and Pranava, is the most sacred symbol of Hinduism, Buddhism and Jainism. It is used both as a symbol and as a sound in religious worship, ritual chanting, performance of sacraments and rituals, meditation and tantra. In Hinduism it is venerated as Brāhman ('Brahma Nada' or 'Pranava Nada') in the form of word (askshara) and sound (shabda). Om is believed by many as "Apaurusheya" (not of human origin).

Initially, in the early Vedic period, because of the sanctity associated with it, the word was kept as a secret and never uttered in public. It was used in private conversations and passed on from the teacher to the disciple or from father to son directly and in secrecy. It was also not used in the rituals. Because it was not permitted to use the word directly, some early Upanishads referred to it indirectly as the udgita (upsound) or pranava (calling out), alluding to its significance in regulated breathing and religious chanting respectively.

The sacred OM is the primordial sound from which the whole creation has manifested. It is compared to the so called scientific big bang theory. The Mandukya Upanishad deals with this topic in detail. The sound Om is divided in four stages or parts. AUM and the silence afterwards. These four represent the four states of human life, viz., the waking, dream, deep sleep and *turiya*. They also represent the three bodies, viz., Gross body, subtle body and causal body and the turiya or transcendental reality. *Turiya* is not a name but an indication for the self which is the subtlest state or the transcendental meditation state in which the body is completely at rest but the mind is fully alert (a state of 'restful alertness'). OM (AUM) is the mystic name for the Hindu Trimurti and represents the union of the three gods: "A" for Brahma, "U" for Vishnu and "M" for Mahadev, which is another name of Shiva.

36.2 'OM' is Primordial

OM or AUM is not just a sound a vibration. It is not just a symbol. It is all that is within our perception and all that is beyond our perception . It is core of our existence. OM was revered before the birth of all the religions in the world. The origin of "Big-Bang" is from the experiments made by some scientists on microwave radiation in the universe. During their studies they were continually getting some unknown radiation from the universe. This radiation associated with the body at a temperature of 3 degrees Kelvin and it is presumed that the radiation must have emanated when Big-Bang took place. Actually, their experiment proved the reverberation of the Big-Bang explosion with which the universe began. Synonymous to this, our scriptures state that the sound OM or AUM – the Pranava mantra – was the first energy created at the time of disturbance of the equilibrium. It has been accepted in Hindu Religion that AUM – the first **primordial** sound energy ('Brahma Nad') emerged in the process of creation. Hence, what the scientific experiments revealed as microwave reverberations during the Big-Bang is already explicitly explained by our scriptures in the form of 'AUM'. "Om is the primordial throb of the universe. It is the sound form of Atma (Consciousness)." – Maitri Upanishad.

36.3 'OM' is Apaurusheya

OM is the soundless sound of existence, which the Zen Buddhists refer to as 'the sound of one-hand clapping'. The sound of 'OM' is known as 'Anahata', which means un-struck sound. All other ordinary sounds in the universe emerge as a result of frictional force between any two or more objects. Therefore, the 'OM' sound cannot be generated by person. It is self-producing sound. It is Apaurusheya (not of human origin). OM stands outside of history: as the distillation of the wisdom of the Vedas, the syllable remains "beyond human origin" (***apauruṣheya***), eternal, prior to everything (Pūrva Mīmāṃsā Sūtra 1.1.27-32).

36.4 'OM' is Perennial

OM is the akshara, which literally means immutable or imperishable, or perennial: the characteristic of the Syllable 'OM' as mentioned in the scriptures subsequent to Rig Veda. Therefore, OM is perennial, meaning that, it timeless, everlasting, which is valid in the past, present and future.

36.5 'OM' is Universal

OM is not related to any particular religion. As stated earlier, 'OM' is revered in many religions in the world: Hinduism, Buddhism, Jainism, Sikhism, and Zoroastrianism, to name a few. It is therefore 'Universal'. Following paragraphs justify this 'Universalism' of OM in details.

36.6 'OM' in Hinduism

36.6.1 OM in Rig Veda

Although the oldest scripture in Hinduism is known to be 'Rig Veda' (the first of the four Vedas), ironically it does not mention about 'OM' directly; rather it indirectly refers to it as 'Akshara' (Rig Veda, 1.164.39).

Richo akshare parame vyoman, yasmin deva adhi vishve nishedhuhu|
Yasthannaveda kim richa karishyathi, yayithath vidu stha ime samasathe||

"Richa is situated in akshara. knowledge is structured in consciousness, the non-changing transcendental basis of all relative existence in which reside the impulses of creative intelligence responsible for the whole manifest universe. He whose awareness is not open to this level of reality, what can these eternal expressions of knowledge accomplish for him?"

OR, in other words:

"He who knows not the eternal Syllable (Akshara) of the Veda, the highest point upon which all the gods repose, what business has he with the Veda? Only its knowers sit here in peace and concord".

The akshara literally means immutable or imperishable, or perennial: the characteristic of the Syllable 'OM' as mentioned in the scriptures subsequent to Rig Veda.

36.6.2 OM in Yajur Veda

Yajurveda Chapter 40 is also called Isha Upanishad. It says:

Om krato smara. Vayur-anilam-amrtam athedam Bhasmantagm sariram,
Om krato smara krtagm smara, krato smara krtam smara.

O men, at the time of death remember OM, the name of God. Think about God and yourself, think about the deeds you performed in your entire life. The vayu takes the soul. And remember that the body is mortal and will be finally destroyed.

"O3m krato smara |"

'O3m' is the highest reality. Here, the number intervening between o and m refers to 3 aspects of 'om' – (1) the sound originating in muladhara, (2) proceeding toward chest and (3) entering and spreading in the head; it spreads in three vyahruti- bhu, bhuvah, svah. Therefore 'OM' is also referred to as 'AUM', where 'A' represents Agni, 'U' represents Vayu, and 'M' represents Aditya.

36.6.3 OM in Aitareya-Brahmana

Om ity asau yo'sau [sûryah] tapati. Aitareya-Brâhmana (5.32)

"That which glows [i.e., the Sun] is Om."

36.6.4 OM in Brihadaranyaka Upanishad

yō ha vai jyēṣhaṅ ca śrēṣṭhaṅ ca vēda jyēṣṭhaśca ha vai śrēṣṭhaśca bhavati prāṇō vāva jyēṣṭhaśca śrēṣṭhaśca || 5.1.1 ||

"Om is Brahman, the Primeval Being. This is the Veda which the knowers of Brahman know; through it one knows what is to be known" .

36.6.5 OM in Chandogya Upanishad

ōmityētadakṣaramudgīthamupāsīta. ōmiti hyudgāyati tasyōpavyākhyānam (1.1.1)

"One should meditate on this syllable: Om. That is the quintessence of the essences, the Supreme, the highest" (Chandogya Upanishad 1.1.1).

Sa esha rasana rasatamah paramah parardhya ashtamo yaddrithah.

(Chandogya Upanishad 1.1.3)

"The syllable OM which is called Udgitha, is the quintessence (means the most perfect) of the essences, the supreme, deserving of the highest place." (Chandogya Upanishad 1.1.3)

This can be said, because Om is the Primal Word, the Original Sound, the First Word "spoken" by God, and by which all that "is" was created, and is being sustained and evolved at this very moment.

"Speech and breath are joined together in the Syllable OM" (Chandogya Upanishad 1.1.6)

"One should meditate on Om.... This sound is that syllable, the immortal, the fearless. having entered this, the gods become immortal, fearless. He, who knowing it thus, praises this syllable, take refuge in that syllable, in the immortal, fearless sound, and having entered it, he becomes immortal, even as the gods became immortal" (Chandogya Upanishad 1.4.1-5).

"The breath is continually sounding Om" (Chandogya Upanishad 1.5.3).

"This is the Udgitha (the song as OM, which uplifts the singer), the most excellent; this is endless. He who, knowing this, meditates on the Udgitha; obtsins progressively the most excellent life and wins the most outstanding worlds." (Chandogya Upanishad 1.9.2).

"The sun is Om" (Chandogya Upanishad 2.20.1).

"As all leaves are held together by a stalk, so is all speech held together by Om. Verily, the Syllable Om is all this–yea, the Syllable Om is all this" (Chandogya Upanishad 2.23.3).

"Even as a great extending highway runs between two villages, this one and that yonder, even so the rays of the sun go to both these worlds, this one and that yonder. They start from the yonder sun and enter into the nadis. They start from the nadis and enter into the yonder sun.... When a man departs from this body, then he goes upwards by these very rays or he goes up with the thought 'Om.' As his mind is failing, he goes to the sun. That, verily, is the gateway of the world, an entering in for the knowers, a shutting out for the non-knowers" (Chandogya Upanishad 8.6.2, 5).

36.6.6 OM in Katha Upanishad

"That word which all the Vedas declare, which all the austerities proclaim, desiring which people practice brahmacharya, that word, to you I shall tell in brief: It is Om. This syllable is, verily, the everlasting Spirit. This syllable is, indeed is the highest end; knowing this very syllable, whatever anyone desires will be his. This support is the best. This support is the highest; knowing this support, one becomes great in the world of Brahma" (Katha Upanishad 1.2.15-17).

36.6.7 OM in Mandukya Upanishad

"Om: this syllable is all this.... All that is the past, the present and the future, all this is only the syllable Om. And whatever else there is beyond the threefold time, that too is only the Syllable Om.... The Self is of the nature of the Syllable Om.... Thus the Syllable Om is the very Self. He who knows it thus enters the [Supreme] Self with his [individual] Self" (Mandukya Upanishad 1, 8, 12).

The Four are letters in AUM represent "A-U-M" and Silence: That Om, though described as having four states, is indivisible; it is pure Consciousness itself. That Consciousness is Om. The three sounds A-U-M (ah, ou, mm) and the three letters A, U, M are identical with the three states of waking, dreaming, and sleeping, and these three states are identical with the three sounds and letters. The fourth state, Turiya is to be realised only in the silence behind or beyond the other three.

Dhanur gṛhīvtā aupàniṣadam mahāstraṁ śaraṁ hy upāsā-niśitaṁ saṁdadhīta, āyamya tad-bhāvagatena cetasā lakṣyaṁ tad evākṣaraṁ, saumya viddhi (2.2.3).

"Taking as the bow the great weapon of the Upanishads [Om], one should place in it the arrow sharpened by meditation. Drawing it with a mind engaged in the contemplation of That [Brahman], O beloved, know that Imperishable Brahman as the target. (Mundaka Upanishad 2.2.3).

36.6.8 OM in Prashna Upanishad

"Satyakama, son of Shibi, asked [the Rishi Pippalada]: 'Venerable Sir, what world does he who meditates on the Omkara until the end of his life, win by That?' To him, he said: 'That which is the Omkara, O Satyakama, is verily the higher and the lower Brahman. Therefore, with this support alone does the wise man reach the one or the other.'… If he meditates on the Supreme Being [Parampurusha] with the Syllable Om, he becomes one with the light, the Sun. He is led to the world of Brahman. He sees the Person that dwells in the body, who is higher than the highest life…. That the wise one attains, even by the Omkara as a support, that which is tranquil, unaging, immortal, fearless, and supreme" (Prashna Upanishad 5:1, 2, 5, 7).

36.6.9 OM in Shvetashvatara Upanishad

"Om has been sung as the supreme Brahman, and in it are the Triad [the individual spirit, the cosmos, and the Cosmic Spirit]. It is the firm support, the imperishable. The knowers of Brahman by knowing what is therein become merged in Brahman, intent thereon and freed from birth" (Shvetashvatara Upanishad 1:7).

"As the form of fire when latent in its source is not seen and yet its seed is not destroyed, but may be seized again and again in its source by means of the drill [a pointed stick whirled to produce fire for the Vedic sacrifices], so it is in both cases. The Self has to be seized in the body by the Pranava. By making one's body the lower friction stick and the Pranava the upper friction stick, by practicing the friction of meditation one may see the hidden God" (Shvetashvatara Upanishad 1:13, 14).

36.6.10 OM in Bhagavad Gita

"O son of Kuntī, I am the taste of water, the light of the sun and the moon, the syllable Pranava (OM) in the Vedic mantras; I am the sound in ether and ability in man." (Bhagavad Gita 7:8).

"Uttering Om, the single-syllabled Brahman, meditating on me, departing thus from his body, he attains the Goal Supreme" (Bhagavad Gita 8:13).

"I am the father of this universe, the mother, the support, and the grandsire. I am the object of knowledge, the purifier and the syllable Om. I am also the Rig, the Sama, and the Yajur [Vedas]." (Bhagavad Gita 9:17).

"Of the great sages I am Bhrgu; of vibrations I am the transcendental om. Of sacrifices I am the chanting of the holy names [japa], and of immovable things I am the Himalayas." (Bhagavad Gita, 10:25).

Thus, the transcendentalists undertake sacrifices, charities, and penances, beginning always with OM, to attain the Supreme. (Bhagavad Gita, 17:24)

36.6.11 OM in Manu Smriti

The Laws of Manu (Manu Smriti) is the oldest code of laws in India.

"The monosyllable Om is the highest Brahman. ...Undoubtedly a Brahmin reaches the highest goal by japa of Om alone, whether he performs other rites or neglects them" (Manu Smriti 2:83, 87).

36.7 'OM' in Buddhism

36.7.1 Avalokitesvara mantra

Oṁ Mani Padme Hūṁ / Om Mani Padme Hum

Avalokiteshvara (or Avalokitesvara) is a Bodhisattva who represents compassion, and his mantra also symbolises that quality. Avalokiteshvara means "The Lord Who Looks Down (in compassion)".

Om has only a mystical meaning — suggesting primordial reality. Mani means jewel, while Padme means lotus. Hum, like Om, has no conceptual meaning. Overall, the mantra is suggestive of the bringing together of the qualities of wisdom (the lotus) and compassion (the jewel).

36.7.2 Manjushri mantra

Manjushri is a Bodhisattva who represents wisdom, and his mantra also symbolises that quality.

Oṁ A Ra Pa Ca Na Dhīḥ

He holds a sword in his right hand — symbolising his ability to cut through delusion. In his left hand, by his heart, he holds the stem of a lotus flower, which bears a book — the Perfection of Wisdom teaching, or Prajnaparamita.

36.7.3 Vajrapani mantra

Om Vajrapani Hum

Vajrapani is a Bodhisattva who represents the energy of the enlightened mind, and his mantra also symbolises that quality. Vajrapani is pictured dancing wildly within a halo of flames, which represent transformation.

He holds a vajra (thunderbolt) in his right hand, which emphasises the power to cut through the darkness of delusion. Vajrapani looks wrathful, but as a representation of the enlightened mind, he's completely free from hatred.

36.7.4 Green Tara mantra

Oṁ Tāre Tuttāre Ture Svāhā / Om Tare Tuttare Ture Svaha
OM ! O Tara! I entreat you, O Tara ! O swift one ! Hail !

36.7.5 Amitabha mantra

Om Amideva Hrih

Om represents the enlightened body, speech, and mind; Ami represents Buddha Amitabha; Dewa represents the deva realms, 6 desire realms, and Brahma realms; Hrih represents the seed syllable of compassion.

Om Ami Dewa Hrih is the sacred mantra of Amitabha (Amitayus) Buddha which protects you from obstacles and dangers and overcomes all hindrances to your success. This chant is also known as "Dharani for pulling out karmic obstructions by the roots and obtaining birth in the Pure Land" or "Rebirth Mantra".

36.7.6 White Tara mantra

White Tara is the Tara associate with compassion and long life. The White Tara mantra is very often chanted with an individual in mind, in order to entreat Tara to bless them with the long life and the compassion that they need to overcome obstacles.

Om Tare Tuttare Ture Mama Ayuh Punya Jñana Pustim Kuru Svaha

Om – can also be reflective of an awareness of the surrounding universe. It is used at the start of many mantras.

Tare – this is representative of salvation from suffering and other forms of mundane dangers. Tara is very often depicted as being one who can alleviate suffering from accidents, crime, and natural disasters.

Tuttare is representative of the delivered down the right spiritual path, and the need for protect from dangers to the spirit. Delusion, hatred, and greed are the three primary spiritual dangers that are responsible for suffering in us all.

Ture – this is representative of the deliverance to the true spiritual path of a bodhisattva. With this syllable, Tara is said to liberate us from the suffering we are inflicted with, while helping us to progress along the path that will allow us to have compassion for others.

Mama means "mine" and is indicative of the desire to possess the qualities of wisdom, happiness, long life, and more. These qualities can be asked for someone else, or for the person reciting the mantra.

Ayuh is representative of long life.

Punya is representative of the merit that is earned from living an ethical life and is said to guide one to a life that is happy and long.

Jnana is representative of wisdom, which is something we all seek.

Pushtim is representative of abundance or an increase in wealth.

Kuru is said to be a mythical land located in the northern regions of the Himalayas but can also be taken to mean "make it so."

Svaha is said to be representative of "allow the meaning of this mantra to take root in my mind."

36.7.7 Shakyamuni mantra

Shakyamuni (the sage of the Shakyan clan) is the historical Buddha, also known as Siddhartha Gautama.

Om muni muni mahamuni shakyamuni svaha

"Om wise one, wise one, great wise one, *to the wise one of the Shakyans* hail!"

36.7.8 Padmasambhava mantra

Padmasambhava was a historical teacher who is said to have finally converted Tibet to Buddhism. He was a renowned scholar, meditator, and magician, and his mantra suggests his rich and diverse nature.

Om Ah Hum Vajra Guru Padma Siddhi Hum

"I invoke you, Vajra Guru, Padmasambhava, by your blessing may you grant us supreme and ordinary realisation."

36.7.9 Bhaisajyaguru (Medicine Buddha) mantra

The Medicine Buddha, or Bhaiṣajyaguru, is as his name suggests connected with healing.

Oṁ bhaiṣajye bhaiṣajye mahābhaiṣajye bhaiṣajyarāje samudgate svāhā

"Bhaisajya" means "curativeness" or "healing efficacy," while "guru" means "teacher" or "master." Thus, he's the "master of healing." He's also known as Bhaisajyaraja, "raja" meaning "king."

The mantra could roughly be translated as "Hail! Appear, O Healer, O Healer, O Great Healer, O King of Healing!"

36.7.10 Vajrasattva mantra

Oṃ vajrasattva samayam anupālaya vajrasattva tvenopatiṣtha dṛdho me bhava sutoṣyo me bhava supoṣyo me bhava anurakto me bhava sarva siddhiṃ me prayaccha sarva karma su ca me cittaṃ śreyaḥ kuru hūḥ ha ha ha ha hoḥ bhagavan sarva tathāgatavajra mā me muñca vajrī bhava mahā samaya sattva aḥ (hūṃ phaṭ)

"Oṃ Vajrasattva! Preserve the bond! As Vajrasattva stand before me. Be firm for me. Be greatly pleased for me. Deeply nourish me. Love me passionately. Grant me siddhi in all things, And in all actions make my mind most excellent. hūṃ! Ha ha ha ha ho! Blessed One! Vajra of all the Tathāgatas! Do not abandon me. Be the Vajra-bearer, Being of the Great Bond! āḥ (hūṃ phaṭ)".

36.8 'OM' in Jainism

In Jainism, Om is considered a condensed form of reference to the Pañca-Parameṣṭhi by their initials A+A+A+U+M (o3m).

The Dravyasamgraha quotes a Prakrit line:

Oma ekākṣara pañca-parameṣṭhi-nāmā-dipam tatkathamiti cheta
"arihatā asarīrā āyariyā taha uvajjhāyā muṇiyā".

AAAUM [or just "Om"] is the one syllable short form of the initials of the five supreme beings [pañca-parameṣṭhi]: "Arihant, Ashiri, Acharya, Upajjhaya, Muni".

By extension, the Om symbol is also used in Jainism to represent the first five lines of the Namokar mantra, the most important part of the daily prayer in the Jain religion, which honours the Pañca-Parameṣṭhi. These five lines are: "(1) veneration to the Arhats, (2) veneration to the perfect ones, (3) veneration to the masters, (4) veneration to the teachers, (5) veneration to all the monks in the world".

The **Namokar (or, navkar**) mantra honours the five Jain Panch Parmeshtis, or great entities.

The five *parmeshtis* are:

- **Arihantas**, (Tirthankars or Jinas), the pure souls, the saints.
- **Siddhas**, liberated souls who are beyond birth and death.

- **Acharyas**, leaders of Jain congregations.
- **Upadhyays,** initiated monks and nuns.
- **Sadhus and Sadhvis**, male and female laypersons (householders).

The Namokar mantra is as follows:

I bow to the Arihantas, the perfected human beings.

I bow to the Siddhas, liberated bodiless souls.

I bow to the Acharyas, the masters and heads of congregations.

I bow to the Upadhyayas, the spiritual teachers.

I bow to the spiritual practitioners in the universe, Sadhus. This five-fold obeisance mantra, Destroys all sins and obstacles, And of all auspicious repetitions, is the first and foremost.

I bow to the enlightened beings;

I bow to the liberated souls;

I bow to religious leaders;

I bow to religious teachers;

I bow to all ascetics of the world.

These five salutations are capable of destroying all sins. And they are the most auspicious of all benedictions.

36.9 Summary of Similarities Between Buddhism and Jainism

There is much that is common between Jainism and Buddhism. Not only were there marked similarities in the careers of the founders of these two schools of philosophy, both of them were contemporary and originated in and around North India. Both possess a common background of Aryan culture. Certain common points in their philosophic content are also striking. Both of them reject the authority of the Vedas and the Vedic priests; Both repudiate the efficacy of ceremonies and rituals; both bitterly condemn animal sacrifices; and both ignore God. Jainism even emphatically denies any Supreme deity or creator, as man is his own architect. To both, distinctions based on birth have no meaning; both subscribe to ahimsa, both believe in transmigration and birth hold that karma experts a definite impact on the future. Both stress on service. Strangely enough, despite their strong regional orientation, both have accommodated many popular beliefs and superstitions.

Following are similarities between Buddhism and Jainism:

1. Both believe in faith and Karma.
2. Both are non-theistic religions.

3. Both had common background of Aryan Culture.
4. Both Founded by Kshatriyas of North India.
5. Both were against Vedas and vedic culture as well as against Brahmanism and also opposed animal sacrifice.
6. Both preached Satya, Ahimsa, Brahmacharya and detachment from material comforts.
7. Both appealed to the socially down-trodden, the Vaishyas who were economically powerful, but were not granted corresponding social status, and the Sudras who were obviously oppressed.
8. Both adopted an identical attitude towards trade. Not surprisingly, the first persons to become the Buddha's lay followers were traders.
9. Both did not follow elaborate rituals and ceremonies and thus were not expensive religions.
10. Despite their protestant character, neither waged a powerful struggle against caste system and untouchability. On the contrary, Buddhism appears to have recognised the phenomenon of untouchability.
11. Buddhism and Jainism tried to improve the position of slaves in some ways. The Dighanikaya advised masters to treat their salves decently. A Jaina text also states that dasas and dash, Karunakaras and Kamarkaris deserves to be well-maintained by their employees.
12. Karakandu, a Pratyekabuddha in both Jainism and Buddhism, is a rare personality that is shared between Jainism and Buddhism. The Jain text Isibhasiyam mentions Vajjiyaputra, Mahakashyap and Sariputra among the rishis.
13. The shared terms include Sangha, Shramana (monk), Shravaka (Householder in Jainism, Buddha's disciple in Buddhism), Jina (Tirthankara in Jainism, Buddha in Buddhism), Chaitya, Stupa, Pudgala (Matter in Jainism, soul in Buddhism) etc. Early Jainism used stupas, although the practice mostly (but not completely) was abandoned later.
14. The Jain community (or Jain sangha) consists of monastics, munis (male ascetics) and aryikas (female ascetics) and householders, śhrāvaks (laymen) and śrāvakīs (laywomen). Buddhism has a similar organisation: the community consists of renunciate bhikkhus and bhikkhunis and male and female laypersons, or śrāvakas and śrāvikas, who take limited vows.

15. Jain and Buddhist iconography can be similar. In north India, the sitting Jain and Buddhist images are in padmasana, whereas in South India both Jain and Buddhist images are in ardha-padmasana (also termed virasana in Sri Lanka). However, the Jina images are always samadhi mudra, whereas the Buddha images can also be in bhumi-sparsha, dharam-chakra-pravartana and other mudras. The standing Jain images are always in khadgasana or kayotsarga asana.

As already summarised above, in Jainism, the way of liberation is the ford (tirtha), and Tirthankaras "those making the ford" (from samsara to moksha) are supreme teachers. Same concept is found in Buddhism which says that through enlightenment (bodhi) an individual crosses the river of samsara and attain liberation. Both religions deny the existence of a creator god. Both reject Vedas. Buddhism and Jainism evince a shared belief in the existence of geographical regions beyond the parameters of Bharatavarsha, access to which could not be gained by ordinary human beings.

36.10 Jainism in Buddhist Texts

36.10.1 Pāli Canon

The Pāli Canon does not record that Mahavira and Gautama Buddha ever met, though instances of Mahavira's disciples questioning Gautama Buddha are to be found in various sutras. For instance, in the Majjhima Nikāya (MN 56), Upāli—one of Gautama Buddha's foremost disciples—is said to have been a disciple of the Mahavira who became a disciple of the Buddha after losing a debate with him. The Buddhists have always maintained that by the time the Buddha and Mahavira were alive, Jainism was already an entrenched faith and culture in the region. According to the Pāli Canon, Gautama was aware of Mahavira's existence as well as the communities of Jain monastics.

Buddhist texts refer to the Mahavira as Nigaṇṭha Jñātaputta. Nigaṇṭha means "without knot, tie, or string" and Jñātaputta (son of Natas), referred to his clan of origin Jñāta or Naya (Prakrit).

The five vows (non-violence, truth, non-attachment, non-thieving, celibacy/chastity) propounded by the 23rd Jain Tirthankara, Pārśva (877-777 BCE), may have been the template for the Five Precepts of Buddhism. Additionally, the Buddhist Aṅguttaranikāya scripture quotes the independent philosopher Purana Kassapa, a sixth-century BCE founder of a now-extinct order, as listing the "Nirgranthas" as one of the six major classifications of humanity.

Buddhist writings reflect that Jains had followers by the time the Buddha lived. Suggesting close correlations between the teachings of the Jains and the Buddha, the Majjhima Nikaya relates dialogues between the Buddha and several members of the "Nirgrantha community".

Indian Buddhist tradition categorised all non-Buddhist schools of thought as pāsaṇḍa "heresy" (pasanda means to throw a noose or pasha—stemming from the doctrine that schools labelled as Pasanda foster views perceived as wrong because they are seen as having a tendency towards binding and ensnaring rather than freeing the mind).

36.10.2 Buddhist Texts in Jain Libraries

According to Padmanabh Jaini, Vasudhara Dharani, a Buddhist work was among the Jainas of Gujarat in 1960s, and a manuscript was copied in 1638 CE. The Dharani was recited by non-Jain Brahmin priests in private Jain homes.

36.11 Similarities between Buddhism and Hinduism

36.11.1 Basic Vocabulary

The Buddha approved many of the terms already used in philosophical discussions of his era; however, many of these terms carry a different meaning in the Buddhist tradition. For example, in the Samaññaphala Sutta, the Buddha is depicted presenting a notion of the "three knowledges" (tevijja) – a term also used in the Vedic tradition to describe knowledge of the Vedas – as being not texts, but things that he had experienced. The true "three knowledges" are said to be constituted by the process of achieving enlightenment, which is what the Buddha is said to have achieved in the three watches of the night of his enlightenment.

36.11.2 Karma

Karma (Sanskrit: from the root kṛ, "to do") is a word meaning action or activity and often implies its subsequent results (also called karma-phala, "the fruits of action"). It is commonly understood as a term to denote the entire cycle of cause and effect as described in the philosophies of a number of cosmologies, including those of Buddhism and Hinduism.

Karma is a central part of Buddhist teachings. In Buddha's teaching, karma is a direct intentional result of a person's word, thought and/or action in life. In Buddhism a person's words, thoughts and/or actions form the basis for good and bad karma: sila (moral conduct) goes hand in hand with the development of meditation and wisdom. Buddhist teachings carry a markedly different meaning from pre-Buddhist conceptions of karma.

36.11.3 Dharma

Dharma (Sanskrit, or Pāli Dhamma) means natural law, reality or duty, and with respect to its significance for spirituality and religion might be considered the way of the higher truths. A Hindu appellation for Hinduism itself is Sanātana Dharma, which translates as "the eternal dharma." Similarly, Buddhadharma is an appellation for Buddhism. The general concept of dharma forms a basis for philosophies, beliefs and practices originating in India. The four main ones are Hinduism, Buddhism, Jainism (Jaina Dharma), and Sikhism (Sikha Dharma), all of whom retain the centrality of dharma in their teachings. In these traditions, beings that live in harmony with dharma proceed more quickly toward, according to the tradition, Dharma Yukam, Moksha, or Nirvana (personal liberation). Dharma can refer generally to religious duty, and also mean social order, right conduct, or simply virtue.

36.11.4 Buddha

The term "Buddha" too has appeared in Hindu scriptures such as the Vayu Purana, where, the sage Daksha calls Lord Shiva Buddha.

36.11.5 Similar symbolism

- **Mudra:** This is a symbolic hand-gesture expressing an emotion. Images of the Buddha almost always depict him performing some mudra.
- **Dharma Chakra:** The Dharma Chakra, which appears on the national flag of India and the flag of the Thai royal family, is a Buddhist symbol that is used by members of both religions.
- **Rudraksha:** These are beads which the devotees, usually monks, use for praying.
- **Tilak:** Many Hindu devotees mark their heads with a tilak, which is interpreted as a third eye. A similar mark is one of the characteristic physical characteristics of the Buddha.
- **Swastika and Sauwastika:** Both are sacred symbols. It can be either clockwise or counter-clockwise and both are seen in Hinduism and Buddhism. The Buddha is sometimes depicted with a sauwastika on his chest or the palms of his hands.

36.11.6 Similar Practices

Mantra

A mantra is a religious syllable or poem, typically from the Sanskrit and Pali language. Their use varies according to the school and philosophy associated with the mantra. They are primarily used as spiritual conduits, words or vibrations that instil one-pointed concentration in the devotee. Other purposes have included religious ceremonies to accumulate wealth, avoid danger, or eliminate enemies. Mantras existed in the historical Vedic religion, Zoroastrianism and the Shramanic traditions, and thus they remain important in Buddhism and Jainism as well as other faiths of Indian origin such as Sikhism.

Yoga

The practice of Yoga is intimately connected to the religious beliefs and practices of both Hinduism and Buddhism. However, there are distinct variations in the usage of yoga terminology in the two religions.

In Hinduism, the term "Yoga" commonly refers to the eight limbs of yoga as defined in the Yoga Sutras of Patanjali, written sometime after 100 BCE, and means "yoking", with the idea that one's individual atman, or soul, would yoke or bind with the monistic entity that underlies everything (brahman). Yoga defines a specific process: it has an emphasis on knowledge and practice. The most basic meaning of this Sanskrit term is with technique. The technique of the different forms of yoga is what makes the practice meaningful. Yoga is not an easy or simple practice, viyoga is what is described as simple. Yoga is difficult in the fact of displaying the faith and meaning of Hinduism. Many Hindus tend to pick and choose between the five forms of yoga because of the way they live their life and how they want to practice it in the form they are most connected to.

In the Vajrayana Buddhism of Tibet, however, the term "Yoga" is simply used to refer to any type of spiritual practice; from the various types of tantra (like Kriyayoga or Charyayoga) to 'Deity yoga' and 'Guru yoga'. In the early translation phase of the Sutrayana and Tantrayana from India, China and other regions to Tibet, along with the practice lineages of sadhana, codified in the Nyingmapa canon, the most subtle 'conveyance' (Sanskrit: yana) is Adi Yoga (Sanskrit). A contemporary scholar with a focus on Tibetan Buddhism, writes that Patanjali was influenced by the success of the Buddhist monastic system to formulate his own matrix for the version of thought he considered orthodox.

Meditation

There is a range of common terminology and common descriptions of the meditative states that are seen as the foundation of meditation practice in both Hindu Yoga and Buddhism. Many scholars have noted that the concepts of dhyana and samādhi - technical terms describing stages of meditative absorption – are common to meditative practices in both Hinduism and Buddhism. Most notable in this context is the relationship between the system of four Buddhist dhyana states (Pali: jhana) and the samprajnata samadhi states of Classical Yoga. Also, many (Tibetan) Vajrayana practices of the generation stage and completion stage work with the chakras, inner energy channels (nadis) and kundalini, called tummo in Tibetan.

36.12 Gautama Buddha in Hinduism

The Buddha has been a formative force in the origins of Hinduism. Regional Hindu texts over the centuries have presented a spectrum of views on Buddhism, possibly reflecting the competition between Buddhism and the Brahmanical traditions.

36.12.1 Avatar of Vishnu

In the Vaishnavite sect of Hinduism, the historic Buddha or Gautama Buddha, is the ninth avatar among the ten major avatars of the god Vishnu. In contemporary Hinduism the Buddha is revered by Hindus who usually consider "Buddhism to be another form of Hinduism".

The adoption of the Buddha in texts relating to Hindu gods, and of Hindu gods in Buddhist texts, is difficult to place chronologically. The myth of the Buddha avatar first appeared in the pre-Gupta period, when orthodox Brahminism was threatened by the success of Buddhism and Jainism, and by foreign invaders. Hindus came to regard the Buddha as an avatar of Vishnu between A.D. 450 and the sixth century, first appearing in the Vishnu Purana (400-500 CE). The replacement of the Buddha as the "cosmic person" within the mythic ideology of Indian kingship occurred at about the same time the Buddha was incorporated and subordinated within the Brahmanical cult of Vishnu.

The Buddha is mentioned as an avatar of Vishnu in the Puranas and the epics such as:

- Harivamsa,
- Vishnu Purana,
- Bhagavata Purana,
- Garuda Purana,
- Agni Purana,
- Naradiya Purana,
- Linga Purana, and
- Padma Purana.

Another important scripture that mentions him as an avatar is Parashara's Brihat Parashara Hora Shastra.

Buddha as an avatar of Vishnu is part of a cosmic cycle, in which the dharma is destroyed in the Kali Yuga, and then restored again in the Satya Yuga, when Vishnu incarnates as Kalki. The Bhavishya Purana incorporates historical facts about dynastical lineages, stating the following:

At this time, reminded of the Kali Age, the god Vishnu became born as Gautama, the Shakyamuni, and taught the Buddhist dharma for ten years. Then Shuddodana ruled for twenty years, and Shakyasimha for twenty. At the first stage of the Kali Age, the path of the Vedas was destroyed and all men became Buddhists. Those who sought refuge with Vishnu were deluded.

Some pre-13th-century Hindu texts, such as the Bhagavata Purana, portray the Buddha as born to lead the asuras, who oppressed the people, away from the Vedic rituals, which they were not worthy to perform. Bhagavata Purana 1.3.24:

Then, in the beginning of Kali-yuga, for the purpose of confusing the enemies of the devas, [he] will become the son of Anjana, Buddha by name, in the Kīkaṭas.

His father is usually called Śuddhodhana, which is consistent with the Buddhist tradition, while in a few places the Buddha's father is named Añjana or Jina. This is due to the fact that in some texts both Buddhism and Jainism are used by Vishnu to mislead the demons, and a confusion of names and doctrines appears, when the Buddha is called the son of Jina, mistakingly mimicking Buddhist texts which refer to the Buddha as Jina (conqueror), a term more often used in Jainism.

Some pre-14th-century Hindu temples include Buddha reliefs with the same reverence they show for other avatars of Vishnu, but though an avatar of Vishnu, the Buddha is rarely worshipped like Krishna and Rama in Hinduism.

36.13 Highlights of Similarities between Jainism and Hinduism

Jainism and Hinduism are two ancient Indian religions. There are some similarities and differences between the two religions. Temples, gods, rituals, fasts and other religious components of Jainism are different from those of Hinduism.

"Jain" is derived from the word Jina, referring to a human being who has conquered all inner passions (like anger, attachment, greed and pride) and possesses Kaivalyagyana (pure infinite knowledge). Followers of the path shown by the Jinas are called Jains. Followers of Brahma, Visnu and Rudra are called Hindus.

Some of the **Similarities** between Hinduism and Jainism are given below:

- Both Hinduism and Jainism believe in reincarnation, i.e. cycle of birth and death.
- Both Hinduism and Jainism believe in non-violence.
- Both Hinduism and Jainism emphasise on consuming a vegetarian diet.
- Both religions give importance to meditation.
- Followers of both religions celebrate festivals like Diwali.
- Both religions have the same concepts as Moksha, Samsara, Karma; although the precise meaning may be different.
- Both religions believe that violence for self-defence is permitted.

36.14 Rama in Jainism

Rama (Rāma), the hero of Ramayana, is described in the Jain scriptures as one of sixty-three illustrious persons, known as Salakapurusa. Among these, there are nine sets of Balabhadra, Vasudeva and Prati-Vasudeva. Rama was the 8th Balabhadra with Lakshmana and Ravana being his Vasudeva and Prati-Vasudeva counterparts. He is described as a young prince who is deprived of his throne and turned into a pauper. While living in exile his wife Sita is kidnapped by Ravana, King of Lanka. Rama then rescues Sita with the help of his brother Lakshmana and King Sugriva. Ravana is killed by Lakshmana (a deviation from the Hindu epic where Rama slays Ravana) and they both go into hell. Rama becomes a Jain monk and his soul attains moksha (liberation from the cycle of birth and death). Sita becomes a Jain nun and is born into heaven as Indra.

The story of Rama in Jainism can be broadly classified into three groups; Samghadasa's version, Vimalsuri's version and Gunabhadra's version.

36.14.1 Sanghadasa's Version

Sanghadasa's version presents only a brief account of Rama's story. [In this version, Dasharatha had three queens; Kaushalya, Kaikeyi and Sumitra. Rama was from Kaushalya, Lakshmana from Sumitra, Bharata and Satrughna from Kaikeyi.

Sita is said to be daughter of Ravana's queen Mandodari. It was predicted that the first child of Mandodari would bring annihilation to the family. Hence, Ravana deserted the child when she was born. The minister who was responsible for this took her in a pearl-box, placed her near a plough and told Janaka of Mithila that the girl is born from the trench. Janaka's queen Dharini became Sita's foster mother.

While in exile, Rama visited a place called Vijanasthana. Surpanakha was dumbstruck at the beauty of Rama and wanted to marry him. However, Rama refused to marry with another person's wife. He, in turn cut her ears and nose after she was scolded by Sita. Surpanakha complained about this to her brothers Khara-Dusana who was killed by Rama on their quest for revenge. Surpanakha then goes to her brother Ravana.

36.14.2 Vimalasuri's Version

Vimalasuri's version is one of the most important and influential Jain stories of Rama. Vimalasuri claims that the Ramayana of Valmiki is filled with illogical and false stories. In his version, Kaikeyi is shown to be a generous and affectionate mother who wanted to stop Bharata from becoming a monk. To do so, she wanted to give him the responsibility of a king. When Rama knew about it, he willingly went into exile. Ravana was also called Dasamukha (ten-headed one) because when he was young, his mother gave him a necklace made of nine pearls. She could see his face reflected ninefold. Hence, he was named thus. In Vimalsuri's Paumachariya, Rama married thrice when he was in exile. His brother Lakshmana married eleven times. Ravana was well known for his abilities in meditation and ascetic practices. He was the king of Rakshasa, a kingdom of civilised and vegetarian people. Sugriva was appointed by his brother Vali to become the king before Vali renounces the world and becomes a Jain monk. Shambuka was accidentally killed by Lakshmana. Ravana had passionate feelings for Sita. Due to the effects of karma (caused because of this vice), he was said to have suffered at the end. Rama's brother Lakshmana kills Ravana. Both Ravana and Lakshmana go to hell for their actions whereas Rama attains moksha (liberation). The vanaras were humans, belonging to a dynasty or clan which has a monkey as their emblem. There are many arguments to which variant is actually authentic.

36.14.3 Gunabhadra's Version

In the story of Gunabhadra, Dasharatha lived in Varanasi. His queen Subala gave birth to Rama and Kaikeyi gave birth to Lakshmana.[21] Sita was born of Ravana and Mandodari. She was subsequently abandoned by Ravana in a place where Janaka was ploughing the field...

Some of the later works which mention the story of Rama are:

- Ramayana of Jinadasa (c. 15th century CE);
- Ramacharitra of Padmadevavijaya Gani (c. 16th century CE);

- Ramacharitra of Somadeva Suri (c. 16th century CE);
- Laghu-Trishashtisalakapurusha Charitra of Somaprabha (c. 15th century CE);
- Padmapurana of Raidhu in Apbhramsha (c. 15th century CE);
- Padma-Ramayana of Nagchandra in Kannada (c. 11th century CE);
- Ramacharita of Devavijayaganir (c. 1596 CE); and
- Laghu-Trishashtisakalapurusha Charitra of Meghvijaya (c. 17th century CE).

36.15 Krishna's Influence on Jainism

Despite their rich theological tradition, Jains could not overlook Krishna's grand persona and assigned him equal status next to that of the Tirthankara.

Shri Krishna cast a magic spell over the minds of innumerable people from all parts of the world, belonging to many creeds and castes, who find themselves impressed with one or the other feature of his magnificent persona and character. In the same strain, the Jains in India were fascinated with Krishna's grand persona, so much so that they recast the Pauranic account of Krishna saga in their own way, as befitting their ideologies. In this context, it seems pertinent to note that in India, religious tradition flows through three major streams of thought — the Vedic or Pauranic, Buddhist, and Jainism.

The latter two streams of thought, however, originated and developed in India outside the pale of Pauranic tradition, but their main aim was confined to delineating and elaborating the theology and mythology surrounding popular Indian deities, such as Shri Krishna or Shri Rama, with the help of assigning different features in their personae character as suitable to their ideals. While pointing out three point of views on Krishna and His interaction with the Jains, let's not lose sight of the fact that from the very beginning, in India they emerged as an important section of Indian society and 8th century BC onwards have contributed a good deal of thought material of Indian civilisation, which is considered a substantial and genuine tradition of the Indian nation.

Similarly, the Jain tradition on Krishna holds great importance for understanding the arch-type of Krishna concept. It is found that the Jains not only included the Krishna concept within their religious fold, but also some other cults and beliefs in their own sect. According to some, the Jains were averse to the encounters of pastoral Krishna, for they hardly talk about it, rather, they relish talking about the oldest tradition on Krishna, which hails him as the Lord of Dwarka and not Gopala Krishna. Further for knowing the Jain tradition on Krishna, the Jain work such as Jaina Harivansha and other Puranic works have to be traversed. These Jain works describe in detail the achievements of Krishna and name him not Krishna but Vasudeva, as is the common practice with the Bhagavatas.

Similarly, the Jains' other descriptions of Krishna's forefathers, Yadavas, and his last days on Earth are in agreement with those of the Puranas, likewise, most of the childhood encounters of Krishna almost find similar versions in the Jain sources. For instance, the Jains also treat Baladeva or Balaram as Krishna's brother and helpmate. The Jains, however, preserve different lists of Krishna's ancestors and descendants. Besides this, even distorted version of Krishna's exploits as given in the Mahabharata and the Puranas is traceable in the Jain sources. According to the Jains, Jarasamdha's killer is Krishna and not the Pandava brother Bhima; Krishna used to remain disgusted with the Pandavas and for that reason they were forced by him to leave Hastinapur and made to settle far off in south. The Jain sources similarly speak differently about Krishna's killer, who was an anonymous fowler according to the Puranas, but according to the Jains, he was Jarakumar or Jarakumar and happened to be Krishna's half-brother and a Yadava prince like him. Here it seems that the idea of an anonymous hunter killing a God could not be acceptable to the Jains, so they invented an idea of the killer of Krishna of equal royal rank and status as that of Krishna. Besides Balarama, Krishna's other nine brothers are referred to by the Jains along with their father, who is named as Andhaka-Vrishni.

With this general note on the transference and innovations in Krishna's personae by the Jains, it may be added that the Jains have provided us a peculiar type of information on Krishna tradition with which they became conversant and fascinated. So much so that they could not desist themselves from including Krishna and his brother among their 63 great personages of the era whom they cherish with great respect and honour. Shri Krishna finds the last position in their list of great personages, whom they call "Shalaka Purushas". They know him as Vasudeva Keshava, the son of Vasudeva. Besides, in Jain tradition, Krishna's 10 forms or incarnations are also popular along with the notions of cowherd Krishna in passing. Moreover, it is interesting to note that the Jains not only agree upon treating their first Tirthankara as Lord Vishnu's great avatara, but even recast the biography of the 22nd Tirthankara Arishtanemi on the pattern of Krishna Saga and declared him as the famous prince of Krishna's Yadava clan and as being related to him as his cousin. The Jains also treat Krishna's Preceptor Ghorangirasa as in the Bhagavata tradition on Krishna.

As a preacher of Gita, Krishna finds a cherished position in the Jain tradition. Among other features of the Jain tradition on Krishna, His role as the Lord of Dwarka or Raivataka is most endearing to the Jains. They abstain from associating Krishna with Mathura and Vrindavan and neither cherish him as Bala Krishna or Gopala Krishna, rather are fond of calling him by the title "destroyer of the vanity of many powerful and proud ones like the wrestlers Charura and Kamsa". The Jains also admire Krishna as the destroyer of Putana, Shakuni bird, vicious bull, and Kaliya.

With regard to the other features of Jain ideology and notion on Krishna, it may be also stated that as they have included Shri Krishna among their 63 personages of high honour, it proves that they look upon him as the great and noble Kshatriya prince, who according to them, was a representative of the ninth black Vasudeva and always accompanied with white Vasudeva who was Baladeva. The Vasudevas, in alliance with the Baladevas, who are also held by the Jains to succeed overpowering the Vishnudvishas who in Krishna's case is Jarasamdha and not Kansa. The Jains also know Krishna as having multitude wives numbering 16,000. The Jains also know Krishna as the son of Vasudeva, who had two wives Devaki and Rohini. Besides Baladeva or Balarama Krishna is said to have another younger brother, Gajasukumar.

Summing up the Jain tradition on Krishna, it can be ascertained that assigning him the role of the ninth Vasudeva and one of the 63 Shalka Purushas, the Jains — although having their rich theological tradition — could not overlook Shri Krishna's manifold personae-features so much so that they included him among their great persons who were worthy of their worship and honour, and also assigned him equal status next to that of the Tirthankara. This Jain contribution towards Krishna concept goes to prove that Krishna's appeal was not only confined to the followers of the Vedic-Brahmanic tradition, but spread beyond among the non-Brahmanic believers and devotees belonging to other schools of thought and discipline like the Jains or others. Besides accepting Krishna as one of the nine Vasudevas, the Jains liberally extend their support to the view which accepts Krishna as belonging to the status of the great chieftains of the age, and one who had obtained supreme glory and was very kind-hearted.

Chapter - 37

Differences between Hindu, Buddhist and Jain Philosophies

37.1 Differences between Hinduism and Buddhism

37.1.1 Founders

The founders of Hinduism and Buddhism are both unlike most major religions. Hinduism has no single founder. It grew out of the overlapping beliefs of the diverse groups who settled in India. The founder of Buddhism was Prince Siddhartha Gautama, a Śramaṇa who subsequently became the Buddha (the enlightened).

37.1.2 God

Gautama Buddha was very ambiguous about the existence of an ultimate reality (Brahman), creator deity (Ishwara) and eternal self (Atman) and rejected them both. Various sources from the Pali Canon and others suggest that the Buddha taught that belief in a Creator deity was not essential to attaining liberation from suffering, and perhaps chose to ignore the theological questions because they were "fascinating to discuss," and frequently brought about more conflict and anger than peace. The Buddha did not deny the existence of the popular gods of the Vedic pantheon, but rather argued that these devas, who may be in a more exalted state than humans, are still nevertheless trapped in the same Samsaric cycle of suffering as other beings and are not necessarily worthy of veneration and worship. The focus of the Noble Eightfold Path, while inheriting many practices and ideologies from the previous Hindu yogic tradition, deviates from the teachings of the Bhagavad Gita and earlier works of the Dharmic Religions in that liberation (Nirvana or Moksha) is not attained via unity with Brahman (the Godhead), self-realisation or worship. Rather, the Buddha's teaching centres around "psychology of desire," that is attaining liberation from suffering by extermination of self-will, selfish desire and passions. This is not to say that such teachings are absent from the previous Hindu tradition, rather they are singled out and separated from Vedic Theology.

The early Buddhist Nikaya literature treats the question of the existence of a creator god "primarily from either an epistemological point of view or a moral point of view". In these texts the Buddha is portrayed not as a creator-denying atheist who claims to be able to prove such a god's nonexistence, but rather his focus is other teachers' claims that their teachings lead to the highest good. The Devadaha Sutta (Majjhima Nikaya 101) states that "while the reader is left to conclude that it is attachment rather than god, actions in past lives, fate, type of birth or efforts in this life that is responsible for our experiences of sorrow, no systematic argument is given in an attempt to disprove the existence of God."

The Buddha (as portrayed in the Pali scriptures, the agamas) set an important trend in nontheism in Buddhism by establishing a somewhat non-theistic view on the notion of an omnipotent god, generally ignoring the issue as being irrelevant to his teachings. Nevertheless, in many passages in the Tripitaka gods (devas in Sanskrit) are mentioned and specific examples are given of individuals who were reborn as a god, or gods who were reborn as humans. Buddhist cosmology recognises various levels and types of gods, but none of these gods is considered the creator of the world or of the human race.

Buddha preaches that attachment with people was the cause of sorrow when 'death' happens and therefore proposes detachment from people. Hinduism though proposes detachment from fruits of action and stresses on performance of duty or dharma, it is not solely focused on it. In Hinduism, Lord Shiva explains 'death' to be journey of the immortal soul in pursuit of 'Moksha' and therefore a fact of life.

While Buddhism says retirement into forest was open to everyone regardless of caste, and although according to the vinaya (the code of conduct for the Sangha) it is not possible to take ordination as a Buddhist mendicant (a Bhikkhu or Bhikkhuni) under the age of 20 or adulthood, this is still viewed as escapism by Hinduism. Pre-Buddhist, non-brahman forest mendicants are criticised in the earliest group of Upanishads. Hinduism allows for this to happen only after performing all dharmas or duties of one's life, starting from studying scriptures, working to support children and family and taking care of aged parents and lastly after all the dharma done retire to the forest and slowly meditate, fast and perform rituals and austerities (tapas), until physical disintegration, and to reach the ultimate truth or Brahman. Buddhism by contrast emphasises realisation by the middle way (avoiding extremes of luxury or austerities), seeing limited value in the rituals and tapas and the danger of their mis-application.

Buddhism explains that attachment is the cause of sorrow in society. Therefore, Buddhism's cure for sorrow was detachment and non-involvement (non-action or negative action). Hinduism on the other hand explained that both sorrow or happiness is due to 'Karma' or past actions and bad karma can be overcome and good karma can be obtained by following dharma or righteous duty (pro-action or positive action) which will ultimately provide 'Moksha' i.e. overcoming the cycle of life and joining Brahman.

Buddhist canonical views about god and the priests are:

Well then, Vasettha, those ancient sages versed in ancient scriptures, the authors of the verses, the utterers of the verses, whose, ancient form of words so chanted, uttered, or composed, the priests of today chant over again or repeat; intoning or reciting exactly as has been intoned or recited-to wit, Atthaka, Vamaka, Vamadeva, Vessamitta, Yamataggi, Angirasa, Bharadvaja, Vasettha, Kassapa, and Bhagu – did even they speak thus, saying: "We know it, we have seen it", where the creator is whence the creator is?

The man depends on god "for his own protection, safety, and security, just as a child depends on his parent." He describes this as a product of "ignorance, weakness, fear, and desire," and writes that this "deeply and fanatically held belief" for man's consolation is "false and empty" from the perspective of Buddhism. The man does not wish to hear or understand teachings against this belief, and that the Buddha described his teachings as "against the current" for this reason. For self-protection the man created god and for self-preservation man created "soul".

In later Mahayana literature, however, the idea of an eternal, all-pervading, all-knowing, immaculate, uncreated and deathless Ground of Being (the dharmadhatu, inherently linked to the sattvadhatu, the realm of beings), which is the Awakened Mind (bodhicitta) or Dharmakaya ("body of Truth") of the Buddha himself, is attributed to the Buddha in a number of Mahayana sutras, and is found in various tantras as well. In some Mahayana texts, such a principle is occasionally presented as manifesting in a more personalised form as a primordial buddha, such as Samantabhadra, Vajradhara, Vairochana, Amitabha and Adi-Buddha, among others.

37.1.3 Caste

The Buddha repudiated the caste distinctions of the Brahmanical religion, by offering ordination to all regardless of caste.

While the caste system constitutes an assumed background to the stories told in Buddhist scriptures, the sutras do not attempt to justify or explain the system. In Aggañña Sutta, Buddha elaborates that if any of the caste does the following deeds: killing, taking anything which is not given, take part in sexual misconduct, lying, slandering, speaking rough words or nonsense, greedy, cruel, and practice wrong beliefs; people would still see that they do negative deeds and therefore are not worthy or deserving respect. They will even get into trouble from their own deeds, whatever their caste (Brahmin, Khattiya, Vessa, and Sudda) might be.

37.1.4 Cosmology and worldview

In Buddhist cosmology, there are 31 planes of existence within samsara. Beings in these realms are subject to rebirth after some period of time, except for realms of the Non-Returners. Therefore, most of these places are not the goal of the holy life in the Buddha's dispensation. Buddhas are beyond all these 31 planes of existence after parinibbana. Hindu texts mostly mentions the devas in Kamma Loka. Only the Hindu god Brahma can be found in the Rupa loka. There are many realms above Brahma realm that are accessible through meditation. Those in Brahma realm are also subject to rebirth according to the Buddha.

37.1.5 Practices

To have an idea of the differences between Buddhism and pre-existing beliefs and practices during this time, we can look into the Samaññaphala Sutta in the Digha Nikaya of the Pali Canon. In this sutra, a king of Magadha listed the teachings from many prominent and famous spiritual teachers around during that time. He also asked the Buddha about his teaching when visiting him. The Buddha told the king about the practices of his spiritual path. The list of various practices he taught disciples as well as practices he doesn't encourage are listed. The text, rather than stating what the new faith was, emphasized what the new faith was not. Contemporaneous religious traditions were caricatured and then negated. Though critical of prevailing religious practices and social institutions on philosophical grounds, early Buddhist texts exhibit a reactionary anxiety at having to compete in religiously plural societies. Below are a few examples found in the sutra:

- Whereas some priests and contemplatives... are addicted to high and luxurious furnishings such as these — over-sized couches, couches adorned with carved animals, long-haired coverlets, multi-coloured patchwork coverlets, white woolen coverlets, woolen coverlets embroidered with flowers or animal figures, stuffed quilts, coverlets with fringe, silk coverlets embroidered with gems; large woollen carpets; elephant, horse, and chariot rugs, antelope-hide rugs, deer-hide rugs; couches with awnings, couches with red cushions for the head and feet — he (a bhikkhu disciple of the Buddha) abstains from using high and luxurious furnishings such as these.

- Whereas some priests and contemplatives... are addicted to scents, cosmetics, and means of beautification such as these — rubbing powders into the body, massaging with oils, bathing in perfumed water, kneading the limbs, using mirrors, ointments, garlands, scents, ... bracelets, head-bands, decorated walking sticks... fancy sunshades, decorated sandals, turbans, gems, yak-tail whisks, long-fringed white robes — he abstains from ... means of beautification such as these.
- Whereas some priests and contemplatives... are addicted to talking about lowly topics such as these — talking about kings, robbers, ministers of state; armies, alarms, and battles; food and drink; clothing, furniture, garlands, and scents; relatives; vehicles; villages, towns, cities, the countryside; women and heroes; the gossip of the street and the well; tales of the dead; tales of diversity [philosophical discussions of the past and future], the creation of the world and of the sea, and talk of whether things exist or not, he abstains from talking about lowly topics such as these...
- Whereas some priests and contemplatives...are addicted to running messages and errands for people such as these — kings, ministers of state, noble warriors, priests, householders, or youths [who say], 'Go here, go there, take this there, fetch that here' — he abstains from running messages and errands for people such as these.
- Whereas some priests and contemplatives...engage in scheming, persuading, hinting, belittling, and pursuing gain with gain, he abstains from forms of scheming and persuading [improper ways of trying to gain material support from donors] such as these. "Whereas some priests and contemplatives...maintain themselves by wrong livelihood, by such lowly arts as: reading marks on the limbs [e.g., palmistry]; reading omens and signs; interpreting celestial events [falling stars, comets]; interpreting dreams; reading marks on the body [e.g., phrenology]; reading marks on cloth gnawed by mice; offering fire oblations, oblations from a ladle, oblations of husks, rice powder, rice grains, ghee, and oil; offering

oblations from the mouth; offering blood-sacrifices; making predictions based on the fingertips; geomancy; laying demons in a cemetery; placing spells on spirits; reciting house-protection charms; snake charming, poison-lore, scorpion-lore, rat-lore, bird-lore, crow-lore; fortune-telling based on visions; giving protective charms; interpreting the calls of birds and animals — he abstains from wrong livelihood, from lowly arts such as these.

- Whereas some priests and contemplatives...maintain themselves by wrong livelihood, by such lowly arts as: determining lucky and unlucky gems, garments, staffs, swords, spears, arrows, bows, and other weapons; women, boys, girls, male slaves, female slaves; elephants, horses, buffaloes, bulls, cows, goats, rams, fowl, quails, lizards, long-eared rodents, tortoises, and other animals — he abstains from wrong livelihood, from lowly arts such as these.
- Whereas some priests and contemplatives... maintain themselves by wrong livelihood, by such lowly arts as forecasting: the rulers will march forth; the rulers will march forth and return; our rulers will attack, and their rulers will retreat; their rulers will attack, and our rulers will retreat; there will be triumph for our rulers and defeat for their rulers; there will be triumph for their rulers and defeat for our rulers; thus there will be triumph, thus there will be defeat — he abstains from wrong livelihood, from lowly arts such as these. Whereas some priests and contemplatives...maintain themselves by wrong livelihood, by such lowly arts as forecasting: there will be a lunar eclipse; there will be a solar eclipse; there will be an occultation of an asterism; the sun and moon will go their normal courses; the sun and moon will go astray; the asterisms will go their normal courses; the asterisms will go astray; there will be a meteor shower; there will be a darkening of the sky; there will be an earthquake; there will be thunder coming from a clear sky; there will be a rising, a setting, a darkening, a brightening of the sun, moon, and asterisms; such will be the result of the lunar eclipse... the rising, setting, darkening, brightening of the sun, moon, and asterisms — he abstains from wrong livelihood, from lowly arts such as these.
- Whereas some priests and contemplatives...maintain themselves by wrong livelihood, by such lowly arts as forecasting: there will be abundant rain; there will be a drought; there will be plenty; there will be famine; there will be rest and security; there will be danger; there will be disease; there will be freedom from disease; or they earn their living by counting, accounting, calculation,

composing poetry, or teaching hedonistic arts and doctrines — he abstains from wrong livelihood, from lowly arts such as these.

- Whereas some priests and contemplatives...maintain themselves by wrong livelihood, by such lowly arts as: calculating auspicious dates for marriages, betrothals, divorces; for collecting debts or making investments and loans; for being attractive or unattractive; curing women who have undergone miscarriages or abortions; reciting spells to bind a man's tongue, to paralyze his jaws, to make him lose control over his hands, or to bring on deafness; getting oracular answers to questions addressed to a mirror, to a young girl, or to a spirit medium; **worshipping the sun, worshipping the Great Brahma**, bringing forth flames from the mouth, invoking the goddess of luck — he abstains from wrong livelihood, from lowly arts such as these.
- Whereas some priests and contemplatives...maintain themselves by wrong livelihood, by such lowly arts as: promising gifts to devas in return for favours; fulfilling such promises; demonology; teaching house-protection spells; inducing virility and impotence; consecrating sites for construction; giving ceremonial mouthwashes and ceremonial bathing; offering sacrificial fires; administering emetics, purges, purges from above, purges from below, head-purges; administering ear-oil, eye-drops, treatments through the nose, ointments, and counter-ointments; practicing eye-surgery (or: extractive surgery), general surgery, pediatrics; administering root-medicines binding medicinal herbs — he abstains from wrong livelihood, from lowly arts such as these.

37.2 Highlights of Differences between Hinduism and Buddhism

Buddhism has a variety of traditions, beliefs and spiritual practices based on teachings of Buddha. Hinduism has been called the oldest religion in the world; many practitioners refer to it as "the eternal way". The differences between Buddhism vs Hinduism given here can help in understanding the basics better, and know their comparisons and similarities thoroughly.

The major differences between Buddhism and Hinduism are:

As per Buddhism, one can reach Nirvana or enlightenment by following the Noble eightfold path. As per Hinduism, one can reach enlightenment by following the path of good deeds, path of devotion and path of knowledge.

- The places of worship of Buddhists are known as Buddhist monasteries, shrines, temples. The places of worship of Hindus are known as Temples.

- Buddha is the founder of Buddhism. Buddhists consider Buddha as the all-transcending sage and highest teacher. Among some sections of Hindus, they consider Buddha as the 9th avatar of Vishnu.
- Tibetan Buddhism has a foremost Spiritual Leader. The title given to the foremost spiritual leader is the Dalai Lama. Dalai Lama is the title given by Tibetan people to the supreme spiritual leader of Yellow Hat or Gelug school of Tibetan Buddhism. Hinduism does not have a concept of having the foremost Spiritual Leader.
- In Buddhism Male Monks are known as Bhikkhus and Female Monks are known as Bhikkhunis. The Monastic Communities in Buddhism are known as Sangha. In Hinduism male monks are known as Yogis, Sages, Rishis, Gurus, Priests, and female monks are known as Sanyasini, sadhvi, swamini.
- The 2 major branches of Buddhism are Hinayana (Theravada) and Mahayana. The 4 largest denominations of Hinduism are Shaktism, Shaivism, Vaishnavism and Smartism.
- The primary language used by Theravada tradition was the Pali language. The primary language used by Mahayana and Vajrayana traditions is Sanskrit. Sanskrit is the primary sacred language of Hinduism. Most of the works of Hindu Philosophy were written in Sanskrit language.
- Some of the most important festivals of Buddhists are Vesak (Buddha's birthday), Parinirvana Day (also known as Nirvana day), Buddha Purnima, Ullambana, Uposatha, Losar (celebrated by Tibetan Buddhists) etc. Holy Days in Hinduism are plenty. There are many important days for worshipping different Gods, some of the most important holy days are Ganesh Chaturthi, Mahashivaratri, Ram Navami, Krishna Janmashtami, Navaratri, Durga Puja etc.
- Some of the most important scriptures are Tripitaka and Gandhara Texts. Tripitaka are composed of 3 sections: Commentaries, Discipline and Discourses. Some of the most important scriptures of Hinduism are Vedas, Bhagavad Gita, Ramayana, Upanishads, Puranas.
- Some of the most important symbols in Buddhism are Conch, Dharmachakra – it is a wheel of dharma, fish, lotus, vase, victory banner, parasol etc. Some of the most important symbols of Hinduism are Om, Swastika etc.

- Buddhism does impart advice on how to maintain a cordial and happy married life. However, Buddhism does not treat marriage as a religious duty. Buddhist monks and nuns follow celibacy all their lives. As per Hinduism, man can marry once. However, in ancient India and in Mythologies there are cases of a man having multiple wives.
- Buddhism does not have a concept of sin. In Hinduism, sins committed deliberately will have to be repaid through Karmic consequences. However, repentance for unintentional sins have been prescribed.
- Vedas were rejected by Buddha as per the dialogues given in Nikayas. In Hinduism, Vedas are considered as very important.
- The Goal of Buddhism is to bring lasting, unconditional happiness. the Goal of Hinduism is freedom from the cycle of birth and rebirth; and ultimately attain moksha or liberation from birth and rebirth.

37.3 Differences between Hinduism and Jainism

- Hinduism believes the Universe was created by Brahma, the creator. Jainism does not believe that the universe was created by one God Brahma, rather Jainism believes the Universe itself is eternal and powerful. Jainism believes it was never created as it is eternal.
- As per Hinduism, Soul was separated from Supreme Soul (Parmatma) and the main purpose of life is to attain moksha i.e. merger of Soul back into the supreme soul. As per Jainism, every soul itself is supreme Soul, hence the objective of life is to separate the soul from bad karma (sinful actions) and attain moksha.
- Hinduism also believes in non-violence, however, if violence is absolutely necessary to achieve victory over evil, then it is permitted, Mahabharata or Ramayana are good examples. Jainism does not believe in violence; it strongly believes only in non-violence.
- The 4 largest denominations of Hinduism are Shaktism, Shaivism, Vaishnavism and Smartism. The 2 important sects of Jainism are Svetambara and Digambara.
- Holy Days in Hinduism are plenty. There are many important days for worshipping different Gods, some of the most important holy days are Ganesh Chaturthi, Mahashivaratri, Ram Navami,

Krishna Janmashtami, Navaratri, Durga Puja etc. one of the most important Jain festivals are Paryushana, Mahavira Janma Kalayanak, Ashtanhika Parv, Nandishwar Ashtanika, Maun agiyaras, Mahamastabhisheka etc.

- In Hinduism many Gods are worshipped, most prominent are Ganapathi, Shiva, Vishnu, Lakshmi, Saraswati, Parvati, Hanuman, Kartikeya etc. In Jainism, 24 Tirthankars, besides some celestial beings are worshipped as Demigods. Mahavira was the 24th Thirthankara of Jainism.
- Hinduism has different castes and classes. In Jainism, there is no division of followers on the basis of castes and classes.
- In Hinduism, one can find people strictly following vegetarian diets as well people who consume non-vegetarian diets. In Jainism, it is strictly forbidden from having non-vegetarian diets including eggs.
- In Hinduism Vedas, Upanishads, Smritis etc. are considered sacred. In Jainism, Vedas and other religious books of Hinduism are not accepted. Jainism has its own sacred scriptures like Agamas and Sutras.
- In Hinduism, animal sacrifices were mostly associated with Shaktism, animal sacrifices were done in ancient times, however, Puranas and Gita forbid animal sacrifice. Animal sacrifices are strictly forbidden in Jainism.
- Hinduism has 4 stages of life: Brahmacharya (student life), Grihastha Ashram (house-holders life), Vanaprastha Ashram (searching for truth), and the final stage Sanyasa Ashram. As per Hinduism Spirituality must be pursued in the last 2 stages of human life. One has to follow Dharma at all stages, but focus on salvation is at the last 2 stages. Jainism does not have different stages of human life; the main focus of entire life is to attain liberation and must be strictly spiritual.

37.4 Differences between Jainism and Buddhism

Jainism has developed and refined the non-violence ('Ahimsa) doctrine to an extraordinary degree where it is an integral part of the Jain culture. Jain vegetarianism, for example, is driven by the principle of not harming any animals and both lay and mendicants are predominantly vegetarian. In Buddhism, Mahayana monks in China, Japan, Korea and Vietnam are vegetarian; however, vegetarianism is not required for lay Buddhists.

In Theravada monastic tradition, a monk should eat whatever is placed in his bowl when receiving food.

Although both Buddhists and Jain had orders of nuns, Buddhist Pali texts record the Buddha saying that a woman has the ability to obtain nirvana in the dharma and Vinaya. According to Digambara Jains, women are capable of spiritual progress but must be reborn as a man in order to attain final spiritual liberation. The religious texts of the Śvētāmbaras mention that liberation is attainable by both men and women.

The Anekantavada doctrine is another key difference between Jainism and Buddhism. The Buddha taught the Middle Way, rejecting extremes of the answer "it is" or "it is not" to metaphysical questions. The Mahavira, in contrast, accepted both "it is" and "it is not", with "perhaps" qualification and with reconciliation.

Jainism discourages monks and nuns from staying in a single place for a long time, with the exception of 4 months in the rainy season (chaturmas). Thus, most of the time the Jain monks and nuns keep wandering, staying in a place for just a few days. Some Theravada Buddhist monks also observe vassa rules, but often they stay in one monastery.

37.5 Highlights of Differences between Jainism and Buddhism

- Rebirth is one of the principal beliefs in Buddhism. It is thought that the endless cycle of birth and re-birth can only be broken by attaining Nirvana (Enlightenment). Jainism believes that the circle of rebirths and deaths will continue due to good or bad deeds until liberation is achieved.
- Scriptures in Buddhism include Tripitaka, which is a vast text consisting of 3 sections: the Discipline, the Discourse and the Commentaries. Main religious texts are called Agamas.
- The principal teaching of Buddhism is that life is suffering and to escape suffering (end cause of desire) one needs to dispel ignorance by realising the Four Noble Truths and practicing the Eightfold Path. Jainism lays emphasis on the respect of all living beings. Liberation from the cycle of rebirths is attained by taking the Five Vows and following the principles of the Three Jewels.
- Sin is not a concept in Buddhism. Sin is defined as harm to others.
- Buddhism is divided into two major sects upon the death of Gautama Buddha. They are the Mahayana and the Theravada. Svetambara and Digambara are the two major sects of Jainism.

- According to some texts in Buddhism, there are beings in heaven but they are bound by “samsara”. They suffer less but they have, not yet achieved salvation. Deities in Jainism are known as “Tirthankaras”. But they are not worshipped in the conventional sense as they are regarded as wise teachers whose teachings must be followed.
- Buddhism was founded in modern-day by Prince Siddhartha (Gautama the Buddha) in the 6th century B.C. Scholars of religion generally hold that Jainism originated in the 7th–5th century BC in Northern India. Mahavira, also known as Vardhamana was the 24th Tirthankara (Spiritual Teacher) of Jainism.
- Buddhism denies the concept of self (jiva) or soul (atman), proposing the concept of no-self (anatta). Whereas Jains believe in the existence of an eternal Jiva (soul).

Bibliography

Adi Sankaracharya's Vivekachudamani, Translated by Swami Madhavananda, Advaita Ashram, Kolkata.

Adi Shankaracharya, "Atma Bodha" (First Publication and English Translation by J. Taylor).

Banerji, Shri Chandra. "Sankhya Philosophy". Hare Press, Calcutta.

Bernard, Theos. "Hindu Philosophy", Philosophical Library, New York, 1947.

Bhavanani, Yogacharya Dr. Ananda Balayogi. "Yoga Sutras of Patanjali: An Overview", : https://www.researchgate.net/publication/241276720

Sri Swami Sivananda, "Bhagavad Gita", Divine Life Society Publication, 2000.

Bilimoria, Purushottama. "Nyaya and Navyanyaya", https://www.researchgate.net/publication/306259158

Bomhard, Allan, "The Original Teachings of the Buddha", https://www.researchgate.net/publication/337707221

Buddhrakkhita, Acharya, "The Dhammapada: The Buddha's Path of Wisdom", Buddhist Publication Society, 1985.

Bukkyo Dendo Kyokai, "The Teaching of Buddha: Wheel of Dharma", 2005.

Chakraborty, Anita (Goswami), "Significance of Vedanta in Modern Indian Thought". PH.D. Thesis submitted to the University of North Bengal, 2002. Chapter · January 2012 https://www.researchgate.net/publication/278665173

Dalai Lama, and Howard C. Cutler, "The Art of Happiness" : A Handbook for Living", 10th Edition, Riverhead Books, 2009.

Datta, Dr. Palto and Mark T Jones. "Karma yoga, its origins, fundamentals and seven life constructs", International Journal of Hinduism & Philosophy (IJHP), 15 Nov 2019, pp. 11-23.

Dudeja, Jai Paul. "An Overview of Primordial, Apaurusheya, Perennial, Universal 'OM' Mantra and Its Scientific Analysis", International Journal of Current Trends in Science and Technology, (ISSN: 0976-9730), Vol. 7, Issue. 9, Sep 2017, pp 20370-20390.

Gokhale, Sarah, "Empty Selves: A Comparative Analysis of Mahayana Buddhism, Jean-Paul Sartre's Existentialism, and Depth Psychology", B.A. Thesis, Wesleyan University, 2013.

Inagaki, Hisao. "The Three Pure Land Sutras", Numata Center for Buddhist Translation and Research, 2003.

Indian Philosophy, School of Inter-Disciplinary and Trans-Disciplinary Studies, Indira Gandhi National Open University, New Delhi, BPYC-131, 2020.

Keith, A. Berriedale. "The Samkhya System", Association Press, 2016.

Lopez, Donald (Ed.), "Buddhist Scriptures", Penguin Books, 2004.

Naicker, Suren, "On the neo-Vedanta as reconceptualised by Vivekananda in his Complete Works: A cognitive linguistic analysis in light of Conceptual Metaphor Theory", Journal of Literary Criticism, Comparative Linguistics and Literary Studies ISSN: (Online) 2219-8237, (Print) 0258-2279.

Nath, Nabaprasad. "Samkhya philosophy of Prakrti an appraisal of samkhya karika of Isvarakrsna", Ph.D. Thesis, Gauhati University, 2009.

Paramahamsa, K. R. "Dvaita Vedanta: Madhva's Vaisnava Theism", Tirumala Tirupati Devasthanams, Tirupati; 2012.

Paramahamsa, K. R. "Visistadvaita: A Philosophy of Religion", Tirumala Tirupati Devasthanams, Tirupati; 2010.

Pathak, Surendra, "Adi Shankaracharya: Contributions and Influences on Sanatana Dharma and Indian Culture", https://www.researchgate.net/publication/303408886

Patriarch, Supreme, "The Jogye Order's Doctrine" Ed by Headquarters of the Jogye Order of Korean Buddhism. Seoul: Jogye Order of Korean Buddhism. 2010.

Powers, John, "Introduction to Tibetan Buddhism", Snow Line Publications, Second Edition, 2007.

Pradhan, Rajat Kumar. "Particle Physics and the Vaisheshika System: A Comparative Analysis", https://www.researchgate.net/publication/281863959

Srinivasachari, P. N. "The Philosophy of Bhedabheda", The Adyar Library, 1950.

Radhakrishnan, S. (Translator), "The Brahma Sutra: The Philosophy of Spiritual Life", George Allen & Unwin Ltd., 1960.

Saksena, Shri Krishna. "Essays on Indian Philosophy", University of Hawaii Press, 1970.

Satchidananda, Murty, K. "Revelation and Reason in Advaita Vedanta", Asia Publishing House, 1959.

Saucier, Melanie. "Worldly and Other-Worldly Ethics: The Nonhuman and Its Relationship to the Meaningful World of Jains", M.A. Dissertation, University of Ottawa, 2012.

Sinha, Nandalal. "The Samkhya Philosophy", Sudhindra Natha Vasu, The Panini Office, Bhuvnesswari Asrama, Bahadurgsnj (Bllababat), 1915.

Sooklal, Anil, "The Neo-Vedanta Philosophy of Swami Vivekananda", 1SSN 1016-5320 - Nidiin. 5. 1993.

Spogli, Freeman, "Introduction of Buddhism to Korea: An Overview" Spice Digest, Fall 2011, http://spice.stanford.edu

Sri Swami Sivananda, "All about Hinduism", The Divine Life Society, Sixth Edition, 1997.

Sri Swami Sivananda, "Narada Bhakti Sutras: Text, Transliteration, Translation & Commentary" Divine Life Society Publication, 1957.

Sri Swami Sivananda, Brahma Sutras, The Divine Life Society, 4th edition, 2008.

Subramanian, Sriram Ganapathi; and Benyamin Ghojogh, "Introduction to the Non-dualism Approach in Hinduism and its Connection to Other Religions and Philosophies", https://www.researchgate.net/publication/342503023

Swami Prabhupada, His Divine Grace A.C. Bhaktivedanta. " Bhagavad-gita As It Is", 1972.

Swami Satchidananda Saraswati, "Salient Features of Shankara's Vedanta", Adhyatma Prakashan Karyalaya, Second Edition, 1990.

Swami Vimuktananda, "Aparokshanubhuti of Self-Realisation of Sri Shankaracharya", Advaita Ashrama, 1938.

Swami Vivekananda, "Bhakti Yoga", http://www.vivekananda.net/PDFBooks/BhaktiYogaS.pdf

Swami Vivekananda, "Jnana Yoga", https://estudantedavedanta.net/Jnana-Yoga-by-Swami-Vivekananda.pdf

Swami Vivekananda, "Karma Yoga", http://www.vivekananda.net/PDFBooks/KarmaYoga.pdf

Swami Vivekananda, "Raja Yoga", http://vivekananda.net/PDFBooks/RajaYoga1920.pdf

Tetiana, Danylova, "Taoism: Eastern Message of Non-Duality", International Electronic Scientific Journal. 2016. Vol. 2, No. 11.

Thanh, Minh; and P.D. Leigh; "Sutra of the Medicine Buddha", International Buddhist Monistic Institute, 2001.

The Dalai Lama, "The Four Noble Truths", Thorsons, 1997.

Todarmalji, Acharyakalp Pt. "Moksha Marg Prakashak (The Illuminator of the Path of Liberation)", Shri Kund-Kund Kahan Tirtha Trust.

Todd, Warren Lee, "A Selfless Response to an Illusory World: A Comparative Study of Śāntideva and Śaṅkara", Ph.D. Thesis, Lancaster University, September 2012.

Ui, H. "Vaisesika Philosophy according to Dasapadartha Sastra", Royal Asiatic Society, 2017.

Vandananjyoti, "Going for Refuge to the Three Jewels", Version 2:1, July 2020.

Venerable Master Hsuan Hua, "The Buddha Speaks of Amitabha Sutra" Buddhist Text Translation Society, 2002. Vol. 2(1), 2014:1-9, www.novaexplore.com

Williams, Paul. "Mahayana Buddhism", Taylor & Francis e-Library, 2008.

Index

P

R

S

Y